Reference Book

Information Relating to

Real Estate Practice,

Licensing and Examinations

Gray Davis
Governor

Maria Contreras-Sweet
Secretary, Business, Transportation & Housing Agency

Paula Reddish Zinnemann
Real Estate Commissioner

LDA — ISBN 0-916478-02-5

Published and Distributed by
State of California, Department of Real Estate

Preface

For the novice and the experienced, individuals preparing for license examination, and as a day-to-day guide in the broad field of real estate, the *Reference Book* is a useful tool.

The *Reference Book* complements another publication available through the California Department of Real Estate entitled *Real Estate Law*. The law book contains the Real Estate Law, Regulations of the Real Estate Commissioner, portions of the Administrative Procedure Act and pertinent excerpts from other California Codes.

It is recommended that real estate brokers and salespersons have a current copy of each volume.

Although the information in the *Reference Book* is believed accurate at the time of publication, persons using the information should check for possible law and procedure changes and other industry developments and trends of more recent date.

To the many individuals and organizations, both public and private, who so generously contributed time, knowledge and interest in preparation and review of this book, we express our sincere appreciation.

DEPARTMENT OF REAL ESTATE

Paula Reddish Zinnemann
Real Estate Commissioner

Location of Offices

Principal Office, Sacramento

2201 Broadway, P.O. Box 187000, Sacramento, 95818
Complaints/Consumer Information .... (916) 227-0864

Licensing:
Information/Renewals, Continuing Education .... (916) 227-0931
Broker Qualifications .... (916) 227-0899
Examination Scheduling.. (916) 227-0900

Mortgage Lending Section .... (916) 227-0770

Subdivisions, P.O. Box 187005, Sacramento, 95818-7005
Subdivisions Office (North) .... (916) 227-0813
Time-Shares, Undivided Interests, Out-of-State
Subdivisions and Subdivision Advertising (only) .... (916) 227-0810

Fresno District Office

2550 Mariposa Mall, Suite 3070, Fresno, 93721-2273
Complaints/Consumer Information .... (559) 445-5009

Los Angeles District Office

320 W. 4th. Street, Suite 350, Los Angeles, 90013-1105
Complaints/Consumer Information .... (213) 620-2072
Subdivisions Office (South) .... (213) 576-6983

Oakland District Office

1515 Clay Street, Suite 702, Oakland, 94612-1402
Complaints/Consumer Information .... (510) 622-2552

San Diego District Office

1350 Front Street, Suite 3064, San Diego, 92101-3687
Complaints/Consumer Information .... (619) 525-4192

www.dre.ca.gov

Past Real Estate Commissioners

Freeman Bloodgood .... 1917 – 1919

Ray L. Riley .... 1919 – 1921

Edwin T. Keiser .... 1921 – 1925

J. R. Gabbert .... 1925 – 1927

Stephen Barnson .... 1927 – 1931

Joseph P. Smith .... 1931 – 1934

J. Mortimer Clark .... 1934 – 1939

Clarence Urban .... 1939 – 1943

Hubert B. Scudder .... 1943 – 1948

D. D. Watson .... 1948 – 1957

F. W. Griesinger .... 1957 – 1959

W. A. Savage .... 1959 – 1963

Milton G. Gordon .... 1963 – 1967

Burton E. Smith .... 1967 – 1971

Robert W. Karpe .... 1971 – 1975

David H. Fox .... 1976 – 1981

E. Lee Brazil 1982

James A. Edmonds, Jr. .... 1983 – 1990

Clark Wallace .... 1991 – 1994

James Antt .... 1995 – 1998

A Word of Caution

Never before has the world of real estate presented so many complexities and challenges to the real estate licensee. Real estate is an exciting business to be in, yet a highly demanding profession.

The real estate agent should guard well the privilege of practicing real estate while avoiding stepping over the sometimes subtle line into the practice of law.

The real estate broker should be the first to recognize that although the field of real estate is highly technical and complicated by the overlapping of numerous areas of knowledge, the legal profession is even more technical, requiring years of preparation and constant study and research.

The phrase "to practice law" and similar expressions are *not* confined to meaning "appearances in court." They include legal advice and counsel and the preparation of legal instruments by which legal rights are secured.

It has been held, for example, that the selection and preparation of a mortgage or deed of trust by a broker in an independent loan transaction in which a fee was charged by the broker was the unlawful practice of law, even though only one transaction was involved.

To the layperson, what appears on the surface to be a minor difficulty may in fact be a complex legal issue, requiring the attention of a competent attorney. Brokers should not attempt to provide advice to clients needing counsel to solve legal problems. Indeed, under the Business and Professions Code, the practice of law by persons who are not members of the State Bar is specifically prohibited.

The foregoing is intended to remind and encourage real estate brokers to be alert for business activity that may require consultation with an attorney and avoid allowing principal or client to place upon them that responsibility which belongs only to a lawyer. Agents endanger their licenses and reputations and do a distinct disservice to customers when they overstep into the attorney's domain

Table of Contents

Chapter   Page

1. The State Department Of Real Estate

Government Regulation Of Brokerage Transactions 1
   The Police Power and the Real Estate Law 1
   Subdivisions 2
   Law Codified 2
   Administration by Commissioner 3
   The Real Estate Advisory Commission 3
   When a Real Estate License is Required 3
   Exemptions From License Requirements 4
   Examinations Required 4
   Applications 4
   Fingerprint Requirement 4
   Proof of Legal Presence 4
   License Term 5

Original Real Estate Broker License 5
   Experience Qualification 6
   Alternate Qualification Methods 7
   Examination for Original Broker License 8

Corporate Real Estate License 8
   Broker-Officers 8
   Corporation Background Statement 8
   Certificate of Qualification - Foreign Corporation 9
   Fictitious Business Name (dba) 9
   Salesperson Licensed to Corporation 9
   Replacing the Designated Broker-Officer 9
   Adding a New Officer as the Designated Officer 9
   Change of Designated Officer When Both Currently Hold
      a Broker-Officer License With Corporation 9
   Change of Main Office or Mailing Address 10
   Change of Corporation Name 10

Original Salesperson License 10
   License Requirements 10

License Renewals – Brokers And Salespersons 11
   Late Renewal 11

Other License Information 12
   Social Security Number 12
   Child Support Obligors 12
   Non-Working Status 13
   Mineral, Oil and Gas Licenses 13
   Partnerships 13
   Restricted License 13
   Fees 13

Continuing Education 14
   Renewal Procedure 14

Table of Contents

Exclusion From CE Requirement 14
List of Approved Sponsors and Their Offerings 14

Miscellaneous Information 14
Main Office Address Change 14
Branch Office 15
Fictitious Business Name 15
Mailing Addresses 16
Non-Resident Information 16
Transfer of Salesperson License 16
Termination of Salesperson for Violation 16
Effect of Revocation or Suspension 17
Loss of License Status 17

Prepaid Residential Listing Service License 17

Enforcement Of Real Estate Law 17
Formal Hearings 18
Violations 18
Other Penalty Sections 21
Examples of Unlawful Conduct - Sale, Lease, or Exchange 22
Examples of Unlawful Conduct - Loan Transactions 24
Regulations 25

Discrimination 25
Age Discrimination - Senior Citizen Housing 26
Housing Discrimination 27
Other State Laws and Regulations 28

Notice Of Discriminatory Restrictions 29
The Federal Rules 29

Subdivisions 30

Department Publications 30

Recovery Account 31

2. The Real Estate License Examinations

Scope of Examination 33
Preparing for an Exam 33
Exam Construction 33
Examination Weighting 34
Exam Outline.. 34
Exam Rules - Exam Subversion 36
Materials 37
Question Construction 37
Multiple Choice Exam 37
Q and A Analysis 37
Sample Multiple Choice Items 38

Table of Contents

3. Trade And Professional Associations

Real Estate Associations And Boards 47
    Realtor® Defined 48
    Multiple Listing Service 49
    Realtist Defined 49

Related Associations 50

Ethics 50

4. Property

Historical Derivations 71
    Freehold Estates 71
    Less-Than-Freehold Estates 71

The Modern View 71
    Land 72
    Things Affixed to Land 72
    Incidental or Appurtenant to the Land 72
    That Which is Immovable by Law 72
    "Modern" Estates 72

Personal Property 73

Fixtures 73

Legal Difference Between Real And Personal Property 73

Land Descriptions 74
    Recorded Map 74
    Description by Township and Section 74
    Metes and Bounds Description 76

Other Discription Methods 78
    Government Lots 78
    Record of Survey 78
    Assessor's Maps 78
    Informal Method 78

5. Title To Real Property

California Adopts A Recording System 79
    Actual v. Constructive Notice 79
    Which Instruments May be Recorded 79
    Purpose of Recording Statutes 79
    When An Instrument is Deemed Recorded 80
    Effect of Recording as Imparting Notice 80
    Priorities in Recording 80
    Special Lien Situations 80

Ownership Of Real Property 81

Separate Ownership 82

Table of Contents

Concurrent Ownership 82
   Tenancy in Common 82
   Joint Tenancy 82
   Community Property 84

Tenancy In Partnership 86

Encumbrances 87
   Definition 87

Mechanic's Liens 87
   Definition 88
   Persons Entitled to a Mechanic's Lien 89
   Property Subject to Mechanics' Liens 89
   Work of Improvement 90
   Lender's Priority 90
   Preliminary 20-Day Notice 90
   Determination of Completion Time 92
   Termination of the Lien 93
   Notice of Nonresponsibility 93
   Release of Lien Bond 94

Design Professional's Lien 94

Attachments And Judgments 94
   Property Subject to Attachment 94
   Judgment 95

Easements 96
   Generally 96
   Appurtenant Easements 96
   Easements in Gross 96
   How Easements Are Created 96
   Easement by Implication of Law 97
   Easement by Prescription 97
   Termination of Easements 97

Restrictions 97
   Distinction Between Covenants and Conditions 98
   Certain Covenants and Conditions Are Void 99
   Covenants Implied in Grant Deed 99
   Deed Restrictions 99
   New Subdivisions 100
   Termination 100
   Zoning Regulations 101

Encroachments 101

Homestead Exemption 101
   Two Homestead Statutes 102
   Declared Homestead 102
   Definitions for Declared Homesteads 102
   Definitions and Terminology from Article 4 102
   Amount of Homestead Exemptions 104

Table of Contents

Contents of the Declaration of Homestead 106
Federal Homestead Act of 1862 108

Assuring Marketability Of Title 109
Abstract of Title 110
Certificate of Title 110
Guarantee of Title 110
Title Insurance 110
Domestic Title Insurance Companies in California 112
Rebate Law 112
Torrens System of Land Registration 113

6. Transfer Of Interests In Real Property

Contracts In General 115
Contract Defined 115

Essential Elements Of A Contract 116
Parties Capable of Contracting 116
Mutual Consent 120
Lawful Object 125
Sufficient Consideration 127

Statute Of Frauds 127
Contracts that Must be Written 127

Interpretation, Performance And Discharge Of Contracts 129
Interpretation of Contracts 129
Performance of Contracts 130
Time 131
Discharge of Contracts 131
Statute of Limitations 131
Remedies for Breach 133
Rescission 133
Damages 133
Specific Performance 134

Real Estate Contracts 136
Provisions in Contracts 137
Options 139
Listing Defined 140
Deposit Receipt 142
Tender Defined 142

Acquisition And Transfer Of Real Estate 142
Will 143
Probate 144
Succession 144
Accession 144
Transfer 146

Table of Contents

7. Principal Instruments Of Transfer

A Backward Look 149
The Pattern Today 149
Deeds In General 149
Acknowledgment 150
Recordation 153
Delivery and Acceptance 154
Types Of Deeds 155
Grant Deed 155
Quitclaim Deed 155
Warranty Deed 155
Trust Deed 155
Reconveyance Deed 156
Sheriff's Deed 156
Gift Deed 156
Void Deeds 156
Voidable Deeds 157

8. Escrow

Definition 159
Essential Elements 159
Escrow Holder 159
Instructions 160
Complete Escrow 160
General Escrow Principles 160
General Escrow Procedures 161
Proration 163
Termination 163
Cancellation of Escrow - Cancellation of Purchase Contract 163
Who May Act As Escrow Agent 164
Escrow Companies Must be Incorporated 164
Audit 164
Prohibited Conduct 165
Realtionship Of Real Estate Broker And The Escrow Holder 165
Designating The Escrow Holder 166
Developer Controlled Escrows - Prohibition 166

9. Landlord And Tenant

Types of Leasehold Estates 167
Dual Legal Nature of Lease 167
Verbal and Written Agreements 168
Lease Ingredients 168
Contract and Conveyance Issues 168

Table of Contents

Rights and Obligations of Parties to a Lease 170
Condemnation of Leased Property 187
Notice Upon Tenant Default 188
Non-Waivable Tenant Rights 188
Remedies of Landlord 188
Disclosures by Owner or Rental Agent to Tenant 190

10. Agency

Introduction 191
Creation Of Agency Relationships 191
Actual Agency 191
Elements of An Agency Agreement 191
Types of Listing Agreements 192
Multiple Listing 193
Ostensible or Implied Agency 193
Compensation 194
Authority Of Agent 194
Express Authority 194
Implied Authority 194
Apparent Authority 195
Emergency Broadens Authority 195
Restrictions On Authority 195
Ratification of Unauthorized Acts 196
Duty to Ascertain Scope of Agent's Authority 196
Power of Attorney 196
Authority to Receive Deposits 196
Dismissal of Broker/Stakeholder From Suit 198
Commingling 198
Agency Disclosure Form 198
Disclosure and Confirmation of Actual Agency Relationships 199
Statutory Limitations and Definitions 200
More on Dual Agency 200
Subagency 200
Delegation of Duties 202
Duties Owed To Principals 202
Loyalty and Confidentiality 202
Fair and Honest Dealing 203
General Disclosure Duties 203
Reasonable Care and Skill 203
Inspection and Disclosures 204
No Secret Profit or Undisclosed Compensation 205
Obligations of Real Estate Salespersons 205
Duties Owed To Third Parties 205
Warranty of Authority 205
Regarding Contracts 206
Regarding Torts 206
Misrepresentation: Fraud v. Negligence 206

Table of Contents

Nondisclosures 207
"Puffing" 207
Torts of the Principal 208
Rights Of Agent 208
   Compensation - Performance Required Under Employment
    Contract 208
Termination Of Agency 211
   When Principal May Revoke Agency 211
   Effect of Termination 211
   Time when Revocation can be Made 211
Special Brokerage Relationships 212
   Probate Sales 212
   Board of Education Sales 213
   State of California Sales 214
Licensee Acting For Own Account 214
Unlawful Employment And Compensation 216
Broker-Salesperson Relationship 217
   Broker-Salesperson Employment Contract 217
   Employer - Employee 217
   Independent Contractor 217
   Liability 218
   Workman's Compensation 218
   Social Security and Income Taxes 218
   Unemployment Insurance 219
   Personal Income Tax - Additional Information 219
   Commission and Deposit Disputes 219
Conclusion 220

11. Impact Of The Penal Code And Other Statutes

   Penal Code 221
   Unlawful Practice of Law 222
   Business and Professions Code 223
   Civil Code 223
   Corporations Code 223

12. Real Estate Finance

Background 225
   Before Deregulation 225
   Deregulation 226
   Reregulation 226
   More Deregulation 226
   California Law 226
   Redesigned Mortgage Instruments 227
   The Fixed-Rate Mortgage 227
   A Forward Look 228

Table of Contents

The Economy 228
    Role of Real Estate in the National Economy 228

The Mortgage Market 231
    Credit 231
    Supply and Demand 231
    Government Intervention Can Redirect Supply 231
    The Primary Mortgage Market 231
    The Secondary Mortgage Market 232
    The "Subprime" Secondary Market 234
    Private Mortgage Insurance 234
    California and the Mortgage Market 235

Overview Of The Loan Process 235

Details Of The Loan Process 237

Federal And State Disclosure And Notice Of Rights 240
    Real Estate Settlement Procedures Act (RESPA) Regulation X ... 240
    Loan Servicing 242

Promissory Notes 243
    The Obligation (Debt) and the Security 243
    Negotiable Instruments 243
    Holder in Due Course Defined 245
    FTC "Holder in Due Course Rule" 245
    Negotiation 245
    Conflict in Terms of Note and Mortgage or Deed of Trust 246

Trust Deeds And Mortgages 246
    Security Interests 246
    In General 246
    Home Mortgage Loan 247
    Differences Between Mortgages and Deeds of Trust 247
    Limitation to Recording of Reconveyance 250
    Required Timely Recording of the Deed of Full Reconveyance ... 250
    Other Characteristics/Essentials of Mortgages and Trust Deeds ... 251

Junior Trust Deeds And Mortgages 252
    Seller Extending Credit 252
    Private Lenders 253
    Usury 253
    General Comments 253
    Balloon Payment Loans 253

Other Types Of Mortgage And Trust Deed Loans 254
    Package Trust Deed 254
    Blanket Trust Deed (Mortgage) 254
    Open-End Trust Deed 254
    Interest-Only Mortgage 254
    Collateralized Junior Mortgage 254
    Tandem (or Piggyback) Loan 254
    Swing Mortgage 255
    Refinance Mortgage 255

Table of Contents

Pledged Savings Account Mortgage 255
Wrap-Around Mortgage or Trust Deed 255
Alternative Financing 256
    Background and Purpose 256
    Graduated Payment Adjustable Mortgage (GPAM) 256
    Adjustable Rate Mortgage (ARM) 256
    Renegotiable Rate Mortgage (RRM) 257
    Shared Appreciation Mortgage (SAM) 257
    Rollover Mortgage (ROM) 257
    Reverse Annuity Mortgage (RAM) 257
Effects Of Security 258
Due On Sale 258
    Recent History of Due-on-Sale Enforcement in California 260
    Enforceability 260
    Other Exceptions 261
    Assumptions May Still be Negotiable 261
    Special Provision 261
Lender's Remedy In Case Of Default 262
    Foreclosure Generally 262
    "One-Action" Rule 262
    Purchase Money Securities 263
    Anti-deficiency Rules 263
    Deficiency Judgments 263
    Reinstatement Rights - Pre-sale 264
    Redemption Rights - Post-Sale 264
    Statute of Limitations 264
    Judicial Sale 265
    Trustee's Sale - "Power of Sale" Foreclosure 265
    The Procedure 265
    Foreclosure Abuses 271
    Statement of Condition of Debt 272
    Annual and Monthly Accounting 272
Basic Interest Rate Mathematics 274
    Principal - Interest - Rate - Time 274
    Compound Interest 275
    The One-Step Formula for Compound Interest 276
    Effective Rate of Interest 276
    Discount Rate 277
    Principal-Plus-Interest 277
    Types of Tables 277
The Tools Of Analysis 278
    Liquidity 278
    Leverage 279
    Activity 279
    Profitability 280

Table of Contents

13. Government Participation In Real Estate Finance

The Federal Housing Administration 281
    Qualifying 281
    Types of Properties and Mortgages 281
    Maximum Loan Amounts 282
    Down Payment 282
    Loan Terms and Prepayment 282
    Mortgage Insurance Premium 282
    Applying for an FHA Loan 283
    Loan Approval 283

Most Frequently Used Fha Programs 283
    Title I - Property Improvement; Manufactured Home Purchase ... 283
    Title II - Home Mortgage Insurance 283

U.S. Department Of Veterans Affairs (VA) 284
    Purpose of VA Loans 284
    Eligibility 284
    Guarantee Amounts 286
    Interest Rates are Negotiable 286
    Funding Fee for VA Home Loans 286
    Loan Classifications and Loan Structure 286
    Manufactured Home (Mobilehome) Loans 286
    Refinancing Existing Loans 287
    Condominiums 288
    When Sales Price Exceeds Amount Shown on VA Certificate of
        Reasonable Value (CRV)... 289
    Down Payment 289
    Discount Points and Prepayment.. 289
    Energy Conservation Measures 289
    Assumability of VA Loans 289
    Release of Liability 289
    Restoration of Entitlement 290
    Supplemental Servicing 290
    Lending Agencies 291
    Procedure 291

California Veterans Farm And Home Purchase Program 291
    Purpose 291
    The First Loan 291
    Benefit Provided 291
    Source of Funds 292
    Interest Rates and Loan Terms 292
    Eligibility 292
    Federal Recapture Tax for Veterans' Revenue Bonds 293
    Refinance Restrictions 294
    Application Procedure 294
    Loan Processing Fees 294
    Secondary Financing 294

Table of Contents

Construction Loans Available 295
Special Loan Conditions 295
Special Loan Programs 295
Subsequent Loan 295
Fire and Hazard Insurance 296
Disaster Coverage 296
Notice 296

14. Non-Mortgage Alternatives To Real Estate Financing

Syndicate Equity Financing 297
Commercial Loan 297
Bonds or Stocks 297
Long-term Lease 297
Exchange 298
Sale-Leaseback 298
Sales Contract (Land Contract) 298

Security Agreements (Personal Property) 300
Uniform Commercial Code (UCC) - Division 9 301
Priorities 302
Failure to File 303
Escrow - Early Filing 303
Fixture Filings 303
Caution 304

15. Mortgage Loans

Broker's Role 305
The Loan Application 305
Advance Fees 305
Title Policy for Lender 306
Usury 306

Article 5 – The Lender 306
Application of Article 5 307
Pooling of Loan Funds 307
Advertising 307
Exception to Article 5 Requirements 308
"Threshold" Criteria 308
Disclosure Statement 308
Disbursing Funds 309
Servicing - Broker Advances 309
Commissioner's Regulations 309

Article 7 – The Borrower 310
Application of Article 7 310
Mortgage Loan Disclosure Statement 310
Disclosures - Case Law 311
Commissions and Other Charges 311

Table of Contents

Balloon Payment 311
Other Restrictions 312
Truth In Lending Act 313
Creditor 313
Exempt Transactions 313
Form of Disclosures 314
Required Disclosures 314
Time of Disclosure 318
Subsequent Disclosure 319
Additional Disclosures Required for High-Rate,
   High-Fee Mortgages 320
Consumer's Right to Rescind 321
Advertising Consumer Credit 322
Administrative Enforcement 324
Civil Liability 325
Criminal Liability 326
Conclusion 326

16. Real Estate Syndicates And Investment Trusts

Real Estate Syndication 327
In General 327
Benefits 327
Syndicate Forms 327
Limited Partnership 328
Regulatory Control of Real Estate Syndicate Offerings 328
Real Estate Investment Trusts 329
Types of REITs 330

17. Appraisal And Valuation

Theoretical Concepts Of Value And Definitions 331
Definition of Appraisal 331
Traditional Approaches to Value 332
The Appraiser's Role in the Real Estate Profession 333
Appraisal Report 334
Laymen's Terms for Appraisal Reports 335
Purposes and Uses of Appraisals 335
Principles Of Valuation 336
Basic Valuation Definitions 339
Value Designations 339
Market Value Defined 339
Legal Definition 340
Value vs. Price 340
Value vs. Cost 340
Purposes and Characteristics of Value 341

Table of Contents

Forces Influencing Value 342
Factors Influencing Value 342
Additional Factors Important for Residential Property 344
Additional Factors Important for Commercial Property 345
Additional Factors Important for Industrial Property 345
Additional Factors Important for Agricultural or Farm Lands 346
Economic Trends Affecting Real Estate Value 346
Regional, National and Global Economics 346
Factors Influencing City Growth and Development 346
Population Trends 347
Neighborhood Analysis 347
Site Analysis And Valuation 348
Legal Data of Site Analysis 348
Physical Factors Involving the Site 349
Methods of Site Valuation 350
Architectural Styles And Functional Utility 353
Architectural Styles 353
Building Quality 356
Functional Utility 357
Functional Utility Checklist 357
Broker's Guidelines for Considering Physical Characteristics
of Real Property for FHA Insurance Purposes 358
The Appraisal Process And Methods 360
Overview of the Appraisal Process 360
The Departure Provision 363
Methods Of Appraising Properties 363
The Sales Comparison Approach 364
Sources of Data 364
The Procedure 365
Application of the Procedure - Residential Sales 366
Cost Approach 369
The Procedure in Brief 369
Cost New Bases 369
Steps in the Cost Approach 370
Depreciation 372
Appraisal and Income Tax Views - "Book" vs. Actual
Depreciation 373
Methods of Calculating Accrued Depreciation 374
Income (Capitalization) Approach 378
Appraiser's and Owner's Viewpoints 379
Capitalization 379
Income Approach Process 381
Determining Net Annual Income 381
Selecting the Cap Rate 382
Capitalizing Net Annual Operating Income 382

Table of Contents

Income Approach Applied 383

Residual Techniques 384
    Property Residual Technique 384
    Building Residual Technique 385
    Land Residual Technique 385
    Finding the Overall Cap Rate - Example 386

Yield Capitalization Analysis 386

Gross Rent Multiplier 388
    Method of Approach in Using the Gross Rent Multiplier 388

Summary 389

Appraisal Of Manufactured Homes (Mobilehomes) 389

Evaluating The Single Family Residence And Small Multi-Family
    Dwellings 390
    New Residence 390
    Older Residence 393

Typical Outline For Writing The Single Family Residence
    Narrative Appraisal Report 395

Conclusion 399

Additional Practice Problems 399
    Applying the Income (Capitalization) Approach 399

The Office Of Real Estate Appraisers (Orea) 402
    Background 402
    Office of Real Estate Appraisers 402
    Real Estate Appraiser Licenses 402
    Terms of Licenses 406
    Renewal Requirements 406
    OREA's Enforcement Division 406
    Additional Information 406

18. Taxation And Assessments

Property Taxes 407
    California's Property Taxes 407
    Property Tax Liens 408
    The Morgan Property Taxpayers' Bill of Rights 408
    Establishing Values 408
    Exemptions 410
    Supplemental Assessments 410
    Postponement (Sections 20581, et seq.) 412
    Tax Sale (Sections 3351 - 3972) 412
    Redemption (Sections 4101, et seq.) 413

Taxation Of Mobilehomes 413

Special Assessments 414
    Benefit Assessments 415

Table of Contents

Certain Assessment Statutes 415
   Vrooman Street Act 415
   Street Improvement Act of 1911 415
   The Improvement Bond Act of 1915 415
   Mello-Roos 416

Federal Taxes 415
   Federal Estate Tax 415
   Federal Tax Liens 415
   Federal Gift Tax and the Unified Credit 416
   Social Security Tax 417
   Unemployment Tax 417

Documentary Transfer Tax 417

State Taxes 418
   Inheritance Tax 419
   Gift Tax 419
   Estate Tax 419

Miscellaneous Taxes 419
   Sales and Use Tax 419
   Real Estate Broker and Mobilehome Sales 420
   Unemployment Insurance Tax 420
   State Tax Lien Law 421

Acquisition Of Real Property 421
   Adjusted Tax Basis 422
   Tax Planning 422

Income Taxation 422
   Federal Income Tax 422
   Depreciation 424
   Home Mortgage Interest Deduction 425
   Mortgage Credit Certificates 425
   Disposition of Real Property - Tax Effects 425
   State Income Tax 428
   Tax Credits Related to Real Estate 428

19. Subdivisions And Other Public Controls

Basic Subdivision Laws 431
   Subdivision Map Act 431
   Subdivided Lands Law 431

Subdivison Definitions 432

Functions In Land Subdivision 433
   Private Professional Services 433
   Planning Commission 433
   Lending Agencies 434
   Title Company 434

Compliance And Goverenmental Consultation 434

Table of Contents

Types Of Subdivisions 434
    Standard 434
    Common Interest 435
    Undivided Interest 437

Compliance With Subdivided Lands Law 437
    Affirmative Standards 438
    Disclosures in Public Report 438
    Filing Notice of Intention/Application 438
    Use of Public Report 438
    Violations - Penalties 438
    Questionnaire Requirements 439
    Subdivision Filing Fees 439
    Where to File 439
    Questionnaire Forms - Contents 439
    Exceptions 440
    Filing Packages 440
    Preliminary Public Report 440
    Amended Public Report 441
    Renewed Public Report 441
    Conditional Public Report 441

Handling Of Purchasers' Deposit Money 441
    Blanket Encumbrance 441
    No Blanket Encumbrance 442
    Impound Requirements - Real Property Sale Contracts 442

Covenants, Conditions And Restrictions 442

Additional Provisions 443
    Material Changes 443
    Special Districts 443
    Special Regulations for Common Interest Subdivisions 444
    Environmental Impact Reports 444
    The California Coastal Act 444
    Mineral, Oil and Gas Subdivisions 444
    Advertising Criteria 444
    Desist and Refrain Orders 445
    Out-of-State Subdivisions 445

Grounds For Denial Of Public Report 445

Subdivision Map Act 446

Preliminary Planning Considerations 446
    Natural Features 446
    Soils Report 446
    Neighboring Property 446
    Drainage 447
    Flood Hazard 447
    Alquist-Priolo Earthquake Fault Zoning Act 447
    Sewage Disposal 448
    Water Supply 448
    Other Utilities 448

Table of Contents

Dedication of Streets and Easements 449
Public Parks and Recreational Facilities 449
Dedication of School Sites 449
Airport within Subdivision 449
Preapplication Conferences 449

Basic Steps In Final Map Preparation And Approval 450

Types Of Maps 450

Tentative Map Preparation 450

Tentative Map Filing 451
Processing the Map 451
Basis for Approval or Denial 451
Appeal 451
Vesting Tentative Maps and Development Agreements 452

Final Map 452
Taxes and Assessments 452
Improvements 452
Final Map Filing 452
Final Map Recordation 453

Parcel Map 453

Other Public Controls 453
State Housing Law 453
Local Building Codes 453
Contractors' State License Law 454

Health And Sanitation 454

Eminent Domain 455
Compensation 455
Severance Damage 453
Procedure 455
Inverse Condemnation 455
Inverse Condemnation for Governmental Regulation 456

Water Conservation And Flood Control 456
Mutual Water Company 456
Public Utilities 457
Special Water Districts 457
Water Pollution Control 458

Interstate Land Sales Full Disclosure Act 458

20. Planning, Zoning, And Redevelopment

The Need For Planning 459

General Plans 459
Preparation 460
Hearings - Adoption or Denial 460
Importance of the General Plan 460
Amendment to General Plans 461

Table of Contents

General Plan Implementation 461
Zoning 462
Zoning and Use Variances 464
Conditional Use Permits 464
California Environmental Quality Act of 1970 (CEQA) 464
Speeding Up Routine Matters 465

Redevelopment 466
Housing Powers, Responsibilities, and Activities
    of Redevelopment Agencies 466
Funding Redevelopment Projects 467

21. Brokerage

Brokerage as a Part of the Real Estate Business 469
Other Specialists 469
Operations 469
Office Size - Management 469
Office Size 469
Career Building 469
The Broker and the New Salesperson 470
Specialization 470
A Broker's Related Pursuits 471

Professionalism 471
Staying Informed - Disclosures.. 471

Mobilehome Sales 472
Permit for Movement 473
Transferring Title (personal property) 473
Additional Information 474

22. Contract Provisions And Disclosures In A Residential Real Estate Transaction

A Basic Transaction 475

A Basic Listing 476
Term 476
Description of the Property 476
Terms of Sale 476
The Broker's Authority 476
The Broker's Duty 477
Broker's Compensation 477
Negotiability of Commission 477
Personal Property 477
Multiple Listing Service (MLS) 478
Deposit 478
Other Provisions 478
Single Agency 478

Purchase Contract/Receipt Of Deposit 479
Date and Place of Buyer's Offer 479

Table of Contents

The Full and Correct Name of the Buyer 479
Description of the Property 479
Purchase Price and Terms 479
Financing 479
Deposit 480
Time Constraints 480
Title and Vesting 480
Prorations 480
Transfer Taxes/Fees 481
Occupancy and Possession 481
Buyer's Inspection of the Property 481
Seller's Representation as to Condition of the Property 481
Smoke Detector(s) 481
Water Heater Bracing 481
Retrofit 482
Governmental Compliance 482
Fixtures 482
Personal Property 482
Home Warranty Plans 482
Septic/Sewer/Well Systems 482
Pest Control 482
Rental Property 483
Repairs and Final Inspection 483
Sale of Buyer's Property 483
Property Destruction or Damage 483
Multiple Listing Service 484
Equal Housing Opportunity 484
Mediation/Arbitration of Disputes 484
Liquidated Damages 484
Attorney's Fees 484
Offer and Acceptance - Contract 484
Disclosures 485
Real Estate Transfer Disclosure Statement 485
Local Option Disclosure Statement 486
Mello-Roos Disclosure 486
Smoke Detector Statement of Compliance 487
Disclosure Regarding Lead-Based Paint Hazards 487
Disclosures Regarding State Responsibility Areas 488
Disclosure of Ordnance Location 489
Disclosure of Geological Hazards and Earthquake Fault Zones ... 489
Environmental Hazard Disclosures 490
Energy Conservation Retrofit and Thermal Insulation Disclosure 491
Special Flood Hazard Area Disclosure and Responsibilities of FEMA .491
Local Requirements Resulting from City and County Ordinances 492
Foreign Investment in Real Property Tax Act 492
Notice and Disclosure to Buyer of State Tax Withholding
    on Disposition of California Real Property 492
Notice Regarding the Advisability of Title Insurance 493

Table of Contents

Visual Inspection 493
Agency Relationship Disclosure 494
No Disclosure Required for Manner/Occurrence of Death;
Affliction of Occupant with AIDS 494
Disclosure of Sale Price Information 494
Seller Financing Disclosure Statement 494
Water Heater Bracing 497

23. Trust Funds

General Information 499
Trust Funds and Non-Trust Funds 499
Why a Trust Account? 500
Trust Fund Handling Requirements 500
Identifying the Owner(S) of Trust Funds 501

Trust Fund Bank Accounts 501
General Requirements 501
Trust Account Withdrawals 502
Interest-Bearing Accounts 502
Commingling Prohibited 503
Trust Fund Liability 505
Summary - Maintaining Trust Account Integrity 507

Accounting Records 507
General Requirements 507
Columnar Records 508
Record of All Trust Funds Received and Paid Out – Trust
Fund Bank Account 508
Separate Record for Each Beneficiary or Transaction 508
Record of All Trust Funds Received - Not Placed in Broker's
Trust Account 509
Separate Record for Each Property Managed 509

Other Accounting Systems And Records 509
Journal 510
Cash Ledger 510
Beneficiary Ledger 510

Recording Process 511

Reconciliation Of Accounting Records 511
Purpose 511
Reconciling the Bank Account Record With the Bank Statement 512
Reconciling the Bank Account Record With the Separate
Beneficiary or Transaction Records 512
Unexplained Trust Account Overages 512
Suggestions for Reconciling Records 512

Documentation Requirements 513
Activities and Related Documents 513

Additional Documentation Requirements 514
Person Signing Contract to be Given Copy 514

Table of Contents

Audits And Examinations 514

Sample Transactions 515

*Questions And Answers Regarding Trust Fund Requirements
and Record Keeping* 524

Summary 524

Exhibits 524

24. Property Management

Professional Organization 537

Property Managers and Professional Designations 538

Functions of a Property Manager 538

Specific Duties Of The Property Manager 539

Rent Schedule 539

Merchandising the Space 540

Maintenance and Purchasing Operations 540

Tenant Relationships 540

Manager as Employer 541

Vacancies 541

Reports to Owner 541

Earnings 541

Management Contract 541

Accounting Records For Property Management 542

25. Developers Of Land And Buildings

Subdividing 543

Developer Builder 544

Home Construction 545

26. Business Opportunities

Definition 547

Agency 547

Small Businesses and the Small Business Administration 547

Form of Business Organization 547

Form of Sale 548

Why an Escrow? 548

Buyer's Evaluation 549

Motives of Buyers and Sellers 549

Counseling the Buyer 549

Satisfying Government Agencies 550

Listings 550

Preparing the Listing 551

Establishing Value 552

Valuation Methods 553

Lease 554

Table of Contents

Goodwill 554
Fictitious Business Name 554
Franchising 555

Bulk Sales And The Uniform Commercial Code 556
Public Notice 556
Sale at Public Auction 557
Escrows 557
Effect of Noncompliance 557
Uniform Commercial Code (Division 9) 558

California Sales And Use Tax Provisions 558
Successor's Liability 559

Alcoholic Beverage Control Act 559
Regulation 559
Transfer of License - Posting of Notice 559
Notice to County Recorder and Escrow Requirement 560

27. Mineral, Oil And Gas Brokerage

History 561

Mineral, Oil And Gas Brokerage 561

1994 – No Separate License Requirements 561
Transactions Requiring a Real Estate License 562
Exempt Transactions 562
Mineral, Oil and Gas is a Technical Field 562
Study References 562
Mineral Oil and Gas Subdivisions 563

28. Tables, Formulas, And Measurements 565

29. Glossary 573

Index 622

1   The California Department of Real Estate

GOVERNMENT REGULATION OF BROKERAGE TRANSACTIONS

As our country's development passed through the pioneering and homesteading stages to urbanization, people across the land found it increasingly difficult to "strike a deal" with strangers for land and homes. There was a real need for an intermediary to provide basic real estate knowledge and services and negotiate transactions. The real estate agent met this need and continues to fill this important role today.

Along with increasing opportunities to provide real estate services to the maturing nation came abuses of the public trust in the form of unethical, illegal or sharp practices by dishonest or incompetent agents operating in a climate of unorganized and often unscrupulous competition. Real estate practitioners themselves began to see the need for government regulation. The public's legitimate interest in the buying, selling, exchanging and financing of real property has led to regulation of the real estate business through the adoption of legislative and administrative controls.

California's Legislature passed the nation's first real estate licensing law in 1917. The courts declared that law to be unconstitutional, based on its conditions compared to the licensing requirements of the Insurance Commissioner. California then adopted the Real Estate Act of 1919, which the State Supreme Court upheld as a reasonable exercise of the power of the state to regulate the conduct of its citizens in the interest of the common good.

All fifty states and the District of Columbia have enacted statutes governing, to some degree, the licensing, regulation and conduct of real estate agents. This type of government regulation and supervision has its foundation in what is known as the police power.

The Police Power and the Real Estate Law

For many people, the phrase "police power" evokes images of police officers, jails and courtrooms. But the police power involves much more than the business of detecting crime and criminals and maintaining public order and tranquility. The following, excerpted from a United States Supreme Court case, gives a useful description of the police power:

"By means of it, the legislature exercises a supervision over matters affecting the commonweal and enforces the observance by each individual member of society of duties which he owes to others and the community at large. The possession and enjoyment of all rights are subject to this power. Under it the state may prescribe regulations promoting the health, peace, morals, education and good order of the people, and legislate so as to increase the industries of the state, develop its resources and add to its welfare and prosperity."

In short, police power is the power of the state to enact laws within constitutional limits to promote the order, safety, health, morals and general welfare of our society.

The police power does not vest arbitrary authority in any legislative body. Laws emanating from exercise of the police power must be necessary and proper for the protection or advancement of a genuine public interest. Neither state nor local authority may impose onerous, unreasonable or unnecessary burdens upon persons, property or business.

Legislation intended to protect the public safety, health and morals may impact the manner of conducting lawful occupations and businesses *without*, of course, taking away the right to be gainfully employed.

For many years, society has benefited from regulation of professions such as law, medicine and dentistry. More recently, many other professions, including real estate, have become subject to regulation beyond that of mere licensing.

The organized real estate industry has been among the strongest supporters of the real estate licensing law. The industry is aware that reasonable regulation of those engaged in the real estate business benefits the public by creating and maintaining professional standards and ethical practices in the conduct of real estate brokerage activities. This, in turn, benefits the industry by creating an orderly market place.

The Real Estate Law exists primarily for the protection of the public in real estate transactions involving the services of an agent. By requiring qualifications for licensing, the law enables the Commissioner to ascertain that persons acting in the capacity of a broker or salesperson meet certain standards of knowledge and honesty and, for the broker license, experience.

The Commissioner's authority is not arbitrary. For the Commissioner to find that an applicant for a license is not honest and truthful there must be facts which justify that conclusion. When an applicant has the qualifications required by law, the Commissioner must issue the license.

Subdivisions
With statutory authority, the Commissioner began regulating the sale or lease of subdivided lands in 1933. Like the 1919 licensing law, the subdivided lands provisions survived the State Supreme Court's test of constitutionality. The court held that the object of the law was the prevention of fraud and sharp practices in a type of real estate transaction particularly open to abuses. The court said the method of furnishing information to real property purchasers, which involved investigation and written disclosure of certain essential facts, was appropriate protection. We call this disclosure document a public report.

Law Codified
On August 4, 1943, the Legislature organized the statutory authority of the Department of Real Estate (DRE) into the two Parts of Division 4 of the Business and Professions Code (hereinafter, the Code). Part 1 (now Sections 10000 to 10580) is titled Licensing of Persons and may be cited as the Real Estate Law. Part 2 (now Sections 11000 to 11200) is titled Regulation of Transactions and may be cited as the Subdivided Lands Law. (Note that these laws are quite different in

purpose and operation from real property law, law of agency, contract law, or other legal aspects of real estate ownership and conveyancing.)

Administration by Commissioner

The Commissioner's mission is to enforce the Real Estate Law and the Subdivided Lands Law in a manner which achieves maximum protection for persons dealing with real estate licensees and for purchasers of subdivided real property. Foremost among the Commissioner's specific duties are: the qualification of applicants and issuance of real estate licenses; the investigation of complaints and, where appropriate, pursuit of formal action against licensees; the investigation of nonlicensees alleged to be performing acts for which a license is required; and the regulation of the sale or lease of subdivision interests. The Commissioner also, through real estate broker and other license requirements, regulates dealings in mineral, oil and gas property and Prepaid Rental Listing Services.

The Real Estate Advisory Commission

The Commissioner appoints the ten members of the Real Estate Advisory Commission. Six are California real estate brokers and four are public members.

The Commission consults with the Commissioner and makes recommendations regarding the functions and policies of the Department and how the Department may best serve the people of the State and recognize the legitimate needs of the industry. After notice of time and place, the Commissioner presides at quarterly meetings of the Commission. At Commission meetings, licensees and members of the public may express their views and make suggestions.

When a Real Estate License Is Required

Sections 10131, 10131.1, 10131.2, 10131.3, 10131.4, 10131.45, and 10131.6 of the Business and Professions Code (hereinafter, the Code) define the scope of a real estate broker's activity. Mortgage loan broker activities may be found in Sections 10131 (d) and 10240, et seq. of Article 7 (known as the Real Property Loan Law). Trust deed transactions and real property sales contract transactions requiring a license are defined in Sections 10131 (e) and Sections 10230-10236.2 (Article 5). Advance fee brokerage activities are defined in Section 10131.2. Mobilehome sales activities requiring broker licensure are described in Section 10131.6 and Prepaid Rental Listing Services provisions are found in Sections 10167-10167.17. Mineral, oil and gas property dealings requiring a broker license can be found in Sections 10131.4 and 10131.45. Section 10132 of the Code defines a real estate salesperson and the acts requiring licensure and employment by a real estate broker.

Without a license, an individual cannot receive compensation for the performance of any of the acts defined as being within the purview of a licensed broker or salesperson. In addition, the law provides penalties for a person who acts or purports to act as a real estate broker or salesperson without being duly licensed. The Commissioner may levy a fine against any real estate broker who is found in a disciplinary hearing to have compensated an unlicensed person for performing activities which require a real estate license. Furthermore, any person who compensates a nonlicensee for performing services which require a license is guilty of a misdemeanor and may also be fined by the courts. (Sections 10138, 10139, 10139.5 of the Code)

Exemptions From License Requirements
Exemptions to the license requirement include: resident managers of apartment buildings and complexes or their employees; short-term (vacation) rental agents; employees of certain lending institutions; employees of real estate brokers for specific, limited functions; lenders making loans guaranteed or insured by an agency of the federal government; certain agricultural associations; licensed personal property brokers; cemetery authorities; certain collectors of payments for lenders or on notes for owners in connection with loans secured directly or collaterally by liens on real property, provided such collectors annually meet exemption criteria; clerical help, etc. (See Sections 10131.01, 10133, 10133.1, 10133.15 10133.2, 10133.3, 10133.35, 10133.4, and 10133.5 of the Code for the license exemptions.)

Examinations Required
The law requires the Commissioner to ascertain by written examination that the license applicant is qualified to act in the capacity of a broker or salesperson. Under no circumstances can the examination requirement be waived. An applicant for a real estate license examination must meet the prerequisite requirements and be scheduled for the applicable qualifying examination. The examination application and fee are valid for a maximum period of two years after the application was filed. No restrictions are placed on the number of times an applicant who fails the qualifying examination may apply for reexamination. Applicants may apply for reexamination by filing the Examination Result Notification (RE 418), or an Examination Change Application (RE 415), and the appropriate examination fee. If the applicant is unsuccessful in passing the examination within the two-year period, the application expires and the applicant will be required to submit a new application and fee, and may be required to submit new qualification documents.

When a qualifying examination is passed, the successful examinee is entitled to apply for a four-year license. The examinations are discussed in more detail in Chapter 2.

Applications
Applications for all examinations and for all licenses issued by the Commissioner must be made on forms furnished by DRE. Forms can be obtained at any of DRE's offices or by writing to the main office in Sacramento. Detailed instructions are furnished with the application forms. An application for an examination or a license may be presented at any of DRE's offices or (preferably) mailed to Sacramento. A license application must be accompanied by the current license fee, one fully completed and classifiable fingerprint card, and the fingerprint processing fee.

Fingerprint Requirement
An applicant for any real estate license must submit one set of classifiable fingerprints, acceptable to the State Department of Justice (DOJ), unless the applicant is currently licensed by DRE or has held a real estate license which expired less than two years ago.

Fingerprints must be submitted through DOJ's Live Scan Program, which involves the electronic taking and transmission of fingerprints to DOJ. A Live Scan Service

Request form (RE237) will be sent to all applicants who successfully complete the real estate examination. Live Scan applicants should take the Live Scan Service Request form to a participating Live Scan service provider. After the Live Scan service provider takes the fingerprints, the applicant must submit to DRE a copy of the RE 237 with Part 4 completed, along with the applicant's completed original license application and the appropriate fee. A list of Live Scan service providers will be provided at the time the license examination is taken, or can be obtained by calling DRE at (916) 227-0931, or by checking the Department of Justice Web site at http://caag.state.ca.us/app/livescan.htm and looking under Contact Information.

Applicants who reside outside California may continue to submit fingerprints in ink using the California license applicant Fingerprint Card (BID 7).

An additional charge of $32.00, payable to DRE, is required for processing fingerprints through DOJ. This fee must be included with the license application and license fee.

Within 90 days after issuance, the Commissioner may suspend without a hearing the license of anyone who procured a license by fraud, misrepresentation or deceit, or made any material misstatement of fact in the application. (Section 10177.1 of the Code)

Proof of Legal Presence
All applicants for a real estate salesperson, broker, officer, mineral, oil and gas broker, or prepaid rental listing service license, must submit proof that they have legal presence in the United States before an original or renewal license can be issued. A proof of legal presence document (i.e., birth certificate, resident alien card, etc.) must be submitted by original and renewal license applicants only one time with a Public Benefits Form (RE205). Please refer to that form for further instructions and information.

License Term
Original broker and salesperson licenses are issued for a four-year period. A broker or salesperson license may be renewed every four years by filing the proper application, fee, and evidence of completion of continuing education. A license may not be renewed which has been revoked as a disciplinary measure or denied or suspended under the provisions of Section 11350.6 of the Welfare and Institutions Code (Family Law - Child Support). The license issued to a salesperson who has not completed the educational requirements outlined under Section 10153.4 within eighteen months of license issuance will be suspended automatically and may not be renewed unless the educational requirements are completed within the original four-year license term.

ORIGINAL REAL ESTATE BROKER LICENSE

The individual broker license entitles a natural person to conduct a brokerage business under his/her own name or, if so licensed, under a fictitious business name.

The applicant for an original real estate broker license must: (1) be at least 18 years old; (2) have had previous experience and education as required by law; (3) be honest and truthful; and (4) pass the qualifying examination. The Real Estate Law requires that every applicant for a real estate broker license must either have been actively engaged as a real estate salesperson for at least two years during the five years immediately preceding the application or prove to the satisfaction of the Commissioner that applicant has general real estate experience which would be the equivalent of two years of full-time experience as a salesperson completed within a similar time period, and must have successfully completed the following statutory three semester-unit (or quarter equivalent) college-level courses:

1. Real Estate Practice	6. And *three* from the following:
2. Legal Aspects of Real Estate	Real Estate Principles
3. Real Estate Finance	Business Law
4. Real Estate Appraisal	Property Management
5. Accounting *or* Real Estate Economics	Real Estate Office Administration
	Escrows
	Advanced Legal Aspects of Real Estate
	Advanced Real Estate Finance
	Advanced Real Estate Appraisal
	Mortgage Loan Brokering and Lending

NOTE: If the applicant completes both Accounting and Economics, only two courses from Group 6 are required.

As an alternative to the experience requirements, the applicant may submit evidence of graduation from a four-year university or college accredited by the Western Association of Schools and Colleges or similar regional accrediting agency recognized by the United States Department of Education, and completion of the required real estate courses.

Some private vocational schools offer these required courses, both in residence (classroom) and through correspondence study. However, only those private schools formally approved by DRE may offer these courses for DRE credit.

Experience Qualification

Many candidates for a real estate broker license base their claims of qualification on two years of experience as a licensed real estate salesperson in California. However, even though DRE's records show the applicant has been licensed for two or more years as a salesperson, that fact does not in itself qualify the applicant. Evidence that an applicant has worked full time as a salesperson for at least two years must be provided by the applicant's employing broker(s), using an Employment Verification (RE 226). The completed verification forms must be mailed with the application. If applicant is unable to obtain certification of experience from the employing broker, experience may be corroborated, on an

Employment Certification (RE 228), by at least two other individuals who were employed in a related real estate field and were in a position to verify the applicant's duties and employment dates, etc. An explanation should be included as to why the employing broker of record cannot verify the salesperson's experience.

The Employment Verification and Employment Certification forms should include sufficient detail to enable DRE to perform an evaluation. DRE may conduct further inquiry in order to evaluate claimed experience.

Alternate Qualification Methods

A claim of equivalent experience, in lieu of the two years of salesperson experience required for the broker examination, may be based on any combination of salesperson experience, equivalent real estate related experience and education, which, considered as a whole, would satisfy the intent of the law.

Claims of equivalent real estate related experience may be made by submitting a completed Equivalent Experience Verification (RE 227). This form must be certified by employers or other responsible parties who have been in a position to verify the applicant's employment status. The verification must include a clear, detailed description of the applicant's duties/activities, as they relate to the general field of real estate. Further information concerning the types of equivalent experience which are considered acceptable for qualification purposes is contained in the most recent edition of the *Instructions to License Applicants* pamphlet that may be obtained at any DRE office or on-line at www.dre.ca.gov.

If an applicant has been licensed as a real estate salesperson in another state, RE 226 must be used to verify previous salesperson experience. If an applicant has been licensed as a real estate broker in another state, two responsible parties, such as other real estate brokers, title officers or loan officers, who have been in a position to verify the applicant's employment status, must complete RE 228. The verification must include a clear, detailed description of the applicant's duties/activities and indicate how the verifier is aware of the applicant's employment record.

Claims of qualification based on a college degree with specialization in subjects relating strictly to real estate must be supported by official transcripts of educational records.

In some instances, applicants may be in a position to claim qualification by combining certain experience and education. For example, the applicant may have been actively engaged as a licensed salesperson in California for one year, had additional experience as an escrow officer or a loan officer, and also had certain education relating to real estate. In such cases, a combination claim for experience can be made.

All claims of experience qualification for real estate broker license, including those based upon two years of full-time work as a licensed salesperson in California, are individually evaluated. The Commissioner decides whether the claim of qualification meets the Commissioner's standards. If the claim is approved, the candidate is scheduled for examination. If rejected, the candidate may eventually qualify for a real estate broker license examination by working the required time as a salesperson. Often a claim of qualification is rejected but the applicant is given a certain amount of credit toward two years as a salesperson. Care in preparing the claim of qualification and the required verification forms will facilitate the experience review process. DRE may conduct further inquiry when evaluating experience.

The applicant who fails to qualify for a license because of lack of experience and/or educational prerequisites is not entitled to a refund of the fee paid with the application. The fee, however, remains to the applicant's credit for two years.

Examination for Original Broker License
All applicants for an original broker license must take and pass a written qualifying examination before the license can be granted.

The appropriate fee must be submitted with a Broker Examination Application (RE 400B). An applicant failing the examination may apply for reexamination and must pay the appropriate fee. There is no limit to the number of reexaminations which may be taken but an application is valid for only two years. A person who fails to pass the examination during this two-year period must file a new application. The application must include documentation which supports the qualification of the applicant.

If an applicant does not take the examination on the date scheduled, or wishes to change the scheduled date, a new examination may be scheduled by completing, signing, and returning the Broker Examination Schedule Notice (RE 401B) to DRE. The rescheduling request may also be made on an Broker Examination Change Application (RE 415B). The first request for a new examination date must be submitted with the appropriate rescheduling fee.

An applicant who passes the examination is notified and may apply for the original broker license.

CORPORATE REAL ESTATE LICENSE

In some cases, brokers will elect to do business as a corporation. A corporation may be licensed as a real estate broker, provided at least one officer of the corporation is a duly qualified real estate broker willing to act as the corporation's responsible designated broker-officer. The corporation must submit, along with the appropriate corporation license application and fee, a *Certificate of Status issued* by the Secretary of State within 30 days prior to the date the application is filed and a statement of officers as filed with the Secretary of State.

Broker-Officers
Each broker who is to act for and on behalf of a corporation as a broker-officer must submit a completed Corporation License Application and the appropriate license fee. Broker-officer applicants who currently hold an officer license for a corporation but have never obtained an individual broker license will be required to furnish evidence of completion of the current continuing education requirements which have been attained within the previous four years.

Corporation Background Statement
The designated officer of an original corporation license applicant must submit a completed Corporation Background Statement (RE 212) for himself or herself and

for each director, the chief executive officer, the president, first level vice presidents, secretary, chief financial officer, subordinate officers with responsibility for forming policy of the corporation and for each natural person owning or controlling more than 10% of the corporation's shares, if that person has been subject to one of the conditions listed in subdivision (a) of Regulation 2746. (See Regulation 2746.) Also, an RE 212 is required whenever there is a change in

corporation officers. A copy of the corporate statement of officers as filed with the Secretary of State, or as amended by corporate resolution to reflect the present corporation officers must be submitted with the RE 212.

Certificate of Qualification - Foreign Corporation
In the case of a foreign corporation, a *Certificate of Qualification is* required, executed within thirty days prior to the date the corporation submits its application.

Fictitious Business Name (dba)
To use any name other than its own, the corporation must submit a copy of a Fictitious Business Name Statement as filed with the county clerk's office in the county where the corporation's principal place of business is located. (Section 10159.5 of the Code)

Salesperson Licensed to Corporation
The corporation must submit a completed Salesperson Change Application (RE 214) for each currently licensed salesperson to be placed in the employ of the corporation.

Replacing the Designated Broker-Officer
The designated broker-officer of a corporation may be replaced by another qualified broker for the balance of the license period by submitting: (a) a completed Corporation License Application (RE 201) and Corporation Background Statement (RE 212); and (b) a copy of the personally signed resignation of the officer leaving the firm, or a copy of the Resolution of the Board of Directors with the corporate seal, or a signed statement giving the date of death of the currently licensed designated broker-officer. To keep the corporation continuously licensed, the RE 201, RE 212, and the resignation documentation must be received in the same package.

Adding A New Officer as the Designated Officer
A new designated officer may be licensed upon receipt of a completed Corporation License Application, Corporation Background Statement, the appropriate license fee and statement that the currently designated broker-officer will remain with the firm as an "additional" officer. Broker-officer applicants without individual broker status will be required to furnish evidence of completion of appropriate continuing education requirements, attained within the previous four-year period. DRE will issue branch licenses to match the term of the new "designated" officer without any additional fee.

Change Of Designated Officer When Both Currently Hold A Broker-Officer License With Corporation
To effect this change, the corporation must submit a completed Corporation Change Application and Corporation Background Statement. No new license

certificate will be issued to either officer. However, if the license terms differ, new branch office licenses will be issued.

Change of Main Office or Mailing Address
Submit a completed Corporation Change Application signed by a licensed officer.

Change of Corporation Name
Submit a completed Corporation Change Application signed by a licensed officer and a copy of the Amended Articles of Incorporation reflecting the name change and bearing the endorsed or filed stamp of the California Secretary of State. If the corporation is currently licensed with a fictitious business name, a copy of the refiled Fictitious Business Name Statement showing the new corporation name as registrant must be submitted.

ORIGINAL SALESPERSON LICENSE

This license is required for an individual who is to be employed as a salesperson under the control and supervision of a licensed broker. The license permits licensed activity only while in the employ of a broker. Salesperson licenses must be available for inspection in the broker's main office (Commissioner's Regulation 2753). The salesperson can be compensated for work as an agent only by the salesperson's employing broker. (Sections 10132 and 10137 of the Code)

License Requirements
A candidate for an original real estate salesperson license must: (1) be at least 18 years old; (2) make application on a form prescribed by the Commissioner; (3) be honest and truthful; and (4) pass a qualifying examination as required. The applicant must, prior to the examination, complete a statutory three semester-unit or four quarter-unit college-level course in real estate principles, and, either prior to issuance of the original license or within 18 months after issuance, complete two additional basic real estate courses selected from the following:

- real estate practice
- real estate appraisal
- accounting
- business law
- property management
- mortgage loan brokering/lending
- legal aspects of real estate
- real estate finance
- real estate economics
- escrows
- real estate office administration

All courses must be three semester-unit or four quarter-unit courses from an institution of higher learning accredited by the Western Association of Schools and Colleges or similar regional accrediting agency recognized by the United States Department of Education, or an equivalent course of study offered by a private vocational school approved by DRE.

The application for a salesperson examination must be made on RE 400A and be accompanied by the appropriate examination fee.

There is no limitation on the number of reexaminations which may be taken by the candidate who fails the qualifying examination. Each examination application must include the reexamination fee.

An applicant who fails to take the examination on the scheduled date may apply for another examination date by completing, signing and submitting the Salesperson Examination Schedule Notice (RE 401A), along with the appropriate fee. The rescheduling request can also be made on a Salesperson Examination Change Application (RE 415A).

An applicant who successfully passes the salesperson examination may apply for a four-year original license by submitting, within one year of the examination date, an application for the real estate salesperson license (RE 202) together with the appropriate license fee, one fully completed classifiable fingerprint card, the fingerprint processing fee, and transcripts showing completion of the remaining required courses. If the applicant does not submit evidence of completion of the two remaining required courses when applying for the license, the applicant must pay a higher license fee and will be issued an 18-month conditional license. If evidence of completion of the remaining two college-level courses is not submitted within 18 months of the date the license is issued, the license will be automatically suspended. The suspension can be lifted by submitting the required course information up to four years from the date the license was issued. If the course information is not submitted by that date, the license may not be renewed and the applicant would have to requalify through the examination process in order to obtain a new license.

LICENSE RENEWALS - BROKERS AND SALESPERSONS

All real estate licenses are issued for a period of four years. A license is renewable without examination upon submittal of the appropriate fee and evidence of completion of the required continuing education. The application for license renewal must be postmarked prior to midnight of the expiration date of the current license to avoid a lapse in licensure and payment of a late renewal fee. For the purpose of determining the date of mailing, postage meter stamps are not considered evidence of a postmark by the U.S. Postal Service.

If a broker's license expires, all licensed activities of the broker must cease and the broker's salespersons are immediately placed in a non-working status. Any branch office licenses are cancelled. The broker must then re-activate the license of each salesperson to the broker's employ by submitting a Salesperson Change Application (RE 214). The broker must re-activate any branch office licenses by submitting a Branch Office Application (RE 203).

An individual with a conditional salesperson license which has been suspended may renew the license only by submitting evidence of completion of the required college-level semester-unit courses within four years of the date the license was issued. These courses are separate from continuing education courses.

Late Renewal

The holder of a license who fails to renew it prior to the expiration of the period for which it was issued may renew it within two years from such expiration by submitting a proper application, evidence of completion of the current continuing education requirements, and the appropriate late renewal fee. Of course, there can be no licensed activity between the date of license expiration and the date of late renewal. A commission may not be claimed without a valid license.

An individual with a conditional salesperson license which has been suspended and who does not submit evidence of completion of the two required college-level semester-unit courses within four years of the date the license was issued may not renew the license on a late basis. (Section 10154 of the Code)

Two years after a license expires, all license rights lapse. The individual will be required to requalify through the examination process before being licensed in real estate.

OTHER LICENSE INFORMATION

Social Security Number
Effective January 1, 1995, an original or renewal license may not be issued to any individual who has not provided a social security number. This requirement applies to real estate broker and officer licenses, real estate salesperson licenses, pre-paid rental listing licenses, and existing mineral, oil, and gas licenses. The requirement does not apply to corporations with regard to a federal tax identification number.

Child Support Obligors
In accordance with Section 11350.6 of the Welfare and Institutions Code, DRE is precluded from issuing or renewing a full-term license if the applicant is on a list of persons (obligors) who have not complied with a court order to provide child support payments. Additionally, a license may be suspended if a licensee's name remains on the list 150 days after notice. Information concerning such individuals is provided to DRE by the Department of Social Services, which obtains the information from the district attorney of each county in California.

A 150-day temporary license may be issued to an otherwise qualified applicant who is on the list of child support obligors. The applicant will be advised that the license applied for cannot be issued unless a release is obtained from the district attorney's office during the 150-day temporary license period. If the applicant fails to submit an appropriate release to DRE from the district attorney's office within the 150-day period, all license rights cease. Only one 150-day temporary license may be issued. License fees submitted are not refundable. In order to be issued another license, all applicable statutory provisions must be met and another licensing fee would have to be submitted. Renewal applicants may have to submit a late renewal fee.

DRE is regularly provided with a supplemental list of obligors which identify individuals who are more than four months delinquent in child support payments and which is matched against DRE's total license population. If there is a match of an existing licensee and the license is not due for renewal for at least six months, the licensee will be advised that the license will be suspended if the delinquency is not cleared within 150 days. The suspension will remain in effect until the delinquency is cleared.

DRE will assess a $95 fee when the name of a license applicant or licensee appears on a child support obligor list or supplemental list.

Non-Working Status

A salesperson may be issued and hold a license (but not perform acts requiring a license) without being in the employ of a broker. The license will be assigned non-working status until DRE is properly notified that the salesperson is employed by a broker.

Mineral, Oil and Gas Licenses

Effective January 1, 1994, DRE no longer issues original mineral, oil, and gas (MOG) broker licenses or permits. MOG activities, as defined in Sections 10507 and 10581 of the Code, can be performed by currently licensed MOG brokers, or by licensed real estate brokers. Licensed MOG brokers may apply for license renewal.

Partnerships

DRE does not issue partnership licenses. A partnership may perform acts for which a real estate broker license is required, provided every partner through whom the partnership so acts is a licensed real estate broker.

Broker members of a partnership formed by written agreement may operate from branch offices of the partnership without obtaining an individual branch office license, provided one member of the partnership is licensed at that location. (Commissioner's Regulation 2728)

A salesperson whose employing broker is a member of a partnership formed by written agreement may perform licensed acts on behalf of the partnership from any branch office maintained by any one of the partners.

Restricted License

There are certain types of restricted licenses sometimes issued by the Commissioner when a license has been suspended, revoked or denied after a hearing. In effect, they are probationary licenses and contain specific restrictions.

The Commissioner can restrict licenses by: term (one month, three months, etc.); employment by a particular broker (for a salesperson); limitation to a certain area or type of activity; requiring detailed reports of each transaction; requiring the filing of a surety bond; other conditions or combinations of conditions.

Fees

License or examination fees must accompany the application for the different types of examination or licenses. Applicants or other interested parties should contact any DRE district office or visit DRE's Web site at www.dre.ca.gov to obtain information on the current examination or license application fees.

By law, fees paid to DRE in connection with licenses and examinations are not refundable (Section 10207). Therefore, a change of mind on the part of the applicant, rejection of a broker license examination application, examination failure or failure to appear to take an examination will *not* result in refund of all or any part of the fee paid.

There are no fees to implement the following: address change; salesperson employment transfer; personal or corporate name change; adding or deleting fictitious business name; branch office; and duplicate license certificate.

Because of statutory mandates, license fees are likely to change frequently. Always check to ensure you are submitting the correct fees.

CONTINUING EDUCATION

All license renewal applicants must prove compliance with the continuing education (CE) requirements. Except for the first renewal of a real estate salesperson, all renewal applicants must satisfactorily complete a total of 45 clock-hours of approved offerings within the four-year period immediately preceding license renewal. See Section 10170, et seq. of the Code.

For current information on the CE requirements, a licensee may contact DRE's Licensing Information Section [P.O. Box 187000, Sacramento, CA 95818-7000, (916) 227-0931] or obtain from any DRE office a copy of the brochure "Instructions to License Applicants."

Renewal Procedure
Information regarding successful completion must be listed on a Continuing Education Course Verification (RE 251) and forwarded with the application for renewal. DRE does not accept an application for license renewal earlier than 60 days prior to the expiration of the license.

Exclusion from CE Requirement
An individual who has been a licensee in good standing for 30 continuous years in this State and who is 70 years of age or older is exempt from the CE requirement.

List of Approved Sponsors and Their Offerings
A list of approved sponsors and their offerings may be reviewed, but not purchased, at any DRE office. You may purchase a list by sending a Request for CE Course List Request (RE 301), along with the fee indicated on that form, to:

Department of Real Estate
Education Section
P.O. Box 187000
Sacramento, CA 95818-7000

MISCELLANEOUS INFORMATION

Main Office Address Change
A broker engaged in activities requiring a license must maintain an office or definite place of business in California. The broker's license and the licenses of any salespersons employed by the broker must be available for inspection by the Commissioner or a designated representative at the broker's principal place of business.

A broker who changes his/her main office address must forward a written notice to DRE in Sacramento not later than the next business day, using a Broker Change Application (RE 204) [or Corporation Change Application (RE 204A)]. No fee is required. The license certificate may be corrected by the licensee by striking out the old address and typing or writing the new address in ink and dating and initialing the change. The broker may obtain a new license certificate reflecting the address change by requesting a duplicate license on RE 204 or RE 204A.

Branch Office

This is the license required for each additional business location if a broker maintains more than one place of business in the State. The branch office license permits full operation from that office and must be available for inspection at the branch location. Branch office licenses may be added or deleted by using RE 203 (Branch Office Application). No fee is required. A new license is issued for each additional branch office.

Fictitious Business Name

An individual or corporate broker can operate under a fictitious business name (dba) after DRE issues a license bearing the fictitious name. Before that license can be issued the individual or corporation must forward to DRE a copy of the fictitious business name statement (FBNS) as filed with the county clerk in the county where the broker maintains the principal business address (See Section 17900 et seq. of the Business and Professions Code). The broker must appear as the registrant on the FBNS. The broker must forward the appropriate change application (RE 204 for individual broker; RE 204A for corporation) to DRE with the FBNS. The addition of a dba to a broker's license does not affect the licenses of the salespersons in the broker's employ.

An application for a license bearing a fictitious business name may be denied if the name:

1. is misleading or would constitute false advertising.

2. implies a partnership or corporation when a partnership or corporation does not exist.

3. includes the name of a real estate salesperson.

4. constitutes a violation of the provisions of Sections 17910, 17910.5, or 17917 of the Code.

5. is the name formerly used by a licensee whose license has been revoked.

6. contains the word or designation "bank," "banker," "trust," "trustee," "trust company," "insurance" or "assurance," "escrow," or "savings."

A broker desiring to use more than one fictitious business name is required to submit a change application (RE 204 or RE 204A) and a copy of the FBNS filed with the county clerk for each fictitious business name. Each fictitious business name is an addition to the existing license, and the right to use it will expire at the same time as the license. The broker's main office license certificate will then display on its face the multiple fictitious business names. All other business locations will be designated as branch offices. A broker may use, and salespersons may work under, any fictitious business name at any business location maintained by the broker.

An FBNS expires at the end of five years from December 31 of the year in which it was filed in the office of the county clerk. When a new statement is required because the prior statement has expired, it need not be published unless there has been a change in the information required in the expired statement.

If a broker or corporation changes the licensed name and has a dba, a new fictitious business name statement must be submitted for each dba, with the new license name shown as the registrant.

Mailing Addresses

All mailings from DRE will be addressed to the mailing address provided by the licensee. A separate mailing address may be provided which is distinct from the business address of record. Brokers are required to notify DRE whenever a change of address occurs for the broker's principal place of business or any branch office not later than the next business day following the change. Salespersons are required to maintain on file the address of the principal place of business of the broker who employs the salesperson. Brokers and salespersons are required to maintain their mailing address of record on file at all times while licensed and during the duration of the two-year late renewal grace period. In order to file a change of address notification, a licensee must forward to DRE the appropriate change application (RE 204 for broker licensees or RE 214 for salesperson licensees) for each license affected. Mailing addresses are public information and are available in a list format.

Non-Resident Information

License applicants or licensees who are out of state residents must file a signed and notarized Consent To Service of Process (RE 234). Brokers are required to maintain a California business address if engaging in licensed activities in California. If a broker does not engage in licensed activities in California, the broker must file an Out of State Broker Acknowledgment (RE 235). Salespersons must be licensed with a California broker if engaging in business in California.

Transfer of Salesperson License

To effect a transfer of employment, a salesperson and the former and new employing brokers must take the following steps:

1. The former employing broker must immediately notify DRE Licensing in Sacramento in writing. (Section 10161.8 of the Code)

2. The former employer gives the transferring salesperson his/her license certificate and signs a Salesperson Change Application (RE 214).

3. Within five days, the salesperson and the new employing broker complete RE 214 (Salesperson Change Application) and send it to the Department of Real Estate, P.O. Box 187003, Sacramento 95818-7003. A new license certificate will not be issued.

Termination of Salesperson for Violation

When a salesperson is terminated by an employing broker for a violation of any of the provisions of the Real Estate Law, the employing broker must immediately file a certified written statement of the facts with DRE. (Section 10178 of the Code)

Effect of Revocation or Suspension

When a real estate broker license is revoked or suspended, the licenses of every real estate salesperson in the broker's employ are automatically canceled. Such salespersons may transfer their licenses to a new employing broker.

Loss of License Status

This may occur when a person holding a license allows two years to elapse from the expiration date without applying for (late) renewal, submitting evidence of completion of the continuing education requirements, and paying the required fee. Loss of license status also occurs if a salesperson is issued a conditional license which is suspended by operation of the law (Section 10153.4 of the Code) and the individual fails to submit evidence of the remaining two required college-level courses within four years from the date the license was issued. A third example of loss of license status occurs if a license is revoked.

PREPAID RENTAL LISTING SERVICE LICENSE (PRLS)

A PRLS is in the business of supplying prospective tenants with listings of residential real property for rent while collecting a fee at the same time or in advance of the time the listings are provided. A PRLS does *not* negotiate rental or lease agreements. Sections 10167-10167.17 of the Code and Regulations 2850-2853 define this activity and contain the PRLS licensing requirements.

ENFORCEMENT OF REAL ESTATE LAW

A licensing and regulatory law is effective only to the extent of its enforcement. The Commissioner, as the chief officer of the Department, is duty bound to enforce the provisions of the Real Estate Law.

The Commissioner shall upon a verified written complaint, or may, upon the Commissioner's own motion, investigate the actions of any person engaged in the business or acting in the capacity of a licensee within this state, and has the power to suspend or revoke the real estate license. The Commissioner also has the authority to deny a license to an applicant if the applicant does not meet the full requirements of the law. Through a screening process (including the fingerprint record) of an applicant for a license, if it is ascertained that the applicant has a criminal record or some other record that may reflect on the applicant's character, an investigation is made by the Commissioner's staff. A formal hearing may be ordered to determine whether or not the applicant meets the requirements of honesty and truthfulness. The Commissioner also has the authority to require evidence of honesty and truthfulness of officers, directors and persons who own or control more than 10% of the shares of the applicant for a corporate real estate brokerage license.

Generally speaking, an investigation of a licensee is based upon a written statement from one who believes he or she has been wronged by a licensee who was acting in the capacity of an agent. The following investigative procedures are followed by the Commissioner's staff: statements are obtained from witnesses, if any; a statement may be obtained from the licensee involved; bank records, title company records and public records are checked as necessary. As part of the investigation, an informal conference may be called, and all parties concerned may be requested to attend for the purpose of determining the validity and seriousness of the complaint. If it appears that the complaint is of a serious nature and that a violation of law has occurred, an accusation is filed and there may be a formal hearing which could result in suspension or revocation of the license.

Formal Hearings

The formal hearing is conducted in accordance with procedures set forth in the Administrative Procedure Act. The accusation or statement of issues is served upon the affected licensee, who is informed of the rights of an accused. In the hearing, the Commissioner becomes the complainant, and brings the charges against the licensee. The original complainant usually becomes a witness. The licensee, known as the respondent in the hearing procedure, may appear with or without counsel. A record is made of the proceedings and the hearing is conducted according to rules of evidence. Testimony is taken under oath. An administrative law judge from the Office of Administrative Hearings hears the case. The Commissioner's case is presented by the Commissioner's counsel. The administrative law judge issues a proposed decision based upon the findings. The Commissioner may reject or accept the proposed decision, or reduce the proposed penalty and make an official decision. The respondent may petition for reconsideration, and has the right of appeal through the courts.

If the charges are not sustained at the hearing, they are dismissed. On the other hand, if the testimony substantiates the charges and they appear to be sufficiently serious, the license of the respondent is suspended or revoked. After a license is revoked, the person affected may not apply for reinstatement of the license until one year has passed.

Representatives of the Commissioner also investigate persons or firms who appear to be operating improperly, or without benefit of a license, or who subdivide land without complying with the subdivision laws enforced by the Commissioner. If sufficient evidence of a violation is obtained, an Order to Desist and Refrain is issued, or a complaint is brought and the parties are prosecuted in a court of competent jurisdiction.

Violations

Sections 10176 and 10177 of the Code constitute the foundation for most license suspensions or revocations. Section 10176 is concerned with the actions of a real estate licensee performing or attempting to perform any of the licensed acts within the scope of the Real Estate Law. As a general rule, the licensee must have been acting as an agent in a real estate transaction before the section will apply. The provisions of some parts of Section 10177, on the other hand, will apply to situations where the licensee was not necessarily acting as an agent. The following is a brief discussion of the various grounds for disciplinary action against a licensee and the reasons for which a real estate license may be denied:

Misrepresentation. Section 10176(a). Many complaints received by the Commissioner allege misrepresentation on the part of the broker or salesperson. Included also as a cause for discipline under this section is failure of a broker or salesperson to disclose to his or her principal material facts of which the principal should be made aware. If the misrepresentation was not important, and the person to whom it was made would have proceeded with the transaction anyway, the misrepresentation probably would not be material. However, an Attorney General's opinion holds that damage or injury need not be present to support an action under this section. The reason is that the California Real Estate Law concerns the conduct of licensees rather than the settling of disputes about damages or injuries between licensees and their clients.

False promise. Section 10176(b). A false promise and a misrepresentation are not the same thing. A misrepresentation is a false statement of fact. A false promise is a false statement about what the promisor is going to do. Many times a false promise is proved by showing that the promise was impossible to perform and that the person making the promise knew it was impossible.

Continued misrepresentation. Section 10176(c). This section gives the Commissioner the right to discipline a licensee for "a continued and flagrant course of misrepresentation or making of false promises through real estate agents or salespersons."

Dual agency. Section 10176(d). Failure to inform all principals that the licensee is acting as agent for more than one party in the transaction.

Commingling. Section 10176(e). Commingling takes place when a broker has mixed the funds of a principal with the broker's own money. (Conversion is misappropriating and *using* principal's funds. Conversion, of course, can be a more serious offense.)

Definite termination date. Section 10176(f). Failure to include a specified termination date on all exclusive listings relating to transactions for which a real estate license is required. The exclusive listing itself must be clear as to expiration.

Secret profit. Section 10176(g). Secret profit cases usually arise when the broker, who already has a higher offer from another buyer, makes a low offer, usually through a "dummy" purchaser. The broker then sells the property to the interested buyer for the higher price. The difference is the secret profit.

Listing-option. Section 10176(h). A licensee who has used a form which is both an option and a listing must inform the principal of the amount of profit the licensee will make, and must obtain the written consent of the principal approving the amount of such profit, before the licensee may exercise the option. This section does not apply where a licensee is using an option only.

Dishonest dealing. Section 10176(i). "Dishonest dealing" is a sort of catch-all section similar in many ways to Section 10177(f). The difference is that under Section 10176(i) the acts must have been those requiring a license, while there is no such need under Section 10177(f).

Signatures of prospective purchasers. Section 10176(j). Brokers must obtain a written authorization to sell from a business owner before securing the signature of a prospective purchaser to any agreement providing for compensation to the broker if the purchaser buys the business.

Obtaining a license by fraud. Section 10177(a). Misstatements of fact in an application for a license; procurement of a license by fraud, misrepresentation, or deceit (e.g., failure to reveal a previous criminal record).

Convictions. Section 10177(b). Criminal conviction for either a felony or a misdemeanor which involves moral turpitude and is substantially related to the qualifications, functions, or duties of a real estate licensee. A court has defined moral turpitude as "everything done contrary to justice, honesty, modesty, or good morals."

False advertising. Section 10177 (c). Includes subdivision sales as well as general property sales.

Violations of other sections. Section 10177(d). This section is the Department's authority to proceed against the licensee for violation of any of the other sections of the Real Estate Law, the Regulations of the Commissioner, and the Subdivided Lands Law.

Misuse of trade name. Section 10177(e). Use of any trade name or insignia of membership in any real estate organization if the licensee is not a member of that organization.

Conduct warranting denial. Section 10177(f). An essential requirement to the issuance of a license is that the applicant be honest and truthful. If any of the acts of a licensee establish that a licensee is not possessed of these characteristics, Section 10177(f) will apply. This section also provides for disciplinary actions when a real estate licensee has either had a license denied or a license issued by another agency of this state, another state, or the federal government, revoked or suspended for acts which if done by a real estate licensee would be grounds for the suspension or revocation of a California real estate license.

Negligence or incompetence. Section 10177(g). The Department proceeds in those cases where the licensee is so careless or unqualified that to allow the licensee to handle a transaction would endanger the interests of clients or customers.

Supervision of salespersons. Section 10177(h). Disciplinary action may result if a broker fails to exercise reasonable supervision over the activities of the broker's salespersons.

Violating government trust. Section 10177(i). Using Government employment to violate the confidential nature of records thereby made available.

Other dishonest conduct. Section 10177(j). Any other conduct which constitutes fraud or dishonest dealing.

Restricted license violation. Section 10177(k). Violation of the terms, conditions, restrictions and limitations contained in any order granting a restricted license.

Inducement of panic selling. Section 10177(l). To solicit or induce the sale, lease, or the listing for sale or lease, of residential property on the grounds, wholly or in part, of loss of value, increase in crime, or decline in the quality of the schools due to the present or prospective entry into the neighborhood of a person or persons of another race, color, religion, ancestry or national origin.

Violation of Franchise Investment Law. Section 10177(m). Violation of any of the provisions of the Franchise Investment Law (Division 5 commencing with

Section 31000) of Title 4 of the Corporations Code) or any regulations of the Corporations Commissioner pertaining thereto.

Violation of Corporations Code. Section 10177(n). Violation of any of the provisions of the Corporations Code or of the regulations of the Commissioner of Corporations relating to securities as specified in Section 25206 of the Corporations Code.

Failure to disclose ownership interest. Section 10177(o). Failure to disclose to buyer the nature and extent of ownership interest a licensee has in property which is the subject of a transaction in which the licensee is an agent for the buyer. Also, failure to disclose such ownership on the part of licensee's relative or special acquaintance *or* entity in which licensee has ownership interest.

Other Penalty Sections
There are additional sections in the Business and Professions Code which provide for the revocation or suspension of licenses. These violations could be included under Section 10177(d) of the law. The following are brief summaries:

Sections 10137 and 10138 - employing or compensating any unlicensed person to perform acts requiring a license.

Section 10140 - false advertising.

Section 10140.6 - advertising of acts which require a license must contain a designation disclosing that the licensee is performing such acts.

Section 10141 - broker must cause notice of sales price to be given to both buyers and sellers within one month after the sale is completed.

Section 10141.5 specifies a broker's responsibility for recording trust deeds.

Section 10142 - licensee must give a copy of any contract to the party signing it at the time it is signed.

Section 10145 specifies licensee's responsibilities in handling trust funds.

Section 10148 requires retention and availability for inspection and copying of all listings, deposit receipts, cancelled checks, trust records, etc. for a three year period.

Section 10160 - brokers shall retain and make available for inspection the licenses of salespersons in the broker's employ.

Section 10161.8 - broker must notify DRE when a salesperson is employed or terminated.

Section 10162 - all active brokers must maintain a definite place of business in the State of California.

Section 10163 - brokers maintaining more than one place of business must first procure branch office license(s).

Section 10165 - failure to make licenses available for inspection and to maintain a place of business.

Section 10167 requires the licensing of individuals, other than real estate licensees, engaged in prepaid rental listing services and makes a willful violation of the law a misdemeanor.

Section 10176.5 - violation of any of the Civil Code Sections (1102, et seq.) which deal with use of the Real Property Transfer Disclosure Statement.

Section 10177.1 - suspension without hearing if license procured by fraud, misrepresentation, deceit, or by the making of any material misstatement of fact in the application for license.

Section 10177.2 violations while performing acts under Section 10131.6 (mobilehome sales).

Section 10177.4 - compensation for referring customers to escrow, pest control, home warranty, title insurer or underwritten title company or controlled escrow company.

Section 10177.5 - final judgment in a civil action against a licensee upon the grounds of fraud, misrepresentation or deceit.

Section 10178 - broker terminates a salesperson for cause and then fails to notify the Commissioner.

Section 10475 - automatic suspension of a real estate license if the Commissioner pays a claim against a licensee from the Recovery Account. No license reinstatement until full reimbursement to the fund, with interest.

Examples of Unlawful Conduct - Sale, Lease, or Exchange
In a sale, lease, or exchange transaction, conduct such as the following may result in license discipline under Sections 10176 or 10177 of the Business and Professions Code:

1. Knowingly making a substantial misrepresentation of the likely value of real property to:

    A. Its owner either for the purpose of securing a listing or for the purpose of acquiring an interest in the property for the licensee's own account.

    B. A prospective buyer for the purpose of inducing the buyer to make an offer to purchase the real property.

2. Representing to an owner of real property when seeking a listing that the licensee has obtained a bona fide written offer to purchase the property, unless at the time of the representation the licensee has possession of a bona fide written offer to purchase.

3. Stating or implying to an owner of real property during listing negotiations that the licensee is precluded by law, by regulation, or by the rules of any organization, other than the broker firm seeking the listing, from charging less than the commission or fee quoted to the owner by the licensee.

4. Knowingly making substantial misrepresentations regarding the licensee's relationship with an individual broker, corporate broker, or franchised

brokerage company or that entity's/person's responsibility for the licensee's activities.

5. Knowingly underestimating the probable closing costs in a communication to the prospective buyer or seller of real property in order to induce that person to make or to accept an offer to purchase the property.

6. Knowingly making a false or misleading representation to the seller of real property as to the form, amount and/or treatment of a deposit toward the purchase of the property made by an offeror.

7. Knowingly making a false or misleading representation to a seller of real property, who has agreed to finance all or part of a purchase price by carrying back a loan, about a buyer's ability to repay the loan in accordance with its terms and conditions.

8. Making an addition to or modification of the terms of an instrument previously signed or initialed by a party to a transaction without the knowledge and consent of the party.

9. A representation made as a principal or agent to a prospective purchaser of a promissory note secured by real property about the market value of the securing property without a reasonable basis for believing the truth and accuracy of the representation.

10. Knowingly making a false or misleading representation or representing, without a reasonable basis for believing its truth, the nature and/or condition of the interior or exterior features of a property when soliciting an offer.

11. Knowingly making a false or misleading representation or representing, without a reasonable basis for believing its truth, the size of a parcel, square footage of improvements or the location of the boundary lines of real property being offered for sale, lease or exchange.

12. Knowingly making a false or misleading representation or representing to a prospective buyer or lessee of real property, without a reasonable basis to believe its truth, that the property can be used for certain purposes with the intent of inducing the prospective buyer or lessee to acquire an interest in the real property.

13. When acting in the capacity of an agent in a transaction for the sale, lease or exchange of real property, failing to disclose to a prospective purchaser or lessee facts known to the licensee materially affecting the value or desirability of the property, when the licensee has reason to believe that such facts are not known to nor readily observable by a prospective purchaser or lessee.

14. Willfully failing, when acting as a listing agent, to present or cause to be presented to the owner of the property any written offer to purchase received prior to the closing of a sale, unless expressly instructed by the owner not to present such an offer, or unless the offer is patently frivolous.

15. When acting as the listing agent, presenting competing written offers to purchase real property to the owner in such a manner as to induce the owner to accept the offer which will provide the greatest compensation to the listing

broker without regard to the benefits, advantages and/or disadvantages to the owner.

16. Failing to explain to the parties or prospective parties to a real estate transaction for whom the licensee is acting as an agent the meaning and probable significance of a contingency in an offer or contract that the licensee knows or reasonably believes may affect the closing date of the transaction, or the timing of the vacating of the property by the seller or its occupancy by the buyer.

17. Failing to disclose to the seller of real property in a transaction in which the licensee is an agent for the seller the nature and extent of any direct or indirect interest that the licensee expects to acquire as a result of the sale. (The licensee should disclose to the seller: prospective purchase of the property by a person related to the licensee by blood or marriage; purchase by an entity in which the licensee has an ownership interest; or purchase by any other person with whom the licensee occupies a special relationship where there is a reasonable probability that the licensee could be indirectly acquiring an interest in the property.)

18. Failing to disclose to the buyer of real property in a transaction in which the licensee is an agent for the buyer the nature and extent of a licensee's direct or indirect ownership interest in such real property: e.g., the direct or indirect ownership interest in the property by a person related to the licensee by blood or marriage; by an entity in which the licensee has an ownership interest; or by any other person with whom the licensee occupies a special relationship.

19. Failing to disclose to a principal for whom the licensee is acting as an agent any significant interest the licensee has in a particular entity when the licensee recommends the use of the services or products of such entity.

Examples of Unlawful Conduct - Loan Transactions
Conduct such as the following when soliciting, negotiating or arranging a loan secured by real property or the sale of a promissory note secured by real property may result in license discipline:

1. Knowingly misrepresenting to a prospective borrower of a loan to be secured by real property or to an assignor/endorser of a promissory note secured by real property that there is an existing lender willing to make the loan or that there is a purchaser for the note, for the purpose of inducing the borrower or assignor/endorser to utilize the services of the licensee.

2. Knowingly making a false or misleading representation to a prospective lender or purchaser of a loan secured directly or collaterally by real property about a borrower's ability to repay the loan in accordance with its terms and conditions.

3. Failing to disclose to a prospective lender or note purchaser information about the prospective borrower's identity, occupation, employment, income and credit data as represented to the broker by the prospective borrower.

4. Failing to disclose information known to the broker relative to the ability of the borrower to meet his or her potential or existing contractual obligations

under the note or contract including information known about the borrower's payment history on an existing note, whether the note is in default or the borrower in bankruptcy.

5. Knowingly underestimating the probable closing costs in a communication to a prospective borrower or lender of a loan to be secured by a lien on real property for the purpose of inducing the borrower or lender to enter into the loan transaction.

6. When soliciting a prospective lender to make a loan to be secured by real property, falsely representing or representing without a reasonable basis to believe its truth, the priority of the security, as a lien against the real property securing the loan, i.e., a first, second or third deed of trust.

7. Knowingly misrepresenting in any transaction that a specific service is free when the licensee knows or has a reasonable basis to know that it is covered by a fee to be charged as part of the transaction.

8. Knowingly making a false or misleading representation to a lender or assignee/endorsee of a lender of a loan secured directly or collaterally by a lien on real property about the amount and treatment of loan payments, including loan payoffs, and the failure to account to the lender or assignee/endorsee of a lender as to the disposition of such payments.

9. When acting as a licensee in a transaction for the purpose of obtaining a loan, and in receipt of an advance fee from the borrower for this purpose, failure to account to the borrower for the disposition of the advance fee.

10. Knowingly making a false or misleading representation about the terms and conditions of a loan to be secured by a lien on real property when soliciting a borrower or negotiating the loan.

11. Knowingly making a false or misleading representation or representing, without a reasonable basis for believing its truth, when soliciting a lender or negotiating a loan to be secured by a lien on real property, about the market value of the securing real property, the nature and/or condition of the interior or exterior features of the securing real property, its size or the square footage of any improvements on the securing real property.

Regulations
The Commissioner has the authority to adopt regulations to aid in the administration and enforcement of the Real Estate Law and the Subdivided Lands Law. The Regulations of the Real Estate Commissioner have the force and effect of the law itself. Licensees and prospective licensees should have a thorough knowledge of the regulations.

DISCRIMINATION

Federal and California laws prohibit discrimination in the sale, rental or use of real property, whether based on sex, race, color, religion, ancestry, national origin, disability or age. These laws apply to persons who sell or rent housing or other real property and to the real estate broker or salesperson involved in such transactions.

The Unruh Civil Rights Act (California Civil Code Section 51, et seq.) declares: "All persons within the jurisdiction of this State are free and equal, and no matter what their sex, race, color, religion, ancestry, national origin or disability are entitled to the full and equal accommodations, advantages, facilities, privileges, or services in all business establishments of every kind whatsoever..."

It is the intent of the Unruh Act to give all persons full and equal accommodations, advantages, facilities, privileges, or services in all business establishments of every kind whatsoever. This law applies to all aspects of real estate activities, including real estate brokerage. An owner/renter of real property cannot discriminate when offering a unit for rent.

Civil Code Section 52 provides monetary remedies to persons who have been discriminated against in violation of the Unruh Act, stating, "Whoever denies, aids, or incites denial, or makes any discrimination or distinction contrary to Section 51 or Section 51.5 [pertaining to business establishments] is liable for each and every such offense for the actual damages, and any amount that may be determined by a jury, or a court sitting without a jury, up to a maximum of three times the amount of actual damage but in no case less than one thousand dollars ($1,000), and any attorney's fees that may be determined by the court in addition thereto, suffered by any person denied the rights provided in Section 51 or 51.5."

Age Discrimination - Senior Citizen Housing
Various cases have held that the Unruh Civil Rights Act applies to age discrimination in apartment rental and condominium properties because they are considered to be businesses subject to this act. In 1984 the Legislature enacted Civil Code Section 51.2 to clarify the holdings in the California Supreme Court cases dealing with the scope of the applicability of the Unruh Civil Rights Act. In the same bill, it enacted Civil Code Section 51.3 to establish and preserve specially designed accessible housing for senior citizens. Additionally, these provisions have been subsequently amended to comply with provisions of the federal law as it pertains to senior citizen housing developments.

Section 51.2 states, in part, that: "Section 51 shall be construed to prohibit a business establishment from discriminating in the sale or rental of housing based upon age. Where accommodations are designed to meet the physical and social needs of senior citizens, a business establishment may establish and preserve such housing for senior citizens, pursuant to Section 51.3, except housing as to which Section 51.3 is preempted by the prohibitions in the federal Fair Housing Amendments Act of 1988 (P.L. 100-430) and implementing regulations against discrimination on the basis of familial status..."

Section 51.3 provides definitions and criteria to be applied for the express allowance for enforcement of legal documents that provide for age limitations for senior citizens housing. This law applies to condominium, stock cooperative, limited-equity housing cooperative, planned development or multi-family residential rental property developed for and initially put into use as housing for senior citizens or substantially rehabilitated or renovated for, and immediately put into use as housing for senior citizens, as described in Section 51.3. The term "senior citizen" is defined as a person 62 years or older or one who is 55 years or older in a senior citizen housing development. A senior citizen housing development is a residential development built, substantially rehabilitated, or substantially renovated for senior citizens and which consists of:

- 70 or more dwelling units built prior to January 1, 1996 (or 150 or more dwelling units built on or after January 1, 1996) in a standard metropolitan statistical area (SMSA) of at least 1,000,000 total residents or 1,000 residents per square mile (1990 census);

- 100 or more dwelling units in an SMSA not exceeding either 399,000 total residents or 999 residents per square mile (1990 census);

- at least 35 dwelling units in any other area.

The law provides standards for the restrictions used for senior citizen housing developments. The restrictions cannot limit occupancy more strictly than to senior citizen residents and "a qualified permanent resident," i.e., a younger spouse or cohabitant or, as an alternative to a spouse, any person who provides primary physical or financial support to the senior citizen. In any such case, the lower age limit is 45 years. This "qualified permanent resident" must have an ownership interest in, or expectation of an ownership interest in, the dwelling unit within the housing development that otherwise limits occupancy based upon age. The qualified permanent resident can remain in residency after the death of the senior citizen or upon dissolution of a marriage with a senior citizen. The restrictions must allow for temporary residency of any non-qualifying person for not less than 60 days per calendar year.

Until January 1, 2000, unless this date is later changed by the legislature, housing developments which were constructed prior to February 8, 1982 can still discriminate by age for senior citizens as an exception to Section 51, if they meet the requirements for senior citizen housing, *except* the criteria that the housing be specifically designed for physical and social needs of senior citizens.

The Unruh Act does not apply to mobilehome developments.

Under the Unruh Act, as well as under case law, restrictions or prohibitions by covenant or condition in written instruments, such as CC&R's, on use, occupancy or transfer of title to real property limiting acquisition, use, occupation of real property because of any of the prohibited classifications are void. (Civil Code Section 51.3)

Housing Discrimination

The Fair Employment and Housing Act (Government Code Section 12900, et seq.) applies to owners of specified types of property, to real estate brokers and salespersons, to other agents and to financial institutions. Sections 12955 and 12980 – 12988 specifically cover housing discrimination. The law prohibits discrimination in supplying housing accommodations because of race, color, religion, sex, marital status, national origin, ancestry, age, familial status or disability. (The phrase "Housing accommodations" is defined as improved or unimproved real property used or intended to be used as a residence by the owner and which consists of not more than four dwelling units. The definition also includes four or fewer owner-occupied housing units that secure a home improvement loan.) The law forbids such discrimination in the sale, rental, lease or financing of practically all types of housing, and establishes methods of investigating, preventing and remedying violations. However, the provisions of Sections 51.2 and 51.3 of the Civil Code, as described above, which establish permissible age criteria for a senior citizen retirement community as an exception to the basic prohibition against age discrimination in housing, also apply to this Act.

Housing discrimination under the Fair Employment and Housing Act is handled by administrative procedures. Complaints are directed to the Department of Fair Employment and Housing and are investigated by its staff. If the Department decides that the law has been violated, and if the person accused of violating the law cannot be persuaded to correct the violation, the Department may file an accusation with the Fair Employment and Housing Commission or bring an action in the Superior Court for an injunction. If the Fair Employment and Housing Commission, after hearing, finds a violation of the law, it may order the sale or rental of the accommodation or like accommodations, if available. It may order financial assistance terms, conditions or privileges previously denied. In addition, it may order payment of punitive damages not to exceed $1,000, adjusted annually in accordance with the consumer price index, and the payment of actual damages. Substantial civil penalties can also be imposed by the Commission. The Department is required to do a compliance review to determine whether its order is being carried out.

The Fair Employment and Housing Act applies to all housing accommodations but does not apply to renting or leasing to a roomer or boarder in a single-family house, provided that no more than one roomer or boarder is to live within the household.

The term "discrimination" includes refusal to sell, rent, or lease housing accommodations, including inferior terms, misrepresentation as to availability, cancellations, etc. For sale or rent advertisements containing discriminatory information are prohibited. Also, discrimination includes failure to design or build a multi-family dwelling of four or more units in a manner that allows disabled persons access and use.

Other State Laws and Regulations
The Housing Financial Discrimination Act of 1977, also known as the Holden Act (Part 6 of Division 24 of the Health and Safety Code, Section 35800 et seq.), prohibits discriminatory loan practices on the part of financial institutions (banks, savings and loan associations, or other financial institutions, including mortgage loan brokers, mortgage bankers and public agencies which regularly make, arrange, or purchase loans for the purchase, construction, rehabilitation, improvement, or refinancing of housing accommodations). See Chapter 12 for further discussion.

No financial institution shall discriminate in their financial assistance wholly or partly on the basis of consideration of conditions, characteristics or trends in a neighborhood or geographic area unless the financial institution can demonstrate that such consideration in a particular case is necessary to avoid an unsafe and unsound business practice.

The Secretary of the Business, Transportation and Housing Agency has issued rules, regulations and guidelines for enforcement of this law and is empowered to investigate complaints regarding lending patterns and practices. Investigation of complaints has been delegated to the state agency which regulates the particular financial institution involved. If a violation is found, the Secretary can order that the loan be made on nondiscriminatory terms or impose a fine of up to $1,000.

Financial institutions are required to notify loan applicants of the existence of this law. Business and Professions Code Section 125.6 contains disciplinary provisions for discriminatory acts by any person licensed under the provisions of the Business and Professions Code.

Commissioner's Regulations 2725(f), 2780 and 2781 deal with discriminatory conduct and proper supervision of real estate licensees in that regard.

Business and Professions Code Section 10177(l) includes the practice of "block busting" as grounds for discipline of a real estate license.

Notice of Discriminatory Restrictions

Effective January, 2000, a county recorder, title insurance company, escrow company, or real estate licensee who provides a declaration, governing documents or deed to any person must provide a specified statement about the illegality of discriminatory restrictions and the right of homeowners to have such language removed. The statement must be contained in either a cover page placed over the document or a stamp on the first page of the document.

The Federal Rules

The Federal Fair Housing Act, Title VIII of the Civil Rights Act of 1968, provides an all-encompassing set of rules prohibiting discrimination on the part of owners of real property and their agents. This law applies to all sales or rentals of residences through the facilities of real estate licensees and to publication, posting, mailing or advertising in violation of this law. Direct refusal of an owner to sell a home because of race is, of course, a violation. This law applies to most rental of dwelling units, except it does not apply to the rental of rooms or units in dwellings of four or fewer living quarters if the owner actually occupies one of the living units as his residence.

Real estate licensees are in violation of this law if they commit any of the prohibited actions, even if there was no intent to discriminate, if the result is proscribed discrimination. The law applies to "blockbusting" and steering of home buyers to different areas on the basis of prohibited classifications.

Wherever federal law is applicable, it is paramount. Title VIII declares that its purpose is to provide "within constitutional limitations...for fair housing throughout the United States." In short, this law applies as thoroughly and as widely as is permissible under the broadest applicable provision of the Constitution and applies even to the most local transactions. This law is enforced by the Secretary of Housing and Urban Development or by civil actions by aggrieved parties or by an attorney general in federal or state court.

Another provision of Title VIII prohibits denial of membership or participation in a real estate board or multiple listing service to a person because of race, color, religion or national origin, or discrimination against a person in terms or conditions of membership. The federal law under Title VIII and relevant cases leads to the following general conclusion for real estate licensees: do not discriminate and, to that end, do not accept restrictive listings or make, print, or publish any notice, statement or advertisement with respect to a sale or rental of a dwelling which suggests discrimination because of race, color, religion, national origin or any other of the prohibited classifications.

The sum of the matter is that there are both a number of state laws and a federal law that apply to discrimination in real estate transactions. Every prohibition of the Unruh Act and the California Fair Employment and Housing Acts remains in effect, and what discrimination they do not prohibit, federal law does. Thus, no one may refuse to sell, lease or rent to another because of race or color, or on the basis of any other prohibited classifications, and no real estate licensee may do so, regardless of the principal's direction. If a principal seeks to restrict a listing on the basis of any of the prohibited classifications, the licensee must refuse to accept the listing.

SUBDIVISIONS

Every broker and salesperson and prospective licensee should be familiar with the extent and purpose of the Commissioner's jurisdiction over the sale or lease of newly subdivided land. Sooner or later the majority of active licensees are associated with the sale of subdivided property or are called on for advice in preparing a subdivision for market.

Sometimes a broker will find that a principal is creating a subdivision without realizing it. The broker should be equipped to protect the principal from violating the law.

When selling subdivided property, the broker must make certain that two important requirements of the subdivision law are observed:

1. Broker must furnish the prospective buyer with a copy of the subdivision public report, obtain a receipt, and give the prospective buyer an opportunity to read the report before the prospect makes an offer to purchase.

2. Broker must handle the deposit or purchase money in accordance with the law.

DEPARTMENT PUBLICATIONS

Although DRE's function as a licensing and law enforcement agency is primarily that of protecting the public, its policy has been to be of assistance to its licensees and to encourage a high level of ethical and professional standards.

To encourage education for licensees, the Department publishes this *Reference Book* and the *Real Estate Law* book, (containing the Real Estate Law, Subdivided Lands Law, Commissioner's Regulations, and pertinent excerpts from the California codes).

DRE also publishes the quarterly *Real Estate Bulletin* which is distributed to all brokers and salespersons. This publication is intended for the education of licensees by keeping them informed of the latest administrative provisions and the current practices in real estate and allied activities.

For information regarding the examination process and the issuance of original licenses, the Department publishes a free pamphlet entitled *Instructions to License Applicants*, available at all district offices.

The Department also publishes several consumer brochures and subdivision guides.

Order forms for the Department's current publications can be obtained at the district offices or by writing to Book Orders, Department of Real Estate, P.O. Box 187006, Sacramento, CA 95818-7006.

RECOVERY ACCOUNT

The Recovery Account is a fund of last resort for a member of the public who has obtained a final civil judgment or criminal restitution order against a real estate licensee based on fraud or certain other grounds and who has been unable to satisfy the judgment through the normal post-judgment proceedings.

For payment to be made, the judgment must be based upon intentional fraud or conversion of trust funds. The licensee must have been properly licensed at the time the cause of action arose, and must have been performing acts requiring a real estate license. The applicant must file the application within one year of the final judgment or criminal restitution order and must show that he or she has made all reasonable efforts to satisfy the judgment from the assets of not only the judgment debtor but also all other persons who may have been liable in the transaction.

When an application for payment is filed, DRE has 15 days to notify the applicant of any deficiencies. After the application is substantially complete, DRE has 90 days within which to pay, compromise, or deny the claim. If an application is denied, the applicant has six months within which to refile with the court which rendered the judgment.

If payment is made, the license of the judgment debtor is automatically suspended until he or she has repaid the amount plus interest. A judgment debtor who filed a timely response may file a writ of mandamus to challenge the suspension of his or her license.

As to a particular transaction/licensee, Section 10474 of the Business and Professions Code sets forth the maximum liability of the Recovery Account.

A portion of license fees are used to fund the Recovery Account.

2 The Real Estate License Examinations

The law requires that the Department of Real Estate (DRE) ascertain, by written examination, the competency of a prospective real estate licensee. DRE cannot waive this examination requirement.

This chapter discusses the examination process in general, details the scope of the examinations and includes practice questions.

A pamphlet titled *Instructions to License Applicants* provides detailed information about examination and licensing procedures. Interested persons may obtain this pamphlet and an application to take an examination by calling or writing any DRE office.

Scope of Examination

Business and Professions Code Section 10153 requires that the real estate examinations test for the following:

- knowledge of the English language, including reading, writing and spelling; and of arithmetical computations used in real estate and business opportunity practices;

- understanding of the principles of real estate and business opportunity conveyancing; the general purposes and general legal effect of agency contracts, deposit receipts, deeds, mortgages, deeds of trust, chattel mortgages, bills of sale, land contracts of sale and leases; and of the principles of business and land economics and appraisals; and

- understanding of the obligations between principal and agent; of the principles of real estate and business opportunity practice and the canons of business ethics pertaining thereto; and of the Real Estate Law, the Subdivided Lands Law and the Commissioner's Regulations.

Preparing for an Exam

Unless a prospective licensee has had experience with the various types of real estate transactions and has *thorough* knowledge of real estate fundamentals, including the obligations of an agent and the laws and regulations governing an agent's activities, it is suggested that *serious* study be undertaken prior to taking the examination. Even persons well-grounded in these areas will find a review extremely valuable.

This book and DRE's *Real Estate Law* book are useful study tools. In addition, public libraries and bookstores have textbooks on California real estate law, practice, finance, economics and appraisal. Real estate courses are available at colleges and private vocational schools.

Exam Construction

DRE's testing program follows guidelines set by the State Personnel Board and other test authorities. Periodically, DRE uses research studies to update the test specifications. Because there are differences in the level and amount of knowledge required of salespersons and brokers, the exams differ in their emphasis and difficulty.

Examination Weighting

DRE attempts to place proper emphasis on the content areas of the examinations. The exact weighting for each subject is included in the *current* edition of DRE's brochure *Instructions to License Applicants*. This publication is also available on-line at the DRE Web site at www.dre.ca.gov.

REAL ESTATE SALESPERSON LICENSING EXAMINATION OUTLINE

Section I - Property Ownership/Land Use Controls
- Classes of Property
- Land Characteristics
- Encumbrances
- Types of Ownership
- Descriptions of Property
- Government Rights in Land
- Public and Private Controls

Section II - Transfer of Property
- Title Insurance
- Deeds
- Escrow
- Reports
- Tax Aspects
- Probate

Section III - Valuation and Market Analysis
- Value
- Methods of Estimating Value/Appraisal Process
- Competitive Market Analysis

Section IV - Financing
- General Concepts
- Types of Loans
- Sources
- Government Programs
- Mortgages/Deeds of Trust
- Financing/Credit Laws

Section V - Laws of Agency/Mandated Disclosures
- Law, Definition & Nature of Agency Relationships, Types of Agencies & Agents
- Creation of Agency & Agency Agreements
- Responsibilities of Agent to Principal
- Responsibilities to Buyer & Third Parties
- Disclosure of Agency
- Disclosure of Acting as Principal or Other Interest
- Termination of Agency
- Commissions and Fees

Section VI - Contracts
- General
- Listing Agreements
- Advance Fee Agreements
- Buyer/Broker Agreements
- Offers/Purchase Agreements
- Counteroffers/Multiple Counteroffers
- Leases as Contracts
- Options
- Rescission and Cancellation Agreements
- Broker/Salesperson Agreements

Section VII - Real Estate Practice
- Trust Accounts
- Fair Housing Laws
- Advertising
- Record Keeping Requirements
- Agent Supervision
- Continuing Education Requirements
- Disciplinary Actions
- Unauthorized Practice of Law
- Specialty Areas

REAL ESTATE BROKER LICENSING EXAMINATION OUTLINE

Section I - Property Ownership/Land Use Controls
- Classes of Property
- Land Characteristics
- Encumbrances
- Types of Ownership
- Descriptions of Property
- Government Rights in Land
- Public & Private Controls

Section II - Transfer of Property
- Title Insurance
- Deeds
- Escrow
- Reports
- Tax Aspects
- Probate

Section III - Valuation & Market Analysis
- Value
- Methods of Estimating Value/Appraisal Process
- Competitive Market Analysis

Section IV - Financing
- General Concepts
- Types of Loans
- Sources

- Government Programs
- Mortgages/Deeds of Trust
- Financing/Credit Laws

Section V - Laws of Agency/Mandated Disclosures

- Law, Definition & Nature of Agency Relationships; Types of Agencies & Agents
- Creation of Agency & Agency Agreements
- Responsibilities of Agent to Principal
- Responsibilities to Buyer and Third Parties
- Disclosure of Agency
- Disclosure of Acting as Principal or other Interest
- Termination of Agency
- Commission and Fees

Section VI - Contracts

- General
- Listing Agreements
- Advance Fee Agreements
- Buyer/Broker Agreements
- Offers/Purchase Agreements
- Counteroffers/Multiple Counteroffers
- Leases as Contracts
- Options
- Rescission and Cancellation Agreements
- Broker/Salesperson Agreements

Section VII - Real Estate Practice

- Trust Accounts
- Fair Housing Laws
- Advertising
- Record Keeping Requirements
- Agent Supervision
- Continuing Education Requirements
- Disciplinary Actions
- Unauthorized Practice of Law
- Specialty Areas

Exam Rules - Exam Subversion

The typical rules for examinations apply: conversation is not permitted; the use of notes or references to texts is strictly forbidden; dishonest practice of any kind will result in a nonpassing grade and may be grounds for denying future examinations.

DRE may deny, suspend, revoke or restrict the license of an applicant or licensee who subverts or attempts to subvert a licensing examination. Conduct which constitutes subversion includes but is not limited to the following:

1. Removing exam material from a test site.
2. Reproducing exam material without authorization.
3. Using paid examinees for the purpose of reconstructing an examination.
4. Using improperly obtained test questions to prepare persons for examination.
5. Selling, distributing, or buying exam material.

6. Cheating during an exam.
7. Possessing unauthorized equipment or information during an examination.
8. Impersonating an examinee or having an impersonator take an examination.

Materials

Only the examination booklet, the answer sheet, a special pencil, and slide rule or silent, battery-operated, pocket-size, electronic calculator without a print-out capability or an alphabetic keyboard are allowed on an examinee's desk, along with the single page of scratch paper (for arithmetical calculations) which DRE will supply and which MUST be turned in with the answer sheet and examination booklet.

Question Construction

Test items are phrased so that they measure the applicant's knowledge without making him or her wonder about their meaning. The questions must not be too difficult, too easy, unimportant or inappropriate for any reason. No question is meant to be a trick or catch question. Words are used according to their commonly accepted meanings.

Multiple Choice Exam

All test items in the real estate exams are multiple-choice. While the examinee may feel that more than one answer has some element of correctness, the examinee must be able to eliminate the incorrect responses and choose the *correct* answer.

Q and A Analysis

The following analyses illustrate the proper approach to exam questions:

Question:

Under no circumstances may a broker:

(a) receive a commission from both buyer and seller
(b) appoint a subagent
(c) misrepresent material facts
(d) sell the principal's property to a relative

Analysis:

(a) *is incorrect.* A broker may receive a commission from both parties provided both buyer and seller have knowledge of the arrangement.

(b) *is incorrect.* A broker may get prior consent from the principal to appoint other brokers as subagents to cooperate in selling the property.

(c) **is correct.** A material misrepresentation is a violation of law.

(d) is *incorrect.* The broker may sell to any purchaser provided the principal has full knowledge.

Question:

A valid bill of sale must contain:

(a) a date
(b) an acknowledgment
(c) the seller's signature
(d) a verification

Analysis:

- (a) *is incorrect.* Although a date is advisable, it is not required.
- (b) *is incorrect.* The law does not require an acknowledgment.
- (c) **is correct.** A bill of sale is an instrument which has been executed (signed) and delivered to convey title to personal property.
- (d) *is incorrect.* Verification means to confirm the correctness of an instrument by an affidavit or oath. Verification may be desirable but not required.

Examinees should be alert for questions phrased in the negative: e.g., "All of the following statements are correct, *except;*" or, "which of the following are *not* ...?" In the following sample question, three of the responses would be correct. However, the answer called for is the *incorrect* statement.

Question:

A valid deed must contain all of the following, *except:*

- (a) the signature of the grantor
- (b) a granting clause
- (c) an adequate description of the property
- (d) an acknowledgment of the grantor's signature

Analysis:

- (a) is *a correct statement.* The grantor is the person who conveys title to another and without the grantor's signature title will not pass.
- (b) is *a correct statement.* The granting clause is necessary to evidence the intent of the grantor.
- (c) *is a correct statement.* The property being transferred must be described so the grantor knows exactly what property is being conveyed to the grantee.
- (d) **is the incorrect statement.** An acknowledgment is necessary for recordation but is not required to make the deed valid.

Sample Multiple Choice Items

The following are examples of the types of questions that appear in the examination. No answers are provided. The results of practice should be checked against appropriate sources.

1. A broker selling a property on which he holds an option should notify the purchaser that he is acting as:
   - (a) an optionor
   - (b) a mortgagor
   - (c) a beneficiary
   - (d) a principal

2. Tax delinquent real property not redeemed by the owner during the five-year statutory redemption period is deeded to the:
   - (a) city
   - (b) county
   - (c) state
   - (d) school district

3. The maximum commission a broker may charge a seller for the sale of residential income property is:
   (a) set forth in the Real Estate Law
   (b) negotiable
   (c) no more that 10 percent of the total sales price
   (d) determined by local custom

4. In a typical percentage lease, rent is calculated as a percentage of:
   (a) assets of the lessee's business
   (b) net sales of the lessee's business
   (c) gross sales of the lessee's business
   (d) net taxable income of the lessee's business

5. The position of trust assumed by the broker as an agent for a principal is described most accurately as:
   (a) a gratuitous relationship
   (b) a trustor relationship
   (c) a fiduciary relationship
   (d) an employment relationship

6. The Federal Housing Administration's role in financing the purchase of real property is to:
   (a) act as the lender of funds
   (b) insure loans made by approved lenders
   (c) purchase specific trust deeds
   (d) do all of the above

7. We call the instrument used to remove the lien of a trust deed from record a:
   (a) satisfaction
   (b) release
   (c) deed of reconveyance
   (d) certificate of redemption

8. Which item would an appraiser use to arrive at a net income for capitalization purposes?
   (a) cost of loans against the property
   (b) allowance for rent loss and vacancies
   (c) federal income tax
   (d) reserve for appreciation of buildings

9. The type of mortgage loan which permits borrowing additional funds at a later date is called:
   (a) an equitable mortgage
   (b) a junior mortgage
   (c) an open-end mortgage
   (d) an extendible mortgage

10. Private restrictions on the use of land may be created by:
    (a) private land use controls
    (b) written agreement
    (c) general plan restrictions in subdivisions
    (d) all of the above

11. As used in real estate practices, the land of a riparian owner borders on:
    (a) a river
    (b) a stream
    (c) a watercourse
    (d) any of the above

12. A quitclaim deed conveys only the present right, title and interest of the:
    (a) grantor
    (b) servient tenement
    (c) grantee
    (d) property

13. If a $54,600 investment in real estate generates gross annual earnings of 15%, the gross monthly return most nearly is:
    (a) $819
    (b) $705
    (c) $685
    (d) $637

14. You are a California real estate broker. A prospect is referred to you by an out-of-state broker and a sale is consummated by you. You want to split your commission with the cooperating broker. Under the California Real Estate Law:
    (a) you may pay a commission to a broker of another state
    (b) you cannot divide a commission with a broker of another state
    (c) you can pay a commission to a broker of another state only if he is also licensed in California
    (d) none of the above

15. A loan to be completely repaid, principal and interest, by a series of regular equal installment payments is a:
    (a) straight loan
    (b) balloon payment loan
    (c) fully amortized loan
    (d) variable rate mortgage loan

16. If the broker, while acting as agent in a sale of real property, misrepresents the principal's property to a buyer, the broker may cause the principal to be subjected to:
    (a) rescission of the sale by the buyer
    (b) a court action for damages by the buyer
    (c) tort liability
    (d) any of the above

17. In a legal sales contract, the seller is often referred to as the:
    (a) trustor
    (b) divisor
    (c) donor
    (d) vendor

18. The instrument used to secure a loan on personal property is called a:
    (a) bill of sale
    (b) trust deed
    (c) security agreement
    (d) bill of exchange

19. Community property is property owned by:
    (a) churches
    (b) husband and wife
    (c) the municipality
    (d) the community

20. An apartment complex cost $450,000. It brings in a net income of $3,000 per month. The owner is making what percentage of return on the investment?
    (a) 7%
    (b) 8%
    (c) 11%
    (d) none of the above

21. A person holding title to real property in severalty would most likely have:
    (a) a life estate
    (b) an estate for years
    (c) ownership in common with others
    (d) sole ownership

22. Under the Federal Truth-in-Lending Law, two of the most critical facts which must be disclosed to buyers or borrowers are:
    (a) duration of the contract and discount rate
    (b) finance charge and annual percentage rate
    (c) carrying charge and advertising expense
    (d) installment payments and cancellation rights

23. Appraisals of single-family dwellings are usually based on:
    (a) capitalization of rental value
    (b) asking prices of comparable houses
    (c) sales prices of comparable properties
    (d) the assessed valuations

24. A contract based on an illegal consideration is:
    (a) valid
    (b) void
    (c) legal
    (d) enforceable

25. The California "standard form" policy of title insurance on real property insures against loss occasioned by:
    (a) a forgery in the chain of recorded title
    (b) liens or encumbrances not disclosed by official records
    (c) rights of parties in possession of the property
    (d) actions of governmental agencies regulating the use or occupancy of the property

26. A house sold for $113,900, which was 11% more than the cost of the house. The cost of the house was most nearly:
    (a) $99,960
    (b) $100,400
    (c) $101,370
    (d) $102,610

27. A secured real property loan usually consists of:
    (a) financing statement and trust deed
    (b) the debt (note) and the lien (deed of trust)
    (c) FHA or PMI insurance
    (d) security agreement and financing statement

28. During escrow, if an unresolved dispute should arise between the seller and buyer preventing the close of escrow, the escrow holder may legally:
    (a) arbitrate the dispute as a neutral party
    (b) rescind the escrow and return all documents and monies to the respective parties
    (c) file an interpleader action in court
    (d) do any of the above

29. Copies of all listings, deposit receipts, canceled checks, and trust records must be retained by a licensed real estate broker for:
    (a) one year
    (b) two years
    (c) three years
    (d) five years

30. Parallel wooden members used to support floor and ceiling loads are called:
    (a) rafters
    (b) joists
    (c) headers
    (d) studs

31. When a loan is fully amortized by equal monthly payments of principal and interest, the amount applied to principal:
    (a) and interest remains constant
    (b) decreases while the interest payment increases
    (c) increases while the interest payment decreases
    (d) increases by a constant amount

32. Joint ownership of real property by two or more persons, each of whom has an undivided interest (not necessarily equal) without right of survivorship, is
    (a) a tenancy in partnership
    (b) a tenancy by the entireties
    (c) a tenancy in common
    (d) a leasehold tenancy

33. A "loss in value from any cause" is a common definition of:
    (a) economic obsolescence
    (b) depreciation

(c) principle of contribution
(d) adverse leverage

34. Which of the following is a lien?
   (a) an easement
   (b) a zoning restriction
   (c) an attachment
   (d) all of the above are liens

35. Of the following, which is the most important reason for a broker to maintain a trust fund account in addition to a regular business account?
   (a) to provide a means of control over the destiny of transactions being negotiated
   (b) it is easier from an accounting point of view
   (c) the bank is responsible for any loss to the trust fund account resulting from embezzlement
   (d) the consequence which could occur should legal action be taken against the broker

36. If an appraiser finds that the fair rent for a vacant parcel of land is $1,400 per month and the interest rate is 11%, what is the approximate indicated land value?
   (a) $109,090
   (b) $138,560
   (c) $152,730
   (d) $210,000

37. Economic obsolescence could result from each of the following, *except:*
   (a) new zoning laws
   (b) a city's leading industry moving out
   (c) misplacement of improvements
   (d) an outdated kitchen

38. Which of the following is an appraiser's primary concern in the analysis of residential property?
   (a) marketability and acceptability
   (b) square foot area
   (c) functional utility
   (d) fixed and operating expenses

39. A subordination clause in a trust deed may:
   (a) permit the obligation to be paid off ahead of schedule
   (b) prohibit the trustor from making an additional loan against the property before the trust deed is paid off
   (c) allow for periodic renegotiation and adjustment in the terms of the obligation
   (d) give priority to liens subsequently recorded against the property

40. In order to evaluate a vacant commercial site, an appraiser decides to use the land residual technique. Here is the information the appraiser gathered:
   Cost new of a proper building - $250,000;
   Estimated net income before recapture - $32,800 per year; interest rate - 8.5%

Estimated remaining economic life of building - 40 years

What is the approximate estimated value of the land using this technique?

(a) $31,000

(b) $47,000

(c) $48,182

(d) $62,353

41. Which of the following types of appraisal reports would be the most comprehensive and detailed?

(a) narrative

(b) form

(c) certificate

(d) letter

42. A contractor obtained a construction loan, and the loan funds are to be released in a series of progress payments. Most lenders disburse the last payment when the:

(a) building is completed

(b) notice of completion is filed

(c) buyer approves the construction

(d) period to file a lien has expired

43. To estimate the value of a parcel of real property, an appraiser concentrated only upon the cost to the buyer of acquiring a comparable, substitute parcel. This estimate approach is most similar to which of the following appraisal methods?

(a) cost

(b) income

(c) market

(d) none of the above

44. Brown purchased a $1,400 note secured by a second mortgage for investment purposes. The seller allowed a 15% discount. The note provided for monthly payments of $122 including interest at 9% per annum over a one-year term. Brown received full payment on the above terms. The yield on Brown's investment, expressed as a percentage, is:

(a) 23%

(b) 31%

(c) 34%

(d) 40%

45. The covenant of quiet enjoyment most directly relates to:

(a) nuisances maintained on adjoining property

(b) possession of real property

(c) title to real property

(d) all of the above

46. An interest in real property may be acquired by either prescription or by adverse possession. The interest resulting from prescription is:

(a) the right to use another's land

(b) a possessory title

(c) an equitable interest

(d) a private grant

47. Generally, the taking of private land by governmental bodies for public use is governed by due process of law and is accomplished through:

(a) exercise of the police power

(b) eminent domain

(c) reverter

(d) escheat

48. Governmental land use planning and zoning are important examples of:

(a) exercise of eminent domain

(b) use of police power

(c) deed restrictions

(d) encumbrances

49. Capitalization is a process whereby an appraiser:

(a) converts income into capital value

(b) determines depreciation reserves

(c) establishes cost of capital investment

(d) finds gross income of equity capital

50. In arriving at an effective gross income figure, an appraiser of rental property makes a deduction for:

(a) real property taxes

(b) repairs

(c) vacancy

(d) depreciation

3   Trade and Professional Associations

In the 1800s, real estate transactions were primarily the result of direct negotiation between buyer and seller, sometimes conducted with the aid of lawyers when transactions were more complicated. As specialization developed within the field of real estate and the mobility of people increased, particularly during the western movement, there was a good deal of unorganized and often unscrupulous real estate competition. Real estate practitioners began to feel the need for some controlling organization. This was first attempted in 1891 and 1892 with the organization of the ambitious but short-lived National Real Estate Association. In 1908, the National Association of Real Estate Associations/Boards (NAREB) was formed by the unification of a nationwide complex of local units or Associations/Boards. On January 1, 1974 this organization officially changed its name to the NATIONAL ASSOCIATION OF REALTORS®. (N.A.R.). Every business and professional group seeks to attain recognition and acceptance by the public. There is the conviction that if members reach professional status, such as that held by lawyers, doctors, clergymen, engineers, and so forth, the standards of business will rise. Yet experience has shown that even in these recognized professional groups, there must be supervision by the organization itself as well as by some government agency. All members of an Association/Board of REALTORS® commit to adhere to the N.A.R. Code of Ethics. All real estate licensees, whether REALTORS® or not, are under the jurisdiction of the California Department of Real Estate.

REAL ESTATE ASSOCIATIONS AND BOARDS

A trade association is a voluntary nonprofit organization of independent and competing business units engaged in the same industry or trade, and formed to resolve the industry's problems, promote its progress and enhance its service.

A real estate association/board is a voluntary organization whose members are engaged in some phase of the real estate business. Real estate licensees who fulfill the membership requirements of a local association of REALTORS® are eligible for REALTOR® or REALTOR-ASSOCIATE® membership. Membership in a local association/board automatically makes one a member in the CALIFORNIA ASSOCIATION OF REALTORS®and the NATIONAL ASSOCIATION OF REALTORS®. Most associations/boards also maintain an "affiliate" classification of membership which is open to financial institutions, trust companies, title companies, escrow companies and others whose duties or interests are related to the real estate business.

The purpose of the CALIFORNIA ASSOCIATION OF REALTORS®is to serve its membership in developing and promoting programs and services that will enhance the members' freedom and ability to conduct their individual businesses successfully with integrity and competency and, through collective action, to promote the preservation of real property rights. The pioneer real estate organizations in California were the San Diego Realty Board organized in 1887 and the San Jose Real Estate Board in 1896. Others followed early in the 1900s. The Berkeley Realty Association/Board was founded in 1902; Los Angeles in 1903; San Francisco in 1905. The California Real Estate Association was formed at Los Angeles in 1905. The name was officially changed to the CALIFORNIA ASSOCIATION OF REALTORS® on January 1, 1975.

The CALIFORNIA ASSOCIATION OF REALTORS®is an organization composed of the members of local associations/boards of REALTORS® throughout the State. In its statement of policy, C.A.R. commits to be responsive to the needs of its members through direct and indirect economic and professional benefits by striving to increase the professionalism, standards and productivity of its members. C.A.R. is dedicated to the protection and preservation of the free enterprise system and the right of the individual to own real property. C.A.R. offers a broad array of valuable products and services to its members. These include: legislative advocacy, legal services, local government relations liaison, standard forms, magazine, economics and research and insurance programs.

REALTOR® Defined

The NATIONAL ASSOCIATION OF REALTORS® unites and unifies the organized real estate interests of the Nation and presents a common cause and program regarding national issues affecting real property. The terms REALTOR®, REALTORS® and REALTOR-ASSOCIATE® as well as the logo "REALTOR®" are collective membership marks owned by NATIONAL ASSOCIATION OF REALTORS®. It is only through membership in the National Association that the right to use the term REALTOR® and its related marks is granted.

A REALTOR® is a person engaged in the real estate business who is a local and state association/board member and therefore a member of the NATIONAL ASSOCIATION OF REALTORS®, is subject to its rules and regulations, observes its standards of conduct, and is entitled to its benefits. REALTOR® members and REALTOR-ASSOCIATE® members are defined in the association's constitution, Article III, Section 1 (C). In California REALTOR® members of local associations/boards are also members of the CALIFORNIA ASSOCIATION OF REALTORS®.

Pursuant to Section 10140.6 of the California Business and Professions Code, a real estate licensee must indicate in real estate advertising that he or she is performing acts for which a license is required. Appropriate designations, such as agent, broker, REALTOR®, and loan correspondent (or abbreviations such as bro., agt.) satisfy the requirement. Licensees entitled to use the term "REALTOR®" must spell out the word in accordance with the N.A.R. trademark guidelines. There are also a few associations/boards in California which are not affiliated with the NATIONAL and the CALIFORNIA ASSOCIATION OF REALTORS®. Only those local associations/boards who are affiliated with N.A.R. may identify themselves as "Associations/Boards of REALTOR®."

Multiple Listing Service

Most associations/boards operate a multiple listing service (MLS) that serves consumers and brokers as a marketing tool. The purpose of an MLS is to provide a means by which authorized MLS broker participants establish legal relationships with other participants by making a blanket unilateral contractual offer of compensation and cooperation to other broker participants. In part, the MLS accumulates and disseminates information to enable authorized participants to prepare valuations of real property. An MLS is a facility for the orderly correlation and dissemination of listing information among the participants so that they may better serve their clients and the public.

California Civil Code Section 1087 defines an MLS as "...a facility of cooperation of agents and appraisers, operating through an intermediary which does not itself act as an agent or appraiser, through which agents establish express or implied legal relationships with respect to listed properties, or which may be used by agents and appraisers, pursuant to the rules of the service, to prepare market evaluations and appraisals of real property." Qualified real estate brokers and certified or licensed appraisers are eligible to be participants in the Multiple Listing Service. A real estate salesperson may obtain access through his/her broker.

An MLS will have local rules and regulations regarding the use of the service, including listing, showing, negotiating, presenting offers and lockbox usage. Most California MLSs use the California Model MLS Rules, approved by C.A.R. Many MLSs are part of a regional MLS or have reciprocal agreements with other MLSs. Some MLSs participate in the statewide reciprocal agreement which allows broader exposure of listings and varying levels of access to other participating MLSs.

REALTIST Defined

The NATIONAL ASSOCIATION OF REAL ESTATE BROKERS, INC. (NAREB) was formed in 1947 in Miami, Florida. NAREB's membership is comprised primarily of African American real estate brokers. NAREB members are known as REALTISTS. The organization has local boards in major cities of most states.

The CALIFORNIA ASSOCIATION OF REAL ESTATE BROKERS, INC. (CAREB), affiliated with the NATIONAL ASSOCIATION OF REAL ESTATE BROKERS, was organized in 1955 and now has eight board affiliates: Associated Real Property Brokers, Oakland; Sacramento Association of REALTISTS, Sacramento; Consolidated Realty Board, Los Angeles; Solano Board of REALTISTS, Fairfield; Inland Valley Board of REALTISTS, Ontario; San Francisco Board of REALTISTS, San Francisco; North Bay Board of REALTISTS, Richmond; and the San Diego Board of REALTISTS, San Diego.

A REALTIST must be a member of a local board as well as a member of the national organization. REALTISTS, nationally and locally, are working for democracy in housing and better housing for the communities they serve.

The NATIONAL ASSOCIATION OF REAL ESTATE BROKERS, INC. has several affiliated institutes, societies and councils. Membership in NAREB is a prerequisite to obtaining membership in any of these groups. The address of the NATIONAL ASSOCIATION OF REAL ESTATE BROKERS, INC. is: 1629 K

Street, N.W., Washington, D.C. 20006. Telephone: 202-785-4477. The address of the CALIFORNIA ASSOCIATION OF REAL ESTATE BROKERS, INC. is: 3725 Don Felipe Dr., Los Angeles, CA 90008.

RELATED ASSOCIATIONS

There are a large number of associated trade and professional bodies which are closely related to the real estate industry, and the average broker will from time to time work with them. These may be divided into two general classes: those related to the construction phase of real estate; and those related to the finance phase. In the former are included the National Association of Home Builders, Building Owners and Managers Association, and the Prefabricated Home Manufacturers Institute. There are, of course, many others.

In the field of real estate finance are associations, such as the American Bankers Association, which have an important impact upon the real estate business through their subsidiary phase of mortgage lending. The U. S. Savings and Loan League, American Savings and Loan Institute, National Savings and Loan League, National Association of Mutual Savings Banks, and Mortgage Bankers' Association are other examples.

ETHICS

The word has its origins in the Greek word *ethos* which means moral custom, use and character. Ethics is usually expressed as a set of principles or values - a standard of conduct by which the individual guides his or her own behavior and judges that of others. It refers then to our conduct, socially and in business, and in attitudes toward others. Whenever one person who has the status of being an expert or knowing a great deal more about a particular field than others assumes the duty of directing the business, health, investment, or general well-being of another on a fee basis, there is vested in such person a high degree of confidence and trust. When one takes advantage of this position of trust to the detriment of another party solely for the purpose of one's own gain, we say that this person is unethical.

Professional courtesy and ethics should not stop at those things which have been sanctioned by law. The individual who tries only to stay on the border of the law, inevitably, at some time, steps across. The course of ethical conduct set forth in the Real Estate Law is that which a licensee must observe. We will now consider what all licensees *should* observe.

The NATIONAL ASSOCIATION OF REALTORS® and its constituent boards and state associations form a composite organization of brokers and salespeople whose objects include providing real estate education, research, and exchange of information for those engaged in the recognized branches of the real estate business for the purpose of raising the standards of real estate practice, and preserving the right of property ownership in the interest of the public welfare; to promote and maintain high standards of conduct in the transaction of the real estate business; and to formulate and promulgate a code of ethics for the members of the Association. To this end, the NATIONAL ASSOCIATION OF REALTORS® Code of Ethics was formulated and adopted. It has the approval of a very large body of brokers in this country. It is recommended that it be carefully studied.

In brief, the Code of Ethics entails adhering to the Golden Rule. It is reproduced below.

Code of Ethics and Standards of Practice
of the
NATIONAL ASSOCIATION of REALTORS®

Effective January 1, 2000

Where the word REALTORS® is used in this Code and Preamble, it shall be deemed to include REALTOR-ASSOCIATES®.

While the Code of Ethics establishes obligations that may be higher than those mandated by law, in any instance where the Code of Ethics and the law conflict, the obligations of the law must take precedence.

Preamble…
Under all is the land. Upon its wise utilization and widely allocated ownership depend the survival and growth of free institutions and of our civilization. REALTORS® should recognize that the interests of the nation and its citizens require the highest and best use of the land and the widest distribution of land ownership. They require the creation of adequate housing, the building of functioning cities, the development of productive industries and farms, and the preservation of a healthful environment.

Such interests impose obligations beyond those of ordinary commerce. They impose grave social responsibility and a patriotic duty to which REALTOR® should dedicate themselves, and for which they should be diligent in preparing themselves. REALTORS®, therefore, are zealous to maintain and improve the standards of their calling and share with their fellow REALTORS® a common responsibility for its integrity and honor.

In recognition and appreciation of their obligations to clients, customers, the public, and each other, REALTORS® continuously strive to become and remain informed on issues affecting real estate and, as knowledgeable professionals, they willingly share the fruit of their experience and study with others. They identify and take steps, through enforcement of this Code of Ethics and by assisting appropriate regulatory bodies, to eliminate practices which may damage the public or which might discredit or bring dishonor to the real estate profession. REALTORS® having direct personal knowledge of conduct that may violate the Code of Ethics involving misappropriation of client or customer funds or property, willful discrimination, or fraud resulting in substantial economic harm, bring such matters to the attention of the appropriate Board or Association of REALTORS®. (Amended 1/00)

Realizing that cooperation with other real estate professionals promotes the best interests of those who utilize their services, REALTORS® urge exclusive representation of clients; do not attempt to gain any unfair advantage over their competitors; and they refrain from making unsolicited comments about other practitioners. In instances where their opinion is sought, or where REALTORS® believe that comment is necessary, their opinion is offered in an objective, professional manner, uninfluenced by any personal motivation or potential advantage or gain.

The term REALTOR® has come to connote competency, fairness, and high integrity resulting from adherence to a lofty ideal of moral conduct in business relations. No inducement of profit and no instruction from clients ever can justify departure from this ideal.

In the interpretation of this obligation, REALTORS® can take no safer guide than that which has been handed down through the centuries, embodied in the Golden Rule, "Whatsoever ye would that others should do to you, do ye even so to them."

Accepting this standard as their own, REALTORS® pledge to observe its spirit in all of their activities and to conduct their business in accordance with the tenets set forth below.

Duties to Clients and Customers

Article 1

When representing a buyer, seller, landlord, tenant, or other client as an agent, REALTORS® pledge themselves to protect and promote the interests of their client. This obligation of absolute fidelity to the client's interests is primary, but it does not relieve REALTORS® of their obligation to treat all parties honestly. When serving a buyer, seller, landlord, tenant or other party in a non-agency capacity, REALTORS® remain obligated to treat all parties honestly. (Amended 1/93)

- **Standard of Practice 1-1**
  REALTORS®, when acting as principals in a real estate transaction, remain obligated by the duties imposed by the Code of Ethics. (Amended 1/93)

- **Standard of Practice 1-2**
  The duties the Code of Ethics imposes are applicable whether REALTORS® are acting as agents or in legally recognized non-agency capacities except that any duty imposed exclusively on agents by law or regulation shall not be imposed by this Code of Ethics on REALTORS® acting in non-agency capacities.

  As used in this Code of Ethics, "client" means the person(s) or entity(ies) with whom a REALTOR® or a REALTORS®'S firm has an agency or legally recognized non-agency relationship; "customer" means a party to a real estate transaction who receives information, services, or benefits but has no contractual relationship with the REALTORS® or the REALTORS®'S firm; "agent" means a real estate licensee (including brokers and sales associates) acting in an agency relationship as defined by state law or regulation; and "broker" means a real estate licensee (including brokers and sales associates) acting as an agent or in a legally recognized non-agency capacity. (Adopted 1/95, Amended 1/99)

- **Standard of Practice 1-3**
  REALTORS®, in attempting to secure a listing, shall not deliberately mislead the owner as to market value.

- **Standard of Practice 1-4**
REALTORS®, when seeking to become a buyer/tenant representative, shall not mislead buyers or tenants as to savings or other benefits that might be realized through use of the REALTORS®'S services. (Amended 1/93)

- **Standard of Practice 1-5**
REALTORS® may represent the seller/landlord and buyer/tenant in the same transaction only after full disclosure to and with informed consent of both parties. (Adopted 1/93)

- **Standard of Practice 1-6**
REALTORS® shall submit offers and counter-offers objectively and as quickly as possible. (Adopted 1/93, Amended 1/95)

- **Standard of Practice 1-7**
When acting as listing brokers, REALTORS® shall continue to submit to the seller/landlord all offers and counter-offers until closing or execution of a lease unless the seller/landlord has waived this obligation in writing. REALTORS® shall not be obligated to continue to market the property after an offer has been accepted by the seller/landlord. REALTORS® shall recommend that sellers/landlords obtain the advice of legal counsel prior to acceptance of a subsequent offer except where the acceptance is contingent on the termination of the pre-existing purchase contract or lease. (Amended 1/93)

- **Standard of Practice 1-8**
REALTORS® acting as agents or brokers of buyers/tenants shall submit to buyers/tenants all offers and counter-offers until acceptance but have no obligation to continue to show properties to their clients after an offer has been accepted unless otherwise agreed in writing. REALTORS® acting as agents or brokers of buyers/tenants shall recommend that buyers/tenants obtain the advice of legal counsel if there is a question as to whether a pre-existing contract has been terminated. (Adopted 1/93, Amended 1/99)

- **Standard of Practice 1-9**
The obligation of REALTORS® to preserve confidential information (as defined by state law) provided by their clients in the course of any agency relationship or non-agency relationship recognized by law continues after termination of agency relationships or any non-agency relationships recognized by law. REALTORS® shall not knowingly, during or following the termination of professional relationships with their clients:

1) reveal confidential information of clients; or

   2) use confidential information of clients to the disadvantage of clients; or

   3) use confidential information of clients for the REALTORS®'s advantage or the advantage of third parties unless:
     a) clients consent after full disclosure; or
     b) REALTORS® are required by court order; or
     c) it is the intention of a client to commit a crime and the information is necessary to prevent the crime; or

d) it is necessary to defend a REALTOR® or the REALTORS®'S
employees or associates against an accusation of wrongful
conduct. (Adopted 1/93, Amended 1/99)

- **Standard of Practice 1-10**
  REALTORS® shall, consistent with the terms and conditions of their real
  estate licensure and their property management agreement, competently
  manage the property of clients with due regard for the rights, safety and
  health of tenants and others lawfully on the premises. (Adopted 1/95,
  Amended 1/00)

- **Standard of Practice 1-11**
  REALTORS® who are employed to maintain or manage a client's property
  shall exercise due diligence and make reasonable efforts to protect it
  against reasonably foreseeable contingencies and losses. (Adopted 1/95)

- **Standard of Practice 1-12**
  When entering into listing contracts, REALTORS® must advise
  sellers/landlords of:

  1) the REALTORS®'s general company policies regarding cooperation
     with and compensation to subagents, buyer/tenant agents and/or
     brokers acting in legally recognized non-agency capacities;
  2) the fact that buyer/tenant agents or brokers, even if compensated by
     listing brokers, or by sellers/landlords may represent the interests of
     buyers/tenants; and
  3) any potential for listing brokers to act as disclosed dual agents, e.g.
     buyer/tenant agents. (Adopted 1/93, Renumbered 1/98, Amended 1/99)

- **Standard of Practice 1-13**
  When entering into buyer/tenant agreements, REALTORS® must advise
  potential clients of:

  1) the REALTORS®'s general company policies regarding cooperation and
     compensation; and
  2) any potential for the buyer/tenant representative to act as a disclosed
     dual agent, e.g. listing broker, subagent, landlord's agent, etc. (Adopted
     1/93, Renumbered 1/98, Amended 1/99)

Article 2

REALTORS® shall avoid exaggeration, misrepresentation, or concealment of
pertinent facts relating to the property or the transaction. REALTORS® shall not,
however, be obligated to discover latent defects in the property, to advise on
matters outside the scope of their real estate license, or to disclose facts which are
confidential under the scope of agency or non-agency relationships as defined by
state law. (Amended 1/00)

- **Standard of Practice 2-1**
  REALTORS® shall only be obligated to discover and disclose adverse
  factors reasonably apparent to someone with expertise in those areas
  required by their real estate licensing authority. Article 2 does not impose

upon the REALTORS® the obligation of expertise in other professional or technical disciplines. (Amended 1/96)

- **Standard of Practice 2-2**
  (Renumbered as Standard of Practice 1-12 1/98)

- **Standard of Practice 2-3**
  (Renumbered as Standard of Practice 1-13 1/98)

- **Standard of Practice 2-4**
  REALTORS® shall not be parties to the naming of a false consideration in any document, unless it be the naming of an obviously nominal consideration

- **Standard of Practice 2-5**
  Factors defined as "non-material" by law or regulation or which are expressly referenced in law or regulation as not being subject to disclosure are considered not "pertinent" for purposes of Article 2. (Adopted 1/93)

Article 3

REALTORS® shall cooperate with other brokers except when cooperation is not in the client's best interest. The obligation to cooperate does not include the obligation to share commissions, fees, or to otherwise compensate another broker. (Amended 1/95)

- **Standard of Practice 3-1**
  REALTORS®, acting as exclusive agents or brokers of sellers/landlords, establish the terms and conditions of offers to cooperate. Unless expressly indicated in offers to cooperate, cooperating brokers may not assume that the offer of cooperation includes an offer of compensation. Terms of compensation, if any, shall be ascertained by cooperating brokers before beginning efforts to accept the offer of cooperation. (Amended 1/99)

- **Standard of Practice 3-2**
  REALTORS® shall, with respect to offers of compensation to another REALTORS®, timely communicate any change of compensation for cooperative services to the other REALTORS® prior to the time such REALTORS® produces an offer to purchase/lease the property. (Amended 1/94)

- **Standard of Practice 3-3**
  Standard of Practice 3-2 does not preclude the listing broker and cooperating broker from entering into an agreement to change cooperative compensation. (Adopted 1/94)

- **Standard of Practice 3-4**
  REALTORS®, acting as listing brokers, have an affirmative obligation to disclose the existence of dual or variable rate commission arrangements (i.e., listings where one amount of commission is payable if the listing broker's firm is the procuring cause of sale/lease and a different amount of commission is payable if the sale/lease results through the efforts of the seller/landlord or a cooperating broker). The listing broker shall, as soon

as practical, disclose the existence of such arrangements to potential cooperating brokers and shall, in response to inquiries from cooperating brokers, disclose the differential that would result in a cooperative transaction or in a sale/lease that results through the efforts of the seller/landlord. If the cooperating broker is a buyer/tenant representative, the buyer/tenant representative must disclose such information to their client. (Amended 1/94)

- **Standard of Practice 3-5**
  It is the obligation of subagents to promptly disclose all pertinent facts to the principal's agent prior to as well as after a purchase or lease agreement is executed. (Amended 1/93)

- **Standard of Practice 3-6**
  REALTORS® shall disclose the existence of an accepted offer to any broker seeking cooperation. (Adopted 5/86)

- **Standard of Practice 3-7**
  When seeking information from another REALTORS® concerning property under a management or listing agreement, REALTORS® shall disclose their REALTORS® status and whether their interest is personal or on behalf of a client and, if on behalf of a client, their representational status. (Amended 1/95)

- **Standard of Practice 3-8**
  REALTORS® shall not misrepresent the availability of access to show or inspect a listed property. (Amended 11/87)

Article 4

REALTORS® shall not acquire an interest in or buy or present offers from themselves, any member of their immediate families, their firms or any member thereof, or any entities in which they have any ownership interest, any real property without making their true position known to the owner or the owner's agent or broker. In selling property they own, or in which they have any interest, REALTORS® shall reveal their ownership or interest in writing to the purchaser or the purchaser's representative. (Amended 1/00)

- **Standard of Practice 4-1**
  For the protection of all parties, the disclosures required by Article 4 shall be in writing and provided by REALTORS® prior to the signing of any contract. (Adopted 2/86)

Article 5

REALTORS® shall not undertake to provide professional services concerning a property or its value where they have a present or contemplated interest unless such interest is specifically disclosed to all affected parties.

Article 6

REALTORS® shall not accept any commission, rebate, or profit on expenditures made for their client, without the client's knowledge and consent.

When recommending real estate products or services (e.g., homeowner's insurance, warranty programs, mortgage financing, title insurance, etc.), REALTORS® shall disclose to the client or customer to whom the recommendation is made any financial benefits or fees, other than real estate referral fees, the REALTORS® or REALTORS®'s firm may receive as a direct result of such recommendation. (Amended 1/99)

- **Standard of Practice 6-1**
  REALTORS® shall not recommend or suggest to a client or a customer the use of services of another organization or business entity in which they have a direct interest without disclosing such interest at the time of the recommendation or suggestion. (Amended 5/88)

Article 7

In a transaction, REALTORS® shall not accept compensation from more than one party, even if permitted by law, without disclosure to all parties and the informed consent of the REALTORS®'s client or clients. (Amended 1/93)

Article 8

REALTORS® shall keep in a special account in an appropriate financial institution, separated from their own funds, monies coming into their possession in trust for other persons, such as escrows, trust funds, clients' monies, and other like items.

Article 9

REALTORS®, for the protection of all parties, shall assure whenever possible that agreements shall be in writing, and shall be in clear and understandable language expressing the specific terms, conditions, obligations and commitments of the parties. A copy of each agreement shall be furnished to each party upon their signing or initialing. (Amended 1/95)

- **Standard of Practice 9-1**
  For the protection of all parties, REALTORS® shall use reasonable care to ensure that documents pertaining to the purchase, sale, or lease of real estate are kept current through the use of written extensions or amendments. (Amended 1/93)

Duties to the Public

Article 10

REALTORS® shall not deny equal professional services to any person for reasons of race, color, religion, sex, handicap, familial status, or national origin. REALTORS® shall not be parties to any plan or agreement to discriminate against a person or persons on the basis of race, color, religion, sex, handicap, familial status, or national origin. (Amended 1/90)

REALTORS®, in their real estate employment practices, shall not discriminate against any person or persons on the basis of race, color, religion, sex, handicap, familial status, or national origin. (Amended 1/00)

- **Standard of Practice 10-1**

  REALTORS® shall not volunteer information regarding the racial, religious or ethnic composition of any neighborhood and shall not engage in any activity which may result in panic selling. REALTORS® shall not print, display or circulate any statement or advertisement with respect to the selling or renting of a property that indicates any preference, limitations or discrimination based on race, color, religion, sex, handicap, familial status or national origin. (Adopted 1/94)

- **Standard of Practice 10-2**

  As use in Article 10 "real estate employment practices" relates to employees and independent contractors providing real-estate related services and the administrative and clerical staff directly supporting those individuals. (Adopted 1/00)

Article 11

The services which REALTORS® provide to their clients and customers shall conform to the standards of practice and competence which are reasonably expected in the specific real estate disciplines in which they engage; specifically, residential real estate brokerage, real property management, commercial and industrial real estate brokerage, real estate appraisal, real estate counseling, real estate syndication, real estate auction, and international real estate.

REALTORS® shall not undertake to provide specialized professional services concerning a type of property or service that is outside their field of competence unless they engage the assistance of one who is competent on such types of property or service, or unless the facts are fully disclosed to the client. Any persons engaged to provide such assistance shall be so identified to the client and their contribution to the assignment should be set forth. (Amended 1/95)

- **Standard of Practice 11-1**

  The obligations of the Code of Ethics shall be supplemented by and construed in a manner consistent with the Uniform Standards of Professional Appraisal Practice (USPAP) promulgated by the Appraisal Standards Board of the Appraisal Foundation.

  The obligations of the Code of Ethics shall not be supplemented by the USPAP where an opinion or recommendation of price or pricing is provided in pursuit of a listing, to assist a potential purchaser in formulating a purchase offer, or to provide a broker's price opinion, whether for a fee or not. (Amended 1/96)

- **Standard of Practice 11-2**

  The obligations of the Code of Ethics in respect of real estate disciplines other than appraisal shall be interpreted and applied in accordance with the standards of competence and practice which clients and the public reasonably require to protect their rights and interests considering the complexity of the transaction, the availability of expert assistance, and, where the REALTORS® is an agent or subagent, the obligations of a fiduciary. (Adopted 1/95)

- **Standard of Practice 11-3**
  When REALTORS® provide consultive services to clients which involve advice or counsel for a fee (not a commission), such advice shall be rendered in an objective manner and the fee shall not be contingent on the substance of the advice or counsel given. If brokerage or transaction services are to be provided in addition to consultive services, a separate compensation may be paid with prior agreement between the client and REALTORS®. (Adopted 1/96)

Article 12

REALTORS® shall be careful at all times to present a true picture in their advertising and representations to the public. REALTORS® shall also ensure that their professional status (e.g., broker, appraiser, property manager, etc.) or status as REALTORS® is clearly identifiable in any such advertising. (Amended 1/93)

- **Standard of Practice 12-1**
  REALTORS® may use the term "free" and similar terms in their advertising and in other representations provided that all terms governing availability of the offered product or service are clearly disclosed at the same time. (Amended 1/97)

- **Standard of Practice 12-2**
  REALTORS® may represent their services as "free" or without cost even if they expect to receive compensation from a source other than their client provided that the potential for the REALTORS® to obtain a benefit from a third party is clearly disclosed at the same time. (Amended 1/97)

- **Standard of Practice 12-3**
  The offering of premiums, prizes, merchandise discounts or other inducements to list, sell, purchase, or lease is not, in itself, unethical even if receipt of the benefit is contingent on listing, selling, purchasing, or leasing through the REALTORS® making the offer. However, REALTORS® must exercise care and candor in any such advertising or other public or private representations so that any party interested in receiving or otherwise benefiting from the REALTORS®'s offer will have clear, thorough, advance understanding of all the terms and conditions of the offer. The offering of any inducements to do business is subject to the limitations and restrictions of state law and the ethical obligations established by any applicable Standard of Practice. (Amended 1/95)

- **Standard of Practice 12-4**
  REALTORS® shall not offer for sale/lease or advertise property without authority. When acting as listing brokers or as subagents, REALTORS® shall not quote a price different from that agreed upon with the seller/landlord. (Amended 1/93)

- **Standard of Practice 12-5**
  REALTORS® shall not advertise nor permit any person employed by or affiliated with them to advertise listed property without disclosing the name of the firm. (Adopted 11/86)

- **Standard of Practice 12-6**
  REALTORS®, when advertising unlisted real property for sale/lease in which they have an ownership interest, shall disclose their status as both owners/landlords and as REALTORS® or real estate licensees. (Amended 1/93)

- **Standard of Practice 12-7**
  Only REALTORS® who participated in the transaction as the listing broker or cooperating broker (selling broker) may claim to have "sold" the property. Prior to closing, a cooperating broker may post a "sold" sign only with the consent of the listing broker. (Amended 1/96)

Article 13

REALTORS® shall not engage in activities that constitute the unauthorized practice of law and shall recommend that legal counsel be obtained when the interest of any party to the transaction requires it.

Article 14

If charged with unethical practice or asked to present evidence or to cooperate in any other way, in any professional standards proceeding or investigation, REALTORS® shall place all pertinent facts before the proper tribunals of the Member Board or affiliated institute, society, or council in which membership is held and shall take no action to disrupt or obstruct such processes. (Amended 1/99)

- **Standard of Practice 14-1**
  REALTORS® shall not be subject to disciplinary proceedings in more than one Board of REALTORS® or affiliated institute, society or council in which they hold membership with respect to alleged violations of the Code of Ethics relating to the same transaction or event. (Amended 1/95)

- **Standard of Practice 14-2**
  REALTORS® shall not make any unauthorized disclosure or dissemination of the allegations, findings, or decision developed in connection with an ethics hearing or appeal or in connection with an arbitration hearing or procedural review. (Amended 1/92)

- **Standard of Practice 14-3**
  REALTORS® shall not obstruct the Board's investigative or professional standards proceedings by instituting or threatening to institute actions for libel, slander or defamation against any party to a professional standards proceeding or their witnesses based on the filing of an arbitration request, an ethics complaint, or testimony given before any tribunal. (Adopted 11/87, Amended 1/99)

- **Standard of Practice 14-4**
  REALTORS® shall not intentionally impede the Board's investigative or disciplinary proceedings by filing multiple ethics complaints based on the same event or transaction. (Adopted 11/88)

Duties to REALTORS®

Article 15

REALTORS® shall not knowingly or recklessly make false or misleading statements about competitors, their businesses, or their business practices. (Amended 1/92)

- **Standard of Practice 15-1**
  REALTORS® shall not knowingly or recklessly file false or unfounded ethics complaints. (Adopted 1/00)

Article 16

REALTORS® shall not engage in any practice or take any action inconsistent with the agency or other exclusive relationship recognized by law that other REALTORS® have with clients. (Amended 1/98)

- **Standard of Practice 16-1**
  Article 16 is not intended to prohibit aggressive or innovative business practices which are otherwise ethical and does not prohibit disagreements with other REALTORS® involving commission, fees, compensation or other forms of payment or expenses. (Adopted 1/93, Amended 1/95)

- **Standard of Practice 16-2**
  Article 16 does not preclude REALTORS® from making general announcements to prospective clients describing their services and the terms of their availability even though some recipients may have entered into agency agreements or other exclusive relationships with another REALTORS®. A general telephone canvass, general mailing or distribution addressed to all prospective clients in a given geographical area or in a given profession, business, club, or organization, or other classification or group is deemed "general" for purposes of this standard. (Amended 1/98)

  Article 16 is intended to recognize as unethical two basic types of solicitations:

  First, telephone or personal solicitations of property owners who have been identified by a real estate sign, multiple listing compilation, or other information service as having exclusively listed their property with another REALTORS®; and

  Second, mail or other forms of written solicitations of prospective clients whose properties are exclusively listed with another REALTORS® when such solicitations are not part of a general mailing but are directed specifically to property owners identified through compilations of current listings, "for sale" or "for rent" signs, or other sources of information required by Article 3 and Multiple Listing Service rules to be made available to other REALTORS® under offers of subagency or cooperation. (Amended 1/93)

- **Standard of Practice 16-3**

  Article 16 does not preclude REALTORS® from contacting the client of another broker for the purpose of offering to provide, or entering into a contract to provide, a different type of real estate service unrelated to the type of service currently being provided (e.g., property management as opposed to brokerage). However, information received through a Multiple Listing Service or any other offer of cooperation may not be used to target clients of other REALTORS® to whom such offers to provide services may be made. (Amended 1/93)

- **Standard of Practice 16-4**

  REALTORS® shall not solicit a listing which is currently listed exclusively with another broker. However, if the listing broker, when asked by the REALTORS®, refuses to disclose the expiration date and nature of such listing; i.e., an exclusive right to sell, an exclusive agency, open listing, or other form of contractual agreement between the listing broker and the client, the REALTORS® may contact the owner to secure such information and may discuss the terms upon which the REALTORS® might take a future listing or, alternatively, may take a listing to become effective upon expiration of any existing exclusive listing. (Amended 1/94)

- **Standard of Practice 16-5**

  REALTORS® shall not solicit buyer/tenant agreements from buyers/tenants who are subject to exclusive buyer/tenant agreements. However, if asked by a REALTORS®, the broker refuses to disclose the expiration date of the exclusive buyer/tenant agreement, the REALTORS® may contact the buyer/tenant to secure such information and may discuss the terms upon which the REALTORS® might enter into a future buyer/tenant agreement or, alternatively, may enter into a buyer/tenant agreement to become effective upon the expiration of any existing exclusive buyer/tenant agreement. (Adopted 1/94, Amended 1/98)

- **Standard of Practice 16-6**

  When REALTORS® are contacted by the client of another REALTORS® regarding the creation of an exclusive relationship to provide the same type of service, and REALTORS® have not directly or indirectly initiated such discussions, they may discuss the terms upon which they might enter into a future agreement or, alternatively, may enter into an agreement which becomes effective upon expiration of any existing exclusive agreement. (Amended 1/98)

- **Standard of Practice 16-7**

  The fact that a client has retained a REALTORS® as an agent or in another exclusive relationship in one or more past transactions does not preclude other REALTORS® from seeking such former client's future business. (Amended 1/98)

- **Standard of Practice 16-8**

  The fact that an exclusive agreement has been entered into with a REALTORS® shall not preclude or inhibit any other REALTORS® from entering into a similar agreement after the expiration of the prior agreement. (Amended 1/98)

- **Standard of Practice 16-9**

  REALTORS®, prior to entering into an agency agreement or other exclusive relationship, have an affirmative obligation to make reasonable efforts to determine whether the client is subject to a current, valid exclusive agreement to provide the same type of real estate service. (Amended 1/98)

- **Standard of Practice 16-10**

  REALTORS®, acting as agents of, or in another relationship with, buyers or tenants, shall disclose that relationship to the seller/landlord's agent or broker at first contact and shall provide written confirmation of that disclosure to the seller/landlord's agent or broker not later than execution of a purchase agreement or lease. (Amended 1/98)

- **Standard of Practice 16-11**

  On unlisted property, REALTORS® acting as buyer/tenant agents or brokers shall disclose that relationship to the seller/landlord at first contact for that client and shall provide written confirmation of such disclosure to the seller/landlord not later than execution of any purchase or lease agreement.

  REALTORS® shall make any request for anticipated compensation from the seller/landlord at first contact. (Amended 1/98)

- **Standard of Practice 16-12**

  REALTORS®, acting as agents or brokers of sellers/landlords or as subagents of listing brokers, shall disclose that relationship to buyers/tenants as soon as practicable and shall provide written confirmation of such disclosure to buyers/tenants not later than execution of any purchase or lease agreement. (Amended 1/98)

- **Standard of Practice 16-13**

  All dealings concerning property exclusively listed, or with buyer/tenants who are subject to an exclusive agreement shall be carried on with the client's agent or broker, and not with the client, except with the consent of the client's agent or broker or except where such dealings are initiated by the client. (Adopted 1/93, Amended 1/98)

- **Standard of Practice 16-14**

  REALTORS® are free to enter into contractual relationships or to negotiate with sellers/landlords, buyers/tenants or others who are not subject to an exclusive agreement but shall not knowingly obligate them to pay more than one commission except with their informed consent. (Amended 1/98)

- **Standard of Practice 16-15**

  In cooperative transactions REALTORS® shall compensate cooperating REALTORS® (principal brokers) and shall not compensate nor offer to compensate, directly or indirectly, any of the sales licensees employed by or affiliated with other REALTORS® without the prior express knowledge and consent of the cooperating broker.

- **Standard of Practice 16-16**
  REALTORS®, acting as subagents or buyer/tenant agents or brokers, shall not use the terms of an offer to purchase/lease to attempt to modify the listing broker's offer of compensation to subagents or buyer's agents or brokers nor make the submission of an executed offer to purchase/lease contingent on the listing broker's agreement to modify the offer of compensation. (Amended 1/98)

- **Standard of Practice 16-17**
  REALTORS® acting as subagents or as buyer/tenant agents or brokers, shall not attempt to extend a listing broker's offer of cooperation and/or compensation to other brokers without the consent of the listing broker. (Amended 1/98)

- **Standard of Practice 16-18**
  REALTORS® shall not use information obtained by them from the listing broker, through offers to cooperate received through Multiple Listing Services or other sources authorized by the listing broker, for the purpose of creating a referral prospect to a third broker, or for creating a buyer/tenant prospect unless such use is authorized by the listing broker. (Amended 1/93)

- **Standard of Practice 16-19**
  Signs giving notice of property for sale, rent, lease, or exchange shall not be placed on property without consent of the seller/landlord. (Amended 1/93)

- **Standard of Practice 16-20**
  REALTORS®, prior to or after terminating their relationship with their current firm, shall not induce clients of their current firm to cancel exclusive contractual agreements between the client and that firm. This does not preclude REALTORS® (principals) from establishing agreements with their associated licensees governing assignability of exclusive agreements. (Adopted 1/98)

Article 17

In the event of contractual disputes or specific non-contractual disputes as defined in Standard of Practice 17-4 between REALTORS® associated with different firms, arising out of their relationship as REALTORS®, the REALTORS® shall submit the dispute to arbitration in accordance with the regulations of their Board or Boards rather than litigate the matter.

In the event clients of REALTORS® wish to arbitrate contractual disputes arising out of real estate transactions, REALTORS® shall arbitrate those disputes in accordance with the regulations of their Board, provided the clients agree to be bound by the decision. (Amended 1/97)

- **Standard of Practice 17-1**
  The filing of litigation and refusal to withdraw from it by REALTORS® in an arbitrable matter constitutes a refusal to arbitrate. (Adopted 2/86)

- **Standard of Practice 17-2**

Article 17 does not require REALTORS® to arbitrate in those circumstances when all parties to the dispute advise the Board in writing that they choose not to arbitrate before the Board. (Amended 1/93)

- **Standard of Practice 17-3**
  REALTORS®, when acting solely as principals in a real estate transaction, are not obligated to arbitrate disputes with other REALTORS® absent a specific written agreement to the contrary. (Adopted 1/96)

- **Standard of Practice 17-4**
  Specific non-contractual disputes that are subject to arbitration pursuant to Article 17 are:

  1) Where a listing broker has compensated a cooperating broker and another cooperating broker subsequently claims to be the procuring cause of the sale or lease. In such cases the complainant may name the first cooperating broker as respondent and arbitration may proceed without the listing broker being named as a respondent. Alternatively, if the complaint is brought against the listing broker, the listing broker may name the first cooperating broker as a third-party respondent. In either instance the decision of the hearing panel as to procuring cause shall be conclusive with respect to all current or subsequent claims of the parties for compensation arising out of the underlying cooperative transaction. (Adopted 1/97)

  2) Where a buyer or tenant representative is compensated by the seller or landlord, and not by the listing broker, and the listing broker, as a result, reduces the commission owed by the seller or landlord and, subsequent to such actions, another cooperating broker claims to be the procuring cause of sale or lease. In such cases the complainant may name the first cooperating broker as respondent and arbitration may proceed without the listing broker being named as a respondent. Alternatively, if the complaint is brought against the listing broker, the listing broker may name the first cooperating broker as a third-party respondent. In either instance the decision of the hearing panel as to procuring cause shall be conclusive with respect to all current or subsequent claims of the parties for compensation arising out of the underlying cooperative transaction. (Adopted 1/97)

  3) Where a buyer or tenant representative is compensated by the buyer or tenant and, as a result, the listing broker reduces the commission owed by the seller or landlord and, subsequent to such actions, another cooperating broker claims to be the procuring cause of sale or lease. In such cases the complainant may name the first cooperating broker as respondent and arbitration may proceed without the listing broker being named as a respondent. Alternatively, if the complaint is brought against the listing broker, the listing broker may name the first cooperating broker as a third-party respondent. In either instance the decision of the hearing panel as to procuring cause shall be conclusive with respect to all current or subsequent claims of the

parties for compensation arising out of the underlying cooperative transaction. (Adopted 1/97)

4) Where two or more listing brokers claim entitlement to compensation pursuant to open listings with a seller or landlord who agrees to participate in arbitration (or who requests arbitration) and who agrees to be bound by the decision. In cases where one of the listing brokers has been compensated by the seller or landlord, the other listing broker, as complainant, may name the first listing broker as respondent and arbitration may proceed between the brokers. (Adopted 1/97)

The Code of Ethics was adopted in 1913. Amended at the Annual Convention in 1924, 1928, 1950, 1951, 1952, 1955, 1956, 1961, 1962, 1974, 1982, 1986, 1987, 1989, 1990, 1991, 1992, 1993, 1994, 1995, 1996, 1997, 1998 and 1999.

Explanatory Notes
The reader should be aware of the following policies which have been approved by the Board of Directors of the National Association of REALTORS:

In filing a charge of an alleged violation of the Code of Ethics by a REALTORS®, the charge must read as an alleged violation of one or more Articles of the Code. Standards of Practice may be cited in support of the charge.

The Standards of Practice serve to clarify the ethical obligations imposed by the various Articles and supplement, and do not substitute for, the Case Interpretations in *Interpretations of the Code of Ethics.*

Modifications to existing Standards of Practice and additional new Standards of Practice are approved from time to time. Readers are cautioned to ensure that the most recent publications are utilized.

CODE OF ETHICS
NATIONAL ASSOCIATION
OF REAL ESTATE BROKERS, INCORPORATED

PART I. RELATIONS TO THE PUBLIC

1. A Realtist is never relieved of the responsibility to observe fully this Code of Ethics.

2. A Realtist should never be instrumental in establishing, reinforcing or extending leased or deed restrictions that limit the use and/or occupancy of real property to any racial, religious or national origin groups.

3. The Realtist realizes that it is his duty to protect the public against any misrepresentations, unethical practices or fraud in his real estate practices, and that he offer all properties on his listing solely on merit and without exaggeration, concealment, deception or misleading information.

4. A Realtist should always avoid offering a property without (a) written authorization of the owner or a person acting in his behalf by power of attorney, (b) fully informing himself of the pertinent facts concerning the property, and (c) advising his client to secure advice of counsel as to the legality of instruments before receiving or conveying title or possession of real property, laws, proposed legislation and public policy relative to the use and/or occupancy of the property.

5. The Realtist should always offer the property at the price the owner has agreed to accept, but never greater.

6. The Realtist should always inform all parties of his own position in the transaction and should not demand or accept a commission from both parties, except with the knowledge and consent in writing and signed by all parties.

7. The Realtist should be diligent in preventing property under his management from being used for immoral or illegal purposes.

8. The Realtist realizes that all contracts and agreements for the ownership, use and/or occupancy of real properties should be in writing and signed by all parties, or their lawfully authorized agents.

9. The Realtist should disclose the fact, if he is purchasing a property to the account of his client and if he has a personal interest in the ownership.

PROFESSIONAL RELATIONS

1. The Realtist should always be loyal to his local Board or Real Estate Brokers and active in its work. The fellowship of his associates and the mutual sharing of experiences are always assets to his own business.

2. The Realtist should so conduct his business as to avoid controversies with his fellow realtists. Controversies between Realtists, who are members of the same local Board of Real Estate Brokers, should be submitted in writing for arbitration in accordance with the regulations of his or her Real Estate Board and not in an action at law. The decision in such arbitration should be accepted as final and binding.

3. Controversies between Realtists who are not members of the same local board should be submitted for arbitration to an Arbitration Board consisting of one arbitrator chosen by each Realtist from the Board of Real Estate Brokers to which he belongs and one other member, or a sufficient number of members to make an odd number, selected by the arbitrators thus chosen.

4. All employment arrangements between broker and salesmen should be reduced to writing and signed by both parties. It is particularly important to specify rights of parties, in the event of termination of employment. All listings acquired by a salesperson during his tenure of employment with the Broker, shall be the exclusive property or right of the employing Broker after such termination.

5. A Realtist should never publicly criticize a fellow Realtist; he should never express an opinion of a transaction unless requested to do so by one of the principals and his opinion then should be rendered in accordance with strict professional courtesy and integrity.

6. A Realtist should never seek information about fellow Realtists' transactions to use for the purpose of closing the transaction himself or diverting the client to another property.

7. When a cooperating Realtist accepts a listing from another Broker the agency of the Broker who offers the listing should be respected until it has expired and the property has come to the attention of the coordinating Realtist from a different source, or until the owner, without solicitation, offers to list with the cooperating Realtist; furthermore, such a listing should not be passed on to a third Broker without the consent of the listing Broker.

8. Negotiations concerning property which is listed with one Realtist exclusively should be carried on with the listing Broker, not with the owner.

9. The Realtist is free to negotiate fees in the lease, sale or exchange of Real Estate. Fees should be based on reasonable compensation for services to be rendered to the client. The Realtist should refrain from making any vestige of unfair competition or making fee structures and/or the advertising thereof in such a manner as to be demeaning to the real estate profession.

10. A Realtist should not solicit the services of any employee in the organization of a fellow Realtist without the written consent of the employer.

11. Signs should never be placed on any property by a Realtist without the written consent of the owner.

ARTICLE I

Name

The name of the organization shall be:

National Association of Real Estate Brokers, Incorporated.

ARTICLE II

Purposes

The purposes of the National Association shall be:

Section 1.   To unite those engaged in the recognized branches of the real estate business, including brokerage, management, mortgage financing, appraising, land development and home building, and allied fields in the United States of America and Canada, for the purpose of exerting effectively a combined influence upon matters affecting real estate interests;

Section 2.   To enable its members to transact their business to better advantage than heretofore, by the adoption of such rules and regulations as they may deem proper;

Section 3.   To promote and maintain high standards of conduct in the transaction of the real estate business;

Section 4.   To formulate and enforce a code of ethics for the members of the National Association of Real Estate Brokers, Incorporated;

Section 5.   To license its members the right to use the term or symbol "Realtist" which is hereby defined as designating a person engaged in the real estate business who is a Board Member or Individual Member of the National Association of Real Estate Brokers, Incorporated, is subject to its rules and regulations, observes its standards of conduct, and is entitled to its benefits; and

Section 6.   To protect the public against unethical, improper or fraudulent practices by the affixing of the term or symbol "Realtist" to advertising matter, stationery, signboards, stock certificates, bonds, mortgages, and other instruments or other material used by or in connection with the real estate business, and to educate the general public to deal only with those persons who have agreed to observe the standards maintained by the National Association of Real Estate Brokers, Incorporated.

ARTICLE III

Membership

Section 1. (a) The members of the National Association of Real Estate Brokers, Incorporated, shall consist of seven (7) classes:

1.   Member Boards
2.   Local Board Members
3.   Associate Members
4.   Individual Members
5.   Allied Members
6.   Life Members
7.   Honorary Members

1.   Member Boards shall consist of local boards of Real Estate Brokers which shall include city, county, or intercounty boards and state associations of Real Estate Brokers.

2.   Local Board Members shall be persons who are certified by a local board as eligible for membership in the National Association of Real Estate Brokers, Incorporated.

Relationship of Real Estate Trade Associations/Boards to the Government and Real Estate Law

While many real estate trade associations/boards have adopted their own codes of ethics and professional conduct and procedures to enforce such codes and conduct, real estate trade associations/boards are private entities and not formally affiliated with or related to the government. In addition, real estate trade associations/boards do not have authority to regulate real estate licensees under real estate licensing laws or otherwise make decisions on civil and criminal law.

4 Property

In English Common Law, the word property referred not to the *thing* owned, but rather to the *rights* which the owner had: the rights to possess, use, encumber, transfer and exclude others. Property consisted of a "bundle of rights" or a "bundle of interests" a person had in a thing, whether the thing was real or personal property.

The early English courts distinguished between lawsuits in which the landowner, if wrongfully ousted, could recover the land itself (the "real thing") and those lawsuits in which the owner could recover only monetary damages. By bringing a "real action," the owner could receive the return of the land, the "real property." An action for monetary damages was called "personal," and the owner's limited interest was labeled "personal property."

In the feudal society of medieval England, an estate was the ownership interest that a person had in the land. The estate was termed a freehold estate when the owner's interest was not subject to certain servile incidents or demands of the overlord. Only an owner of a freehold estate could bring a real action. Therefore, only freehold estates were regarded as real property. A freehold estate was of indefinite duration. A less-than-freehold estate was an interest of specified duration.

Freehold Estates

A freehold estate could be an estate in fee or a life estate. An estate in fee could be either absolute or qualified.

An *estate in fee simple absolute* was the largest estate recognized by the law. Among other rights, its owner controlled its disposition, including the right to will it. Upon disposition, this estate could become *qualified* by a condition. For example, grantor A could sell the estate to grantee B on the condition that the property be used as a hostel for itinerant musicians. If B changed the use, A could reenter the property and terminate B's estate. Hence, B's fee/estate could be defeated and was termed *fee simple defeasible.*

A *life estate* would be created if grantor A conveyed real property to B for the life of B *or* the life of some other person, with the initial grant controlling disposition of the estate upon the death of B (or the death of the other person). Again, this was a freehold because its duration was not fixed in specified temporal terms (i.e., months or years).

Less-Than-Freehold Estates

Less-than-freehold estates were the rights of tenants who rented or leased real property. These estates were personal property.

THE MODERN VIEW

Today, we think of property as the *thing* (not the *rights*) owned. Property is either real or personal. Real property consists of:

1. Land;

2. Anything affixed and regarded as a permanent part of the land;

3. That which is incidental or appurtenant to the land; and

4. That which is immovable by law.

Land

Land includes the soil, rock, and other substances that compose the material of the earth. It also includes space. Not just the space on the surface of the earth, but also the space beneath it to the center of the earth and the space above it to the top of the sky.

The courts have recognized a public right to the use of airspace above private land as a "highway" available to all so long as such use does not unreasonably interfere with the landowner's enjoyment of the property. The courts also recognize the fluid and "fugitive" or moving nature of subsurface oil and gas. The right of the landowner to drill vertically into his or her land for the purpose of capturing these substances is a valuable part of what is included in the ownership of land, but this does not include any right to drill slantwise under a neighbor's land for this purpose.

Things Affixed to Land

These include buildings, bridges and trees, as well as anything that is affixed to them (e.g., the doors of a building, permanently installed cabinets, or built-in appliances).

Incidental or Appurtenant to the Land

This form of real property includes anything which is by right used with the land for its benefit.

Examples are watercourses or easements/rights of way over adjoining lands and even passages for light, air, or heat from or across the land of another. Another example is stock in a mutual water company. When such stock is "appurtenant to the land," ownership of the stock may not be transferred unless the land is transferred with it.

Crops

A tenant's crops (emblements), industrial growing crops and things attached to or forming part of the land which are agreed to be severed before sale or under a contract of sale, shall be treated as goods.

"Modern" Estates

Section 761 of the California Civil Code (enacted in 1872) classifies estates in real property, with respect to duration, as:

1. Estates of inheritance or perpetual estates;

2. Estates for life;

3. Estates for years; or

4. Estates at will.

PERSONAL PROPERTY

Personal property is any property that is not real property. It includes money, movable goods or chattels, evidences of debt and choses (things) in action.

"Choses in action" is a legal phrase used to describe the right to recover money or other personal property through a judicial proceeding. It includes the right to recover something under a contract (e.g., money owed on a note) and the right to recover damages for a tort or private wrong

FIXTURES

Fixtures are items of personal property which are attached to the land in such a manner as to be considered part of the real property.

The courts have utilized five general tests to determine whether or not a given piece of personal property is a fixture. These are:

1. **The intention** of the person incorporating the personal property into the land.

2. The **method** by which the property is incorporated into the land. The degree of permanence of the annexation is significant. For example, if the attachment is by cement and plaster, the item so attached is likely to be classified as a fixture.

3. The **adaptability** of the personal property so attached for *ordinary* use in connection with the land. If well adapted, the item is probably a fixture.

4. The existence of an **agreement** between the parties involved as to the nature of the property affixed to the land. If there is a clear agreement, the status of the attached item is not likely to be an issue.

5. The **relationship** between the person who adds or annexes the article and the person with whom a dispute arises as to its character. This would usually involve seller and buyer or landlord and tenant.

Buyers and lenders inspecting property in contemplation of purchase or loan are justified in assuming that whatever is attached to the land or building and is essential for its use will be part of the conveyance/security. The contract should state clearly any desired exceptions.

A tenant may, during the term of the tenancy, remove from the premises anything the tenant has affixed thereto for purposes of trade, manufacture, ornament or domestic use, *provided* the removal can be accomplished without damage to the premises. This exception does not apply if the thing has, by the manner in which it is affixed, become an integral part of the premises.

LEGAL DIFFERENCES BETWEEN REAL AND PERSONAL PROPERTY

The following are important legal differences between real and personal property:

1. To be enforceable, an agreement for the sale of real property must ordinarily be in a writing signed by the party to be charged. An agreement for the sale of personal property must be in writing if the amount or value of the property exceeds $500.

2. For the most part, the laws of the situs state govern the transfer of title to real

property. Commercial sales of personal property are subject to federal and state laws.

3. The state has provided by law a system for recording documents or instruments affecting the title or interest in real property.

4. Tax laws often distinguish between real and personal property. To the property owner and the taxing authority, the distinction may be one of considerable importance.

LAND DESCRIPTIONS

Every parcel of land sold, leased or mortgaged must be properly identified or described. These descriptions are often referred to as *legal descriptions*. A good description is said to be one which describes no other piece of property but the one involved in the transaction.

The three most common methods of describing property are: by recorded map; by U. S. Government section and township; and by metes and bounds.

Recorded Map
In California, the Subdivision Map Act (Government Code Sections 66410 et seq.) requires the mapping of all new subdivisions. The map shows the relationship of the subdivision to other lands and each parcel in the subdivision is delineated and identified. When accepted by county or city authority, the map is filed in the county recorder's office. Documentation can then describe any lot in the subdivision by indicating the lot number, the block, and the map. The description also includes the name of the city, county and state. For example:

"Lot 14, Block B, Parkview Addition (as recorded July 17, 1956, Book 2, Page 49 of maps), City of Sacramento, County of Sacramento, State of California."

Description by Township and Section
In the township and section system, we begin with *base lines*, which are horizontal, and *meridians*, which are vertical.

This system establishes a grid of vertical lines ("ranges") and horizontal lines ("township" lines). The lines are six miles apart. A square created by intersections is therefore six miles on each side and contains 36 square miles. Each of these squares is called a township. (In order to correct for the spherical shape of the Earth, additional *guide meridians* are run every 24 miles east and west of the *meridian* and *standard parallels* are run every 24 miles north and south of the *base line*. These are known as *correction lines.*)

In land descriptions, we move "townships" (north or south) from a principal base line and "ranges" (east or west) from a principal meridian,

California has three sets of base lines and meridians: the Humboldt Base Line and Meridian in the northwestern part of the State; the Mt. Diablo Base Line and Meridian in the central part of the State; and the San Bernardino Base Line and Meridian in the southern part of the State.

The description "township 4 north, range 3 east, Humboldt Base Line and Meridian" directs us to the township which is 4 townships to the north from the Humboldt Base Line and 3 townships to the east from the Humboldt Meridian.

Here is a township, with its 36 (square mile) sections numbered and further divided so that the smallest squares are quarters of quarter sections, each containing 40 acres.

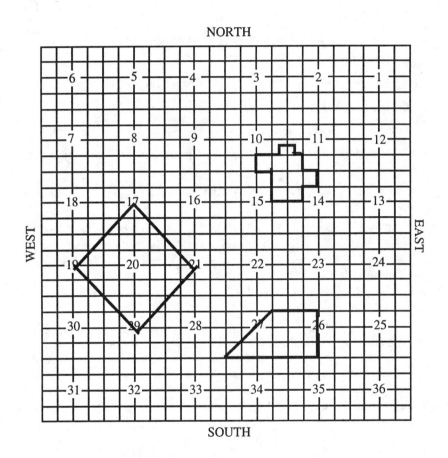

NORTH

WEST

EAST

SOUTH

The following mathematical observations may aid understanding of section/township descriptions:

- a township is a square, six miles on each side;

- a township contains 36 sections;

- each of the 36 sections in a township is a square, one mile on each side;

- a mile is 5,280 feet;

- a square mile is 27,878,400 square feet (5,280 x 5,280);

- an acre is 43,560 square feet;

- each section in a township is 640 acres (27,878,400 divided by 43,560);

- a half-section is 320 acres;

- a quarter-section is 160 acres; and

- a quarter of a quarter-section (the smallest squares in the township plat) is 40 acres.

The following is the description for the diamond-shaped figure on the township on the preceding page.

Beginning at the NE. corner of SW. 1/4 of Sec. 17, thence southeasterly to the NW. corner of the SE. 1/4 of Section 21, thence southwesterly to the SE. corner of the NW.1/4 of Sec. 29, thence northwesterly to the SW. corner of the NE. 1/4 of Sec. 19, thence northeasterly to the point of beginning.

The description is linear, delineating the boundaries of the figure by connecting four points.

For practice, the reader may want to write out the descriptions of the other two figures. The description of the figure in the upper right can begin: "The SE 1/4 of the NE 1/4 of the SE 1/4, and the S 1/2 of the SE 1/4 of Section 10;" If the reader can locate and shade that portion, the reader can write the rest of the description in like fashion.

The description of the third figure can begin as follows: "Beginning at the NW corner of the SE 1/4 of the NE 1/4 of Section 27, thence due east 3,960 feet,". [Each side of a quarter of a quarter section measures 1,320 feet (5,280 ÷ 4). The line/side described therefore measures 1,320 feet x 3 = 3,960 feet.]

Metes and Bounds Description

A "metes and bounds" description may be necessary when the property referred to is not covered by a duly recorded map and is shaped so as to make it impractical to describe by section and township. Some metes and bounds descriptions are lengthy and difficult for anyone but a civil engineer or surveyor to understand. A complex metes and bounds description is a burden to county recorders and assessors.

A *metes and bounds* description starts at a fixed point of beginning and follows, in detail, the boundaries of the land described in courses and distances from one point to another until returning to the point of beginning. If a mistake is made at the point of beginning, the description is worthless.

Metes are measures of length: feet, yards, etc.

Bounds are measures of boundaries, both natural and manmade: e.g., rivers and roads. Landmarks (trees, boulders, creeks, fences, roads and iron pipes, etc.), referred to as monuments, are often used in such descriptions.

Older descriptions of this type used markers that have disappeared, been moved or otherwise been altered, making the descriptions indefinite. Thus, since markers are subject to destruction and disappearance they should be used only where necessary and every identifying feature should be designated.

Here is a drawing and metes and bounds description of a regular parcel (front and rear dimensions and sides are the same).

Plat Map
Lots 1 to 8, block 10, tract 1502

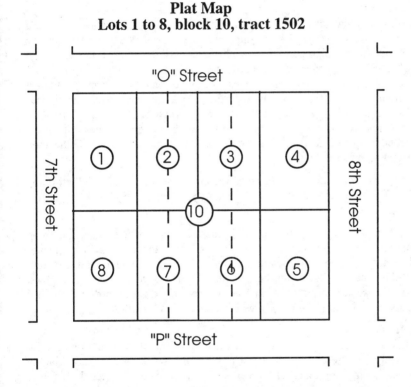

Beginning at a point on the southerly line of "O" Street, 150 feet westerly of the SW corner of the intersection of "O" and 8th Streets; running thence due south 300 feet to the northerly line of "P" Street; thence westerly along the northerly line of "P" Street, 100 feet; thence northerly and parallel to the first course, 300 feet, to the southerly line of "O" Street; thence easterly along the southerly line of "O" Street, 100 feet, to the point or place of beginning.

OTHER DESCRIPTION METHODS

Government Lots

In the original government survey system, lakes, streams and other features were sometimes encountered which created fractional pieces of land less than a quarter section in size. These fractional segments were identified by number. The specific lot number then became the legal description for that land parcel and these parcels were called *government lots.*

Today, acreage lost due to township correction lines and unascertainable errors is placed in the quarter sections bordering the western and northern boundaries of a township. These geographical divisions which would otherwise qualify as quarter-quarter sections are also referred to as "government lots." A government lot does not necessarily contain a standard number of acres.

Record of Survey

After establishing points or lines, a land surveyor or civil engineer who has made a survey in conformity with land surveying practices must file a record of survey relating to boundaries or property lines with the county surveyor in the county in which the survey was made. This record of survey map discloses: (1) material evidence of physical change which does not appear on any map previously recorded in the office of the county recorder; (2) a material discrepancy with information of record with the county; (3) any evidence that might result in alternate positions of lines or points; and (4) the establishment of lines not shown on a recorded map which are not ascertainable from an inspection of the map without trigonometric calculations.

The county surveyor, after examining a record of survey map filed with the surveyor's office, shall then file it with the county recorder.

Assessor's Maps

The county assessor may prepare and file in the assessor's office an accurate map of any land in the county and may number or letter the parcels in a manner approved by the board of supervisors. Section 327 of the Revenue and Taxation Code provides "that land shall not be described in any deed or conveyance by a reference to any such map unless such map has been filed for record in the office of the county recorder of the county in which such land is located."

Informal Method

In the absence of a title report, it is often found convenient to refer to a specific parcel of realty by street number, name (e.g., "The Norris Ranch"), or blanket reference (e.g., "my lot on High Street"). These methods are legal, but title companies will not ordinarily insure title involving such a description.

If there is doubt about the correct property description method to be used, a person should consult with a licensed engineer or surveyor or with a title company.

5 Title to Real Property

In California, the basic principles now followed governing title to real property were derived from England's Common Law. In the absence of some specifically applicable constitutional or statutory provisions, the Common Law prevails.

CALIFORNIA ADOPTS A RECORDING SYSTEM

One of the first acts of the legislature of the new state was to adopt a recording system by which evidence of title or interest could be collected in a convenient and safe public place, so that those planning to purchase or otherwise deal with land might be presumed to be informed about the ownership and condition of the title. This system was designed to protect innocent lenders and purchasers against secret conveyances and liens and to allow the title to the real property to be freely transferable. The California Legislature adopted a recording system modeled after the system established by the original American Colonies. It was strictly an American device for safeguarding the ownership of land.

Actual v. Constructive Notice
Actual notice consists of express information of a fact. Constructive notice means notice given by the public records. By means of constructive notice, people are presumed to know the contents of recorded instruments.

Which Instruments May Be Recorded
The Recording Act of California provides that, after being acknowledged, any instrument or judgment affecting the title to or possession of real property may be recorded.

The word "instrument" as used in the Recording Act means "some paper signed and delivered by one person to another, transferring the title to, or giving a lien on, property or giving a right to a debt or duty." (Hoag v. Howard, Cal. 564.) "Instrument" does not necessarily include every writing purporting to affect real property. Instrument does include deeds, mortgages, leases, land contracts, deeds of trust and agreements between or among landowners.

Purpose of Recording Statutes
The general purpose of recording statutes is to permit (rather than require) the recordation of any instrument which affects the title to or possession of real property, and to penalize the person who fails to take advantage of recording. Because of recording, purchasers and others dealing with title to property may in good faith discover and rely upon the ownership as shown by the recorded instruments. While the Recording Act does not specify any particular time within which an instrument must be recorded, priority of recordation will ordinarily determine the rights of the parties if there are conflicting claims to the same parcel of land.

Instruments affecting real property must be recorded by the county recorder in the county within which the property is located. If the property lies in more than one county, the instrument, or certified copy of the record, must be recorded in each county in which the property is located in order to impart constructive notice in the respective counties.

If it is necessary to record a document written in a foreign language, the recorder will file the foreign language instrument with a certified translation. In those counties in which a photographic method of recording is employed, the foreign language instrument and the translation may be recorded and the original instrument returned to the party seeking recordation.

When an Instrument is Deemed Recorded
Generally, an instrument is recorded when it is duly acknowledged or verified and deposited in the recorder's office with the proper officer and marked "filed for record." It is the duty of the recorder to number the instrument in the order in which it is deposited, include the year, month, day, hour and minute of its reception, and indicate at whose request it was "filed for record." The contents of the document are transferred to its appropriate book of records upon the page endorsed on the document, and the original document is returned to the party who left it for recording. The recorder indexes all recorded documents in alphabetical order according to the names of the grantors and grantees or mortgagors or mortgagees, and name or nature of the document. They are also indexed by date of recording and the recording reference.

Effect of Recording as Imparting Notice
The courts have ruled that the benefits of a recording statute are not available to one who takes title with *actual* notice of a previously executed though unrecorded instrument. For example, possession of land by one other than the seller is actual notice to an intending buyer sufficient to place a duty on the intending buyer to inquire about the possession. Despite the recording statutes and the assurance they give about the status of title, a prudent purchaser will always inspect the premises in person or through a trusted agent.

There are many types of unrecorded interests which a prospective purchaser may discover during a physical inspection of property. For example, a pathway or sewer line may mean adjoining owners have an unrecorded easement. Lumber or recent carpentry work may mean certain persons have a right to file mechanics' liens.

The recording laws do not protect the party "first to record" against the foregoing, nor do standard-form title insurance policies cover the situations described above.

Priorities in Recording
The California statute of priorities in recording encourages prompt recording of conveyances and prohibits use of the constructive notice doctrine as an aid to proven fraud. Only innocent parties are protected by the recording laws.

Not all liens on real property rank in priority according to their respective dates of recording. For example, with respect to the same parcel of property, A executed a mortgage in favor of B dated June 1 and recorded June 20. A executed a mortgage in favor of C dated June 10 and recorded June 15. C's mortgage will be superior in priority to B's only if C did *not* have, on or prior to June 15, notice of B's mortgage.

Special Lien Situations

The subject of liens and encumbrances is discussed later in detail but it will be helpful to note here the impact of the recording laws on this subject.

A lender will often agree to make "future advances" as a part of a secured loan transaction. Another lien (for example, a second deed of trust or mechanic's lien) may intervene between the time of recordation of the original lender's mortgage or deed of trust and the time of a future advance. A question of priority is then posed.

If the terms of the original loan transaction require the lender to make further advances (e.g., an installment payment under a construction loan), these "obligatory advances" have the same priority as the original deed of trust, regardless of intervening liens.

In other cases, the lender may have the privilege of advancing more money to the borrower but is not required to do so. This "optional advance" dates only from the time it is made unless the lender can show lender received no actual or constructive notice of intervening liens.

Mechanics' liens relate back to the time of the commencement of the construction work as a whole. Thus, a deed of trust must be executed, delivered, and recorded prior to commencement of any work at all in order to assure its priority.

Liens for real property taxes and other general taxes, as well as special county and municipal taxes and assessments are superior in priority to the lien of any mortgage or trust deed regardless of the date of execution or delivery or recording.

Provided they are bona fide encumbrances, trust deeds and mortgages recorded prior to general federal tax liens or state tax liens are superior in priority to those liens.

Persons having priority may by agreement waive this priority in favor of others. An agreement to do this is called a "subordination agreement." These agreements are often executed in connection with deeds of trust to subordinate a landowner's purchase-money deed of trust to a construction loan. Without such priority of claim for payment against the real property, the building contractor might refuse to expend time and materials on the project.

A mortgage or trust deed given for the purchase price of real property at the time of the conveyance has priority over all other liens created against the purchaser, subject to operation of the recording laws.

Two or more deeds of trust recorded at the same time (concurrently) may contain on the face of each deed of trust a recital about which deed of trust is intended by the parties to be first, second, third, etc. in priority. The recitals can be effective subordination agreements.

OWNERSHIP OF REAL PROPERTY

All property has an owner, either the government - federal, state or local — or some private party. Very broadly, an estate in real property may be owned in the following ways:

1.   Separate ownership;

2. Concurrent ownership;
   a. Tenancy in common;
   b. Joint tenancy; and
   c. Community property.

SEPARATE OWNERSHIP

Separate ownership means ownership by one person. Being the sole owner, one person alone enjoys the benefits of property and is subject to the accompanying burdens, such as the payment of taxes. A sole owner is free to dispose of property at will, and normally only a sole owner's signature is required on the deed of conveyance.

CONCURRENT OWNERSHIP

Concurrent ownership or co-ownership means simultaneous ownership of a given piece of property by two or more persons. The several types of concurrent ownership are:

Tenancy in Common

Tenancy in common exists when two or more persons are owners of undivided interests in the title to real property. It is created if an instrument conveying an interest in real property to two or more persons does not specify that the interest is acquired by them in joint tenancy or in partnership or as community property.

Example: Interests of such tenants in common may be any fraction of the whole. One party may own one-tenth, another three-tenths, and a third party may own the remaining six-tenths. If the deed to cotenants does not recite their respective interests, the interests will be presumed to be equal.

There is a unity of possession in tenancy in common. This means each owner has a right to possession and none can exclude the others nor claim any specific portion for himself or herself alone. It follows that no tenant in common can be charged rent for the use of the land unless otherwise agreed to by all the cotenants. On the other hand a tenant in common who receives rent for the premises from a third party, must divide such profits with the other tenants in common in proportion to the shares owned. By the same token, payments made by one tenant in common for the benefit of all may normally be recovered on a proportionate basis from all. These might include moneys spent for necessary repairs, taxes, and interest and principal under a trust deed.

Any tenant in common is free to sell, convey or mortgage the tenant's own interest as he or she sees fit, and the new owner becomes a tenant in common with the others. Sometimes this may be impractical, and the tenant may force a sale of the entire property by filing an action in court known as a "partition action." As there is no right of survivorship, the undivided interest of a deceased tenant in common passes to his or her heirs or devisees who simply take the tenant's place among the owners of the property in common.

Joint Tenancy

Joint tenancy exists if two or more persons are joint and equal owners of the same undivided interest in real property. We regard this as a fourfold unity: interest, title, time, and possession. Joint tenants have one and the same interest, acquired by the same conveyance, commencing at the same time, and held by the same possession.

The most important characteristic of joint tenancy is the right of survivorship which flows from the unity of interest. If one joint tenant dies, the surviving joint tenant (or tenants) immediately becomes the sole owner. Thus, joint tenancy property cannot be disposed of by will nor does it become part of the estate of a joint tenant subject to probate. Further, the surviving joint tenant is not even liable to creditors of the deceased who hold unforeclosed liens on the joint tenancy property. The words "with the right of survivorship" are not necessary for a valid joint tenancy deed, although they are often inserted.

The creditors of a living joint tenant may proceed against the interest of that tenant and force an execution sale. This would sever the joint tenancy and leave title in the execution purchaser and the other joint tenant as tenants in common.

Exceptions. California appellate courts have accepted and enforced the common law rule that if any one of the four unities — time, title, interest or possession — is lacking, a tenancy in common, not a joint tenancy, exists. By statute, however, a joint tenancy may be created:

1. By transfer from a sole owner to himself or herself and others as joint tenants.

2. By transfer from tenants in common to themselves or to themselves, or any of them, and others as joint tenants.

3. By transfer from joint tenants to themselves, or any of them, and others as joint tenants.

4. By transfer from a husband and wife (when holding title as community property or otherwise) to themselves, or to themselves and others, or to one of them and to another or others as joint tenants.

5. By transfer to executors of an estate or trustees of a trust as joint tenants.

Severance. A joint tenant may sever the joint tenancy as to his or her own interest by a conveyance to a third party, or to a cotenant. If there are three or more joint tenants, the joint tenancy is severed as to the interest conveyed but continues as between the other joint tenants as to the remaining interests. If title is in A, B and C as joint tenants and A conveys to D, then B and C continue as joint tenants as to a two-thirds interest and D owns a one-third interest as tenant in common. If A and B only are joint tenants and B conveys to C, then A and C own as tenants in common. Also, partition may be had by joint tenants. If the partition cannot be made without prejudice to the owners, a court may order sale of the property and division of the proceeds.

In some circumstances, a severance will not terminate the right of survivorship interest of the other joint tenants in the severing joint tenant's interest. Nor, under the circumstances set out in Civil Code Section 683.2, may a severance contrary to a written agreement of the joint tenants defeat the rights of a purchaser or encumbrancer for value and in good faith and without knowledge of the written agreement.

On death of a joint tenant, the joint tenancy is automatically terminated. Nevertheless, for record title purposes, the following must be recorded in the county where the property is located:

- A certified copy of a court decree determining the fact of death and describing the property; OR

- A certified copy of the death certificate or equivalent, or court decree determining the fact of death, or letters testamentary or of administration or a court decree of distribution in probate proceedings. With each of these alternatives, it is customary to attach an affidavit which identifies the deceased as one of the joint tenants of the property.

The pros and cons of joint tenancy. On the plus side, the major advantage of joint tenancy is the comparative simplicity of vesting title in the surviving joint tenant (or joint tenants). The title delay of upward from six months involved in probate proceedings is avoided. Although certain legal costs are ultimately involved in formally terminating the joint tenancy, the customary commissions and fees payable to executors or administrators and to attorneys are avoided.

A further advantage of joint tenancy is that the survivor holds the property free from debts of the deceased tenant and from liens against the deceased tenant's interest. This can work an injustice to creditors, but a diligent creditor can usually take appropriate precautionary steps to avoid such loss, or may have access to other assets of the decedent.

On the other hand, in many situations joint tenancy is a pitfall for the ignorant or unwary.

The supposed advantages may be imaginary. A joint tenant may not want the other (surviving) joint tenant to get the title free and clear; the saving in probate fees is at least partly offset by costs of terminating the joint tenancy, and, indeed, may be completely offset by added taxes; the probate delay is not unreasonably long; and there may in fact be no creditors to worry about. Moreover, the joint tenant gives up the right to dispose of his or her interest by will.

Giving advice about the way to hold title to real property is ill-advised because tax and other consequences may result from holding title in one form or another.

Community Property

Community property basically consists of all property acquired by a husband and wife, or either, during a valid marriage, other than separate property. Separate property of either the husband or the wife is not community property.

Separate property of a married person includes:

1. All property owned before marriage.

2. All property acquired during marriage by gift or inheritance.

3. All rents, issues and profits of separate property, as well as other property acquired with the proceeds from sale of separate property. For instance, if a wife owned a duplex prior to marriage, the rents from the duplex would remain her separate property. If she sold the duplex and bought common stock,

the stock and dividends would be her separate property. It would have to be clearly and unequivocally identifiable as separate property, and separate records should be maintained to make certain any separate property is not commingled with the community property in any way. Very often husband and wife deliberately or casually allow their separate property to merge with community property in keeping with their intentions.

4. Earnings and accumulations of a spouse while living separate and apart from the other spouse.

5. Earnings and accumulations of each party after a court decree of separate maintenance.

6. Property conveyed by either spouse to the other with the intent of making it the grantee's separate property.

It should be recalled that a husband and wife may hold property as joint tenants. Yet, even when title is held in joint tenancy, it is possible (e.g., by separate written agreement) to own the assets as community property. The record title may not be controlling in light of off-record agreements showing other intentions of the parties. Joint tenancy property owned by married persons may, in fact, be considered separate property.

Management and control. Each spouse has equal management and control of community property. An exception exists if one of the spouses manages a community personal property business. That spouse has sole management and control of that business. Community property is liable for the debts of either spouse contracted after marriage. Community property is liable for a debt contracted prior to marriage, except that portion of the community property comprised of the earnings of the other spouse.

Neither spouse may make a gift of community property without the consent of the other. Neither spouse may encumber the furniture, furnishings, or fittings of the home, or the clothing of the other spouse or minor children without the written consent of the other spouse. Both must join in the conveyance, encumbrance or leasing of community real property.

If real property is owned by more than one person, licensees should obtain all necessary signatures to the contract at the time the owners sign the listing and acceptance.

Each spouse has the right to dispose of his or her half of community property by will. Absent a will, title to the decedent's half of the community property passes to the surviving spouse.

Joint tenancy and community property. Considerable confusion surrounds the status of some family homes in California since husband and wife may acquire their home with community funds but proceed to take record title "as joint tenants." It is not generally understood that some of the consequences of holding title in joint tenancy are entirely different from the consequences of holding title as community property.

The California courts are aware of this problem and have established the rule that the true intention of husband and wife as to the status of their property shall prevail over the record title. Ambiguity results from the specific circumstance of having the record title in joint tenancy while the true character of the property which husband and wife intended is community property. This transition might be accomplished by appropriate agreement in writing, or even by a deed from themselves as joint tenants to themselves "as community property."

Among themselves, the rights and duties of joint tenants are generally the same as among tenants in common, with the vital exception of the rule of survivorship. A joint tenant may borrow money and as security execute a mortgage or deed of trust on his/her interest just as a tenant in common may. This does not destroy the joint tenancy, but if the borrower should default, and the mortgage or deed of trust should be foreclosed while the borrower is still alive, the joint tenancy would be ended (severance) and a tenancy in common created. Most lenders would hesitate to make such a loan. If the borrower dies before the mortgage is paid off or foreclosed, the surviving joint tenant gets title free and clear of the mortgage executed by the deceased joint tenant.

TENANCY IN PARTNERSHIP

Tenancy in partnership exists if two or more persons, as partners, own property for partnership purposes. Under the Uniform Partnership Act, the incidents of tenancy in partnership are such that:

1. A partner has an equal right with all other partners to possession of specific partnership property for partnership purposes. Unless the other partners agree, however, no partner has a right to possession for any other purpose.

2. A partner's right in specific partnership property is not assignable except in connection with the assignment of rights of all the partners in the same property.

3. A partner's right in specific partnership property is not subject to attachment or execution, except on a claim against the partnership.

4. On death, a partner's right in specific partnership property vests in the surviving partner (or partners). The rights in the property of the last surviving partner would vest in the decedent's legal representative. In either case, the vesting creates a right to possess the partnership property only for partnership purposes.

5. A partner's right in specific partnership property is not subject to dower or curtesy (both have been abolished in California by statute) nor allowance to widows, heirs, or next of kin. Even when married, a partner's right is not community property. On the other hand, a partner's interest in the partnership as such (that is, a partner's share of profits and of surplus) is governed by community property rules for some purposes.

These incidents make sense because two or more persons are attempting to carry on a business for profit. Without these incidents, continuity and unified, efficient operation would be difficult. Partners are not, however, prevented from owning different fractional parts of the business. Thus, although each partner has unlimited liability to third parties for firm debts, each partner's interest in profits and losses may be any percentage agreed upon. Partners may also structure the business relationship as a partnership in many different ways. By agreement, one partner may have greater authority than the other partners.

ENCUMBRANCES

In this section, we examine the principal types of encumbrances which may be imposed on a given parcel of land without destroying the owner's estate.

Definition

An encumbrance may be defined very generally as any right or interest in land, possessed by a stranger to the title, which affects the value of the owner's estate but does not prevent the owner from enjoying and transferring the fee.

There are two categories of encumbrances: those affecting title and those affecting condition or use of property.

Encumbrances that affect title. Most notably, these are liens. A lien is defined as a charge imposed on property and made security for the performance of an act, typically the payment of a debt/promissory note. Liens may affect real or personal property and may be voluntary (e.g., a home mortgage to secure a loan) or involuntary (e.g., imposed by law for overdue taxes). A lien may be specific, affecting only a particular property (e.g., a trust deed, or a mechanic's lien on a given property) or general, affecting all property of the owner not exempt by law (e.g., a money judgment, or a lien for overdue state or federal income taxes).

Encumbrances that affect the physical condition or use of the property. These are easements, building restrictions and zoning requirements, and encroachments.

A buyer will commonly accept a deed to encumbered property, with the price adjusted accordingly. Often, the encumbrance is not objectionable; for example, an easement for utility wires. But sometimes a buyer may insist that the encumbrance be removed or cleared from the public record before the transaction closes.

Cloud on the title. A "cloud on the title" is defined as any outstanding claim or encumbrance which would, if valid, affect or impair the owner's title to a particular estate. While the cloud remains, the owner is prevented from conveying marketable title.

Examples are: a mortgage paid off but without official recordation of that fact; an apparent interest in the property which remains because one of a group of heirs fails to sign the deed on sale of the property; or a notice of action (a lis pendens) which remains on the public record even after plaintiff and defendant have agreed to dismissal of the court action. Removal of a cloud may require time and patience. Meanwhile, closing will be postponed until the owner obtains a title insurance policy without reference to the cloud.

MECHANIC'S LIEN

California law expressly provides that persons furnishing labor or material for the improvement of real estate may file liens upon the property affected if the persons furnishing labor or material are not paid. Thus, an unpaid contractor, or a craftsman employed by the contractor to work on a building project but who has not been paid by the owner or contractor may protect their right, as an unpaid contractor or craftsman employed by a contractor, to get paid by filing a lien against the property in a manner prescribed by law. The same right is held by any person who has furnished material such as lumber, plumbing, or roofing if the claim is not paid. It is because of the possibility of these liens being recorded that an owner employing a contractor sometimes requires that a bond be furnished to guarantee payment of possible mechanics' lien claims.

Definition

A lien is a charge imposed in some way, other than by a transfer in trust upon specific property by which it is made security for the performance of an act. A mechanic's lien is a lien which secures payment to persons who have furnished material, performed labor, or expended skill in the improvement of real property belonging to another.

It is helpful to keep in mind while reading and thinking about this material on mechanics' liens that:

• The mechanic's lien claimant's fundamental objective is to get paid; and

• The claim of mechanic's lien is the claimant's security used to reach the objective of payment.

To convert the security for the lien into money requires:

1. Timely recordation of a notice and claim of lien (one document) in the county recorder's office in which the work of improvement is located;

2. Perfection of the recorded notice and claim of lien by the filing of an action (a lawsuit) in the right court ;

3. Recordation of a lis pendens;

4. Timely pursuit of the lawsuit to judgment; and

5. Enforcement of that judgment by a mechanic's lien foreclosure sale.

Origin. The basic lien rights of mechanics, materialmen, artisans and laborers is found at Article XIV, Section 3 of the State Constitution:

"Sec. 3. Mechanics, persons furnishing materials, artisans, and laborers of every class, shall have a lien upon the property upon which they have bestowed labor or furnished material for the value of such labor done and material furnished; and the Legislature shall provide, by law, for the speedy and efficient enforcement of such liens."

The statutes enacted pursuant to this constitutional provision are in Title 15 Division 3, Part 4, of the Civil Code, commencing with Section 3082.

The theory. The mechanic's lien law is based on the theory that improvements to real property contribute additional value to land; therefore, it is only equitable to impose a charge on the land equal to such increase in value. This charge may exist in the absence of any direct contract relationship between the lien claimant and the landowner. The lien must, however, be founded upon a valid contract with the contractor, subcontractor, lessee or vendee. Also, ordinarily the lien is valid only to the extent of labor and materials furnished for and actually used in the job.

Public policy. The mechanics' lien statutes and the decisions of the courts interpreting and construing them reflect a strong public policy of according extraordinary rights to unpaid contributors of services and material in the property they were instrumental in improving and in the funds intended for payment for the improvements. The rights of these unpaid contributors accrue and may be enforced against the property even though the owner of the property has not contracted with the claimant and has no personal liability to him.

The mechanic's lien device is the traditional remedy giving security to people who improve the property of others. However, owners are given means within the California statutes to protect against the burdening of their land with improper liens. The basic elements of California's system of protection for mechanics' lienors and owners are:

1. Mechanic's lien;

2. Stop notice on private work;

3. Stop notice on public work;

4. Payment bond on private work;

5. Payment bond on public work;

6. Contractor's license bond; and

7. Notice of nonresponsibility.

Persons Entitled to a Mechanic's Lien

The constitutional guarantee of the right to a mechanic's lien is accorded mechanics, artisans, and laborers. However, such lien rights have been extended by statute to all persons and laborers of every class performing labor upon, providing skill or other necessary services on furnishing materials, for, leasing equipment to be used upon, furnishing appliances, teams, or contributing power to a work of improvement. (Section 3110 of the Civil Code) Persons specifically entitled to mechanics' liens by virtue of the constitution and the statutes include the following:

Mechanics	Registered Engineers
Materialmen	Licensed Land Surveyors
Contractors	Machinists
Subcontractors	Builders
Lessors of Equipment	Teamsters
Artisans	Draymen
Architects	Union Trust Fund (Section 3111 Civil Code)

Property Subject to Mechanics' Liens

The property which may be subject to a claim of mechanic's lien should be considered to be that property described in a recorded claim of mechanic's lien. Perhaps the only safe exception to this is real property owned and used by the public. No lien for work or material attaches to a "public work." [*Los Angeles*

Stone Co. v. National Surety Co., 178 C 247, 173 P 79 (1918)] In situations in which private enterprise undertakes improvement of public lands, a claim of lien could be sustained against the improvement, although it would be invalid as to the land. [Western Electric Co. Inc. v. Colley, 79 CA 770, 251 P 331 (1926)]

With every statutory increase in the designation of those contributors of services and material entitled to a claim of mechanic's lien, there has usually been a corresponding broadening of the property interests which may be subjected to a claim of mechanic's lien. Today, under appropriate circumstances, a claim of mechanic's lien may attach to only a building or structure; only to land beneath a building or structure; to both land and the building or structure; or, to a parcel of land upon which there is no structure.

Public works. This discussion of the mechanic's lien law applies only to private works of improvement. Sections 3179 through 3214 and Sections 3247 through 3252 of the Civil Code should be consulted in connection with any question or problem arising from the contribution of labor or material to a public work of improvement. A "public work of improvement" means any work of improvement contracted for by a public entity. "Public entity" means the state, Regents of the University of California, a county, a city, district, public authority, public agency, and any other political subdivision or public corporation in the state.

Work of Improvement
Mechanics' liens are triggered by the commencement of a work of improvement. A work of improvement is defined in Section 3106 of the Civil Code as including the construction, alteration, addition to, or repair of a building or structure. The structure could be a bridge, ditch, well, fence, etc. It may also include activities not directly associated with a building or structure such as seeding, sodding, planting, or grading.

Lender's Priority
If commencement of work has occurred on a project prior to recordation of a deed of trust, all mechanics' liens are prior to the recorded deed of trust. The lender's margin of security for repayment of a construction loan is jeopardized by the commencement of work on the project prior to recordation of the deed of trust. If any mechanic's lien claimant can show that commencement of work occurred prior to recordation of the lender's deed of trust, all mechanic's lienors will take priority over the lender if the project real property is sold at sheriff's sale. (Civil Code Section 3134)

Preliminary 20-Day Notice

The right to claim a lien and to assert the privileges of a mechanic's lien claimant is dependent on compliance with numerous statutory procedural requirements.

The initial step in the perfection of a claim of mechanic's lien for all claimants, except one under direct contract with the owner, one performing actual labor for wages or an express trust fund as defined in Civil Code Section 3111, is to give the preliminary 20-day notice specified in Section 3097 of the Civil Code. That is, before recording a mechanic's lien, the lien claimant gives a written notice to certain persons, depending on the relationship of the lien claimant to the work of improvement and the owner of the real property on which the work has been done or will be done. The notice may be given any time after the contract has been entered into, but it must be given no later than 20 days after claimant has first furnished labor, services, equipment or materials to the job site. The preliminary 20-day notice is preliminary to the recording of a mechanic's lien. It is a prerequisite to the validity of a claim of mechanic's lien. The persons who are entitled to *receive* the notice depends on the relationship of the mechanic's lien claimant to the owner of the property. Thus,

1. If the claimant has a direct contract with the owner, the notice needs to be given only to the construction lender, if any, or to the reputed construction lender, if any (Section 3097(b) of the Civil Code).

2. If the claimant does not have a direct contract with the owner, the notice is required to be given to the following (Section 3097 (a) of the Civil Code):

   a. The owner, or reputed owner;

   b. The original contractor, or reputed contractor; and

   c. The construction lender, or reputed construction lender.

   d. Any subcontractors with whom the claimant has contracted.

The purpose of the notice is to inform the owner, original contractor, and construction lender, prior to the time of recording a claim of lien, that the improved property may be subject to liens arising out of a contract to which they are parties. [Wand Corp. v. San Gabriel Valley Lumber Co. 236 CA2d 855, 46 Cal. Rptr. 486 (1965)]

The preliminary 20-day notice shall contain all of the following:

1. Name and address of the person furnishing the labor, service, equipment, or materials and an estimate of the total price thereof;

2. Name of the person who contracted for purchase of the labor, service, equipment, or materials;

3. Common street address of the job site, sufficient for identification; and

4. A general description of the labor, service, equipment, or materials furnished, or to be furnished.

An up-to-date form should be used since a failure to use a current form that complies with the statute may cause the court to disregard the preliminary 20-day notice. [Harold James Inc. v. Five Points Ranch, Inc., 158 CA3 1, 204 CR 494 (1984)]

Every written contract entered into between a property owner and an original contractor shall provide space for the owner to enter his name and address of residence and place of business. The original contractor must make available the name and address of residence of the owner to any person seeking to serve a preliminary 20-day notice. (Section 3097 (m) of the Civil Code)

If one or more construction loans are obtained after commencement of construction, the property owner must provide the name and address of the construction lender or construction lenders to each person who has given to the property owner a preliminary 20-day notice. (Section 3097 (n) of the Civil Code)

Filing preliminary 20-day notice [Civil Code Section 3097(o)]. Each person serving a preliminary 20-day notice may file (not record) that notice with the county recorder in which any portion of the real property is located. The filed preliminary 20-day notice is not a recordable document and, hence, is not entered into the county recorder's indices which impart constructive notice. Filing of the preliminary 20-day notice does not impart actual or constructive notice to any person of the existence (or contents) of the filed preliminary 20-day notice. No duty of inquiry on the part of any party to determine the existence or contents of the preliminary 20-day notice is imposed by the filing.

The purpose of filing the preliminary 20-day notice is limited. It is intended to help those who filed the preliminary 20-day notice get notice (from the county recorder by mail) of recorded notices of completion and notices of cessation. Once the county recorder's office records either a notice of completion or cessation, it must mail to those persons who filed a preliminary 20-day notice, notification that a notice of completion or cessation has been recorded and the date of recording. (Section 3097 (o) (2) of the Civil Code)

Failure of the county recorder to mail the notification to the person who filed the preliminary 20-day notice or failure of those persons to receive notification shall not affect the period within which a claim of lien is required to be recorded.

The index maintained by the recorder of filed preliminary 20-day notices must be separate from those indices maintained by the county recorder of those official records of the county which by law impart constructive notice.

Determination of Completion Time
Fixing the time of completion, to the exact day, is critical to establishing whether or not a given claim of lien has been recorded within the time limit fixed by law. The determination of completion can be complex under California law. Generally, any one of the following alternatives is recognized by the law as equivalent to completion:

1. Occupation or use by the owner or owner's agent, accompanied by cessation of labor thereon;

2. Acceptance by the owner or owner's agent of the work of improvement;

3. A cessation of labor thereon for a continuous period of 60 days; or

4. A cessation of labor thereon for a continuous period of 30 days or more, if the owner records in the county recorder's office a prescribed notice of cessation (Section 3092, Civil Code).

If the work of improvement is subject to acceptance by any public entity, the completion date is considered as the date of acceptance or a cessation of labor for a continuous period of 30 days.

Thereafter the owner may file the notice of completion. If properly drawn, it will show the date of completion, the name and address of the owner, the nature of the interest or estate of the owner, a description of the property (which includes the official street address of the property if it has one), and the name of the original contractor, if any. If the notice is given only of completion of a contract for a particular portion of the total work of improvement, then the notice will also generally state the kind of work done or materials furnished. The notice of completion should be filed with the recorder of the county where the property is situated within 10 days after completion of the work of improvement.

A mechanic's lien may be filed:

1. By the *original contractor* within 60 days after the date of filing for record of the notice of completion. An original contractor is one who contracts directly with the owner or owner's agent to do the work and furnish materials for the entire job, or for a particular portion of the work of construction. Not uncommonly, the owner may enter into different original contracts, such as for plumbing, painting or papering. A material supplier, as such, is not an original contractor.

2. By *any claimant, other than the original contractor*, within 30 days after filing for record of the notice of completion.

3. If the notice of completion is not recorded, by *any claimant* within 90 days after completion of the work of improvement.

It should be noted that if there are two or more separate contracts and a notice of cessation or of completion is properly recorded as to one of them, the other contract cannot be tagged to it to extend the time in which the contractor thereunder may file a lien.

Termination of the Lien
Voluntary release of a mechanic's lien, normally after payment of the underlying debt, will terminate the lien. But even in the absence of release, the lien does not endure indefinitely. If a mechanic's lien claimant fails to commence an action to foreclose the claim of lien within 90 days after recording the claim of lien and if within that time no extended credit is recorded, the lien is automatically null, void and of no further force and effect. (Section 3144(b), Civil Code) When credit is extended for purposes of this limitation, it may not extend for more than one year from the time of completion of the work. Moreover, a notice of the fact and terms of the credit must be filed for record within the 90-day lien period.

If the lien is foreclosed by court action, there may ultimately be a judicial sale of the property and payment to the lienholder out of the proceeds.

Notice of Nonresponsibility
The owner or any person having or claiming any interest in the land may, within 10 days after obtaining knowledge of construction, alteration, or repair, give notice that he or she will not be responsible for the work by posting a notice in some conspicuous place on the property and recording a verified copy thereof. The notice must contain a description of the property; the name of the person giving notice and the nature of his/her title or interest; the name of the purchaser under the contract, if any, or lessee if known; and a statement that the person giving the notice will not be responsible for any claims arising from the work of improvement. If such notice is posted, the owner of the interest in the land may not

have his/her interest liened, provided the notice is recorded within the ten-day period.

The validity of a notice of nonresponsibility cannot be determined from the official county records since they will not disclose whether compliance has been made with the code requirements as to posting on the premises. If such posting has not been made, a recorded notice affords no protection from a mechanic's lien.

Release of Lien Bond
Owners and contractors disputing the correctness or the validity of a recorded claim of mechanic's lien may record, either before or after the commencement of an action to enforce the claim of lien, a lien release bond in accordance with the provisions of Civil Code Section 3143. A proper lien release bond, properly recorded, is effective to "lift" or release the claim of lien from the real property described in the lien release bond as well as any pending action brought to foreclose the claim of lien.

DESIGN PROFESSIONAL'S LIEN

Effective January 1,1991, California Civil Code Sections 3081.1 through 3081.9 provide for the filing of a design professional's lien.

For this purpose, a design professional is defined as a certificated architect, a registered professional engineer, or a licensed land surveyor.

If a landowner defaults under a contract with a design professional, the statutes provide that the design professional may mail to the landowner a statement of the default and a demand for payment. Subsequently, the design professional may record a notice of lien against the real property on which a work of improvement is planned to be constructed and to which the design professional supplied services pursuant to a written contract with the landowner.

The statutes provide for enforcement of a design professional's lien in the same manner as a mechanic's lien.

ATTACHMENTS AND JUDGMENTS

Property Subject to Attachment
Attachment is the process by which real or personal property of a defendant in a lawsuit is seized and retained in the custody of the law as security for satisfaction of the judgment the plaintiff hopes to obtain in the pending litigation. The plaintiff gets the lien before entry of judgment, and thus is somewhat more assured of availability of the defendant's property for eventual execution in satisfaction of the claim if judgment is indeed awarded to the plaintiff.

The purpose of an attachment is to protect a plaintiff who is a prospective judgment creditor against attempts by the defendant/debtor to transfer or dissipate the property subject to the attachment, and thus, in so dissipating the property, frustrate efforts to obtain satisfaction of a judgment subsequently obtained. The property seized and held under the attachment process constitutes an asset, or assets, which a judgment creditor may cause to be sold through execution proceedings in satisfaction of the judgment.

An attachment has always been referred to as a harsh remedy because it imposes a lien on the defendant's property and deprives him or her of absolute dominion and control over it for so long as it takes the court to adjudicate the plaintiff's claim. It is because of the deprivation of the defendant's right to dispose of defendant's attached property that the procedural framework of the attachment process has not been adopted to accommodate time consuming complex legal issues or disputes. Instead, the attachment process is based on the theory that the existence of a debt owed by the defendant to the plaintiff is conceded and that the principal function of the court is merely to ascertain the amount of that debt. This is why the right of a plaintiff to an attachment lien before trial has been historically confined to actions arising out of contracts, express or implied, for the payment of money.

Section 488.720 of the Code of Civil Procedure introduces a novel method of tempering the harsh consequences of an attachment lien and preventing its abuse. If, in noticed proceedings before the court, the value of the defendant's interest in the property sought to be attached can be shown to be clearly in excess of the amount necessary to satisfy plaintiff's claim, the court may order a release of as much of the property as it considers excess security.

Prejudgment attachments of the property of a natural person (individual) have been limited by case law and statute to claims arising out of the conduct of a business, trade or profession. There are numerous other limitations on obtaining a prejudgment attachment.

Exempt from attachment and execution. As a matter of public policy, certain property is exempt from attachment or execution when proper claim is made for exemption. (Code of Civil Procedure Sections 487.020 and 706.010, et seq.)

The most important exemption is the homestead, and the formalities of declaration of homestead by the owner are discussed later in this chapter.

Judgment

A final judgment is the final determination of the rights of the parties in an action or proceeding by a court of competent jurisdiction. There is, of course, always a possibility that either party will appeal, and the judgment might subsequently be reversed or amended. Comparatively few judgments are appealed, but even for those which are not, the judgment is not truly finalized until the time to appeal or seek other procedural legal relief has elapsed.

A simple money judgment does not automatically create a lien. However, as soon as a properly certified abstract of the judgment is recorded with the recorder of any county, it becomes a lien upon all real property of the judgment debtor located in that county. It extends, moreover, to all real property the debtor may thereafter acquire, in that county, before the lien expires. The lien of a lump sum money judgment normally continues for ten years from the date of entry of the judgment or decree.

As with the lien on attachment, a judgment lien is discharged if enforcement of the judgment is stayed on appeal and the defendant executes a sufficient undertaking (promise or security) or deposits in court the requisite amount of money.

EASEMENTS

Generally

Having considered various types of liens which are encumbrances affecting the title to property, we now direct our attention to encumbrances which affect the physical condition or use of the property. Easements, probably the most common of this category, are ordinarily rights to enter and use another person's land or a portion thereof within definable limits. Therefore, an easement is a right, privilege or interest limited to a specific purpose which one party has in the land of another.

Easement rights are often created for the benefit of the owner of adjoining land. The benefitted land is called the "dominant tenement," and the land subject to the easement is described as the "servient tenement." Unless the easement is specifically described to be "exclusive," its creation does not prevent the owner of the land from using the land and the portion covered by the easement in a way which does not interfere with the use of the easement.

Appurtenant Easements

Typical statutory easements (or land burdens or servitudes as they are also known) include: a right of ingress and egress (a right to go on the land and to exit from the land); the right to use a wall as a party wall; the right to receive more than natural support from adjacent land or things affixed thereto. These easements, when attached to a "dominant tenement," are considered "appurtenant" thereto, and pass automatically upon transfer of the dominant tenement without explicit mention in the instrument of transfer. "Appurtenant" means "belonging to." Civil Code Section 801 lists a variety of easements. Civil Code Section 801.5 provides for a solar easement.

Easements in Gross

It is possible to have an easement which is not appurtenant to particular land. Thus A, who owns no land, may have a right-of-way over B's land. Public utilities frequently enjoy easements to erect poles and string wires over private lands, yet own no related dominant tenement. Such easements are technically known as easements in gross, and are personal rights attached to the person of the easement holder and not attached to any specific land, yet in reality they encumber someone's land and in effect constitute an interest therein.

If the instrument creating an easement is unclear, the following factors are useful in determining whether the easement is appurtenant or in gross: (1) if the easement can fairly be construed as being attached to the land it will be so construed; (2) the intention of the parties and the right created are important considerations; and (3) outside evidence may be considered.

How Easements Are Created

Easements may be created in various ways, such as by express grant, express reservation, implied grant or implied reservation, agreement, prescription, necessity, dedication, condemnation, sale of land with reference to a plat, or estoppel.

Normally, easements arise in one of three ways. Either they are expressly set forth in some writing (such as a deed or a contract) or they arise by implication of law or by virtue of long use. Those created by deed must comply with the usual requirements of any deed and may arise either by express grant to another or by express reservation to oneself.

While the most common method of creating an easement is by express grant or reservation in a grant deed, written agreements between adjoining landowners often are used. The only person who can grant a permanent easement is the fee owner of the servient tenement or a person with the power to dispose of the fee.

Easement by Implication of Law

Civil Code Section 1104 contains the rule for implied grants. Certain conditions must exist at the time a property is conveyed before an easement by implied grant will have effect. An easement by necessity is one example of an easement by implication, but an easement by necessity differs somewhat in its requirements from other easements by implication.

The "way of necessity" is generally recognized whenever a transfer occurs which truly "landlocks" a parcel of real estate and there is no method of access whatsoever, except over the servient tenement retained by the seller, or over the land of a stranger.

Another implied easement is recognized when land in one ownership is divided, and at the time of division one portion is being used for the benefit of the other portion, e.g., a sewer lateral.

Easement by Prescription

Continuous and uninterrupted use for five years will create an easement by prescription where such use is hostile and adverse (i.e., without license or permission from the owner), open and notorious (i.e., the owner knows of the use or may be presumed to have notice of the use), exclusive (i.e., although use is not necessarily by one person only, it is such as to indicate to the landowner that a private right is being asserted), and under some claim of right. Also, if any ad valorem or other relevant real property taxes are assessed separately against the easement, these must be paid by the easement claimant.

Termination of Easements

Easements may be extinguished or terminated in several ways, including express release, legal proceedings, nonuse of a prescriptive easement for five years, abandonment, merger of the servient tenement and the easement in the same person, destruction of the servient tenement, and adverse possession by the owner of the servient tenement. An easement obtained by grant cannot be lost by nonuse.

RESTRICTIONS

A very common type of encumbrance is the restriction, which, as the name suggests, in some way restricts the free use of the land by the owner. Commonly, restrictions are referred to as the covenants, conditions, and restrictions (CC&Rs) or the declaration.

Restrictions are generally created by private owners, typically by appropriate clauses in deeds, or in agreements, or in general plans of entire subdivisions. A restriction usually assumes the form of a *covenant*—a promise to do or not to do a certain thing—or a *condition*. Zoning is an example of a public use restriction on the use of land.

Distinction Between Covenants and Conditions

A covenant is essentially a promise to do or not to do a certain thing. It is generally used in connection with instruments pertaining to real property, and is created by agreement. Typically it is embodied in deeds, but it may be found in any other writing. For example, a tenant might covenant in a lease to make certain repairs, or a buyer might covenant to use certain land only for a retail grocery store. A mere recital of fact, without anything more, is not a covenant.

A condition, on the other hand, is a qualification of an estate granted. Conditions, which can be imposed only in conveyances, are classified as conditions precedent and conditions subsequent. A condition precedent requires certain action or the happening of a specified event before the estate granted can vest (i.e., take effect).

A familiar example is a requirement found in most of the installment contracts of sale of real estate. All payments shall be made at the time specified before the buyer may demand transfer of title. If there is a condition subsequent in a deed, the title vests immediately in the grantee, but upon breach of the condition, the grantor has the power to terminate the estate. This is termed a forfeiture, since the title may revert or be forfeited to the creator of the condition without payment of any consideration.

Covenants and conditions are distinguishable in two further respects, in regard to the relief awarded and second, as to the persons by or against whom they may be enforced.

Relief awarded. As to the first, while a condition affects the estate created, and the failure to comply with it may result in a forfeiture of title, the only remedy to a breach of covenant is an action of damages or an injunction. Breach of a condition may prevent any right arising in favor of the breaching party, or destroy a right previously acquired, but does not subject the breaching party to liability and damages. Breach of covenant, while it gives rise to a right of actual damages, does not necessarily excuse the other party from performance.

Enforcement. As to the second difference, a covenant normally does not bind successors of the promisor who may become owners of the affected land. However, some covenants "run with the land" (i.e., they bind the assigns of the covenantor or promisor and vest in and benefit the assigns of the covenantee or promisee), or they may be binding and effective by statute or in equity. Conditions, on the other hand, always run with the restricted land into the indefinite future.

How construed. Whether a particular provision is a condition or covenant is a question of construction. Since the law abhors forfeitures, the courts ordinarily will construe restrictive provisions as covenants only, unless the intent to create a condition is plain. The use of the term "condition" or "covenant" is not always controlling. The real test is whether the intention is clearly expressed and the enjoyment of the estate conveyed was intended to depend upon the performance of a condition; otherwise, the provision will be construed as a covenant only.

For instance, the deed reciting that it is given upon the agreement of the grantee to do or not to do a certain thing implies a covenant and not a condition. So also with a recital that the land conveyed is or is not to be used for certain purposes.

Certain Covenants and Conditions Are Void

Covenants and conditions that are unlawful, impossible of performance, or in restraint of alienation are void.

A condition that a party shall not marry is void, but a condition to give use of property only *until* marriage is valid. A condition against conveying without the consent of the grantor, or for only a specified price, is void as in restraint of alienation. In such cases, title passes free of the condition subsequent. Title does not pass at all if a condition precedent is impossible to perform or requires the performance of a wrongful act. However, if the act itself is not wrong, but is otherwise unlawful, the deed takes effect and the condition is void.

Covenants Implied in Grant Deed

When the word "grant" is used in any conveyance of an estate of inheritance or fee simple, it implies the following covenants on the part of the grantor (and grantor's heirs or successors in interest) to the grantee (and grantee's heirs, successors and assigns):

1. That the grantor has not already conveyed the same estate or any interest therein to any other person;

2. That the estate is free from undisclosed encumbrances made by the grantor, or any person claiming under grantor. As noted earlier, encumbrances include liens, taxes, easements, restrictions, conditions.

Thus, a grant deed by a private party is presumed by law to convey a fee simple title unless it appears from the wording of the deed itself that a lesser estate was intended. Moreover, if a grantor subsequently acquires any title or claim of title to the real property which grantor had purported to grant in fee simple, that after-acquired title usually passes by operation of law to the grantee or grantee's successors.

Deed Restrictions

Restrictions imposed by deeds, or in similar private contracts, may be drafted to restrict, for any legitimate purpose, the use or occupancy of land. The right to acquire and possess property includes the right to dispose of it or any part of it, and to impose upon the grant any legal restrictions the grantor deems appropriate. However, the right may not be exercised in a manner forbidden by law. Restrictions prohibiting the use of property on the basis of race, color, sex, religion, ancestry, national origin, age (generally), disability, sexual orientation, marital status, familial status, or source of income are unenforceable under state and federal law. In addition, conditions considered unreasonable or "repugnant to the interest created" are prohibited by Section 711 of the Civil Code.

Restrictions may validly cover a multitude of matters: use for residential or business purposes; character of buildings (single family or multiple units); cost of buildings (e.g., a requirement that houses cost more than $100,000); location of buildings (e.g., side lines of five feet and 20-foot setbacks); and even requirements for architectural approval of proposed homes by a local group established for that purpose.

Unless the language used in the deed clearly indicates that the grantor intended the conditions or restrictions to operate for the benefit of other lots or persons, the restrictions run to the grantor only, and a quitclaim deed from the grantor, or grantor's heirs or assigns, is a sufficient release. However, if the language used in the deed shows that the conditions or restrictions were intended for the benefit of adjoining owners, or other lots or owners in the tract, quitclaim deeds must be obtained from all owners of lots having the benefit thereof, as well as from the grantor or grantor's heirs or assigns, in order to release them.

Notice of Discriminatory Restrictions

Effective January, 2000, a county recorder, title insurance company, escrow company, or real estate licensee who provides a declaration, governing documents or deed to any person must provide a specified statement about the illegality of discriminatory restrictions and the right of homeowners to have such language removed. The statement must be contained in either a cover page placed over the document or a stamp on the first page of the document.

New Subdivisions

In contrast to zoning ordinances, private contract restrictions need not promote public health, general public welfare or safety. They may be intended to create a particular type of neighborhood deemed desirable by the tract owner and may be based solely on aesthetic conditions. As might be expected, the most common use of restrictions today is in new subdivisions. The original subdivider establishes uniform regulations as to occupancy, use, character, cost and location of buildings and records a "declaration of restrictions" when the subdivision is first created. Thereafter, all lot owners, as among themselves, may enforce the restriction against any one or all of the others, provided the restrictions have been properly imposed.

In some cases, when land is originally subdivided, arrangement is made in the nature of a covenant whereby a perpetual property owners' association is formed, to be governed by rules and regulations set forth in an agreement signed by all new lot purchasers. Such associations are often given the power to amend tract restrictions from time to time to correspond with community growth. They may have the power to revise building restrictions pertaining to certain blocks of lots in the development, impose architectural restrictions and make other authorized requirements from time to time.

Termination

Restrictions may be terminated by

1.   expiration of their terms;

2.   voluntary cancellation;

3.   merger of ownership;

4.   act of government; or

5.   changed conditions (i.e., a court finds that the restrictions should be terminated because the conditions which the restrictions addressed have changed).

Restrictions usually have either a fixed termination date or one which becomes effective on recordation of a cancellation notice by a given percentage of the lot owners.

Zoning Regulations

Restrictions on the use of land may be imposed by government regulation as well as by private contracts.

The governing authority of a city or county has the power to adopt ordinances establishing zones within which structures must conform to specified standards as to character (including aesthetic considerations) and location, and to prohibit buildings designed for business or trade in designated areas. However, zoning restrictions, to be valid, should be substantially related to the preservation or protection of public health, safety, morals or general welfare. They must be uniform and cannot be discriminatory or created for the benefit of any particular group. Public authorities may enjoin or abate improvements or alterations which are in violation of a zoning ordinance, but only the use of the land, not the title, is affected.

ENCROACHMENTS

Adjoining owners of real property often find themselves involved with real estate law because of *encroachments* in the form of fences or walls and buildings extending over the boundary line. The party encroaching on a neighbor may be doing so with legal justification. The person who encroached may have gained title to the strip encroached on by adverse possession, or may have acquired an easement by prescription or possibly by implication.

On the other hand, the encroachment may be wrongful. If it is, the party encroached upon may sue for damages and a court may require removal of the encroachment.

Note: If the encroachment is slight (e.g., measurable in inches), the cost of removal great, and the cause an excusable mistake, a court may deny removal and award dollar damages.

HOMESTEAD EXEMPTION

The principal purpose of the *homestead exemption* is to shield the home against creditors of certain types whose claims might be exercised through judgment lien enforcement. Few areas of California real property law are more misunderstood by lay persons.

Obligations unaffected by the declaration. Over the years the homestead exemption amount has been increased from time to time, with the type of homestead determining the actual amount of the exemption. However, the validity of a homestead depends not only upon the recordation of the homestead declaration but on certain off-record matters as well, e.g., actual residency in the declared homestead dwelling at the time the declaration is recorded and an actual interest in the "dwelling."

The homestead declaration does not protect the homestead from all forced sales; e.g., it is subject to forced sale if a judgment is obtained: (1) prior to the recording of the homestead declaration; (2) on debts secured by encumbrances on the premises executed by the owner before the declaration was filed for record; and (3) obligations secured by mechanics', contractors', subcontractors', laborers', materialmen's or vendors' liens on the premises. Voluntary encumbrances by the owner of the homestead are not affected by a declaration of homestead. A mortgage or deed of trust is an example of a voluntary encumbrance.

Two Homestead Statutes

Articles 4 and 5 of Chapter 4, Division 2, Title 9, Part 2 of the California Code of Civil Procedure (Sections 704.710-704.995) contain, respectively, the residential homestead exemption and the declared homestead

While both articles deal with granting homeowners homestead protection from the claims of certain creditors, the articles seem to be mutually exclusive. Article 4 provides protection to homeowner debtors who meet the requirements but have not filed a declaration of homestead. Article 5 concerns homeowners who undertake the actual filing of a homestead declaration. In either case, there is protection against certain judgment liens to the amount of the exemption afforded by law.

The following discussion concerns primarily the declared homestead under Article 5.

(**NOTE:** A probate homestead also exists in California. See Probate Code Sections 60 and 6520 through 6528.)

Declared Homestead

A dwelling in which an owner or his or her spouse resides may be selected as a declared homestead by recording a homestead declaration in the office of the county recorder of the county where the dwelling is located. From and after the time of recording, the dwelling is a declared homestead.

Definitions for Declared Homestead

A "declared homestead" is the dwelling described in a homestead declaration and a "declared homestead owner" includes both (1) the owner of an interest in the declared homestead who is named as a declared homestead owner in a homestead declaration recorded pursuant to Article 5 and (2) the declarant named in a declaration of homestead recorded prior to July 1, 1983 pursuant to former law (Civil Code) and the spouse of such declarant.

"Dwelling" means any interest in real property (whether present or future, vested or contingent, legal or equitable) that is a "dwelling" as defined in Section 704.710 of Article 4 of this code, but does not include a leasehold estate with an unexpired term of less than two years or the interest of the beneficiary of a trust.

"Homestead declaration" includes both (1) a homestead declaration recorded pursuant to Article 5 and (2) a declaration of homestead recorded prior to July 1,1983, pursuant to former (Civil Code) law.

"Spouse" means a "spouse" as defined in Section 704.710 of Article 4.

Definitions and Terminology from Article 4

Some of the terminology for declared homesteads depend for their meaning on definitions from Article 4, which covers a residential exemption if there is no filing of a homestead declaration document. The definitions are:

1. **"Dwelling"** means a place where a person actually resides and may include but is not limited to the following:

a. A house together with the outbuildings and the land upon which they are situated;

b. A mobilehome together with the outbuildings and the land upon which they are situated;

c. A boat or other waterborne vessel;

d. A condominium, as defined in Section 783 of the Civil Code;

e. A Planned Development, as defined in Section 11003 of the Business and Professions Code;

f. A stock cooperative, as defined in Section 11003.2 of the Business and Professions Code; and

g. A community apartment project, as defined in Section 11004 of the Business and Professions Code.

2. **"Family unit"** means any of the following:

a. The judgment debtor and the judgment debtor's spouse if the spouses reside together in the homestead.

b. The judgment debtor and at least one of the following persons who the judgment debtor cares for or maintains in the homestead:

(1) The minor child or minor grandchild of the judgment debtor or the judgment debtor's spouse or the minor child or grandchild of a deceased spouse or former spouse.

(2) The minor brother or sister of the judgment debtor or judgment debtor's spouse or the minor child of a deceased brother or sister of either spouse.

(3) The father, mother, grandfather, or grandmother of the judgment debtor or the judgment debtor's spouse or the father, mother, grandfather, or grandmother of a deceased spouse.

(4) An unmarried relative described in this paragraph who has attained the age of majority and is unable to take care of or support himself or herself.

c. The judgment debtor's spouse and at least one of the persons listed in paragraph (2) who the judgment debtor's spouse cares for or maintains in the homestead.

3. **"Homestead"** means the principal dwelling (1) in which the judgment debtor or the judgment debtor's spouse resided on the date the judgment creditor's lien attached to the dwelling, and (2) in which the judgment debtor or the judgment debtor's spouse resided continuously thereafter until the date of the court determination that the dwelling is a homestead. Where exempt proceeds from the sale or damage or destruction of a homestead are used toward the acquisition of a dwelling within the six-month period provided by Section 704.720, "homestead" also means the dwelling so acquired if it is the principal dwelling in which the judgment debtor or the judgment debtor's spouse resided continuously from the date of acquisition until the date of the court

determination that the dwelling is a homestead, whether or not an abstract or certified copy of a judgment was recorded to create a judgment lien before the dwelling was acquired.

4. **"Spouse"** does *not* include a married person following entry of a judgment decreeing legal separation of the parties, or an interlocutory judgment of dissolution of the marriage, unless such married persons reside together in the same dwelling.

Amount of Homestead Exemption

The amount of the homestead exemption is the same under Articles 4 and 5 and is based upon the debtor's status at the time the creditor's lien is recorded. The current protected homestead exemption value and the protected homestead exemption values for several years past are as follows:

When Recorded On and after	Head of Family	Others	Persons 65 and Older See a, b, c and d below
January 1, 1985 ....$45,000		$30,000	
Jan. 1, 1981 to Dec. 31, 1984 45,000		30,000	$45,000
Jan. 1, 1979 to Dec. 31, 1980 40,000		25,000	40,000
Jan. 1, 1977 to Dec. 31, 1978 30,000		15,000	30,000
Jan. 1, 1971 to Dec. 31, 1976 20,000		10,000	20,000
Nov. 10, 1969 to Dec. 31, 1970 15,000		7,500	15,000

Creditors having a right to execute on a homestead cannot be prejudiced by subsequent increases in the statutory exemption value. The statutory definition of the protected value is the actual cash value of the dwelling over and above all liens and encumbrances on it at the time of levy of execution. In other words, the homestead protects the owner's equity in the dwelling.

a. Amendment effective January 1, 1985

California Code of Civil Procedure Section 704.730 was amended effective January 1, 1985 to provide that the homestead exemption shall be $55,000 if the judgment debtor or spouse of judgment debtor residing on the homestead is 65 years of age or older, or physically or mentally disabled and unable to engage in substantial gainful employment. The amendment makes it clear that the exemption amount is a combined exemption amount if both spouses are jointly obligated under the judgment.

Creditors are interested in knowing the dollar amount of the owner's protected equity in homestead property because it determines whether or not they can enforce their claim against it. In cases where the owner's protected equity in homestead property exceeds the statutory exemption limit, it becomes of significance in the reporting and insuring of titles to real property protected by a homestead.

b. Amendment effective January 1,1987:
Code of Civil Procedure Section 704.730 was amended effective January 1, 1987 raising the homestead exemption to $60,000 if the judgment debtor is either 65 years of age or older or a person physically or mentally disabled (and as a result unable to engage in substantial gainful employment).

c. Amendment effective January 1, 1989:

1. Code of Civil Procedure Section 704.730 was amended effective January 1, 1989, raising the homestead exemption to $75,000 if judgment debtor is either 65 years of age or older or a person physically or mentally disabled and as a result of that disability unable to engage in substantial gainful employment.

2. The amendment effective January 1, 1989 also permitted a homestead exemption of $75,000 if the judgment debtor is a person 55 years of age (or older); has a gross income of not more than $15,000 (or if the judgment debtor is married, a gross annual income, including the gross annual income of the debtor's spouse, of not more than $20,000); and sale is an involuntary one.

d. Amendment effective January 1, 1991:
Effective January 1, 1991, the three categories of homestead exemptions in Code of Civil Procedure Section 704.730 were changed in the amount of the exemption only. The new amounts are:

1. From $30,000 to $50,000 (704.730 (a)(1))

2. From $45,000 to $75,000 (704.730 (a)(2))

3. From $75,000 to $100,000 (704.730 (a)(3))

Again, in reliance on any of the above statutes, creditors having a right to execute on a homestead cannot be prejudiced by subsequent increases in the statutory exemption value.

e. Amendments effective January 1, 1998

1. Code of Civil Procedure Section 704.730(a)(3) has been amended effective January 1, 1998. By amendment, the homestead exemption is raised to $125,000 if judgement debtor is either:

   • 65 years of age or older, or

   • Physically or mentally disabled and unable to engage in substantial gainful employment.

2. Code of Civil Procedure Section 704.730(a)(3) has been amended effective January 1, 1998. By amendment, the homestead exemption is raised to $125,000 if the judgment debtor is:

   • a person 55 years of age or older,

- with a gross income of not more than $15,000 (or if the judgement debtor is married, a gross annual income, including the gross annual income of the debtor's spouse, of not more than $20,000), and

- the sale is an involuntary one.

3. C.C.P. 704.730(a)(1) is now $50,000

4. C.C.P. 704.730(a)(2) is now $75,000

Contents of the Declaration of Homestead

1. A recorded homestead declaration will contain all of the following:

    a. The name of the declared homestead owner. A husband and wife both may be named as declared homestead owners in the same homestead declaration if each owns an interest in the dwelling selected as the declared homestead.

    b. A description of the declared homestead.

    c. A statement that the declared homestead is the principal dwelling of the declared homestead owner or such person's spouse, and that the declared homestead owner or such person's spouse resides in the declared homestead on the date the homestead declaration is recorded.

2. The homestead declaration shall be executed and acknowledged in the manner of an acknowledgment of a conveyance of real property by at least one of the following persons.

    a. The declared homestead owner.

    b. The spouse of the declared homestead owner.

    c. The guardian or conservator of the person or estate of either of the persons listed in Paragraph (1) or (2). The guardian or conservator may execute, acknowledge, and record a homestead declaration without the need to obtain court authorization.

    d. A person acting under a power of attorney or otherwise authorized to act on behalf of a person listed in paragraph (1) or (2).

3. The homestead declaration shall include a statement that the facts stated in the homestead declaration are known to be true as of the personal knowledge of the person executing and acknowledging the homestead declaration. If the homestead declaration is executed and acknowledged by a person listed in paragraph (3) or (4) of subdivision (b), it shall also contain a statement that the person has authority to so act on behalf of the declared homestead owner or the spouse of the declared homestead owner and the source of the person's authority.

The definition of "dwelling" for purposes of Article 5 means an interest in real property that is a dwelling as defined in Section 704.710 but excludes a leasehold estate with an unexpired term of less than two years at the time of the filing of the homestead declaration. Thus a "dwelling" that is personal property (boat, waterborne vessel or mobilehome not affixed to land) appears to be excluded under Article 5.

The law does not set a limit on the amount of land that may be contained in the homestead "dwelling" property, ownership interest and occupancy by the owner or owner's spouse at the time of filing the declaration being the principal governing factors.

Where unmarried persons hold interests in the same "dwelling" in which they both reside, they must record separate homestead declarations if each desires to have a valid homestead.

Under previous law, a person who was a "head of household" was entitled to qualify for the amount of the greater exemption. Under current law, the amount of the exemption will depend upon whether or not the judgment debtor qualifies as a "family unit."

Declarations recorded prior to July 1, 1983. Any declaration of homestead filed prior to July 1,1983, remains valid, but the effect is limited to the effect given a homestead declaration under current statutes, i.e., the previously filed declaration must be qualified under present law.

Effect of recording - how terminated. When a valid declaration of homestead has been filed in the office of the county recorder where the property is located, containing all of the statements and information required by law, the property becomes a homestead protected from execution and forced sale, except as otherwise provided by statute, and it remains so until terminated by conveyance, abandoned by a recorded instrument of abandonment, or sold at execution sale.

A homestead declaration does not restrict or limit any right to convey or encumber the declared homestead.

To be effective, the declaration must be recorded; when properly recorded, the declaration is prima facie evidence of the facts contained therein; but off-record matters could prove otherwise.

Rights of spouses. A married person who is not the owner of an interest in the dwelling may execute, acknowledge, and record a homestead declaration naming the other spouse who is an owner of an interest in the dwelling as the declared homestead owner but at least one of the spouses must reside in the dwelling as his or her principal dwelling (Sections 704.920 and 704.930(a) (3) and (b) (2)), at the time of recording.

Either spouse can declare a homestead on the community or quasi-community property, or on property held as tenants in common or joint tenants, but cannot declare a homestead on the separate property of the other spouse in which the declarant has no ownership interest. A homestead cannot be declared after the homeowner files a petition in bankruptcy. (Note: "Quasi-community property" refers to real property situated in this state acquired in any of the following ways: (1) By either spouse while domiciled elsewhere which would have been community property if the spouse who acquired the property had been domiciled in this state at the time of its acquisition. (2) In exchange for real or personal property, wherever situated, which would have been community property if the spouse who acquired the property so exchanged had been domiciled in this state at the time of its acquisition.)

If a husband and wife own separate interests as separate property, each spouse qualifies for his or her own exemption but the combined exemptions cannot exceed the amount that is due to a "family unit." A declaration intended to be for the "joint benefit" of both spouses, one or both spouses must qualify as a "family unit."

After a decree of legal separation or interlocutory judgment of dissolution of marriage, if a spouse no longer resides on the property, the spouse cannot declare a homestead on the property.

Levy and execution sale. When an execution for the enforcement of a judgment is levied on a homestead dwelling, the judgment creditor must follow specific procedures.

Within 20 days after a writ of execution is levied and the creditor is notified of this fact, the creditor must apply to the court where the judgment was rendered for an order to execute the sale of the property (Section 704.760).

The value of the property is determined by the court. The court may appoint an appraiser and will consider other evidences of value in order to set a minimum bid for the property. Creditors must prove sufficient value to receive the minimum bid or the court may not make a finding for the sale.

If the court makes an order for sale of the dwelling upon a hearing at which neither the judgment debtor's spouse nor attorney debtor or spouse appeared, then within 10 days after the order for sale, the creditor must serve a copy of the order and statutory notice of sale on the debtor. The property is not sold if no bid is received at least equal to the court's prescribed minimum bid (which is a sum at least equal to the amount needed to pay all liens and encumbrances on the property, the amount of the homestead exemption, and the lien of the judgment creditor enforcing the lien), and the creditor cannot subject the property to an additional order for sale for at least one year (Section 704.800).

After the sale, the proceeds of sale are distributed as follows: (a) to discharge all liens and encumbrances on the property recorded prior to the judgment lien; (b) to the owner/debtor for the amount of the homestead exemption; (c) to costs of execution; (d) to the amount due the judgment creditor; and finally (e) balance to owner/debtor.

The proceeds from the execution sale are exempt for 6 months after the debtor receives the proceeds. If reinvested in a new "dwelling" and a new declaration of homestead is recorded within this 6 month period, the new filing has the same effect as though recorded on the date the prior declaration was recorded. (Section 704.960(b))

Federal Homestead Act of 1862

The declared homestead discussed above has nothing to do with the term "homesteading" as applied to filings on federal lands whereby a person acquired title to acreage by establishing residence or making improvements upon the land.

The purpose of the Federal Homestead Act of 1862 was to encourage settlement of the nation. Except for Alaska, homesteading was discontinued on public lands in 1976 when, because all the good agricultural land had already been homesteaded/deeded, Congress recognized that the Homestead Act had outlived its usefulness and passed the Federal Land Policy and Management Act of 1976, which immediately repealed the old law as to all states except Alaska.

ASSURING MARKETABILITY OF TITLE

Casual reflection on the nature of title to real property and its use and transfer must lead to the conclusion that establishing marketable title is often a complex and difficult undertaking. The term itself has no universally accepted meaning. It does not mean a perfect title, but rather one which is free from plausible or reasonable objections. In effect, the title is marketable (or merchantable) if there is reasonable assurance as to the extent of the rights involved. The title must be such that a proper court would compel the buyer to accept it, if asked to decree specific performance of the sale contract.

Establishing a marketable title is especially important whenever land is transferred for consideration, and when, in connection with such transfer or otherwise, money is loaned with land as security. The prospective buyer or lender would be reluctant to commit funds to the transaction without some assurance of getting what was bargained for. Buyers of real property expect some assurance that there are no hidden interests in the real property they propose to buy.

For example: One uses the surface, another extracts subsurface minerals, and a third controls the air space above the surface; since much land is of comparatively high value, especially in urban areas where the growth and concentration of population have placed a premium on parcels of land and consequently the land has been divided and subdivided and recombined into a patchwork measured in feet and sometimes even in inches; since the persons who own or deal with land are themselves subject to a variety of laws which determine the extent of their rights (e.g., probate, dissolution, guardianship, bankruptcy, business association laws); and since creditors and others may burden the real property with a variety of encumbrances.

Who owns what? Essentially, then, the problem is one of determining all the important facts with reference to who owns what interests or rights in the title to a particular parcel of land. Actual possession of the property has always been important and helpful in providing the answer. But possession may be by someone other than the owner, and transfers may be made without taking possession. Hence, the documentary record of ownership in the county recorder's office of the county in which the parcel is located assumes great significance. Reliance on recorded documents is encouraged by the official recording system under which deeds and other instruments affecting title may be recorded with the recorder of the county in which the land is situated. Thus a "chain of paper title" could be traced back to the original conveyance from the government. However, recordation is not compulsory, nor is it always properly done. Records may be erroneous, or sometimes may even reflect fraudulent and unenforceable transactions. When done thoroughly and conscientiously, the resulting records over the years become a complicated history in themselves, yet they may be woefully incomplete for purposes of determining the status of the title in question. This is so for a variety of reasons.

For example: In an intestate transfer, a qualified heir might have inadvertently been excluded; or a transfer, valid on its face may have been made by a person incompetent because of age or mental condition. Then too, other official records (e.g., tax records and records of court judgments) may profoundly affect the picture. In short, title to land and marketability of that title depend not only on recorded facts of title transfer, but also on a vast array of extraneous information outside of the documents recorded in the county recorder's office.

Abstract of Title

As might be expected under such complex circumstances, historically the individual buyer or lender was ill-equipped to make the necessary *investigation* of the status of the title to property. They soon came to rely on the title specialist who made a business of studying the records and preparing summaries or abstracts of title of all pertinent documents discovered in the search. An abstract of title is a summary statement of the successive conveyances and other facts (appearing in the proper place in the public records) on which a person's title to real property rests. The abstract of title and a lawyer's opinion of the documents appearing in the abstractor's "chain of title" were the basis of our earliest attempts to establish marketable title. This method still exists today, with modern refinements.

Certificate of Title

In time, abstractors accumulated extensive files of abstracts and other useful data, including "lot books" wherein references to recorded documents were systematically arranged according to the particular property affected, and "general indices" wherein landowners were listed alphabetically together with information concerning them and affecting titles (e.g., probates and property settlements).

These files came to be known as "title plants" and provided classified and summarized histories of real estate transactions and of other activities which affect or might affect ownership of the land in the areas covered. With the growth and improvement of title plants and increased proficiency of examiners employed by the abstractors, the formal abstract of title for delivery to the customer and the related legal opinion were sometimes dispensed with completely. The abstract company would simply study its records and furnish the customer with a certificate of title in which it stated that it found the title properly vested in the present owner, subject to noted encumbrances. The certificate plan has strictly limited use today, for it was a transitional method of assuring titles.

Guarantee of Title

The next step was the guarantee of title under which the title insurance company did more than certify the correctness of its research and examination.

Thus, the company provided written *assurances* (not insurance) about the title to real property. The coverage was usually limited to a particular condition of title, a certain period of time, and a certain kind of information. This meant it was engaged in the insurance business and generally was subject to regulation as such.

Title Insurance

As already noted, the public records may be incomplete or erroneous and do not necessarily disclose shortcomings arising from forgery, incompetence, and failures to comply with legal requirements. Accordingly, the policy of title insurance was developed as the culmination of the quest for a reliable and marketable title as well as compensation for incorrect assurances which cause a covered loss. Although still covering most risks which are a matter of public record, it alone extends protection against many nonrecorded types of risks, depending on the type of policy purchased. The title insurance company continues to utilize the title plant to conduct as accurate a search of the records as possible and seeks to interpret correctly what it finds in the records. But its unique contribution is the protection it affords against risks which lie outside the public records.

Standard policy. In addition to risks of record, the standard policy of title insurance protects against:

- off-record hazards such as forgery, impersonation, or lack of capacity of a party to any transaction involving title to the land (e.g., a deed of an incompetent or an agent whose authority has terminated, or of a corporation whose charter has expired);

- the possibility that a deed of record was not in fact delivered with intent to convey title;

- the loss which might arise from the lien of federal estate taxes, which is effective without notice upon death; and

- the expense, including attorneys' fees, incurred in defending the title, whether the plaintiff prevails or not.

The standard policy of title insurance does *not* however protect the policyholder against defects in the title known to the holder to exist at the date of the policy and not previously disclosed to the insurance company; nor against easements and liens which are not shown by the public records; nor against rights or claims of persons in physical possession of the land, yet which are not shown by the public records (since the insurer normally does not inspect the property); nor against rights or claims not shown by public records, yet which could be ascertained by physical inspection of the land, or by appropriate inquiry of persons on the land, or by a correct survey; nor against mining claims, reservations in patents, or water rights; nor against zoning ordinances.

These limitations are not as dangerous as they might appear to be. To a considerable degree they can be eliminated by careful inspection by the purchaser or his or her agent (lenders) of the land involved, and routine inquiry as to the status of persons in possession. However, if desired, most of these risks can be covered by special endorsement or use of extended coverage policies at added premium cost.

ALTA Policy (for lenders). In California, many loans secured by real property have been made by out-of-state insurance companies which were not in a position to make personal inspection of the properties involved except at disproportionate expense. For them and other nonresident lenders, the special ALTA (American Land Title Association) Policy was developed. This policy expands the risks normally insured against to include: rights of parties in physical possession, including tenants and buyers under unrecorded instruments; reservations in patents; and, most importantly, unmarketable title. The new ALTA Loan Policy (10-17-92) also covers recorded notices of enforcement of excluded matters (like zoning), as well as recorded notices of defects, liens, or encumbrances affecting title that result from a violation of matters excluded from policy coverage.

Extended coverage. The American Land Title Association has adopted an owner's extended coverage policy (designated as ALTA Owner's Policy [10-17-92]) that provides to buyers or owners the same protection that the ALTA policy gives lenders. But note that even in these policies no protection is afforded against defects or other matters concerning the title which are known to the insured to exist at the date of the policy yet have not previously been communicated in writing to the insurer, nor against governmental regulations concerning occupancy and use. The former limitation is self-explanatory; the latter exists because zoning regulations concern the condition of the land rather than the condition of title.

For homeowner's (1 to 4 residential units) a new CLTA/ALTA policy was developed in 1998; (ALTA Homeowner's Policy (10-17-98), and CLTA Homeowners Policy (6-2-98). The two policies are identical with one exception: the CLTA policy provides a form of Subdivision Map coverage, while the ALTA policy makes the Map Act coverage optional. The idea of the new policies is to provide homeowners with a form of extended coverage. The new policies contain for the first time, maximums payable under certain categories of coverages and small deductibles payable by the insured. Both policies incorporate protection against certain risks that conventionally were available only to lenders and only by endorsement.

Domestic Title Insurance Companies in California
Section 12359 of the Insurance Code of California requires that a title insurance company organized under the laws of this State have at least $500,000 paid-in capital represented by shares of stock. Section 12350 requires that the insurer deposit with the Insurance Commissioner a "guarantee fund" of $100,000 in cash or approved securities to secure protection for title insurance policy holders. A title insurer must also set apart annually, as a title insurance surplus fund, a sum equal to 10 percent of its premiums collected during the year until this fund equals the lesser of 25 percent of the paid-in capital of the company or $1,000,000. This fund acts as further security to the holders and beneficiaries of policies of title insurance.

Policies of title insurance are now almost universally used in California, largely in the standardized forms prepared by the California Land Title Association, the trade organization of the title companies in this State. Every title insurer must adopt and make available to the public a schedule of fees and charges for title policies. Today, it is the general practice in California for buyers, sellers and lenders, as well as the attorneys and real estate brokers who serve them, to rely on title insurance companies for title information, title reports and policies of title insurance.

Rebate Law
Title insurance companies are required to charge for preliminary reports under the terms of legislation adopted at the 1967 general session of the California Legislature. The rebate law requires title insurance companies to not only charge for reports, but also to make sincere efforts to collect for them except in certain defined circumstances.

Title insurance companies can still furnish "the name of the owner of record and the record description of any parcel or real property" without charge.

The statute extends the anti-commission provisions of Section 12404 of the Insurance Code to prohibit direct or indirect payments by a title insurance company to principals in a transaction as a consideration for title business.

Thus, the law prohibits a title insurance company from paying, either directly or indirectly, any commission, rebate or other consideration as an inducement for or as compensation on any title insurance business, escrow or other title business in connection with which a title policy is issued.

Torrens System of Land Registration
The Torrens system of land title registration, patterned after the system of registering titles to ships, was adopted by California in 1914 as the Land Title Act and provided for registration after a court decree in an action similar to a quiet title suit.

Always optional, the system never became popular and its use was confined almost exclusively to the southern counties. In 1955, the Torrens Act was repealed. All Torrens instruments were incorporated into the records of the county recorders, with the result that Torrens papers were included in the record chain of title and imparted constructive notice of their contents.

However, the repealing act provided that the records of the county recorder, after April 30, 1955 (thus including former Torrens registrations) would not have any greater or other effect as constructive notice or otherwise than they would have had prior to April 30, 1955. Because of this provision, a Torrens title which was defective because a documentary evidence of title had been recorded rather than registered was not cured by the repeal of the Act. For this reason, rules of practice governing the issuance of evidences of title to property once registered under the Torrens system cannot be ignored. As examples:

- If a deed to registered land was recorded instead of registered prior to April 30, 1955, the title would be unmarketable both before and after the repeal of the Act; and

- A recorded but unregistered deed of trust would not be a lien upon registered land prior to April 30, 1955 and the passage of the Act would not serve to elevate it to a status constituting constructive notice.

In both of the above examples, the defects in the title could be cured by re-recording the document after April 30, 1955. Title to real property formerly in the Torrens system that is not burdened with the defect just mentioned may be conveyed by grant deed. The grant deed may be recorded in the conventional way.

6   Transfer of Interests in Real Property

CONTRACTS IN GENERAL

Probably no other phase of the law is as important to parties who are transferring real estate, real estate brokers and salespersons as the law of contracts. Every transaction of any consequence almost invariably includes one or more contracts. It is important, therefore, to understand their nature and to be well acquainted with some of the broad rules governing contract creation, operation and enforcement.

In this chapter we consider contracts in general. Chapter 7 focuses on contracts used most frequently in the real estate business.

Contract Defined

Any term as broad in its application as "contract" is difficult to define with precision. California's Civil Code states: "A contract is an agreement to do or not to do a certain thing." The American Law Institute offers this definition: "A contract is a promise or a set of promises for the breach of which the law gives a remedy, or the performance of which the law in some way recognizes as a duty." Still another authority on the subject, Corbin, submits a definition which combines the foregoing two versions: "A contract is an agreement between two or more persons consisting of a promise or mutual promises which the law will enforce, or the performance of which the law in some way will recognize as a duty." This latter can serve as our working definition, and its meaning will be clarified later when we analyze the essential elements of a contract.

Classification. It will be helpful to review certain terms which are commonly used to classify contracts. With reference to *manner of creation,* a contract may be *express* or *implied.*[*]

In an express contract, the parties declare the terms and put their intentions in words, either oral or written. In an implied contract, however, the agreement is shown by acts and conduct rather than words. (In a hurry, you enter the corner drugstore, where you have an account, pick up a pack of gum, wave it at the clerk; the clerk nods and you leave. There is an implied contract that you will pay for the gum later.)

With reference to *content of the agreement,* a contract may be *bilateral* or *unilateral.* A bilateral contract is one in which the promise of one party is given in exchange for the promise of the other party. (A tells B, "I'll give you $300 if you will promise to paint my house" and B so promises.) In a unilateral contract, on the other hand, a promise is given by one party to induce some actual performance by the other party. The second party is not bound to act but if the second party acts, the former is obligated to keep the promise. (A offers a reward of $100 to anyone

---

[*] Contract implied in fact should be distinguished from contract implied in law. A contract implied in law evidences obligations created by law for reasons of justice. A contract implied in law would be the foundation of an employee's claim against a deceased employer's estate for overtime wages.

who will find and return A's lost dog. B does not make any promise but just happens to find and return the dog. A must pay B $100.)

With reference to *extent of performance,* a contract may be *executory* or *executed.* In an executory contract, something remains to be done by one or both parties. In an executed contract, both parties have completely performed.

Finally with reference to *legal effect,* contracts may be classified as *void, voidable, unenforceable,* or *valid.* A *void* agreement is not a contract at all. It lacks legal effect (e.g., an agreement to commit a crime; or, in California, an attempt by a minor under 18 to make a contract relating to real property). A *voidable* contract is one which is valid and enforceable on its face, but one which one or more of the parties may reject (e.g., certain contracts of minors are voidable at the option of the minor; a contract induced by fraud may be voided by the victim). An *unenforceable* contract is valid, but for some reason cannot be proved or sued upon by one or both of the parties (e.g., a contract that cannot be enforced because of the passage of time under the statute of limitations). A *valid* contract is one that is binding and enforceable. It has all the essential elements required by law.

ESSENTIAL ELEMENTS OF CONTRACT

Under the Civil Code of California it is essential to the existence of a contract that there be:

1. Parties capable of contracting;
2. Their consent;
3. Lawful object; and
4. A sufficient consideration.

It may be helpful to add a fifth requirement which is present only in certain contracts: a proper writing.

Parties Capable of Contracting
For a valid contract, there must be two or more parties who have at least limited legal capacity. Generally everyone is fully capable of contracting, except persons who are subject to certain limitations [unemancipated minors, persons of unsound mind, aliens and persons deprived of civil rights (e.g., convicts)].

Minors. A minor is a person under the age of 18 years. A minor is either unemancipated or emancipated (set free from parental control/supervision) under the Emancipation of Minors Law.

An unemancipated minor (hereafter "minor") cannot give a delegation of power, make a contract relating to real property or any interest therein, or relating to any personal property not in the minor's immediate possession or control. With certain statutory exceptions, a minor may disaffirm any contracts entered into during minority or for a reasonable time after reaching majority. In case of a minor's death within that period, the minor's heirs or personal representatives may disaffirm any contract into which the minor entered.

A minor is deemed incapable of appointing an agent; therefore, a delegation of authority (e.g., a power of attorney) is absolutely void. A real estate broker could not serve as agent of a minor to buy or sell. A broker could represent an informed adult in dealing with a minor, but the client must be willing to hazard the possibility of having the contract voided. Difficulty can be forestalled by negotiating in real property with or for a minor only through a court-appointed guardian. For the minor's protection, such negotiations cannot be concluded by the guardian without court approval.

Emancipation of Minors Law. Under this law (Family Code Sections 7000, et seq.) emancipated minors have certain powers to deal with real property and are considered as being over the age of majority for certain purposes, including: entering into a binding contract to buy, sell, lease, encumber, exchange, or transfer any interest in real or personal property; conveying or releasing interests in property.

An emancipated minor is a person under 18 years of age who has entered into a valid marriage (even though terminated by dissolution) or is on active duty with any of the armed forces of the United States of America or has received a declaration of emancipation by petitioning the superior court of the county where he or she resides.

Brokers dealing with minors must proceed cautiously and should seek the advice of their attorney.

Incompetents. California law provides that after the incapacity of a person of unsound mind has been judicially determined, no contract can be made with such person until restoration to capacity. Similarly, a person who is entirely without understanding but has not been judicially declared incompetent has no power to contract.

In dealing with incompetents concerning real property, proper procedure calls for appointment of a guardian and court approval of the guardian's acts.

Note: Both minors or incompetents, however, may acquire title to real property by gift or by inheritance. They may convey, mortgage, lease or acquire real property pursuant to a superior court order obtained through appropriate guardianship or conservatorship proceedings.

Aliens. In California, resident or nonresident aliens have essentially the same property rights as citizens. Section 671 of the Civil Code provides that "any person, whether citizen or alien, may take, hold, and dispose of property, real or personal, within this state." In the federal law, however, there are certain restrictions on the property rights of aliens.

Convicts. Persons sentenced to imprisonment in state prisons are deprived of such of their civil rights as may be necessary for the security of the institution in which they are confined and for the reasonable protection of the public.

Convicts do not forfeit their property. They may acquire property by gift, inheritance or by will, under certain conditions, and they may convey their property or acquire property through conveyance.

Individual proprietors. The bulk of the nation's business is conducted by *individual proprietors,* by ordinary *partnerships,* by *corporations,* and, more recently, by *limited partnerships* and *limited liability companies.* The first category presents no special problems. The owner who is a sole proprietor takes title in his or her own name, or, if married, the spouse may join as a grantee.

Partnership. In a partnership, two or more persons carry on a business as co-owners. The partnership may exist if such intention can be proven whether or not the partners have reduced their agreement to a formal writing. The more important characteristics of a *partnership* are: its lack of separate capacity to deal independently from its members (with certain exceptions hereafter noted); customary equal participation of members in management; co-ownership of partnership assets; individual interest of each partner in profits and surplus; and the mutual agency relationship between partners making each the agent of the others insofar as partnership business is concerned.

Partnership property constitutes the originally invested and subsequent partnership acquisitions. The best practice in investing in property usually is to take title in the name of the partnership itself. However, title may also be taken in the individual name of one or more partners, or in the name of a third party as trustee for the partnership. Although any authorized partner may then dispose of the property, it is customary for all partners to execute the instrument of transfer.

If property is acquired in the partnership name, it should not be transferred until a "GP-1 form" is filed with the Secretary of State and then recorded in the recorder's office showing the names of the partnership and its members.

The Uniform Partnership Act of 1994 became effective January 1, 1997. All partnerships formed prior to January 1, 1997 remained governed by the old Uniform Partnership Act (Corporations Code Section 15001, et seq.) until January 1, 1999. On that date, the old Uniform Partnership Act was repealed and all partnerships were governed by the Uniform Partnership Act of 1994 (Corporations Code Section 16100, et seq.).

Of course, if title to real property is in an individual's name, both the individual and such person's spouse should sign the instrument of transfer.

In order to enjoy some of the benefits of incorporation yet retain the partnership form, it is possible to form a *"limited partnership."* This can be achieved only by filing a formal certificate. Limited partners may not allow their names to be used in the business and may not participate in the control of the business. If all legal requirements are met, the limited partners are not responsible for partnership debts beyond their investment. At least one partner must be a general partner with unlimited liability.

Limited liability companies. The Beverly-Killea Limited Liability Company Act (California Corporations Code Sections 17000–17705) allows the formation of limited liability companies. It became effective, generally, in September of 1994.

To form a limited liability company, two or more persons must enter into an operating agreement and must execute and file articles of organization with the California Secretary of State.

The name of a limited liability company must contain, at the end, either the words "limited liability company" or the abbreviation "LLC". The words "limited" and "company" may be abbreviated to "Ltd." and "Co.," respectively.

Subject to any limitations contained in the articles of organization and to compliance with any other applicable laws, a limited liability company may engage in any lawful business activity, except the banking, insurance, or trust company business. (Corporations Code Section 17002)

Corporations Code Section 17101 sets forth the liability of members of a limited liability company. In part, the liability parallels that of shareholders in a corporation, while the company is treated as a partnership for tax purposes.

Corporations. The more important characteristics of a *corporation* are: separate capacity to deal with property independently from its members; centralized control in a board of directors; liability of shareholders normally limited to the amount of their investment; freely transferable shares; and continued existence regardless of death or retirement of its shareholders.

Although a corporation may take title to property in its own name, it is an "artificial person" created by law, and must function through human agents. Accordingly, corporate control is vested in the board of directors and so it becomes important to have some evidence of the board's decision in connection with the proposed property transaction. The decisions of the board are usually in the form of resolutions authorizing certain officers to deal with the corporate property. It should be noted that since a corporation has perpetual existence, it is not permitted to take title to property in joint tenancy with right of survivorship.

Note: Some corporations are organized on a nonprofit basis. Members of such a *nonprofit corporation* are not personally liable for the debts or obligations of the corporation, and in many respects such an organization is similar in operation to a regular corporation. A board of directors controls its property and conducts its affairs. The corporation may enter into contracts and acquire and dispose of real or personal property in its own name.

Nonprofit associations. Sometimes transactions in real property will involve *nonprofit associations*: loosely knit, unincorporated associations of natural persons for religious, scientific, social, educational, recreational, benevolent or other purposes. Members of such associations are not personally liable for debts incurred in acquisition or leasing of real property used by the association, unless they specifically assume such liability in writing. These nonprofit organizations may, by statute, hold such property in the group name as is necessary for business objects and purposes and may so hold nonessential property for 10 years.

When an unincorporated association proposes to dispose of property, the conveyance should, in the case of benevolent or fraternal societies or associations, be executed by its presiding officer and recording secretary under seal after resolution duly adopted by its governing body. In the case of other incorporated associations for which no other provision is made by statute, conveyances may be executed by the president or other head, and secretary, or by other specific officers so authorized by resolution. Such an association may record a statement setting forth its names and the persons authorized to execute conveyances. California Corporations Code Sections 20003 through 24007 govern unincorporated associations organized under California law.

Personal representative. A final category of parties to contracts, and one of considerable importance, is that of *personal representatives of decedents*. A person who leaves a will may names an *executor* or *executrix* to carry out its provisions. If a person dies intestate or fails to name an executor, the probate court will appoint an *administrator* to administer the estate. The acts of these officials are generally subject to court supervision. Real estate agents usually come in contact with executors and administrators when the latter are interested in selling a parcel of real estate belonging to the estate.

Mutual Consent

The second element of a valid contract is that the parties who have capacity to contract shall properly and *mutually consent* or assent to be bound. This mutual consent is normally evidenced by an offer of one party and acceptance by the other party. *An offer* expresses the offeror's willingness to enter into the contract. It must of course be *communicated* to the offeree. It must, moreover, manifest a *contractual intention.* There need not be a true "meeting of minds" of the parties, for they are bound only by their apparent intentions outwardly manifested by words or acts. Courts cannot read minds, and secret or unexpressed intentions, hopes and motivations are immaterial. However, the assent must be genuine and free, and if it is clouded or negated by such influences as fraud or mistake the contract may be voidable at the option of one or both parties, depending on the circumstances.

Sometimes when negotiating a contract, some of the terms might be left for future determination or there might be a condition which must be met before the parties become obligated (this may be called a "condition precedent"). In any of these situations, it is usually held that there have been only preliminary negotiations, mutual consent has not been reached and a binding contract has not come into existence. In such cases even the courts cannot guess what the parties will mutually agree upon.

Definite contract terms. Finally, the offer must be *definite and certain* in its terms. The precise acts to be done must be clearly ascertainable. Courts cannot make contracts for the parties, nor fix terms and conditions. The offer must be "nonillusory" in character, that is it must actually bind the offeror if it is accepted.

If the offeror could cancel or withdraw at pleasure without reasonable notice, the offer would be illusory. Another example would be an offer/promise completely within the offeror's control to perform or not to perform, such as an offer to buy a property "contingent upon obtaining a $100,000 loan." Without more conditions and specificity, the offeror might not even apply for a loan. To avoid illusion, clauses in the contract should carefully specify the details of the condition and should contain promises by both parties to provide some semblance of mutuality. A clause in a deposit receipt conditioning the offer upon the obtaining of a loan by the offeror should include the amount of the loan the buyer desires, interest rate, monthly installments, how secured, type (i.e., FHA, VA or conventional), an agreement by the buyer to use best efforts to procure such a loan and an agreement by the seller to cooperate in such efforts.

On many occasions, California courts have refused to enforce contracts because of uncertainty.

In one case, a broker provided in a deposit receipt that there was to be a first deed of trust in a fixed amount to a bank, and a second to the seller for the balance. Interest in each case was fixed. Then the contract stated "total monthly payments including interest, to be $95." Specific performance was denied because the deposit receipt was silent as to what portion of the $95 was to be paid to the bank and what to the seller.

Another agreement was drawn which was certain in all particulars except that it provided that the balance of the purchase price was to be evidenced by a first and second mortgage. The agreement was silent as to the amount of each mortgage and the uncertainty was critical because the parties disagreed as to the amounts of each mortgage. The court refused to enforce the agreement.

Another contract was found to be too uncertain because it was silent as to the rate of interest on the deferred balance and as to the date of maturity of the indebtedness.

Uncertainty and insufficiency were found in which a form was used containing a provision that an "extension of time for 30 days may be granted by (blank)". Since either party could extend, the court held that no one was in fact authorized.

Provisions in a contract that the property is to be improved with streets, water system, other utilities, and paved boulevards are too indefinite for enforcement. The court will not determine where the streets are to run, or how many there are to be, or the area to be covered or how they are to be constructed.

Description of property. The problem of certainty and definiteness may be acute in connection with land identification. A broker may not have the deed by which the owner acquired property, or the title report or policy connected with it. The contract must, however, contain such a description, or at least include a unique aspect of the property agreed to be sold so that it can be exactly ascertained. Where the broker has a former title policy or a preliminary report, he should refer to the description by the title company's name and policy number. From such a mention or reference, it can be ascertained what property is meant. Oral evidence may be resorted to in court for the purpose of identifying the description, but not for the purpose of ascertaining and locating a missing description, or one too uncertain to be identified.

For example, it is very common to describe property by the street and house number: No. 19, 10th Street, city, county and state. Usually, this will be sufficient. However, if the seller has a large property with more than one building on it, or an adjoining lot, the description would be insufficient. "My house and lot on 10th Street, between A and B Streets" would be sufficient provided the owner had no other house and lot on that block. "My land consisting of 96 acres located about four miles northeast from Porterville, California" was held sufficient to enable the court to determine what land was meant, because that was all that the seller had in that vicinity.

Termination of offer. The hope of the offeror is that the other party will accept and a contract will be formed. But the offeror does not want to wait indefinitely, and need not. The offer may be terminated in any one of a number of ways:

1. Lapse of Time. The offer is revoked if the offeree fails to accept it within a time period prescribed in the offer. If the offer does not include a deadline for acceptance, the lapse of a reasonable time without communication of acceptance may cause the offer to be considered to have been revoked. What is a reasonable time is a question of fact dependent upon the circumstances.

2. Communication of Notice of Revocation. This can be done anytime before the other party has communicated acceptance and is effective even if the offeror said the offer would be kept open for a stated period of time which has not yet elapsed. If the offeree pays to keep the offer open for a prescribed period of time, we have an *option* and the offeror must abide by its terms.

Sometimes an offer is made to sell and the person to whom the offer is made later acquires reliable information that the property has been sold to another party. This, too, constitutes a revocation.

3. Failure of offeree to fulfill a condition prescribed by the offeror or to accept in a prescribed manner. If the offeree makes a qualified acceptance (as by changing the price), in effect a counteroffer is made and the original offer is dead. It cannot later be accepted, unless revived by the offeror repeating it. Thus the roles of the parties are exchanged, and the counteroffer itself may then be terminated like an original offer. It should be noted here that this discussion of offer and acceptance, and the rest of the discussion as to formation of contracts, may not apply to contracts between merchants for the sale of goods. These are governed by the California Uniform Commercial Code.

4. Rejection by the offeree. An unequivocal rejection ends the offer, but simple discussion and preliminary bargaining do not do so when they involve no more than inquiries or suggestions for different terms.

5. Death or insanity of the offeror or offeree causes revocation of the offer.

Acceptance. Acceptance is the proper assent by the offeree to the terms of the offer.

Obviously, the person to whom the offer is made must have knowledge of it before he or she can accept. Acceptance by anyone other than the offeree is not possible. Most contracts are bilateral, but interesting problems arise in connection with the less common unilateral variety where the offeror asks for action, not a promise. Normally, when the requested act is performed, the offer is automatically accepted. But if the offeree doesn't intend an act to be an acceptance, or if there is no knowledge of the offer, there can be no acceptance and no contract. This sort of thing might happen when one returns a lost dog without even seeing the ads offering a reward for its return.

Acceptance must be absolute and unqualified, for if it modifies the terms of the offer in any material way, it becomes a counteroffer. As already noted, this terminates the original offer. Indeed, if the acceptance is too late or otherwise defective, the person making the offer cannot waive the delay or defect and treat the relationship as a binding contract.

Acceptance must be expressed or communicated, though it may be sufficient without actually being received by the person making the offer. Silence cannot be regarded as an acceptance of an offer ordinarily, because the party making the offer cannot force the party to whom an offer is made to make an express rejection. Silence may amount to an acceptance when the circumstances or previous course of dealing with a party places the party receiving the offer under a duty to act or be bound. Acceptance may be made by implication as by the acceptance of a consideration tendered with an offer.

Acceptance of an offer must be in the manner specified in the offer, but if no particular manner of acceptance is specified, then acceptance may be by any reasonable and usual mode.

A contract is made when the acceptance is mailed or put in the course of transmission by any other prescribed or reasonable mode (e.g., by deposit of a telegram for transmission). This is so even though the letter of acceptance is lost and never reaches the party making the offer, as the acceptance has been placed in the course of transmission by the offeree.

Genuine assent. The final requirement for mutual consent is that the offer and acceptance be genuine. The principal obstacles to such *genuine or real assent* are fraud, mistake, menace, duress or undue influence. If any one of these obstacles is present, the contract may be voidable and a party to the alleged contract may seek rescission (restoring both parties to their former positions) or dollar damages or possibly reformation of the contract to make it correct.

Fraud. Fraud may be either actual or constructive in nature. Normally, fraud exists when a person misrepresents a material fact while knowing it's not true, or does so with careless indifference as to its veracity. A person must misrepresent with the intent to induce the other person to enter the contract, and the other must rely thereon in entering the contract. "Material fact" means an important fact which significantly affects the party's decision to enter into the contract.

Civil Code Section 1572 lists the following five acts which would be deemed *actual fraud* when done by a party to a contract or with his or her connivance with intent to induce another to enter into the contract, or even simply to deceive such other party:

1. The suggestion, as a fact, of that which is not true, by one who does not believe it to be true;

2. The positive assertion, in a manner not warranted by the information of the person making it, of that which is not true though the person believes it to be true;

3. The suppression of that which is true, by one having knowledge or belief of the fact;

4. A promise made without any intention of performing it; or,

5. Any other act intended to deceive.

Ordinarily, misrepresentation of law does not amount to actionable fraud, no doubt because everyone is presumed to know the law. Nevertheless, this may be actionable fraud where one party uses superior knowledge to gain an unconscionable advantage, or where the parties occupy some sort of confidential relationship, even though the guilty party is not a strict fiduciary.

Constructive fraud. Constructive fraud as defined in the Civil Code may consist of first, any breach of duty which, without an actual fraudulent intent, gains an advantage for the person in fault or anyone claiming under that person by misleading another to the other's prejudice or to the prejudice of anyone claiming under the other person. Second, it may consist of any such act or omission as the law specifically declares to be fraudulent without respect to actual fraud. The element of reliance is essential, and where it is shown that no commitments were made until independent investigation by others, there can be no action claiming fraud. Negligent misrepresentation has also been held to be a species of fraud.

A distinction should be made between fraud in the inception or execution, and fraud in the inducement of a contract. For example, if the promisor knows what he or she is signing and the consent is induced by fraud, the contract is *voidable* by the promisor; but if the fraud goes to the inception or execution of the agreement so that the promisor is deceived as to the nature of his or her act and actually does not know what is being signed, and does not intend to enter into a contract at all, it is *void*. Where the contract is voidable, it is binding until rescinded, while if the contract is void, a formal act of rescission is not necessary.

If one signs a contract without reading it and therefore fails, through carelessness or negligence, to familiarize oneself with the contents of a written contract prior to its execution, relief is denied. Where such failure or negligence is induced by the false representation and fraud of the other party to the contract so that its provisions are different from those set out, the court, even in the absence of a fiduciary or confidential relationship between the parties, may reform or cancel the instrument.

A party to a contract who has been guilty of fraud in its inducement is not relieved of the effects of the fraud by any stipulation in the contract, either that no representations have been made or that any right which might be grounded upon them is waived. Such a stipulation or waiver will be ignored, because the fraud renders the whole agreement voidable, including the waiver provisions.

False representations. Where false representations are made by an agent and the contract contains a recital limiting the agent's authority to make representations, the innocent principal may, by certain stipulations, be relieved of liability in a court action for damages for fraud and deceit, but the defrauded third party may nevertheless rescind the contract. The guilty agent may, of course, be liable in damages for the wrongful act.

Mistakes. Another possible obstacle to genuineness of assent is mistake. Where both parties are mistaken as to the identity of the subject matter of the contract, there can be no contract. Where the subject matter of the agreement has, unknown to the parties, already ceased to exist, so that performance of the contract would be impossible, there is no contract.

Mutual agreement as to the subject matter is the basis of a contract. If the parties to an agreement consent thereto, a contract results. However, the contract may be voidable if there is a substantial mistake as to some basic or material fact which induced the complaining party to enter into it. Negligence of the injured party does not in itself preclude release from mistakes, unless the negligence is gross, as where the party simply fails to read the agreement. One who accepts or signs an instrument which is on its face a contract is deemed to assent to all of its terms and cannot escape liability on the ground of not having read it. This is true only in the absence of such influences as fraud, undue influence, or duress.

Mistakes are classified in the Civil Code as mistakes of fact or of law. A *mistake of fact is* one consisting of ignorance or forgetfulness of a fact material to the contract, but which is not caused by the neglect of a legal duty on the part of the person making it. Or it may consist in the mistaken belief in the existence of a thing material to the contract, or a belief in the past existence of such a thing, which has not existed. A *mistake of law,* on the other hand, is described as one which arises from a misunderstanding of the law by all parties involved, all making substantially the same mistake while thinking they knew and understood the law.

A mistake may also be a misunderstanding of law by one party, which the other party is aware of but does not rectify.

Duress, menace, undue influence. Sometimes a contract may be rendered voidable because it was entered into under the pressure of duress, menace or undue influence. All three, in effect, deprive the victim of the free exercise of will, and so the law permits such person to void the contract, as well as other remedies under the law.

Duress involves coercion or confinement. While duress is technically the unlawful confinement of persons or property, modern case law has expanded duress to include unlawfully depriving a person of the exercise of free will. Economic compulsion or duress may result in a finding that a contract provision is unconscionable.

Menace consists of a threat to commit duress, but also includes threat of unlawful and violent injury to a person or the person's character.

Undue influence is unfair advantage taken by someone who has the confidence of another, or who holds a real or apparent authority over another. It may involve taking an unfair advantage of another's weakness of mind, or in taking a grossly oppressive and unfair advantage of another's necessities or distress. Undue influence is most frequently encountered in connection with contracts between persons in confidential relationships, where the victim is justified in assuming the other party will not act contrary to the victim's welfare. The relationships which usually fall within this rule include trustee and beneficiary, broker and principal, attorney and client, guardian and ward, parent and child, husband and wife, physician and patient, employer and employee.

Lawful Object
Assuming now that parties are capable of contracting and have properly manifested their consent through an offer and acceptance, the validity of their agreement might still be attacked on grounds of legality. The contract must be legal in its formation and operation. Both its consideration and its object must be lawful. The object refers to what the contract requires the parties to do or not to do. Where the contract has but a single object, and that object is unlawful in whole or in part, or is impossible of performance, the contract is void. If there are several distinct objects, the contract is normally valid as to those parts which are lawful. An object is not lawful that is contrary to an express provision of the law, or contrary to the policy of express law.

In general the law will lend its resources to neither party involved in an illegal contract. Thus if a contract is executory and illegal, neither party may enforce it; if it is executed, neither party may rescind and recover consideration. But sometimes the law which was violated was designed to protect one of the parties; or the parties are not equally blameworthy; or one party repents and calls the deal off before any part of the illegal object has been realized. In such cases, the law will provide appropriate relief.

Common violations. The objects and consideration of a contract must be legal and not violate some specific prohibition of the law. If such violation does occur, its effect upon the contract may depend upon the particular statute involved. Two types of situations in the real estate field involving statutory violations are:

1. Contracts of unlicensed "brokers" or "general contractors." These persons are not permitted to enforce their contracts.

2. Forfeiture clauses in deposit receipts, contracts of sale and leases.

(A contract clause which specifies a fixed amount of damages in the event of a breach is known as a liquidated damages clause. Except as discussed below, a liquidated damages clause is presumed valid unless the party seeking to invalidate the provision proves that it was unreasonable under the circumstances existing at the time the contract was made.

A liquidated damages clause is void if the liquidated damages are sought to be recovered from: (1) a party to a contract for the retail purchase or rental of personal property or services primarily for that party's personal, family, or household purposes; or (2) a party to a lease of real property for use as a dwelling by that party or his or her dependents.

Special rules apply to liquidated damages provisions in contracts for the purchase of residential real property. These rules are explained below in the Section entitled "REAL ESTATE CONTRACTS."

Special rules apply to liquidated damages clauses in construction contracts with certain government entities, making provisions for amounts to be paid for each day of delay in construction valid unless manifestly unreasonable at the time the contract was made.)

3. Contracts by which one is restrained from engaging in business may be void, although a person selling goodwill may promise the buyer not to compete within a reasonably limited area for a specific period of time.

4. Persons may not generally avoid responsibility for their own fraud or negligence merely by so providing in a contract.

5. A contract calling for the payment of interest in excess of the California Constitution's current limits may be usurious depending upon the identity of the lending entity and the purpose of the loan. If such a contract is usurious, that portion of the contract relating to the payment of interest is void.

6. In addition to the foregoing, brokers must be careful to comply with the numerous regulatory measures incorporated in the Real Estate Law. Specific violations may prevent enforcement of a listing contract. It should be noted that violations of law not only affect the enforceability of the contract involved, but may also subject the violator to criminal punishment.

Sufficient Consideration

Even if the agreement meets all the requirements of a valid contract already discussed, it may fail because of the lack of sufficient consideration. In general, every executory contract requires consideration. The consideration may be either a benefit conferred, or agreed to be conferred, upon the person making the promise, or any other person; or a detriment suffered or agreed to be suffered. It may be an act of forbearance or a change in legal relations. It is the price bargained for and paid for a promise, and it may, of course, be a return promise. If a valid consideration exists, the promise is binding even though some motive other than obtaining a consideration induced the promisor to enter into the contract.

Ordinarily, the nature of the consideration is reflected in the written agreement of the parties. The consideration must have some value. A purely moral obligation may under some circumstances be consideration. There is no requirement of adequacy to make the contract enforceable. Thus, an option to purchase valuable property may be given for consideration of one dollar or some other nominal sum. It is only in an action for *specific performance* that the amount is important, and in this event the equitable remedy will be denied unless an adequate consideration is proved. Also, gross inadequacy of consideration may be a circumstance which, together with other facts, will tend to show fraud or undue influence.

In a unilateral contract, a promise of the offeror is consideration for an act or forbearance sought from the offeree. In a bilateral contract, a promise of one party is consideration for the promise of another, and generally any valid promise, whether absolute or conditional, is sufficient consideration for another promise.

STATUTE OF FRAUDS

Contracts That Must Be Written

The law is more concerned with substance than with form. With reference to form, it is generally immaterial whether a contract is oral or written or even manifested by acts or conduct. Thus all contracts may be oral except those specially required by a statute to be in writing.

Most contracts which by statute are required to be in writing are referred to as coming under the Statute of Frauds. The Statute of Frauds was first adopted in England in 1677 and became part of the English common law. Subsequently, it was introduced into this country and has been codified in California. The purpose of the California Statute of Frauds is to prevent perjury, forgery and dishonest conduct on the part of unscrupulous people in proving the existence and terms of certain important types of contracts.

The statute provides that certain contracts are invalid, unless the contract or some note or memorandum of the contract is in writing and subscribed (i.e., signed) by the party to be charged or by his or her agent. Under Section 1624 of California's Civil Code, contracts that are required to be in writing are:

1. An agreement that by its terms is not to be performed within a year from the making thereof;

2. A special promise to answer for the debt, default, or miscarriage of another, except in the cases provided for in Civil Code Section 2794;

3. An agreement for the leasing for a longer period than one year or for the sale of real property, or of an interest therein. Such agreement, if made by an agent of the party sought to be charged, is invalid, unless the authority of the agent is in writing, subscribed by the party sought to be charged;

4. An agreement authorizing or employing an agent, broker, or any other person, to purchase or sell real estate, or to lease real estate for a longer period than one year, or to procure, introduce, or find a purchaser or seller of real estate or a lessee or lessor of real estate where such lease is for a longer period than one year, for compensation or a commission;

5. An agreement which by its terms is not to be performed during the lifetime of the promisor;

6. An agreement by a purchaser of real property to pay an indebtedness secured by a mortgage or deed of trust upon the property purchased, unless assumption of said indebtedness by the purchaser is specifically provided for in the conveyance of such property.

7. A contract, promise, undertaking, or commitment to loan money or to grant or extend credit, in an amount greater than one hundred thousand dollars ($100,000), not primarily for personal, family, or household purposes, made by a person engaged in the business of lending or arranging for the lending of money or extending credit. For purposes of this section, a contract, promise, undertaking, or commitment to loan money secured solely by residential property consisting of one to four dwelling units shall be deemed to be for personal, family, or household purposes.

Relates to remedy. It should be noted that the Statute of Frauds relates to the remedy only and not to the substantial validity of the contract. Thus, the contract which fails to comply with the statute is not void but merely *unenforceable*. This, of course, is an important distinction. It is effective for all purposes until, in an attempt to enforce it by action, its invalidity is urged. Moreover, the statute is a defense only and cannot be the basis for affirmative action. It has been held that significant partial performance can excuse the lack of a writing.

When a contract has been fully performed, the Statute of Frauds does not apply and may not be invoked for any reason.

The note or memorandum required by the statute may be in any form since its purpose is simply evidence of the contract. It may consist of one paper, or even a series of letters. It must however contain all the material terms of the contract so that a court can determine to what the parties agreed. It must, of course, bear the signature of the party to be charged or held to the agreement. The other party bringing the action can always add his or her signature later.

Real estate applications of the statute. It is readily apparent that several very important sections of the Statute of Frauds apply to persons dealing in real estate. Practically all contracts for the sale of any interest in real property must be in writing. This includes assignment of a percentage of the proceeds of oil produced from designated lands. It would embrace any and all instruments creating liens, such as trust deeds, mortgages, leases for periods of longer than one year, rights to rights of way through property and any and all encumbrances incurred or suffered by the owners, or by operation of law. "By operation of law" means judgments, attachments, or restrictions placed on the property by legislative bodies, zoning ordinances, and other such means.

The statute does not apply to a lease for a year or less.

Commissions. The Statute of Frauds provides that in order for a broker to collect a commission when earned, the contract providing for a commission must be in writing and signed by the party to be charged: e.g., a property owner who employs the broker to produce a buyer; or a buyer who employs the broker to find a suitable property.

The Statute of Frauds is applicable to situations where the lease of real estate for a period longer than one year is involved. A broker who is commissioned to seek a lessee of property for a term longer than one year cannot rely upon an oral agreement to collect a commission. If the broker is successful in negotiating the lease, the contract with the lessor must be in writing or there must be reliable written evidence thereof in order to sustain a claim of commission.

It has been held that the moral obligation to pay for services performed under oral authorization is sufficient consideration to support a promise of compensation contained in escrow instructions later drawn up. It also has been held that these provisions have no application to an oral agreement between brokers to share a commission to be earned as a result of the sale or exchange of real estate.

The Statute of Frauds invalidates any unwritten agreement by a purchaser of real property to pay an indebtedness secured by a mortgage or deed of trust upon that property unless assumption of the indebtedness is specifically provided for in the property conveyance.

INTERPRETATION, PERFORMANCE AND DISCHARGE OF CONTRACTS

The majority of all contracts are properly performed and discharged or executed without legal complications. If difficulties arise, the parties themselves, or with the aid of legal counsel, will typically work out an amicable settlement. But the courts remain available for the resolution of conflicts between contracting parties that cannot be so settled. Set forth below are some of the rules which guide the courts in their *interpretation* of contracts.

Interpretation of Contracts

In general, contracts are interpreted so as to give effect to the mutual intention of the parties as it existed at the time of contracting, insofar as that intention is ascertainable and lawful. A contract may be explained by reference to the circumstances under which it was made, and the matter to which it relates. But the language of the contract governs its interpretation, if the language is clear and explicit and does not involve an absurdity. Obviously the language should be reduced to writing, for the wiles of the unscrupulous are infinite, and the memory of every man and woman is finite and fallible.

Fortunately, as noted earlier, most contracts of interest to real estate brokers must be in writing under the Statute of Frauds. A broker can render valuable service by seeing to it that the writing clearly expresses the intention of the parties. But when a written contract fails to express the real intention of the parties because of fraud, mistake or accident, the courts will seek to discover the real intention and disregard the erroneous parts of the writing.

The execution of a contract in writing, whether the law requires it to be written or not, supersedes all the negotiations and stipulations concerning this matter which preceded or accompanied the execution of the instrument. When a contract is partly written and partly printed, written parts control the printed part, and the parts which are purely original control those which were copied from a form. If the two are absolutely contradictory, the latter must be disregarded.

Modification or alteration of a contract is a change in the obligation by a modifying agreement which requires mutual assent. A contract in writing may be altered by a new contract in writing, or by an executed oral agreement, and not otherwise.

Parol evidence rule. Parol evidence refers to prior oral or written negotiations or agreements of the parties, or even oral agreements contemporaneous with their written contract. The parol evidence rule prohibits the introduction of any extrinsic evidence (oral or written) to vary or add to the terms of an integrated written instrument such as a deed, contract, will, etc. This rule helps to finalize agreements with certainty, and it discourages fraudulent claims. On the other hand, the courts will permit such outside evidence to be introduced when the written contract is incomplete or ambiguous, or when necessary to show that the contract is not enforceable because of mistake, fraud, duress, illegality, insufficiency or failure of consideration, or incapacity of a party.

Under the *"parol evidence rule,"* when a contract is expressed in a writing which is intended to be the complete and final expression of the rights and duties of the parties, parol evidence is not admissible as evidence.

Where the parties come to an agreement by mistake or fraud, and the written instrument does not express their agreement correctly, it may be reformed or revised by the court on the application of the party agreeing to it, provided that this can be done without prejudice to rights acquired by third persons in good faith and for value.

Performance of Contracts
In connection with *performance* of contracts, it is not uncommon to find a party who would prefer to drop out of the picture without terminating the contract. Under proper circumstances this may be accomplished by assignment or by *novation.*

Assignable contract. Whether the contract is assignable depends upon its nature and terms. Ordinarily, either a bilateral or a unilateral contract is assignable unless it calls for some personal quality of the promisor, or unless it expressly or impliedly negates the right to assign. The contract might expressly provide that it shall not be assigned or it may contain provisions which are equivalent to such expressed stipulations, or it may require consent to assign.

The effect of assignment is to transfer to the assignee all of the interest of the assignor. The assignee stands in the shoes of the assignor, taking assignor's rights and remedies, subject to any defenses which the obligor has against the assignor, prior to notice of the assignment. Where the subject matter of the assignment involves reciprocal rights and duties, the assignor may transfer the benefit and may divest himself or herself of all rights, but cannot escape the burden of an obligation by a mere assignment. The assignor still remains liable to the obligee; even if the assignee assumes the obligation, the assignor still remains secondarily liable as a surety or guarantor, unless the obligee releases the assignor.

The assignment carries with it all the rights of the assignor, thus the assignment of a note carries with it any incidental securities such as mortgages or other liens.

In some cases the original contracting party who wants to drop out completely may do so by *novation.*

Novation is the substitution by agreement of a new obligation for an existing one, with intent to extinguish the latter. The substitution may be a new obligation between the same parties, and/or a new party, either a new debtor or a new creditor. A novation requires an intent to discharge the old contract and, being a new contract, it requires consideration and other essentials of a valid contract.

Where one party is indebted to another and the creditor takes a promissory note for the sum owed, this does not discharge the original debt unless the parties expressly so agree, or unless such intention is clearly indicated. No particular form is required ordinarily for a novation. It may be written or implied from conduct where the intent sufficiently appears.

Time

The question of time is often significant in contracts. By statute, if no time is specified for the performance of an act required to be performed, a reasonable time is allowed. If the act is in its nature capable of being done instantly, it must be performed immediately upon being exactly ascertained, unless otherwise agreed.

If the last day for the performance of any act provided by law to be performed within a specified period of time shall be a holiday, then such period is extended to the next day which is not a holiday.

Discharge of Contracts

In the matter of *discharge* of contracts, there are two extremes, *full performance* and *breach of contract.* Between these extremes are a variety of methods of discharge of the contract including the following:

1. By part performance;

2. By substantial performance;

3. By impossibility of performance;

4. By agreement between the parties;

5. By release;

6. By operation of law; and

7. By acceptance of a breach of the contract.

Statute of Limitations

The running of the *Statute of Limitations* will bar any legal action seeking relief for a breach of contract. Civil actions can be commenced only within the periods prescribed by statute after the cause of action shall have accrued. The policy of the law is to aid the vigilant. The person who "sleeps upon his rights" may be barred from relief by this statute. The following is a summary of some of the clauses which are of special interest to real estate brokers.

Actions which must be brought within 90 days. Civil actions for the recovery of or conversion of personal property such as baggage alleged to have been left at a hotel, boarding house, lodging house, furnished apartment house or furnished bungalow court, shall be commenced within 90 days from and after the departure of the owner of the personal property.

Within six months. An action against an officer, or officer defacto, to recover any goods, wages, merchandise or other property seized by the officer in an official capacity as tax collector, or to recover the price or value of any such goods or other personal property, as well as for damage done to any person or property in making any such seizure. Also actions on claims against a county which have been rejected by the board of supervisors.

Within one year. An action for libel, slander, injury or death caused by wrongful act or neglect of another, or by a depositor against a bank for the payment of a forged or raised check.

Within two years. An action upon a contract, obligation or liability not founded upon an instrument in writing (other than open book accounts, accounts stated, and open, current and mutual accounts, where the limit is *four* years); or an action founded upon a contract, obligation or liability, evidenced by a certificate or abstract or guaranty of title of real property or by a policy of title insurance; provided, that the cause of action of such contracts shall not be deemed to have accrued until the discovery of the loss or damage suffered by the aggrieved party thereunder.

Within three years. Included are: an action upon a liability created by statute, other than a penalty or forfeiture; an action for trespass upon or injury to real property; an action for taking, detaining, or injuring any goods or chattels, including actions for the recovery of specific personal property; an action for relief on the grounds of fraud or mistake. (Cause of action does not accrue until discovery by the injured party of the facts constituting the fraud or mistake.)

Within four years. An action upon any contract, obligation or liability founded upon an instrument in writing except an action upon any bonds, notes or debentures issued by any corporation or pursuant to permit of the Commissioner of Corporations, or upon any coupons issued with such bonds, notes or debentures, if such bonds, notes or debentures shall have been issued to or held by the public, where the limit is *six* years; also provided that the time within which any action for a money judgment for the balance due upon an obligation for the payment of which a deed of trust or mortgage with power of sale upon real property or any interest therein was given as security, following the exercise of the power of sale in such deed of trust or mortgage, may be brought shall not extend beyond *three* months after the time of sale under such deed of trust or mortgage.

An action to recover:

1. Upon a book account whether consisting of one or more entries;

2. Upon an account stated, based upon an account in writing;

3. A balance due upon a mutual, open and current account, provided that where an account stated is based upon an account of one item, the time shall begin to run from the date of said item, and where an account stated is based upon more than one item, the time shall begin to run from the date of the last item.

Within five years. An action for mesne profits (i.e., profits accruing between the time an owner acquires title and actually takes possession). Also, an action for the recovery of real property.

Within ten years. An action upon a judgment or decree of any court of the United States or of any state within the United States.

In connection with the Statute of Limitations, an action is commenced when the complaint is filed with a court of competent jurisdiction.

Remedies for Breach
As a final possibility, a contract may be discharged by simple *acceptance of breach*. If one party fails to perform, the other may accept the contract as ended, concluding either that recoverable damages are too limited to justify litigation or that the other party is "judgment proof" (without sufficient assets to satisfy a judgment.

On the other hand, the victim of a breach of contract may not be willing to accept the breach. That person has a choice of two, and sometimes three, courses of action:

1. Unilateral rescission.

2. Action for dollar damages.

3. Action for specific performance.

Rescission
To rescind because of breach requires diligent compliance with the following statutory rules:

- One must rescind promptly after discovering the facts which justify rescission; and,

- One must restore to the other party everything of value received from the other party under the contract, or must offer restoration upon condition that the other party do likewise, unless the latter is unable or positively refuses to do so.

If a court awards rescission, it may require that the rescinding party make any compensation to the other which justice may require. It should be noted, however, that a party having the right to rescind may independently accomplish a completed rescission, terminating further liability and discharging the contract.

Damages
Whenever a party to a contract is a victim of breach, such party has suffered a detriment and may recover compensation therefor in money, which is called damages. This party is entitled to interest (now 10% per annum) thereon from the day the right to recover is vested. If the contract itself stipulates a legal rate of interest, that rate remains chargeable after the breach as before, and until superseded by a verdict or other new obligation.

Damages for breach of contract must be reasonable, and exemplary damages which serve to punish the defendant are not allowed normally unless a strong showing of bad faith can be made. The measure of damages normally is the amount which will compensate the party aggrieved for all the detriment proximately caused thereby, or which in the ordinary course of things would be likely to result therefrom. Sometimes, when the breach has caused no appreciable detriment, hence no dollar damages, the court will award "nominal damages" (e.g., $1).

The detriment caused by the breach of an agreement *to convey* an estate in real property is deemed to be the price paid and the expenses properly incurred in examining the title and preparing the necessary papers, with interest thereon. In case of bad faith, added to the above is the difference between the price agreed to be paid and the value of the estate agreed to be conveyed, at the time of the breach, and the expenses properly incurred in preparing to enter upon the land. On the other hand, the detriment caused by the breach of an agreement *to purchase* an estate in real property is deemed to be the excess, if any, of the amount which would have been due to the seller, under the contract, over the value of the property to the seller.

Sometimes, especially in building contracts, the parties will anticipate the possibility of a breach: e.g., a delay in completion beyond a promised date. The parties may specify in the contract the amount of damage to be paid in the event of the breach. Such *liquidated damage* agreements will be enforced by the courts provided the amount specified is not so excessive as to constitute a penalty, and provided it would be impractical or extremely difficult to fix the actual damage and normally only if the contract expressly provides that liquidated damages shall be the only remedy available in the event of breach of the contract.

Specific Performance
Generally where dollar damages at law cannot provide an adequate remedy, equity will take jurisdiction and order the defendant to perform the contract. (Sometimes, equity may also enforce a promise to forbear from doing something by granting an *injunction.*)

Requirements to compel performance. Specific performance is especially important in the real estate business in connection with contracts for the transfer of interests in land. Since every piece of land is unique, the law presumes that the breach of an agreement to transfer real property cannot be relieved adequately by money compensation. For specific performance to be available as a remedy, however, certain other requirements must normally be met before the court will compel a party to perform a contract.

If specific performance is to be ordered, the remedy must be mutual. However, by statute, even if the agreed counter-performance would not be specifically enforceable, specific performance may be compelled if: (a) specific performance would otherwise be an appropriate remedy, and (b) the agreed counter-performance has been substantially performed or can be assured. Brokers dealing with prospective oil land and oil leases are familiar with a contract provision stating that the lessee may at any time before or after discovery of oil on the property quitclaim the same or any part thereof to the lessor, whereupon the rights and obligations of the parties to the lease shall cease. Such a clause giving the lessee the right to abandon robs the contract of mutuality. It therefore cannot be specifically enforced.

An option for the purchase of real estate where there is a consideration therefor is specifically enforceable although the owner cannot at that time compel its exercise. Neither can the owner withdraw the option during the time agreed upon. Upon the written exercise of the option by the buyer according to its terms, there is then created a contract of sale. It is this contract that gives rise to the remedy of specific performance. It is not uncommon for an optionee or other person who may not have signed a contract to bring suit thereon for its specific performance. The fact that the party brings such a suit establishes mutuality, because by it one subjects oneself to and agrees to abide by the decree of the court.

Obligations which cannot be specifically enforced. By statute, the following obligations cannot be specifically enforced: (1) to render personal service; (2) to employ another in personal service; (3) to perform an act which the party has not power lawfully to perform when required to do so; (4) to procure the consent of any third person; and (5) an agreement the terms of which are not sufficiently certain to make the precise act which is to be done clearly ascertainable.

Thus husband and wife must join in executing any instrument by which community real property or any interest therein is sold, conveyed, or encumbered, or is leased for a longer period than one year.

Note: The right of a purchaser in good faith without knowledge of the marriage relation where one spouse alone holds the record title to the real property may be established without the other spouse's signature.

Since an agreement to procure the consent of a spouse or any third person cannot be specifically enforced, it is exceedingly important to get the signature of the other spouse. In fact, the signatures of both spouses to any contract relating to community real property should be secured.

Frequently this failure to procure the signature of the other spouse is cured by the seller putting into escrow the deed signed by both husband and wife or by the buyer putting into escrow a deed of trust signed by both. Where that is done the original want of mutuality is cured, provided it is done before an attempt is made to withdraw from the contract by the other party. It is not wise to rely upon this possibility, or even probability. The alert real estate broker will in the beginning obtain the signatures of all parties.

It is not uncommon that there are two owners to property other than husband and wife. It is therefore necessary to get the signatures of all of the owners because the buyer could not compel specific performance of the contract as to one-half of the property where it is contemplated that the whole is to be sold.

Adequate consideration — assent by fraud — merchantable title. Specific performance cannot be enforced against a party to a contract if such party has not received adequate consideration. This doctrine does not require that the highest price obtainable must be procured. It means that a price that is fair and reasonable under the circumstances must be obtained. If a higher price is offered during the negotiations, it must be presented.

Thus in one California case the broker signed up a buyer at $30,000, knowing that $35,000 had been offered for the property. Inadequacy was held to defeat the buyer's suit in specific performance. The court also called attention to the law which requires perfect good faith on the part of agents, not only in form but in substance.

Furthermore, to entitle plaintiff to use the equitable remedy of specific performance, he or she must show that the contract as to the defendant is just and reasonable. The court denied specific performance in one case because the seller was not given adequate security to insure the payment of the balance of the price.

Specific performance cannot be enforced against a party to a contract if his or her assent was obtained by misrepresentation, concealment, circumvention, or unfair practices of any party to whom performance would become due under the contract, or by any promise of such party which has not been substantially fulfilled. This is likewise true if such assent was given under the influence of mistake, misapprehension, or surprise.

Note: Where the contract provides for compensation in case of mistake, the mistake, if correctable, may be compensated for, and the contract specifically enforced in other respects.

A buyer is always entitled to receive a merchantable title. Therefore, if the seller cannot give the buyer a title free from reasonable doubt, the seller cannot specifically enforce such an agreement. This does not mean title need be merchantable at the time the original agreement was executed, but at the time it becomes the duty of the seller to convey. If there are encumbrances known to the parties, subject to which it is agreed the title will be conveyed, these encumbrances should be described in the contract and will not block specific performance.

REAL ESTATE CONTRACTS

Real estate contracts include: (1) contracts for the sale of real property or of an interest therein; (2) agreements for leasing of realty for a longer period than one year; and (3) agreements authorizing or employing an agent or broker to buy or sell real estate for compensation or a commission.

These contracts are essentially like any other contract except that they must be in writing and must be signed by the party to be charged to make them valid under the Statute of Frauds. Thus as we have seen in the discussion on contracts in general, there must be: (1) *parties capable of contracting; (2) their consent (i.e., genuine offer and acceptance); (3) a lawful object; and (4) sufficient consideration.*

In the usual real estate sales transaction, the prospective buyer states the terms and conditions under which the buyer is willing to purchase the property. These terms and conditions constitute the offer. If the owner of the property agrees to all of the terms and conditions of the offer it is an acceptance which results in the creation of a contract. It makes no difference whether the offer comes from the seller or the buyer; if the negotiation finally leads to a definite offer on the one side and unconditional acceptance on the other side, a contract has been effected. All that is legally required to complete the contract for the sale of real property is to reduce the terms and conditions to writing, and to have the parties sign the contract.

Provisions in Contracts

Forms such as listing agreements (authorization to sell), deposit receipts, exchange agreements, and other real estate contracts for the sale or exchange of real estate should contain the following provisions:

1. The date of the agreement;

2. The names and addresses of the parties to the contract;

3. A description of the property;

4. The consideration;

5. Reference to creation of new mortgages (or trust deeds) and the terms thereof; the terms and conditions of existing mortgages, if any;

6. Any other provisions which may be required or requested by either of the parties;

7. The date and place of closing the contract.

A contract of sale normally calls for the preparation of a deed to convey the property. It is executory in that when the deed is properly *signed and delivered* to the purchaser the contract is executed.

Handling deposit on property in a sale. *An earnest money deposit by a prospective purchaser of real property is trust funds.* The deposit must be handled by the broker as prescribed by the Real Estate Law and the regulations.

Section 10145 of the Real Estate Law provides that the broker who receives trust funds must place the funds into a trust fund account in a bank or other recognized depository if the broker does not place the funds into a neutral escrow or into the hands of the broker's principal.

The regulations of the Commissioner spell out the procedures to be followed by a broker who elects to hold the funds uncashed or place the earnest money deposit into broker's trust fund account until acceptance. The contract usually provides that upon acceptance, the deposit will be immediately placed into an independent escrow or title company.

The provision of law which purports to sanction the handing over of all varieties of trust funds to a principal by the broker poses some real dilemmas for brokers when the trust funds in question are in the form of deposits toward purchase. The problems for the broker are particularly troublesome in those transactions where there has been an alleged breach by the buyer of what appears to be a binding contract to purchase the real property. Since the law apparently permits a broker to hand over an earnest money deposit to the seller as soon as there has been an acceptance of the offer to purchase, unless the terms of the contract provide otherwise, can the broker who has the money in his or her trust fund account refuse to turn it over to the seller upon demand when the seller concludes that the buyer has breached the contract?

There is no legal authority that provides a clear-cut answer to this question. There are those knowledgeable of the Real Estate Law in California who contend that the broker holds the earnest money deposit after an apparent acceptance of the contract as an escrow holder rather than as an agent of the seller. While the Department does not accept this proposition, it does recognize that the broker is in a very difficult position when a transaction falls apart and either or both parties make demand for the earnest money. To avoid having to make a decision as to who is entitled to an earnest money deposit and later possibly be held liable or subject to disciplinary action for having made the wrong choice, the broker is probably well advised to file an interpleader action and deposit the funds with the court in which the action is brought. If, as noted above, the trust funds have already been placed into an independent escrow upon acceptance, the funds may be held there pending resolution of the dispute.

Forfeitures. Contracts for the sale of real property frequently include a provision that a deposit toward purchase made by a prospective buyer shall be divided between the seller and the broker if the prospective buyer breaches the contract through no fault of the seller or broker. Such provisions for the forfeiture of the deposit by the buyer in case of breach come within the definition of liquidated damages clauses.

If the contract is for the purchase and sale of residential real property, defined as a dwelling of not more than four residential units and the buyer intends to occupy the dwelling or one of the units as a residence, the following rules apply:

1. These special rules apply only to amounts actually prepaid, in the form of deposit, downpayment, or otherwise.

2. If the amount paid pursuant to the liquidated damages clause does not exceed 3% of the purchase price, the clause is valid unless the buyer proves that the amount paid is unreasonable.

3. If the amount actually paid pursuant to the liquidated damages clause exceeds 3% of the purchase price, the clause is invalid unless the party seeking to enforce it proves that the amount paid is reasonable.

4. The provision must be separately signed or initialed by each party to the contract, and if it is a printed contract, the provision must be set off in ten point bold type or contrasting red print in eight point type.

These rules do not apply to real property sales contracts, as defined in Civil Code Section 2985.

Effect of seller's death on real estate contract. If the contract is entered into for the sale or purchase of real estate, and before the time of taking title the seller dies, a real problem ensues. A real estate contract properly drawn usually contains a provision which states that all the terms of the contract are to be binding upon the heirs, executors, administrators, and the assigns of the respective parties.

In the event this wording is used, the buyer's rights are the same against the heirs, executors, administrators, or assigns of the seller as the buyer had against the seller. Under these circumstances buyer may compel the seller's heirs, administrators, executors, or assigns specifically to perform the contract.

Uniform Vendor and Purchaser Risk Act (Civil Code Section 1662). Occasionally, after a contract is made for the purchase and sale of real property, a fire or other disaster destroys or seriously damages the property. Who shall take the loss? Under California's Uniform Vendor and Purchaser Risk Act, any contract made in this state for the purchase and sale of real property shall be interpreted as including an agreement that the parties shall have the following rights and duties unless the contract expressly provides otherwise:

1. If, when neither the legal title nor the possession of the subject matter of the contract has been transferred, all or a material part thereof is destroyed without fault of the purchaser or is taken by eminent domain, the seller cannot enforce the contract, and the purchaser is entitled to recover any portion of the price paid;

2. If, when either the legal title or the possession of the subject matter of the contract has been transferred, all or any part thereof is destroyed without fault of the seller or is taken by eminent domain, the purchaser is not thereby relieved from a duty to pay the price, nor entitled to recover any portion thereof that has been paid.

Options

Since an option is a form of contract, the requirements for the enforceability of real estate contracts in general apply. Some consideration, even though it might be only 25¢ on a $100,000 parcel of real estate, must in fact pass from optionee to optionor. A mere recital of consideration alone is insufficient. Provisions of a lease, however, are themselves sufficient consideration to support an option contained in it. Option contracts typically "run from" seller to buyer. That is, in exchange for consideration paid by the buyer, the seller is deprived of the right and power to revoke the basic offer to sell. The buyer, in effect, purchases an agreed amount of time in which to accept or reject the seller's underlying offer concerning the property. Thus, the underlying offer is rendered irrevocable for the period specified in the collateral option contract.

Although option rights are usually assignable unless there is a restriction to the contrary, they do not give the optionee any "interest in the land." For this reason, the optionee cannot "mortgage" his or her rights. The holder of an unexercised option does however have an interest for which the holder may be entitled to compensation on condemnation of the land.

The option may be given either alone or in connection with a lease of the property. It may be in either the customary form of an exclusive right to purchase or lease, or in the form of a privilege of first right of refusal to purchase or lease. The option will terminate automatically upon expiration of the time specified without "exercise" by the optionee. Additionally, the termination of a lease containing an option also usually terminates the option. A renewal of the lease may, however, renew the option. The specific lease situation must sometimes be carefully examined, since the option provisions and the lease provisions may be divisible.

An option to purchase real property is a written agreement whereby the owner of real property agrees with the prospective buyer, that such buyer shall have the right to purchase the property from the owner at a fixed price within a certain time. Terms of financing, payments, etc., should be set forth in such agreement. The prospective buyer at buyer's option may comply with all the terms of the agreement or be relieved from the terms of the agreement without the owner having recourse to legal procedure for damages or specific performance. The option does not bind the optionee to any performance. It merely gives the optionee a right to demand performance. Time is of the essence in an option and is usually strictly construed. If no time is specified, a reasonable time is implied.

In the event an option is recorded by the optionee, but is not exercised before or on the date of the expiration of the option, the optionee should remove the effect of the option from the records by recording a quitclaim deed.

The broker usually does not earn a commission for having secured a client who takes an option, as the broker's right of commission does not arise unless the option is exercised.

Listing Defined

A listing is a written contract by which a principal employs an agent to do certain things (e.g., sell real property) for the principal. Therefore an agent holding a listing is always bound by the law of agency and has certain fiduciary obligations to the principal that do not exist between two principals.

Net listing. In a net listing the compensation is not definitely determined, but a clause in the contract usually permits the agent to retain as compensation all the money received in excess of the selling price accepted by the seller. Under the Real Estate Law failure of an agent to disclose the amount of agent's compensation in connection with a net listing is cause for revocation or suspension of license. This must be done prior to or at the time the principal binds himself or herself to the transaction. The agent is also required by the Real Estate Law to reveal to both buyer and seller, in writing within one month of the closing of the transaction, the selling price involved. The law permits this information to be disclosed by the closing statement of the escrow holder, and this is the usual practice.

A net listing is perfectly legitimate, but it may give rise to a charge of fraud, misrepresentation and other abuses. Accordingly, if a net listing is used, the commission arrangement should be thoroughly explained to the principal.

Open listing. An open listing is a written memorandum signed by the party to be charged (usually the seller of the property) which authorizes the broker to act as agent for the sale of certain described property. Usually no time limit is specified for the employment, although open listings can provide for a definite term. The property is identified by a suitable description, and generally the terms and conditions of sale are set forth.

Open listings are the simplest form of written authorization to sell. They may be given concurrently to more than one agent, and usually the seller is not required to notify the other agents in case of a sale by one of them in order to prevent liability of paying more than one commission. Where several open listings are given, the commission is considered to be earned by the broker who first finds a buyer who meets the terms of the listing, or whose offer is accepted by the seller. If the owner personally sells the property, the owner is not obligated to pay a commission to any of the brokers holding open listings. The sale of the property under such an agreement is considered to cancel all outstanding open listings.

Exclusive agency listing. An exclusive agency listing is a contract containing the words "exclusive agency." The commission is payable to the broker named in the contract and if the broker or any other broker finds the buyer and effects the sale, the broker holding the exclusive listing is entitled to a commission.

If a broker other than the broker holding the exclusive agency listing is the procuring cause of the sale, the owner may be liable for the payment of two full commissions if the procuring broker has some type of written agreement with the seller. Because the listing refers to an *agency* and the owner is not an agent, the owner may personally effect the sale without incurring liability for commission to the broker holding the exclusive agency listing.

Exclusive right to sell listing. Another form of listing is the "exclusive right to sell." Under such listing, a commission is due the broker named in the contract if the property is sold within the time limit by the said broker, by any other broker, or by the owner. Frequently, this listing also provides that the owner will be liable for a commission if a sale is made within a specified time after the listing expires to a buyer introduced to the owner by the listing broker during the term of the listing. The real estate broker is usually obligated under the terms of the listing contract to furnish a list of the names of persons with whom the broker has negotiated during the listing period within a specified number of days after the expiration of the listing.

The "exclusive right" and the "exclusive agency" type of listing must be for a definite term, with a specified time of termination. If a broker does not provide for this, the broker's license is subject to disciplinary action under the California Real Estate Law.

Multiple listing service. A multiple listing service is a cooperative listing service conducted by a group of brokers, usually members of a real estate board. The group provides a standard "multiple listing" form which is used by the members. It is usually an "Exclusive Authorization Right to Sell" listing form and provides, among other things, that the member of the group who takes the particular listing is to turn it in to a central bureau. From there it is distributed to all participants in the service and all have the right to work on it. Commissions earned on such listings are shared between the cooperating brokers, with the listing broker providing for the division of commission in each listing sent to other participants.

When broker is entitled to commission. Ordinarily the broker is entitled to a commission when the broker produces a buyer ready, willing and able to purchase the property for the price and on the terms specified by the principal, regardless of whether the sale is ever consummated. Contracts may expressly provide that no commissions are payable except on a completed sale or on an installment of the purchase price when paid by the buyer, and such a provision controls in the absence of fraud or prevention of performance by the principal. The broker must be the procuring cause of the sale. It is not sufficient that the broker merely introduces the seller and buyer, if they are unable to agree on the terms of the sale within the time period of the agency.

The broker may, however, have a cause of action for the payment of commission if, within a specified time after expiration of the listing, the property is sold to a buyer introduced by the broker during the term of the listing contract.

Deposit Receipt

California brokers use a deposit receipt when accepting earnest money with an offer to purchase real property. This is a receipt for the money deposited and, more importantly, the basic contract for the transaction. It should set forth all the basic factors which are included in a contract of sale, including arrangements for financing. It should contain a complete understanding among the buyer, seller, and broker as to the return of the deposit in the event the offer is not accepted, and provisions for disposition of deposit money should the buyer fail to complete the purchase.

Some of these provisions are incorporated by standard clauses in the deposit receipt forms. The terms and conditions written into the offer must be done with extreme care by the broker or salesperson.

Agent must give copies of contracts. The real estate license law provides that brokers and salespersons must give copies of documents and agreements to the persons signing them at the time the signature is obtained. The law not only applies to copies of listing contracts and deposit receipts, but to any document pertaining to any of the acts for which one is required to hold a real estate license.

Tender Defined

A tender in a real estate transaction is an offer by one of the parties to the contract to carry out that party's part of the contract. A tender is usually made at the time for closing of escrow (i.e., concluding the transaction). If one of the parties defaults or is unable to carry out his or her contractual obligation, the other party makes the tender. (If the seller, an offer of the deed and a demand for payment of the balance of the purchase price. If the purchaser is ready, an offer of the money required and demand for the deed.) In the event of litigation arising out of some dispute between the buyer and the seller, the party who made the tender can rightfully claim that he or she was ready, willing and able to go through with the deal, and that the other party defaulted. If both parties were in default, neither may recover any damages from the other. Whether the parties made a tender is a question of fact which must be established by competent evidence.

The person to whom the tender is made must specify any objections at the time or they are waived. The tender of performance, when properly made, has the effect of placing the other party in default if the other party refuses to accept it and the party making the tender may rescind or sue for breach of contract or for specific performance.

ACQUISITION AND TRANSFER OF REAL ESTATE

Usually, acquisition of property by one party entails a transfer from another party, and so we consider acquisition and transfer together.

The basic distinction between real and personal property is not taken into account in the broad statutory statement of how "property" is acquired. In the following discussion, however, the methods by which real property is acquired or transferred are emphasized.

The Civil Code states that there are five ways to acquire property: will, succession, accession, occupancy, and by transfer as follows:

1. By will:
   a. Formal or witnessed will.
   b. Holographic will.
   c. California Statutory will.
   d. California Statutory will with Trust.

2. By succession:
   a. Of separate property.
   b. Of community property.

3. By accession:
   a. Through actiocren (alluvion or reliction).
   b. Through avulsion.
   c. Through addition of fixtures.
   d. Through improvements made in error.

4. By occupancy:
   a. Abandonment.
   b. Prescription.
   c. Adverse possession.

5. By transfer:
   a. Private grant.
   b. Public grant.
   c. Gift (to private person or to public, by dedication).
   d. Alienation by operation of law or court action (partition, quiet title, foreclosure, declaratory relief).

6. By marriage.
7. By escheat.
8. By eminent domain.
9. By equitable estoppel.

Will

Property accumulated during life may be disposed of at death to designated beneficiaries. The instrument to achieve this disposition of property is called a will. The execution of a will during life has no effect on property interests; the instrument only becomes effective at death. This is the distinguishing feature between wills and other instruments creating property interests such as deeds and contracts. The latter two instruments create some present interest and are not dependent upon the fact of death to be effective.

Types of wills. The types of wills permitted by law are the *witnessed will, holographic will, statutory will* and *statutory will with trust.* The first is a formal written instrument signed by the maker and declared to be the maker's will in the presence of at least two witnesses who, at the maker's request and in the maker's presence, also sign the will as witnesses. This document should be prepared by an attorney. A holographic will is one entirely written, dated and signed in the testator's own handwriting. No other formalities are required. Statutory wills are prepared in accordance with a format authorized by statute.

When a person dies, title to his or her real property passes directly to the beneficiaries named in the will, or to the heirs if the decedent left no will. Title, however, is not marketable or insurable because the law provides that on death all property is subject to the temporary possession of the executor or executrix, administrator or administratrix, with a few exceptions. Legal title is also subject to the control of the probate court for purposes of determining and liquidating creditors' claims and for establishing the identity of the heirs, devisees, and legatees of the estate.

Probate

Probate procedure commences with a "petition for probate" of a will or for letters of administration if there is no will. A hearing is held and a representative is appointed to handle the estate. This person is referred to as an executor or executrix if there is a will or an administrator or administratrix if there is no will or if no personal representative is named in the will.

Notice to creditors is then published, giving all creditors four months within which to file their claims. An inventory and appraisement of the estate listing all the assets is filed with the county clerk. During administration of the estate, the representative may sell estate property subject to court approval only.

After the time for filing creditors claims has expired, the representative files an accounting of all receipts and disbursements and requests court approval of same. Finally, the representative petitions the court to approve distribution of the remaining assets to the proper heirs and devisees. Small estates may be exempt from probate administration or subject to special summary procedures.

Succession

If a person dies without leaving a will, the law provides for disposition of decedent's property. This is called *intestate succession.* A large number of special rules are included in the law depending upon the character of the property and the relationship of the next of kin. In the simplest cases, *separate* property is divided equally between a surviving spouse and one child, or split one-third to the surviving spouse and one-third to each of two children, etc. One-half of the *community* property belongs to the surviving spouse and the other half is subject to disposition by the decedent's will. If there is no will, the decedent's half of the community property remaining after payment of his or her liabilities goes to the surviving spouse.

Accession

By accession, an owner's title to improvements or additions to his/her property may be extended as a result of either man-made or natural causes. For example, a fixture may be annexed to a building by a tenant, or a neighbor may affix a wall or a building in such a way to the landowner's property without agreement to remove the improvement so as to extend the landowner's title to the improvement.

By natural causes, through *accretion,* the owner of a riparian property (i.e., located along a moving body of water such as a river or stream) or littoral property (located beside a pond, lake or ocean) may acquire title to additional land by the gradual accumulation of land deposited on the owner's property from the shifting of the river or the ocean's action. The land increase by this build-up of sediment (or alluvium) is called *alluvion.* The gradual recession of water, leaving permanently dry land is *accession* caused by *reliction.* Rapid washing away of land is called *avulsion.*

Addition of fixtures. Acquisition of title by addition of fixtures occurs when a person affixes something to the land of another without permission and/or an agreement permitting removal of it. The thing so affixed belongs to the owner of the land, unless the owner requires the former tenant to remove it.

Improvements made in error. At one time there was no compensation for the innocent person who mistakenly improved someone else's real property (e.g., built a house on another's lot). However, the Legislature changed this in 1953 by amendment of Civil Code Section 1013.5. The change permits a person who affixes improvements to the land of another in good faith and erroneously believing because of a mistake of fact or law that he or she has a right to do so to remove the improvements upon payment of damages to the owner of the land and any other persons having an interest therein who acquired the interest in reliance on the improvements.

Abandonment. Abandonment is the voluntary surrender of possession of real property or a leasehold with the intention of terminating one's possession or interest and without assigning the interest to another. If the owner of a leasehold interest (i.e., the lessee) abandons the property, the landlord reacquires possession and full control of the premises. Mere non-use is not abandonment.

Prescription. An easement created by prescription is analogous to adverse possession. Although only the right to use someone else's land results, a property interest is thus acquired.

Adverse possession. The actual physical possession of property has always been accorded considerable weight in connection with a variety of rights and obligations. Immediately upon occupying property, an adverse possessor acquires a title to the property good against all the rest of the world except the state and the true owner. Such occupation may ripen into *legal* title by adverse possession if the possession is:

1. by actual occupation;

2. open and notorious;

3. hostile to the true owner's title;

4. under claim of right or color of title;

5. continuous and uninterrupted for a period of five years;

6. accompanied by payment of all real property taxes for a period of five years.

Since title by adverse possession cannot be traced from the county recorder's office, it is neither marketable nor insurable until perfected by court decree.

Title by adverse possession cannot usually be acquired against a public body.

Transfer

Property is acquired by transfer when, by an act of the owner or of law, title to property is conveyed from one person to another. It is the variations of transfer which are of primary concern to real estate brokers.

Private grant. Conveyancing, for consideration, of title to real property by private grant is very important to a real estate broker and is discussed in Chapter 7.

Gift. An owner of property may voluntarily transfer it to another person without demanding or receiving consideration. If the gift is real property, it would normally be conveyed by a deed.

Public dedication. Real property intended for public use can be acquired by a governmental body for such use in any one of three ways: common law dedication, statutory dedication, and deed.

Common law dedication requires that the landowner's conduct evidence an intent to devote the land to some public use, as by executing a deed describing a boundary as being a "street." To be effective, the public must accept this dedication by local ordinance or by public use.

The most common example of statutory dedication takes place under the Subdivision Map Act when a landowner records a map on which certain areas are expressly dedicated to the public for streets and parks, etc.

Dedication by deed is generally used in specific situations not involving subdivisions created under the Subdivision Map Act. Usually, only an easement is transferred. However, many local governments now require deeds so that fee title, rather than an easement, is acquired. This method avoids title problems arising upon abandonment.

Alienation by court action. There are a variety of situations in which courts establish legal title regardless of the desires of the record owners.

Any person may sue another who claims an adverse interest in real property. This type of proceeding is called a *quiet-title action* and is the usual way of clearing tax titles, titles based upon adverse possession and the title of a seller under a forfeited recorded contract of sale.

A co-owner of property may sue the other co-owners, requesting a severance of the respective interests. If the property cannot practically be divided physically, as is usually the case, the court may order a sale, transfer title to the buyer, and divide the proceeds among the former owners. This proceeding is called a *partition action.*

A person holding a lien based upon contractual delinquency may ask that the court order sale of the property, transfer of title to the purchaser, and application of the sales proceeds to the unpaid balance due under the contract. This is called a *foreclosure action.* Mortgage and mechanic's lien foreclosures are examples.

A person may, in cases of actual controversy, bring an action to determine his/her rights and obligations under any written instrument. A judicial declaration of rights in advance of an actual tortious incident enables the parties to shape their conduct so as to avoid a breach. This *declaratory relief action* is often used to construe deeds, restrictions or homesteads, or to determine rights under an oral contract.

Execution sale. A plaintiff in an action who obtains a money judgment against a defendant can take appropriate steps to get a *writ of execution.* This court order directs the sheriff (or marshal or constable) to satisfy the judgment out of property of the debtor. Real property belonging to the debtor, and not exempt from execution, is seized by the officer and sold at public auction.

The buyer receives a certificate of sale and, if no redemption is made within the time allowed by statute (usually 12 months), the officer executes and delivers a deed to the buyer.

Forfeiture. An owner may impose a *condition subsequent* in a deed. If the condition is breached, the grantor or grantor's successor has the power to terminate the estate and reacquire title. Similarly, the owner may impose a *special limitation* in a deed. If the stated event occurs or the prescribed status fails to endure, the estate automatically terminates and the grantor or his or her successor reacquires title. In both cases, property is acquired by forfeiture with no need for consideration.

Marriage. Under California law, marriage does not effect a transfer of title to property. However, *subsequent* earnings and acquisitions of husband and wife, or either, during marriage, when not acquired as separate property, are *community property.* Each spouse has a present, existing and equal interest in such property.

Escheat. Escheat is the legal process by which title to property vests in the state, usually for lack of heirs or want of legal ownership. Since a presumption exists that some heirs capable of taking title exist in every case, the process of escheat is not automatic. Escheat proceedings can be based on an action initiated by the Attorney General or on a decree of distribution by a probate court.

Eminent domain. By eminent domain, a governmental entity takes private property for public use, paying compensation based on fair market value.

Equitable estoppel. Equity and good conscience sometimes require that title to real property be transferred if justice is to be done. The former owner is barred or estopped from denying the title of the innocent claimant.

For example, if an owner permits a friend to appear to the world as the owner of certain property, and an innocent third party buys the land from that apparent owner, the true owner is barred by the doctrine of equitable estoppel from claiming ownership.

Similarly, if a person has no title, or a defective title or an estate smaller than the one purported to be conveyed, but later acquires full title or estate, or perfects the title, the grantee (or grantee's successor) gets the after-acquired title by way of estoppel.

7   Principal Instruments Of Transfer

A Backward Look

Under the early English common law, ownership of real property was transferred by a technique called "feoffment." This involved delivery of possession, which was termed "livery of seizin." No writing or deed was involved. The transfer was actually effected by a delivery of the land itself or something symbolical of the land, such as a twig, a stone, or a handful of dirt.

Another early method of transfer was by a statement usually made before witnesses in view of the land to the effect that possession was transferred, followed by entry of the new owner. Again, no written instrument was at first required. An interest in land which was not capable of actual possession (termed an incorporeal right), such as an easement, was transferred by a deed called a "deed of grant."

A *"conveyance by a release"* was a deed given to transfer an estate or interest in land, but no *"livery of seizin"* could be given until the new owner took possession, which involved a multiplicity of formalities. A release was also used for the purpose of extinguishing a right in the land and corresponds to its modern descendant, the quitclaim deed.

A recording system was unknown to the early common law. Ownership was a matter of common knowledge and transfer was not often made except by descent from father to son on the father's death.

The method of making land transfers in California under Spanish and Mexican rule was somewhat similar to that of the common law. It was early held by the Supreme Court of California that land could not be conveyed under Spanish and Mexican laws without an instrument in writing, unless conveyance of the land was made by an executed contract in which actual possession was delivered at the time of sale by entry upon the premises and the doing of certain ceremonial acts (which in a sense were like "livery of seizin" at common law). The ancient "livery of seizin" is symbolized today by the delivery of the deed, not the property, by the grantor to the grantee. The deed is the now the symbol of title.

The Pattern Today

Today, Californians most often transfer title to real property by a simple written instrument, *the grant deed*. The word "grant" is expressly designated by statute as a word of conveyance. (Civil Code Section 1092) A second form of deed is the *quitclaim deed*. It resembles the common law *"conveyance by a release."* Other types of deeds are the warranty deed, the trust deed, the reconveyance deed, the sheriff's deed, and the gift deed.

DEEDS IN GENERAL

When properly executed, delivered and accepted, a deed transfers title to real property from one person (the *grantor*) to another person (the *grantee*). Transfer may be *voluntary*, or *involuntary* by act of law, such as a foreclosure sale.

There are several different essentials to a valid deed:

1. It must be in writing;

2. The parties must be properly described;

3. The parties must be competent to convey and capable of receiving the grant of the property;

4. The property conveyed must be described so as to distinguish it from other parcels of real property.;

5. There must be a granting clause, operative words of conveyance (e.g., "I hereby grant");

6. The deed must be signed by the party or parties making the conveyance or grant; and

7. It must be delivered and accepted.

Contrary to the law and established custom in other states, the expression "to have and to hold" (called the "habendum clause" of a deed) is not necessary, nor are witnesses or seal required. The deed should be dated, but this too is not necessary to its validity.

Any form of written instrument containing the essentials above set out will convey title to land. A typical grant deed may be in the form as follows:

"I, John A. Doe, a single man, grant to Emma B. Roe, a widow, all that real property situated in Sacramento County, State of California, described as follows: Lot 21, Tract 62, recorded at Page 91 of Book 7 of Maps of Sacramento County, filed January 21, 1965. Witness my hand this tenth day of October, 1983.

　　　(Signed) John A. Doe"

Usually, a deed is executed for consideration, but this is not essential for a valid transfer. Moreover, even when consideration is given for the property, this point need not be mentioned in the deed. However, it should be noted that lack of consideration may affect the rights of the grantee as against the rights of certain third parties because the recording statutes are intended to protect bona fide purchasers.

For example, a transfer made without consideration by a grantor who is or will thereby be rendered insolvent, is fraudulent as to grantor's creditors and those creditors may have the deed set aside in a court action.

A deed need not be acknowledged, nor need it be recorded. However, both *acknowledgment* and *recordation* are part of the standard operating procedure in real estate transfers for very good reasons.

Acknowledgment

An acknowledgment is a formal declaration before a duly authorized officer, such as a notary public, by a person who has executed an instrument that such execution is his or her act and deed. The piece of paper (or form) executed by the officer before whom the formal declaration was made (for example, the grantor in a grant deed) is a Certificate of Acknowledgment. This certificate is either printed right on the grant deed itself or is a separate piece of paper which is stapled to the grant deed. The acknowledgment of a writing is a way of proving that the writing was in fact signed (or executed) by the person who purported to sign (or execute) the writing. Moreover, an acknowledgment is a safeguard against forgery and false impersonation. Duly acknowledged writings are entitled to be introduced into evidence in litigation without further proof of execution.

Many instruments are not entitled to be recorded unless acknowledged. Unless by statute an acknowledgment is made essential to the validity of an instrument, the instrument itself is valid between the parties and persons having actual notice of it, though not acknowledged. The time of acknowledgment is almost invariably immaterial if the rights of innocent third parties do not intervene.

Where acknowledgments may be taken and by whom. Anywhere within the state, proof or acknowledgment of an instrument may be made before a justice, retired justice or clerk of the Supreme Court, or District Court of Appeal, or the judge or retired judge of a superior court, or, after September 17, 1959, a notary public. (Before that date a notary could not act outside the notary's own county.)

In this state and *within the city, county, city and county, or district for which the officer was selected, or appointed,* acknowledgment of an instrument may be made before either: a clerk of a municipal or justice court; a county clerk; a court commissioner; a judge or retired judge of a superior, municipal or justice court or certain other local officials. (Civil Code Section 1181)

Acknowledgments may be made and taken by any deputy of the foregoing, duly authorized by law. Also, certain military officers are authorized to take acknowledgments of persons serving in the armed forces. (Civil Code Section 1183.5)

The principal form of acknowledgement authorized by California law is provided for in Civil Code Section 1183.5. An acknowledgment taken outside this state, must be in accordance with the forms, provisions, and laws of this state. If not, it should have attached thereto a certificate of a clerk of the court of record of the county or district where the same was taken, or of a consul or consular agent of the U.S., or judge if in a foreign country. The certificate of acknowledgment must state that it is in accordance with the laws of the state, the United States or the foreign country in which it was taken and that the officer taking the same was authorized by law to do so and that the signature is true and genuine.

A form of acknowledgment called an "Apostille" may be used in California to authenticate a certificate of acknowledgment drafted in a foreign country.

If the certificate of acknowledgment is sufficient in other respects, it will not be invalidated by a mistake in the date or even by the absence of a date. It is sufficient that such date appears by evidence within the instrument itself and, in the absence of proof to the contrary, it may be presumed that the acknowledgment was taken on the date of the execution of the instrument or at least before the recordation thereof.

Where the date of the deed is subsequent to that of the acknowledgment, the later date may be taken as the true date of the deed. The certificate must be authenticated by the signature of the officer followed by the name of his or her office. An official seal must be affixed if the officer is by law required to have a seal.

In California, a notary public is required to have a seal on which must be engraved the words "notary public," the name of the county, name of the notary and the State Seal. A notary is required by law to keep adequate records of all notary actions taken and to have record evidence for the proper identification of the person making an acknowledgment of his/her signature.

Acknowledgments taken by officers having an interest in the transaction. In general, case law has consistently provided that officers who take an acknowledgment of a writing should not have a direct financial interest in the transaction. The purpose of the prohibition is to discourage fraud, and if an acknowledged instrument discloses on its face that such conflict of interest exists, it has been held the recorded instrument does not impart constructive notice of its contents.

No reliance should be placed on instruments acknowledged before an officer who is known to have, or who may reasonably be expected to have, a direct financial or beneficial interest in the transaction. For example: an officer acknowledging his own signing of a document or instrument; an officer acknowledging a mortgagor's execution of a mortgage naming the officer as mortgagee; and an officer acknowledging a deed in which he or she is named as grantee.

An acknowledging officer who is one of several grantors or mortgagors may properly acknowledge signing of the instrument by the other grantors or mortgagors, but his or her own signing must be acknowledged by a different officer.

Effective January 1, 1978 the following statutes became effective with respect to the acknowledgments taken by notaries public:

• *Government Code Section 8224*

A notary public who has a direct financial interest in a transaction shall not perform any notarial act in connection therewith. Transactions covered include the following:

1. Financial transactions in which the notary public is named, individually, as a principal.
2. Real property transactions in which the notary public is named, individually, as grantor, grantee, mortgagor, mortgagee, trustor, trustee, beneficiary, vendor, vendee, lessor or lessee.

• *Government Code Section 8224.1*

A notary public shall not take the acknowledgment or proof of instruments in writing executed by him or by her.

Certain instruments must be acknowledged by affected party. California law protects property owners from unwarranted or unauthorized encumbrance of their property on the official records. Most instruments affecting real property must be executed and acknowledged or proved by the owner of the property before the instrument is eligible for recordation.

Among such instruments, besides conveyances, mortgages and trust deeds, are agreements for sale, option agreements, deposit receipts, commission receipts or any affidavit which quotes or refers to these instruments.

Any instrument transferring or encumbering community property must be executed by both the husband and the wife.

Recordation

While recording a deed does not affect its validity, it is extremely important to record since recordation protects the grantee. If a grantee fails to record, and another deed or any other document encumbering or affecting the title is recorded, the first grantee is in jeopardy. The recording system is established to show the sequence of transfers or other actions affecting property, and it is foolish to fail to avail oneself of the privilege of recording.

Possession of property also gives notice of the rights of persons in possession. A person buying real property should not rely entirely on a title policy, but should investigate to see if somebody is in possession and find out what their rights are. The occupants might be in possession under a partly paid contract of purchase and sale, or they could be in possession under a lease that gave them an option to buy.

Consistency of names in title instruments. Complete record title to land cannot be established unless the various instruments in a chain of title in the recorder's office show direct connection by name between the different owners. Any substantial variation between the name of the grantee in one instrument and the name of the grantor in the next instrument executed by that grantee will, irrespective of the fact that identity may be shown by "off record" evidence, render the title defective. Furthermore, the subsequent instrument executed by the grantor of that grantee cannot impart constructive notice of its contents to a third person.

A legal name of an individual consists of one personal, or given, name and one surname/family name. The old common law recognized but one given name and frequently disregarded middle names or initials. It has been stated that the insertion or omission of, or mistake or variance in a middle name or initial is immaterial. However, while the omission or addition of a middle name or initial in an instrument affecting real property is generally considered immaterial, a variance in middle names or initials may result in defective record of title.

Change of name. With limited exceptions, a person in whom title to real estate is vested who afterwards has a name change must, in a conveyance of the real estate, set forth the name in which he/she took title. For example: If a single woman acquires title as "Mary Doe" and later marries a man whose last name is Smith, she should convey the property as "Mary Doe Smith, formerly Mary Doe" (or "who acquired title as Mary Doe").

Generally, any conveyance, though recorded as provided by law, which does not comply with the foregoing provision does not impart constructive notice of the .contents to subsequent purchasers and encumbrancers, but the conveyance is valid as between the parties thereto and those who have actual notice. To correct a situation in which an incorrect name has been used in a transfer of title, it is advisable to clear title by filing a special action and proceeding under Section 770.020 of the California Code of Civil Procedure.

Party in title instrument cannot be fictitious but may use fictitious name. A deed to a purely fictitious person (false or feigned name) is void, but a deed to an actual person under a fictitious name by which he or she is known or which this person assumes for the occasion is valid. If the grantee is misnamed in the deed, the error can be corrected by a second deed to the same grantee under the true name. The grantee designated in the deed must be a person in existence, either natural or artificial, and must be capable of taking title to the land, for a deed to a dead person is void. A deed to the estate of a deceased person is questionable. A deed to the administrator of the estate of a deceased person, if the administrator is duly nominated, appointed and acting, conveys title to the heirs or devisees of the deceased, subject to administration of the estate.

For example: A better mode of granting deeds to an estate, and one which has been approved by most title companies would be "to the heirs or devisees of John Doe, deceased, subject to the administration of his estate."

Delivery and Acceptance
A deed is of no effect unless delivered. But delivery in this context means more than a turning over of the physical possession of the document. The grantor must have the *intention* to pass title immediately. It is possible in some cases to have a legal delivery without the instrument actually being handed to the grantee, if the grantor has the requisite intent to transfer title.

That intention is not present if A gives B a deed but tells B not to record it until A's death, both parties believing the deed is ineffective until recorded. Nor is such intention present in the typical case of cross-deeds between husband and wife placed in a joint safe-deposit box with the understanding that the survivor will record his or her deed.

The law presumes a valid delivery if the deed is found in the possession of the grantee or is recorded, but such presumption is rebuttable. A deed may be entrusted to a third party (such as an escrow agent) with directions that it be delivered to the grantee upon the performance of designated conditions. The deed itself may contain conditions. But with reference to delivery, by statute, a grant cannot be delivered to the grantee conditionally. Delivery to the grantee, or to the grantee's agent as such, is necessarily absolute, and the instrument takes effect immediately, discharged of any condition on which the delivery was made which is not expressed in the deed. (Or, no delivery may have occurred and the deed may be found to be void.) The grantor attempting a conditional delivery should withhold transfer of the deed to the grantee until the conditions are satisfied; or incorporate the conditions in the deed itself; or deposit the deed into an escrow with appropriate instructions. Transfer of a deed conditioned on the grantor's death is ineffective as an attempted testamentary disposition failing to meet the requirements of a will.

A duly executed deed is presumed to be delivered as of its dated date. The dated date of a deed is often different from its recorded date. Possession or the rights thereto must be given when the deed is delivered.

Ordinarily, a deed cannot be given effect unless it is accepted by the grantee. An exception to this rule is made when the grantee is a minor or mentally incompetent. Acceptance of a deed may be shown by acts, words or conduct of the grantee showing an intent to accept. A deed to a governmental entity must ordinarily contain (either on the face of the deed itself or on a separate sheet attached to the deed) a certificate of acceptance.

TYPES OF DEEDS

Grant Deed

Because of inclusion of the word "grant" in a grant deed, the grantor impliedly warrants that he or she has not already conveyed to any other person and that the estate conveyed is free from encumbrances done, made or suffered by the grantor or any person claiming under grantor, including taxes, assessments and other liens. This does not mean that the grantor warrants that grantor is the owner or that the property is not otherwise encumbered. The grant includes appurtenant easements for ingress and egress and building restrictions. The grantor's warranty includes encumbrances made during grantor's, but no other individual's, possession of the property. It conveys any title acquired after the grantor has conveyed the title to the real property (after-acquired title), generally. Observe that these warranties carried by a grant deed are not usually expressed in the grant deed form. They are called "implied warranties" because the law deems them included in the grant whether or not explicitly expressed in the deed

Quitclaim Deed

A quitclaim deed is a deed by which a grantor transfers only the interest the grantor has at the time the conveyance is executed. There are no implied warranties in connection with a quitclaim deed. This type of deed guarantees nothing and there is no expressed or implied warranty that grantor owns the property or any interest in it. Moreover, a quitclaim deed does not convey any after-acquired title. A quitclaim deed effectively says, "I am conveying all the title that I have in the property described in this quitclaim - if I have, in fact, any title."

A quitclaim deed is generally used to clear some "cloud on the title." A "cloud on the title" is some minor defect in the title which needs to be removed in order to perfect the title. Deeds of court representatives, such as guardians, administrators, and sheriffs, usually have the effect of a quitclaim pursuant to court order.

Warranty Deed

A warranty deed contains express covenants of title. Warranty deeds are uncommon in California, no doubt because of the almost universal reliance in this state on title insurance to evidence marketable title.

Trust Deed

A trust deed (or deed of trust) is a 3-party security instrument conveying title to land as security for the performance of an obligation. There are three parties to a trust deed: borrower *(trustor)*, lender *(beneficiary)*, and a third party, called a *trustee*, to whom legal title to the real property is conveyed. The trustee holds the legal title in trust for the beneficiary and has the power to sell the property if the trustor does not fulfill the obligations as recited in the instrument. The trustee also possesses power to reconvey the legal title to the trustor provided the beneficiary requests a reconveyance of that title. This event occurs if the promissory note is paid in full.

A trustor signing the trust deed retains what is called an equitable title. That is, the trustor enjoys the right of possession and can do with the property whatever the trustor pleases so long as the trustor does not jeopardize the interest of the lender (beneficiary).

Business and Professions Code Section 10141.5 requires that a real estate licensee record a deed of trust within one week after closing of a transaction or deliver it to the beneficiary with a written recommendation that it be recorded or deliver it to the escrow holder. Failure of a real estate licensee to carry out the duties prescribed in Section 10141.5 does not affect the validity of the transfer of title to the real property.

Reconveyance Deed

A reconveyance deed is an instrument conveying title to property from a trustee back to the trustor on termination of the trust. This title is held by the trustee until the note or obligation is fully paid. Then, when the beneficiary issues a "Request for Full Reconveyance," the trustee executes the reconveyance to the borrower. Termination of the trust usually occurs when the promissory note is paid in full.

Sheriff's Deed

A sheriff's deed is a deed given to a party on the foreclosure of property, levied under a judgment for foreclosure on a mortgage or of a money judgment against the owner of the property.

The title conveyed is only that acquired by the state or the sheriff under the foreclosure and carries no warranties or representations whatsoever.

Gift Deed

A grantor may make a gift of property to the grantee, and use a grant deed form or a quitclaim deed form for the purpose. Grantor may, but need not, say in the deed that grantor makes the transfer because of love and affection for the grantee.

A gift deed made to defraud creditors may be set aside if it leaves the debtor/grantor insolvent or otherwise contributes to fraud. (Uniform Fraudulent Transfer Act, Civil Code Sections 3439 through 3439.12)

Void Deeds

Deeds that are void and pass no title even in favor of a bona fide purchaser for value include:

1. A deed from a person whose incapacity has been judicially determined, e.g., a deed from a person for whom a conservator has been appointed (Civil Code Section 40);

2. Forged deeds *(Meley v. Collins,* 41 Cal. 663);

3. A deed from a person under 18 years and not emancipated;

4. A deed executed in blank, where the name of the grantee has been inserted without authorization or consent of the grantor *(Trout v. Taylor,* 220 Cal. 652); and

5. A deed purely testamentary in character, i.e., when the grantor intends that the deed not become operative until his death.

Voidable Deeds

Deeds which are not void, but are voidable and pass title subject to being set aside in appropriate judicial proceedings include:

1. A deed from a person of unsound mind whose incapacity has not been determined *(Hughes v. Grandy*, 78 Cal. App. 2nd, 555);

2. Prior to March 4, 1972, a deed from a person over 18 years of age and under 21 years of age, except a deed from a lawfully married person 18 years of age or older (Family Code Sections 6700, 6701, 6710). Family Code Section 6701(b) limits the authority of a minor to "make a contract relating to real property or any interests therein". Since any person 18 or over, and under 21, who was lawfully married was deemed to be an adult for the purposes of dealing in property, it may be necessary to determine the legality of the marriage. If the person was married outside of California, and the marriage was valid by the laws of the state or the county in which the same was contracted, the marriage was valid in California. If the person was married in California, the age of the person will determine the procedure necessary to effect a valid marriage. (Family Code Sections 301 and 302.)

8   Escrow

An escrow is essentially a small and short-lived trust arrangement. It has become almost an indispensable mechanism in this state for the consummation of real property transfers and other transactions such as exchanges, leases, sales of personal property, sales of securities, loans, and mobilehome sales. This chapter discusses the real estate sale escrow.

Definition

California Civil Code Section 1057 provides this description of an escrow:

> "A grant may be deposited by the grantor with a third person, to be delivered on the performance of a condition, and, on delivery by the depositary, it will take effect. While in the possession of the third person, and subject to condition, it is called an escrow."

And, in Section 17003 of the Financial Code:

> "Escrow means any transaction wherein one person, for the purpose of effecting the sale, transfer, encumbering or leasing of real or personal property to another person, delivers any written instrument, money, evidence of title to real or personal property, or other thing of value to a third person to be held by such third person until the happening of a specified event or the performance of a prescribed condition, when it is then to be delivered by such third person to a grantee, grantor, promisee, promisor, obligee, obligor, bailee, bailor, or any agent or employee of any of the latter."

Essential Elements

The two essential requirements for a valid sale escrow are a binding contract between buyer and seller and the conditional delivery of transfer instruments to a third party. The binding contract can appear in any legal form, including a deposit receipt, agreement of sale, exchange agreement, option or mutual escrow instructions of the buyer and the seller.

Escrow Holder

An escrow holder is the depositary, agent, or impartial third person having and holding possession of money, written instruments, or personal property to be held until the happening of designated conditions. (Once these conditions are met and performed the escrow agent is generally released from liability.) According to Financial Code Section 17004, "escrow agent" is any person engaged in the business of receiving escrows for deposit or delivery.

The escrow holder acts to ensure that all parties to the transaction comply with the terms and conditions of the agreement as set forth in the escrow instructions. The escrow holder may also coordinate the activities and professional services involved in the transaction, such as the activities of the lender and the title company as well as those between the buyer, seller and broker.

Instructions

The conditional delivery or transfer is accompanied by instructions to the escrow holder to deliver the instruments and funds respectively on the performance of the stipulated conditions. There are two forms of escrow instructions employed: bilateral (i.e., binding on both buyer and seller) and unilateral (separate instructions of buyer and seller). Since the escrow instructions implement and may also supplement the original contract, both are interpreted together if possible. If, however, the instructions contain terms in conflict with the original contract, the instructions, constituting the later contract, usually control.

When instructions have been signed by the parties to the escrow, neither party may unilaterally change the escrow instructions. The parties may, by mutual agreement, change the instructions at any time and one party may waive the performance of certain conditions, provided the waiver is not detrimental to the other party to the transaction.

While an escrow holder can be held liable for violating written instructions, the escrow holder is really only a stakeholder, not legally concerned with controversies between the parties. As such, an escrow holder is entitled to file an action of interpleader to require litigation of controversies.

Complete Escrow

Properly drawn and executed escrow instructions become an enforceable contract. An escrow is termed "complete" when all the terms of the instructions have been met.

Escrow Principles

The following are major escrow principles:

1. Escrow instructions must contain mutuality and the understanding of the principals to the escrow. Properly drawn instructions are clear and certain as to the intentions of the parties, the duties of the escrow holder, and the fact that it is the principals themselves who must perform the escrow contract by complying fully with the instructions. The escrow holder does not have, and must not exercise, *discretionary* authority.

2. The escrow holder does not act as a mediator or advisor, or participate in customer controversy, or arbitrate disputes. Instructions are drawn so that the parties to the escrow make the promises, perform, and put the escrow holder in a position to close the escrow.

3. The escrow holder is prohibited from offering legal advice and must suggest that disagreeing parties consult an attorney (or real estate broker if it is a transaction matter that may be negotiated).

4. Escrow is a limited agency relationship governed by the content of the escrow instructions. As agent for *both* parties, the escrow holder acts only upon specific *written* instructions of the principals. When the escrow is closed, the escrow holder becomes agent for *each* principal with respect to those things in escrow to which the parties have respectively become completely entitled.

5. When all parties to the escrow have signed mutual (identically conforming) instructions, the escrow becomes effective. If only one party has signed, that

party may terminate the proposed escrow at any time prior to the other party's signing.

6. The escrow holder must avoid vague or ambiguous terms and provisions in instructions and documents.

7. The escrow holder must forward immediately to the title company any document which is to be recorded and furnish a copy to any concerned party, so that the document's sufficiency can be determined. This will help avoid delay in closing escrow.

8. Documents and funds not contemplated by the escrow instructions should not be accepted by the escrow holder without authorization of the principals.

9. The escrow trust account must be maintained with extreme care. Overdrawn accounts (debit balances) are strictly forbidden.

10. Escrows are confidential in nature. The escrow holder must not give out any information to third parties concerning an escrow without approval of the escrow principals.

11. The escrow holder is the agent of the principals to the escrow. Legally, any facts known by the escrow agent are imputed to the principals. Any detrimental or new material information, previously undisclosed, made known to the escrow holder and affecting the principals should be disclosed to them for their instructions in the matter.

12. The escrow holder must maintain a high degree of trust, efficient customer service, and good customer relations.

13. The escrow holder must remain strictly neutral, not favoring either party. The escrow holder must not advise either party, as any gain to the one will likely be detriment to the other.

14. The escrow holder must maintain records and files on a daily basis, to be sure that a procedure is not overlooked. Neat and orderly files, complete with check sheets, will help insure smooth progression toward closing.

15. Before closing an escrow, the escrow holder must audit the file, accounting for all items to be handled, recorded and delivered, including cleared funds.

16. The escrow holder must not disburse any funds from an escrow account until all items such as checks, drafts, etc. have cleared, and thus have become available for withdrawal. This "holding period" may range from 1 to 10 days, depending on the type and location of lender.

17. Closing and settlement must be prompt, using forms which are simple and clear.

GENERAL ESCROW PROCEDURES
(may vary according to local custom)

Basic escrow procedures include the following:

1. *Prepare Escrow Instructions* on the escrow holder's printed form. All principals to the escrow sign instructions which fully set forth the understanding of the parties to the transaction. Usually accompanied by an

initial deposit. For a home purchase, the mutual instructions of the principals set forth:

- the purchase price and terms;
- agreement as to mortgages;
- how buyer's title is to vest;
- matters of record subject to which buyer is to acquire title;
- inspection reports to be delivered into escrow;
- proration adjustments;
- date of buyer's possession of the property;
- documents to be signed by the parties, delivered into escrow, and recorded;
- disbursements to be made, costs and charges and who pays for them; and
- date of closing.

2. *Order Title Search* on the subject property, resulting in a "Preliminary Report" from the title company. The escrow holder examines this report carefully for items not contemplated in the escrow instructions. The seller must clear any such item or it must be brought to the attention of the buyer "for information" and "expression of desire in the matter."

3. *Request Demands and/or Beneficiary Statements* from any lenders of record. The necessary document will be:

- a "Demand for Pay-off" if an existing loan is to be paid in full through escrow; or
- a "Beneficiary Statement" if buyer is purchasing "subject to" or assuming a loan.

4. *Accept Structural Pest Control Report and Other Reports* (such as plumbing or roofing inspections) into escrow and obtain, as instructed, any necessary approvals from the parties in connection with the reports/inspections. Hold the reports (and any funds associated therewith) for delivery to the proper party, or recording, at close of escrow.

5. *Accept New Loan Instructions and Documents* if the buyer is obtaining new financing. Obtain buyer's approval/execution of the documents. Satisfy all lender's instructions prior to using the lender's funds to complete the transaction.

6. *Accept Fire Insurance Policies and Complete Settlement* by:

- accepting and delivering any fire insurance policy and transferring the insurance if so instructed by the parties;
- making all prorations (e.g., property taxes and insurance) as instructed by the parties;
- completing the accounting (settlement) details and informing the principals that escrow is ready to proceed.

7. *Request Closing Funds.* The law prohibits disbursal of funds from an escrow account until all items such as checks, drafts, etc. have cleared and become available for withdrawal.

8. *Audit File in Preparation for Closing* by:
   - accounting for all funds (Cash Reconciliation Statement) and documents;
   - determining that the parties have complied with all escrow instructions.

9. *Order Recording* by authorizing the title company to run the seller's title to date and record the necessary documents, provided no change has occurred in the seller's title since issuance of the preliminary title report.

10. *Close Escrow*, after confirming recording, by:
    - preparing settlement statements for buyer and seller;
    - disbursing all funds; and
    - delivering documents to the party or parties entitled thereto.

Proration

The seller is the beneficial owner of the property until close of escrow. If possession is delivered at some time other than at the close of escrow, the principals may agree to adjust the proration date since possession normally indicates beneficial ownership. If possession is delivered sometime after close of escrow, the parties may agree to proration of taxes, rent and/or assessments, along with prepaid items for which the buyer becomes responsible upon recording of the deed, such as interest on a new loan or prepaid fire insurance obtained by buyer.

Termination

Escrows are voluntarily completed by full performance and closing or terminated by mutual consent and cancellation. It has been held that compliance with escrow instructions must be achieved within the time limit set forth in the escrow agreement and the escrow holder has no authority to enforce or accept performance after the time limit provided in the instructions. When the time limit provided in the escrow instructions has expired and either party to the escrow has not performed in accordance with the terms of the escrow agreement, the parties may cancel escrow and are entitled to the return of their respective property and documents. The escrow holder does not have authority to determine that a principal has not performed. Therefore, clear and precise instructions from the principals are necessary.

Cancellation of Escrow - Cancellation of Purchase Contract

Cancellation of escrow may not also cancel a purchase contract. In *Cohen v. Shearer (1980)* 108 C.A. 3d 939, a Court of Appeal decided that cancellation of an escrow by mutual agreement of the parties did not rescind the purchase contract between them.

Therefore, a real estate broker seeking to carry out the principal's decision to cancel a contract of purchase or sale should be sure the other party to the contract agrees in writing to do precisely that and not simply settle for written advice to cancel the escrow. As happened in the *Cohen* case, if a purchase agreement is not canceled along with the escrow, either party to the agreement may retain the right to specific enforcement of the contract or for the recovery of damages.

WHO MAY ACT AS ESCROW AGENT

The Escrow Law (Division 6 of the California Financial Code) provides that escrow agents must be licensed by the Commissioner of Corporations. However, banks, savings and loan associations, title insurance companies, trust companies, attorneys and real estate brokers have exemptions from the licensing requirements of the Escrow Law.

The exemption for real estate brokers [Section 17006 (a)(4) of the Financial Code] applies to any broker licensed by the Real Estate Commissioner while performing acts in the course of or incidental to a real estate transaction in which the broker is a party or in which the broker is an agent performing an act for which a real estate license is required.

The Department of Corporations has interpreted Section 17006 (a)(4) to mean that:

1. the exemption is personal to the broker and the duties, other than ministerial functions, cannot be delegated by the broker;
2. in a purchase and sale transaction, if the broker is not a party, he must be the selling or listing broker;
3. the exemption is not available for any association with other brokers for the purpose of conducting escrows; and
4. when the broker's escrow business is a substantial factor in the utilization of the broker's services, the escrow business is not "incidental to a real estate transaction."

A broker cannot advertise that he or she conducts escrows without specifying in the advertisement that such services are only in connection with the broker's real estate brokerage business.

A broker may not use a fictitious name or a corporate name containing the word "escrow," or advertise in any other manner which would tend to be misleading to the public.

A real estate broker who conducts an escrow under the exemption must maintain all escrowed funds in a trust account and keep proper records. The broker must follow the provisions of Commissioner's Regulations 2950 and 2951.

Escrow Companies Must Be Incorporated

An individual cannot be licensed as an escrow agent. A corporation duly organized for the purpose of conducting an escrow business must hold the license. Applicants for escrow licenses must be financially solvent and furnish a surety bond in the amount of $25,000 or more, based upon yearly average trust fund obligations. All officers, directors, trustees, and employees having access to money or negotiable securities in the possession of the corporate licensee must furnish a bond of indemnification against loss. All money deposited in escrow must be placed in a trust account which is exempt from execution or attachment.

AUDIT

An escrow agent is required to keep accurate accounts and records which are subject to examination by the Commissioner of Corporations. The corporation must also, at its own expense, submit annually an independent audit prepared by a Certified Public Accountant or Public Accountant.

PROHIBITED CONDUCT

No escrow agent licensee may disseminate misleading statements or describe as an "escrow" any transaction which is not included under the definition of "escrow" in the Financial Code.

A licensed escrow agent may not pay fees to real estate brokers or others for referral of business. Such prohibited "fees" would include gifts of merchandise or other things of value.

An escrow agent cannot disburse a real estate broker's commission prior to closing of the escrow.

Escrow licensees may not solicit or accept escrow instructions, or amended or supplemental instructions, containing any blank to be filled in after signing or initialing. They may not permit any person to make any addition to, deletion from, or alteration of an escrow instruction unless it is signed or initialed by all persons who had signed or initialed the instructions. Escrow licensees are charged by law with delivering, at the time of execution, a copy of any escrow instruction, or amended or supplemental instruction, to all persons executing it. However, escrow instructions, being confidential, may not be disclosed to nonparties.

A real estate broker may not nominate an escrow holder as a condition precedent to a transaction, but may suggest an escrow holder if requested to do so by the parties.

RELATIONSHIP OF THE REAL ESTATE BROKER AND THE ESCROW HOLDER

A real estate broker should always consult the escrow officer before telling the principals that escrow will close on a certain date. An escrow includes a myriad of details, any of which could cause delay. Submission of accurate documents will expedite closing. Some suggestions:

1. As far as possible, make certain that the deposit receipt reflects the entire intentions of the principals.

2. When opening escrow, bring the recorded grant deed whereby the seller acquired the property or the seller's title policy. These documents establish the correct legal description and the manner in which seller holds title to the property.

3. Remember that all escrow instructions and amended instructions must be in writing. If the buyers are planning to be away, the broker should check with the escrow officer before they leave to determine if their absence will in any way hold up closing of escrow. If a small amount of money is due from the buyers, the broker cannot offer to put up the money or instruct the escrow officer to deduct the amount from the broker's commission. The escrow officer cannot do this. The buyer may be deliberately withholding the deposit of closing funds until seller performs some condition known only to the principals. To accept "buyer's closing funds" from any party other than buyer is to force an escrow to close against the understanding of the parties.

4. Furnish escrow with the correct spelling of buyer's name, address and telephone number. Buyer's and seller's business phone numbers should be included.

5. Be sure the escrow officer knows how buyer wants to take title. Brokers, salespersons or escrow officers should not assist with this decision, as it may involve legal and tax consequences.

6. Give escrow holder names and addresses of all lenders or loan servicing agents and the loan numbers. Many lenders, and FHA, require a 30-day advance payoff notice or seller may be subject to additional charges on any loan payoff.

7. Check with the seller regarding bonds or other liens on the property. Those not being assumed may be paid before opening the escrow.

8. If new financing has not been arranged before escrow is opened, notify the escrow officer immediately when the loan has been obtained.

9. Before escrow is opened, determine how fire insurance is to be handled. (The buyer may want to do business with buyer's insurance agent or a certain company. The seller's policy may include other property and the seller may not want it transferred or totally canceled.)

10. Be aware of the escrow holder's time requirement relating to non-cash deposit of funds. Checks must clear before the escrow holder can make disbursements.

DESIGNATING THE ESCROW HOLDER

Because selection of an escrow holder is not usually critical to either principal in a transaction, real estate brokers have in the past played a large role in deciding where a transaction would be escrowed. In recent years, however, there has been an increasing effort on the part of federal and state regulators to minimize the influence of the broker in selection of the escrow holder. The rationale is that buyers and sellers have the right, and should have the opportunity, to compare escrow services and charges and, if they so desire, negotiate between themselves as to where escrow will be held.

DEVELOPER CONTROLLED ESCROWS - PROHIBITION

Civil Code Section 2995 prohibits any real estate developer (defined as any person or entity having an ownership interest in real property which is improved by such person or entity with single-family dwellings which are offered for sale to the public) from requiring, as a condition precedent to the transfer of real property containing a single-family residential dwelling, that escrow services effecting such transfer be provided by an escrow entity in which the developer has a "financial interest." The phrase "financial interest" means ownership or control of 5 percent or more of the escrow entity. A developer who violates this statute is liable for damages of $250 or three times the charge for escrow services, whichever is greater, plus attorney's fees and costs. Any waiver of this prohibition is against public policy and therefore void.

9   Landlord and Tenant

The distinguishing feature of a leasehold interest is the right to exclusive possession and use of real property, for a fixed period of time, held by the lessee (or "tenant"). The lessor (or "landlord"), having parted with this right to exclusive possession, merely holds the basic title (the "reversion") during the existence of the lease. Hotel guests, licensees and employees may all be privileged to use a given space under certain contractual conditions, but since none of these has an exclusive right to possession, they are not governed by the laws regulating the relationship of landlord and tenant.

A leasehold estate itself is *chattel real.* Although the lessee has an estate/interest in real property, the estate is in fact a form of personal property, governed by laws applicable to personal property.

Types of Leasehold Estates
Most authorities classify leases into four categories, based on the lease term:

Estate for years;

Estate from period to period (periodic tenancy);

Estate at will; and

Estate at sufferance.

Estate for years. An *estate for years* is one which is to continue for a definite period fixed in advance by agreement between landlord and tenant. The name is somewhat misleading because the period may be for less than a year, measured in specific days, weeks, or months.

Estate from period to period. An *estate from period to period* (or periodic tenancy) is one which continues for periods of time (typically year-to-year, month-to-month, or week-to-week) as designated by landlord and tenant in their agreement. The most common periodic tenancy is the month-to-month tenancy.

Estate at will. An *estate at will* is one which is terminable at the will or unilateral decision of either party with no designated period of duration. Tenancies at will are uncommon because the landlord's acceptance of periodic rents causes the tenancy to be treated like a periodic tenancy (Civil Code Section 1946). By statute, California and certain other states have modified the potentially summary and abrupt conclusion of such estates to require advance 30-day notice of termination by either party.

Estate at sufferance. An *estate at sufferance* is one in which the tenant who has rightfully come into possession of the land retains possession after the expiration of the term. For example, a tenant who holds over after the expiration of a lease would be deemed to be holding an estate at sufferance.

Dual Legal Nature of Lease
A lease is an oral or written agreement that creates and governs, by express or implied terms, a landlord-tenant relationship. A lease has two characteristics, each of which has its own set of rights and obligations:

1. a conveyance by the landlord to the tenant of an estate in real property covering the premises leased (which creates "privity of estate" between the landlord and tenant); and

2. a contract between the landlord and tenant which governs both the landlord's delivery and maintenance of the premises and the tenant's possession of, use of, and payments for the premises (which creates "privity of contract" between the landlord and tenant).

Verbal and Written Agreements

A lease with a term of one year or less may be created by verbal agreement. However, for the sake of clarity and to reduce the risk of disagreement (both during the lease term *and* after tenant's surrender of the premises), all leases, even those with month-to-month terms, should be reduced to written form.

California's Statute of Frauds requires a lease to be in writing if it either:

1. has a term longer than one year; or

2. has a term less than one year which expires more than one year after the agreement is reached.

An example of a lease with a term of less than one year that must be in writing is a lease for a ten month term that begins three months from the date when an agreement is reached. Although one might automatically assume that the lease would not need to be in writing since it is for a term of less than one year, the contractual relationship (which will exist during the three month "pre-tenancy" period *and* the ten month term of lease) will actually be maintained for thirteen months.

Unwritten leases that are for a term of longer than one year or that expire more than one year after the agreement is reached are unenforceable. If a tenant enters into possession under an unenforceable lease, the tenant becomes a tenant at-will.

Lease Ingredients

No particular words, form, or language are required to create an oral or written lease. However, the words used must:

1. evidence the landlord's and tenant's intent to create a landlord-tenant relationship (which intent is apparent from either the parties' acts or deeds, or the language of a written agreement);

2. identify the parties;

3. describe the premises leased;

4. specify the time, amount, and manner of rental payments; and

5. establish a definite term.

Contract and Conveyance Issues

In light of its dual character of being a contract and a conveyance, an enforceable lease must satisfy specific laws with respect to:

1. the creation and interpretation of a contract; and

2. the prerequisites for the transfer of an interest in real property.

Contract specifics. The general rules regarding the creation of a lease (and contract), in addition to those governing whether or not there must be a writing, include:

1. mutual assent of landlord and tenant (i.e., an offer and an acceptance);

2. mutuality of obligation (i.e., neither party may have an unrestricted right to withdraw from the lease);

3. legal capacity of each party to contract (which, in general, excludes minors, persons of unsound mind, and persons deprived of their civil rights); and

4. lawful object (e.g., use does not violate health and safety regulations or criminal statutes). Although a lease may, indeed, have a lawful object, specific provisions within the lease may be deemed against public policy and therefor void. For example, residential leases that waive tenant procedural rights (such as the right to receive a notice of default) or rights regarding security deposits; or waive any future course of action against the landlord.

As a contract, a written lease is construed according to the intent of the parties, as gathered from the language of the lease and the performance of the parties under the lease, and in accordance with the rules of interpretation of contracts. Furthermore, like other written contracts, the executory (yet to be performed) provisions of a written lease may not be orally modified. Rather, such provisions must be modified in a writing signed by all parties to the original lease. To the extent that the parties mutually agree to modify the lease with respect to fully performed lease obligations, such modifications become *executed* modifications of the lease.

Leases are presumed to be for month-to-month tenancies unless otherwise set forth in writing or construed from the surrounding circumstances (also known as parol evidence), and except for rental of lodgings and dwelling houses (Civil Code Sections 1943 and 1944). In addition, although certain tenancy agreements clearly need not be in writing to be enforceable, when a lease is negotiated in Spanish and is for a residential unit, the lease must be written in Spanish.

Execution, delivery and acceptance. In general, a written lease must be executed, delivered, and accepted before it may be enforced according to its express terms. However, a lease signed and delivered by the landlord is enforceable by the tenant even if the tenant fails to sign the lease. On the other hand, if the tenant takes possession of the premises or pays the stipulated rent, having still failed to sign the lease, the tenant's acceptance of the landlord's delivery of the executed lease and premises is presumed and the landlord may then enforce the lease provisions against the tenant. The lease must be fully executed, however, before the landlord may enforce the lease's special contractual covenants (e.g., a covenant to repair) against the tenant.

Recording. A lease (or memorandum thereof summarizing key provisions) may be recorded in the official public records of the county in which the leased premises are situated. However, even an unrecorded lease is enforceable between the parties and against any party who, with notice of the tenant's interest, receives an interest in the property in which the premises are situated. If a lease term exceeds one year and the lease is not properly recorded, and if the tenant's possession under the lease does not give a bona fide purchaser notice of the tenant's on-going tenancy, that tenancy becomes subject (and subordinate) to the bona fide purchaser's interest in the leased premises.

Rights and Obligations of Parties to a Lease

A number of matters should be considered before entering into a lease agreement. Many of these are relatively unimportant in an oral month-to-month tenancy, but become increasingly important in the case of written leaseholds for a longer period of time. Since these subjects are each covered in considerable detail by contract provisions of the instrument, each written lease must be studied to determine the rights and obligations of the parties involved. Some of the more important aspects of a lease are:

1. term of lease;
2. rent;
3. security deposit;
4. possession, maintenance, and improvements;
5. liability of parties for injuries resulting from condition of premises;
6. transfer of interest in leased premises;
7. special covenants, conditions and provisions; and,
8. termination.

Term of lease. The lease term is that period of time during which the tenant may occupy the premises. Since the lease term is an essential element of a lease, if the lease fails to specify its term, a specific period of time will be implied as a matter of law, and the length of that period of time hinges on the nature of the lease and the circumstances surrounding it.

A lease term need not commence with full execution of the lease, and it ordinarily is based on a fixed or computable period. On some occasions, however, the length of a tenancy is either:

1. conditioned on the occurrence of an event which may trigger the commencement of the lease term, terminate the lease term, or both; or
2. based on the life of the landlord.

A common example is a term which commences upon the landlord's completion of certain improvements to the premises and/or delivery thereof to the tenant. If, however, a lease is to commence upon the occurrence of a future event, the lease becomes invalid if the term does not commence within 30 years of full execution of the lease.

Where the parties fail to specify the lease term, the term is determined in accordance with the following statutory presumptions, each of which applies to a certain type of rental property:

1. For lodgings, dwelling-houses, and residential properties, the period of time adopted for the payment of rent. For example, if rental payments are due on a monthly basis, the lease term is equal to one month. If the lease fails to address the period adopted for rental payments, the tenancy is presumed to be for one month.

2. For agricultural or grazing properties, one year.

3. For all other properties where there is no custom or usage on the subject, the tenancy is for one month unless otherwise designated in writing.

Even if the landlord and tenant do specify a lease term or the term is implied by statute, the following statutory restrictions will supersede and limit the lease term:

1. A lease for agricultural or horticultural purposes cannot have a term exceeding 51 years.

2. A lease for any town or city lot cannot have a term exceeding 99 years.

3. A lease of land for the production of minerals, oil, gas, or other hydrocarbon substances cannot have a term exceeding 99 years.

4. A lease of property owned by an emancipated minor or an incompetent person cannot have a term longer than a probate court may authorize.

A *lease renewal* creates a new and distinct tenancy. Accordingly, the parties should execute an entirely new instrument.

A *lease extension* is a continuation in possession under the original lease. A lease extension may also occur if the tenant holds over with permission from the landlord. Indeed, if a tenant remains in possession of the premises after expiration of the lease term and the landlord accepts rental payments, the parties are presumed to have renewed the lease on the same terms and conditions on a month-to-month basis if rent is payable monthly, and in no event longer than one year.

A contractual right to extend or renew a lease is an irrevocable offer by the landlord to lease the premises in the future on specific terms. Such a right to extend or renew a lease is within the Statute of Frauds and, therefore, if the original lease is covered by the Statute of Frauds or if the lease, as extended, would be covered by the Statute of Frauds, the renewal or extension must be in writing to be enforceable.

To be enforceable, lease provisions for the extension or renewal of a lease must be reasonably specific and contain all of the material terms. A provision on terms "to be mutually agreed upon" is generally unenforceable. An unexercised option to extend the term for a specified period does not create a property right until it is exercised unequivocally and in strict accordance with its terms. Whether specified in the lease or not, an option hinges on the continued viability of the lease and must be exercised prior to expiration or earlier termination of the lease.

A lease that is limited to the hiring of residential real property and provides for an automatic renewal or extension of the lease if the tenant either remains in possession after lease expiration or fails to give notice of intent not to renew, is voidable by the party who did not prepare the lease. Provided, however, that such a lease is valid if, in a printed lease, the automatic renewal clause is printed in 8-point boldface type and a recital of inclusion of the automatic renewal clause appears in 8-point boldface type immediately above the signature line.

Rent. Rent is the consideration paid for possession, use, and enjoyment of leased property. A tenant's obligation to pay rent arises from either the express terms of a lease (privity of contract) or a tenant's mere occupancy of the premises where no gift is intended (privity of estate).

Through privity of contract, a tenant is bound by a covenant to pay rent even if the tenant never enters into possession of the premises. Through privity of estate, even if a lease does not specify the terms for payment of rent, an obligation to pay rent arises out of a tenant's occupancy of the premises (again, assuming no gift is intended).

Since, by statute, the term "rent" includes "charges equivalent to rent," rental payments need not be paid in currency (unless otherwise specified in the lease), but may be made in the form of goods, crops, and any other product or other consideration agreed upon by the parties.

Unless there is either a course of dealing between the parties or a lease provision to the contrary, rental payments are due at the end of each successive holding period or term (e.g., at the end of the day, week, month, quarter, or year). In addition, in the absence of any lease provision to the contrary, rental payments must be delivered to the demised premises. Most commercial and residential leases, however, specifically provide for payment of rent in advance of the period covered by such payment and provide for payment of rent to a specific address.

Rent paid by check constitutes payment of rent conditioned on the landlord presenting the check to the drawee bank, and the tenant's obligation to pay rent is merely suspended until the check is presented to the drawee bank. If, however, the tenant knows that there are insufficient funds to honor the check at the time of delivery to the landlord, the tenant's obligation to pay rent is not suspended and the landlord may, immediately after the rent is due, sue for the payment of rent or commence eviction proceedings. In addition, although the landlord is liable for any loss caused by its delay in presenting a rental check to the drawee bank, the landlord's acceptance of a rental payment by check does not prejudice its right to sue for collection of rent or to evict the tenant for failure to pay rent.

A *late charge* is enforceable by the landlord if the amount specified in the lease is reasonably related to the landlord's anticipated administrative costs and loss of interest caused by the late payment. However, since forfeiture of a lease is a drastic remedy, when a lease does provide for a late charge the landlord may not have the right to terminate the lease solely because of a late rental payment.

In general, rent that is paid in advance is due on a specific date and is not apportionable. However, if, after prepayment of rent, the lease is terminated due to the fault of the landlord (thereby causing a "constructive eviction"), or if the lease provides for apportionment of rent, the rule against apportionment is inapplicable. If rent is not prepaid and the lease is terminated prior to the expiration of the term, the tenant is liable for that portion of the rent due for the time during which the tenant had the right to occupy the premises.

Unless otherwise specified in the lease or unless terminated prior to the expiration of the lease term (for example, due to complete destruction or condemnation of the premises, or the tenant's death), a tenant must pay rent throughout the term of the lease and thereafter until the tenant returns possession of the premises to the landlord. If the tenant tenders possession of premises to the landlord upon the expiration of the lease, the tenant's rental obligation terminates at that time.

A tenant's obligation to pay rent is generally deemed an "independent" lease obligation: i.e., independent of the landlord's lease obligations to the tenant. Therefore, even if the landlord fails to honor its lease obligations (e.g., fails to perform its maintenance obligations), the tenant must continue to pay rent according to the provisions of the lease.

In contrast, if the landlord breaches a material covenant of the lease, the tenant's obligation to pay rent may be abated or terminated. For example, in a residential lease, if the landlord fails to honor the implied warranty of habitability (which is deemed so material that it cannot be waived by the tenant), the tenant is deemed constructively evicted and may remain in possession and abate rental payments in proportion to the impairment of use and enjoyment of the premises. In addition, if a residential or commercial tenant is actually or constructively evicted from the premises as a result of events not caused by the tenant, such as partial condemnation or lack of access to the premises (and assuming that the risk of such occurrence is not allocated to the tenant in the lease), the tenant's rental obligations terminate if (and only if) the tenant vacates the premises.

Generally, if the leased premises are taken by government power or eminent domain, the lease will be terminated as of the date of taking (unless the lease specifically provides otherwise), and the tenant's obligation to pay rent shall cease. However, if only a portion of the leased premises is taken and the remaining portion is still usable for the purpose for which it was leased, the tenant must continue to pay rent according to the terms of the lease agreement. Thus, it may be advisable for the parties to provide in the lease for a proportional abatement of rent if the leased premises are partially taken; and to specify what portion of the premises (e.g., 50%), if taken, will constitute a complete taking and terminate the tenant's obligation to pay rent.

Security deposit. A security deposit secures a tenant's performance of lease obligations. It constitutes assurance to the landlord that, in the very least and to the extent of the security deposit, the tenant's monetary obligations will be satisfied.

Although a security deposit is generally cash deposited with the landlord, other forms are often used in commercial transactions: letters of credit and certificates of deposit. In addition, a security deposit may generally be categorized pursuant to the terms of the lease as:

1. prepaid rent (generally for rent payable at the end of the term);
2. a forfeitable security deposit (forfeited in its entirety upon a tenant default specified in the lease);
3. a non-forfeitable security deposit (refunded at the end of the term, less debits attributable to specified tenant defaults); or
4. a bonus for lease execution (non-refundable).

In any event, a security deposit is held by the landlord for the benefit of the depositing tenant, and a tenant's claim to the security deposit has priority over claims of all the landlord's creditors except a trustee in bankruptcy.

In a residential lease, notwithstanding the specific terminology (e.g., "advance payment," "fee," or "charge") or the purpose designated (e.g., a "cleaning" or "security" deposit) used to describe a tenant's monetary deposit to secure performance under the lease, the money deposited is a refundable security deposit. Any purported waiver by a tenant of the right to a refund of the security deposit (less allowable debits attributable to the tenant's defaults as specified in the lease) is null and void.

A landlord may require that the tenant pay, regardless of the purpose therefor and in addition to the first month's rent, a maximum of:

- two months' rent in the case of an unfurnished residential property;
- three months' rent in the case of a furnished residential property.

If, however, the term of the lease is six months or longer, the landlord may collect an advance payment of up to six months' rent.

Within three weeks after a tenant vacates and surrenders the premises, the residential landlord must:

1. give the tenant (by personal service or first-class mail, postage pre-paid) an itemized written statement setting forth the amount of the original security deposit and the basis for and amount of any deduction therefrom; and

2. refund the balance of the security deposit.

If the landlord sells the residential property or transfers its interest in the premises, the landlord may transfer the security deposit (less any lawful deductions) to the new landlord. In the event of any such transfer, the landlord must (by personal delivery or first-class mail, postage prepaid) give the tenant written notice specifying the amount of the transfer, itemizing the deductions, and identifying the successor landlord by name, address, and telephone number. Alternatively, the landlord may return the security deposit to the tenant, less any lawful deductions, with a statement itemizing the deductions therefrom. The successor residential landlord has the same rights and obligations with respect to a security deposit as the original landlord.

The existence of a security deposit creates a debtor/creditor relationship between the landlord and tenant. Consequently, the landlord has a personal obligation to return the security deposit (less any lawful deductions). If the original landlord fails to satisfy either statutory alternative set forth immediately above, both the original landlord and the successor landlord remain personally liable to the tenant for the amount of the deposit (less any lawful deductions).

If the landlord retains any portion of the deposit in bad faith, the landlord is liable for actual damages, a statutory penalty not exceeding $600, and interest thereon at the rate of 2 percent per month from the due date until paid. In addition, the landlord may be liable for punitive damages.

The law governing commercial property security deposits is less onerous to landlords in each of the following material respects (and is otherwise similar to that governing residential property security deposits):

1. There is no maximum on the amount of the security deposit.

2. When rent is the only deduction from the security deposit, the remaining balance, if any, must be returned within two weeks of the tenant vacating and surrendering the premises. However, if the landlord makes bona fide deductions (e.g., for cleaning or damage), the landlord has up to 30 days

(unless otherwise agreed to by the parties) to refund the balance and no written itemization is required.

3. Following the landlord's transfer of the property, the successor landlord will not be liable for return of any security deposit (or prepaid rent) paid to the prior landlord unless those funds are actually transferred to the successor landlord. Absent such transfer, the tenant must recover from the prior landlord.

4. If the landlord fails to return the security deposit in a timely manner, the statutory penalty is $200.

Possession, maintenance and improvements. In a *commercial lease*, the landlord's right of entry to perform maintenance obligations should be set forth in the lease. If not, a landlord would likely be permitted access to the premises to perform obligations under the lease, following reasonable advance notice.

In contrast, a landlord may enter premises rented to a residential tenant only in specific situations, at certain times, and after giving (or attempting to give) advance notice.

Specifically, a landlord may enter a dwelling unit only:

1. in case of emergency;

2. to make necessary or agreed repairs, decorations, alterations, or improvements;

3. to supply necessary or agreed services;

4. to show the dwelling to prospective or actual purchasers, mortgagees, tenants, workmen, or contractors;

5. where the tenant has abandoned or surrendered the premises; or

6. pursuant to court order.

A landlord may not abuse the right of access or use it to harass the tenant. Any purported waiver or modification by tenant of the statutory protection in this regard is null and void.

Except for cases of emergency, unless the tenant has abandoned or surrendered the premises or the tenant consents at the time of entry, a landlord may only enter the dwelling unit during normal business hours. Unless it is impracticable to do so, the landlord must give the tenant reasonable notice of intent to enter the premises. Twenty four hours advance notice is presumed to be reasonable absent evidence to the contrary.

While a landlord's limited right of entry is defined by statute, a tenant's remedy against a landlord who fails to honor the statutory requirement is not specified in the statute. A tenant may, however, pursue either: the common law remedy for breach of the implied warranty of quiet enjoyment, including invasion of privacy and intentional infliction of emotional distress; or the statutory remedy of relief from harassment under California Code of Civil Procedure Section 527.6.

Similarly, a landlord's remedy against a tenant for failure to permit access (after providing the requisite notice) is not defined by statute. Denied access, the landlord may have to seek entry under court order.

The essence of a tenant's leasehold interest is possession, or the right to possess, the leased premises. In every lease, the law implies a covenant on the part of the landlord to provide the tenant with possession and "quiet enjoyment" of the premises. This "covenant of quiet enjoyment" constitutes a warranty by the landlord that the landlord will not take any action or make any omission which disturbs a tenant's right to possession and quiet enjoyment of the premises. The covenant does not protect the tenant from the acts of third parties over whom the landlord has no control.

A landlord can breach the covenant of quiet enjoyment in various ways, some of which are:

1. causing a tenant to be "evicted," i.e., physically removed from the leased premises under circumstances where the tenant otherwise has the legal and contractual right to possession.

2. denying a tenant access to the premises.

3. causing or permitting a third party who has paramount title to physically oust the tenant. For example, if a lender forecloses upon the landlord's property pursuant to a mortgage which is senior to the tenant's lease (and there is no "non-disturbance" agreement between the tenant and the lender), the lease is extinguished and the foreclosing lender has the right to evict the tenant. This would constitute a breach of the covenant by the landlord, even though it is the lender rather than the landlord actually evicting the tenant.

4. any disturbance, caused either directly by the landlord or by a person or circumstance within the landlord's legal control, of the tenant's use or possession of the leased premises whereby the property is rendered wholly or substantially unsuitable for the use for which it was leased. For example: a landlord's attempt to lease the property to a third party; harassing the tenant or making unwarranted threats of expulsion; making extensive and unwarranted alterations to the leased property which materially and adversely interfere with the tenant's use and enjoyment thereof; or failing to make necessary repairs to the premises. Of course, a tenant cannot establish a constructive eviction if the tenant, by wrongful or negligent action, causes the defects in the premises.

It must be emphasized that a tenant must have a legal right to possession of the premises in order to make a claim of breach of the covenant of quiet enjoyment. Thus, if a landlord evicts a tenant through proper legal procedures following a default by the tenant under the lease, the tenant no longer has a legal right to occupy the premises and eviction would not constitute a violation of the covenant of quiet enjoyment.

For many years, the courts held that a tenant relying on the doctrine of constructive eviction must surrender possession of the premises in order to escape the obligation to pay rent. This rule still applies to leases of commercial buildings. However, the California Supreme Court has held that there is no obligation to vacate the premises in order to avoid the obligation to pay rent where the leased premises is a dwelling. Instead, the California Supreme Court held that there exists an implied warranty of habitability from the landlord to the tenant that the premises will be maintained in a condition to meet *bare living requirements*, and that if the landlord breaches this implied warranty the tenant will remain liable for the reasonable rental value of the premises in the condition existing at the time of the violation as long as the tenant continues to occupy the premises. A condition which renders a dwelling partially or entirely uninhabitable, however, does not *automatically* give the tenant the right to reduce or cease paying rent. Before the tenant may be entirely or partially absolved from the obligation to pay rent, or may vacate the premises, the tenant must have given notice to the landlord of the defects which allegedly render the premises uninhabitable or unusable and the landlord must have failed to cancel or cure such defects within a reasonable time following receipt of tenant's notice. If a tenant vacates the leased premises or pays a reduced rent based upon even a good faith belief that the condition of the premises supports a claim of constructive eviction, such tenant does so at the risk that a court may deny the allegation that the premises are totally or partially uninhabitable. In such circumstances, a court may rule that the tenant violated the lease by failing to pay the full amount of rent owed under the lease, entitling the landlord to the same remedies as if a tenant simply defaulted in the obligation to pay rent, including ordering that the tenant be evicted from the premises and awarding the landlord damages against the tenant for the reasonable rental value of the premises for the remainder of the lease term.

A landlord of a residential dwelling has a legal duty to keep the dwelling in a habitable condition. Civil Code Section 1941.1 sets forth the following criteria:

1. Effective waterproofing and weather protection of roof and exterior walls, including unbroken windows and doors;

2. Plumbing or gas facilities which conformed to applicable law in effect at the time of installation, maintained in good working order;

3. A water supply approved under applicable law, which is under the control of the tenant, capable of producing hot and cold running water, or a system which is under the control of the landlord which produces hot and cold running water, furnished to appropriate fixtures and connected to a sewage disposal system approved under applicable law;

4. Heating facilities which conformed with applicable law at the time of installation, maintained in good working order;

5. Electrical lighting, with wiring and electrical equipment which conformed with applicable law at the time of installation, maintained in good working order;

6. Building, grounds, and appurtenances at the time of commencement of the lease or rental agreement in every part clean, sanitary, and free from all accumulations of debris, filth, rubbish, garbage, rodents, and vermin, and all areas under control of the landlord kept in every part clean, sanitary, and free from all accumulations of debris, filth, rubbish, garbage, rodents, and vermin;

7. An adequate number of appropriate receptacles for garbage and rubbish, in clean condition and good repair at the time of the commencement of the lease or rental agreement, with the landlord providing appropriate, serviceable receptacles thereafter, and being responsible for the clean condition and good repair of such receptacles under his control; and

8. Floors, stairways, and railings maintained in good repair.

There are other statutory provisions which affect the landlord's maintenance obligations. For example, the California Health and Safety Code requires that every dwelling intended for human occupancy have an operable smoke detector. The landlord is responsible for installing and maintaining the smoke detector, but if a smoke detector is operable when the tenant takes possession, the tenant has a duty to inform the landlord if it becomes inoperable.

It is not always clear that a landlord's failure to maintain constitutes a breach of the implied warranty of habitability. A court will decide this on a case-by-case basis. Generally, if a unit falls into disrepair but still meets basic living requirements, the court will find that the landlord has not breached the warranty. Serious housing code violations, lack of adequate heat, serious rodent infestation, or extremely unsafe utilities or appliances are examples of factors upon which courts will base a finding that the implied warranty of habitability has been breached.

In cases where a landlord breaches the implied warranty of habitability, a tenant is not obligated to give the landlord notice and an opportunity to correct the conditions causing the breach of this warranty prior to exercising the tenant's remedies. Moreover, when this warranty is breached, a tenant is temporarily relieved of its obligation to pay rent until the deficient conditions are corrected. However, a court will ultimately determine the rental value of the premises in the substandard condition and the tenant will be obligated to pay that rent. Accordingly, a court will often require the tenant to deposit with the court the rent the tenant otherwise would have paid the landlord until the dilapidated condition is repaired and the court has determined the extent of the tenant's rental obligation for the period in which the property was in substandard condition. Alternatively, the tenant can exercise the same remedy available for breach of the covenant of quiet enjoyment, vacate the property, and be relieved of the obligation to pay rent for the remainder of the lease term. In either case, the tenant can seek to recover monetary damages from the landlord for breach of the implied warranty of habitability. However, as with the covenant of quiet enjoyment, a tenant who exercises his remedies for breach of this warranty does so at the risk that the court will not agree that the warranty has been breached.

Civil Code Section 1941.2 provides that if a tenant fails in certain affirmative obligations and the failure "contributes substantially" to a condition which renders the property uninhabitable or interferes substantially with the landlord's repair obligations, the landlord has no duty to repair the condition. The tenant's obligations under Section 1941.2 are as follows:

1. Keep his/her part of the property as clean and sanitary as the condition of the property permits (unless the landlord has expressly agreed in writing to do so);

2. Dispose of rubbish, garbage, and other waste from the dwelling in a clean and sanitary manner (unless the landlord has expressly agreed in writing to do so);

3. Properly use the plumbing, electrical and gas fixtures and keep them as clean and sanitary as their condition permits;

4. Not permit any person on the property with the tenant's permission to willfully or wantonly destroy, deface, damage, impair, or remove any part of the structure or dwelling unit or the facilities, equipment, or appurtenances thereto; nor may the tenant do any such thing; and

5. Occupy the property as an abode, using for living, sleeping, cooking, or dining purposes only those portions which were designed or intended to be so used.

In addition to the implied covenant of habitability and the landlord's maintenance obligations expressed in a lease agreement, the California State Housing Law and various local housing codes require the landlord to keep a dwelling in good condition in accordance with specified structural, plumbing, electrical sanitation, fire and safety standards. Local government departments are generally empowered to investigate complaints and require the landlord to make needed repairs and/or to impose a fine upon the landlord.

If the landlord fails to maintain a residential property in a condition fit for human occupancy, the tenant may give the landlord notice to repair the premises. If, after receipt of tenant's notice, the landlord fails within a reasonable time to make the repairs necessary, the tenant has the statutory right to either:

1. spend up to one month's rent in repairs (only twice in any twelve-month period); or

2. abandon the premises, in which case the tenant is relieved from the requirement of paying additional rent and the performance of other conditions of the lease. (See Cal. Civil Code § 1942.)

Generally, *in non-residential leases*, the landlord is *not* under any *implied* obligation to make repairs or to maintain the leased premises in a tenantable condition. The respective obligations of landlord and tenant with respect to maintenance and repair are typically addressed in their lease agreement. For example, it is common in a lease for a commercial building for the landlord to be obligated to maintain and repair the "structural elements" of the building (i.e., the foundation, exterior walls, roof supports and roof), and for the tenant to agree to maintain the remainder of the building, including interior, plumbing, electrical, heating, ventilation, and air conditioning systems. In the absence of a specific covenant obligating the landlord to maintain or repair the premises, the tenant is deemed to have taken the premises in "as is" condition and to have assumed the obligation to maintain the premises in a safe condition.

Closely related to the landlord's and tenant's maintenance obligations under a lease is the obligation to cause the premises to comply with laws existing as of the time the lease is entered into or enacted at any time during the term of the lease.

In the non-residential context, the lease agreement should specify which party shall bear the responsibility of complying with governmental laws and regulations affecting the leased premises, whether enacted before or after the lease date. If the law does not explicitly place upon the landlord the obligation to comply with its provisions, courts will look to the language of the lease agreement to determine where this responsibility lies. However, the lease agreement will not necessarily be dispositive on the issue of who will ultimately have to bear the time, expense, and effort necessary to bring the premises into compliance with applicable law. Using the terms of the lease as a starting point, pursuant to the California Supreme Court case of *Brown v. Green* (8 Cal. 4th 812, 35 Cal. Rptr. 2d 598 1994), courts will endeavor to analyze the relevant provisions of the lease in light of certain circumstantial factors in order to determine the "probable intent" of the parties in entering into the lease. Among these factors are the length of the lease term, the cost of compliance in relation to the rent, the nature of the repair (i.e., structural v. non-structural), the extent to which the tenant's enjoyment of the premises will be interfered with during the period in which the necessary alterations are made, and the likelihood that the parties, in entering into the lease, contemplated that the particular law or regulation would become effective.

Governmental mandates affecting leased premises can be enacted at any time during the lease term and compliance can be extremely expensive. Examples of governmental compliance issues which have been of great significance to landlords and tenants include: the requirement that asbestos or other toxic substances be removed from the leased premises; the requirement that the leased premises be reinforced for seismic safety; and the requirement that alterations be made to the leased premises to comply with the Americans With Disabilities Act. In light of the ambiguity in the standards set forth in *Brown v. Green*, it is important that both parties consider the potential impact of unforeseen governmental mandates and address the issue accordingly in drafting the lease.

The terms of the lease should address to what extent, if any, the landlord and the tenant have the right and/or obligation to make alterations or improvements to the leased premises. A lease should also specify whether or not the tenant has the right and/or the obligation to remove certain improvements upon the expiration or termination of the lease. Upon installation of fixtures or improvements in the premises, the issue arises as to the ownership thereof. Unless the landlord and tenant agree otherwise, many improvements and fixtures installed in a leased premises will as a matter of law be deemed "permanent" and will become part of the premises (and thus the landlord's property) upon the expiration of the term. Thus, if a lease is not clear as to the nature of certain improvements which a tenant desires to make to the premises, the tenant should first attempt to establish an understanding with the landlord, perhaps entering into a separate agreement concerning such improvements. Otherwise, the tenant may not have the right to remove its fixtures or improvements upon the expiration of the lease term; or, the tenant may be obligated to remove certain fixtures or improvements which the tenant wanted to leave in the premises. The general rule that improvements will become part of the premises has been modified by statute in California in cases where a tenant has installed fixtures for the purposes of trade, manufacture, ornamental or domestic use. Such fixtures may be removed by the tenant during or upon expiration of the term of the lease unless they have become an integral part of the premises through the manner in which they are affixed and if removal cannot be accomplished without injury to the leased property.

The law in its current state leaves much room for honest differences of opinion between the landlord and tenant as to the characterization of fixtures and other improvements installed in the leased premises. It is therefore preferable for the landlord and tenant to provide in advance by agreement for the disposition of fixtures.

Liability of parties for injuries resulting from condition of premises. Depending on the circumstances, both residential and non-residential landlords may be held liable for injuries to tenants resulting from the condition of the premises. A residential landlord can be held liable on simple negligence grounds for injuries resulting from potentially hazardous conditions or defects in the premises existing at the time of renting the premises to the tenant if such conditions or defects could have been discovered by a reasonable inspection of the premises. Thus, if such an inspection would have revealed a potentially dangerous condition (e.g., a slippery bathtub or staircase), the landlord may be held liable for failing to take corrective measures to mitigate the condition. Merely warning a tenant will probably not be sufficient to protect the landlord from liability.

In addition, if a dangerous condition or defect does not exist at the commencement of the rental term but arises later, a residential landlord has a duty to repair such condition or defect after receiving notice from the tenant thereof. Failure to make such repair could subject the landlord to liability for injuries arising from such defect or condition.

The law pertaining to a residential landlord's liability for a "latent" defect in the premises (i.e., a defect which is not discoverable by a reasonable, diligent inspection of the premises) existing at commencement of the rental term, has changed significantly. Previously, in the case of *Becker v. IRM Corp.* (38 Cal. 3d 454, 213 Cal. Rptr. 213 1985), the California Supreme Court held that a residential landlord was "strictly liable" for injuries to tenant resulting from a "defective" shower door which shattered, in spite of the fact that the "latent defect" in the premises (i.e., the fact that the shower door was made of regular glass, as opposed to tempered glass), would not have been discoverable by a reasonable inspection of the premises. Under such a ruling, a thorough, diligent inspection of the premises would not insulate a residential landlord from liability for injuries to a tenant resulting from the defective condition. However, in *Peterson v. Superior Court* (10 Cal. 4th 1185, 43 Cal. Rptr. 2d 836 1995), the California Supreme Court reversed its earlier holding in *Becker* and returned to the rule that a landlord will only be liable for injuries resulting from defects in residential premises existing as of the commencement of the rental term if the landlord is negligent in failing to discover and correct the defect in the premises. Thus, while a landlord may still be liable if a court finds that a defect should have been discovered and corrected by the landlord, the ruling in *Peterson* should provide residential landlords with some relief from liability for defects which are not readily discoverable.

In leases of non-residential premises, a landlord generally will not be liable for injuries sustained by tenants resulting from defects in the leased premises. However, the landlord will be liable for injuries resulting from the landlord's failure to correct such defects if the lease:

1. places the obligation on the landlord to maintain all or a portion of the premises (e.g., making the landlord responsible for maintenance of the roof and structure);

2. contains an affirmative covenant requiring the landlord to correct or repair a defective item; or

3. gives the landlord control over a defective item or the area containing the defective item (e.g., defective or dangerous sidewalk in common areas of shopping center or office building which landlord controls).

Additionally, the landlord may be held liable for resulting injuries if the landlord:

1. is under a statutory duty to repair the defective condition;

2. knows of or has reason to know of a "latent" defective condition and fails to disclose it to the tenant or to adequately repair it; or

3. agrees to make a repair but does so negligently or fails to even make the repair.

Transfer of interest in leased premises by landlord. Unless prohibited by the terms of the lease, a landlord may transfer its interest in leased property to a third party. Following such transfer, the lease will remain in force and effect and the new landlord and the tenant will generally have the same rights and obligations with respect to each other as did the prior landlord and tenant. However, an exception to this principal is set forth in California Civil Code §823, which provides that successor landlord will not be liable for violations caused by the prior landlord of covenants against encumbrances or relating to title or possession of the premises.

Transfer of interest in leased premises by tenant. Unless a lease expressly prohibits the tenant from transferring its interest in the premises, the tenant may "assign" (i.e., transfer its entire remaining interest in the premises for the remainder of the lease term) or "sublease" (i.e., transfer its right to a portion of the premises, or its right to the entire premises for less than the entire remaining lease term) its interest in the premises to any third party. Leases usually will either prohibit the tenant from subleasing or assigning its interest in the lease or, more often, prohibit it without the landlord's consent. Since the law favors the transferability of a tenant's leasehold rights, prohibitions against subleasing or assigning are construed strictly against the landlord. Nevertheless, courts generally have held that a prohibition in a lease against assigning or subleasing without the landlord's consent will be valid if such consent is exercised in a reasonable manner.

Regardless of whether a transfer is *called* an "assignment" or a "sublease," the *nature of the transfer* will determine whether it will be legally treated as an assignment or a sublease. An assignment of a tenant's interest in a lease does not relieve the tenant from its liability under the lease, unless the landlord expressly agrees to do so. The original tenant will remain liable under the lease throughout the remainder of the lease term. Likewise, the successor tenant (the "assignee"), and each succeeding assignee will remain liable to the landlord throughout the term. However, the extent of this remaining liability of an assignee depends on whether the assignee expressly assumed the obligations of the assignor. If there is an express assumption, an assignee will be fully liable under the lease. If, instead, there is an assignment without an express assumption by the assignee, the assignee will be liable for certain obligations which derive from its "privity of estate" or its occupancy of the premises, such as the payment of rent and the duty to maintain, but will not be liable for purely contractual obligations under the lease, such as the obligation to pay the landlord's attorney's fees in the event of litigation between the parties.

Likewise, in a sublease the original tenant remains liable to the landlord for all obligations under the lease and for all acts or omissions committed by the subtenant. However, because there is neither "privity of contract" nor "privity of estate" between a subtenant and a landlord, a subtenant generally has no direct obligation to the landlord. The subtenant's rights are derived entirely through the tenant. Thus, although a landlord has no right to enforce the provisions of the lease directly against a subtenant, the landlord *can* enforce them against the tenant, and if the landlord terminates the tenant's lease for default, whether it was the tenant or the subtenant who performed the act or omission leading to the default, the subtenant's rights in the premises will be simultaneously extinguished. Nevertheless, in some cases a landlord's consent to a sublease, or a subtenant's assumption of the obligations of the tenant contained in the lease, creates a sufficient "direct" relationship to enable the parties to enforce the terms of the lease against one another.

Termination. A lease automatically *expires* by its own terms at the end of the term specified in the lease. If neither party commits a breach or other act justifying a termination of the lease, the tenancy will continue until the term expires. If the tenancy is for a specified term (i.e., estate for years), the tenancy ends at the expiration of the term without notice or any other act or deed by either party.

In addition, since a lease is a contract, it may be *rescinded* by a party if that party enters into the lease in reliance upon the other party's fraud or by either party if the parties enter into the lease in reliance upon a mutual mistake.

A lease is *terminated* only when a landlord or tenant exercises a specific right set forth in the lease or prescribed by statute, or when a lease-terminating event occurs that is not within the control of either the landlord or the tenant.

In general, a lease may be terminated for any of the following reasons:

1. notice;
2. destruction of the premises;
3. commercial frustration of purpose;
4. merger of estates;
5. death of a party;
6. insolvency or bankruptcy of the tenant;
7. insolvency or bankruptcy of the landlord;
8. exercise of option to terminate;
9. tenant's or landlord's breach of a condition or covenant;
10. illegal use of the premises; or
11. abandonment and surrender of the premises.

[Notwithstanding any lease provision to the contrary, a lease may *not* be terminated for any reason which contravenes public policy, including, without limitation: retaliatory eviction (e.g., retaliation by the landlord for tenant's reporting to governmental authorities the landlord's health or safety code violations); discrimination against children or physically disabled persons; or discrimination based on race, creed, color, national heritage, or sex.]

Termination by notice. Although a tenant at sufferance is not entitled to notice and a tenant under a lease with a specified term is not required to give or entitled to receive notice, either party to a tenancy at will or a periodic tenancy may terminate a lease by giving notice thereof to the other in accordance with the terms and provisions of the lease.

A tenancy at will may be terminated by not less than 30 days' written notice, regardless of whether the tenancy is created orally (and is an unenforceable lease), under no agreement, or otherwise.

Periodic tenancies, on the other hand, may be terminated by either party by written notice equal to the term of the tenancy or 30 days, whichever is less. For example, if a tenant pays rent weekly, one week's advance notice is sufficient, and if a tenant pays rent only bi-annually, 30 days' written notice is sufficient. Notwithstanding the foregoing, a lease for an unspecified term may provide for termination upon as little as 7-days' advance written notice. In a month-to-month tenancy, the tenant's notice of termination need not correspond to the due date for rent. For example, if rent is payable in advance monthly and due on the first of the month, the tenant can give written notice on the tenth of a month and move out on the tenth of the following month. The tenant will be liable, of course, for rent for the first 10 days of the following month.

It should be noted that the foregoing termination rights may be modified by specific statutory limitations on a landlord's ability to terminate tenancies without cause pursuant to local rent control ordinances, laws pertaining to publicly-owned and federally assisted housing projects, and mobilehome tenancies.

Destruction of the premises. If neither party assumes the duty to repair or rebuild, either party may terminate the lease upon complete destruction of the premises (so long as the party seeking to terminate the lease is not a cause of the destruction). If the premises are only partially destroyed (due to no fault of the tenant), the tenant may terminate the lease upon delivery of written notice to the landlord if a substantial portion of the premises is damaged or if a material portion of the premises necessary for tenant's use is damaged. Unless the lease provides otherwise, however, a tenant may not terminate the lease if the damage or destruction occurs to a part of the property not actually leased by the tenant; e.g., a ground lessee may not terminate a lease if a building situated on the leased land is damaged or destroyed.

If damage or destruction occurs and the lease continues in effect (either because neither party has the right to terminate the lease or neither party elects to do so), the tenant may not apportion rent if the lease does not permit apportionment and rent is required be paid in advance, even if the premises are uninhabitable. Of course, if the tenant is entitled to exercise a right to terminate, a shrewd tenant desirous of staying in the premises would probably threaten to exercise its right to terminate if the landlord would not permit a retroactive apportionment of rent.

If a commercial landlord assumes an unconditional obligation to repair or rebuild the leased premises in the event of damage or destruction (as contrasted with an obligation merely to repair and maintain the premises), the tenant cannot terminate the lease. A landlord's general covenant to repair and maintain the premises, however, does not preclude the tenant from exercising a right to terminate when the premises are totally destroyed. In addition, if a commercial lease gives the tenant a right to terminate the lease within a certain period of time after the damage or destruction occurs, the tenant may terminate the lease within that time-frame, even if the landlord has commenced the repair or rebuilding.

Frustration of commercial purpose. Although a tenant may lease property for a specific purpose, the tenant may not terminate the lease because that purpose is frustrated. However, if the lease specifies and limits the tenant's use of the premises, the tenant may be excused from performance and terminate the lease if the tenant may no longer use the premises for the purpose specified in the lease.

A tenant's right to terminate for frustration of purpose, however, is only available in cases of extreme hardship. Indeed, the tenant's purpose must be completely frustrated. A "significant" or "material" frustration (e.g., the tenant's purpose becomes more difficult or less profitable) is not sufficient to justify termination. In addition, the tenant must not have assumed the risk of the occurrence of the intervening event (regardless of how unimaginable the event was at the time of entering into the lease), the intervening event must have been unforeseeable at the time of entering into the lease, and the intervening event must be uncontrollable by the tenant at the time of its occurrence.

Merger of estates. When a landlord acquires the leasehold estate (e.g., by tenant's assignment of the lease and surrender of the premises to landlord), or the tenant acquires title to the premises superior to that of the landlord (and there is no intervening estate), the landlord's fee simple ownership interest in the property and the tenant's leasehold interest are deemed to "merge" as a matter of law. In such a case, the lease is terminated and the tenant is relieved of its obligation to pay rent.

Death of a party. A lease terminable at the will of the landlord and tenant is terminated upon the death (or incapacity) of either party upon delivery of written notice to the other of such death (or incapacity). Although written notice is not required to terminate a tenancy at will or at sufferance upon the death of either party, if the landlord desires to terminate the lease upon the death of the tenant, the landlord must file and prosecute against the tenant an unlawful detainer action. In the absence of a provision to the contrary contained in the lease, a lease for a fixed term is not terminable or terminated upon the death of either party.

Insolvency or bankruptcy of tenant. In light of the "automatic stay" imposed on a bankrupt's financial and legal affairs, as long as a tenant has an interest in a lease a landlord may not, without prior bankruptcy court approval, recover possession of the bankrupt tenant's premises or evict the tenant therefrom.

The trustee in bankruptcy must, however, accept or reject a bankrupt's leases within a certain period of time (which period varies according to the nature of the property and the bankruptcy filing). If the trustee fails to do so within the specified time-frame, the lease is deemed rejected.

While the trustee decides whether to reject or confirm the lease, the landlord may petition the bankruptcy court for relief from the automatic stay (which requires a showing of either inadequate protection or both that the tenant lacks equity in the premises and the lease is not essential to the reorganization). During that time, the court may enforce specific lease provisions, including, without limitation, provisions regarding payment of rent and maintenance of the premises.

A lease is generally breached if a trustee rejects it. After rejection, the landlord can proceed with unlawful detainer proceedings to recover possession. In addition, as soon as a plan of reorganization is filed and the automatic stay is removed, the landlord may employ remedies for defaults which occurred after the bankruptcy petition.

Insolvency or bankruptcy of landlord. A trustee's power to reject leases entered into by a now bankrupt landlord is limited to:

• leases that would not, under federal bankruptcy law, be binding on a bona fide purchaser;

• situations where rejection would provide substantial benefit to the bankrupt's estate and other creditors.

If the trustee elects to reject a lease, the tenant may treat the lease as terminated or may remain in possession of the premises as permitted under state law.

Exercise of option to terminate. A lease may provide that it is terminable at the election of a particular party (or either party) upon: the occurrence or non-occurrence of a particular event (e.g., sale of the premises); the passage of time; or simply the party's election, for no particular reason at all. Such options to terminate may be exercised only by the delivery of notice from the terminating party to the other in strict accordance with the terms and provisions specified in the lease, regardless of statutory notice requirements for termination of leases.

Tenant's or landlord's breach of a condition or covenant. A *condition* is a prerequisite to a party's performance. If the condition does not occur, the party whose performance is conditioned need not perform. The non-occurrence of a lease condition entitles the party whose performance is conditioned to terminate the lease. A *covenant*, however, is a promise to do or not do a certain act. If the promise is not honored, the non-breaching party is generally only entitled to remedies for breach of lease (such as suing for damages or injunctive relief), which are usually less drastic than termination.

Lease provisions are often construed as both conditions and covenants. Because of the severity of the remedy for breach of a condition (termination), a court is likely to construe an ambiguous provision as merely a covenant. In addition, conditions are narrowly construed, and even if a condition is breached, the breach must generally be material or substantial to warrant the remedy of termination and forfeiture.

On the other hand, some *covenants* are so material to the efficacy of the lease that their breach justifies termination and forfeiture. For example, a landlord's implied covenant of habitability in a residential lease and a tenant's express covenant to not assign a lease or use the premises for unlawful purposes are deemed so material that their breach may warrant termination and forfeiture of the lease.

A landlord's and tenant's covenants to one another are the inducements by each of them to the other to enter into the lease transaction, and to the extent that covenants are not merely incidental or subordinate to the main purposes of the lease, they are mutual. Accordingly, a landlord's and tenant's covenants to one another are deemed dependent obligations, and each party's performance of its covenants is a condition precedent to its right to recover for the breach of a covenant by the other party. For example, if a landlord fails to continue to provide quiet possession of the premises or constructively evicts the tenant, the tenant may elect to terminate the lease.

There is, however, one significant exception to the doctrine of dependent covenants: if the tenant fails to pay rent, the landlord must continue to honor its lease obligations (e.g., the promise to maintain and repair the premises) and, conversely, if the landlord fails to honor its lease obligations, the tenant must continue to pay rent. This exception, however, does not apply to the landlord's implied covenant of habitability for residential premises. If the landlord breaches the implied covenant of habitability, the tenant may withhold rent until the landlord satisfies its maintenance and repair obligations.

Illegal use of the premises. A tenant's occasional use of the premises for an illegal purpose is not grounds for termination unless the lease specifically provides therefor, though the landlord may seek alternative remedies against the tenant. Only an illegality that specifically relates to the use of the premises may justify a termination of the lease.

Abandonment and surrender of the premises. A surrender of the premises (and termination of the lease), by mutual agreement of landlord and tenant, occurs upon an actual abandonment of the premises by the tenant and acceptance of them by the landlord. Upon surrender, the leasehold and fee title estates are merged, and the tenant remains liable for only its "pre-surrender" obligations.

A surrender may occur by express mutual agreement between the landlord and tenant, or by implication and operation of law. If a lease is surrendered and that lease is required by the Statute of Frauds to be in writing, the surrender must also be in writing, unless the surrender either occurs by an executed oral agreement or operation of law.

For example, a surrender by implication and operation of law occurs if a tenant abandons the premises and tenders it to the landlord, and thereafter the landlord relets the premises to a new tenant. In this scenario, the landlord will be deemed to have accepted the abandoned premises from the original tenant and that lease is automatically terminated, even without a writing, and the landlord will be estopped from asserting that the premises were not surrendered since it took actions inconsistent with such an assertion.

Condemnation of Leased Property
If a leased property is condemned under a proceeding in eminent domain, the tenant is ordinarily released from all of his obligations under the lease agreement, including the obligation to pay rent. If the premises are only partially taken and the portion of the property which has not been condemned may still be used by the tenant for the purpose for which it was leased, the tenant must continue to pay rent according to the terms of the lease agreement.

Notice Upon Tenant Default

If a landlord desires to terminate a lease upon the tenant's default, the landlord must comply with requirements set forth in the California Code of Civil Procedure. The required written notice must specify that the tenant must, within three days, either comply with the terms of the lease (if the breach is of a nature which can be cured by the tenant) or vacate and surrender the premises. Compliance with this procedural requirement is a prerequisite to the filing of an unlawful detainer action.

Service. The notice of default may be served:

1. by personal delivery on the tenant;

2. if the tenant is absent from the premises and from the tenant's usual place of business, by leaving a copy with a person of suitable age and discretion at the tenant's residence or place of business *and* mailing a copy to the tenant at the tenant's residence; or

3. if the tenant's place of residence or business address cannot be ascertained, or if a person of suitable age and discretion cannot be found, by affixing a copy in a conspicuous place on the premises, delivering a copy to the person occupying the premises, *and* mailing a copy to the tenant at the premises.

It must be noted that delivery of a notice in accordance with the statutory requirements does not automatically terminate the lease. See the discussion below regarding unlawful detainer actions.

Non-Waivable Tenant Rights

Any provision in a residential lease executed after January 1, 1976, which purports to modify or waive any of the following tenant rights is void and unenforceable:

1. A tenant's rights with respect to the security deposit, as set forth in California Civil Code Section 1950.5;

2. A tenant's rights with respect to limitations on the landlord's ability to enter the premises, as set forth in California Civil Code Section 1954;

3. A tenant's right to assert a cause of action against the landlord which may arise in the future;

4. A tenant's right to a notice, as provided by law;

5. The procedural rights available to a tenant in any litigation involving the tenant's rights and obligations under the lease;

6. A tenant's right to have the leased premises maintained in a habitable condition and in compliance with all applicable health, safety, environmental, and other laws, rules, regulations, and ordinances; and,

7. A tenant's right to have the landlord exercise a duty of care to prevent personal injury or personal property damage where that duty is imposed by law.

Remedies of Landlord

Right to maintain lease in effect. In the event the tenant is in default in rental payments, the landlord may sue for each installment as it becomes due. (Civil Code Section 1951.4) This is true whether the tenant remains in possession or abandons the premises.

In any suit by the landlord to collect unpaid rent, the tenant may assert certain defenses, such as any right of the tenant contained in the lease to withhold or offset rent due to landlord's failure to comply with the lease, or the landlord's breach of the implied warranty of habitability.

In any event, this remedy is usually unsatisfactory to the landlord from a financial standpoint, and is thus not often used.

Termination of lease. If a tenant breaches the obligation to pay rent or any other obligation under the lease, and fails to cure the violation or quit the premises after three days' notice from the landlord, the landlord can terminate the lease under Civil Code Section 1951.2, and receive damages resulting from the breach. Where the tenant abandons the property, the landlord usually retakes possession for the tenant's account and relets the premises to others. At the end of the term, the landlord sues the old tenant for damages in the amount of the difference between the lease rental and the lesser amount actually obtained by reletting. On the other hand, where the tenant refuses to give up possession although in default in rental payments, the landlord normally serves a three-day notice and files an unlawful detainer action as a means to regain possession of the premises.

Unlawful detainer. A landlord who seeks to oust a defaulting tenant from possession of the premises may bring an action in ejectment (which is a long process), or the more common and expeditious procedure of unlawful detainer. Because of the complexities involved in properly prosecuting an unlawful detainer, the landlord is likely to employ an attorney or reputable eviction service.

The remedy of unlawful detainer is available against a tenant who:

1. holds over after expiration of the term for which the property has been let.

2. continues in possession after default in payment of rent.

3. continues in possession after neglect or failure to perform conditions or covenants of the lease or agreement under which the property is held, including any covenant not to assign or sublet.

4. commits waste or causes a nuisance upon the leased premises.

5. fails to quit (i.e., leave/vacate) after giving written notice of intention to terminate lease.

In most cases, a three-day notice to cure a breach or quit is required. In instances where a breach of a lease cannot be cured, the three-day notice need not give the tenant the option to cure the breach.

The purpose of the unlawful detainer procedure is to provide a landlord with a relatively quick and direct means of regaining possession of leased premises following a tenant default in instances where the tenant refuses to vacate voluntarily. It is intended to encompass all claims a landlord may have against the tenant resulting from the tenant's default. Nevertheless, in connection with granting the landlord possession of the leased premises, a court in an unlawful detainer proceeding can award the landlord damages for rent owing up through the date of the court's judgment. A landlord cannot recover in an unlawful detainer proceeding rent which would have been owed by the tenant under the lease after the date of the unlawful detainer judgment. If the landlord desires to recover post-judgment rent or other damages from the tenant (e.g., losses resulting from tenant's physical damage to the premises), the landlord must do so in a separate proceeding.

Because possession is the focus of an unlawful detainer proceeding, if a tenant relinquishes possession of the leased premises to the landlord prior to the commencement of the unlawful detainer trial the case is converted into an ordinary civil lawsuit for damages and will not receive priority on the court's calendar as would an unlawful detainer proceeding.

A defendant/tenant in an unlawful detainer proceeding has five days from service of the summons in which to file an answer with the court, or judgment will be entered in favor of the landlord. In the tenant's answer, the tenant must raise any affirmative defenses it may have to the landlord's unlawful detainer, or they will be deemed waived. The most common defenses to an unlawful detainer action are allegations that:

1. the landlord has not complied with the procedural requirements for an unlawful detainer (e.g., failure to properly serve tenant with a three-day notice);

2. the landlord has breached the implied warranty of habitability;

3. the unlawful detainer was brought in retaliation for some lawful exercise of the tenant's rights (e.g., tenant's reporting landlord to governmental authorities for violation of building or health codes); or

4. the landlord is evicting the tenant on the basis of the tenant's race or some other form of prohibited discrimination.

After granting judgment in favor of the landlord in an unlawful detainer proceeding, the court will authorize the local sheriff or other evicting authority to remove the tenant and the tenant's property from the premises. A landlord is not permitted to enter the premises and forcibly remove the tenant or the tenant's property.

Disclosures by Owner or Rental Agent to Tenant

The owner of every multi-unit dwelling or a party signing a rental agreement on such owner's behalf must disclose the name and address of each person authorized to manage the premises and to receive process for notices and demands on behalf of the owner. In the case of an oral rental agreement, on written demand by the tenant, the owner or person acting on the owner's behalf must furnish the tenant with a written statement containing such information, which must be kept current. The statutory requirement to furnish a tenant with this information is enforceable against a successor owner or manager.

If the party who enters into a rental agreement on behalf of the owner fails to comply with the above provisions, such person is deemed an agent of each person who is an owner for the purpose of service of process, notices and demands and for the purpose of performing the obligations of the owner under the law and the rental agreement. It should be noted that the law provides for optional methods of disclosure. A printed or typed written notice containing the required information may be placed in every elevator and in one other conspicuous place. Where there are no elevators, notices must be posted in at least two conspicuous places.

10 Agency

INTRODUCTION

The primary purpose of this chapter is to provide a general understanding of the concepts of agency and fiduciary duty so that real estate licensees may better fulfill their responsibilities to the public.

The concepts of agency and fiduciary duty are quite old, being derived from Common Law. According to Civil Code Section 2295 (enacted in 1872), "An agent is one who represents another, called the principal, in dealings with third persons. Such representation is called agency." In an agency relationship, the principal delegates to the agent the right to act on his or her behalf, and to exercise some degree of discretion while so acting.

CREATION OF AGENCY RELATIONSHIPS

A principal and agent can create an agency relationship by:

- agreement between them;
- by ratification;
- by estoppel; or
- as the result of the conduct of the parties and the agent's inherent relationship with third parties (i.e., ostensible or implied agency).

(Regarding ratification and estoppel, see the discussion titled "AUTHORITY OF AGENT" below.)

Actual Agency

Most often, a real estate broker and a principal in a real property or real property secured transaction place the broker in the capacity of *agent* by an express agreement. This is called an actual agency. (Civil Code Section 2299)

A broker has a duty to know and understand the agency relationship being constructed. The broker must be certain that the employment agreement with the principal (typically termed a "listing") is in a correct form and is constructed according to the circumstances and in a fair manner.

An agency agreement must be in writing for the agent to enforce a commission claim based upon a breach of contract. [Civil Code Section 1624(d)]

Elements of an Agency Agreement

An agency agreement/listing typically includes:

1. the names of the parties;
2. effective identification of the property;
3. terms and conditions of the anticipated sale, lease or loan;
4. the amount of commission or other compensation to be paid;

5. the expiration date of the agency (An exclusive listing *must* include a definite, specified date of final and complete termination.); and

6. signatures of the parties to the listing.

In addition, an agency agreement/listing concerning the sale of residential property of one to four units, or a mobilehome, must contain, immediately before the commission clause, a statement in ten point boldface type or larger that commission amounts are not set by law but are negotiable between seller and broker. Business and Professions Code Section 10147.5 sets forth the exact wording which must be used. A real estate broker may deem it prudent to include such a statement in all transactions where the broker is acting within the course and scope of the real estate license.

Types of Listing Agreements
The four kinds of listing agreements most commonly used are:

*   the open listing;
*   the exclusive agency listing;
*   the exclusive right to sell listing; and
*   the net listing.

Open listing. An open listing is the least restrictive of the four principal kinds of listing agreements, and is distinguished by the fact that the owner retains the right to revoke the listing at any time, to sell the property him or herself, or to list the property with another broker. Open listings often generate questions regarding a real estate broker's claim to a commission because the sale of the property by either the owner or any subsequently hired agent could defeat the original broker's right to a commission.

Exclusive agency. An exclusive agency is an agreement by which the owner agrees to employ a particular real estate broker to solicit prospective buyers, tenants/lessees, or lenders. Under an exclusive agency listing, the broker's right to a commission is protected as against other brokers for the duration of the listing agreement. However, under an exclusive agency agreement, the owner retains the right to sell, encumber or rent/lease the property on his or her own and, in that event, the owner can terminate the agency agreement and the broker has no claim to a commission or other compensation.

Exclusive right to sell. The exclusive right to sell listing affords a real estate broker the greatest protection and makes him or her the sole agent for the sale of the property. The broker is entitled to a commission provided only that the property is sold during the listing period, regardless of who procures the buyer. Under an exclusive right to sell agreement, the owner relinquishes both the right to list the property with other agents and the right to defeat the broker's claim for a commission by selling the property him or herself. An exclusive right listing may also be used in a rental or loan transaction.

Net listing. A net listing is one which contemplates the seller realizing certain net proceeds. The real estate broker's commission is any sum received in excess of the seller's net. For example, if the seller enters into a net listing with a broker for a $100,000 net, the broker would receive no commission if the net proceeds of the sale are $100,000 or less. On the other hand, if the net proceeds of the sale are $125,000, the broker is entitled to a commission of $25,000. This type of listing has more to do with the type of compensation than with whether it is exclusive or not.

Unilateral and bilateral agreements. An agreement can be classified as either unilateral or bilateral. A unilateral agreement is one in which one party makes a promise to induce some act or performance by the other party, but the latter can act or not act as he chooses. For example, in an open listing the seller agrees to pay compensation to a real estate broker who procures a buyer, but there is no obligation on the part of any broker to do so.

A bilateral agreement is one in which a promise by one party is given in exchange for a promise by the other party. For example, an exclusive right to sell listing includes a broker's promise to use due diligence in attempting to find a buyer. In exchange, the seller promises to pay the broker a commission if the broker is successful.

Multiple Listing
A multiple listing service (MLS) is a means by which information concerning individual listings is distributed to all participants and subscribers of the service. For example, assume a seller lists property for sale with a broker. Pursuant to the listing, the broker transmits to the MLS information about the property which includes information such as the type of property, its size, location, listed price and other relevant information as well as the compensation offered to other brokers who procure a buyer. The MLS publishes the information in a database and sometimes in book format.. Other brokers throughout the region are thereby made aware of the listing and can show the property and contact the listing agent on behalf of prospective buyers.

When a resultant sale closes, the listing broker makes good on his unilateral offer to split the commission with the selling broker.

Ostensible or Implied Agency
An agency relationship can result from the conduct of the parties even though there is no express employment agreement and regardless of the source of compensation. Agency relationships created from the actions or conduct of the parties are known as ostensible or implied agencies.

For example, a listing broker can unintentionally become the agent of the other principal to a transaction by leading the buyer to believe they are negotiating on behalf of or advocating the interest of the buyer when presenting the offer to the seller, or when processing the transaction to close of escrow. [To act as an undisclosed agent of the other principal (i.e., without the informed consent of both parties), may subject the broker to administrative discipline and/or loss of commission, and may be grounds for rescission of the transaction. [Business and Professions Code Section 10176(a) and (d)]

(See also "AUTHORITY OF AGENT" below.)

Compensation

Compensation is not essential to the creation of an agency. One may undertake to act gratuitously as an agent and still be held to certain standards demanded of an agent for compensation. Under the Real Estate Law, one who acts as a gratuitous agent does not need a real estate license. However, in any transaction subject to the Real Estate Law, and where there is an *expectation* of compensation, regardless of the form, time, or source of payment, a license is required. (Business and Professions Code Sections 10130, et seq.)

Compensation, or the expectation of compensation, is viewed broadly. For instance, benefits arising out of a joint venture relationship, or even out of the sharing of overhead, have been held to be sufficient compensation to establish licensed activity.

AUTHORITY OF AGENT

An agent has authority to:

•   Do everything necessary, proper or usual in the ordinary course of business to effect the purpose of the agency; and

•   Make representations as to facts, not including the terms of the agent's authority, on which the agent's right to use his or her authority depends, and the truth of which cannot be determined by the use of reasonable diligence on the part of the person to whom the representation is being made. (Civil Code Section 2319)

Actual authority is that authority a principal intentionally confers upon the agent, or intentionally, or by want of ordinary care, allows the agent to believe that he or she possesses. (Civil Code Section 2316) Ostensible authority is that authority a principal intentionally, or by want of ordinary care, causes or allows third persons to believe that the agent possesses. (Civil Code Section 2317) Ostensible authority is sometimes referred to as apparent or implied authority.

Express Authority

Again, express authority is created by a contract which completely and precisely delineates those activities the agent is authorized to undertake. For example, if the principal authorizes the agent to acquire a particular single-family residence for $100,000, the agent has express authority to do precisely that and nothing else. The agent would not have express authority to purchase the house for $105,000 or to purchase a different house.

Implied Authority

Implied authority exists because it is often impractical or even impossible for the principal to specifically delineate every aspect of the agent's authority. Implied authority may be derived from express authority and exists to the extent that it is reasonably necessary to accomplish the objectives of the agency. In the example above, the agent had express authority to purchase a particular property at a certain price. The agent might have implied authority to set time limits for performance of the agreement, receive notifications from the seller, waive conditions in the agreement and possibly undertake efforts to obtain financing for the buyer.

Implied authority cannot conflict with express authority but it may exist where there is no relevant grant of express authority. The determination of whether implied authority has been given usually involves determining the custom and practice of the community and whether the specific act was reasonably necessary for achieving the objectives for which the agency relationship was created.

Apparent Authority

Apparent authority depends not upon the express or implied agreement between principal and agent, but upon the reasonable expectations of third parties who have been led to believe that the agent is authorized to act on behalf of the principal. Apparent authority is distinctly different from actual or express authority and is sometimes referred to as ostensible authority by *estoppel.* Ostensible authority by estoppel arises when the principal, by words or conduct, leads a third party to believe that another person is his agent.

In other words, apparent or ostensible authority will arise and the principal could be estopped to deny the existence of the agency, or the scope of the agent's authority, when the principal's actions have created the appearance of authority in the agent and a third party reasonably relies, to his/her detriment, upon this authority. The most common causes of questions concerning apparent authority are the principal's placement of a limitation upon the normal and ordinary authority of the agent and failure to communicate this limitation to a third party dealing with the agent.

Liability of principal to third parties. The principal is liable to persons who have sustained injury through a reasonable reliance upon the ostensible, whether implied or apparent, authority of an agent. The act of the agent can never alone establish ostensible authority, but silence upon the part of the principal who knows that an agent is holding himself or herself out as vested with certain authority may give rise to liability of the principal.

Emergency Broadens Authority

An agent has expanded authority in an emergency, including the power to disobey instructions where it is clearly in the interests of the principal, and where there is no time to obtain instructions from the principal. An example of this authority occurs in the relationship between a property manager and an owner when an immediate repair or replacement is required to protect the property and to provide necessary services to the tenant.

Restrictions on Authority

An agent who is given the power to sell real property for a principal also possesses the power to give the usual covenants of warranty unless there are express restrictions in this regard in the agent's agreement with the principal. Also, an agent can never have authority, either actual or ostensible, to do an act which is known or suspected by the person with whom the agent deals to be a fraud upon the principal. Unless specifically authorized, an agent has no authority to act in the agent's own name except when it is in the usual course of business for the agent to do so.

An agency to sell property does not carry with it the authority to modify or cancel the contract of sale after it has been made. A limited agency as created between a seller and a real estate broker to sell the property ordinarily empowers the real estate broker to find a buyer, but does not authorize the agent to enter into a contract to convey title to the property on behalf of the principal.

An agent who has authority to collect money on behalf of his or her principal may endorse a negotiable instrument received in payment only where the exercise of this power is necessary for the performance of the agent's duty and where the principal has specifically granted the power to endorse the instrument. Where an agent is expressly authorized to collect money, the agent may accept a valid check and the agent's receipt of the check on behalf of the principal will be considered payment to the principal.

Ratification of Unauthorized Acts

Occasionally, a person may act as agent without authority to do so, or an agent may act beyond the scope of the agent's authority. The alleged principal may not be bound by such acts. A principal may under certain circumstances *ratify* the acts of the agent and thus become bound. Not only must the principal intend to ratify, but:

1. The agent must have professed to act as a representative of the principal.

2. The principal must have been capable of authorizing the act both at the time of the act and at the time of ratification.

3. The principal must have knowledge of all material facts unless ratification is given with the intention to ratify no matter what the facts are.

4. The principal must ratify the entire act of the agent, accepting the burdens with the benefits.

5. The principal must ratify before the third party withdraws.

Generally, an act may be ratified by any words or conduct showing an intention on the part of the principal to adopt the agent's act as the principal's own. Once ratified, the legal consequences are the same as though the act had been originally authorized.

Duty to Ascertain Scope of Agent's Authority

No liability is incurred by the principal for acts of the agent beyond the scope of the agent's actual or ostensible authority. A third party who deals with an agent and knows of the agency is under a duty to ascertain the purpose and scope of the agency.

Power of Attorney

A power of attorney is a written instrument giving authority to an agent. The agent acting under such a grant of authority is generally called an "attorney in fact." A *special* power of attorney authorizes the attorney in fact to do certain prescribed (limited) acts on behalf of the principal. Under a *general* power of attorney, the agent may transact all of the business of the principal. Powers of attorney are strictly construed and ordinarily where an authority is given partly in general and partly in specific terms, the general authority is limited to acts necessary to accomplish the specific purposes set forth.

Authority to Receive Deposits

Virtually all listing agreements now give express authority to the broker to accept an earnest money deposit on behalf of the seller. The authority granted a listing broker also applies to any subagents of the seller. The authority, however, would not apply to a broker who is acting only as an agent of the buyer.

Except for a check to be held uncashed until acceptance of the offer, as discussed below, a broker must place funds accepted on behalf of another into the hands of the owner of the funds, into a neutral escrow depository or into a trust fund account in the name of the broker as trustee at a bank or other financial institution not later than three business days following receipt of the funds by the broker or the broker's salesperson.

In those cases where a down payment has been paid to the broker and not deposited in escrow, title to such payment vests in the seller when the seller accepts the purchase contract. Further, where an agreement for sale of real property provides that a deposit with the broker is to become a part of the down payment when the seller puts in escrow a deed evidencing good title, the deposit becomes the seller's property when the deed is put in escrow. Similarly, money received by seller's agent under a deposit receipt with a valid liquidated damages clause is generally (in the case of the buyer's breach) not recoverable by the buyer.

The rationale behind this rule is that money received by a broker as agent or subagent for the seller belongs to the seller when the offer has been accepted. In general, the broker may not return the funds to the buyer without the consent of the seller.

Check. A broker who accepts a check (or promissory note) as an earnest money deposit must make full disclosure to the seller.

If a buyer has given a check to the broker as an earnest money deposit with written instructions to hold the check until acceptance of the offer, the buyer's instructions should be followed. But the seller must be informed in writing that the buyer's check is being held and not negotiated. This disclosure should be given to the seller no later than the actual presentation of the offer to the seller.

During the time between receipt of the check by the broker and acceptance of the purchase offer by the seller, the broker must record receipt of the check on broker's trust fund records and hold the check in a safe place. (Real Estate Commissioner's Regulations 2831 and 2832)

California law has held that a post-dated check may be considered the equivalent of a promissory note. Therefore, a broker should not accept a post-dated check from a buyer since this may result in mischaracterization of the form of earnest money deposit without adequate disclosure to the seller.

As our society more often uses electronic transfer of funds, other forms of earnest money deposits may well be used in real property transactions. Full and complete disclosure to the seller is required of the form, amount, and disposition of the earnest money deposit.

Promissory note. While checks are universally accepted as equivalent to cash in business transactions, promissory notes are not. The maker of a check represents that sufficient funds are in the bank account upon which the check has been drawn, and failure to have such money may be a crime. The maker of a note does not represent that he or she has sufficient money to pay as the note requires, and failure to pay is generally not a crime.

A broker violates the Real Estate Law if he/she directly or impliedly misrepresents to broker's principal/seller that a purchaser has given cash or a check as an earnest money deposit when in fact the broker has accepted a non-negotiable promissory note.

Escrow depository. When a buyer deposits earnest money directly into a neutral escrow, the delivery is conditional. While it may be argued that the buyer retains title to the money until the conditions have been performed, the escrow holder will generally not return the earnest money deposit to the buyer without concurrence of the seller. If a transaction does not close as agreed, it is the obligation of buyer and seller to insure that all funds deposited into escrow are given to the person who is entitled to the money.

If the buyer and seller are unable to resolve a dispute regarding an earnest money deposit, the escrow holder may file an interpleader action seeking declaratory relief from the court. The cost of such action will typically be deducted from the earnest money deposit.

If buyer and seller perform as agreed, the escrow holder becomes the agent of the seller as to the purchase money and the agent of the buyer as to the deed. At closing, the escrow holder delivers the money to the seller and the deed to the buyer.

Dismissal of Broker/Stakeholder From Suit
A real estate broker may be named as a defendant in a law suit for recovery of money the broker is holding as a trustee in a transaction. If the only relief sought against one of several defendants is payment of a stated amount of money, such defendant may, after notice to the other parties, apply to the court for an order of discharge from liability and dismissal from the action. Again, this is known as an interpleader action. The defendant broker must deposit with the clerk of the court the money in dispute. The court may then dismiss the suit as to defendant broker.

A broker need not wait to become a defendant in a lawsuit. If there is a fund disputed by two or more persons, the holder of the fund may file an interpleader action and deposit the fund with the court. The pleading would allege that the holder has no interest in the fund, and it would require the other parties to litigate their claims. The holder of the fund may be awarded attorney fees and costs.

Commingling
An agent who places a client's money in the agent's personal bank account is guilty of commingling and risks attachment of the funds for personal claims against the agent. Except for a check to be held until acceptance, a real estate broker must, within three business days of receipt, place all funds received on behalf of principals in a trust account, neutral escrow depository or into the hands of the principal who is entitled to them. If the broker fails to do so, the broker's license may be subject to disciplinary action by the Commissioner. A salesperson should immediately deliver all deposits into the hands or into the control of salesperson's broker, or as may be instructed by the broker.

Agency Disclosure Form
Sections 2079.13, et seq. of the Civil Code establish an agency disclosure format for sale transactions involving residential property improved with one to four

dwelling units. This disclosure format also applies to leases of such residential property for longer than one year and to sale of a mobilehome under authority of a real estate broker's license. A "sale" includes an exchange of the property, or a sale by real property sales contract as defined in Civil Code Section 2985.

The agency disclosure form sets forth disclosure obligations and describes certain duties a licensee owes to a principal in a real property transaction, whether the broker is the seller's agent, the buyer's agent, or a dual agent. The text of the form is set forth in Section 2079.16 of the Civil Code. Sections 2079.13 through 2079.15, inclusive, and 2079.17 through 2079.24, inclusive, must be printed on the back of the form.

The listing broker (or his or her agent, whether salesperson or broker associate) must deliver the form to the seller before entering into a listing agreement. The selling broker (or his or her agent) must provide the form to the seller as soon as practical and before presenting the offer. If the selling broker does not deal face to face with the seller, the form may be delivered by the listing broker. The agency disclosure form may also be delivered to the seller by certified mail. The selling broker must deliver the form to the buyer as soon as practical before the buyer signs the offer to buy. If the offer is not prepared by the selling broker, the form must be delivered to the buyer no later than the next business day following receipt of the offer from the buyer. [Civil Code Section 2079. 14 (d)]

(A broker associate is a real estate broker who has entered into a written contract to act as the salesperson/agent of another broker in connection with acts requiring a real estate license and to function under the employing broker's supervision. As used in this chapter, the term "salesperson" includes "broker associate.")

A broker must obtain a receipt from the principal receiving the disclosure. When the disclosure form is delivered by certified mail, no further receipt is required. If a seller or buyer refuses to sign the receipt, the broker or his or her agent must "set forth, sign, and date a written declaration of the facts of the refusal." (Civil Code Section 2079.15)

The disclosures are essentially as follows:

- the duty of utmost care, integrity, honesty and loyalty in dealings with the agent's principal;
- the duty to exercise skill and care in performance of the services rendered by the agent;
- the duty to act honestly and without fraud or deceit and to act fairly and in good faith; and
- the duty to disclose all material facts known to or which should be known to the agent affecting the value or desirability of the property not known to or readily observable by the parties to the transaction.

Disclosure and Confirmation of Actual Agency Relationships
As soon as practicable, a listing agent must disclose to the seller whether the listing agent is acting exclusively as the seller's agent, or as a dual agent representing both the seller and the buyer.

As soon as practicable, a selling agent must disclose to the buyer and seller whether the agent is acting exclusively as the buyer's agent, exclusively as the seller's agent, or as a dual agent representing both the buyer and seller. The term "exclusively" is generally understood to mean the agent acting for the principal in that transaction as contrasted with the dual agency in the same sales contract and does not mean the listing or selling agent does not have other clients. It does not preclude, for example, the listing broker from representing other sellers or the selling agent from representing other buyers.

The disclosed agency relationships must be confirmed in writing, either in the purchase agreement or in separate writings executed or acknowledged by seller, buyer, and agent(s), prior to or coincident with execution of the contract.

These disclosure requirements and the form of the written confirmations are contained in Civil Code Section 2079.17.

Statutory Limitations and Definitions
In addition to establishing disclosure requirements, Civil Code Sections 2079.13, et seq. impose various limitations on the conduct of, and add definitions regarding the performance of, the *agency* role of the real estate broker acting in a sale transaction. Among such limitations and definitions are the following:

1. A listing broker who is also a selling broker is a dual agent and cannot be the agent of the buyer only. (Civil Code Section 2079.18)

2. The source of compensation to a broker does not in and of itself determine who is that broker's principal. (Civil Code Section 2079.19)

3. A real estate broker functioning as a dual agent may not disclose to the seller that the buyer is willing to pay more than the buyer's written offer to purchase, nor may a dual agent disclose to the buyer that the seller will take less than that which is set forth in the listing agreement, without the express written consent of the party authorizing the disclosure. (Civil Section 2079.21)

4. A listing broker may also be the selling agent without necessarily becoming a dual agent. (Civil Code Section 2079.22)

Section 10176(d) of the Business and Professions Code requires that a licensee may act for more than one party to any real estate transaction only with the knowledge or consent of all parties to the transaction.

When applying Section 10176(d), it is prudent for licensees to get written consent and not rely on knowledge of the parties alone.

More on Dual Agency
Dual agency arises where the listing broker who is the actual agent of the seller becomes also the actual agent, or ostensible or implied agent, of the buyer.

Dual agency also commonly arises when two salespersons associated with the same broker undertake to represent two or more parties to a transaction. The real estate broker is then a dual agent.

Although dual agency is a common practice in California, a real estate broker who represents both parties must act with extreme care.

In any dual agency situation, the broker owes fiduciary duties to both principals. Dual agents face a particular difficulty with the elements of fiduciary duty which involve loyalty and confidentiality. Typical examples arise in connection with the negotiation of price and terms between seller and buyer and negotiation of loan amount and terms between lender and borrower.

The Legislature recognized this conflict when enacting Section 2079.21 of the Civil Code. That section states, in part: "A dual agent shall not disclose to the buyer that the seller is willing to sell the property at a price less than the listing price, without the express written consent of the seller. A dual agent shall not disclose to the seller that the buyer is willing to pay a price greater than the offering price, without the express written consent of the buyer."

A form of dual agency which has not been specifically addressed in the disclosure statutes is a broker's presentation of offers on behalf of two different buyers. This can easily happen when a broker is showing the same property to two prospective buyers and both buyers want the broker to write an offer on the property. The situation becomes even more complex if buyer A is in contract and buyer B makes a back-up offer. Buyer A's position is almost certainly weakened and buyer A would have reason to claim that the real estate broker breached fiduciary duties and obligations by participating in the offer by buyer B. A broker should not represent two buyers on the same property without the clear, informed and unequivocal consent of both parties.

Subagency

Real property transactions frequently involve cooperation between two brokers. The legal principles which govern the field of subagency are particularly complex. This is due, at least in part, to the different relationships which exist between the brokers and the principals to the transaction.

A critical element in determining relationships between the parties is whether the principal has agreed to allow the listing broker to delegate some portion of his or her authority to another. A listing usually provides that the listing broker may cooperate and share commissions with other brokers to carry out the purpose and scope of the agency.

When another agent is appointed by the listing broker *with* the express or implied authority of the principal, the second broker becomes the subagent of the principal. On the other hand, where the listing broker appoints another broker *without* the consent of the principal, the second broker becomes the agent of the listing broker.

The acts, errors and/or omissions (negligence) of a cooperating broker who is the authorized subagent of the seller may be imputed to the seller. For example, certain negligent acts of the cooperating broker may be imputed to the seller and the seller may be liable to third parties under the legal theory of respondeat superior.

Likewise, when the cooperating broker is the agent of the listing broker, the negligent acts of the cooperating broker may be imputed to the listing broker and the listing broker may be liable to third parties, again under the legal theory of respondeat superior.

(Remember, pursuant to Civil Code Section 2079.19, the payment of compensation does not *necessarily* determine the nature of the agency relationship between the parties.)

Delegation of Duties

Agents commonly delegate certain of their duties and their responsibilities to others. Unless specifically forbidden by the principal, the general rule is that such delegation is allowed.

The powers which may be delegated by an agent to others are generally limited to the following:

* purely mechanical acts;

* acts the agent cannot do alone and the subagent can lawfully perform; and

* acts which common practice has established may be delegated or which the principal authorizes to be delegated.

(Civil Code Section 2349)

When delegating a power to another, the agent must exercise care in delegating the authority and in choosing and appointing the delegee. Although an agent may not be authorized to assign a *duty of performance* to another, the agent may nevertheless be authorized to delegate the *actual performance* of such duty to others, and thereby discharge the duty through performance of the delegee. Although most agency agreements do not require the *personal performance* of the original agent, the original agent will typically remain liable for the acts delegated to others.

DUTIES OWED TO PRINCIPALS

An agency relationship creates a fiduciary duty owed by the agent to the principal within the course and scope of the agency and the authority granted by the principal. The fiduciary duty owed by real estate brokers to their principals has been compared by the courts to the duty owed to the beneficiaries by a trustee under a trust.

Fiduciary duties include: loyalty; confidentiality; the exercise of utmost care (and in certain fact situations, reasonable care); full and complete disclosure of all material facts; the obligation to account to the principal; the obligation to act fairly and honestly and without fraud or deceit; and the duty to "explain" and "counsel" about that which has been disclosed, thereby helping the principal make an informed and considered decision to buy, sell, lease, exchange, borrow or lend.

A salesperson owes a duty to the principal equivalent to the duty owed by the real estate broker for whom the salesperson acts.

Loyalty and Confidentiality

A real estate broker owes duties of loyalty and confidentiality to the broker's principal. The broker is prohibited from personally profiting by virtue of the agency relationship, except through receipt of compensation for services rendered by the broker in accordance with the terms of the employment agreement. This fiduciary duty is the most significant aspect of the agency relationship.

A broker may not unite his or her role as an *agent* with his or her *personal* objectives in a transaction without disclosure to, and consent from, the principal. The act of an agent within the course and scope of the agent's authority is the act of the principal. In exercising that authority, the agent is dealing with property or other matters of grave concern to the principal. As a fiduciary, a real estate broker performing as an *agent* is bound by law to exercise, among other duties, the utmost good faith, loyalty and honesty.

Fair and Honest Dealing

A real estate broker who is the agent of a principal owes a duty of fair and honest dealing to the other party to the transaction. This duty includes the obligation to make a complete and full disclosure of all material facts. A real estate broker owes this duty of full disclosure even though the broker is not the agent and fiduciary of the party to whom the disclosures are made. This is a duty which the courts have held to exist by reason of the agent's status as a real estate broker. (*Lingsch v. Savage* 1963 213 Cal. App. 2d 729, 736)

The duty of disclosure may also be found to exist by way of the agent's fiduciary obligation to the party on whose behalf the disclosures are being made. Any misrepresentation or material concealment on the part of the agent may afford the other party grounds for rescission or damages.

General Disclosure Duties

In a fiduciary relationship, it is the duty of the agent to make full disclosure of all material facts relating to the subject matter of the agency. For example, the courts have held that negotiating a sale to the real estate broker's wife without making a full disclosure to the principal is a violation of the duty to disclose all material facts. A later case was concerned with the failure of the real estate broker to disclose to the seller that the buyer was the broker's mother-in-law.

The court stated that where a seller's real estate agent is obligated to disclose to the agent's principal the identity of the buyer, and where the buyer is not the agent but has with the agent such blood, marital or other relationship which would suggest a reasonable possibility that the agent could be indirectly acquiring an interest in the property, such relationship is a material fact which the agent must disclose to the agent's principal.

An agent's duty includes full disclosure and explanation of facts necessary for the principal to make an informed and intelligent decision. In *George Ball Pacific, Inc. v. Coldwell Banker & Co.* (1981 117 Cal. App. 3d 248), the court found that the broker had made an inaccurate representation when he arranged a lease without knowing whether the lessor owned the property being leased.

Reasonable Care and Skill

An agent has a duty to use reasonable care and skill (and depending upon the fact situation, utmost care) to obey directions of the employer, and to render an accounting to the principal. The language in Civil Code Section 2079.16 requires "a fiduciary duty of utmost care, integrity, honesty and loyalty." The reasonable care and skill standard applies to the party in the transaction who is not the agent's principal. Whether the standard is utmost or reasonable will depend upon the fact situation and the relationship between the agent and the principal. A gratuitous agent (i.e., one who is not paid for the agent's services) cannot be compelled to perform the undertaking, but such an agent who actually enters upon performance must obey instructions and is bound to exercise the utmost good faith in dealing with the principal.

Although real estate brokers as agents and fiduciaries are obligated to fully disclose to a principal all material facts which might influence the principal's decision concerning any real property or real property secured transaction, they should be aware of a California Attorney General's opinion (Op. 69/263). This Opinion explains that *race, creed or color is not a material fact* and should not be disclosed, even though the furnishing of such information is at the request of the principal.

Inspection and Disclosures

Listing and selling brokers have an affirmative duty to conduct a reasonably competent and diligent inspection of the residential property listed for sale, and to disclose to prospective purchasers all facts materially affecting the value or desirability of the property that such an investigation would reveal.

After the *Easton v. Strassburger* decision, Civil Code Sections 2079, et seq. were enacted to describe this duty of inspection as follows:

1. A real estate broker has a duty to the buyer of residential real property of one to four units (including manufactured homes) to conduct a reasonably competent and diligent visual inspection of the property offered for sale and disclose to the buyer all facts materially affecting the value or desirability of the property that such an investigation would reveal, if the broker has a written listing contract with the seller to find a buyer or is a broker who acts in cooperation with such a broker to find a buyer.

2. This duty also applies to leases of such residential property with an option to buy and to real property sale contracts as defined in Civil Code Section 2985.

3. The standard of care owed by a broker is the degree of care that a reasonably prudent real estate licensee would exercise and is measured by the degree of knowledge through education, experience, and examination, required to obtain a real estate license.

4. The inspection to be performed does not include areas that are reasonably and normally inaccessible to such an inspection. If the property is a unit in a planned development, condominium or stock cooperative, the inspection does not include more than the unit offered for sale, if the seller complies with Section 1368 of the Civil Code, which requires a seller of such properties to furnish the buyer with copies of covenants, conditions, and restrictions, by-laws, delinquent assessments and penalties, etc.

5. In no event shall time for commencement of legal action for breach of duty imposed by this article exceed two years from the date of possession, which means the date of recordation, the date of close of escrow, or the date of occupancy, whichever comes first.

6. The inspection to be performed also does not include an affirmative inspection of areas off the site of the subject property, or public records or permits concerning the title or use of the property.

Transfer Disclosure Statement. The results of the brokers' inspections will be included on the Real Estate Transfer Disclosure Statement required by Civil Code Section 1102.3.

Professional liability insurance. Section 11589.5 of the Insurance Code provides that no insurer who provides professional liability insurance for persons licensed under the Real Estate Law shall exclude from coverage under that policy liability arising from breach of the duty of the licensee arising under Article 2 (starting with Section 2079) of Chapter 3 of Title 6 of Part 4 of Division 3 of the Civil Code. (An insurer may exclude coverage of liability arising out of a dishonest, fraudulent, criminal, or malicious act, error, or omission committed by, at the direction of, or with knowledge of the insured.)

Buyer's duty. Nothing in this disclosure law relieves a buyer or prospective buyer of the duty to exercise reasonable care to protect themselves including those facts which are known to or within their diligent attention and observation.

No Secret Profit or Undisclosed Compensation
The courts have unequivocally held that an agent *cannot*:

- acquire any secret interests adverse to the principal;
- make a secret personal profit out of the subject of the agency; or
- conceal the agent's interest in the property being conveyed or encumbered.

If an agent is aware of the amount at which a property may be sold and purchases at a lower amount, reselling and pocketing the difference, the agent will be compelled to disgorge the secret profit.

Claiming or receiving a secret profit or any form of undisclosed compensation is cause for discipline under Business and Professions Code Section 10176(g). The obligation to disclose all compensation regardless of the form, time, or source of payment is imposed upon real estate licensees whether acting in a real property or real property secured transaction.

Obligations of Real Estate Salespersons
A real estate salesperson is the agent of a broker and is subject to the same duties and obligations arising out of the fiduciary relationship between the broker and the broker's principal.

A salesperson must disclose to the broker's principal all the information the salesperson has which may affect the principal's decision. Failure to fulfill this obligation could result in disciplinary action against the salesperson's license and may result in disciplinary action against the license of the employing broker. Moreover, a broker will generally be held liable for damages for acts and omissions of the broker's salesperson.

DUTIES OWED TO THIRD PARTIES

Warranty of Authority
If an agent acts in the name of the agent's principal with authority given by the principal, the principal is bound by the agent's act. When the agent acts without authority or in excess of the agent's authority, the agent may be held liable for resulting damages for having breached the agent's implied warranty of authority.

While the agent warrants the agent's own authority, the agent does not impliedly warrant the authority of the principal (e.g., the principal's authority or capacity to contract).

Regarding Contracts

When a contract is negotiated and executed by an agent in the name of the principal, the agent will not ordinarily be held liable for performance of the contract. If, however, there is a lack of authority on the part of the agent, the agent is liable for performance of the contract as a principal. The agent could also be personally liable for performance of the contract if the agent fails to reveal the name of the principal or the fact that the agent is acting in an agency capacity.

The manner in which an agent signs a contract with a third party on behalf of the agent's principal may be significant in determining whether the agent has any personal liability to the third party. Ordinarily, an agent should enter the name of the principal as the contracting party and should then sign the instrument "by" himself or herself as agent for that principal.

Regarding Torts

Torts are private wrongs committed upon the person or property of another and arising from a breach of duty created by law rather than by contract. An agent is liable to third parties for the agent's own torts whether the principal is liable or not. Where a person misrepresents his or her authority to act as agent for another, such person may be liable in tort to the third party who relies on the representation to the third party's detriment.

Real estate brokers and their salespersons are constantly making representations to prospects concerning property being offered for sale. A representation may be merely an expression of opinion or "puffing" on the part of the licensee but it may be reasonably understood by a prospective buyer to be a representation of fact and thus a part of the contract if agreement is reached.

Material representations which are false or misleading may result in liability of the real estate broker. The same may be said with respect to failure on the part of the broker to disclose material facts about the property to a prospective buyer. In addition to incurring liability for damages to the buyer, a broker guilty of overt misrepresentations or failure to disclose material facts may be subject to license discipline by the Department of Real Estate.

Misrepresentation: Fraud v. Negligence

Misrepresentation may be either fraudulent or negligent. The principal may be vicariously liable in damages for the broker's misrepresentations even where the principal was not the source of the erroneous information conveyed by the broker acting as the principal's agent.

Certain misrepresentations, even though made by an agent with no bad intent, are defined by law as actual fraud if they are positive assertions of that which is not true made in a manner not warranted by the information of the person making the representation, notwithstanding that such person believes it to be true. Constructive fraud, as defined in the California Civil Code, includes any breach of duty which, without an actually fraudulent intent, gains an advantage to the person in fault, or anyone claiming under him or her, by misleading another to his or her prejudice, or to the prejudice of anyone claiming under him or her.

Thus, in the area of misrepresentations, the dividing line between fraud and negligence is often blurred and yet there may be a significant difference in the agent's exposure in damages depending upon whether the misrepresentation is found to be negligent or fraudulent. If found by a court or jury to be fraudulent, punitive damages can be awarded against the person making the misrepresentation. Remember, a real estate broker acting as an *agent* in a real property or real property secured transaction may make no representation without a reasonable basis for believing the representation is true; may assert no half-truths; and may not assert a series of independent truths which when interconnected are expressly or inferentially misleading.

Furthermore, if a fraud judgment is entered against a real estate broker based on the broker's performance of acts for which a real estate license is required, disciplinary action may be taken against the broker based solely on the civil judgment. (*California Real Estate Loans, Inc. v. Wallace* 1993 18 Cal. App. 4th 1575) If, on the other hand, the broker's misrepresentation is found to be no more than negligent, a case against the broker for negligence would have to be heard at the administrative level where the standard of proof required in order to discipline is convincing proof to a reasonable certainty as opposed to the preponderance-of-evidence standard in a civil negligence action.

Nondisclosures
Civil liability of a real estate broker for misrepresentation and the possibility of disciplinary action against the licensee may arise from the broker's failure to disclose as well as from overt misstatements. Liability for failure to disclose may result where the broker has knowledge of facts materially affecting the value, desirability, or intended use of the property, and which facts the broker does not convey to the prospective buyer knowing that the buyer does not have the same information.

Cases imposing a duty of disclosure oftentimes involve concealment by the seller of latent defects in the property. These cases have held that the real estate broker acting as an agent of the seller and the seller have a duty to disclose facts materially affecting the value, desirability, or intended use of property, if the broker knows that the buyer is unaware of these facts and they are not within the buyer's diligent attention, including inspection of the property. The courts have sometimes referred to such non-disclosure as negative fraud.

"Puffing"
Even in some situations where a licensee honestly believes that representations to the prospective buyer are nothing more than "puffing" or "sales talk," a problem may develop if the impression made upon the buyer is that the representation is one of fact. Persons of limited expertise and sophistication may tend to rely upon such statements and to purchase property as a result of such reliance.

A statement by a licensee that a house was "in perfect shape," while obviously not literally true, has been described by an appellate court as a representation of a material fact.

Torts of the Principal
While an agent is personally liable for torts which the agent commits, regardless of the liability or absence of liability of the principal, the agent cannot be held liable for torts committed by the principal. For example, if the principal supplies the agent with false information concerning the property and the agent passes this information along to a prospective buyer in reasonable reliance upon its truth, the agent is not liable to the buyer for what amounts to republishing the misrepresentation.

RIGHTS OF AGENT

Compensation - Performance Required Under Employment Contract
Generally. To be entitled to a commission in a sale transaction a broker must:

- produce a buyer ready, willing and able to purchase upon the terms and at the price stipulated by the seller; or

- secure from a prospective buyer an offer upon terms and conditions which the seller subsequently accepts.

In the first situation, a real estate broker's right to compensation is based upon the written listing. The listing agreement requires that the broker produce an offer by a buyer ready, willing and able to purchase on the seller's listing terms. A ready and willing buyer denotes one who is prepared to enter into a binding contract while an able buyer is one who has the financial ability to consummate the transaction at the proper time.

From the broker's standpoint, a listing agreement is very much result oriented. The broker's right to a commission is not dependent upon the amount of work put into finding a buyer and negotiating a "meeting of the minds" of buyer and seller. If the broker expends *no* time and effort on behalf of the principal and yet is able to produce a buyer who is ready, willing and able to purchase on the terms specified in the listing contract, the broker is the procuring cause and has earned the compensation.

Lawful condition. The payment of a commission under a listing contract may be made dependent on any lawful condition. A seller may be relieved from the obligation to pay a commission if it appears from the language of the contract that payment was contingent upon the happening of a condition that did not occur. The burden is on the broker to establish that he or she has earned a commission. If the fulfillment of a condition is prevented by the fraud or bad faith of the seller, or through collusion between the seller and other parties, the broker may recover compensation even if the condition has not been met.

If broker performs within time limit broker is entitled to commission. Revocation of a broker's authorization cannot operate to deprive the broker of the compensation contracted for, or its equivalent in damages, for nonperformance of the owner's contract if, within the time specified in the listing agreement, the broker has found a buyer ready, willing and able to purchase upon the price and terms in the listing. The principal will not be relieved from liability by a capricious refusal to consummate a sale where the principal's voluntary act precludes the possibility of performance on the principal's part. This is based upon the familiar principle that no one can avail himself or herself of the nonperformance of a condition precedent who has occasioned its nonperformance. It is also well settled that a principal cannot discharge an agent pending negotiations by the agent with a prospective buyer, then effect a sale to that buyer without liability to the agent.

Agreement between brokers. An agreement between brokers cooperating in the sale of real property for a division of the commission is not illegal nor against public policy. It will be construed and enforced the same as other contracts not required to be in writing but no partnership or joint venture is created by such an agreement.

Right of principal to secure buyer. Where the listing is an open one, sale by the owner of the property to a person who has not been referred to the owner by the broker does not violate the listing agreement and creates no liability to the broker on the part of the owner. If there is no termination date in an open listing, the owner may not seek to take advantage of a failure on the part of the broker to produce a person willing to purchase on the terms of the listing by attempting to deal directly with the agent's prospect.

An agency contract which provides that the agency is irrevocable for a fixed time does not prevent the owner from selling the property within that time to a person with whom the agent has had no prior negotiations.

Commission as negotiated. The amount of commission is set out in a broker's contract of employment. In the absence of any evidence of incapacity to read or any fraud to prevent the reading of it, the party signing the written contract is bound by its express terms and conditions. Ordinarily, the compensation of the broker is negotiated at a certain percentage of the purchase price obtained by the owner. If no amount of compensation is mentioned in the contract of employment, the law recognizes an implied promise on the part of the owner to pay the usual or customary commission charged in the neighborhood for like services.

Both the listing agreement and the deposit receipt usually expressly provide for payment of a commission if the owner accepts an offer procured by the broker at a price which is less than the price specified in the listing agreement.

Listing agreement - no deposit receipt contract. When agency is executed. A broker has earned a commission when, within the life of the contract, the broker has fulfilled the terms of the agency contract. As stated before, a buyer produced must be ready, willing and able to purchase upon the terms and conditions specified in the listing. The readiness and willingness of a person to purchase real property may be shown by an offer to purchase from that person. Unless such person has made an offer to the seller to enter into such a contract, this person cannot be regarded as a person ready, willing and able to buy. The buyer and seller must be brought into communication with each other. Merely putting a prospective purchaser on the track of property which is on the market does not entitle the broker to the commission contracted for and even though a broker opens negotiations for the sale of the property, the broker will not be entitled to a commission if the broker ultimately fails to induce the prospective buyer to make an offer on the property. The obligation assumed by the broker is to achieve a "meeting of the minds" of the buyer and seller as to the price and other terms for the transaction.

Deposit receipt contract—no listing. On occasion, the only written agreement containing a promise to pay a commission to the broker is in the contract to purchase between buyer and seller. In order to protect a right to a commission, the broker should attempt to obtain a separate agreement for the payment of a commission even if it is a listing that is written up to terminate within hours after an offer is presented. If a seller refuses to enter into such a separate agreement, the broker will have to rely upon the deposit receipt agreement. Then, a question may arise concerning the seller's obligation to pay a commission if the sale of the property is not consummated. Whether or not there is an enforceable obligation on the part of the seller will often depend upon the wording of the commission clause in the deposit receipt.

Both listing agreement and deposit receipt contract. A broker's right to a commission usually flows from an employment contract/listing. The execution of a contract to sell is nevertheless significant in that it evidences the fact that the agent has produced an offer that is acceptable to the owner.

Sale to broker's prospect after termination of listing. A broker's negotiations during the life of a listing with a prospect who ultimately purchases the property does not necessarily entitle the broker to a commission. Special circumstances may nevertheless dictate that the agreed commission be paid to the broker. For example, where the sale is consummated directly by buyer and seller after expiration of the listing on the same terms as proposed through the broker or with only a price reduction to the buyer, there is every reason to believe that the broker was the procuring cause of the sale and is entitled to the agreed compensation.

A broker may include a protective clause in a listing agreement. Under this clause, the seller agrees to pay a commission to the broker if the property is sold within a certain time period after expiration of the listing to a person with whom the broker negotiated while the listing was in effect. Ordinarily, a listing contract which includes such a protective clause requires that the broker give to the owner, within a prescribed number of days after expiration of the listing, a list of prospective purchasers with whom the broker has negotiated.

Even if the broker did not negotiate with anyone during the term of the listing, the seller may waive expiration of the contract by encouraging the broker to continue efforts to find a buyer. If the broker continues in reliance upon such a waiver and does produce an offeror to whom the property is ultimately sold, broker may be entitled to a commission.

Breach of contract v. tort theory. The obligation to pay compensation to the broker must be in writing. The broker's right to compensation and the amount are usually set forth in the listing agreement. A real estate broker can act upon a letter received from an owner, whether voluntarily sent by the owner or in answer to the broker's solicitation. When relying upon letters, the broker should be very careful to see that the letter contains an employment clause or authorizes the broker to find a buyer and describes the compensation the broker is entitled to receive as a result of accomplishing the purpose and scope of the agency.

Statutory and case law have been interpreted to mean that a broker is not entitled to recover a commission under a breach of contract theory unless there is a signed agreement between the broker and the principal. The agreement can be a listing agreement, some other form of agency agreement, or the agreement to pay the commission may be set forth in the purchase agreement itself.

TERMINATION OF AGENCY

Ordinarily, an agency may be terminated by the acts of one or both of the parties or by operation of law. An agency is also terminated by the expiration of its term, the accomplishment of the purpose for which the agency was established, the extinction of its subject matter, or the death or incapacity of either principal or agent.

When Principal May Revoke Agency
Because the relationship between a principal and agent is a personal one, founded on trust and confidence, the principal has an absolute power under the law to revoke the agency at any time.

Nevertheless, while the principal in most circumstances has an absolute *power* to revoke, the principal does not necessarily have the *right* to do so and may be liable for breach of contract if revocation is without good cause. If the agency was created by a recorded instrument containing a power to convey or execute instruments affecting real property, revocation of the agency is not effective unless it is in writing, acknowledged, and recorded in the same place as the instrument creating the agency.

Effect of Termination
According to Civil Code Section 2355, notice of termination of an agency relationship must be given to third persons if the agency is terminated as a result of expiration of the term, extinction of the subject matter, or the agent's death, incapacity or renunciation. If the agency is in fact terminated in any of the ways enumerated in Section 2355, the former agent is still an ostensible agent as to those third persons who have not received notice of termination. If the agency is terminated through the death or incapacity of the principal or by the principal's express act of revocation, it is effective as to third persons even though they have no notice.

Time When Revocation Can Be Made
As a rule, unless a real estate broker's authority is coupled with an interest in the property, the broker's authorization may be revoked at any time by the principal. A real estate broker's right to earn a commission under a listing agreement is not considered to be an interest in the contract which precludes termination by death, incapacity or revocation on the part of the principal. This is true even if the broker is given a particular time within which to perform under the terms of the listing agreement. On the other hand, the courts have recognized circumstances where the contract of agency is irrevocable because the licensee has an interest in the property which is the subject matter of the agency.

The principal's termination of the agency relationship by revocation may give a real estate broker a right to damages for breach of contract or to compensation pursuant to the terms of the listing agreement. Withdrawal of the property from the market by the owner prior to expiration of the listing is an example of a de facto revocation which may give the broker a cause of action for agreed compensation under the listing contract. The California Supreme Court has held that a clause in an exclusive listing contract providing for payment of a commission to a real estate broker on withdrawal of the property from sale by the principal does not constitute an unenforceable penalty under California law. If the listing is an open one, a sale negotiated by the owner or by a broker terminates the listing and notice of termination need not be given to brokers other than the broker who has presented the offer which has been accepted.

In the event an open listing specifies no fixed term of employment, the listing normally may be revoked by the owner at any time without liability prior to production of a ready, willing and able buyer by the broker. If a fixed term is specified, it is possible that, despite revocation by the owner, the commission will be earned if the broker produces such a buyer within the specified time.

Exclusive listing agreements must contain a definite, specified date of final and complete termination. If the listing does not contain a definite termination date, the listing is unenforceable by the real estate broker and the claim, demand or receipt of any fee under the agreement by the broker may be a basis for license discipline. See Section 10176(f) of the Business and Professions Code.

SPECIAL BROKERAGE RELATIONSHIPS

From time to time a broker may have occasion to make a sale of property included in the estate of a decedent. Less frequently, a broker may represent a Board of Education or the State of California.

Probate Sales

The representative of the estate of a decedent may initiate a probate sale by seeking offers to purchase directly or through one or more brokers. (Probate Code Section 10150) The executor or administrator may sell the real property of an estate where it is found to be in the best interests of the estate. Whether the sale is public or private, it must be advertised by publication or posting of notice. (Probate Code Sections 10300, et seq.) Acceptance of an offer by the estate representative is subject to probate court confirmation. The representative of the estate of the decedent may, with court permission, grant an exclusive right to sell the property for a period of not to exceed 90 days. (Probate Code Section 10150)

The broker's compensation and the court confirmation procedure are set forth in Probate Code Sections 10160, et seq. Initial information concerning the property, the broker's compensation, and the court confirmation procedure, if any, can be furnished by the attorney for the estate. If a bank or trust company has been appointed representative, interested persons may apply directly to the trust office of the institution for information. If a public administrator is the estate representative, inquiry may be made at that office. The broker should ask about the Independent Administration of Estates and whether the administrator is entitled to sell the property without the court's confirmation but with notice to all beneficiaries. (Probate Code Sections 10400, et seq.)

An offer to purchase must be for a price which is not less than 90% of the property's appraised value (appraisal date within one year of sale) and it must conform to statutory requirements, the rules of the local superior court governing probate sales and the terms stated in the public notice of sale. The court will attempt to establish that the executor or administrator of the estate has exposed the property to the market. (Probate Code Sections 10160, et seq.)

When an offer has been received which the representative has accepted subject to court confirmation, the representative will petition the court to confirm the sale. When the court has set the matter for hearing, any interested person may bid at the time of the hearing. To open the bidding there must be an increase over the bid returned to the court for confirmation which is at least 10% of the first $10,000 bid and 5% of the bid in excess of $10,000. Once the bidding has been opened, the court in its discretion may permit the bidding to continue on lesser raises until it declares a bid to be the highest and best obtainable. The sale will then be confirmed by the court to the maker of that bid. (Probate Code Sections 10000, et seq.)

The person making the offer returned to court for confirmation, and the broker representing that person, should attend the confirmation hearing whether or not that person plans to participate in higher bidding for the property. All prospective bidders and brokers should be familiar with local rules of court governing advance bidding, deposits required and similar matters. Ordinarily, after court confirmation of a sale, normal escrow procedures are used to consummate the transaction on the terms and conditions approved by the court.

Payment of commissions to brokers participating in probate sales is generally within the discretion of the probate court, subject to certain standards prescribed by statute. For example, Section 10162 of the Probate Code provides that the compensation of the agent producing a successful bidder shall not exceed one-half of the difference between the amount of the bid in the original return and the amount of the successful bid, provided that the limitation shall not apply to any compensation of the agent holding a contract with the estate representative pursuant to Section 10150 of the Probate Code.

It is important that the broker who procures the offer which is accepted by the estate representative and returned to court for confirmation have a written contract with the representative. In the case of an overbid in open court at the confirmation hearing, it is a matter of importance to the broker that the court be informed that a licensed broker has produced the bid in question. If a purchaser not represented by an agent has his overbid confirmed, the listing broker may receive a full commission on the original bid only. (Probate Code Section 10162.5)

In its order confirming the sale, the court will set forth the amount of commission to be paid and the division of the commission if more than one broker is to be compensated. (Probate Code Sections 10160, et seq.) Needless to say, where an agent is also the purchaser, the court will carefully examine "the substantiality" of the agent's acts in putting together "the best deal" for the estate, especially where the agent expects a commission. (*Estate of Levinthal v. Silberts* 1980 105 Cal. App. 3d 691)

Board of Education Sales
The Education Code provides that the governing body of any school district may pay a commission to a licensed real estate broker who procures a buyer for real

property sold by the board. The sealed bid for the property must be accompanied by the name of the broker to whom the commission is to be paid and by a statement of the rate or amount of the commission.

In the event of a sale on a higher oral bid to a purchaser procured by a qualified licensed real estate broker, other than the broker who submitted the highest written proposal, the board will allow a commission on the full amount for which the sale is confirmed.

Note: One-half of the commission on the amount of the highest written proposal will be paid to the broker who submitted it, and the balance of the commission on the purchase price to the broker who procured the purchaser to whom the sale was confirmed.

State of California Sales

From time to time, the State of California has real property for disposal. When bids received for this property, after advertising, do not equal its appraised value, the Department of Finance may authorize employment of a licensed real estate broker to effect the sale on a commission basis. This procedure does not apply to surplus real property of the State Division of Highways.

LICENSEE ACTING FOR OWN ACCOUNT

A real estate licensee will sometimes act in a real property transaction for his or her own account. Because of professional background and contacts, a licensee is oftentimes more aware than most people of investment and profit opportunities in such transactions. An effort to exploit these opportunities to personal advantage may involve legal or ethical matters to be carefully considered by the licensee.

When acting for his or her own account, a broker or salesperson is obliged to act honestly and fairly, in good faith, and without fraud or deceit. These duties and obligations are expected of all parties to agreements.

In certain fact situations, a broker or salesperson acting as a principal has additional duties to the other party to the transaction. An example is a broker or salesperson acting as a principal in a transaction who is also an arranger of credit pursuant to Civil Code Sections 2956 - 2957. Licensees who are principals in such transactions must prepare and complete a seller financing disclosure statement to be delivered to the other principal.

Oftentimes, complaints to the Department of Real Estate result from the efforts of licensees to secure profits in real property transactions by purporting to act as principals. In this connection, they have resorted to the use of options, net listings, guaranteed sales, and other types of agreements which combine features of a listing with an obligation or right imposed upon or given to the licensee to act as a principal. The use of options, net listings, and guaranteed sales is neither illegal nor unethical in California so long as a full disclosure of the licensee's involvement in the transaction and the legal effect of such an agreement is explained to the person(s) with whom the licensee is transacting business. The other party to the transaction must be advised and understand that the licensee may be acting as a principal, and potentially as both an agent and a principal in the transaction, rather than simply as an agent.

When a real estate licensee is acting only as a principal in a transaction, the other party should be aware that dealings with the licensee are at "arms-length" and not that of an *agent* and principal.

Since the broker or salesperson holds himself or herself out as a real estate licensee, the broker or salesperson must be careful when acting as a principal only, or as both an *agent* and a principal. It is easy for the public to misunderstand the role of the licensee because the contacts between them usually arise out of the marketing activities of the licensee. For example, office signs, signs on properties, stationery, newspaper advertisements and business cards are all illustrations that the broker or salesperson is acting or intending to act in a licensed capacity. Therefore, care must be taken to dispel the agency image if the licensee chooses to act as a principal only in a real property or real property secured transaction.

Also, it is important for the licensee to disclose and explain fact situations where the licensee may be acting both as a principal and an *agent*. An example of such a fact situation occurs when a licensee lists his or her property on a multiple listing service, soliciting buyers through that medium, and the real estate firm with whom the licensee is associated later becomes the agent of the buyer. Another example is a real estate broker who undertakes, on behalf of a borrower, to solicit a lender to make a loan. If the broker later decides to make the loan him or herself or with broker-controlled funds, clear disclosure of the broker's changing role should take place.

It is particularly important for a licensee who starts out as an agent in a transaction and then switches status to that of a principal to make a clear and distinct disclosure of the change before the transaction is consummated. It is advisable to create a written record of the disclosure. In fact, it may not be possible to discharge the responsibilities inherent in the agency relationship in the middle of a transaction. The usual result is that the licensee will be acting both as a principal and as an *agent* of the other principal in the transaction. The licensee must be scrupulous in informing the other principal of the inherent conflicts of interest when the licensee is acting as a principal.

Various court decisions indicate that the burden of proof under these circumstances is upon the licensee to show that the principal was fully informed of this change of status. Obviously, such disclosures must be made in writing. [Civil Code Section 2079.17 and Business and Professions Code Sections 10176(a) and (d)] Vague or ambiguous disclosures will not be sufficient notice of a change of status by the licensee from *agent* to principal only.

Option to purchase by the broker as an agent. A somewhat similar situation arises when a broker who is employed as an *agent* to find a buyer of real property obtains an option to purchase the property which runs concurrently with the agency. In such a case, the broker cannot ignore the interests of the principal and the broker may not take advantage of the fiduciary relationship with the principal.

The law is well summarized in *American Jurisprudence*: "If a broker employed to sell property is also given...an option to purchase the property himself, he occupies the dual status of agent and purchaser and he is not entitled to exercise his option except by divesting himself of his obligation as an agent by making a full disclosure of any information in his possession as to the prospect of making a sale to another."

Disclosure of conflicts and profits by the broker as an agent. In the language of *The Restatement of Agency*: "Before dealing with the principal on his own account ... an agent has as a duty, not only to make no misstatements of fact, but also to disclose to the principal all relevant facts fully and completely. A fact is relevant if it is one which the agent should realize would be likely to affect the judgment of the principal in giving his consent to the agent to enter into the particular transaction on the specified terms. Hence, the disclosure must include not only the fact that the agent is acting on his own account but also all other facts which he should realize have or are likely to have a bearing upon the desirability of the transaction from the viewpoint of the principal." [Restatements (Second) of Agency § 390]

The very nature of combining listings, options, and guaranteed sale agreements places a licensee in a position where he or she must exercise the utmost caution to avoid violating the fiduciary duties and obligations owed to the principal. Additional problems arise in this context because the Real Estate Law and general principles of agency require that the licensee make full disclosure to the principal of any compensation, commission or profit claimed or taken by the licensee with respect to the transaction. [Business and Professions Code Section 10176 (g)]

UNLAWFUL EMPLOYMENT AND COMPENSATION

It is unlawful for any licensed real estate broker to employ or compensate, directly or indirectly, any person for performing any of the acts for which a license is required who is not a licensed real estate broker, or a real estate salesperson licensed under the broker employing or compensating him or her; provided, however, that a licensed real estate broker may pay a commission to a broker of another state. No real estate salesperson shall be employed by or accept compensation from any person other than the broker under whom he or she is at the time licensed. It is unlawful for any licensed real estate salesperson to pay any compensation for performing any of the acts within the scope of the Real Estate Law to any real estate licensee, except through the broker under whom he or she is at the time licensed. (Business and Professions Code Section 10137)

The prohibition against sharing commissions with unlicensed persons applies only to a payment made by a licensee to a nonlicensee as compensation for the performance of acts for which a real estate license is required. Thus, payment of a portion of a commission by a licensee to a principal in the transaction does not constitute a violation of Section 10137, but if there is a commission rebate to the buyer in the transaction that fact must be disclosed by the agent to the seller who has paid the commission. (Business and Professions Code Sections 10138, 10139, and 10139.5)

BROKER - SALESPERSON RELATIONSHIP

Broker - Salesperson Employment Contract
Commissioner's Regulation 2726 requires that a real estate broker have a written agreement with each of his or her salespersons, whether licensed as a salesperson or a broker under a broker-salesperson arrangement. An employment contract between broker and salesperson may be instrumental in establishing the relationship between them, but only to the extent that the provisions do not conflict with the relationship as mandated by the Real Estate Law, other statutes, and applicable case law. The details of the association, including supervision, duties and compensation, must be spelled out in the contract and adhered to in practice.

Employer - Employee
An employee is defined in the Labor Code as one who renders personal service to the employer and who performs the service under the direction and control of the employer. An employee works for his or her employer, while an agent not only does this but also acts for and in the place of the principal for the purpose of making agreements and thus bringing the principal into legal relationships with third persons. Thus, a filing clerk in an office or a machinist in a factory would be an ordinary employee. A broker normally would not be classified as an employee. For purposes of the Real Estate Law and the Civil Code, a real estate salesperson is an employee of the real estate broker under whom he or she is licensed. If the broker is a corporation, the salesperson is an agent of the corporation, not of the supervising qualifying broker in his or her individual capacity. (*Walters v. Marler* (1978) 83 Cal.App.3d 1,147 Cal. Rptr. 655)

Independent Contractor
An independent contractor is one who, in rendering services, exercises an independent employment or occupation and is responsible to the principal only for the results of his or her work. For the most part, an independent contractor sells final results rather than time, and the methods of achieving those results are not subject to the control of the principal. An independent contractor may also be an agent of the principal. For instance, a real estate broker is typically an independent contractor acting as an *agent* of the principal for a defined limited purpose.

An important factor in establishing independent contractor status is that the contractor determines the method of accomplishing the work for which the contractor has been engaged. Salespersons are usually characterized as independent contractors of the broker for purposes of state and federal income tax reporting and sometimes for certain other purposes such as Workers' Compensation Insurance coverage. (See, for example, Unemployment Insurance Code Section 650 and 26 U.S.C. Section 3508.) Accordingly, salespersons are agents and employees of the supervising broker in connection with dealings with the public but may, at the same time, be independent contractors for income tax reporting and certain other purposes.

To maintain independent contractor status for income tax reporting and related labor law purposes, it is necessary for the supervising broker to specify in contracts with salespersons that the associates are independent contractors and not employees for income tax reporting purposes. However, the real estate broker must distinguish between the implementation of independent contractor status of salespersons for tax reporting, Workman's Compensation, or other labor-related purposes and the broker's duty to supervise those salespersons under the Real Estate Law. Moreover, the independent contractor status does not diminish the broker's responsibilities and civil liabilities for the conduct of the broker's salespersons. (Business and Professions Code Sections 10032, 10132, 10177(h) and 10159.2)

Liability

Even though an employer or principal may not be personally at fault, they can be held liable in damages for the negligent conduct of their employees or agents who act within the general course and scope of their employment or agency. This liability finds its most notable illustrations in cases involving automobile accidents of employees while driving on the employer's business. If the wrongdoer is an independent contractor for all purposes, the person who hired him or her would not ordinarily be liable for injuries caused by the negligence of the independent contractor. Brokers may wish to consider carrying general liability and errors and omission insurance covering their salespersons and office personnel regardless of their contractual and employment relationships with the supervising broker.

Workman's Compensation

Under the California Workman's Compensation Act, a broker may not necessarily be required to carry workers' compensation insurance covering salespersons. However, failure to carry such coverage may result in the broker's liability if a court later concludes that the real relationship between the parties for the purposes at issue was that of employer and employee. The broker will minimize the risks inherent in the uncertainties of the law in this field by carrying workers' compensation insurance.

Social Security and Income Taxes

A similar situation arises under the Federal Insurance Contributions Act and the Internal Revenue Code. A broker may submit to the District Director of Internal Revenue employment agreements and detailed data as to operating methods and obtain a ruling whether the salespersons are considered employees under these laws. The existing exemptions available to real estate brokers have extended primarily to brokerage sales and related services. Real estate brokers who are engaged in a broad list of licensed and nonlicensed activities may wish to review with legal counsel the effect of these activities upon the available exemptions from employer and employee relationships for tax reporting purposes. (26 U.S.C. Section 3508; IRS Rev. Rulings 76-136 and 76-137; and California Attorney General Opinion 59 Ops. A.G. 369)

The consequences of mischaracterizing the relationship in this context are serious. For example, if the IRS rules that the salespersons are employees for income tax reporting purposes, the supervising broker may be liable for income taxes due from the salespersons which should have been withheld by the broker and paid to the IRS. Interest and penalties will typically be added. Supervising brokers should obtain the advice of a CPA and/or qualified tax attorney when establishing policies and procedures in this regard.

Unemployment Insurance
For purposes of maintaining unemployment insurance coverage, the California Unemployment Insurance Act excludes from the definition of employee brokers and salespersons paid solely by commission. (Unemployment Insurance Code Section 650) If the IRS rules in a given fact situation that salespersons are employees of the supervising broker for income tax reporting purposes, EDD is likely to follow the IRS ruling and impose the same relationships.

Personal Income Tax - Additional Information
In recent years, the IRS has challenged the exemption available to real estate licensees under 26 USC Section 3508 when the activities involved are other than general sales brokerage and related services (mortgage brokerage, mortgage banking, and special project brokering such as new subdivision sales). Real estate licensees may still be treated as independent contractors for both federal and state personal income tax purposes, depending upon the fact situation.

This issue has been addressed in part by the Federal Tax Equity and Fiscal Responsibility Act (TEFRA) and amendment of Section 650 and addition of Section 13004.1 to the California Unemployment Insurance Code. Under these laws, real estate licensees functioning on behalf of a supervising real estate broker, in certain fact situations, are and remain exempt from treatment as employees for income tax reporting and other labor-related purposes provided that certain conditions are met.

Section 13004.1 provides that an individual will not be considered an employee for *state income tax purposes* if all of the following conditions are met: (1) the individual is licensed by the Department of Real Estate and is performing brokerage services as a real estate licensee on a commission basis; (2) substantially all remuneration for such services is related directly to sales or other output rather than the number of hours worked; and (3) the real estate services are performed pursuant to a written agreement between the individual and the supervising broker which includes a provision that the individual will not be treated as an employee with respect to those services for state tax reporting purposes. Similar standards apply for establishing independent contractor status for federal income tax purposes.

Again, it is important to understand that the characterization of independent contractor status for state and federal income tax reporting purposes has no effect upon the supervising (individual or corporate) broker's civil or public liability for the conduct or misconduct of salespersons.

Commission and Deposit Disputes
The Real Estate Commissioner has no authority regarding commission disputes between licensees or between a licensee and his/her principal.

A commission dispute between (listing and selling) brokers is a civil matter.

A real estate salesperson (or broker acting in the capacity of a salesperson) involved in a commission dispute with his/her broker may contact the Labor Commissioner. In determining jurisdiction, the Labor Commissioner will consider the salesperson's status as either employee or independent contractor. If the salesperson is an independent contractor, the dispute must be settled in a court of competent jurisdiction or through arbitration.

The Real Estate Commissioner has no authority to determine the proper disposition of a deposit in a failed real estate transaction. The Commissioner does not take the place of a court of law and does not give legal advice.

CONCLUSION

The subjects of agency and fiduciary duty are quite complex. Hopefully, the discussion in this chapter has enchanced the reader's knowledge of the duties and obligations owed to their principals by real estate brokers and their salespersons.

11 IMPACT OF THE PENAL CODE AND OTHER STATUTES

Penal Code

Violations of the Penal Code (PC) are of interest to real estate licensees because such offenses may be committed by clients or by others with whom licensees come into contact. If there is doubt as to whether a transaction involves a crime, a licensee should obtain legal advice.

For the most part, grand (as opposed to petty) theft is committed when the value of the money, labor, or real or personal property taken exceeds four hundred dollars ($400). Theft of certain farm crops, farm animals and real property severed from land is defined as grand theft at values below $400. (PC 484, 487a through 487g, 488)

Some examples of real estate related crimes are:

1. Diversion of construction funds from the intended purpose; use of a false voucher to obtain construction loan funds. (PC 484b, 484c)

2. Copying without permission, and with intent to use, documents owned by a title company. (PC 496c)

3. Removal of a structure from mortgaged real property, or after a foreclosure sale, with intent to defraud or to injure the mortgagee or purchaser. (PC 502.5)

4. Fraudulent appropriating or secreting of trust funds by a broker or other fiduciary. (PC 506)

5. Failure by debtor, upon sale of property covered by a security agreement, to pay to the secured party the amount due under the security agreement (or the proceeds, whichever is less). (PC 504b)

6. Obtaining property from another by a threat to accuse that person or members of his or her family of a crime or to expose their secrets. (PC 518, 519)

7. Making or recording a deed, knowing the maker has no title; being a party to a fraudulent conveyance of land. (PC 531a)

8. Making or procuring a false financial statement to benefit oneself or another person in obtaining credit. (PC 532a)

9. Offering or giving parcels of real property by means of winning numbers at any drawing or with admission tickets, and collecting fees in connection with the land transfer. (PC 532c)

10. Giving a kickback of construction funds. (PC 532e)

11. Selling the same land twice to different persons. (PC 533)

12. Willful concealment by a married person of the necessity for concurrence of a spouse in the sale or mortgaging of land. (PC 534)

13. A broker or agent who "holds out" on a principal, or renders a principal a false accounting, commits a misdemeanor. (PC 536, 536a)

14. Except for posting legal notices, placing advertising signs on public or private property without permission. (PC 556, 556.1, 556.2)

15. Bribing a lender to obtain credit; accepting the bribe. (PC 639, 639a)

16. Signing the name of another person, or of a fictitious person, without authority to do so; falsely making, altering, forging or counterfeiting documents such as leases, deeds or checks; passing such documents as true and genuine, with intent to defraud. (PC 470, 473)

Unlawful Practice of Law

Sections 6125 and 6126 of the California Business and Professions Code prohibit the practice of law by persons who are not members of the State Bar.

In 1943, in *People v. Sipper* (61 CA 2d 844), the California District Court of Appeal stated that the practice of law is the doing and performing of services in a court of justice in any matter pending therein throughout its various stages and in conformity with the adopted rules of procedure. The court recited the larger traditional definition that includes legal advice and counsel and the preparation of legal instruments and contracts by which legal rights are secured, although such matters may not be pending in a court.

In the Sipper case, a married couple had asked the real estate broker "to make out a paper to protect Mrs. Hetman for the money" which they had borrowed from her in order to pay off the indebtedness on their real property. The defendant broker proceeded to prepare a trust deed, and later a mortgage. He charged $15 for his services, later reducing the charge to $10.

The appellate court held that the trial jury was justified in concluding that the defendant broker undertook to, and did, advise his clients as to the kind of legal document that they should execute in order to secure the loan. He made a charge which clearly indicated "...that he considered he was called upon to do something more than the mere clerical work of typing in certain furnished information on a blank form." This was practicing law.

Significantly, the court stated that if the defendant "...had only been called upon to perform and had only undertaken to perform the clerical service of filling in the blanks on a particular form in accordance with information furnished by the parties, or had merely acted as a scrivener to record the stated agreement of the parties to the transaction, he would not have been guilty of practicing law without a license."

In discussing this problem, an authoritative encyclopedia of California law, *California Jurisprudence*, states that, "...an established business custom sanctions the activities of real estate and insurance agents in drawing certain agreements in business transactions in which they take part in their respective professional capacities." The editors then quoted an article by Robert L. Lancefield (29 California Law Review 602) which stated: "While these actions are technically within the usual definition of practice of law, they are generally recognized as proper where:

- the instrument is simple or standardized;

- the draftsman or intermediary does not charge any fee for such work (other than his regular commission for the transaction); and,

* the drafting is incidental to his other activities in the transaction."

Selection and use of a form by the broker may sometimes require a lawyer's help.

Business and Professions Code

The Department of Real Estate publishes the *Real Estate Law*, a book which includes the many Business and Professions Code Sections which regulate real estate licensees.

Civil Code

The Civil Code (CC) proscribes various acts relative to real property sales contracts. A real property sales contract (sometimes called a contract of sale or a land installment contract) is defined as an agreement to convey title to land upon satisfaction of specified conditions set forth in the contract and which does not require conveyance within one year of formation of the contract.

Some examples of violations involving contracts of sale are:

1. Without the buyer's consent, the seller under an unrecorded contract of sale encumbers the land in an amount exceeding the present contract balance. (CC 2985.2)

b. While there is a payment due an obligation secured by the land, a seller under a contract of sale appropriates a payment received from the buyer to any purpose except payment on that obligation. This does not apply to any difference between the payment received by the seller and the amount due on the seller's obligation. (CC 2985.3)

c. Failure by the seller under a contract of sale to apply to those purposes pro rata tax and insurance payments received from the buyer. (CC 2985.4)

(The Department of Real Estate's *Real Estate Law* book includes these and other Civil Code sections which are of interest to real estate licensees.)

Corporations Code

Some of the activities which constitute crimes under the Corporations Code relate to the sale of securities. A conspiracy to violate the California Corporate Securities Act is a crime. (PC 182; Corporations Code Section 25540)

The sale of fractionalized interests in promissory notes secured by deeds of trust may result in the sale of corporate securities subject to qualification or exemption with the California Department of Corporations. Without such qualification or exemption, the sales are illegal and the broker or offeror could be convicted of a crime.

12 Real Estate Finance

BACKGROUND

Finance is the lifeblood of the real estate industry. Developers, contractors, real estate brokers (REBs) and mortgage loan brokers (MLBs) must understand how real estate is financed.

Traditional sources of loan funds are the depository institutions: savings and loan associations, savings banks, commercial banks, thrift and loans, and credit unions. Other sources are insurance companies and non-institutional sources such as mortgage bankers, finance lenders, MLBs, private individuals, pension funds, mortgage trusts, investment trusts and securitized pools of mortgage loans.

Recent California legislation has characterized certain non-depository institutions as institutional lenders for defined purposes. These include: mortgage bankers, finance lenders, pension funds in excess of $15,000,000 in assets, mortgage trusts, investment trusts and securitized pools of mortgage loans which have either been qualified or registered for intra- and/or interstate issuance of public offerings, or which have met qualified exemption statutes and rules for issuance as private placements.

The secondary mortgage market (investors purchasing real estate loans originated by other lenders) has surpassed loan sources which dominated real estate lending prior to the 1990s. The significant financial collapse and consolidation of the savings and loan industry has contributed to this change. In the early 1980s, there were approximately 4,022 savings and loans in the United States. As of 1994 approximately 1,535 were left, with only a few being regulated by the State of California.

Before Deregulation

Partially because of the unstable market forces prevailing over the last 25 to 30 years, institutional financial intermediaries/lenders such as savings and loan associations, savings banks, commercial banks, credit unions, and thrift and loans experienced reductions in profitability. Unregulated non-depository institutions (e.g., uninsured money market funds) drew savings deposits away from regulated depository institutions by paying investors higher rates of interest.

During the late 1970's, many institutional lenders were holding low-interest loan portfolios which steadily declined in value. At the same time, they were unable to make enough higher-interest loans to achieve acceptable profit levels. This happened in part because of the decline in personal savings, appreciating property values, and increasing interest rates. Many potential home buyers could not qualify for higher-rate loans and/or were unable to make required down payments.

Across the country, forced postponements of home ownership occurred except for transactions involving transferable first loans and seller-assisted financing. Subdividers and builders cut production. In late 1980 the prime interest rate reached 21.5%. On September 14, 1981, the interest rate for FHA and VA single-family home loans reached 17.5%. Tight money, stringent credit underwriting, and high interest rates made mortgage money scarce and expensive. Potential private and government sector borrowers were forced to bid for available loan funds.

Deregulation

The foregoing led to a period of deregulation, the process whereby regulatory restraints upon the financial services industry are reduced or removed. Deregulation has extended to California law and leveled the playing field for California licensed and chartered lenders.

Significant deregulation commenced with the Depository Institutions Deregulation and Monetary Control Act of 1980 and continued through the Depository Institutions Act of 1982, also known as the Garn - St. Germain Act.

Re-regulation

Re-regulation occurred as a result of substantial losses in the savings and loan industry. Re-regulation began with the Financial Institutions Reform, Recovery and Enforcement Act of 1989 (FIRREA) and continued with a significant number of amendments to both the Real Estate Settlement Procedures Act (RESPA) and the Consumer Credit Act, also known as the Truth in Lending Act (TILA).

FIRREA was designed to "bail out" the savings and loan industry and re-regulate federal financial institutions.

More Deregulation

More recently, Congress has returned to deregulation. An example is the Financial Institutions Regulatory Relief Act (FIRRA), also known as the Paper Reduction Act of 1996. FIRRA has terminated the Savings Association Insurance Fund (SAIF) and transferred insurance of those deposits to the Bankers Insurance Fund (BIF). The BIF operates under the Federal Deposit Insurance Corporation (FDIC).

With deregulation, the differences once separating the products, services, and purposes of savings and loans and commercial banks have been for the most part eliminated. Savings institutions now compete for business and profits with few government restrictions. Some experts in the financial world believe that depository institutions which survive this competition will be larger, more diverse, and more efficient than the lending institutions of the past.

Credit unions have been merging so that some have hundreds of millions of dollars in assets. Currently, approximately 7,244 credit unions control 205 billion in assets, 181 billion in deposits, and 120 billion in loans. (Commercial banks control 4.4 trillion in assets, 3.1 trillion in deposits, and 2.7 trillion in loans.)

California law

Among recent changes at the California State level has been consolidation of the licensing of finance lenders, effective July 1, 1995, into the California Finance Lenders Law. A single license, the California Finance Lender (CFL) has replaced three licenses: personal property brokers, consumer finance lenders, and commercial finance lenders.

In addition, in 1996, the California Legislature created a new license category for mortgage bankers either originating or servicing loans in this state. The new licensees are known as residential mortgage lenders (RMLs). Several hundred firms are now licensed under this law. CFLs and RMLs are licensed and regulated by the Department of Corporations (DOC).

Some mortgage bankers are still licensed as REBs and continue to operate their non-residential commercial business under the regulation of the Department of Real Estate. MLBs now deliver to lenders approximately 50% of the real estate loans secured by one to four residential units.

In 1996, the California Legislature passed legislation consolidating regulation of depository institutions into a new Department of Financial Institutions. This department replaces the Department of Banking and the (former) Department of Savings and Loans and will acquire from the Department of Corporations regulatory oversight of both state-chartered thrift and loans and credit unions.

California industrial loan companies, known as state thrift and loans, have also experienced significant restructuring. These institutions were legislatively required to switch from a California-based insurance fund to the FDIC. With this switch has come more regulatory oversight including stricter loan underwriting guidelines. Diminished profits followed the restructuring and the result has been the merger of many of these institutions into larger institutions which are able to function within the current regulatory climate and competitive market of the 1990s.

Redesigned Mortgage Instruments
Unstable economic conditions caused national and California legislators, consumers, lenders, and real estate industry representatives to explore a whole catalog of issues having to do with making alternative mortgage instruments available to home purchasers.

In 1970, legislation was passed and regulations adopted in California authorizing variable-rate mortgages (VRMs). The interest rate of a VRM changes with increases or decreases in a published index.

In 1980, State legislation authorized renegotiable rate mortgages (RRMs) in which the borrower has an option to either prepay or renew the residential loan at three or five year intervals. Generally, renewal of the loan is subject to renegotiation of the interest rate. The lender must offer a fixed-rate mortgage as an option to the RRM.

The California Legislature authorized adjustable rate mortgages (ARMs) in 1981, allowing for the interest rate to adjust periodically, by a set margin, to a certain index. Again, a lender was required to also offer a fixed-rate mortgage when offering an ARM.

Basically, adjustable mortgages result in borrowers contributing extra amounts to lenders' inflow of funds during periods of tight money and high interest rates.

The Fixed-Rate Mortgage
The use of alternative financing instruments, also authorized under preemptive federal law, constituted a major change in the traditional lender-borrower relationship in that the risk of changes in the market rate of interest was shifted from the lender to the borrower. However, marketplace competition, including FHA and VA loans, has resulted in continued availability of fully amortized, long-term, fixed-rate mortgages.

A Forward Look

Deregulation and the proliferation of alternative mortgage plans have been largely responsible for the restructuring of our housing finance system.

As always, the most important issue facing both mortgage lenders and borrowers is the availability and affordability of mortgage funds.

As legislators, lenders, and consumers address complex challenges and opportunities, more changes will occur in the lending process, including electronic loan origination.

The increased involvement of RMLs, CFLs, and MLBs in residential loan origination's is likely to continue. What remains to be seen is how much more consolidation will occur among these licensees, and if not consolidation, how many of these licensees will affiliate horizontally into what are now known as Affiliated Business Arrangements (ABAs).

THE ECONOMY

America's economic system is a regulated capitalistic system. Although individuals, partnerships and corporations own and control property and the means of production of goods and services, the government intervenes and influences general economic trends in an attempt to ensure reasonable competition and a viable, growing, fair and equitable economy.

Role of Real Estate in the National Economy
Real estate plays four major roles in our economy:

Net worth. Land and improvements make up a very large portion of the total net worth of the United States.

Income flow. As we see on the circular flow chart of our economy (next page), money is paid for the use of real estate (rent) and for the raw materials, labor, capital and management used in construction work of all kinds.

Major employer. The real estate industry (brokerage, construction, management, finance, etc.) is a major employer.

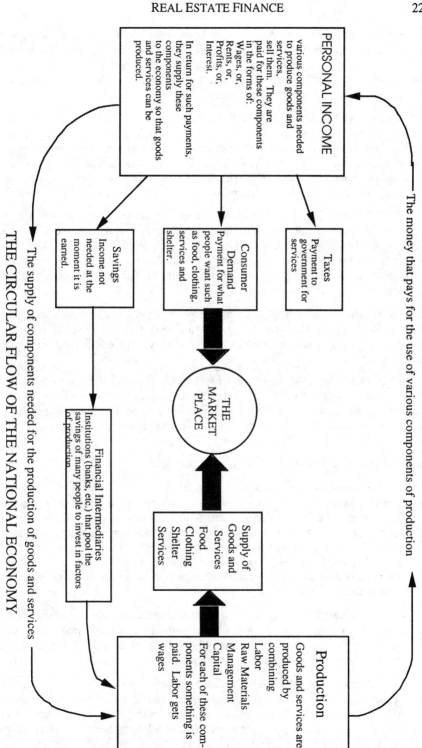

THE CIRCULAR FLOW OF THE NATIONAL ECONOMY

PERSONAL INCOME

various components needed to produce goods and services, sell them. They are paid for these components in the forms of: Wages, or, Rents, or, Profits, or, Interest.

In return for such payments, they supply these components to the economy so that goods and services can be produced.

Taxes
Payment to government for services

Consumer Demand
Payment for what people want such as food, clothing, services and shelter.

Savings
Income not needed at the moment it is earned.

Financial Intermediaries
Institutions (banks, etc.) that pool the savings of many people to invest in factors of production.

THE MARKET PLACE

Supply of Goods and Services
Food
Clothing
Shelter
Services

Production
Goods and services are produced by combining
Labor
Raw Materials
Management
Capital
For each of these components something is paid. Labor gets wages

The money that pays for the use of various components of production

The supply of components needed for the production of goods and services

Appreciation and inflation. After having been in decline for much of the 1990s, residential real estate values are stabilizing and in many markets increasing. Income producing properties began to decline following the Tax Reform Act of 1986. Depending upon the area, values fell between 25% and 50% from their peak. Income producing properties are also again increasing in value.

Federal Reserve Bank System. The Federal Reserve Bank System (the Fed) is the nation's central bank. Its chief responsibility is to regulate the flow of money and credit to promote economic growth with stability. The goal is a monetary policy which encourages high employment, stable price levels and a satisfactory international balance of payments. This monetary policy attempts to counteract inflation, recession or any other undesirable shift in the economy.

The Fed's Board of Governors formulates monetary policy and shares responsibility for its application with the 12 Federal Reserve Banks. The governors are appointed by the President of the United States and confirmed by the Senate for 14-year terms, the long terms being intended to insulate the governors from outside pressures. The Chairman and Vice Chairman of the Fed are appointed by the President for four-year terms.

Monitoring the money supply. To avoid the peaks and valleys and "boom or bust" business cycles that spawn liquidity and credit crises, the Fed monitors economic conditions and controls the supply of money and credit. This is a delicate balancing act.

If The Fed makes too little credit available, borrowers may bid against each other for available funds and drive up the cost of borrowing. People then buy and borrow less, investments and sales decline, and a recession may follow. On the other hand, too much available credit translates into over stimulation of the economy and invites inflation.

To accomplish its goals, the Fed uses three basic tools:

- **Reserve requirements.** Member banks must set aside and keep as reserves a certain percentage of each deposit. By raising or lowering this reserve requirement, the Fed increases or decreases the amount of money in circulation. An increase in reserve requirements means banks have less money to lend, interest rates will likely increase, and borrowing and spending will slow. Conversely, a lessening of the reserve requirement increases lending funds and should lead to lower interest rates. Borrowing and spending can then be expected to increase.

- **Discount rates.** The discount rate is the interest rate the Fed charges on money it lends to a member bank. A decrease in the discount rate may encourage bank borrowing, increasing deposits which the bank may loan to businesses and consumers. An increase in the discount rate will have the opposite effect.

- **Open market operations.** The Fed also uses open market operations (buying and selling of government securities) to influence the amount of available credit. When the Fed buys government securities, cash is deposited into sellers' bank accounts, increasing reserves and allowing banks to extend more credit to borrowers. If the Fed sells securities, the opposite effect occurs.

Office of Thrift Supervision (OTS). Created pursuant to the restructuring required by FIRREA, the OTS regulates federally chartered savings and loans.

[FIRREA also reorganized the Federal Deposit Insurance Corporation (FDIC) into four offices and two subagencies. The four offices are the Deposit Insurance Fund (DIF), the OTS, the Resolution Trust Corporation (RTC), and the Resolution Funding Corporation (RFC). Under DIF are two insurance funds: the Bank Insurance Fund (BIF) and the Savings Association Insurance Fund (SAIF). These two funds are to be combined pursuant to the Financial Institutions Regulatory Reform Act of 1996.]

THE MORTGAGE MARKET

Money serves as a medium of exchange. The potential to exchange money for goods and services can be stored. This is called savings. Savings are the primary source of funds for lending.

If the value of money is relatively stable, people are more inclined to save, since their stored capacity to exchange (with interest) is not being eroded by inflation.

Credit
"Credo" is a Latin word which means "I believe." A lender loans money believing that it will be paid back as agreed. Therefore, the lender grants, or extends, "credit."

Supply and Demand
The supply of capital is finite. Real estate borrowers must always compete with government, business, and other consumers for available funds. If mortgage money is in short supply, mortgage interest rates rise. One cause is placement of potential mortgage money in other markets which are paying higher interest rates.

Government Intervention Can Redirect Supply
Between late 1989 and the middle 1990s, a "credit crunch" occurred in a portion of the real estate market primarily because the federal government, through re-regulation and capital reserve requirements imposed under FIRREA, redirected mortgage lending by financial institutions.

The capital reserves then required for residential mortgage loans secured by one-to-four residential units were from 2% to 4%, depending primarily on whether or not the loan was insured or guaranteed by a federal agency. The reserve requirements for income-producing properties jumped to as much as 8%.

Accordingly, lenders rushed to make residential loans and avoided loans secured by commercial, industrial, and residential income properties. The flow of capital to residential mortgages helped cause "refinance mania" during the early and mid-1990s.

The Primary Mortgage Market
The Primary Mortgage Market consists of savings and loan associations, banks, other institutions and mortgage bankers that originate mortgage loans by lending funds directly to borrowers.

Participants in the Primary Mortgage Market replenish their funds by selling loans in the Secondary Mortgage Market.

Federal Housing Administration (FHA). This agency insures loans made by approved lenders. See discussion in Chapter 13.

Veterans Administration. This agency guarantees loans made to veterans for housing, farms or businesses. See discussion in Chapter 13.

Department of Veterans Affairs. This agency assists qualified California veterans with the purchase of housing and farms. See discussion in Chapter 13.

Mortgage bankers. Mortgage bankers are privately owned companies that are often affiliated with banks or savings and loans. Mortgage bankers generally originate conventional (including "subprime") or FHA/VA loans.

In California, mortgage bankers are typically licensed as either Residential Mortgage Lenders (RMLs) or California Finance Lenders (CFLs). Some remain licensed as real estate brokers (REBs); however, the real estate broker's license is oriented toward the status of an agent arranging a loan on behalf of another or others, and not the status of a lender making a loan.

Mortgage bankers may continue to service loans they have sold, sell the servicing to purchasers of loans, or sell the servicing separately.

The Secondary Mortgage Market
Participants in the Secondary Mortgage Market buy loans originated in the Primary Mortgage Market and also buy and sell among themselves.

Two types of purchases normally occur in the Secondary Mortgage Market:

• the purchase of individual mortgages; and

• the purchase of (securitized) blocks or pools of loans.

Federal National Mortgage Association (FNMA-Fannie Mae). Fannie Mae provides a secondary market for FHA and VA loans and, since the early 1970s, conventional mortgages originated by approved lenders.

Fannie Mae's sources of funds are: borrowing; selling long-term notes, mortgage-backed securities (MBS) and debentures in the capital markets; issuing and selling its own common stock; and earnings from its mortgage portfolio, including fees.

Fannie Mae purchases graduated payment mortgages (GPMs), conventional fixed-rate first and qualifying second mortgages secured by one-to-four family homes, and a variety of ARMs. Fannie Mae also has a resale/refinance plan whereby lenders offer borrowers blended below-market interest rates or new loans at competitive interest rates.

FNMA's mortgage-backed securities (MBS) plan involves a lender selling a block or pool of mortgages in exchange for a like amount of securities which represent undivided interests in that pool of loans and may be sold or retained by the lender. FNMA provides 100% guaranty of full and timely payment of interest and principal to the security holder.

While FNMA is the largest investor in the secondary market, it delegates most underwriting and servicing responsibilities to approved sellers/servicers.

FNMA has played a major role in development of standardized loan origination documents, including the 1003 loan application form, promissory notes and deeds of trust and the uniform residential appraisal report.

Fannie Mae has a 15-member board of directors, 10 elected by shareholders and 5 appointed by the President of the United States.

Government National Mortgage Association (GNMA-Ginnie Mae). Ginnie Mae is a government corporation which administers mortgage support programs which could not be carried out in the private market place. Ginnie Mae increases liquidity in the secondary mortgage market and attracts new sources of funds for residential loans. Ginnie Mae does not purchase mortgages. Rather, it adds its guarantee to mortgage-backed securities issued by approved lenders. GNMA's three major activities are:

- Mortgage-Backed Securities (MBS) Program;

- Special Assistance Functions; and

- Management and Liquidation Functions.

Through the MBS Program, GNMA guarantees securities issued by financial intermediaries and backed by pools of mortgages. Mortgage bankers, savings institutions, commercial banks and other approved types of financial intermediaries are all issuers of securities. Security holders receive a pass through of principal and interest payments on the pool of mortgages, less amounts to cover servicing costs and certain GNMA fees. Ginnie Mae guarantees that the securities holders will receive payments of principal and interest as scheduled, as well as unscheduled recoveries of principal. Because of the Federal guaranty (pledge of full faith and credit of the U.S. Government), GNMA mortgage-backed securities are considered by many to be as safe, as liquid, and as easy to hold as Treasury securities.

The MBS programs of FNMA and GNMA have benefited all regions of the country by increasing the flow of funds from the securities market to the residential mortgage market and from capital-surplus to capital-short geographical areas.

Under the Special Assistance Functions, GNMA purchases certain types of mortgages to provide support for low-income housing and to counter declines in mortgage lending and housing construction.

Under the Management and Liquidation Functions, GNMA manages and liquidates (sells) portfolios of federally-owned mortgages.

The President of the United States appoints the President of GNMA, who acts under the direction of the Secretary of the Department of Housing and Urban Development (HUD).

Federal Home Loan Mortgage Corporation (FHLMC - Freddie Mac - or, The Mortgage Corporation). FHLMC increases the availability of mortgage credit for the financing of urgently needed housing by developing, expanding and maintaining a nationwide secondary market primarily for conventional loans originated by savings and loans, thrift institutions, commercial banks, mortgage bankers and other HUD-approved mortgagees.

Freddie Mac finances most of its mortgage purchases through the sale of mortgage Participation Certificates (PCs).

Through its Standard Programs, Freddie Mac buys:

• whole loans and participation interests in conventional l-to-4 family loans with both fixed and adjustable rates;

• home improvement loans; and

• multifamily whole loans and participation interests.

The mortgages purchased in the Standard Programs are generally less than one year old. FHLMC underwrites the loans delivered under its purchase commitments, and typically rejects only a small percentage of the loans submitted. Mortgages with loan-to-value ratios above 80 percent generally must carry private mortgage insurance.

Freddie Mac's Guarantor or "Swap" Program gives primary mortgage lenders an added source of liquidity during periods when the yield on mortgage portfolios of predominantly older loans is lower than the cost of funds for many lenders. Lenders may thus convert a low yield portfolio into highly liquid securities which can be sold or used as collateral for borrowing.

FHLMC is an independent stock company and functions in direct competition with FNMA.

Freddie Mac has an 18-member board of directors, 13 of whom are elected by FHLMC's stockholders; 5 are appointed by the President of the United States.

The "Subprime" Secondary Market
Securitization of mortgages into pools underwritten by Wall Street investment bankers has accelerated in recent years. These securitized pools are made up of mortgages known in the industry as "subprime." "Subprime" loans are those that will not qualify for sale to FNMA or FHLMC and cannot be securitized into a pool guaranteed by GNMA. Much of the growth is in low down payment mortgages made to home buyers who have poor credit. Conventional lenders, who traditionally ignored these borrowers, are now participating in the "subprime" residential mortgage market and benefiting from the higher interest rates involved.

Private Mortgage Insurance
Private Mortgage Insurance Companies (MICs) provide mortgage insurance for conventional loans, making these loans perhaps more attractive in the Secondary Mortgage Market. Private mortgage insurance enables borrowers to obtain loans with higher loan-to-value ratios and purchase better homes with smaller down payments. Mortgage insurance reduces the risk to the lender and to the investor.

MICs have underwriting standards which conventional lenders must meet so that investors will purchase the loans. A MIC may buy the insured loans and issue securities in the name of the MIC or a subsidiary.

MICs may also provide servicing of loans sold in the secondary market.

California and the Mortgage Market

The following characteristics make California attractive to suppliers of mortgage money from all over the world:

1. High demand for mortgage money.

2. A large, and usually growing, population.

3. Wide diversification of industry.

4. Generally high employment and prosperity.

5. Large financial depository institutions.

6. Presence of experienced and highly efficient mortgage loan correspondents (mortgage bankers).

7. Common usage of title insurance and escrow rather than settlement.

8. Predominant use of trust deeds with power of sale rather than mortgages as a legal basis to secure real estate loans.

9. The existence of financial institutions and sophisticated licensed lenders which will package mortgages together for sale with a guaranteed rate of return and no servicing problems to the institutional investor or government enterprise.

OVERVIEW OF THE LOAN PROCESS

There are four steps to obtaining a real estate loan:

- application

- analysis

- processing

- closing

The application. Historically, application forms varied from lender to lender. Now, however, a "standard" form for residential mortgage loan applications is commonly used: the FHLMC/FNMA 1003. Even FHA and VA use this form.

A loan application package consists of:

- the loan request;

- borrower information;

- property or collateral information;

- credit analysis;

- lender's action (approval or disapproval); and

- processing check list.

The loan request. This is a written request by the prospective borrower giving the borrower's name, setting forth the amount and terms of the requested loan, the purpose of the loan, and how and when it will be repaid.

The federal Equal Credit Opportunity Act prohibits discrimination based on age, sex, race, marital status, color, religion or national origin. Senior citizens, young adults and single persons must be considered in light of income adequacy, satisfactory net worth, job stability and satisfactory credit rating, and credit guidelines are to be applied to each potential borrower in the same manner.

Borrower information. The following information helps the lender gauge the borrower's ability and willingness to repay the loan:

1. Purpose of the loan (home purchase, investment, refinance).

2. Type and duration of employment. If under 2 years, or type of employment appears unstable, further investigation is usually needed.

3. Other income: e.g., rents, annuities, royalties, etc.? How much? (Other sources of income are often not fully counted because they are usually less stable than full-time jobs.) Does spouse work? There can be no discrimination against income of spouse.

4. How many dependents must be supported by the borrower and for how long? Children help stabilize a borrower in one way but also add considerably to financial obligations.

5. What are the borrower's living expenses? How much of gross income is available for loan payments, taxes and insurance? How much are borrower's other installment payments and liabilities?

6. What happens to the loan in the event the borrower becomes disabled or dies? Is there sufficient insurance?

7. What previous experience has the lender had with borrower?

8. What is applicant's debt repayment record? What kind of credit and other references does the borrower have? Many lenders rely heavily on the findings of credit reporting services. Telephone check-ups made by the lender to other creditors of the prospective borrower can be revealing.

9. Type, location, value, encumbrances and repayment schedules for other real property applicant owns.

10 Borrower's other assets: bank and savings accounts, personal property, etc.

Property information. The property may have to function for quite some time as security for the loan. For this reason the lender is very much interested in the trend of the collateral's value and not just its status today.

This section will elicit the following information:

1. Specific identification of the property, including legal description and street address.

2. Title information: vesting, claims, encumbrances, liens, mortgages, etc.

3. Description of land and type of improvements, including work done within the last 90 days that might be subject to Mechanics' Liens.

4. Original price and terms; date purchased; taxes; zoning; assessments. If income property, operating income and expenses for several years and amount of income which will be available to support loan repayment.

5. Present value, trends, etc. (The appraisal is usually made after interview with borrower.)

Credit analysis. The lender will gauge the ability and willingness of the borrower to repay the loan based on:

- information contained in the application and supporting documents;

- information developed by the lender in checking the credit and character of the prospective borrower;

- verification of employment, bank deposits, etc.; and

- a personal interview.

Lender's action. Typically, approval or disapproval of the loan.

Processing check list. After loan approval, the lender will use a check list of steps and documentation necessary to close the loan.

DETAILS OF THE LOAN PROCESS

Processing the application. The prospective borrower should complete the application accurately and entirely to avoid needless delays and facilitate processing and closing.

With the completed application, the lender begins to process the loan.

Interview. Some lenders and government agencies deem necessary an initial interview with the prospective borrower. Some lenders interview the borrower by telephone or electronically. Telephonic and electronic interviews are particularly useful with borrowers who qualify for the "prime" or "A" residential mortgage market. Borrowers who are able to qualify only for the "subprime" or "A through C" or "B & C" mortgage market often require a face-to-face interview. Personal interviews with the borrower are important for the following reasons:

- Ensure accuracy of the application and enable the loan officer to make a personal assessment of the borrower and bring into play long experience as a judge of people.

- Help the loan officer evaluate the loan proposal and make certain the applicant understands the terms of the loan as proposed. Is it a sound loan for the borrower to carry? If it is not sound for the borrower it is not sound for the lender.

- Learn more about the property that will secure the loan. This information may be helpful to the appraiser in the appraisal function.

- Discuss loan costs. Often a prospective borrower is unaware of the various costs (notary, recording and legal fees, title, credit and appraisal reports, insurance) involved in obtaining a loan. (Under the Real Estate Settlement Procedures Act (RESPA), which is applicable to most federally-related mortgage loans to be secured by 1-to-4 residential units, good faith loan cost estimates and a special information booklet must be furnished the applicant within 3 business days of the loan application. Some lenders and brokers prefer to deliver the disclosures and booklet at the time of the loan application.)

Appraisal report. A staff or independent appraiser evaluates the property and estimates present market value and the value trend. The relationship between the amount of the proposed loan and the estimate of fair market value of the property is the "loan-to-value" ratio. Most lenders base their loans on price or value, whichever is lower.

Credit analysis. A lender will use a standard of ability to repay. Some lenders require that the applicant's fixed monthly expenses not exceed 30-35 percent of net monthly income. Other lenders use a ratio (e.g., 4 to 1) of the borrower's gross income to the proposed monthly loan payment.

An FHA lender will require gross monthly income, less long-term monthly debt payments, of 3-1/2 to 4 times the monthly mortgage payment (including impounds).

Lenders in the "prime" mortgage market generally prefer that not more than 25% to 28% of an applicant's gross income be spent for housing.

For income property, an insurance company may require that 50 percent of the gross income of the property be sufficient to pay the mortgage payments and real estate taxes.

Some institutions use Gross Annual Income Multipliers: i.e., the price of a property should not exceed 2-1/2 (or 3 or 4) times the borrower's annual gross income from salary. Again, such a ratio would be used in the "prime" mortgage market.

The issue of *willingness* to pay is also crucial to credit analysis. The lender will check the prospective borrower's department store charge accounts, oil company charge accounts, and other suppliers of credit to determine if the borrower pays bills on time.

Automated underwriting, where credit is granted almost as soon as the application is received, requires instant credit analysis. To this end, lenders use computer-generated credit scores as mathematical representations of an applicant's credit standing.

Numerous credit reporting agencies exist. However, these agencies or bureaus obtain their information from three sources: TRW, Trans Union, and Equifax. Each source has its own name for the credit scores it issues. Equifax calls its score a Beacon and Trans Union calls it an Empirica Score. TRW uses the name FICO Score. (FICO is an acronym for Fair, Isaac and Company.)

Loan committee. Some lenders operate with a Loan Committee of experienced senior officers who consider loan applications recommended to them by loan officers who have screened the applications with borrower interviews, appraisal reports, and credit analyses.

If the committee approves a loan application, the file then goes to the Loan Funding Department.

Closing the loan. The mechanics of closing will vary. For the sale of a residence, an escrow holder is usually handling a sale transaction between seller and buyer and a loan transaction between lender and buyer/borrower. During escrow, the escrow holder will typically furnish the lender with a certified copy of the signed sale escrow instructions, together with any amendments thereto, and other documents the lender requires. These may include:

1. Preliminary Report showing condition of the title, claims against the title, conditions, covenants, restrictions, encumbrances, etc.

2. Appraisal report estimating the market value of the property for loan underwriting purposes.

3. Survey, if applicable, showing the exact location of the property.

4. Soils report, If obtained, showing the condition of the soil and sub-soil, topography, flood and slide hazards, etc.

5. Payoff Demand showing the exact amount due if an existing loan is to be paid off. If an existing loan is to remain, a Beneficiary Statement is needed to verify existing loan terms, etc.

6. Tax report showing the exact amount of taxes due as of escrow closing date, to determine proration.

7. Insurance report for proration and insurance coverage purposes, including proper endorsements.

8. For income property, a statement showing rent paid in advance, security deposit, etc.; again, for proration purposes.

9. Contractors report and contract for new construction, showing cost breakdown, building plans and specifications, etc.

10. Geologic Hazard Report showing any known geologic or seismic hazards which affect the property.

11. Structural pest control, roofing, electrical, foundation, or generalist reports describing the condition of the property improvements.

12. Loan documents and disclosures and notices of rights, including the note and deed of trust, any riders or addenda thereto, any separate agreements between the lender and the borrower, lender's escrow instructions, disclosures and notices of rights required to be made or given by lenders or brokers.

The escrow holder then awaits confirmation that the lender is ready to fund the loan.

Recordation. When all instructions have been complied with, the lender places the loan funds in escrow. The escrow holder disburses funds as required and records the appropriate documents in the county recorder's office.

FEDERAL AND STATE DISCLOSURE AND NOTICE OF RIGHTS

Various federal and state disclosure laws and regulations apply to lenders who make, and brokers who arrange, real estate loans, especially when the securing property is 1 to 4 residential units.

Most notable of these laws and regulations are:

- the federal Consumer Credit Act also known as the Truth In Lending Act (TILA), implemented by Regulation Z;

- the Federal Real Estate Settlement Procedures Act (RESPA), implemented by Regulation X; and

- the state mortgage disclosure law known as Article 7 of the Business Professions Code, implemented by Title 10, Chapter 6, Section 2840, et seq. of California Code of Regulations.

Chapter 15 includes discussions of TILA and Article 7.

Real Estate Settlement Procedures Act (RESPA) Regulation X

RESPA, enforced by HUD, requires that borrowers, buyers and sellers receive closing cost information (estimates of fees, costs and commissions) for federally related loans used to purchase or refinance real property improved with one to four residential units, provided the property includes the principal residence of the buyer/borrower. An exemption exists for a loan secured by residential property of twenty-five or more acres.

A residential loan is "federally related" if made by a federal depository institution, a HUD-approved mortgagee, or a person who annually makes a million dollars or more in mortgage loans secured by real property improved with one to four residential units.

RESPA requires that a Good Faith Estimate (GFE) of loan costs, etc. be given to the borrower at the time of loan application or within three business days of the originating broker's or lender's receipt of the application. RESPA also requires the HUD-1 or HUD-1a closing statement be made available to the borrower at least one day before closing. RESPA imposes limitations on the payment of unauthorized referral fees (kickbacks) and regulates how affiliated entities may refer business/transactions to each other when those activities are subject to RESPA.

Computerized Loan Origination (CLO). Prior to June 7, 1996, real estate brokers benefited from an exemption permitting them to charge fees for limited borrower services: pre-qualifying, counseling, and matching available loan products to borrower qualifications and needs. The CLO had to meet certain federal standards and be accompanied by delivery of an advance notice describing the intended services and fees. If the standards were met, the broker was able to charge a negotiated fee, without direct regard to its relationship to the services provided. If the standards were not met, the fees charged by the broker were required to be reasonably related to the services provided. (Because of the fiduciary duty owed by a real estate broker to the borrower, this distinction was irrelevant under California law.)

HUD has withdrawn from CLOs both the required notice and the qualified exemption for payment of compensation to brokers. This change will likely eliminate the use of limited service CLOs.

Affiliated Business Arrangements. Affiliated Business Arrangements (ABAs or AFBAs), formerly called Controlled Business Arrangements, occur when affiliated service providers refer borrowers to each other in transactions subject to RESPA. ABAs include entities with a defined percentage of common ownership. This common ownership may be held by shareholders or by an entity common to both (e.g., a holding company). This may also apply to associated relationships where one entity exercises control over, or shares control with, the other (i.e., by joint venture, partnership or, in certain fact situations, a common business plan). If one service provider benefits financially by referring borrowers to another service provider, the cautious approach is to assume that the referral is subject to ABA disclosures.

Unless the affiliated entities or associated relationships are structured pursuant to an acceptable division of labor or services agreement, the ABA must function through a separate entity which may not be a division of either of the affiliated parties. HUD has required adequately capitalized separate entities to be either corporations or partnerships. The preferred option is that of a corporation. The separate entity must accept its own business risk, be licensed if required, and have, among other attributes, its own facilities and employees.

A component of an ABA, whether a separate entity or structured pursuant to an acceptable division of labor agreement, may be paid for performing compensable loan services when engaged in loan originations. HUD has made it clear that *sham* entities will not be recognized. They will be treated as a *ploy* for avoiding the unauthorized payment of referral fees.

When a face-to-face interview occurs with the borrower or when written or electronic referral is made to the borrower, the ABA disclosure must be delivered to the borrower at or before the time of the referral and the lender must keep a record of the delivery. After a face-to-face interview, the lender must attempt to obtain a written receipt from the borrower for the ABA disclosure. If the borrower refuses to sign the receipt, the lender must note the refusal in the business records.

If an ABA referral is made telephonically, the substance of the ABA disclosure must be given during the conversation, together with an explanation that a written disclosure will follow within three business days of the conversation. A record of the telephone discussion and mailing of the ABA disclosure must be included in the lender's records. Finally, if a referral is made by a lender to an affiliated lender, the ABA disclosure may be delivered to the borrower no later than the settlement booklet is delivered. Again, the lender should retain a record of this delivery.

HUD authority for cooperative agreements. In February 1995, HUD responded by letter to an inquiry from the Independent Banker's Association of American (IBAA) regarding agreements dividing loan origination services/compensation between IBAA members and other service providers. HUD provided an opinion letter which allowed division of labor or service agreements between service providers in certain fact situations. Before this letter, HUD generally refused to recognize any cooperative loan brokerage agreements in loan transactions subject to RESPA. Brokers may now share the performance of compensable services when originating RESPA loans.

A written agreement is necessary between brokers, describing the services each will perform. Each broker must perform at least six identifiable functions (or 5 plus the loan application for the broker representing the borrower). The division of compensation among cooperating brokers must be reasonably related to the services each performs. Likewise, agreements between brokers and lenders to share origination functions must be based upon performance by the brokers of compensable services for fees which are reasonably related to the services provided. Such agreements will not work between real estate and mortgage brokers, or between real estate brokers and lenders, if the loan transactions are FHA insured.

Bona fide HUD employee exemptions. In 1997 HUD modified the limitations imposed on payment of referral fees or fee-splitting in RESPA loan transactions. The modifications apply to payments which are made by employers to bona fide employees, (recipients of W-2 tax forms). The employer/employee relationship must be neither a *sham* nor established on a temporary basis to *circumvent* the intent of the regulation. HUD has outlined the following general exemptions for payments made by employers to bona fide employees:

- Payments for generating business for the employer, or for providing services in the loan origination process.

- Payments to marketing employees and managerial employees (employees not providing services) for referrals to the employer or another provider within an ABA. (The latter must include an ABA notice.)

- Payments to managerial employees based upon criteria relating to performance, as long as the payments are not on a per loan basis.

Independent contractor limitations. Independent contractor relationships are not subject to the same exemptions. Accordingly, loan representatives who are independent contractors of a mortgage firm must perform compensable loan services to be compensated in RESPA loan transactions. The compensation paid to independent contractors must be reasonably related to the services they provide and should be evidenced by a division of labor agreement between the mortgage firm and its independent contractors.

Loan Servicing
Whether the loan servicing function is an independent operation or part of the lender's overall organization, the service operation must strive to assure the lender the expected yield on the investment, protect the investment from loss, and provide good and prompt service.

A servicing operation should have a written agreement with its principal, including the servicer's responsibilities and compensation. This is true even if the servicing operation is part of the lender's organization. The agreement may discuss collections, forwarding of payments, late charges, defaults, foreclosures, insurance, etc. In certain situations, including servicing under a real estate broker's license, a written agreement is required by law.

Monthly collections. A major problem in loan servicing is the flood of payments arriving during the first ten days of each month. Two possible solutions are:

- computerized processing of loan payments;

- staggering loan payment schedules so that some payments are due on the first or 10th of the month, while others are due on the 15th or 20th, etc.

Delinquencies. Loan servicing software is available to quickly identify loan delinquencies and establish the length of delay in the receipt of payment. These software applications are capable of identifying and delivering various notices to borrowers including pre-notice of default, notice of default and notice of trustee's sale.

Statute of limitations. A borrower has three years from the date of occurrence to bring an action against a lender for failure to timely disclose transfer of loan servicing and other loan servicing issues. The limit is one year from the date of occurrence for a lender's unauthorized payment of referral fees (kickbacks) or the forced use of a title insurance company.

PROMISSORY NOTES

The Obligation (Debt) and the Security
Real property loans are customarily evidenced by the borrower's signing the loan obligation (the promissory note or promise to pay) and the security instrument (the trust deed or mortgage).

The promissory note is the prime instrument and if there are conflicts in the provisions of the note and trust deed, generally the terms of the note are controlling.

Negotiable Instruments
A negotiable instrument is a written unconditional promise or order to pay a certain amount of money at a definite time or on demand. The promissory note exemplifies the instrument involving a promise and the draft and bank check are examples of instruments involving orders. Bank checks are the most common variety of negotiable instruments. Drafts (also known as bills of exchange and trade acceptances) are similar "three-party paper," except that they do not necessarily involve a bank.

Promissory notes constitute "two-party paper." The maker promises to pay the payee a specified amount of money. There are five basic kinds of notes in general use with the mortgage and trust deed:

1. A straight note calling for payment of interest only during the term of the note, with the principal sum becoming due and payable on a certain date.

2. An installment note calling for periodic payments on the principal, the payments being separate from the interest payments.

3. An installment note demanding periodic payments of fixed amounts, including both interest and principal. These are referred to as amortized payments.

4. An adjustable rate note with an interest rate that varies depending upon changes in an agreed upon index.

5. A demand note which does not become due until the holder makes demand for its payment.

Negotiable instruments are freely transferable in commerce. They are typically accepted as virtual equivalents of cash, yet the hazards of handling large sums of cash are avoided. However to be regarded as a negotiable instrument the document must conform strictly to the statutory definition. Thus a negotiable promissory note must be:

1. signed by the maker or drawer;

2. an unconditional promise or order to pay a sum certain in money and no other promise, order, obligation or power given the maker or drawer;

3. payable on demand or at a definite time; and

4. payable to order or bearer.

Every one of the listed elements must be present if the instrument is to qualify as a negotiable instrument. If any one is missing the document may still be valuable and transferable like an ordinary contract. As such the transferee or assignee receives no more benefits than the transferor had. Defenses which were good against the assignor are good against the assignee.

It is possible in the case of negotiable instruments that the transferee may receive more benefits than the transferor had. If the holder of the instrument transfers it to a third party who is a bona fide purchaser for value, that third party enjoys a favored position provided the third party takes the note as a *holder in due course* (without notice of defect or dishonor and absent a continual business relationship with the transferor). This holder in due course status facilitates trade and commerce because persons are more willing to accept such instruments without careful investigation of the maker's credit or of the circumstances surrounding creation of the instrument.

Holder in due course status is limited if the loan transaction is subject to the federal Truth In Lending Act (TILA). Transferees of such loans are liable to the maker if:

• Violation of the Truth-in-Lending Act is apparent on the face of the disclosure statement or the loan document (e.g., Reg. Z final disclosure shows the amount of the broker's commission to be $2,000.00 and the HUD-1 lists the commission as $5,000.00); or

• The assignment was voluntary, as opposed to involuntary (e.g. private investor dies and the estate inherits the loan or a court orders the loan assigned pursuant to a writ of execution).

Finally, loans which are subject to section 32 of Regulation Z of TILA are subject to a broader assignee liability standard: i.e., assignees of high cost and high fee loans do not benefit from standing as a *good faith purchaser* or a *holder in due course*.

Holder in Due Course Defined

A holder in due course is one who has taken a negotiable instrument (a) for value, and (b) in good faith, and (c) without notice that it is overdue or has been dishonored or of any defense against or claim to it on the part of any person. A holder in due course may be a person who has taken the instrument through a prior holder in due course, or, for that matter, through a person who was not a holder in due course.

Notice may be obtained in many ways, including defects on the face of the instrument and actual knowledge of dishonor or of a defense, but mere recording of an instrument does not give notice to prevent the holder from being in due course. (Commercial Code Section 3302)

FTC "Holder in Due Course Rule"

State law governing the rights of a holder in due course has been limited by the so-called "holder in due course rule" of the Federal Trade Commission (16 Code of Federal Regulations, Part 433, Preservation of Consumer's Claims and Defenses, 1977). Under this rule, any holder of a consumer credit contract is subject to all claims and defenses which the consumer could assert against the seller of goods or services obtained under the consumer credit contract or obtained with proceeds from the consumer credit contract. This rule has limited application in the field of promissory notes secured by liens on real property. It appears to be applicable only in the context of a home improvement contract secured by a deed of trust on the home. A typical example would be a siding contract. The normal promissory note secured by deed of trust used to finance the purchase or construction of improvements on residential or other real property is apparently not subject to the FTC holder in due course rule.

Negotiation

Negotiation is the transfer of an instrument in such form that the transferee becomes a holder. If the instrument is payable to order it is negotiated by delivery with any necessary endorsement; if payable to bearer it is negotiated by delivery. An exception to the requirement of delivery of the instrument is set forth in Section 10233.2 of the Business and Professions Code. Under this section, a real estate broker acting as a servicing agent of the note holder may perfect delivery by retaining possession of the promissory note or collateral instruments and documents, provided the deed of trust or assignment of the deed of trust or collateral documents in favor of the note holder is recorded in the office of the county recorder of the county in which the security property is located and the note is made payable to the note holder who is the lender or the assignee or endorsee.

An endorsement must be written by or on behalf of the holder and on the instrument or on a paper so firmly affixed thereto as to become a part thereof. An endorsement on a paper so affixed shall be valid and effective even though there is sufficient space on the instrument to write the endorsement.

An endorsement is effective for negotiation only when it conveys the entire instrument or any unpaid residue. If it purports to do less, it operates only as a partial assignment.

There are various types of endorsements, including:

1. Blank: the holder simply signs his or her name on the back of the note.

2. Special: the holder writes "Pay to the order of (named transferee)" and then signs.

3. Restrictive: the holder restricts future negotiation, as by writing "Pay to the order of _____ State Bank, for deposit only" and then signs.

4. Qualified: the holder adds the words "Without Recourse" to what would otherwise be a simple blank or special endorsement. This means that if the maker refuses to pay, the endorser will not be liable for the amount. Actually, such qualified endorsement does not eliminate the endorser's contingent liability on certain warranties implied by law. That is, by negotiating a note by simple delivery, or by endorsing the instrument, such individual still warrants that (a) the instrument is genuine and what it purports to be; (b) the transferor has good title to the instrument; (c) all prior parties had capacity to contract; and (d) The transferor does not know any fact that would impair the validity of the instrument or render it valueless.

It should be noted that when negotiation is by delivery only, the above warranties extend only in favor of the immediate transferee. Negotiability of a note is not affected by inclusion of a clause adding court costs and reasonable attorney's fees in the event litigation becomes necessary to collect; nor by inclusion of an acceleration clause which provides that default in one of a series of payments makes the entire principal amount immediately due. These and similar provisions actually make the note more acceptable to lenders.

Conflict in Terms of Note and Mortgage or Deed of Trust
The lien of a mortgage is a mere incident of the debt or obligation. Where there is a conflict in the note and mortgage provisions the provisions of the note will generally control. A mortgage or deed of trust gives no additional validity to an unenforceable note. The two instruments are to be construed together, and if a mortgage or deed of trust contains an acceleration clause, exercising it will cause the note to become due even though the note contains no such clause. However, since July 1, 1972, in every new mortgage or deed of trust on property containing four or fewer residential units, any provision accelerating the debt must be uniformly set forth in both note and mortgage to be valid.

TRUST DEEDS AND MORTGAGES

Security Interests
"Security interest" is a term designating the interest of the creditor in the property of the debtor. Certain assets of the borrower are set aside so that the creditor can reach or sell them if the debtor defaults on his or her obligation. The document that describes the rights and duties of the lender and the borrower is called a security instrument. Mortgages and deeds of trust are security instruments.

In General
The deed of trust is the security instrument most frequently used in California real estate transactions.

Early distinctions between the legal and economic effects of the mortgage and deed of trust have diminished considerably. Now both security instruments are basically subject to the same antideficiency limitations and reinstatement and redemption privileges before a foreclosure sale, and are also subject to the same judicial or nonjudicial procedures and restrictions. The same rules are generally applicable to both instruments, except when applying post foreclosure sale possession and redemption.

For a lender, the principal remaining advantage of the trust deed over the mortgage is that the trust deed's power of sale (nonjudicial action) is typically not outlawed by time (although subject to periodic renewal), while a mortgage remains subject to the statute of limitations (four years). For the borrower, the principal advantage of the mortgage over the trust deed may be the right of redemption and possession following a judicial foreclosure.

Unless indicated otherwise, references to "mortgage," "mortgagor," or "mortgagee" in this discussion include "trust deed," "trustor," or "beneficiary," and vice versa.

Home Mortgage Loan
A home mortgage loan is a debt, for any purpose, incurred by a private borrower, which is secured by a mortgage or other lien on the borrower's title to residential real property. If the borrower fails to pay, the creditor can look to the property, or its proceeds of sale, for payment (by judicial foreclosure or trustee's sale if the mortgage has a power of sale). A first mortgage is one that has priority over any other mortgage or lien on the property. A foreclosure by the holder of a first mortgage will wipe out all subordinate liens on the property. Junior lien holders in such circumstances are "sold out" juniors.

Differences Between Mortgages and Deeds of Trust
Mortgages and deeds of trust differ in several respects:

• Parties	• Reinstatement
• Title	• Redemption
• Statute of Limitations	• Deficiency Judgment
• Remedy	• Satisfaction

As to the parties. In a mortgage there are typically two parties: a mortgagor and a mortgagee. The mortgagor (borrower) gives the mortgagee (lender) a lien upon the mortgagor's property as security for the loan advanced by the mortgagee.

In a deed of trust there are three parties: the trustor (borrower), the trustee (third party), and the beneficiary (lender). The trustor conveys title to the trustee to hold until the trustor performs or defaults under the terms of the note. The trustee's function is to reconvey the property to the trustor when the loan is paid in full or, upon default by the trustor, to foreclose upon the property at the request of the beneficiary.

As to title. A mortgage does not convey title; it creates a lien. In a deed of trust, technical legal title for a limited purpose is conveyed to a trustee. In both cases, possession and equitable title remain with the borrower.

As to the statute of limitations. In the case of a mortgage, an action to foreclose is barred when the statute of limitations of four years has run on the note.

In a deed of trust, the rights of the creditor against the property are not ended when the statute has run on the note, for the trustee has title and can still sell to pay off the debt.

As to remedy. In a mortgage, the only remedy of the mortgagee is foreclosure, unless the mortgage contains a power of sale, in which event such power may be exercised. In a deed of trust, alternative remedies of trustee's sale or judicial foreclosure are permitted.

As to reinstatement. Under a mortgage, the mortgagor and certain other persons listed in Civil Code Section 2924c may reinstate the loan by curing the default at any time before the judicial decree of foreclosure by paying all delinquencies, including advances made by the mortgagee to a senior lienor (lenders), plus all costs and fees incurred because of the foreclosure action. Persons permitted by statute to cure a default are the mortgagor or his successor in interest, any mortgagee or beneficiary under a junior mortgage or trust deed, or any other person having a subordinate lien or encumbrance of record.

Reinstatement under a trust deed (or mortgage under a power of sale) is the same, except reinstatement must be made prior to five business days preceding the date of the trustee's sale or the date of any postponed sale if the power of sale is exercised.

Under either security instrument, the lender's right to accelerate payment of the debt on default is limited by the statutory right of reinstatement.

As to redemption. Code of Civil Procedure Section 729.020 provides that property sold subject to the right of redemption may be redeemed only by the judgment debtor or his successor in interest. Junior lienors are no longer entitled to redeem and have their liens reattach, but must sue as an unsecured creditor.

The redemption period is three months after the sale date if the sale proceeds are sufficient to pay the secured indebtedness plus interest and costs of foreclosure. The redemption period is one year after the sale date if the sale proceeds do not satisfy the amount of the debt plus interest and costs. However, if the mortgagee waives or is prohibited from obtaining a deficiency judgment, there is no longer any right of redemption according to Code of Civil Procedure Section 726 (the one action rule).

Under a trust deed or a mortgage with power of sale, the debtor in most cases has a statutory right of reinstatement after default up to five business days prior to the date of the trustee's sale or the date of any postponed sale and the right of redemption thereafter to the conclusion of the trustee's sale. No right of redemption applies following the trustee's sale. The sale is absolute.

As to deficiency judgment. A deficiency judgment is a personal judgment against a debtor for the difference between the unpaid balance of the secured debt (plus interest and costs and fees of sale) and the amount of the actual proceeds of the sale. California law places restrictions on deficiency judgments.

Where a mortgagee or beneficiary elects to foreclose the security by power of sale rather than by judicial foreclosure, a deficiency judgment is automatically barred under Code of Civil Procedure Section 580d. Section 726 of the same code sets certain limits for a deficiency judgment; and Section 580b of that code prohibits deficiency judgments when specified purchase money secured loans are involved.

A purchase money obligation may arise by:

- a seller extending credit to a purchaser and taking back from the purchaser a note secured by a trust deed on the property regardless of the nature of the security property; or

- a third party lender advancing cash to the purchaser to pay all or part of the purchase price of the security property which is the intended residence of the borrower and which consists of 1 to 4 residential units.

Usually, a seller extending purchase money credit cannot obtain a deficiency judgment if the buyer defaults and a foreclosure sale fails to bring sufficient proceeds to pay off the seller's note. An exception to this rule exists in the sale of a property to a developer for commercial development and the seller subordinates his purchase money lien to the lien of the purchaser/developer's construction loan. Thereafter, upon default of the purchaser/developer, the vendor loses his security interest after sale or foreclosure under the senior lien. Code of Civil Procedure Section 580b will not be applied to bar recovery by the junior vendor/lienor of the unpaid balance of the purchase price of the property.

A person lending cash may obtain a deficiency judgment unless the loan was to pay all or part of the purchase price of a residential dwelling consisting of 1 to 4 units to be occupied entirely or in part by the purchaser.

Where a deficiency judgment is permitted, the beneficiary must first look to the security to satisfy the debt through a judicial foreclosure before seeking a deficiency judgment, except a "sold-out junior" (lien holder) may sue directly on the note.

It should be noted that a purchase money mortgage or trust deed given for all or part of the purchase price of real property at the time of its conveyance has priority over all other private liens created by or against the purchaser's security, subject to the operation of the recording laws. This rule protects even third persons who furnished money, but only when it is loaned for the express purpose of paying for the property. (Civil Code Section 2898)

As to satisfaction. When any mortgage has been satisfied, the mortgagee or the assignee of the mortgagee must initiate the discharge procedure and shall execute a certificate of the discharge thereof, as provided in Civil Code Section 2939 and shall, within 30 days of satisfaction, record or cause to be recorded, except as explained below, such certificate in the office of the county recorder in which the mortgage is recorded. The mortgagee shall then deliver, upon written request of the mortgagor, the original note and mortgage to the person making such request. (Civil Code Section 2941)

When the obligation secured by any deed of trust has been satisfied, the beneficiary or the assignee of the beneficiary shall execute and deliver to the trustee the original note and deed of trust, a request for a full reconveyance and such other documents as may be necessary to reconvey the deed of trust. The trustee shall, within 21 calendar days after receipt of all necessary documents, instructions and fees, execute and record or cause to be recorded, except as provided below, a full reconveyance in the office of the county recorder in which the deed of trust is recorded. The trustee shall then deliver, upon the written request of the trustor, the original note and deed of trust to the person making such request and a copy of the reconveyance shall be delivered to the beneficiary, its successor in interest, or its servicing agent if known. (Civil Code Section 2941)

Limitation to Recording of Reconveyance

Pursuant to Civil Code Section 2941, the mortgagee or trustee shall not record or cause the certificate of discharge or the deed of full reconveyance to be recorded when any of the following circumstances exist:

1. The mortgagee or trustee has received written instructions to the contrary from the mortgagor or trustor, or the owner of the land (as the case may be), or from the owner of the obligation or debt secured by the deed of trust or his or her agent, or escrow holder.

2. The certificate of discharge or deed of full reconveyance is to be delivered to the mortgagor or trustor, or the owner of the land (as the case may be), through an escrow to which the mortgagor, trustor, or owner is a party.

3. Personal delivery is not for the purpose of causing recordation and the certificate of discharge or deed of full reconveyance is to be personally delivered with receipt acknowledged by the mortgagor or trustor or owner of the land, as the case may be, or their agent if authorized by mortgagor or trustor or owner of the land.

Required Timely Recording of the Deed of Full Reconveyance

If a deed of full reconveyance is not issued and recorded within 60 calendar days of satisfaction of the debt, the beneficiary, upon receipt of a written request by the trustor or trustor's heirs, successors in interest, authorized agent thereof, or assignee, may execute and acknowledge a document pursuant to Civil Code Section 2934a substituting another as trustee and issue a deed of full reconveyance.

If a deed of full reconveyance is not executed and recorded either in accordance with the previous paragraph or within 21 days of the trustee's receipt of all documents, instruments, instructions and fees necessary to effect the reconveyance, then within 75 calendar days of satisfaction of the debt or obligation a title insurance company may prepare and record a release of the obligation. The release shall be deemed, when recorded, to be the equivalent of a reconveyance of the deed of trust. However, at least 10 days prior to issuance and recording of a full release pursuant to this paragraph, the title insurance company shall mail by first-class mail, with postage prepaid, the intention to release the debt or obligation to the trustee, trustor, and beneficiary of record, or their successor in interest of record, at the last known address for each party.

The release shall set forth:

1. the name of the beneficiary;

2. the name of the trustor;

3. the recording reference to the deed of trust;

4. a recital that the obligation or debt secured by the deed of trust has been paid in full; and

5. the date and amount of payment.

Sanctions and penalties. Failure to comply with Civil Code Section 2941 makes the violator liable to the person affected for all damages sustained by reason of the violation. Further, the violator must forfeit to that person the sum of $300. In addition, Civil Code Section 2941.5 provides that every person who willfully violates Section 2941 is guilty of a misdemeanor punishable by a fine of not less than $50 nor more than $400, or by imprisonment in a county jail not to exceed 6 months, or by both such fine and imprisonment.

Fees for services rendered. A trustee, beneficiary or mortgagee may charge a reasonable fee to the trustor or mortgagor or the owner of the land for services involved in the preparation, execution and recordation of the full reconveyance including, but not limited to, document preparation and forwarding services, plus any additional official fees that may be required (e.g., notary and recording).

Fees charged for the foregoing are not to exceed $65 plus official fees. These fees are conclusively presumed to be reasonable. It is important to note that such fees cannot be charged prior to the opening of a bona fide escrow, or more than 60 days prior to full satisfaction of the debt or obligation secured by the deed of trust or mortgage.

Other Characteristics/Essentials of Mortgages and Trust Deeds
The parties and the property must be adequately identified in the instruments and the instruments signed and delivered. The parties should be named in the security instrument in the same manner they are named in the note. Acknowledgment of the security instrument is necessary for recording purposes.

A valid mortgage or trust deed must have a valid underlying debt or obligation, meaning the obligation must have consideration, otherwise the security instrument secures nothing because apart from the debt the security instrument has no meaning and no lien attaches to the property.

One security instrument can secure several debts or obligations (whether present or future), and one debt or obligation can be secured by several security instruments on several parcels of land. Notes in series which are secured by a single deed of trust or more than one deed of trust of equal priority, or notes providing fractionalized interests to non-exempt investors are securities requiring either issuance pursuant to a qualified exemption or pursuant to a permit from the Department of Corporations or the Securities and Exchange Commission (depending upon whether the securities are to be issued intra- or both intra- and interstate).

Unless prohibited by law, fractional interests as well as the entire fee interest may be mortgaged, but lenders are generally reluctant to lend on partial estates. No requirement exists that the trustor be the debtor. One person may give a mortgage or trust deed to secure the debt of another, or as a guaranty. However, the debtor and trustor are usually the same person.

A transaction which is really a mortgage transaction disguised to appear otherwise (grant deed to secure a loan, for example) will be subject to the "one form of action" and antideficiency rules.

A mortgagee or beneficiary under a power of sale will usually prefer the publicly held, privately conducted foreclosure sale (trustee's sale) if the real property is valuable enough to satisfy the debt and expenses of sale because the power of sale eliminates the debtor's right of redemption subsequent to the sale. If the property's sale will not satisfy the debt, the lender/creditor will generally initiate a judicial sale and seek a deficiency judgment following the foreclosure sale, if a deficiency judgment is allowable. The remedy is the creditor's choice.

JUNIOR TRUST DEEDS AND MORTGAGES

It is often necessary to obtain junior financing (secondary financing) to complete a transaction where the first trust deed loan plus buyer's down payment are not sufficient to meet the purchase price. Two non-institutional or non-licensed sources have been available for junior financing: sellers and private lenders. In recent years, institutional and licensed lenders have become active in the making of junior loans.

Seller Extending Credit
A seller who receives a substantial portion of the purchase price in cash from the proceeds of the first loan plus the buyer's down payment may be willing to extend credit to the purchaser usually, because of the increased risk, at an interest rate higher than that of the first loan.

When a seller "carries the paper," the extension of credit is called a "purchase money" trust deed. This financing method is often used when a seller wants to receive income spread out over a period of time instead of lump-sum cash or when an existing mortgage is to be assumed and seller extends credit for a portion of the purchase price. Such liens are used most often in periods of tight money.

Sellers accepting a junior lien may either retain it or sell it, with or without the services of a mortgage broker, to a permanent investor. The principal balance is usually discounted anywhere from 10 to 50 percent, depending upon the risk of the loan (due date, amount, interest rate, borrower stability, property securing the lien, and whether the loan includes due-on-sale, late charge or prepayment penalty provisions).

Disclosures required. Since July 1, 1983, where there is a transaction involving a purchase money lien on dwellings for not more than 4 families with the seller extending credit to the purchaser and there is "an arranger of credit" (typically a real estate broker), certain specific disclosures must be made by the arranger of credit to both seller and buyer. Also, the seller is to make certain disclosures to the purchaser with respect to information within the seller's knowledge and the purchaser is to disclose certain information (credit worthiness) within the purchaser's knowledge to the seller. Chapter 22 includes a discussion of these disclosures.

Private Lenders

Private persons may loan money directly or work through a mortgage broker because of the usury exemption, convenience and additional services provided. These direct lenders are usually persons desiring higher returns on their funds for higher risks. Individuals acting for their own account are subject to fewer laws and regulations, but must still operate within the laws of this state governing lending and usury.

Private lenders must receive a disclosure from the mortgage broker pursuant to Sections 10232.4 and 10232.5 of the Business and Professions Code prior to committing their funds to the loan transaction or to the purchase of a promissory note and purchase money lien. The borrower must receive a disclosure from the mortgage broker, pursuant to Sections 10240 and 10241 of the Business and Professions Code, prior to becoming obligated to complete the loan transaction. Chapter 15 includes a discussion of these disclosures.

Usury

In California, the passage of Proposition 2 in 1979 made significant changes to the constitutional provisions on usury. Now all loans secured in whole or in part by liens on real property and made or arranged by a licensed real estate broker are exempt from the usury law. Private individuals making such loans without a broker are controlled by the usury law. However, federal law preempts state constitutional and statutory interest ceilings on most federally related real property loans.

General Comments

Private lenders are usually highly subjective about loan decisions, make most of their loans on single-family residences within a geographic area known to lender and loans are for relatively small amounts with terms of three to five years. These loans are called "hard money" loans, meaning the lender actually gives cash to the borrower as opposed to the situation in which a seller extends credit only to a purchaser. The cost of such junior loans must of course be borne by the borrower and can prove to be a burden. Real estate brokers as fiduciaries have a duty not to make or arrange a loan which will obviously end in financial difficulty for a borrower who does not have the ability to meet mortgage payments from an overstrained budget.

With few exceptions, government loan programs prohibit the placing of junior liens on the real property concurrently with the recording of the government first mortgage lien. FHA permits no concurrent junior financing.

Balloon Payment Loans

Often in California when a "hard money" lender makes a loan or when a seller takes back a junior purchase money note and trust deed, the monthly payments do not amortize the loan. The last payment, called a balloon payment, is a substantial payment of principal and interest. Loans with balloon payments are usually short-term: i.e., three to five years.

Section 2924i of the Civil Code requires the holder of a balloon payment loan secured by an owner-occupied dwelling of four or fewer units to give 90 to 150 days notice of the due date of the balloon payment. Construction loans, loans for which creative financing disclosures have been made, seller "carry backs," and loans made before January 1, 1984 are exempt from this requirement.

Certain "hard money" real property loans negotiated by real estate brokers (junior loans under $20,000 or first loans under $30,000) against nonowner-occupied dwellings with a loan term of less than three years (six years or less for owner-occupied) must provide for substantially equal installment payments over the loan term. No installment, including the final installment, can be greater than twice the amount of the smallest installment. This requirement does not apply to a purchase money note given back to a seller on account of the purchase price.

OTHER TYPES OF MORTGAGE AND TRUST DEED LOANS

Package Trust Deed
A package trust deed involves a loan on real property that is secured by more than just the lot and basic structure. It includes fixtures (appliances, carpeting, drapes, air conditioning unit) and perhaps items of personal property.

Blanket Trust Deed (Mortgage)
A blanket trust deed is a loan which covers more than just one parcel of property. Usually, the loan contains a "release clause" providing for release of a particular parcel upon the repayment of a specified portion of the loan. Typical use is in connection with a tract of homes built on speculation. Initially, one blanket trust deed covers the entire tract. When a home is sold, a separate loan (take-out loan) is made to the buyer covering only that buyer's new home and all or a portion of the proceeds of the new loan is paid against the blanket loan to obtain release of the sold property. Blanket trust deeds are often used in connection with construction loans to builders.

Open-End Trust Deed
An open-end trust deed involves a loan arrangement whereby additional amounts of money may be lent in the future without affecting the loan's priority. In California, the law provides that these additional amounts are considered as part of the original loan if the loan contract *requires* the lender to advance additional funds, as opposed to the advance(s) being optional on lender's part.

Interest-Only Mortgage
An interest-only mortgage is a balloon payment mortgage loan in which the monthly payments only cover the accrued interest. The unpaid balance, which remains constant, is due and payable on an agreed date, often in one to five years, or upon some other event (e.g., receipt of the proceeds from the sale of another property, or an agreed increase in the debtor's earnings), whichever first occurs.

Collateralized Junior Mortgage
A collateralized junior mortgage involves an arrangement whereby a secured loan is pledged as collateral (security) for a loan in a lesser amount.

Tandem (or Piggyback) Loan
A tandem loan, usually used in residential income type financing, occurs when two lenders share in making a single loan. For example, one lender supplies 60% of the loan funds and a participating lender supplies 25% of the funds. This is another form of junior mortgage financing. The purpose is to grant a higher than usual "loan-to-value" loan.

Swing Mortgage

A swing mortgage is a temporary loan made on a borrower's equity in his present home (which will be sold), or on the equity in both the present and the "contemplated" home (which will be purchased) for use as the down payment on the contemplated residence.

Refinance Mortgage

A refinance loan is one made to replace an existing loan. It usually is an obligation of the same debtor or debtors and it remains secured by the same property. In most cases:

- some additional credit is extended;

- the interest rate is adjusted to more closely reflect (if not equal) the current market interest rate;

- a new schedule of payments is arranged; and

- the lender and borrower may desire to substitute a basically different kind of mortgage (e.g., a variable rate mortgage in place of a conventional fixed-rate mortgage).

(Note: Under most circumstances, the character of the mortgage may be changed from that of a purchase money mortgage to a non-purchase money mortgage.)

Pledged Savings Account Mortgage

Under the pledged savings account mortgage, also known as the flexible loan insurance program mortgage, or FLIP, part of the borrower's down payment is used to fund a pledged savings account. The savings account is maintained as cash collateral for the lender and a source of supplementary payments for the borrower during the first (usually five) years of the loan. Interest on the account is usually paid to the borrower.

Wrap-Around Mortgage or Trust Deed (Also Called an Over-Riding or All-Inclusive Trust Deed - AITD)

Before discussing this type of financing, a word of caution. Anyone planning to use this security device should make sure the existing loan can be legally combined with (wrapped by) the new loan. Most institutional loans contain acceleration or alienation provisions (due-on-sale clauses) in their loan documents which preclude the transfer of the property to a new owner without lender approval. The advice of legal counsel is recommended to assure that all parties receive what they bargained in an AITD situation.

During periods of credit shortages and/or "tight-money," it is virtually impossible for some potential buyers to qualify for conventional loans and for other borrowers to refinance an existing loan on investment real estate to raise additional capital. Refinancing may be a practical impossibility in a number of cases because: no prepayment of the existing debt may be provided for in the debt contract; prepayment penalties often make refinancing too costly; or, if the existing loan is eliminated, there is no possibility of obtaining the desired financing to complete the sale.

These buyers and sellers may decide to use the AITD technique.

An AITD, like a junior mortgage, does not disturb the existing loan, yet the debtor is able to borrow an additional amount against the property. After the wrap-around mortgage loan has been arranged, the new lender assumes payment of the existing mortgage while giving a new, increased loan at a higher rate of interest to the borrower. The amount of the wrap-around mortgage includes the unpaid principal balance of the existing loan plus the new loan funds (or the amount of the purchase price being "carried back" by the seller).

The borrower makes payment on the new loan to the new lender, who makes payment to the holder of the prior loan. The new loan "wraps around" the existing loan. This method is also used to finance a sale of real estate where the purchaser has only a small down payment. The buyer executes a wrap-around mortgage to the seller who will collect a larger mortgage payment from buyer and continue to make payments on the old loan. The interest rate spread causes a profit for the lender or seller.

ALTERNATIVE FINANCING

Background and Purpose
In a stable economic environment (i.e., one involving low inflation and relatively constant market interest rates), the long-term fixed-rate mortgage is the typical financing vehicle for the purchase of residential real property.

Uncertainty regarding future inflation and interest rates can complicate matters for both lenders and borrowers. As people continue to build, sell, and purchase homes, the terms of home mortgages reflect economic realities and expectations and the periodic reluctance of lenders, investors and borrowers to accept long-term fixed-rate loans.

Loans that involve balloon payments, interest reset options, shared appreciation at resale, etc. have ramifications that are not readily apparent to most people. This section discusses some of the alternatives to the fixed-rate loan.

Graduated Payment Adjustable Mortgage (GPAM)
A GPAM provides for partially deferred payments of principal at the start of the loan term. There are a variety of plans. Usually, after the first five years of the term, the principal and interest payments increase substantially to pay off the loan during the remainder of the term (e.g., 25 years). This loan may be appropriate for borrowers who expect salary increases in the coming years. A GPAM involves negative amortization (i.e., increase in principal) in the early years of the loan. Thus, early sale of the home could require that the borrower repay more than the original amount of the loan. This could be a problem if the property has not increased in value.

Adjustable Rate Mortgage (ARM)
An ARM is a mortgage loan which provides for adjustment of its interest rate as market interest rates change. Thus, an ARM is called a fluctuating or floating rate mortgage.

An ARM's interest rate is linked to an index that reflects changes in market rates of interest. A variety of published indexes are used: e.g., the Cost-of-Funds Index published by the Office of Thrift Supervision, and the Federal Reserve Discount Rate.

Because ARM rates can increase over the term of the loan, ARM borrowers share with lenders the risk that interest rates will rise. This sharing permits the lender to charge a lower initial interest rate than would be charged for a fixed-rate mortgage.

Renegotiable Rate Mortgage (RRM)

An RRM is a long-term mortgage (up to 30 years) comprised of a series of short-term loans. The loans are renewable after specified periods (e.g., every three years, every four years, or every five years). Both the interest rate and the monthly payment remain fixed during periods between renegotiation/renewal.

Any change in the interest rate, limited by law, is based on changes in an index. If the borrower declines renewal after any period, the remaining balance is due.

Shared Appreciation Mortgage (SAM)

A shared appreciation mortgage (SAM) gives the lender the right to an agreed percentage of the appreciation in the market value of the property in exchange for an initial below-market interest rate. These loans are usually not available in markets where properties are not appreciating in value.

Rollover Mortgage (ROM)

The ROM (currently used extensively in Canada) is a renegotiated loan wherein the interest rate (and, hence, the monthly payment) is renegotiated, typically every five years. Consequently, the mortgage rate is adjusted every five years consistent with current mortgage rates, although monthly payments are amortized on a 25 or 30 year basis. Monthly payments are calculated in the same manner as a conventional mortgage, with the term decreasing in increments of five years to permit full payment at maturity specified at loan origination.

Reverse Annuity Mortgage (RAM)

Elderly homeowners often face the reverse problem of young families in that their incomes are relatively low and, although they own their homes free and clear, they must move in order to utilize their equity for living expenses. Under a reverse annuity mortgage, the lender pays the borrower a fixed annuity, based on a percentage of the value of the property. The borrower is not required to repay the loan for 15 or 20 years or until a specified event such as death or sale of the property, at which time the loan is paid (e.g., through a probate sale). In effect, a RAM enables a retired couple to draw on the equity of their home by increasing their loan balance each month. No cash payment of interest is involved, as the increase in the loan balance each month represents the cash advanced, plus interest on the outstanding balance.

Summing up. Alternative mortgages are not suitable to everyone. It is very important that those who recommend such plans, or who contemplate using them personally, have a good understanding of the potential risks and drawbacks as well as the benefits. A temporary solution to a financing problem may turn out to be a long-term detriment to the borrower and/or lender.

Real estate licensees should use caution when advocating the use of innovative financing techniques and be prepared to explain benefits and risks to their clients. Furthermore, innovative financing techniques generally should not be pursued without the advice of legal counsel. Alternative financing is not something that a licensee and his or her principal should learn together through trial and error.

EFFECTS OF SECURITY

Having subjected property to the lien of a trust deed or mortgage, the debtor must further submit to various incidents or effects of this security arrangement. Some of the more important effects refer to:

1. assignment of the debt by the creditor;

2. transfer of the property by the borrower;

3. satisfaction of the debt;

4. lien priorities; and

5. acceleration due to default.

Assignment of debt by the creditor. The assignment of a debt secured by a mortgage carries with it the security. An attempted assignment of the mortgage without the note transfers nothing to the assignee, but a transfer of the note without the mortgage gives the assignee the right to the security.

An assignment of a mortgage or deed of trust may be recorded and recordation gives constructive notice to all persons. After the note has been transferred and the assignment of the mortgage has been recorded, the debtor is not protected if he continues making payment to the original creditor. (Note: Recent federal and state changes require notice to the debtor of any transfer of servicing agent - RESPA and Civil Code Section 2937.)

Business and Professions Code Section 10234 requires every licensee negotiating a loan secured by a trust deed or an assignment of a trust deed, to cause the trust deed or assignment to be recorded, or when delivering these instruments to the lender or assignee, to give written recommendation that the trust deed or assignment be immediately recorded.

Transfer of property by the borrower. When mortgaged real property is transferred, the purchaser either obtains new financing (and the old mortgage is paid off), buys the property "subject to" the existing loan, or "assumes" the loan. Taking title "subject to" the existing loan generally results in no personal liability to the purchaser. Despite the grant, the seller will (except in purchase money mortgage fact situations) remain personally liable to the lender for the loan repayment. If a purchase money loan is involved, in the event of a default no deficiency judgment could be obtained and the lender would be required to look only to a sale of the security property to recover the amount of the debt.

If the loan terms do not include a due-on-sale clause and as long as the purchaser makes the loan payments in a timely manner, no problem should occur for the original signer and maker of the loan. If the buyer defaults and the loan is not a purchase money loan, the lender can look to the seller/maker for payment, even years after the transfer was made. The seller may also suffer a loss of credit status due to the purchaser's failure to make the payments.

Under a loan assumption, the buyer becomes the principal debtor and the seller either may remain liable to the lender as a continuing maker, or may become liable to the lender as surety for any deficiency resulting after the sale of the property. The safest arrangement for the seller is to ask the lender for a substitution of liability, relieving the seller of all liability in consideration for assumption of the debt by the buyer.

Caution regarding due-on-sale. Proposed loan transfers, whether as the result of assumptions or taking title "subject-to," must be very carefully considered in light of the Supreme Court ruling allowing the nation's federal lenders to automatically enforce due-on-sale provisions in their loans and the effects of the Garn-St. Germain or Depository Institutions Act of 1982. The federal act limited, and in 1985 eliminated, except in certain fact situations, automatic transfers of all other types of loans with due-on-sale provisions. Covert transfers, no matter how structured, are not acceptable practice and are to be avoided by real estate licensees.

Offset statement. In transactions involving an assignment of an existing mortgage or trust deed to an investor, an offset statement is customarily obtained for the benefit of the investor. The information included in the offset statement is typically the unpaid balance of note, date to which interest is paid, interest rate, payment amount and due date, the maturity/due date of loan, and whether or not the property owner has any claims which do not appear in the instrument being purchased by the investor. The offset statement is in addition to the beneficiary statement from the lender. Together, the offset and beneficiary statements confirm to the person purchasing the existing loan the nature of the obligation of the property owner (mortgagor) to the new holder of the mortgage (assignee).

Satisfaction of the Debt. See the discussion of this earlier in the chapter under the heading "**As to satisfaction.**"

Lien priorities. Ordinarily, different liens upon the same property have priority according to the time of their creation. Notice is an important element in the determination of priority. Notice may be actual or it may be constructive from recordation, thus giving notice of the lien to subsequent purchasers and encumbrancers for value.

County and municipal tax liens are paramount and prior to an existing mortgage. Where there are successive tax liens, they are generally prior in the inverse order of their creation; that is, those attaching last are superior to the earlier ones. See Government Code Section 53930, et seq., as to the effect of successive special assessments. Such taxes and special assessments are on a parity of equal rank. When delinquent, a deed to any agency for taxes will not wipe out the other liens in favor of other agencies.

Acceleration clause. Trust deeds and mortgages generally contain a clause giving the lender the right to declare the full amount of debt due and payable upon default in payment of an installment, taxes, or interest or the happening of a certain event such as failure to maintain the property.

Also, a "due-on-sale" clause, which is a form of an acceleration clause, gives the lender the right or option to insist that a mortgage be paid off or renegotiated when the title to the mortgaged property changes ownership. When mortgage funds are available at acceptable interest rates, new buyers ordinarily obtain new financing and the owner pays off the existing loan. In times of scarce money and escalating interest rates, buyers prefer to assume or take "subject to" the existing mortgage. Lenders generally do not want to be "locked" into long-term, lower-than-market-rate loans. Often, lenders will argue that they must not only watch the value of their old loans decline but also are forced to pay higher interest rates to depositors who otherwise would withdraw funds and seek higher returns in other investments.

The issue of a lender's right to automatically enforce a "due-on-sale" provision upon transfer of the mortgaged property has been resolved as previously indicated in favor of the lender, as a result of a 1982 United States Supreme Court decision and 1982 federal regulations and law, with specified exceptions. Of course, loan documents containing no due-on-sale clause are not affected, and security properties usually, but not always, remain transferable without the lender's consent when encumbered by this type of loan security document.

DUE-ON-SALE

Recent History of Due-on-Sale Enforcement in California
The California Supreme Court ruled in *Wellenkamp v. Bank of America* (1978 21 Cal. 3d 943) that a state-chartered institutional lender could not automatically enforce a due-on-sale provision in its loan documents to accelerate payment of a loan when residential property securing the loan is sold by the borrower. Under this ruling an institutional lender had to demonstrate that enforcement was necessary to protect against impairment of its security or the risk of default (credit considerations).

In its opinion, the court reviewed prior decisions having to do with enforceability of due-on-sale clauses, particularly *La Sala v. American Savings and Loan Association,* (1971) 5 Cal. 3d 864, and *Tucker v. Lassen Savings and Loan Association,* (1974) 12 Cal. 3d 629. In *La Sala,* further encumbering of real property through a second loan was found to be insufficient justification for acceleration of the maturity date. In *Tucker,* sale of the property under a real property sales contract (installment contract) was held to be insufficient justification.

A flurry of California court cases followed *Wellenkamp* addressing issues it left unresolved, such as the applicability of Wellenkamp to private lenders, commercial as well as residential property, and federal regulations preempting state laws on due-on-sale provisions. The *Wellenkamp* rule was found applicable, and it generally prevailed.

However, federally-chartered banks and savings and loan associations successfully asserted that the validity and automatic exercise of due-on-sale provisions is applicable to them. This contention was upheld by the United States Supreme Court in *Fidelity Federal Savings and Loan Association v. de la Cuesta* (1982 458 US 141).

On October 15, 1982, the *Garn-St. Germain Depository Institutions Act of 1982* became effective. As mentioned previously, with certain exceptions the law makes due-on-sale provisions in real property secured loans automatically enforceable by all types of lenders, including non-institutional private lenders.

The federal law preempts state laws and judicial decisions which restrict enforceability of due-on-sale provisions in financing instruments, and assures that due-on-sale clauses in real property loans originated after October 15, 1982, can be automatically enforced. In addition, FHA and VA have since implemented rules and regulations restricting the transferability of the loans they insure, guarantee, or indemnify.

Enforceability

The following concerns the automatic enforceability of due-on-sale provisions in loan instruments:

1. Federally-chartered savings and loan associations may automatically enforce due-on-sale clauses in promissory notes and deeds of trust which they originated while federally chartered.

2. With certain exceptions of limited application, all loans originated after October 15, 1982 may be accelerated, upon transfer of the property securing the loan, if the security instrument includes a due-on-sale clause.

3. As of October 15, 1985, with very few exceptions, loan transfers without the consent of the lender no longer exist in California.

Other Exceptions

Notable exceptions to automatic enforceability of due-on-sale clauses enumerated under the law include, among others, the following:

1. creation of a junior deed of trust or lien on property which is not related to a transfer of the rights of occupancy when the security property is an owner occupied residence;

2. transfer of the property to a joint tenant;

3. transfer to a relative of a borrower resulting from the death of the borrower; and

4. transfer into an inter vivos trust of which the borrower is a beneficiary if it does not relate to a transfer of rights of occupancy of the property.

Assumptions May Still Be Negotiable

The Garn-St. Germain Act specifically encourages lenders to allow loan assumptions at a blended or below-market rate of interest and nothing in Garn is to be interpreted to prohibit any such assumptions.

Brokers should proceed cautiously in any transaction in which a buyer is proposing to take title "subject to" an existing loan. Such transactions should be reviewed by legal counsel in advance of consummation.

Lender may still require buyers to satisfy credit standards and complete customary credit forms. If the buyer refuses to provide the information within 15 days of the lender's written request, the lender may enforce the due-on-sale provision in its loan.

Special Provision

A clause in any trust deed or mortgage that provides for acceleration of the due date upon sale, conveyance, alienation, lease, succession, assignment or other transfer of property (containing four or fewer residential units) subject to the trust deed or mortgage is invalid unless the clause is printed, in its entirety, in both trust deed or mortgage and the promissory note or other document evidencing the secured obligation. (Civil Code Section 2924.5)

LENDER'S REMEDY IN CASE OF DEFAULT

Foreclosure Generally

Foreclosure is a legal procedure used to terminate the right, title and interest of a mortgagor or trustor in real property by selling the encumbered property and using the sale proceeds to satisfy the liens of creditors.

A mortgage without a *power of sale* can only be foreclosed judicially (i.e., by court proceeding). A mortgage or a deed of trust which contains a *power of sale* may be foreclosed nonjudicially by trustee's sale. Most security instruments in California expressly provide for *power of sale,* thus providing the choice of a trustee's sale or judicial foreclosure sale.

Where anti-deficiency judgments are sought and permitted by law, foreclosure must be by judicial proceedings and a creditor may proceed with both a foreclosure and an action to obtain a deficiency judgment in the same judicial action.

As a general rule, procedural requirements in effect at the time the foreclosure is begun will govern, even if the requirements change. (Code of Civil Procedure Section 725a, et seq.)

"One-Action" Rule

Under California law, the "one-action" rule applies for recovery of any debt or enforcement of any right secured by a mortgage on real property. (Code of Civil Procedure Section 726)

The "one-action" rule requires the mortgagee or beneficiary to first foreclose the property before seeking a personal money judgment against the debtor for the deficiency, if this latter action is permitted under the anti-deficiency rules. Only after the security has been exhausted may the unpaid creditor seek a personal judgment against the trustor/mortgagor.

There are specific exceptions to the "one-action" rule, such as the "sold out junior beneficiary" and "worthless-security" exceptions.

Where a junior lien holder on a property foreclosed by a senior lien holder holds a *non-purchase money* security which has become worthless because the junior creditor no longer has a lien on the property, the "sold out" junior may sue the debtor directly on the note. However, a "sold-out" junior beneficiary or mortgagee is prohibited from suing on a *purchase money note* following a foreclosure sale by a senior mortgagee or trust deed holder because a judgment would result in the equivalent of a deficiency judgment.

If a property is "legally" worthless, (i.e., nonexistent or not actually owned by the mortgagor, or in a situation in which foreclosure would be meaningless because the security has been destroyed or has become valueless without any act by the creditor) or where fraud is involved, the creditor is not limited to the "one-action" rule. Under such circumstances, the creditor may sue directly on the note and need not first foreclose. California Financial Code Section 7460 limits the damages available to the lender in fraud actions where the security property is or was the occupied residence of the borrower.

"Worthless security" does not include a loss in property value or security value due to marketplace or economic declines. Should an opinion of value of the security property be required, the mortgagee or beneficiary must first foreclose to have the court determine "economic worthlessness" and whether a writ of attachment may be granted.

Purchase Money Securities
Code of Civil Procedure Section 580b prohibits deficiency judgments with limited exceptions where "purchase money" securities are involved. For this purpose, "purchase money" means (1) credit extended by a seller to a buyer with the seller "carrying back" a promissory note executed by the buyer and secured by a trust deed on the property being purchased as a part of the purchase price, or (2) a third-party lender advancing funds to a buyer to be used to pay all or part of the purchase price of a dwelling of not more than four units to be occupied in part or entirely by the buyer.

Thus, buyer protection against deficiency judgments is limited by the type of real property purchased. Certain creditors are denied and other creditors may obtain a deficiency judgment. As previously indicated, where third-party money is advanced to enable a buyer to purchase a residential dwelling (1-4 units) in which buyer will reside, the lender is typically barred from obtaining a deficiency judgment. However, if the third-party lender loans funds to enable a buyer to purchase residential property over 4 units, or to purchase investment or commercial property, or raw land, or residential property of 1-4 units *not intended to be buyer occupied,* the lender may seek a deficiency judgment against the buyer when foreclosing judicially.

Anti-deficiency Rules
When a mortgagee or beneficiary elects to "foreclose" under a *power of sale,* there is a complete bar against a deficiency judgment.

Under a judicial foreclosure, if a deficiency judgment is permitted following a judicial sale, the sale is subject to redemption (buy-back) by the debtor within three months if the proceeds of the sale were adequate to satisfy the amounts owing. Otherwise, the redemption period is one year after the sale. Only after the security has first been exhausted may the creditor sue the debtor for the balance owing on the note.

Deficiency Judgments
Purchase money anti-deficiency provisions also apply to installment land contracts, and to instruments determined to be, in fact, security devices (disguised mortgages, for example, equitable liens).

Transactions falling outside the provisions of Code of Civil Procedure Section 580b (i.e., non-purchase money transactions) depend upon a "purpose" scrutiny and a security property and related analysis by the court to determine if a deficiency judgment will be allowed where third-party lenders are involved.

A borrower generally cannot waive at the time of executing the loan the protections granted by law. Subsequent to signing the loan documents, a borrower may under limited fact situations execute a waiver of rights concerning the protections granted against deficiency judgments or the "one-action" rule.

Reinstatement Rights - Pre-sale

Under a judicial foreclosure, a trustor or mortgagor or his or her successor in interest, any beneficiary under a subordinate trust deed or mortgage, or any other person having a subordinate lien or encumbrance of record, may reinstate the loan at any time before entry of judgment by restoring the loan (usually to its installment-payment basis) by paying the delinquencies and advances on the debt plus costs and fees. Thereupon, all foreclosure proceedings terminate and the loan continues in full force and effect as if no such acceleration proceeding had taken place.

Under a trustee's sale, the statutory right of reinstatement for the individuals named above ends five business days prior to the date of the trustee's sale or of any postponed sale.

Redemption Rights - Post-Sale

Under a judicial foreclosure, only the judgment debtor or his or her successor in interest may redeem from a foreclosure sale. All junior lien holders are eliminated under the law effective July 1, 1983. (Code of Civil Procedure Section 729.020) As mentioned previously, the redemption period is three months if the sale proceeds satisfy the debt plus interest and costs of the action. If sale proceeds are insufficient to do this, the redemption period is one year. (Code of Civil Procedure Section 729.030) If the creditor waived the deficiency judgment or it was prohibited, there is no right of redemption. [Code of Civil Procedure Section 726(e)]

During the redemption period permitted under the judicial sale, the judgment debtor or tenant in the property is entitled to remain in possession but must pay rent to the buyer at the foreclosure. Often a mortgage or deed of trust permits the mortgagee or trustee to take possession upon default under the "assignment of rents" provision and manage the property, pay expenses, and collect the rent, applying the net proceeds to the maintenance of the property and to preserve the lender's security.

Under the trustee's power of sale foreclosure, no post-sale redemption right exists.

Statute of Limitations

Civil Code Section 2911 provides that a lien is extinguished by time if an action on the underlying debt or obligation is not brought within the time limits stated. Judicial foreclosure actions must be filed within four years after maturity of the obligation or any installment payment. Both a mortgage and trust deed secure a written debt or obligation that if not performed creates a cause of action for four years following the default. The mortgage, being only a lien, is extinguished without action by the mortgagee four years after default. (The rule is four years from and after: the date the last payment was due; the maturity date; the date the debt was last acknowledged by the mortgagor; or the date of the default under the loan terms, whichever is the later.) The power of sale under a mortgage is also lost for inaction.

However, a deed of trust grants the trustee all of the trustor's right, title and interest in the trust property. Even though the statute of limitations bars an action on the note, the power of sale continues unaffected by the passage of time, except the requirement to periodically renew certain deeds of trust.

Judicial Sale

The court form of foreclosure, a judicial foreclosure, is usually sought when a mortgagee or beneficiary wants to obtain a deficiency judgment. The mortgagee or beneficiary must be mindful of whether a deficiency judgment against the debtor will be sought before concluding the foreclosure remedy. Depending upon the sale results, i.e., the sale proceeds are either sufficient to pay the debt in full or insufficient to do so, the statutory period of redemption for the debtor is either three months or one year from the date of the sale.

The process. The judicial foreclosure sale process involves:

- filing a complaint and notice of action (lis pendens) which will bind all persons acquiring liens or interests in the property during the pendency of the action;

- a summons served on the parties whose interests are to be eliminated, such as the trustor or his successor in interest and junior lien holders;

- the trial, after which the judgment is entered (decree of foreclosure and order of sale);

- the recording and serving by the Sheriff of Notice of Levy followed by the Notice of Sale.

The Notice of Sale cannot be earlier than 120 days after recording and serving of the Notice of Levy if a deficiency judgment is barred or waived.

Where a deficiency judgment is available, the property is sold subject to the one-year redemption period, the 120-day notice period is not required and only a 20-day Notice of Sale is needed. The 20-day Notice of Sale must be made by posting the Notice of Sale in a public place and on the property at least 20 days before the sale and by publishing the notice once a week for three weeks in a newspaper of general circulation in the city or judicial district in which the property or any part of it are located. The notice must also be mailed to all defendants at their last known address and to any other person who has requested to be notified.

The sale. The sale is to be held between 9 a.m. and 5 p.m. on a business day in the county where the property or some of it is located. The foreclosing creditor, debtor, junior lien holders and others may bid at the sale. The foreclosing creditor may credit-bid up to the amount owed him, and cash bid in excess of the debt. All other bidders must bid cash except that a bidder may, if the bid price exceeds $5,000, deposit with the party conducting the sale the greater of $5,000 or 10 percent of the bid amount, and pay the balance within ten days of the sale, plus interests and costs, and damages if he fails to pay and a second sale is required.

After the sale. The Sheriff issues the highest bidder a prescribed Certificate of Sale stating the title is subject to any redemption privilege of the debtor. The certificate operates to transfer title to the purchaser. The purchaser receives no rights to possession for the period of redemption, but does have the right to receive rents. The title received by the highest bidder is subject to any senior liens but free of any junior liens. The Certificate of Sale is recorded.

Sale proceeds are applied to costs of lawsuit and attorney fees; selling expenses; amount due beneficiary; junior lien holders in order of priority; and finally the excess to the debtor.

If the debtor does not redeem the property within the 3-month or 1-year (if a deficiency judgment has been obtained) redemption period, the Sheriff will issue a Deed of Conveyance containing special recitals concerning the foreclosure and sale and will record the deed. The grantee receives all right, title and interest of the trustor as of the date the trust deed or mortgage foreclosed upon was recorded. The grantee may now evict the trustor or tenant in possession.

A creditor seeking a deficiency judgment must file application in the court case within three months of the sale for a determination of the deficiency. If the court enters a deficiency judgment against the trustor or mortgagor and the beneficiary or mortgagee records it, the judgment becomes a lien upon all property owned by the debtor or acquired by him or her within ten years of the entering of the judgment ruling.

If a debt is secured by both real and personal property, the creditor may foreclose upon the real property under the power of sale and bring a separate action on the personal property security.

Trustee's Sale - "Power of Sale" Foreclosure
The alternative method of foreclosure is called a "trustee's sale" or "power of sale." Usually, a corporate trustee is the entity initiating and handling the proceedings for the beneficiary or mortgagee. It is important that all statutory provisions governing the sale be complied with, as any irregularity may invalidate the sale. The "power of sale" is based upon Civil Code Section 2924, et seq., which is procedural and not substantive law.

Unless a mortgagor or trustor files suit contesting the sale, or obtains a court injunction (for example, to determine whether a valid lien exists, or whether there is a default, or the amount of the default), the court system may be entirely bypassed in a trustee's sale. Under the existing statutes, the time required between filing of the Notice of Default and Sale and the actual sale date allows the debtor time to seek a judicial trial or injunction to establish underlying facts. Of course, after the trustee's sale, the mortgagor, trustor, or any other party affected by the sale may bring an action to set aside the sale, usually on procedural grounds, even though the sale is characterized as absolute.

Generally. No security instrument can be foreclosed at a trustee's sale unless it contains a "power of sale" provision. Without a power of sale, the mortgage or trust deed must be judicially foreclosed; however, the power of sale may be an independent document as long as it is properly integrated.

In a trustee's sale, no deficiency judgments are permitted, nor does the debtor have post-sale redemption rights. However, during the statutory reinstatement period (Civil Code Section 2924, et seq.), the debtor or any other party with a junior lien or encumbrance of record on the real property may in most fact situations reinstate (bring current and restore) the debt accelerated by the creditor because of the default.

Reinstatement restores the loan to its installment-paying or other basis by curing the default and paying all costs and fees incurred by the creditor, who must then terminate the foreclosure action.

After the statutory reinstatement period, the debtor may still redeem (buy back) the property and avert the foreclosure sale by paying off the entire debt, plus interest and costs, fees, advances and any damages to the creditor, at any time within five business days prior to the date of the trustee's sale or any sale. This is the exercise of the trustor's "equity of redemption" privilege.

Special rules. Special rules apply in trustee's sales involving bankruptcy, substitution of trustee, federally insured or guaranteed loans, individuals in military service, senior citizens, and Unruh Act mortgages (on single-family owner-occupied residences arising from a contract for goods or services). The advice of legal counsel should be obtained in advance of proceeding with a foreclosure involving any of the foregoing fact situations.

The Procedure

The beneficiary notifies the trustee of the default (usually a failure to make specified installment payments of principal and interest or make a balloon payment) and delivers the original note and trust deed to the trustee along with receipts, payment records and other evidence of advances made by the beneficiary to protect the security (e.g., payments to senior lenders, or taxes, fire insurance, etc.). The beneficiary signs a document for the trustee usually entitled Declaration of Default and requests foreclosure be started by the trustee.

(Any one beneficiary in a "fractionalized" trust deed may initiate the foreclosure. Further, Section 2941.9 has been added to the Civil Code regarding fractionalized trust deed holders or holders of notes in series. Section 2941.9 establishes a process through which all beneficiaries under a trust deed may agree to be governed by beneficiaries holding more than 50% of the record beneficial interest of the note. The parties must agree in writing to majority rule and each fractionalized note holder or holder of a note in series must be noticed of the action taken. The agreement between the note holders must be in the form of an affidavit and is to be acknowledged and recorded.)

The beneficiary furnishes the date of the original default to the trustee. The trustee normally obtains a title company foreclosure guaranty report showing the present condition of the record title, parties in interest and encumbrances. The trustee then prepares, records, mails and publishes the Notice of Default and Election to Sell as prescribed by statute (Civil Code Section 2924, et seq.).

Notice of default and election to sell. The Notice of Default must be executed by the beneficiary or the trustee and must state an election on the part of the beneficiary to declare the entire debt due because of the default. (Absent this declaration, the full amount owing on the debt cannot be collected at the foreclosure sale.) The Notice should make it clear that unless the default is noncurable, the trustor or the successor trustor may reinstate and cure the default prior to five business days immediately before the date of the trustee's sale or any postponed sale.

The Notice of Default is recorded in the office of the county recorder where the real property, or some of it, is located at least three months before Notice of Sale is given. Within ten days after recordation of the Notice of Default, a copy of the Notice containing the recording information must be sent by certified or registered mail to all persons who have requested notice and to the trustor at his or her last known address.

If there has been no request for notice by the trustor, or the request by the trustor includes no address, then the Notice of Default must be published weekly for four weeks in a newspaper of general circulation in the proper jurisdiction starting within ten days of the recording date, or the notice may be personally delivered to the trustor.

The Notice of Default, and also the Notice of Sale, are valid if the foreclosure statutes have been strictly followed, whether or not the trustor (mortgagor) has actual knowledge of the notices.

The Notice of Default must also be sent within one month of recording by registered or certified mail to persons listed in Civil Code Section 2924b even though they have not recorded a request to receive notice. These persons are: successors in interest to the trustor or mortgagor; a beneficiary or mortgagee of any junior recorded trust deed or mortgage or the assignee of such beneficiary or mortgagee; the vendee of any contract of sale, or the lessee of any lease of the interest being foreclosed which is junior to the security instrument being foreclosed, or to the successor in interest to such vendee or lessee; to the State Controller if a recorded lien for postponed property taxes exists against the property; and such other parties as are required by law.

Notice of sale. If the loan is not reinstated, the trustee issues a Notice of Trustee's Sale, the content and form of which is prescribed by Civil Code Section 2924f(b). The Notice of Sale sets a sale date not sooner than twenty days after the recording date of the Notice of Sale. Actual practice usually requires a longer time (e.g., 31 days), especially if federal tax lien notice requirements are to be met or other justifiable delays are encountered. In any event, the sale date is set to allow time for the required recording, publication, posting and mailing of the Notice of Trustee's Sale.

The Notice of Sale must be recorded at least fourteen days, and mailed by registered or certified mail to the trustor and other persons requesting/receiving notice of default at least twenty days, before the sale (Civil Code Section 2924b). The notice must be published once a week over a period of at least twenty days in a newspaper of general circulation in the city, county or judicial district where the real property, or any part of it, is located. Three publications of the notice not more than seven days apart are required. The notice must be posted for at least twenty days in at least one public place in the city, judicial district, or county of the sale, and in a conspicuous place on the property (a door, if possible, if the property is a single-family residence).

If the loan has not been reinstated by the debtor, a partial payment accepted by the beneficiary may not terminate the foreclosure. The beneficiary, however, should be careful when accepting partial payments to set forth in writing:

- whether it is the intention of the parties that the partial payment constitute a reinstatement and therefore a cure of the default; or

- whether the partial payment is to be construed to be part of a work-out agreement providing a plan for payment of all delinquencies and related costs and expenses; or

- whether the partial payment has been received without any effect on the foreclosure process, thereby permitting the beneficiary to proceed with foreclosure as though no payment has been received.

The sale. The sale is to be conducted at a public auction by the trustee, or auctioneer named by the trustee, on any business day between 9 a.m. and 5 p.m. in a public place in the county where the property, or some part of it, is located. All bids must be for payment in cash, cashier's check from a qualified lender specified in the code, or "a cash equivalent which is authorized by law or has been designated in the Notice of Sale as acceptable to the trustee." (Civil Code Section 2924h)

Until the auction bidding concludes, the debtor or any junior lien holder may still redeem the property by paying off the defaulted loan in full, plus all fees, costs and expenses permitted by law. Reinstatement of a monetary default under the terms of an obligation secured by a deed of trust or mortgage may be made at any time within the period commencing with the date of recordation of the Notice of Default, until five business days prior to the date of sale set forth in the initial recorded notice of sale. As previously stated, the reinstatement period revives as a result of a postponed sale where the postponed sale date is more than five business days subsequent to the initial sale date. [Civil Code 2924c, subdivision (e)]

Any person, including the debtor, creditor or a junior lien holder may bid. Only the selling beneficiary (holder of the debt being foreclosed) may credit-bid or offset up to the amount of the debt owed the creditor plus interest and costs. Junior lien holders may not credit-bid the amount of their junior liens. However, the amount bid by the junior lien holder would serve to reduce any potential liability that the trustor had to the junior lien holder. Further, the junior lien holder, who controls the senior lien being foreclosed, is not entitled to purchase the security property at a depressed price and then sue the trustor for deficiency under their now sold out junior promissory note.

A trustee may reject all bids if the trustee believes they are all inadequate. At the trustee's discretion, the sale may be postponed and a new sale date at the same location announced. Bid fixing, restraining from bidding or the offering or accepting of consideration for not bidding at a trustee's sale ("chilling the bidding process") is unlawful and subjects the participants to fine, imprisonment, or both. [Civil Code Section 2924h(f)] The trustee may postpone a sale, by announcement at the time and place of sale, up to three times, for other compelling reasons given in the statutes. If there are more postponements, a new Notice of Sale must be published, recorded, mailed and posted.

After the sale. The successful bidder receives a Trustee's Deed to the property containing special recitals giving notice of compliance with the foreclosure statutes to protect the purchaser and subsequent purchasers. The title conveyed is without covenant or warranty that there are no title defects and relates back in time to the date the trustor signed the trust deed. The Trustee's Deed passes to the purchaser the title then held and any after-acquired title of the trustor, not the trustor's title as of the sale date.

However, title will remain subject to certain liens:

- federal tax liens filed more than thirty days before the date of the trustee's sale unless the proper twenty-five day notice has been given the Internal Revenue Service;

- assessments and real property taxes; and

- valid mechanic's liens.

Even with proper notice to the IRS, the federal government may have the right for 120 days following the trustee's sale to redeem the property by paying the amount advanced by the successful bidder.

Provided that the beneficiary successfully makes a "full credit bid" (bids the full amount of unpaid principal and interest and any charges, penalties, costs, expenses, attorneys' fees, and advances that may be lawfully due and owing to the beneficiary), the sale eliminates the debt and obligation of the trustor. Whether a beneficiary full credit bids or underbids, completion of a trustee's sale will extinguish the mortgage or trust deed lien securing the debt and obligation in favor of a beneficiary, and will extinguish any junior liens and encumbrances (e.g., mortgages, deeds of trust, judgment liens, easements, and leases which do not have priority over the lien which has been foreclosed or which do not evidence a tenancy subject to a local rent control ordinance).

A beneficiary may elect to underbid when the beneficiary anticipates a collateral action against the debtor/trustor or a claim against a third party for part payment of the amount due and owing to the beneficiary. A beneficiary may elect to proceed with a legal action for fraud, waste or malicious destruction of the security against the debtor/trustor, or third parties, or, for example, if a casualty loss has occurred to the security property for which insurance coverage is available, a beneficiary would underbid and then file a claim against the insurer under the terms of the insurance policy to recover the cost of damage to the property as part of the amount due the beneficiary.

Liens or encumbrances, including real property taxes, which are senior to the foreclosed trust deed remain on the security property. The title is free of any right of redemption by the debtor/trustor and the debtor/trustor has no further rights or interest in the security property absent a successful legal action to set aside or void the trustee's sale. Further, a Petition in Bankruptcy may be filed by the debtor/trustor which may permit either the debtor/trustor or a trustee in the bankruptcy to void the foreclosure sale and return the security property to the estate of the debtor/trustor. Also, a transaction involving residential real property in foreclosure may be voidable and may be rescinded by the debtor/trustor within two years from the date of such transaction upon written notice if unconscionable advantage has been taken of the debtor/trustor. (See Civil Code Section 1695.14.)

The successful bidder and purchaser is entitled to immediate possession of the security property and may evict the debtor-trustor by instituting an Unlawful Detainer action subsequent to delivery of a three-day Notice to Quit. In the event the occupant is a tenant who occupies under the terms of a lease junior to the foreclosed lien and who does not occupy pursuant to any local rent control ordinance, the purchaser at the foreclosure sale may evict the tenant subsequent to the delivery of a thirty-day Notice to Vacate and thereafter, if the tenant fails to vacate, by instituting an Unlawful Detainer action subsequent to the delivery of a three-day Notice to Quit. Some attorneys recommend concurrently delivering a thirty-day and a three-day notice to tenants occupying the foreclosed property.

If a tenant occupies pursuant to a lease agreement that is senior in priority to the foreclosed lien or whose occupancy is subject to the provisions of a local rent control ordinance, the successful purchaser should seek legal advice before taking any action to evict the tenant or otherwise terminate the occupancy of the tenant. On the other hand, if the lease is subordinate in priority to the foreclosed lien, the leasehold interest may be extinguished as a result of the foreclosure sale.

Disposition of sale proceeds. The trustee distributes the foreclosure sale proceeds in the following order:

- to trustee's fees, costs and sale expenses;

- to beneficiary to satisfy the full amount of unpaid principal and interest and any charges, penalties, costs, expenses, attorney's fees, and advances that may be lawfully due and owing;

- to junior lien holders in order of priority, whether matured or not;

- any surplus to the debtor/trustor.

If either a junior lien holder or the debtor/trustor disputes the distribution of funds, the trustee should file an interpleader action and have the court decide the issue.

Foreclosure Abuses

In 1979, corrective legislation was passed aimed at home-equity purchasers and mortgage foreclosure consultants. (Civil Code Sections 1695, et seq. and 2945, et seq.) These laws provide protection for homeowners who are in default on loans secured by their residences.

Civil Code Section 1695, et seq. (Home Equity Sales Contracts) requires that a contract for the sale of a residence in foreclosure to a person (an equity purchaser) who does not intend to occupy the property contain specified provisions. The law allows rescission of such contracts under specified conditions. Further, an equity purchaser who violates Section 1695.6 or Section 1695.13 may be liable for actual damages, exemplary damages in an amount not less than three times the equity seller's actual damages, attorney's fees and costs, and equitable relief. A criminal conviction for violation of Section 1695.6 (or for any practice which operates as fraud or deceit upon the equity seller) may result in a fine of not more than $10,000 and/or a jail sentence of not more than one year.

The law establishes a presumption that a grant to an equity purchaser with an option for the equity seller to repurchase is a loan rather than a sale transaction.

Because of the specific requirements of the Home Equity Sales Contract Law, the standard real estate purchase contracts and receipts for deposits customarily used in the real estate brokerage business are not acceptable for use in home equity sales when the real property is in foreclosure. Accordingly, a real estate licensee should seek the advice of legal counsel to prepare the proper contract forms and for advice regarding the manner in which such sales must be conducted.

Civil Code Sections 2945, et seq. (Mortgage Foreclosure Consultants) address the problem of consultants who represent that they can assist homeowners who are in foreclosure, often charge high fees, frequently secure the payment of their fees by a deed of trust on the residence in foreclosure and have been known to perform no service or essentially a worthless service to the homeowner.

The law requires that contracts for services of foreclosure consultants contain specified provisions. The law allows rescission of such contracts under certain conditions and makes violation of the provisions relating to such contracts a crime.

It is illegal for any person to take "unconscionable advantage" of any property owner in foreclosure. While real estate licensees may, under certain circumstances, be exempt from the provisions of the Mortgage Foreclosure Consultants law, a licensee should proceed with an abundance of caution when dealing with owners of property where a Notice of Default has been recorded and/or a home-equity sales contract is being considered. Among other requirements, the real estate licensee must act within the course and scope of his or her license, must not accept any advance fees, and must not acquire any interest in the residence in foreclosure. Again, the real estate licensee should seek the advice of legal counsel prior to representing a seller of residential real property that is subject to a Notice of Default. Representing an equity purchaser may be difficult due to the bonding requirement because the bonds have been proven to be unavailable.

Statement of Condition of Debt

Pursuant to Civil Code Section 2943, any time before or within two months after the recording of a notice of default under a deed of trust or mortgage with power of sale, or before thirty days prior to entry of a decree of judicial foreclosure, the debtor, trustor or mortgagor or entitled person (as defined in the law) may make written demand of the beneficiary or mortgagee for a written beneficiary statement showing:

1. the amount of the unpaid balance of the obligation secured by the mortgage or deed of trust and the interest rate, together with the total amounts, if any, of all overdue installments of either principal or interest, or both;

2. the amounts of periodic payments, if any;

3. the date on which the obligation is due in whole or in part;

4. the date to which real estate taxes and special assessments have been paid to the extent the information is known to the beneficiary;

5. the amount of hazard insurance in effect and the term and premium of such insurance to the extent the information is known to the beneficiary;

6. the amount in an account, if any, maintained for the accumulation of funds with which to pay taxes and insurance premiums;

7. the nature and amount, if known, of any additional charges, costs or expenses paid or incurred by the beneficiary which have become a lien on the real property involved; and

8. whether the obligation secured by the mortgage or deed of trust can or may be transferred to a new borrower.

Section 2943 of the Civil Code also provides that the mortgagee or beneficiary may make a charge not to exceed $60 for furnishing the beneficiary statement, except when the loan is insured by FHA or guaranteed by the Department of Veterans Affairs. Whether the charge may be imposed and how much the charge may be will addressed in the deed of trust.

Within 21 days of receipt of the written demand, the beneficiary or his or her authorized agent shall prepare and deliver the statement together with a complete copy of the note or other evidence of indebtedness. In addition, if requested, the beneficiary or his or her authorized agent shall furnish a copy of the deed of trust or mortgage at no additional charge.

A penalty of $300 and liability for damages is prescribed for willful failure on the part of the beneficiary or mortgagee to deliver the statement within 21 days. The beneficiary may reasonably require that the entitled person produce evidence that they are eligible to make the request pursuant to the terms of the law and may demand payment of the fee at the time of request.

Civil Code Section 2943 was also amended to include the definition and use of pay-off demand statements as distinct from beneficiary statements. The beneficiary statement is intended to provide information when the loan may be transferred to a buyer of the security property. The pay-off demand statement details amounts owing for purposes of loan pay-off. While the beneficiary statement may not be requested subsequent to 60 days following the recordation of notice of default, the pay-off demand statement may be requested anytime except following the first publication of the notice of a trustee sale or of the hearing of a court supervised sale.

As is the case with a request for beneficiary statement, the beneficiary must respond to a request for a pay-off demand statement within 21 days of receipt and the failure of a beneficiary to timely respond may subject the beneficiary to an automatic $300 sanction plus actual damages and attorney's fees.

The fee for a pay-off demand statement is the same as the fee for a beneficiary statement. Failure to specifically identify whether the statement being requested is a beneficiary statement or a pay-off demand statement will allow the beneficiary to "default" to the pay-off demand statement.

Annual and Monthly Accounting
Under Section 2954 of the Civil Code, any mortgagor, trustor, or vendee under a mortgage, trust deed, or real property sales contract may make a written request of

the lender or vendor for a statement of condition of account. A statement is to be provided within sixty days after the end of each calendar year. The statement includes an itemized accounting of money received for interest and principal repayment and received and held in or disbursed from an impound or trust account, if any, for payment of property taxes, insurance premiums, or other purposes relating to the property. The debtor is entitled to receive one statement for each calendar year without charge.

A monthly statement or passbook showing money received for interest and principal and received and held in and disbursed from an impound or trust account constitutes compliance with this requirement.

Where a written request for accounting is on file with the mortgagor, trustor, or vendee, the monthly rate of payment for impound or trust accounts cannot be increased until the itemized accounting of the condition of the account, a statement of the new monthly rate of payment, and an explanation of the factors necessitating the increase each have been furnished.

BASIC INTEREST RATE MATHEMATICS

The practice of real estate requires an understanding of the means by which we calculate values such as mortgage interest and principal, monthly payments, prorations, yields, etc. Although calculators, computers and charts will do the work, a real estate practitioner must know the underlying concepts and formulas and, indeed, may occasionally need to derive correct values without assistance.

Principal - Interest - Rate - Time
Principal is the amount of money on which interest is paid, usually the loan amount. Interest is termed "simple" or "compound." Simple interest is interest paid only on the principal owed; compound interest is interest paid on the principal plus accrued interest.

The basic simple interest formula has four components: interest (I), principal (P), rate (R) and time (T).

$$I = P \times R \times T \quad \text{or} \quad I = PRT$$

To calculate one of these values, you must know the other three.

Example. Find the interest on $2500 for 7 years at 13%.

$I = PRT$

$I = \$2500 \times .13 \times 7$

$I = \$325 \times 7$

$I = \$2275$

Example. How much money must be loaned to receive $2275 interest at 13% if the money is loaned for 7 years?

$I = PRT$. As with any equation, if we do the same thing to both sides, it remains an equation. If we want to solve for P, we simply divide both sides of the equation by RT. Thus, $I \div RT = PRT \div RT$, which simplifies to $I \div RT = P$, which rearranges to:

$P = I \div RT$

$P = \$2275 \div .13 \times 7$

$P = \$2275 \div .91$

$P = \$2500$

Compound Interest

Compound interest is interest on the total of the principal plus accrued interest. For each time period, called the conversion period, interest is added to the principal to form a new principal amount and each succeeding time period has an increased principal amount on which to compute interest. Conversion periods may be monthly, quarterly, semi-annual or annual.

The compound interest rate is usually an annual rate and must be changed to "interest rate per conversion period" or "periodic interest rate." The formula to find compound interest is $I = P \times i$, "i" being the annual interest rate divided by the conversion periods per year.

Example. How much interest will $5000 earn in 3 years if interest compounds annually at 12%?

$I = P \times i$

Because interest compounds annually, the number of conversion periods per year is 1. Therefore, $i = .12 \div 1 = .12$.

$I = \$5,000 \times .12$

First year's interest: $I = \$5,000 \times .12 = \$600$.

To calculate the second year's interest, we add the first year's interest to the $5000 principal and again multiply by "i."

Second year's interest: $I = \$5,600 \times .12 = \$672$.

To calculate the third year's principal, we add the second year's interest to $5,600 principal and again multiply by "i."

Third year's interest: $I = \$6,272 \times .12 = \$752.64$. Add to $6,272 principal.

With interest compounding annually at 12%, $5,000 will grow to $7,024.64 ($5,000 + $600 + $672 + $752.64) in three years.

Example. How much interest will a $1,000 investment earn over 2 years at 16% interest compounded semi-annually?

Since the conversion period is semi-annual, the periodic interest rate is 16% divided by two: $i = 8\%$.

1.	Original principal amount	$1,000.00
2.	Interest for 1st period ($1,000 x .08)	80.00
3.	Balance beginning 2nd period	1,080.00

4. Interest earned for 2nd period ($1,080 x .08) .... <u>86.40</u>

5. Balance beginning 3rd period 1,166.40

6. Interest for 3rd period ($1,166.40 x .08) .... <u>93.31</u>

7. Balance beginning last period 1,259.71

8. Interest for last period ($1,259.71 x .08) .... <u>100.78</u>

9. Compound principal balance 1,360.49

Therefore, I for 2 years = $1,360.49 - $1,000 = $360.49.

Note that annual *simple* interest would be $40.49 less ($1,000 x .16 x 2 = $320 simple interest).

The One-Step Formula for Compound Interest
The above method for calculating compound interest is far too tedious for actual practice. Compound interest tables will give the answer quickly.

Further, the formula for computing compound interest is:

$S = P (1 + i)^n$

S = the sum; the compounded amount (principal and interest)

P = the original principal amount (the present value of S)

i = the interest rate divided by the number of conversion periods per year

n = the number of conversion periods in the term

Example. You deposit $100 in a savings account paying 6% interest compounded quarterly. How much interest do you earn in one year?

S = compounded sum being sought

$P = \$100$

$i = 6\% \div 4 = 1\ 1/2\% = .0150$

$n = 4$ (the number of conversion periods in the one-year term)

$S = P (1 + i)^n$

$S = 100 (1 + .0150)^4$

$S = 100 (1.0150) (1.0150) (1.0150) (1.0150)$

$S = 100 (1.0613634)$

$S = \$106.14$

The total interest is $6.14. [Simple interest ($100 x 6%) would be $6.]

Effective Rate of Interest
The "nominal" or "named" interest rate is the rate of interest stated in the loan documents. The effective interest rate is the rate the borrower is actually paying, commonly called the annual percentage rate (APR). The difference depends on how many times a year the interest is compounded. For example, 6% compounded semi-annually produces $6.09 per $100. Therefore, 6% is the nominal rate and 6.09% is the effective rate. A rate of 6% converted semi-annually yields the same interest as a rate of 6.09% on an annual basis.

Discount Rate

When the loan proceeds disbursed by the lender are less than face value (the original principal sum stated in the promissory note), the lender has deducted "up front" a loan fee and perhaps discount points as compensation for making the loan on the agreed terms. The borrower thus receives less than must be repaid under the contract. This lending practice is called "discounting." loans. Real estate lenders discount loans by collecting "points" in advance to increase yield. (Sometimes under a bank's commercial loan terms, the *total* interest is deducted in advance before the loan proceeds are given to the borrower. This method is usually associated with short-term bank loans.)

When interest tables are unavailable, it is possible to *approximate* effective interest cost when discounting occurs. Here is the procedure:

i = approximate effective interest rate (expressed as a decimal)

r = contract interest rate (expressed as a decimal)

d = discount rate (expressed as a decimal)

P = principal of loan (expressed as the whole number 1 for all dollar amounts)

n = term (years, periods, or fraction thereof)

The formula for approximating the effective rate of interest on a discounted real estate loan is written:

$$i = r + [(d \div n) \div (P-d)]$$

Example. What is the approximate effective interest on a $60,000 mortgage loan, with a 20-year term, contract rate of 12% per annum, if the loan is discounted 3% so that only $58,200 is disbursed to the borrower?

$$i = .12 + [(.03 \div 20) \div (1 - .03)] = .12 + .0015 \div .97 = .121546 = 12.15\%$$

Principal-Plus-Interest

Another manner of figuring interest is the Principal-Plus-Interest or the "interest extra" approach. Here the borrower makes a fixed payment on the principal each time *plus* paying the interest on the unpaid balance. Since the interest is different each time, the total payment is different each time. This method is not widely used in California in the case of first mortgages or trust deeds. It is occasionally found in secondary financing.

Types of Tables

The mathematics of financing is generally done with appropriate tables, formulas and calculators. Courses dealing with these subjects are available in most communities.

The following tables are used in real estate finance:

Amortization tables. These are commonly available in booklet form from various title companies, escrow companies, and banks. They indicate the monthly payment needed for periodic repayment of a loan, with interest.

Discount or present worth tables. Money has time value. A dollar in cash today is worth more than the payment of the same dollar a year from now. Or, to phrase it another way, a dollar to be paid in one year is worth less than a dollar paid today. But how much less? That depends on the rate of interest money would normally earn in that year. By checking a Present Worth Table we can determine how much less a payment in the future is worth today.

Proration table. This is simply a table that gives the number of days between various dates. It is used to prorate (adjust or divide between principals) items such as interest, insurance premiums, and rent.

Remaining balance table. This table shows the remaining balance of a loan expressed as a percentage of the original loan amount, using the following data: original loan amount, interest rate, age of loan, and original term of loan.

Mortgage yield tables. We use this table to determine yield on a mortgage at a specified discount or discount at a specified yield.

Balloon payment table. We use this table to determine the unpaid balance due on a loan before it has been amortized. Loans, especially second trust deed loans, often have terms of five years but are amortized over twelve or fifteen years, resulting in a lump sum (balloon) payment due at the end of five years.

Compound interest table. This table shows the six functions of $1 and annual constants for monthly payment loans. Arranged often in six columns with each column being one of the compound interest (future value) or annuity (present value) functions.

Constant annual percent tables. An annual constant is the sum of twelve (12) monthly payments expressed in percent of a principal loan amount. When multiplied times the loan amount, the annual loan payment may be determined. Remaining term of a loan, remaining loan balance, and interest rate of a loan may also be determined by use of a constant annual percent table.

Depreciation tables. These tables show the amount of depreciation that is deductible each year for properties with varying economic lives. There is usually a set for each economic life in terms of years and each set has columns devoted to the various methods of calculating depreciation (straight line, declining balance, and sum-of-the-years'-digits).

The amount of depreciation is usually expressed as a percentage of the depreciable value of the improvement.

THE TOOLS OF ANALYSIS - INCOME PROPERTY

The tools of analysis most commonly used to evaluate loan proposals for investment/income properties fall into four main categories: liquidity, leverage, activity and profitability.

Liquidity

A loan officer must determine how able a borrower is to pay bills as they come due. Current assets are compared to current liabilities. A liquidity ratio of 2 to 1 (current assets are twice the liabilities) or better is recognized as safe and acceptable by most lenders. Cash and accounts and notes receivable due within one year are "current" assets; liabilities due or payable within one year are considered "current."

Leverage

Leverage is the ability of the borrower/investor to control a large investment with a small amount of his or her own equity capital and a large amount of other people's money. The more money borrowed in relation to value of the property, the greater the leverage. Leverage tests reveal how much of the total financing for the project is supplied by the owner and how much is supplied by creditors such as the mortgage lender.

Debt-to-equity ratio. Leverage tests in connection with analysis of a borrower's financial statements are completed by comparing the owner's equity interest and the total value of the capital investment to the long term debt and the value of the total capital investment. The purpose is to find how much of the total investment is ownership and how much is debt. To determine the original equity ratio, divide the down payment by the purchase price. To determine the debt ratio, divide the loan amount by the purchase price.

It is common for equity investors to seek debt ratios in excess of 75-80%. Lenders, looking at risk factors, carefully scrutinize loan proposals to assure a safe equity ratio based on property characteristics and borrower's repayment record. The rule of thumb ratio for debt to equity ratio will be something between 3:1 and 4:1. The borrower often wants a more extreme ratio because it reduces the amount of his or her own money that is being risked. Real estate investment examples have been presented where ratios of 1 to almost 0 are achieved by borrowers. This is usually a very dangerous situation for the lender. An exception of course would be where the repayment of the loan is guaranteed or insured by some reputable third party in the transaction, such as the FHA or VA or a financially strong company such as a major chain store or oil company.

Some lenders are willing to risk entering a high debt to equity loan situation in anticipation of market prices going up, which automatically achieves growth in the owner's equity and a more moderate ratio is automatically achieved. Experience has repeatedly shown that this expectation is not always borne out, especially in unstable economic conditions.

Coverage of fixed expenses is a test of how many times net income before income taxes and fixed expenses (gross income minus operating expenses) will cover the fixed expenses. It reveals how low income can drop before the property (or the borrower) will be unable to meet the fixed expenses such as real estate taxes, insurance, license and permit fees.

Net income after operating expenses is divided by fixed expenses to get this ratio. If the ratio is 1:1, the net income after operating expenses is just barely able to cover the fixed expenses.

Activity

Activity tests are designed to reveal just how hard and effectively assets are working. There are several tests for this but the most widely used is the income to total asset ratio. This ratio is found by dividing total income by the value of total assets.

Profitability

Profitability tests are designed to see how much net profit results from the operation. The following are several of a variety of ratios and tests that are used to inquire into profitability.

Return on net worth. This is the ratio of net profit (after taxes) to the net worth of the project. This will yield a percentage return on investment which can be compared with the return available from other investments of comparable risk.

Yield analysis. This is a form of analysis well suited to determining profitability of real estate projects because it is relatively easy to compute and takes into consideration three factors unique in their combination to real estate investment: cash return, equity return, and tax shelter.

It involves dividing the total return (net spendable cash income, principal reduction of mortgage loans, and tax shelter) by the investor's equity.

13 Government Participation in Real Estate Finance

This chapter discusses three government programs which are very important to the California real estate industry:

1. the mortgage insurance program of the Federal Housing Administration;
2. the mortgage guaranty program of the United States Department of Veterans Affairs; and
3. the mortgage loan program of the California Department of Veterans Affairs.

The reader should be aware that the programs offered by these agencies change regularly.

THE FEDERAL HOUSING ADMINISTRATION

The Federal Housing Administration (FHA) is part of the U.S. Department of Housing and Urban Development (HUD). Since 1934, FHA has offered mortgage insurance programs which help people obtain financing for homes. (HUD Web site: http://www.hud.gov/)

FHA mortgage insurance allows a homebuyer to make a modest down payment and obtain a mortgage for the balance of the purchase price. The loan is made by a bank, savings and loan association, mortgage company, credit union, or other FHA-approved lender. FHA insures the loan and pays the lender if the borrower defaults on the mortgage. (Of course, if the property is readily saleable at a price which exceeds the amount of the loan including all charges, the lender will undoubtedly sell the property and not apply for FHA funds.) Because of this insurance, the lender may offer more liberal terms than the prospective homeowner might otherwise obtain.

Qualifying
A person with a satisfactory credit history, enough cash to close a loan, and sufficient steady income to make the monthly payments should be able to qualify for an FHA-insured mortgage.

For the most part, FHA mortgages are limited to owner-occupied properties. One exception is the rehabilitation insurance program, which is available to investors.

Special terms are available to qualified veterans. The veteran must present a *Certificate of Veterans Status* from the Department of Veterans Affairs. There is no limit on the number of times an eligible veteran can use this FHA privilege.

Types of Properties and Mortgages
Primarily, FHA insures mortgages for:

1. the purchase of existing and newly built single family homes and condominiums;
2. home improvements;
3. the purchase and repair of houses needing rehabilitation;

4.   the purchase of two-, three-, and four-unit properties; and

5.   the refinancing of existing mortgages.

An FHA-insured loan can be fixed rate, adjustable rate, graduated payment, or growing equity.

A fixed rate mortgage features an interest rate which stays the same for the term of the loan. The payment will also remain constant unless amounts included for taxes and insurance change.

With an adjustable rate mortgage (ARM), the interest rate and payment may increase or decrease during the life of the loan. The initial interest rate on an FHA ARM will stay the same for the first twelve or eighteen months, as specified in the note. Thereafter, the rate will vary with the 1-year Treasury Constant Maturities Index but cannot increase or decrease more than one percent in any year or five percent over the life of the loan.

A graduated payment mortgage (GPM) allows the borrower to make lower payments during the early years of the loan. Then the payments increase annually for several years before leveling off and remaining constant for the balance of the loan term. Because the lower beginning payments do not cover all the interest then due, the loan balance actually increases (negative amortization) during the early years. A GPM may be appropriate for a person who expects his/her income to rise as the years go by and the loan payments increase.

A growing equity mortgage (GEM) requires payments which increase during the early years of the loan, with all of the excess applied to reduce the balance owed. A GEM features early payoff and a reduction in the total amount of interest paid.

Maximum Loan Amounts
Maximum loan amounts for FHA-insured loans vary with the cost of housing. Real estate licensees and their clients should consult with HUD-approved lenders or the local HUD Field Office as to the maximum loan amount for a certain area.

Down Payment
Most FHA programs require a down payment of between 3 and 5 percent of the total cost of the home. The total cost is the purchase price plus closing costs. Total cost does not include prepaid items such as real estate taxes and hazard insurance.

Loan Terms and Prepayment
The costs associated with a loan can vary significantly from one lender to another. FHA does not establish minimum or maximum amounts for interest rates, discount points, and other fees/closing costs for the loan. Rather, these are all negotiable between the borrower and lender. There is no prepayment penalty.

Mortgage Insurance Premium
FHA charges a premium to insure a mortgage. The premiums are used to pay lenders if/when borrowers default on FHA-insured mortgages.

On most FHA-insured mortgages, the borrower must pay an up-front mortgage insurance premium (MIP) and an annual MIP as well. The up-front MIP can be financed into the mortgage.

Applying for an FHA Loan

Having selected a lender, the borrower will fill out a loan application and meet with a loan officer. The borrower will provide his/her most recent bank statement and pay stub, picture identification, proof of social security number, and fees for appraisal and credit report.

Loan Approval

Many lenders are authorized to approve FHA mortgage applications without submitting any paperwork to FHA. These Direct Endorsement Lenders handle most FHA-insured loans. In some cases, however, FHA reviews information submitted by the lender and determines whether the property and the borrower are acceptable risks for an FHA-insured mortgage.

MOST FREQUENTLY USED FHA PROGRAMS

FHA derives its authority to insure mortgage loans from the National Housing Act. This act has eleven main subdivisions called "titles." Real estate licensees and their principals will be concerned mostly with Titles I and II.

Title I - Property Improvement; Manufactured Home Purchase

Title I authorizes FHA to insure lending institutions against loss on loans made to finance alterations, repairs, and improvements to existing structures, and the building of small new structures for nonresidential use.

These loans are made by private lending institutions to borrowers with satisfactory incomes and credit records.

The property can be single-family, multi-family, or non-residential.

A Title I loan may also be used for the purchase of a manufactured home and/or a lot for a manufactured home, so long as the manufactured home is to remain personal property. If the manufactured home is attached to a foundation, and thus real property, a Title II, Section 203(b) loan must be used.

Title II - Home Mortgage Insurance

Section 203(b) of Title II is the most commonly used FHA single family program. Using this program, a borrower may purchase a new or existing one- to four-family home in an urban or rural area. A 203(b) mortgage may have a term of 10, 15, 20, 25, or 30 years.

Section 234(c) provides mortgage insurance for the purchase of a unit in a condominium project. FHA must first approve the project. In part, FHA conditions this approval on an owner-occupancy rate of at least 51 percent.

Section 203(k) authorizes mortgage insurance for the purchase (or refinance) and rehabilitation of a home which is at least one year old. A portion of the loan proceeds are placed in an escrow account and released as rehabilitation progresses. Rehabilitation may involve moving the home to a new foundation at a different site. Also, a Section 203(k) mortgage may be used to convert a non-residential building to residential use or to change the number of family units in a building.

A **Section 203(h)** loan can help a person whose home has been damaged or destroyed because of a major disaster, as declared by the President of the United

States. The loan may be used to purchase a new or existing home. No down payment is required.

Section 203(i) authorizes mortgage insurance for rural properties. This could include a farm house on at least 2.5 acres of land adjacent to an all-weather road.

Section 220 allows mortgage insurance for rehabilitation of dwellings with up to eleven family units or to build new dwellings in urban redevelopment areas.

Section 220(h) authorizes insured improvement loans for dwellings with up to eleven family units in urban areas.

Section 221(d)(2) provides home mortgage insurance for low and moderate income families or families displaced by urban renewal, code enforcement, condemnation or by a major disaster.

Section 222 authorizes mortgage insurance for those on active duty with the Department of Transportation (Coast Guard) or the Department of Oceanic and Atmospheric Administration. There is no up front mortgage insurance premium and the employing agency pays the monthly mortgage insurance premium directly to HUD as long as the borrower remains in active service. The borrower must have a certificate of eligibility from the employing agency.

Section 223(e) involves properties in older, declining urban areas.

Section 237 authorizes mortgage insurance for low and moderate income families who are unable to meet normal underwriting standards because of their credit history. To qualify, the borrower(s) must obtain counseling from a HUD-approved agency. These agencies provide budget, debt management, and related counseling services.

Section 238(c) provides mortgage insurance for repair, rehabilitation, or purchase of a home near any military installation in a federally impacted area. The Secretary of Defense must certify the need for additional housing in the area.

Section 240 deals with purchase of a home on leased land.

U.S. DEPARTMENT OF VETERANS AFFAIRS (VA)

Previously known as the Veterans Administration, the United States Department of Veterans Affairs guarantees loans made to eligible veterans by institutional lenders (mortgage companies, savings and loans, banks). We continue to call these VA (not DVA) loans. A VA guaranty on such a loan helps protect the lender against loss if the payments are not made. The intention is to encourage lenders to offer veterans more favorable loan terms. (Benefits Web site: http://www.vba.va.gov)

Purpose of VA Loans
A VA loan will enable a qualified veteran to:
1.   buy, build, alter, repair or improve a home or condominium (including a farm residence to be occupied by the veteran as a home);
2.   buy a mobilehome with or without the lot; or
3.   refinance an existing mortgage on a dwelling owned and occupied by the veteran.

Eligibility

The following individuals are eligible for VA loans:

1. A veteran of active military duty during World War II, the Korean Conflict, Vietnam Era, or Post-Vietnam Era, provided the veteran was discharged or released from active duty under conditions other than dishonorable after active duty of 90 days or more (or because of a service-connected disability), any part of which was during one of the following periods:

    September 16, 1940 to July 25, 1947;

    June 27, 1950 to January 31, 1955; or

    August 5, 1964 to May 8, 1975.

2. A veteran of active duty entirely within the period July 25, 1947 and prior to June 27, 1950 or during any part of the periods after January 31, 1955 and prior to August 5, 1964 or after May 8, 1975 and prior to September 7, 1980 (for enlisted personnel; October 16, 1981 for commissioned officers), provided the veteran was discharged or released from active duty under conditions other than dishonorable from a period of continuous active duty of 181 days or more (or for a service-connected disability). Absent discharge or release, a veteran must have served on continuous active duty at least 181 days.

3. A veteran who originally enlisted in a regular component of the Armed Forces after September 7, 1980 (after October 16, 1981 for a commissioned officer), provided the veteran completes the lesser of twenty-four continuous months of active duty or the full period for which the person was called or ordered to active duty. These minimum service requirements do not apply to individuals still on active duty or those who are discharged or released from active duty for convenience of the U.S. Government, hardship, or a service-connected disability.

4. Any member of the Women's Army Auxiliary Corps who served for at least 90 days and who was honorably discharged therefrom for disability incurred in the line of duty. (This applies only to persons so discharged from the Women's Army Auxiliary Corps prior to the integration of that corps into the Women's Army Corps.)

5. Certain United States citizens who served in the armed forces of a government allied with the United States in World War II.

6. Unremarried surviving spouses of an above-described eligible person who died as the result of service or service-connected disabilities.

7. Service personnel who have served at least 181 days in active duty status, even though not discharged, while their service continues without a break.

8. The spouse of any member of the armed forces serving on active duty who is listed as missing in action, or is a prisoner of war and has been so listed for a total of more than 90 days.

Reservists and National Guard members activated on or after August 2, 1990 for the Persian Gulf Conflict may also be eligible. Questions regarding eligibility should be directed to VA at 1-800-827-1000. VA has two publications which will also be of assistance: "VA-Guaranteed Home Loans for Veterans" (VA Pamphlet 26-4) and "To the Home-Buying Veteran" (VA Pamphlet 26-6). These may be obtained by writing to:

Department of Veterans Affairs
810 Vermont Avenue NW
Washington, D.C. 20420

Guarantee Amounts
For current guaranty amounts, the veteran or agent should contact the VA or a lender who funds VA loans.

Interest Rates Are Negotiable
The interest rate on a VA loan is negotiable between lender and borrower.

Funding Fee for VA Home Loans
VA collects a funding fee for each loan. The fee varies with the amount of the down payment and the status of the borrower (active duty/veteran/reservist). The fee is payable for both VA home and mobilehome loans with the following exceptions:

- veterans receiving VA compensation for service-connected disabilities;
- veterans who elected to receive service retirement pay in lieu of VA compensation; and
- surviving spouses of veterans who died in service or from a service-connected disability.

The funding fee may be included in the loan and paid to VA from loan proceeds without regard to limiting the loan amount to the reasonable value of the property.

Loan Classifications and Loan Structure
VA loans are classified as real estate loans. A real estate loan is any loan used to purchase real property, improved or to be improved. A VA loan may be:

1. a traditional 30-year mortgage with a fixed-rate and term.

2. a Graduated Payment Mortgage, amortized in a manner which allows lower initial monthly payments. The monthly payment increases annually by a fixed percentage during the first five years. At the beginning of the sixth year, the payments become level and remain so.

3. a Temporary Interest Rate Buydown loan, providing that funds be held in an escrow account to subsidize monthly mortgage payments for a set period of time. Most buydown plans run from 3 to 5 years and the escrowed funds may be paid by buyer or seller.

4. an Adjustable Rate Mortgage, with annual interest rate increase limited to one percent. The maximum increase in the interest rate over the life of the loan is five percent.

5. a Growing Equity Mortgage, with a gradual increase in monthly payments. All of the increase is applied to the principal balance of the loan, resulting in growing equity and accelerated amortization.

Manufactured Home (Mobilehome) Loans
A qualified veteran may use a VA loan for the purchase of a manufactured home.

To be eligible for a VA loan, a single-wide manufactured home must be at least 40 feet x 10 feet (400 square feet). A double-wide must be at least 35 feet x 20 feet (700 square feet).

Elimination of the requirement that a veteran have maximum entitlement available for use in order to obtain a loan enables use of remaining entitlement for any eligible purpose, including a manufactured home loan, except that a veteran who obtains a guaranteed loan to purchase a manufactured home may not use remaining entitlement to obtain another manufactured home without first disposing of the previously acquired manufactured home.

The maximum term of a loan for the purchase of a single-wide manufactured home, with or without a lot is 20 years and 32 days.

The maximum term of a loan for the purchase of a double-wide manufactured home without a lot is 23 years and 32 days; with a lot, 25 years and 32 days.

Location. A manufactured home may be located on any VA-approved rental site, or any lot owned or to be purchased by the veteran which has been determined to be acceptable by the VA. A veteran must make certain that the lot location does not conflict with any zoning laws prohibiting manufactured homes. The VA guarantees loans to veterans for the purchase of manufactured homes that are permanently affixed to a foundation, provided the foundation meets VA requirements and the unit and land are taxed as real estate.

Interest rates. The interest rate for a VA manufactured housing loan is negotiable.

Assumability. A VA loan on a manufactured home cannot be assumed unless the purchaser qualifies from a credit standpoint. If the veteran sells the manufactured home and permits the buyer to assume the loan obligation, the veteran will remain liable on the loan unless application is made to VA for a release from liability on the loan and VA grants the release in writing. Further, the veteran will not be eligible to use VA loan entitlement for purchase of another manufactured home until the manufactured home loan is paid in full, regardless of whether or not VA grants the release from liability.

If, however, the buyer obtains new financing in connection with the sale and the VA loan is paid in full, the veteran will have no further liability on the loan and will be eligible to use his or her VA loan entitlement for other purposes.

Refinancing Existing Loans

Veterans may refinance existing mortgage loans or other liens of record on a dwelling owned and occupied by them. Any discount points paid in connection with such refinancing must be reasonable in amount and may be added to the loan, as may back taxes and assessments. The amount of loan may not exceed 90% of VA's reasonable value plus funding fee.

Under the refinancing loan guarantee, a loan may be made:

- solely to refinance the sum due the holder of an existing mortgage loan or other lien indebtedness; or

- to refinance an existing mortgage loan or other lien indebtedness and to provide the veteran with funds for a purpose acceptable to the lender.

A veteran can refinance a VA loan with another VA loan provided:

1. The interest rate of the loan must be less than the interest rate of the loan being refinanced, except that an adjustable rate loan can be refinanced with a fixed

rate loan even if the interest rate on the fixed rate loan is higher than the rate currently in force on the adjustable rate loan.

2. The new loan must be secured by the same dwelling or farm residence as secured the loan being refinanced and such dwelling or residence must be owned and occupied by the veteran or his/her spouse.

3. The amount of the loan may not exceed an amount equal to the sum of the balance of the loan being refinanced and such closing costs (including any discount points permitted) as may be authorized by the Secretary.

Term. Interest rate reduction refinancing loans may have a term of up to 10 years longer than that of the original loan, to a maximum of 30 years and 32 days.

A refinance loan shall be deemed to have been obtained with the guaranty entitlement used to obtain the loan being refinanced. Therefore, the loan may be guaranteed without regard to the amount of outstanding guaranty entitlement available for use by the veteran, and the amount of the veteran's guaranty entitlement shall not be charged as a result of any guaranty provided for such purpose.

Surviving spouse. If a veteran is deceased and the veteran's surviving spouse is a co-obligor under an existing VA loan, the surviving spouse is entitled to refinance the loan with another VA loan. Like a veteran, the surviving spouse will be permitted to pay a reasonable discount in connection with obtaining a VA loan to refinance an existing VA home or mobilehome loan.

Condominiums

VA guarantees loans for the purchase of one-family residential units in a project converted or proposed to be converted to condominium ownership, provided the governing documents for the project meet VA Regulations and the project or unit has been approved by VA on or after July 1, 1979. The VA approach to this program area is intended to be of sufficient flexibility to provide protection to veterans as potential homeowners and to VA as guarantor while assuring the viability of the program. The following definitions apply to this program:

• **Existing Condominium.** A condominium project originally built and sold as a condominium where all on-site and off-site improvements were completed prior to appraisal by VA.

• **Converted Condominium.** A project or structure not originally built or sold as a condominium but subsequently converted to a condominium and approved by VA on or after July 1, 1979.

• **Proposed Condominium.** A condominium project that is to be constructed or is under construction.

• **High-Rise Condominium.** A condominium project which is a multi-story elevator building.

• **Low-Rise Condominium.** A condominium in which all or part of a living unit extends over or under another living unit. Such a project may contain one or more elevators. (Also known as a garden apartment project.)

• **Horizontal Condominium.** A condominium project in which generally no part of a living unit extends over or under another living unit. These (detached, semi-detached, row, and quadruplex) projects are designed in a manner similar to most planned developments.

When Sales Price Exceeds Amount Shown on VA Certificate of Reasonable Value (CRV)

Prior to signing an offer or contract creating a legal obligation to pay a purchase price or cost which exceeds the amount shown on a CRV, a veteran must be informed of the reasonable value established by VA. If a veteran signs a sales agreement before the CRV is available, the contract must provide that if the purchase price exceeds the VA reasonable value, the veteran may either affirm the contract and complete the transaction or withdraw from the transaction and receive a refund of the deposit without further legal liability or obligation.

Down Payment

In the case of a home or condominium loan, the VA does not usually require a down payment. The lender, however, may require one. A VA loan cannot exceed the VA reasonable value plus funding fee. Any difference must always be paid by the veteran in cash from personal resources.

VA usually requires a 5 percent down payment for manufactured homes. However, a lender may require a larger down payment.

Discount Points and Prepayment

The payment of loan discount points is a matter for negotiation between the buyer, seller, and lender. There is no prepayment penalty.

Energy Conservation Measures

A VA loan may be used to improve a dwelling or farm residence with solar heating/cooling or some other qualified residential energy conservation measure. The interest rate on such a loan is negotiable between the veteran/borrower and the lender.

Assumability of VA Loans

There are limitations on the assumability of VA loans. Loans for which commitments have been made on or after March 1, 1988 are not assumable unless:

1. the lender is notified of the proposed assumption prior to the transfer;
2. the loan is current;
3. the new purchaser has agreed to assume full liability for the repayment of the loan and all the veteran's obligations under the original loan documents; and
4. the new purchaser qualifies from a credit standpoint.

A lender is permitted to charge a fee in connection with processing an assumption request.

Release of Liability

For VA loans closed on or after March 1, 1988, all sales must be approved through a Release of Liability process. For a loan closed prior to March 1, 1988, a veteran/seller should request the necessary forms and instructions for release of liability prior to conveying title to a purchaser who assumes the VA loan. This request must be made to the VA office that guaranteed the loan.

VA Pamphlet 26-68-1, "Selling Your GI Home," is available at all VA Regional Offices. Lenders, title and escrow companies, real estate licensees and service organization representatives are urged to order the pamphlet for distribution to veterans.

Veterans are reminded that they are still legally liable to the Government on their VA loan even though they sell the property and the loan is assumed, *unless* VA releases the veteran in writing from liability.

Veterans should be certain that anyone assuming their VA loan agrees in writing on the sales agreement that he is willing to apply and qualify for the veteran's release of liability prior to the veteran conveying title to the property.

In the event the assuming purchaser of the veteran's VA loan does not qualify for assumption of the loan, the veteran and the assuming purchaser will be notified of such by the VA.

If the person buying the veteran's property obtains other financing and the VA loan is paid in full at close of escrow, the veteran may then have loan guaranty eligibility restored. However, a Release of Liability alone will not automatically restore entitlement. See "Restoration of Entitlement" below.

Restoration of Entitlement
VA can restore a veteran's entitlement to loan guaranty benefits after the property has been disposed of and the prior loan has been paid in full. Even if the property has not been sold, there can be a *one-time* restoration if the veteran has repaid the prior VA loan in full. After this one-time restoration, a future restoration must be preceded by disposal of all property previously financed with VA loans.

VA can restore a veteran/seller's entitlement and release the veteran from liability to VA when an immediate veteran/transferee has agreed to assume the outstanding balance on the loan and consented to use of his/her entitlement to the same extent that the entitlement of the veteran/transferor was used originally. The veteran/transferee and the property must otherwise meet the requirements of the law.

If VA has suffered a loss on a loan, the loss must be paid in full before entitlement can be restored.

Supplemental Servicing
VA is committed to assisting veterans who find themselves in temporary financial difficulty and default on their VA loan payments.

While VA does not relieve mortgagees of their primary loan servicing responsibilities, VA conducts appropriate supplemental servicing without specific requests from mortgagors or mortgagees. When a loan becomes three months delinquent, holders are required to file a Notice of Default showing the amount delinquent, the types of contact made with the mortgagor, the reason(s) for default, a summary of the holder's servicing activities, and a recommendation as to whether further indulgence is warranted. Upon receipt of this Notice of Default, a VA loan guaranty technician reviews it for adequacy of servicing and to ascertain whether any personal supplemental servicing should be undertaken at that time. At minimum, contact is made with the veteran/borrower by letter. This contact serves the two-fold purpose of communicating, at an early date, VA's interest in having the veteran make satisfactory arrangements to pay the arrearage and of providing the veteran with the name and address of the VA's Regional Office of jurisdiction, as well as the name and telephone number of a responsible VA loan servicing supervisor. If personal supplemental servicing is warranted and provided, it is the VA's objective to assist the borrower through financial counseling and the development of special repayment plans to reinstate the loan to good standing.

Lending Agencies

Any bank, savings and loan association, insurance company, mortgage company, or other lending agency may make a VA loan.

Procedure

The first step for the veteran planning to negotiate a veteran's guaranteed loan is to find the property. If a deposit is paid to bind the deal, the deposit agreement usually provides for the return of the deposit in case of failure to obtain a VA loan. The next step is to present the proposition to a bank or other lending agency. Every veteran carries a potential loan guaranty in his or her discharge papers. Supervised lenders and non-supervised automatic lenders approved by VA may process and complete most loans, automatically committing VA to a guaranty.

The property is then checked by an appraiser who must be one of a panel qualified by VA. VA's CRV (cost: $350 minimum) then goes to the prospective lender and this bank or lending agency decides whether it will approve and make the loan.

Web site: http://www.vba.va.gov/bln/loan/veteran.htm

CALIFORNIA VETERANS FARM AND HOME PURCHASE PROGRAM

Purpose

In recognition of veterans' sacrifice and service, the California Legislature established the Veterans Farm and Home Purchase Program (Cal-Vet) in 1921. The program provides low-cost, low-interest financing so that an eligible veteran can purchase a home, farm or mobilehome in California for use as a primary residence. (Cal VA Web site: http://www.ns.net/cadva)

The First Loan

Owen W. Myers, a 100% disabled World War I veteran, obtained the first Cal-Vet loan on June 30, 1922. The loan enabled Mr. Myers to purchase a home on the east side of Los Angeles for $4,120.00. The twenty-year loan, at 5% interest, required payments of $25.94 per month. Mr. Myers paid the loan in full in fifteen years.

Benefit Provided

The Cal-Vet program can fund a home, farm, or mobilehome loan under a contract of sale arrangement. Loan costs and down payment are low. The maximum loan amount varies with the type of property (home, farm, manufactured home), the purchase price and the cost of housing in the area/county. (The highest home loan amount is currently $250,000.) A veteran/borrower or agent should contact Cal-Vet for current information in this regard.

Up to an additional $5,000 in loan amount may be granted for a home equipped with an active solar energy heating device.

Source of Funds

Cal-Vet loan funds are obtained through the sale of both State of California general obligation bonds and veterans' revenue bonds. These bonds are repaid by veterans participating in the loan program.

Interest Rates and Loan Terms

The interest rate on Cal-Vet loans is variable, depending on bond expenses and program administration costs. The interest rate has never been above 8 percent.

By law, Cal-Vet must review the interest rate once each year. Ninety days' written notice must precede any increase in the interest rate.

New Cal-Vet loans are initially based on a 30-year loan term for single family residences. A more limited term may be necessary in individual cases. A loan for the purchase of a mobilehome in a park will normally have a repayment period between 10 and 20 years, depending upon the age, quality and condition of the mobilehome and certain characteristics of the park.

A veteran may make a written request for a shorter loan term. The term of a loan does not affect the interest rate.

Eligibility

Basic laws governing eligibility:

1. Release from active duty under honorable conditions.
2. At least 90 days service on active duty, unless:
    a. discharged because of a service-connected disability;
    b. eligibility to receive a campaign or expeditionary medal; or
    c. called to active duty from the Reserve or National Guard due to a Presidential Executive Order during a time when the United States was engaged in a military conflict and released under honorable conditions after serving less than 90 days. Note: Service solely for training does not qualify.

Unless the United States government authorized a campaign or expeditionary medal for the veteran's period of active duty, at least one day of active service must have been during one of the following "war" periods:

*   **Operation Restore Hope.** Veterans who served or worked in direct support to troops in Somalia (regardless of the number of days on active duty).

*   **Operation Desert Shield and Operation Desert Storm.** August 2, 1990 through a date yet to be determined.

*   **Vietnam Era.** August 5, 1964 through May 7, 1975.

*   **Korean Period.** June 27, 1950 through January 31, 1955.

*   **World War II.** December 7, 1941 through December 31, 1946.

A veteran who was called to active duty from the Reserve or National Guard by Presidential Executive Order while the United States was engaged in a military conflict need not have served in the theater of operations, or have received a campaign or expeditionary medal, or have served 90 consecutive days on active duty to be eligible for Cal-Vet benefits.

Active duty personnel need only provide a statement of satisfactory performance from the military indicating their character of service and verifying their qualifying dates of service.

Veterans who are eligible for military retirement, or receiving military retirement pay, may have dual eligibility if they purchased a farm or home through Cal-Vet while on active military duty. The original purchase contract must have been paid in full and the veteran must have served during more than one period for which eligibility is granted. Veterans with active duty during more than one period for which eligibility is granted, with a break in service between the periods of eligibility, also may have dual eligibility.

Cal-Vet may also acquire an assignment of an Indian veteran's leasehold or beneficial interest in trust land for the purpose of entering into a contract with the Indian veteran for the acquisition of a home, farm, or mobilehome on trust land.

The un-remarried surviving spouse of an eligible veteran may apply for a Cal-Vet loan if the veteran:

1. died after filing an application for a Cal-Vet loan;

2. died, before or after discharge from active duty, from injuries sustained in the line of duty; or

3. is being held as a prisoner of war or has been designated by the armed forces as missing in action.

The pertinent military service documents (primarily the DD-214 discharge document) must establish eligibility. If necessary, Cal-Vet may require additional evidence.

Military service solely for the purpose of processing, physical examination, or training does not qualify the veteran for a Cal-Vet loan. A student at a military academy who fails to complete the course of study and does not serve on active duty cannot qualify.

Federal Recapture Tax for Veterans' Revenue Bonds

Recipients of Cal-Vet loans funded from proceeds of veterans' *revenue* bonds may be subject to a Federal recapture tax. This tax would become due only if:

1. the property were sold or refinanced during the first nine full years following the funding of the Cal-Vet loan;

2. there was a gain on the sale; and

3. the veteran (seller) has current income above a specified threshold.

The purpose of the federally imposed tax is to repay the government for some of the tax exempt benefits associated with revenue bond funds. It should be noted that, due to the way the federal law is written, very few veterans pay recapture tax.

There is no recapture tax liability if the Cal-Vet loan is funded from the proceeds of veterans' *general* obligation bonds.

Refinance Restrictions

Under federal law, Cal-Vet loan funds are rarely used to refinance existing loans. The exceptions are:

- interim loans (bridge loans or similar temporary initial financing);
- construction period loans.

It is the responsibility of the veteran to assure that interim or construction financing complies with federal law governing refinancing.

Application Procedure

In order to qualify, a completed Cal-Vet loan application must be received in the local district office prior to completion of the purchase or acquisition of an interest of record in the property to be financed with a Cal-Vet loan.

The above rule does not apply if:

1. the veteran has an interest of record in a building site;
2. the dwelling has not been completed, and
3. a certificate of occupancy has not been issued.

Cal-Vet will prequalify potential loan applicants at local district offices at no cost to the veteran. Prequalification will determine if the veteran is militarily eligible and financially qualified for the loan amount requested, and provide an estimated monthly payment. A copy of the DD214 will assist with the prequalification process.

Cal-Vet requires that the eligible applicant be qualified financially for the loan requested. District offices may provide credit guideline information prior to submission of a loan application.

A loan application package, as well as assistance in completing the forms, can be obtained from any Cal-Vet office, or from local County Veteran Services Offices.

After a completed loan application package is received, Cal-Vet can process a typical loan request in 35 calendar days or less.

Loan Processing Fees

Cal-Vet charges a $50 application fee. There are no "points" charged to the buyer or seller. The only other fee collected prior to close of escrow is for completion of the appraisal. If a Cal-Vet appraiser performs the property appraisal, the cost will be $300. Fees charged by outside appraisers may vary. The appraisal fee must be paid at the time the appraisal is conducted.

Secondary Financing

Cal-Vet may consent to secondary financing at the time of purchase to supplement the Cal-Vet loan. The combined financing cannot exceed 90 percent of the appraised value of the property. Also, the secondary lender must subordinate to Cal-Vet's interest by completing and returning Cal-Vet's subordination agreement.

This document must be submitted before a loan package can be forwarded for funding.

Construction Loans Available
Cal-Vet provides funds to purchase a building site and construct a home.

Cal-Vet must approve the site that is owned, or will be purchased, by the veteran. Qualifying sites include: undeveloped sites/acreage; lots in subdivision developments; sites in non-profit, self-help developments; and sites on Indian trust lands where the Indian veteran can assign a leasehold or beneficial interest in the site. Condominiums, duplexes, townhouses, farms, and mobilehomes in parks do not quality.

Construction of the structure must be performed by a California licensed contractor. The contractor will be required to purchase a surety performance and payment bond.

Special Loan Conditions
The veteran, or a member of the veteran's immediate family, as defined by law, must occupy the property within sixty days after signing a Cal-Vet loan contract and must continue to reside in the property as the principal place of residence until the loan is paid in full or the property is sold.

There are two possible exceptions to the residency requirement. An exception concerning farm properties will be considered only if the veteran will be personally cultivating, harvesting crops or tending livestock. An exception can also be considered after the veteran has purchased and occupied a property and has then shown good cause for not residing in the home. This would require a signed Cal-Vet Waiver of Occupancy. All requests for a Waiver of Occupancy must be submitted in writing and must comply with Federal laws governing the use of tax-exempt bonds.

The transfer, assignment, encumbrance or rental of Cal-Vet property is prohibited without Cal-Vet's prior written consent.

If a Cal-Vet loan is prepaid in full within the first two years, the purchaser shall pay two percent of the original loan amount as a prepayment or service charge.

Special Loan Programs
Some veterans may qualify for specialized Cal-Vet loans. These include deferred principal payment loans for purchasers meeting certain income criteria, and conditional commitment loans to purchase homes in need of rehabilitation.

Subsequent Loan
A veteran may apply, under the same terms and conditions described above, for a subsequent Cal-Vet loan if the veteran:

1. has sold a Cal-Vet property;
2. has divested his/her interest in a Cal-Vet property through divorce or dissolution of marriage; or,
3. has dual eligibility (active duty during more than one qualifying service period) and a previous Cal-Vet loan has been paid in full.

Fire and Hazard Insurance

With the exception of condominium units with master insurance policies and mobilehomes, Cal-Vet contracts with insurance companies for fire and hazard insurance on all Cal-Vet properties. Broad coverage, including protection against abnormal earth movement, is provided on dwellings and appurtenant structures. The veteran must pay a deductible, currently $100.00, on each insured loss/claim. Premium payment is included in the monthly installment.

Disaster Coverage

The Cal-Vet Disaster Indemnity and Catastrophe Program provides low cost protection against some perils not covered by fire and hazard insurance. Covered perils include earthquake and flood. All Cal-Vet purchasers are required to participate in this program, with payment billed each spring. For each loss, the deductible is $250.00.

Notice

Up-to-date information may be obtained by calling Cal-Vet Home Loans at 800-952-5626, on the Net at http://www.ns.net/cadva, or any local Cal-Vet office.

14 Non-mortgage Alternatives to Real Estate Financing

There are a variety of ways to acquire real estate interests without using mortgage financing. With the exception of the real property sales contract, these methods are available only to large financiers, very strong tenants or substantial institutions.

An all-cash purchase is an obvious alternative to mortgage financing. However, it is often difficult for an individual to raise substantial sums of money and protect against unlimited liability.

Syndicate Equity Financing
Syndicates afford small investors opportunities to invest in high-yield real estate. A syndicate offers knowledge of values and the ability to find, organize and manage a successful venture.

Commercial Loan
A straight bank loan can be used to purchase real property. The borrower obtains the loan based on good credit or on some type of collateral (stocks, bonds, personal property) other than the real property.

Bonds or Stocks
Large, well-rated corporations can sell stocks or general obligation bonds in order to purchase real property without using a mortgage.

Long-term Lease
This is a good approach if the property is usable *as is*. If the lessee is leasing only the land and has to pay for construction of improvements, the investment will probably be larger than buying improved property with a mortgage.

Advantages to the tenant are:

- One hundred percent of rent is deductible as expense. (If property was owned, only the improvements would be depreciable.)

- Money freed for other uses can frequently be used more advantageously.

- Tenant's total debt load is not increased.

Disadvantages to the landlord are:

- Often cannot find good tenants willing to lease.

- Tenant having a high credit rating at beginning of lease may go "sour" in a few years.

- Tenant may improve property with special purpose development and then go bankrupt

- Tenant may go bankrupt before completing construction, leaving landlord with unsaleable and unleasable property.

Exchange

A trade or exchange of properties can be an alternative to mortgage financing, if the properties are not mortgaged and the trade is made without financing.

Sale-Leaseback

A sale-leaseback is a popular option for companies with excellent credit. Also termed *purchase-lease, sale-lease, lease-purchase* or *leaseback.*

Some advantages of sale-leaseback to seller/lessee are:

1. Property is suited to needs.
2. Working capital not tied up in fixed assets.
3. Since leases are not considered long-term liability, rent is 100 percent tax deductible. Lease term is often longer than mortgage. Balance sheet looks better and credit is enhanced.
4. Often more capital can be raised than by borrowing.
5. Writing off 100 percent of lease payments is frequently better than depreciation since the land cannot be depreciated.
6. By selling property at profit after development, seller acquires immediate use of additional cash. Repayment is actually in rent paid over time in constantly inflating dollars.
7. For companies working under government contracts that call for cost plus a fixed fee, rent is an allowable expense item but mortgage interest is not. (This is why many aircraft, electronic, and other defense plants are leased rather than owned.)

Some advantages of sale-leaseback to buyer/lessor are:

1. Transaction results in a long-term, carefree investment.
2. Property is likely to appreciate.
3. Usually, the lease payments are higher than the mortgage payments. Lease payments will pay off the mortgage and lessor will still have title to the property.
4. Investment will not be paid off prematurely, as mortgages often are through refinancing. Investor will not have to seek another good investment to replace the one prematurely paid off.
5. Lease terms often give lessor a claim against other assets of the lessee in the event of a default.

Sales Contract (Land Contract)

A real property sales contract is an instrument by which the seller (vendor) agrees to convey title to real property after the buyer (vendee) has met certain conditions specified in the contract and which does not require conveyance within one year.

If a buyer can make only a small down payment and monthly installments, a real property sales contract may be appropriate.

This device, variously designated "Installment Sales Contract," "Agreement to Convey," "Agreement for Purchase and Sale," "Land Sale Contract," or "Land

Contract of Sale," must meet the requirements set forth in Section 2985, et seq. of the California Civil Code.

Historically, the primary advantage of this instrument to a seller was the ease with which seller could eliminate purchaser's interest in the event of default. This advantage was considerably weakened by the court's conclusion, in *Barkis v. Scott* (34 Cal. 2d 116, 208 P. 2d 367), that California Civil Code Section 3275 was a sufficient barrier to harsh and unreasonable foreclosure proceedings. After *Barkis v. Scott,* other cases have expanded the remedies of defaulting vendees to include even willfully defaulting persons.

When selling a parcel of land under a sales contract which is not recorded, the seller is prohibited from otherwise encumbering the parcel to an aggregate amount exceeding the amount due under the contract without the written consent of the purchaser.

A real property sales contract must recite the number of years to complete payment and, if a tax estimate is made, the basis for it.

When selling real property under a real property sales contract, the seller must apply installment payments first to payment(s) due on an obligation(s) secured by the property. The seller must hold in trust payments received for taxes and insurance and use those funds only for those purposes, unless the payor and the holder of an encumbrance on the property agree to some other use of those funds.

A real property sales contract for purchase of real property in a subdivision must clearly set forth the legal description of the property, all the existing encumbrances at the date of the contract and the terms of the contract.

Except in the special area of large land developments, the advantage which a land contract may have held as a security device seems to have dissipated in favor of the use of a deed of trust with power of sale.

Disadvantages to buyer. The disadvantages of a sales contract to the buyer are:

1. The contract may include covenants restricting its assignment or transfer.

2. Most financial institutions regard a land contract as poor collateral.

3. Buyer has no assurance that the seller has good title at the time the contract is made. The buyer cannot rescind the contract for this reason.

4. If, prior to full performance by the buyer and conveyance by deed, the seller is:

     adjudicated a bankrupt;

     dies, with title passing to heirs; or

     is adjudicated an incompetent;

    the buyer can expect time-consuming, frustrating, and expensive litigation before obtaining a deed and policy of title insurance.

5. After full performance, the buyer may receive defective title or no title at all, although normally the contract will require delivery of a policy of title insurance. The buyer may have to pay the premium for this.

Many of these disadvantages are largely eliminated by using a contract secured by a deed of trust or a three-party instrument, where a trustee is appointed in the same way as in a deed of trust, coupled with title insurance insuring the equitable title of the vendee and the legal title of vendor.

Prepayment. A buyer shall be entitled to prepay all or any part of the balance due on any real property sales contract entered into on or after January 1,1969 with respect to the sale of land which has been subdivided into a residential lot or lots which contain a dwelling for not more than four families. Provided, however, that the seller, by an agreement in writing with the buyer, may prohibit prepayment for up to a 12-month period following the sale. Any waiver by a buyer of this provision is contrary to public policy and thus unenforceable and void but would not affect the validity of the remainder of the contract.

SECURITY AGREEMENTS
PERSONAL PROPERTY SECURED TRANSACTIONS
UNIFORM COMMERCIAL CODE - DIVISION 9

Agents in real estate transactions involving both personal and real property must be familiar with the transfer and encumbrance of personal property. Because it is often difficult to determine whether or not a particular item affixed to real property is a fixture, the obligation should be secured by both a trust deed/mortgage and a personal property security instrument (mixed security).

Upon default and foreclosure of real property, Code of Civil Procedure Sections 580(b), 580(d) and 726 prevent or limit a deficiency judgment. No antideficiency limitation exists in a personal property foreclosure.

Business opportunities. Business opportunity brokers are routinely involved in personal property transactions which must fully satisfy the Bulk Sales Law (Uniform Commercial Code, Division 6) and the secured transaction statutes (Uniform Commercial Code, Division 9). Assets of a business are commonly used as collateral to create a security interest in the seller or lender.

Just as a trust deed or mortgage encumbers real property as security for an obligation (debt), a "security agreement" creates a security interest in personal property.

To protect "or perfect" the interest created by a security agreement, as against other security interests and/or lien creditors or subsequent purchasers, a Financing Statement (UCC-l) is usually filed. In most cases, a security interest is *perfected* when it has attached and been properly filed with the appropriate filing officer (the Secretary of State in Sacramento or the appropriate county recorder).

A security interest *attaches* when:

- there is agreement by the parties that it attach;
- value has been given; and
- the debtor has acquired rights in the collateral.

Once *perfected,* the secured party's interest is protected against the debtor's other creditors.

The Financing Statement should not be confused with the actual security agreement. The security agreement creates the security interest.

Although a written agreement is not necessary where the collateral is in the possession of the secured party as a pledge, a security interest is usually not enforceable unless there is a written security agreement, signed by the debtor, describing the collateral.

Uniform Commercial Code (UCC)—Division 9

Division 9 (entitled "Secured Transactions, Sale of Accounts, Contract Rights and Chattel Paper") of the Uniform Commercial Code (UCC) contains the unified and comprehensive scheme for regulation and control of the sale, creation and priority of all liens and security interests in personal property. It covers a transaction in any form which is intended to create a security interest in personal property, including goods, documents, installments, chattel paper, accounts or contract rights and similar items. The security interest gives the secured party the right to foreclose and apply the sale proceeds toward the satisfaction of the secured obligation if the debtor defaults.

Purpose of the UCC. The basic purpose of the Uniform Commercial Code is to provide a simple and unified structure within which the immense variety of secured financing transactions can be completed.

As amended over the years, the UCC comprises a uniform, clear and easily available set of rules for the conduct of commercial intra- and interstate transactions.

Filing system. Under the UCC, a *Financing Statement*, properly filed, perfects a security interest. Absent a filed *Financing Statement*, subsequent purchasers without actual knowledge of the security interest might acquire property free of the prior security interest. On the other hand, a secured party who does file is in most cases protected from the interests of subsequent purchasers. UCC records are indexed by the true name of the debtor.

Place of filing. The proper place to file in order to perfect a security interest is as follows:

- When the collateral is consumer goods, in the office of the county recorder in the county of the debtor's residence or, if the debtor is not a resident of this state, in the office of the recorder of the county in which the goods are kept.
- When the collateral is crops growing or to be grown, timber to be cut or minerals or the like (including oil and gas) or accounts subject to subdivision (5) of Section 9103, in the office where a mortgage on the real estate would be recorded.
- In all other cases, in the office of the Secretary of State.

The proper place to file in order to perfect a security interest in collateral, including fixtures, of a transmitting utility is the office of the Secretary of State. This filing also constitutes a fixture filing as to the collateral described therein which is or is to become fixtures.

For filing purposes, the residence of an organization is its place of business if it has one or its chief executive office if it has more than one place of business.

The proper place to file a financing statement as a fixture filing is in the office where a mortgage on the real estate would be recorded.

Any subsequent filings such as *Statements of Continuation, Termination, Release, Assignment* and *Amendment* must be filed in the same location as the original *Financing Statement.*

Erroneous filing. A filing made in good faith in an improper place or not in all of the places required is nevertheless effective with regard to any collateral as to which the filing complied with the requirements and is also effective with regard to collateral covered by the financing statement against any person who has knowledge of the contents of the financing statement.

Change in debtor's/collateral's location. A filing which is made in the proper place in this state continues effective even though the debtor's residence or place of business or the location of the collateral or its use, whichever controlled the original filing, is thereafter changed.

Proper filing. Presentation for filing of a *Financing Statement,* tender of the filing fee and acceptance of the statement comprise filing under the code.

Duration of filing. A *Financing Statement* is effective for five years from the date of filing. For extension, the secured party must file a *Continuation Statement* any time within the six-month period preceding expiration. Succeeding *Continuation Statements* may thereafter be filed in the same manner to continue the effectiveness of the original Financing Statement.

Filing information. If the Standard Form UCC-1 or UCC-2 is used for filing, the filing officer will note the file number and date and hour of filing and return the acknowledged copy to the person or firm indicated in the box at the bottom of the standard form. If a non-standard form is used, the filing party must request an acknowledgment and send the filing officer a duplicate copy of the form filed, which will be acknowledged and returned.

The Secretary of State will furnish a certificate showing whether there is on file in its office any presently effective *Financing Statement,* naming the *Debtor* and, if there is, giving the date and hour of filing of each such statement and the names and addresses of each secured party named therein. This information and copies of the pertinent financing statements may be obtained by filing a *Request for Information* or Copies form (UCC-3) with the Secretary of State.

Priorities
One purpose of the Uniform Commercial Code Division 9 is to give lien rights to providers and installers of fixtures. A provider's perfected security interest in fixtures has priority over the conflicting interests of owners and subsequent encumbrancers [Section 9313 (4)].

A secured creditor who is first to make a proper filing has priority, regardless of when his/her claim arose. However, Sections 9301(2) and 9312(4) grant sellers special priority on purchase money security interests when perfected within 10 days of the purchaser's receiving possession of the collateral.

Section 9312 of the UCC sets forth the basic rules of priority among conflicting security interests in the same collateral and Section 9313 gives the priority rules for liens of a trust deed and other fixture filings.

Failure to File

If a Financing Statement is not filed, subsequent purchasers and secured parties without actual knowledge of it take the property free of the prior security interest. Section 9201 provides, however, that the (unperfected) Security Agreement is still valid between the debtor and secured party.

Escrow - Early Filing

A Financing Statement may be filed before a security agreement is made or before a security interest otherwise attaches. In an escrow for a bulk sales transaction there is often need to promptly perfect a seller's purchase money security interest to establish priority over other liens which will be perfected when the legal ownership changes. An escrow holder often files a Financing Statement to perfect the seller's interest before escrow closes. (If escrow fails to close, the escrow holder files a UCC-2 Termination Statement to remove the UCC-1 from the record.)

Fixture Filings

Under the UCC, tangible personal property includes "goods" and personal property deemed fixtures under the law, meaning goods which are so related to particular real property that an interest in them arises under real estate law. However, ordinary building materials to be incorporated into a building are not deemed fixtures.

A security interest in fixtures can be created by (1) specific provisions included in a trust deed or mortgage secured by the real property or (2) a fixture filing in the form of a Financing Statement. Both must be recorded in the county where the real property is located.

In either case, to qualify as a fixture filing, the instrument must contain:

1. a description of the goods which are or will become fixtures;

2. a legal description of the real property;

3. a statement that the goods are, or will become, fixtures; and

4. an assertion that the statement will be recorded in the county where the real property is located.

A fixture filing in the form of a Financing Statement is a lien on the fixture for 5 years from the date of filing, unless a Continuation Statement is recorded prior to expiration to extend the Financing Statement/lien an additional 5 years. A fixture filing in the form of a trust deed or mortgage is effective as long as the trust deed or mortgage remain a lien.

As to enforcement, a fixture filing in the form of a Financing Statement is enforced according to the provisions for personal property secured interests in the UCC. If the fixture filing is contained in a trust deed or mortgage, the secured party has the option of proceeding under the UCC to enforce the lien or by foreclosure proceedings under the trust deed/mortgage to enforce the lien on both the real and the personal property.

UCC 9402 provides:

- a Financing Statement form to be used as a fixture filing;
- the formal requisites of a Financial Statement; and
- amendments and contents of a mortgage to be used as a Financing Statement.

A copy of a security agreement signed by the debtor is sufficient as a Financing Statement if it contains all the information required by Section 9402.

Caution

This discussion of the Uniform Commercial Code should not serve as a substitute for:

- statutory analysis when dealing with specific problems;
- consultation with legal counsel on legal matters; or
- proper financial advice on banking or financing problems.

15 Mortgage Loans

This chapter explores the role of the real estate licensee in arranging loans, or sales of loans, secured by real property. It also discusses the federal Truth in Lending Act and Regulation Z.

NOTE: *Unless otherwise stated, "Department" means the Department of Real Estate and statutory references are to sections of the Business and Professions Code.*

Broker's Role

Mortgage brokers may negotiate loans for property owners who are unable to obtain financing from more conventional sources. A broker negotiates such a loan through a private lender. The phrase "hard money" means cash, as opposed to a loan for the purchase of a property.

The Loan Application

A broker negotiating a loan must obtain information from the applicant which the broker knows will be required by the private lender, including the borrower's ability and willingness to repay the loan. Knowing a lender's guidelines serves the interests of both the lender and the borrower. Those contemplating brokering loans must ascertain the policies and guidelines of their prospective investors.

The following is the type of information the broker will need:

1. Address of the property.
2. Requested loan amount and purpose of the loan.
3. Is the property currently owned or is it being purchased?
4. If being purchased, the purchase price; if currently owned, borrower's estimate of value.
5. How long owned?
6. The vested ownership of the property.
7. Is the property encumbered? What are the loan balances, payment amounts and names and addresses of lenders.
8. Any assessment or unpaid taxes?
9. Any other liens?
10. Borrower's income and debts.

A standard FNMA/FHLMC or similar loan application will usually elicit the necessary information. A credit report and property appraisal will also be necessary.

Advance Fees

A broker may wish to collect money in advance from a loan applicant to cover the cost of services to be performed in arranging the loan. Money collected "up front" is an advance fee. An advance fee may only be collected pursuant to an agreement previously approved by the Department of Real Estate. Commissioner's Regulation

2970 sets forth the basic contents of an advance fee agreement. The broker must also submit, for the Department's prior approval, all advertising materials used in conjunction with an advance fee arrangement.

Any real estate broker who contracts for or collects advance fees from a principal must deposit the funds into a trust account. Advance fees are not the broker's funds. Amounts may be withdrawn for the benefit of the broker only when actually expended for the benefit of the principal or five days after verified accounts have been mailed to the principal. If advance fees are not handled in accordance with the Real Estate Law, it will be presumed that the broker has violated Penal Code Sections 506 and 506a. Penalties and fines may result.

The Department does not treat as advance fees funds collected in advance for appraisal and credit reports as long as the broker collects as near as possible the exact amount(s) necessary and refunds any excess as soon as it is identified. Though not treated as advance fees, these funds *are* trust funds.

Title Policy for Lender
A primary concern is that the borrower has good title to the real property which would secure the loan. Once a lender decides that serious consideration can be given to a loan application, the lender will usually request a preliminary report from a title insurance company. This "prelim" includes:

1. a description of the property;

2. the owner of record;

3. taxes, bonds and assessments then owing;

4. reference to recorded covenants, conditions and restrictions affecting the property; and

5. certain other "exceptions" which will not be insured and, therefore, often must be cured before the loan will be granted.

When all objections to title are resolved to the satisfaction of the lender, a title policy insuring the interest of the lender must ordinarily be obtained before the loan is funded. In this policy, the title insurer guarantees to defend the lender against actions founded upon claims of encumbrances or title defects which were known, or should have been discovered, by the title insurer when the policy was issued.

Usury
A loan, arranged extension, forbearance, or refinancing of a loan in which a broker had originally been compensated (even though not being specifically compensated for arranging new credit terms), secured in whole or in part by a lien on real property and made or arranged by a licensed real estate broker is exempt from the usury law. Private individuals making such loans without a broker are controlled by the usury law.

ARTICLE 5 - THE LENDER

The Real Estate Law imposes certain duties and restrictions on real estate licensees who broker mortgage loans or, as either principal or agent, buy, sell or exchange existing promissory notes secured by real property or existing real property sales contracts. Since trading in real property sales contracts is relatively rare, this chapter generally focuses on the deed of trust as a security device. Virtually everything said about the purchase, sale and exchange of loans secured by real property is true with respect to real property sales contracts.

For the sake of simplicity, the phrase "promissory note secured by a deed of trust" is frequently abbreviated to "deed of trust" or "trust deed."

Application of Article 5

The passage of Proposition 2 in November 1979 eliminated interest rate limits on real property loans "made or arranged" by real estate brokers. The Legislature responded in 1981 and 1982 by extensive additions to the Real Estate Law, specifically to Articles 5 (Transactions in Trust Deeds and Real Property Sales Contracts) and 7 (Real Property Loans).

Article 5 (Sections 10230 - 10236.2) is basically applicable to brokering either the funding of mortgage loans by private, noninstitutional investors or the buying, selling or exchanging of trust deeds on behalf of private, noninstitutional investors. The provisions of Article 5 apply also to real estate licensees who engage as principals in buying from, selling to or exchanging deeds of trust with the public, and to brokers who make agreements with the public for the collection of payments or the performance of services in connection with deeds of trust.

Pooling of Loan Funds

Banking or pooling of lenders' or purchasers' funds, commonly referred to as multi-lender or fractionalized loans, is prohibited except as authorized by permit issued pursuant to the provisions of the Corporate Securities Law which is administered by the Department of Corporations. A multi-lender loan may be exempt under Corporation Commissioner's Regulation 260.105.30. Before arranging any multi-lender loan or pooling investor funds, a broker should contact the Department of Corporations.

Advertising

Section 10235 proscribes false, misleading or deceptive advertising by a real estate licensee engaged in the business of brokering loans or the sale of existing trust deeds. An advertisement cannot imply a yield or return on a promissory note different from the interest rate of the note itself unless the advertisement sets forth both the actual interest rate and the difference (discount) between the outstanding principal balance of the note and the price at which it is being offered for sale.

Article 5 also prohibits a real estate licensee from offering or advertising any premium, gift or other inducement to a prospective note purchaser, borrower or lender. (Section 10236.1) The Department does not consider rebates or reductions in the costs and fees of the loan to be a violation. For example, a broker can offer free appraisals as long as no other fees or costs are increased to allow for this inducement.

Real Estate Commissioner's Regulation 2848 implements the statutory provision against false, misleading or deceptive advertising in areas of mortgage loan brokerage and the marketing of trust deeds. A broker must also disclose license status and regulatory agency in all advertising for loans. A disclosure of "Real Estate Broker, CA. Dept. of Real Estate" in a broker's mortgage loan advertising complies. (Regulation 2847.3)

Exception to Article 5 Requirements

The provisions of Article 5 do not apply to negotiation of a loan or sale or exchange of a trust deed by a real estate licensee in connection with a real property sale or exchange transaction in which the broker acted as an agent, unless the broker also had a direct or indirect monetary interest as a party.

"Threshold" Criteria

Except as otherwise provided in the law, a real estate broker, acting as agent for others, meets the "threshold" criteria if he/she intends or expects in any 12-month period to do any of the following:

1. Negotiate any combination of 20 or more of the following transactions pursuant to subdivision (d) and (e) of Section 10131 or Section 10131.1 in an aggregate amount of more than $2,000,000:

   a. loans or sales of real property sales contracts or promissory notes secured by liens on real property or on business opportunities;

   b. as the owner, the sale or exchange of real property sales contracts or promissory notes secured by liens on real property or business opportunities; or

2. Make collections of payments in an aggregate amount of $500,000 or more on behalf of owners of promissory notes secured directly or collaterally by real property or owners of real property sales contracts; or

3. Make collections of payments in an aggregate amount of $500,000 or more on behalf of borrowers on promissory notes secured directly or collaterally by liens on real property or lenders (sellers) on real property sales contracts.

A threshold broker must notify the Department in writing within 30 days that the broker meets the threshold criteria. Failure to inform the Department may result in a fine of up to $10,000 and license revocation.

A broker who meets the threshold criteria must file with the Department an annual report within 90 days after the end of the broker's fiscal year and a quarterly trust fund status report within 30 days after each of the broker's first three fiscal quarters.

Loans or sales negotiated by a broker, or for which the broker collects payments, are not counted in determining whether the broker meets the threshold criteria if the lender or purchaser is an institutional lender or if the loan or sale is under the authority of a securities permit issued by the Department of Corporations. Generally speaking, only those brokers dealing with private investors and small pension trusts will satisfy the threshold criteria. (Section 10232)

Disclosure Statement

Sections 10232.4 and 10232.5 require that a real estate broker furnish a non-institutional lender or purchaser of a trust deed with a disclosure statement setting forth:

1. the loan terms;

2. pertinent information about the borrower (identity, occupation, income, credit data, as represented to the broker by the prospective borrower);

3. pertinent information about the property which will secure the loan, including address or other means of identification, fair market value, age, size, type of construction and description of improvements;

4. provisions for loan servicing;

5. pertinent information concerning all encumbrances which are currently liens against the property and which the borrower discloses as prospective liens.

The statement must be delivered before the lender (or purchaser of a note) becomes obligated to complete the loan (or purchase).

A real estate broker who advertises for or solicits funds from the public that are to be used for the broker's direct or indirect benefit must submit the format of the disclosure statement to the Department prior to any solicitation and then an individual statement to each prospective lender or purchaser before the broker accepts any funds from the person solicited. (Section 10231.2)

Disbursing Funds
Unless a lender has given written authorization to the broker, the broker may not disburse loan funds until after recording the trust deed which conveys the property to a trustee as security for the loan. If the lender has given the broker authority to release funds prior to recordation, the securing trust deed must be recorded, or delivered to the obligee with a written recommendation for immediate recordation, within ten days following disbursement of loan funds. The broker is similarly responsible for the execution and recordation of the assignment of a real property sales contract or deed of trust when the sale of the contract or trust deed has been negotiated by the broker.

Servicing - Broker Advances
A real estate broker servicing a note or contract may advance his or her own funds to protect the security of the note being serviced, including an advance to pay debt service on a senior note secured by the same real property. If the broker does advance funds for taxes, hazard insurance or debt service on a senior note secured by the same real property, the broker must, within ten days, give written notice of the advance to the beneficiary of the note being serviced. (Section 10233.1)

Retention of funds. If a broker receives funds from the obligor (borrower) in payment of a promissory note or contract, as is ordinarily the case when servicing the note or contract for the obligee (lender), the broker may not retain the funds for more than sixty days without written authorization from the obligee. The authorization from the obligee may not provide for payment of interest to the broker on funds retained by the broker. Moreover, the agreement between the broker and the obligee (or obligor) authorizing the broker to service the instrument must be in writing.

Commissioner's Regulations
Real estate licensees active in the mortgage loan business should be familiar with Commissioner's Regulations 2845 (interpretative opinion request); 2846 (approved lender/purchaser disclosure statement); 2846.5 (report of annual trust fund accounts review); 2847, 2847.3 and 2848 (advertising); and 2849.01 (annual report format).

ARTICLE 7 - THE BORROWER

The Real Estate Law has long required the licensing of one who negotiates, for another and for compensation, a loan secured by real property. The statutory scheme now found in Article 7 of Chapter 3 (Sections 10240 - 10248.3) was enacted to curb a variety of abuses: exorbitant commissions; inflated costs and expenses; short term loans with large balloon payments; and misrepresentation or concealment of material facts by licensees negotiating loans. Article 7 is variously referred to as the Real Property Loan Law, the Mortgage Loan Brokers' Law and the Necessitous Borrowers' Act.

Application of Article 7

Except for the disclosure statement requirement, Article 7 applies only to loans secured by real property which includes a dwelling. For this purpose, a dwelling is a single dwelling unit in a condominium or cooperative or a parcel containing only residential units if the total number of units on the parcel is four or less. (Sections 10240.1 and 10240.2)

Except for its disclosure statement, late charges, and loan prepayment provisions, Article 7 applies only to first trust deed loans under $30,000 and junior trust deed loans under $20,000. (Section 10245)

Article 7 applies only to loans made or negotiated by real estate brokers acting within the meaning of subdivision (d) of Section 10131 (the basic definition of a real estate broker) or subdivision (b) of Section 10240. Subdivision (b) of Section 10240 brings under Article 7 loan transactions in which a broker solicits a borrower with express or implied representations that the broker will arrange a loan as an agent but in fact makes the loan with the broker's own funds.

Mortgage Loan Disclosure Statement

The Mortgage Loan Disclosure Statement is at the heart of Article 7. The statement's purpose is to provide a prospective borrower with information concerning the important features of a loan.

A real estate broker negotiating, or, under the circumstances described above, making, a mortgage loan of any kind or in any amount to be secured directly or collaterally by a lien on real property must present a completed Mortgage Loan Disclosure Statement to the prospective borrower within 3 days of receipt of a completed written loan application or before the borrower is obligated to take the loan, whichever is earlier. A broker (or, of course, a salesperson employed by the broker) must obtain the borrower's signature on the statement prior to the time that the borrower becomes obligated to complete the loan. In addition, if the loan is subject to Article 7, the licensee must certify in the statement that the loan complies with Article 7.

Section 10241 sets forth the information that must be included in the statement. The form of the statement must be approved by the Commissioner prior to its use. The Commissioner has established two approved forms in Regulations 2840 and 2840.1. RE Forms 882 and 883 can be obtained at any Department office.

The disclosure statement set forth in Commissioner's Regulation 2840.1 is believed to satisfy the disclosure requirements of the federal Real Estate Settlement Procedures Act.

Broker-controlled funds. Both forms of the Mortgage Loan Disclosure Statement provide for disclosure that the broker anticipates that the loan will be made with broker-controlled funds. The phrase "broker-controlled funds" means funds owned by the broker, by the broker's spouse, child, parent, grandparent, brother, sister, father-in-law, mother-in-law, brother-in-law or sister-in-law, or by any entity in which the broker alone or together with any of the above relatives has an ownership interest.

Disclosures - Case Law

In *Realty Projects, Inc. v. Smith* (1973 32 C.A. 3d 204), the court held that the statutory obligation of a licensee to act fairly and honestly demanded that the licensee inform prospective borrowers of the difference between commissions and other charges for loans in amounts subject to the Real Property Loan Law as against loans not covered by that law. While the court referred to the respondent/licensee as the agent of a prospective borrower, the court did not rely upon an agency theory in reaching its decision regarding the disclosure duty. Rather, the duty was declared to stem simply from the respondent's status as a licensee.

In the case of *Wyatt v. Union Mortgage Co.* (1979 24 C.A. 3d 773), the court held that a mortgage loan broker's duty to disclose information about late charges and the effective interest rate of a loan was based upon a fiduciary relationship between the broker and the prospective borrower.

Commissions and Other Charges

Article 7 limits the amount that may be charged as commission or fees for arranging or making a loan and as "costs and expenses" of making the loan. (Again, these limitations do not apply to a first loan of $30,000 or more or a junior loan of $20,000 or more.) The maximum commissions for loans subject to Article 7 are:

1. First loans:
   a. 5 percent of the principal of a loan of less than 3 years;
   b. 10 percent of the principal of a loan of 3 years or more;

2. Second or other junior loans:
   a. 5 percent of the principal of a loan of less than 2 years;
   b. 10 percent of the principal of a loan of at least 2 years but less than 3 years;
   c. 15 percent of the principal of a loan of 3 years or more.

Costs and expenses of making a loan subject to Article 7, including appraisal fees, escrow fees, notary and credit investigation fees (but excluding actual title charges and recording fees) charged to a borrower cannot exceed 5 percent of the loan or $390, whichever is greater, to a maximum of $700. The amount charged cannot exceed the actual costs and expenses paid, incurred or reasonably earned. No charge can exceed the amount customarily charged for the same or comparable service in the community where the service is rendered. (Regulation 2843)

Balloon Payment

A balloon payment is defined as an installment payment that is greater than twice the amount of the smallest installment payment required by the promissory note.

Generally, no loan subject to Article 7 may have a balloon payment if the term of the loan is less than 3 years.

If the property securing the loan is an owner-occupied dwelling, a balloon payment is not permissible if the term of the loan is 6 years or less. As in the case of the 3-year balloon payment provision, the restriction does not apply to a promissory note given back to the seller by the purchaser of the dwelling place on account of the purchase price.

The Mortgage Loan Disclosure Statement includes a notice regarding balloon payments. Section 10241.4 requires an expanded disclosure if provisions have been made, or will be sought, for extension, refinancing or renegotiation of an Article 7 loan which includes a balloon payment.

Other Restrictions

Other restrictions on loans subject to Article 7 include:

1. A mortgage loan broker is prohibited from charging or negotiating any loan servicing or loan collection fee to be paid by the borrower.

2. A borrower may not be required to purchase credit life or credit disability insurance as a condition of obtaining a loan.

3. A licensee may collect only one premium for credit life or credit disability insurance provided through duly licensed agents. Only borrowers whose earnings are reasonably relied upon by the lender for repayment of the loan may be insured.

4. Regardless of the amount of the loan, charges for late payment of an installment are limited to 10 percent (or $5, whichever is greater) of the principal and interest part of the installment payment. If a payment is made within ten days of its due date, no late charge may be imposed.

5. Regardless of the amount of the loan, the penalty that may be charged to a borrower for prepayment is limited if the security for the loan is a single family, owner-occupied dwelling. No charge may be assessed for a prepayment made more than seven years from the date of the loan. During the first six years of the loan, twenty percent of the principal balance of the loan may be paid off during any 12-month period without penalty. The maximum prepayment penalty allowed is six months' interest on the amount prepaid above 20 percent of the unpaid principal balance. This provision applies to loans of any dollar amount if negotiated by a real estate licensee for compensation.

6. The term of an exclusive right to secure financing cannot exceed 45 days.

TRUTH IN LENDING ACT

The Truth in Lending Act (hereinafter, the Act) became effective July 1, 1969. The principal purpose of the Act is to promote the informed use of consumer credit by requiring creditors to disclose credit terms in order to enable consumers to make comparisons between various credit sources. To implement the Act, the Board of Governors of the Federal Reserve System issued a regulation known as Regulation Z.

After a decade of experience with the Act and Regulation Z, it became clear that the requirements placed too great a burden on creditors, provided too many disclosures for consumers, and fostered too much litigation. This prompted Congress to amend the Act in 1980 by passing the Truth in Lending Simplification and Reform Act. To reflect the amendments to the Act the Federal Reserve Board substantially revised Regulation Z. Compliance with the simplified Act and revised Regulation Z became mandatory on October 1, 1982.

At the time revised Regulation Z was promulgated, the Federal Reserve Board adopted model disclosures for closed-end transactions such as purchases of real property, and model language for certain other disclosures. The Board also announced that its staff would no longer provide written responses to individual requests for interpretations of the Regulation, but would issue a staff commentary from time to time to address questions of interpretation.

Creditor
The creditor is responsible for furnishing Truth in Lending disclosures to the consumer. Regulation Z defines a creditor as a person who extends consumer credit more than 25 times a year or more than 5 times a year for transactions secured by a dwelling. The credit extended must be subject to a finance charge or be payable by written agreement in more than four installments. Another requirement that must be met to render a person a creditor is that the obligation be initially payable on its face or by agreement to that person.

In its definition of "creditor," revised Regulation Z included "arranger of credit," which it defined as a person who initially arranged for the extension of credit by persons who did not meet the "creditor" definition. The Federal Reserve Board, in considering the necessity for a more specific description of the type of activity which would constitute "arranger of credit," inquired whether real estate brokers who arrange seller financing of homes should be considered "arrangers of credit." In 1982, Congress resolved the question by passing the Garn-St. Germain Depository Institutions Act, which amended the Truth in Lending Simplification and Reform Act of 1980 by deleting "arranger of credit" from the definition of "creditor." To implement the amendment, the Federal Reserve Board amended revised Regulation Z by removing "arranger of credit" from the "creditor" definition, effective October 1, 1982. The effect of the Board's action is to release real estate brokers or other arrangers of credit from the responsibility for providing Truth in Lending disclosures unless such persons otherwise come within the definition of "creditor."

Exempt Transactions
There are two basic types of transactions that are exempt from coverage under Regulation Z. The first exemption is for credit extended primarily for a business,

commercial, or agricultural purpose. If property is not, or is not intended to be, owner-occupied, and the creditor extends credit to acquire, improve, or maintain a rental property, regardless of the number of family units, the transaction will be considered to be for a business purpose.

Special rules apply for credit to acquire, improve, or maintain rental property that is, or will be, owner-occupied within a year. If the property contains more than two family units and the purpose of the credit is to acquire the property, the credit is deemed to be for a business purpose. However, if the credit is extended to improve or maintain the property, it is deemed to be for a business purpose if it contains more than four housing units. These rules should not be construed to prevent an extension of credit for property containing fewer than the aforesaid prescribed number of units from being considered business credit. Credit involving fewer numbers of units may be considered business credit depending on the circumstances of the transaction.

The second exemption is for credit over $25,000. The dollar limitation does not apply if the loan is secured by real property, or by personal property which is used or expected to be used as the consumer's principal dwelling.

See Section 226.3 of Regulation Z, 12 C.F.R. § 226.3.

Form of Disclosures

Regulation Z requires all Truth in Lending disclosures concerning the credit sale or loan to be grouped together and segregated from other information. The Regulation prohibits the inclusion of any information not directly related to the disclosures required by Regulation Z. It also provides that any itemization of the amount financed be made separately from the other required disclosures. In addition, Regulation Z requires that the terms "finance charge" and "annual percentage rate" be more conspicuous than other required disclosures.

The disclosures may be segregated by putting them on a separate sheet of paper, or if the disclosures are on a contract or other document they may be set off from other information by outlining them in a box or by printing them in a different type style, with bold print dividing lines, or with a different color background. The portion of the sale or loan document that contains these disclosures is commonly called "the federal box."

Before its revision, Regulation Z required that all Truth in Lending disclosures be made on one side of a page. Under revised Regulation Z, the Truth in Lending disclosures must be separate from everything else, but may be continued from one page to another.

Regulation Z contains several model forms, including forms which contain disclosures required for transactions involving loan assumptions, variable rate mortgages, and graduated payment mortgages. Lenders may duplicate these forms or modify them by including disclosures required for particular transactions.

See Section 226.17 of Regulation Z.

Required Disclosures

There are as many as eighteen disclosures required by Regulation Z for closed-end credit transactions such as mortgage loans. A creditor is only required to make those disclosures that are relevant to a particular transaction. The disclosure statement must have simple descriptive phrases next to five of the most important items disclosed. These items are: the amount financed, the finance charge, the annual percentage rate, the total of payments, and, in credit sales, the total sale price. Regulation Z provides suggested phrases for the five required terms. These phrases are not required to be used verbatim.

The following is a summary of the required disclosures:

Identity of creditor. The creditor making the disclosures must be identified.

Amount financed. Regulation Z requires the use of the term "amount financed" together with a brief description of the term. The suggested phrase is "the amount of credit provided to you or on your behalf."

Itemization of amount financed. The disclosure of the itemization of the amount financed may be eliminated in those cases where good faith estimates of settlement costs have been supplied for transactions subject to the Real Estate Settlement Procedures Act (RESPA). If the transaction is not subject to RESPA, the creditor must either provide a written itemization of the amount financed, or provide a statement that the consumer has the right to receive a written itemization of the amount financed together with a space for the consumer to indicate whether an itemization is desired. However, many state laws require that the creditor provide the itemization even if the consumer does not specifically request it. The itemization must be separate from the "federal box."

Finance charge. Regulation Z requires the use of the term "finance charge" together with a brief description such as "the dollar amount the credit will cost you."

The requirement that the components of the finance charge be itemized has been eliminated from revised Regulation Z. In fact, the new rules prohibit creditors from itemizing the finance charge with the other disclosures. Only the total amount may be given. In addition, Regulation Z requires the disclosure of the finance charge in all real estate transactions. Prior to its revision, Regulation Z did not require either the total dollar amount of the finance charge or the total of payments to be disclosed on a first loan to finance the purchase of the borrower's dwelling.

The finance charge must include any charge payable directly or indirectly by the consumer and imposed directly or indirectly by the creditor as incident to or a condition of the extension of credit. Regulation Z provides examples of charges that must be included in the finance charge and examples of charges that are excluded from the finance charge.

Charges of particular importance in real estate and residential mortgage transactions which Regulation Z lists among those charges included in the finance charge are:

1. interest;
2. loan fees, assumption fees, finder's fees and buyer's points;
3. investigation and credit report fees;
4. premiums for mortgage guaranty or similar insurance; and
5. borrower-paid mortgage broker fees.

Charges which are not finance charges include seller's points and the following fees when charged in a transaction secured by real property or in a residential mortgage transaction (which may include the purchase of a mobilehome), if they are bona fide and reasonable in amount:

1. fees for title examination, abstract of title, title insurance, property survey, and similar purposes;

2. fees for preparing loan-related documents;

3. notary, appraisal, credit report, and pest infestation and flood hazard inspection fees;

4. amounts required to be paid into escrow or trustee accounts if the amounts would not otherwise be included in the finance charge; and

5. third-party closing agent fees (including those charged by settlement agents, attorneys, and escrow and title companies).

Annual percentage rate. The disclosure of the annual percentage rate requires the use of that particular term together with a brief description such as "the cost of your credit as a yearly rate." In a regular transaction, the disclosed annual percentage rate is considered accurate if it is not more than 1/8 of 1 percentage point above or below the actual annual percentage rate determined. However, in an irregular transaction, the annual percentage rate is considered accurate if it is not more than 1/4 of 1 percentage point above or below the actual annual percentage rate determined. Irregular transactions include multiple advances, irregular payment periods (other than an odd first period), or irregular payment amounts (other than an odd first or final payment).

Variable rate. If the annual percentage rate may increase within a term of one year or less after consummation in a transaction secured by the consumer's principal dwelling, there must be disclosure of:

1. the circumstances under which the rate may increase;

2. any limitations on the increase;

3. the effect of an increase; and

4. an example of the payment terms that would result from an increase.

If the annual percentage rate may increase within a term greater than one year after consummation in a transaction secured by the consumer's principal dwelling, there must be disclosure of:

1. the fact that the transaction contains a variable-rate feature; and

2. a statement that variable-rate disclosures have been provided earlier.

Payment schedule. The creditor must disclose the number, amounts, and timing of payments scheduled to repay the obligation. Regulation Z provides for an abbreviated disclosure of payment schedule for transactions in which a series of payments vary solely because of the application of a finance charge to the unpaid principal balance. This situation arises most frequently in graduated payment mortgages or in mortgages where mortgage insurance premiums are based on the unpaid principal balance. In these transactions creditors need to disclose only the amount of the largest and smallest payments in the series and that the other payments may vary.

Total of payments. Regulation Z requires the creditor to use the term "total of payments" as well as a brief description such as "the amount you will have paid when you have made all scheduled payments." The total of payments (which is the sum of the payments disclosed in the payment schedule) must be disclosed for all real estate transactions under revised Regulation Z.

Demand feature. Regulation Z requires that if the obligation has a demand feature, that fact be disclosed. This disclosure is required only for a demand feature contemplated by the parties as part of the legal obligation. Transactions that convert to a demand status as a result of the consumer's default are not within the purview of this requirement. Nor is a due-on-sale clause.

Total sale price. In a credit sale (a sale in which the seller is a creditor) Regulation Z requires the use of the term "total sale price" together with a brief description such as "the total price of your purchase on credit, including your down payment of $___."

Prepayment penalties and rebates. Creditors are required to make a disclosure of the existence of a penalty on prepayment in full. Even if a creditor does not charge a prepayment penalty, a statement to that effect must be included. However, this disclosure is only required if the finance charge is computed from time to time by application of a rate to the unpaid principal balance. In any other type of transaction, a statement must be included indicating whether the consumer is entitled to a rebate of any portion of the finance charge in the event of prepayment. It is no longer necessary to disclose a particular method of rebate, such as the rule of 78s.

Late payment charge. A disclosure is required only for those charges imposed before maturity due to a late payment. The disclosure may reflect the fact that late charges may be determined as either a percentage or a specified dollar amount.

Security interest. Regulation Z requires the creditor to disclose what security interest is or will be retained in the property purchased in the transaction or other property. In transactions in which the credit is being used to purchase the collateral, the creditor is required to give only a general identification such as "the property purchased in this transaction." In the revision of Regulation Z, the requirement that a security interest in after-acquired property must be disclosed was deleted.

Insurance. If charges for credit life, accident, health, or loss-of-income insurance are excluded from the finance charge, there must be a disclosure of the premium and that the insurance is not required to obtain credit, and the consumer must sign or initial a request for the insurance. If the charges for property insurance are excluded from the finance charge there must be a disclosure setting forth the cost of the insurance if obtained from the creditor and stating that the insurance may be obtained from a person of the consumer's choice. The disclosure may be made on the disclosure form, or, at the creditor's option, on a document different from the disclosure form.

Certain security charges. If disclosed, taxes and fees paid to a public official with respect to a security interest may be excluded from the finance charge. The charges may be aggregated, or may be broken down by individual charge. No special form is required for this disclosure, which could be labeled "filing fees and taxes." This disclosure may be made on the disclosure form, or, at the creditor's option, on a document different from the disclosure form.

Reference to contract terms. Regulation Z requires that creditors include in their disclosures a statement that refers consumers to appropriate contract documents for information about non-payment, default, the right to accelerate the maturity of the obligation, and prepayment rebates or penalties. At the creditor's option, the statement can also include a reference to the contract for more information about security interests and the creditor's assumption policy.

Assumption policy. In a residential mortgage transaction, the creditor must state whether a subsequent purchaser of the dwelling from the consumer may be permitted to assume the remaining obligation on its original terms.

Required deposit. An example of a required deposit is a savings account created as a condition of a loan. If a creditor requires the consumer to maintain the deposit as a condition of the extension of credit, the creditor must state that the annual percentage rate does not reflect the effect of the required deposit.

See Section 226.18 of Regulation Z.

Time of Disclosure

Regulation Z requires disclosures to be made before consummation of the credit transaction, which is usually the time of closing. Consummation is defined as the time that a consumer becomes contractually liable on a credit obligation as determined by state law. In some situations, special variable rate and other disclosures (discussed below) must be provided at an earlier point in time.

Certain residential mortgage transactions. Creditors, as a whole, have been encouraged, through liberalized provisions on estimates in the revised Regulation Z, to use early disclosures in order to enable consumers to have ample time to shop for credit. However, creditors involved in residential mortgage transactions subject to the Real Estate Settlement Procedures Act, known as RESPA, are required to make Regulation Z disclosures before consummation, or deliver or place them in the mail within three business days after receiving the consumer's written application, whichever is earlier. If the estimates turn out to be inaccurate, it may be necessary to make another disclosure at consummation.

See Sections 226.17(b), 226.17(f), and 226.19(a) of Regulation Z.

Certain variable-rate transactions. If the annual percentage rate may increase after consummation in a transaction secured by the consumer's principal dwelling with a term greater than one year, the following disclosures must be provided at the time an application form is provided or before the consumer pays a nonrefundable fee, whichever is earlier:

1. the booklet titled *Consumer Handbook on Adjustable Rate Mortgages* published by the Board and the Federal Home Loan Bank Board, or a suitable substitute; and

2. a loan program disclosure for each variable-rate program in which the consumer expresses an interest.

Redisclosure. In general, an event occurring after delivery of the disclosures to the consumer, which renders the disclosures inaccurate, does not result in a violation of Regulation Z and does not require redisclosure. However, if disclosures are given before the date of consummation and a subsequent event makes them inaccurate prior to consummation, redisclosure is required before consummation, if the actual annual percentage rate is above or below the disclosed rate by more than 1/8 of 1 percent in a regular transaction, or more than 1/4 of 1 percent in an irregular transaction, as described above.

If redisclosure is required, the creditor has the option of providing the consumer with either a complete set of new disclosures or a disclosure of *only* the terms that vary from those originally disclosed.

Subsequent Disclosure

After consummation, three events require the creditor to make disclosures: refinancing, assumption, and variable-rate adjustments.

Refinancing. Regulation Z states that a "refinancing" is a new transaction requiring new disclosures to the consumer, and that a refinancing occurs when an existing obligation is satisfied and replaced by a new one undertaken by the same consumer. In addition, the Regulation sets forth examples of what does not constitute a refinancing, which include, among others: (1) a renewal of a single payment obligation with no change in the original terms; (2) a reduction in the annual percentage rate with a corresponding change in the payment schedule; and (3) a change in the payment schedule or a change in collateral requirements as a result of the consumer's default or delinquency.

Assumption. Regulation Z states that an "assumption" is a new transaction requiring new disclosures to the consumer, and that an assumption occurs when a new party becomes obligated on an existing obligation. Whenever a creditor agrees in writing to accept a new consumer as a primary obligor on an existing residential mortgage transaction, before the assumption occurs the creditor must make new disclosures to the new obligor based on the remaining obligation. The mere addition of a guarantor to an obligation for which the original consumer remains primarily liable does not constitute an "assumption."

See Sections 226.17(e), 226.19 and 226.20 of Regulation Z.

Variable-rate adjustments. Certain new disclosures are required when an adjustment is made to the interest rate (with or without an accompanying change in the payment rate) in a variable rate transaction secured by the consumer's principal dwelling and with a term greater than one year. The creditor must provide the following information at least once each year during which an interest rate adjustment is implemented without an accompanying payment change, and at least 25 but not more than 120 calendar days before a payment is due at a new level:

1. the current and prior interest rates;
2. the index values on which the current and prior interest rates are based;
3. the extent to which the creditor has foregone any interest rate increase;
4. the contractual effects of the adjustment, including the new payment amount and the loan balance; and

5.   the payment (if different from the payment disclosed above) that would be required to fully amortize the loan at the new interest rate over the remaining loan term.

Additional Disclosures Required for High-Rate, High-Fee Mortgages

The "Home Ownership Equity Protection Act of 1994" amended the Truth in Lending Act to establish new requirements for certain loans with high rates and/or high fees. The requirements do not apply to loans to purchase or initially construct a consumer's principal dwelling, to reverse mortgages, or to home equity lines of credit. Loans are covered if they meet the following tests: (1) the annual percentage rate exceeds by more than 10 percentage points the rate on Treasury notes of comparable maturity; or (2) the total fees and points exceed the larger of 8 percent of the total loan amount or $424 (for 1997 - dollar amount adjusted annually by the Federal Reserve Board, based on changes in the Consumer Price Index). The amendments primarily affect refinancing and home equity installment loans that also meet the definition of a high-rate or high-fee loan.

In addition to the other Truth in Lending Act disclosures described above, high-rate or high-fee loans, also referred to as "Section 32 mortgages," must include the following disclosures:

1.   a written notice stating that the loan need not be completed, even though the consumer has signed the loan application and received the required disclosures;

2.   a warning that failure to make required payments could result in the consumer losing the home;

3.   disclosure of the APR and regular payment amount; and

4.   in the case of variable rate transactions, a statement that the interest rate and monthly payment may increase, as well as the amount of the single maximum monthly payment (based on the maximum interest rate).

The consumer has three business days to sign the loan agreement after receiving the Section 32 disclosures.

The 1994 amendments also ban the following features from high-rate, high-fee loans:

1.   all balloon payments for loans with less than five-year terms (with an exception for bridge loans of less than one year used by consumers to acquire or construct a home);

2.   negative amortization;

3.   default interest rates higher than predefault rates;

4.   rebates of interest upon default calculated by any method less favorable than the actuarial method;

5.   a prepayment schedule that consolidates more than two periodic payments that are to be paid in advance from the proceeds of the loan; and

6.   most prepayment penalties, including refunds of unearned interest calculated by any method less favorable than the actuarial method.

Creditors also are prohibited from engaging in a pattern or practice of lending based on the collateral value of property without regard to the consumer's ability to repay the loan. In addition, proceeds for home improvement loans must be disbursed either directly to the consumer, jointly to the consumer and home improvement contractor, or, in some instances, to the escrow agent.

See Section 226.32 of Regulation Z.

Consumer's Right to Rescind

As a general rule, the right of rescission applies to all consumer credit transactions where the obligation is secured by a lien against the consumer's principal dwelling. A consumer can have only one "principal dwelling" at a time. Since the definition of a dwelling is not limited to real property, transactions involving mobilehomes can be rescindable even if they are treated as personal property under state law.

Exemptions. There are a number of important exemptions applicable to residential real estate transactions. One of these exemptions concerns "residential mortgage transactions." Under this exemption, the right of rescission does not apply to transactions made to finance acquisition or initial construction of the consumer's principal dwelling and secured by that dwelling, regardless of lien status. In other words, second mortgages for the purpose of financing an acquisition are no longer subject to the right of rescission.

Another exemption is for a refinancing by the same creditor of a loan already secured by the principal dwelling, provided no new money is advanced. If new money is advanced, the transaction is rescindable to the extent of the new money if the loan is secured by the consumer's principal dwelling. This exemption is most likely to arise in connection with renewals, extensions, or refinancing of balloon notes.

By restricting the right of rescission to transactions in which the secured property is currently used as the consumer's principal dwelling, revised Regulation Z has exempted from the rescission requirements loans secured by property that is expected to be used as other than a principal dwelling, such as vacant lots, vacation homes, and retirement homes.

Notice of right to rescind. The creditor must provide each consumer entitled to rescind (any consumer with an "ownership interest" in the principal dwelling subject to the security interest) with two copies of the notice of right to rescind. Creditors are not required to use any specific language when making rescission disclosures. Regulation Z contains a model rescission form that meets the requirements.

Rescission period. The consumer has the right to rescind until midnight of the third business day following the last to occur of these events:

1. consummation of the transaction;
2. delivery of all material Truth in Lending disclosures; or
3. delivery of the notice of right to rescind. A business day is any calendar day, except Sundays and federal legal holidays.

Waiver of right to rescind. Regulation Z provides that the consumer may waive the right to rescind if the consumer determines that the extension of credit is needed to meet a bona fide personal financial emergency. To waive the right, the consumer must give the creditor a dated written statement that describes the emergency and specifically waives the right to rescind. The use of preprinted waiver forms is prohibited by the Regulation.

See Section 226.23 of Regulation Z. (A parallel provision exists in Section 226.15 of Regulation Z for liens against principal dwellings securing open-end credit.)

Advertising Consumer Credit

Anyone placing an advertisement for consumer credit must comply with the advertising requirements of the Truth in Lending Act and Regulation Z. Thus, real estate brokers and home builders who place ads must comply even if they are not creditors in the financing being advertised.

Disclosures in credit advertisements must be made "clearly and conspicuously." This standard requires that disclosures be made in a reasonably understandable form, but does not prescribe the type size or the placement of disclosures in the ad.

An advertisement may state specific credit terms only if the creditor is actually prepared to offer those terms. A creditor may advertise terms that will be offered for only a limited period, or terms that will become available at a future date.

Advertising the rate of finance charge. If the finance charge in a credit advertisement is expressed as a rate, it must be stated as an "annual percentage rate," using that term or the abbreviation "APR." If a component of that finance charge is interest computed at a simple annual rate, that rate *may* also be included. However, it must not be displayed more conspicuously than the annual percentage rate. For example, an advertisement for mortgage credit may include the contract rate of interest together with the annual percentage rate, which reflects insurance, discounts, points, and other charges, as well as interest.

Variable rate mortgages. If the annual percentage rate offered may be increased after consummation of the transaction, the advertisement must state that fact. An advertisement for a variable rate mortgage with an initial annual percentage rate of 9% that may vary after settlement without any limit could be advertised as "9% annual percentage rate, subject to increase after settlement." This disclosure may be used for any type of mortgage instrument with a variable interest rate. It may not be used in advertisements of graduated payment mortgages that have a fixed interest rate and payments that may increase during the loan. Fixed-rate "buydowns" and "step-rate" mortgages are also *not* variable rate mortgages. These mortgages involve different interest rates in effect during the life of the loan, all of which are known at settlement. A variable rate transaction involves future interest rates unknown at settlement.

The Official Staff Commentary to Regulation Z, which is published by the staff of the Federal Reserve Board, sets forth special rules for advertising rates other than simple annual or periodic rates, i.e., for "buydowns" and "payment" or "effective" rates.

Buydowns. A seller or creditor may advertise a reduced simple interest rate resulting from a "buydown" so long as the advertisement shows the limited term to which the reduced rate applies and the simple interest rate that applies to the balance of the term, as well as the annual percentage rate that is determined in accordance with the commentary to Section 226.17(c) of Regulation Z. (Where more than one reduced rate applies, the advertisement must show each rate and the respective term for which each rate is effective.) The advertisement may also show the effect of the buydown on the payment schedule without triggering additional disclosures under Section 226.24(c) of Regulation Z.

Discounted variable rates. Adjustable rate mortgages (ARMs) often have a first-year "discount" or "teaser" feature in which the initial rate is substantially reduced. In these loans, the first year's rate is not computed in the same way as the rate for later years. Often the "spread" or "margin" that is normally added to an "index" (such as the one-year Treasury-note rate) to determine changes in the interest rate in the future is not included in the first year of a discounted ARM offered by a creditor. Special rules, similar to those for buydowns, apply to advertising a discounted variable rate. An advertisement for this type of plan can show the simple interest rate during the discount period, as long as it also shows the annual percentage rate. However, in contrast to buydowns, the ad need not show the simple interest rate applicable after the discount period. For example, a plan with a low first year's interest rate (8%), but with a 10.25% rate in subsequent years, and additional credit costs, could be advertised as follows: "8% first-year financing. APR 10.41%. APR subject to increase after closing." As in buydowns, the annual percentage rate in discounted plans is a composite figure that must take into account the interest rates that are known at closing. In the above example, the disclosed APR must reflect the 8% rate for the first year, as well as, for example, the 10.25% rate applicable for the remainder of the term, plus any additional credit costs (such as buyer's points). An ad for a discounted variable-rate loan, like an ad for a buydown, may show the effect of the discount on the payment schedule during the discount period *without* triggering other disclosures. An example of a disclosure that complies with Regulation Z is: "Interest rate only 8% first year. APR 10.50% subject to increase. With this discount, your monthly payments for the first year will be only $587."

Payment or effective rates. In some transactions, particularly some graduated payment loans, the consumer's payments for the first few years of the loan may be based upon an interest rate lower than the rate for which the consumer is liable (a situation referred to as "negative amortization"). As with buydowns, special rules apply when the "effective" or "payment" rates are advertised for such transactions. The following information must be included in any advertisements containing effective rates: (1) the "effective" or "payment" rate; (2) the term of the reduced payments; (3) the "note rate" at which interest is actually accruing; and (4) the annual percentage rate. The advertised annual percentage rate must take into account the interest for which the consumer is liable, even though it is not paid by the consumer during the period of reduced payments. This type of financing could be advertised as: "An effective first-year rate of only 7-1/2 percent. Interest being charged at 10-1/2 percent. 10-3/4% APR." In contrast to an ad for a buydown or a discounted variable rate, an ad for an "effective" or "payment" rate may *not* show the monthly payments without triggering the disclosures listed in the following section.

Advertising terms that require additional disclosures. If only the annual percentage rate is disclosed, additional disclosures are not required. If, however, an advertisement contains any one of the following terms, the ad must also disclose other credit terms:

1. the amount or percentage of any downpayment;
2. the number of payments or period of repayment;
3. the amount of any payment; or
4. the amount of any finance charge.

These provisions apply even if the so-called "triggering term" is not stated explicitly but may be readily determined from the advertisement. An ad that states "80% financing" implies that a 20 percent down payment is required. However, an ad that states "100% financing" requires no further disclosures because no downpayment is required.

If any triggering term is used, then the following three disclosures must also be included in the advertisement:

1. the amount or percentage of the down payment;
2. the terms of repayment; and
3. the "annual percentage rate," using that term or the abbreviation "APR." If the annual percentage rate may be increased after consummation of the credit transaction, that fact must be disclosed.

Regulation Z also permits the advertiser to substitute examples of one or more typical extensions of credit for required disclosures that are specific to a particular transaction. Where typical examples are used, the advertisement must contain all of the terms that apply to each example. The examples must be typical of the credit terms that are actually available.

See Section 226.24 of Regulation Z.

The Official Staff Commentary to Regulation Z provides additional guidance and illustrative examples of these general rules. It also prescribes special rules for advertising complex transactions such as graduated payment mortgages and wrap-around loans.

In addition, the Federal Trade Commission publishes a manual for business entitled "How to Advertise Consumer Credit: Complying with the Law." This manual is available from the U.S. Government Printing Office.

Administrative Enforcement

The Federal Trade Commission enforces the Truth in Lending Act and Regulation Z with respect to real estate brokers, mortgage loan brokers, mortgage bankers, and other creditors and advertisers not regulated by the following federal agencies, which have jurisdiction over the indicated financial institutions:

Comptroller of the Currency (national banks);

Federal Deposit Insurance Corporation (FDIC - insured banks that are not members of the Federal Reserve System);

Federal Reserve Board (state member banks of the Federal Reserve System),

Office of Thrift Supervision (Federally-insured savings institutions and members of the Office of Thrift Supervision System not insured by FDIC); and

National Credit Union Administration (federally chartered credit unions).

The FTC may determine that a creditor or advertiser has violated the law and order the creditor or advertiser to cease and desist from further violations. Violations of such an administrative order may result in an $11,000 civil penalty each day the violation continues.

If creditors or advertisers engage in practices which they know the Commission has previously determined to be unfair or deceptive, the Commission may file an action in federal district court seeking penalties of up to $11,000 for each violation.

In addition, where a creditor inaccurately discloses an annual percentage rate or finance charge, the FTC can require the creditor to adjust the accounts of persons to whom credit was extended to assure that the obligors will not be required to pay a finance charge in excess of the finance charge actually disclosed or the dollar equivalent of the disclosed annual percentage rate, whichever is lower. Section 108(e) of the Truth in Lending Act sets forth the conditions under which these administrative restitution cases may be brought, as well as defenses the creditor can assert in such cases.

Civil Liability

Under the amended Truth in Lending Act, a creditor may be liable to a consumer for a statutory penalty of twice the amount of the finance charge, with a minimum of $100 and a maximum of $1,000. Statutory liability applies only to seven specific violations: Failing to properly disclose the right of rescission, where applicable; and the improper disclosure of the amount financed, the finance charge, the annual percentage rate, the total of payments, the payment schedule, or the security interest taken by the creditor. In addition, the creditor is liable for actual damages suffered by the consumer and, if the consumer prevails, for the consumer's reasonable attorney's fees and costs. The creditor can avoid such liability if it notifies the consumer within 60 days after discovering the error and adjusts the account to reflect the correct annual percentage rate or finance charge, provided the consumer has not instituted suit, or the creditor has not received written notice of its error, prior to its notification.

Creditors are not liable for violations that were unintentional and resulted from bona fide errors. They must show that they have procedures reasonably adapted to prevent such errors. Examples of bona fide errors include clerical, calculation, computer malfunction and programming, and printing errors. Errors of legal judgment do not qualify as bona fide errors.

Creditors are deemed to be in compliance with the nonnumerical disclosure provisions of the Truth in Lending Act if the creditor: (1) uses any appropriate model form or clause as published by the Federal Reserve Board; or (2) uses any such model form or clause and changes it by (a) deleting any information that is not required by the Act, or (b) rearranging the format, if in making such deletion or in rearranging the format, the creditor does not affect the substance, clarity, or meaningful sequence of the disclosure.

See Sections 105(b) and 130 of the Truth in Lending Act.

Criminal Liability

A creditor is also subject to a fine of not more than $5,000 or imprisonment for not more than one year, or both, for willfully and knowingly violating the Act or Regulation Z by giving false or inaccurate information, failing to provide required disclosures, or consistently understating the annual percentage rate.

See Section 112 of the Truth in Lending Act.

Conclusion

The foregoing summary of the Truth in Lending Act and Regulation Z incorporates the Federal Reserve Board's official staff commentary issued in October, 1981, and the updates to the commentary through March, 1996. The summary is intended to be a guide to the new law; it does not cover all contingencies. Anyone needing additional information may contact the Federal Trade Commission, 11000 Wilshire Blvd., Suite 13209, Los Angeles, California 90024. Telephone number: (310) 235-4040.

16 Real Estate Syndicates and Investment Trusts

REAL ESTATE SYNDICATION

Real estate syndication offers the opportunity to channel private savings into real estate investments for which other financing is not available. It has been a popular method of financing the purchase and sale of properties in the higher price ranges.

The term "syndication" has no precise legal significance. It is a descriptive term for an organization or combination of investors pooling capital for investment in real estate. The responsibility, obligation and relationship of the syndicator to the investment group and the investors to each other are determined principally by the form of organization.

Real estate licensees have been active in real estate syndication for years. This follows naturally from licensees' involvement as agents in purchase and sale transactions. When confronted with a listing or other opportunity to sell property requiring financing that could not be handled by a single purchaser, a real estate broker might turn to others for pooling of capital necessary to consummate the purchase.

In General

A typical real estate syndication combines the money of individual investors with the management of a sponsor, and has a three-phase cycle: origination (planning, acquiring property, satisfying registration and disclosure rules, and marketing); operation (sponsor usually manages both the syndicate and the real property); and liquidation or completion (resale of the property).

Benefits

Virtually every real estate broker or developer has been at some time in a controlling position with respect to an expensive piece of property that appears to offer extremely favorable opportunities for profit to the purchaser. All too often the investment outlay on such a purchase is more than any single client can manage. The real estate licensee who understands the methods of syndication can turn what would otherwise have been a frustrating and unrewarding situation into a profitable transaction for both the licensee and the investors.

By pooling limited financial resources with others who are similarly situated, a small-scale investor is afforded an opportunity to participate in ownership and operation of a piece of property that is too much to handle singly or in a joint venture with one or two others.

Syndication also offers professional management which might not otherwise be economically feasible for the small investor. Professional management, the basic commodity that the syndicator has to offer, is crucial to successful syndication.

Syndicate Forms

Selecting the form of organization involves practical as well as legal and tax considerations. Each of the available entities has advantages and disadvantages. The corporate form insures centralized management as well as limited liability for the investors but is seldom utilized in modern syndicates because of its negative tax features. The general partnership (joint venture) avoids the double taxation normally involved in a corporate entity but the unlimited liability provision and lack of centralized management militate against its use. The limited partnership combines nearly all of the advantages of the corporate and partnership forms. It has the corporate advantages of limited liability and centralized management and the tax advantages of the partnership. Consequently, the limited partnership form of organization is the one most frequently selected for real estate syndicates.

Another form of business, the limited liability company, was added in 1994 and includes liability limitation similar to that afforded shareholders of a corporation.

Limited Partnership
Under the California Revised Limited Partnership Act, a limited partner is not liable as a general partner unless the limited partner is also named as a general partner in the certificate of limited partnership or the limited partner participates in control of the business (Corporations Code Section 15632). If the limited partnership agreement otherwise satisfies certain tax requirements, the limited partnership is taxed as a partnership rather than as an association taxable as a corporation.

Regulatory Control of Real Estate Syndicate Offerings
The increasing use of syndicates to invest in real estate in California led to the enactment of the Real Estate Syndicate Act (Business and Professions Code Sections 10250, et seq.) in 1969. Operative January 2, 1970, this law was applicable only to noncorporate syndicates owned beneficially by 100 persons or less which were formed for the sole purpose of investing in real property. Jurisdiction over these offerings was transferred from the Department of Corporations to the Department of Real Estate. Jurisdiction over other syndicate offerings (e.g., oil and gas syndicates) remained with the Department of Corporations.

Effective January 1, 1978, the Real Estate Syndicate Act was repealed and the regulation of offerings of all real estate syndicate interests was again vested in the Department of Corporations.

A given form of business for pooling investment money may constitute a securities offering for which the organizers must seek a permit or exemption from the Department of Corporations.

The 1977 legislation also added Section 25206 to the Corporations Code, enabling real estate brokers to engage in the sale of real estate syndicate security interests without having to obtain a broker-dealer license from the Department of Corporations. The legislation also added a provision to the Real Estate Law making it the basis for disciplinary action against a real estate broker if he/she violates certain provisions of the Corporations Code or the regulations of the Corporations Commissioner in transactions involving the sale, exchange or trade of real estate syndicate interests in which the broker is permitted to engage under the Corporations Code. Real Estate Brokers seeking to engage in the sale of security interests in real estate syndicates should also consult Department of Corporations Release No. 62-C (July 2, 1980).

Persons desiring detailed information concerning the offer and sale of interests in real estate syndicates should seek such information from the Department of Corporations.

REAL ESTATE INVESTMENT TRUSTS

A real estate investment trust (REIT) is a trust or corporation that serves as a conduit for the real estate investments of its shareholders.

In 1960, the *Real Estate Investment Trust Act* (Public Law 86-779 - Internal Revenue Code Section 856 et seq.) provided a vehicle by which investors who prefer real estate to security investments could receive substantially the same tax benefits as mutual funds and other regulated investments. Thus, if a REIT distributes 95 percent or more of its ordinary income to shareholders, it is taxed, at corporate rates, on only the retained earnings.

Some of the other advantages which REITs now share with stock investment companies are: (1) pooling of funds to take advantage of big investment opportunities; (2) the best possible legal counsel; and, (3) the added safety and probability of higher returns from widely diversified investment projects.

A REIT is accorded special tax treatment because most of its income is received from real estate and distributed to the shareholders. Along with this tax advantage, REITs are subject to qualifications and limitations, including:

1. Must not hold property primarily for sale to customers in the ordinary course of business.

2. Must be beneficially owned by at least 100 investors.

3. No five, or fewer, persons may hold more than 50 percent of the beneficial interests.

4. The beneficial interest must be evidenced by transferable shares or certificates of interest.

5. In California, each share or certificate of interest must carry with it an equivalent vote.

6. Investments must account for a minimum of 95 percent of the trust's gross income.

7. Seventy-five percent of gross income must come from real estate investments.

8. Less than 30 percent of the trust's gross income may result from short-term gains on sales of stock or securities held for less than six months plus sales (but not involuntary conversions) of real estate held less than four years.

9. Accounting period must be the calendar year.

Because the usual penalty for not meeting the qualifications is the loss of REIT status, it is suggested that licensees contact the IRS for the most current tax law involving REITs.

Types of REITs

REITs are categorized as equity trusts, mortgage trusts (short-term or long-term) or combination (balanced) trusts.

An *equity trust* owns real property (residential, commercial, or industrial) and its chief source of income is rent. It may buy or construct buildings, develop real estate projects, lease properties, collect rent, and place mortgages on its properties. It is prohibited by law from holding any property primarily for sale to customers. It takes depreciation on its properties and distributes at least 95 percent of its net income to its shareholders.

An equity trust's internal sources of growth capital are refinancing of its mortgage debt and retaining of capital gains when property is sold. External sources are the public sale of its securities, acquisition of properties in exchange for its securities, and short-term bank loans.

Mortgage trusts invest their assets in short-term or long-term mortgages or other liens against real property. Their primary source of income is from interest earned from their mortgage portfolios or from commissions and discounts on mortgages purchased.

A short-term mortgage trust's investment objective stresses 6 to 24-month construction and development loans, usually funded through use of commercial paper or bank loans. Maximum profits are realized by continual increase of short-term leverage, thereby netting the spread between the trust's cost of funds and its contractual lending rates.

The investment objectives of a long-term mortgage trust emphasize 20 to 30-year amortized loans, including equity participation loans.

Equity trusts and mortgage trusts both outnumber *combination trusts*, which are able to develop property, own property, lease property, provide mortgage financing and land development loans, etc.

There are many other technical and involved provisions spelled out in federal law, Internal Revenue Service rulings, and the California Corporations Commissioner's regulations. To be properly informed beyond the general picture presented here, licensees should contact the State Department of Corporations.

17 Appraisal and Valuation

Property valuation may be considered the heart of all real estate activity. Only a practical understanding of real estate values will enable real estate brokers and salespersons to carry out their functions in a useful and dependable manner in serving their clients and in meeting their obligations to the general public.

Brokers and salespersons should have a good understanding of: the theoretical concepts of value; the forces which influence value; and the methods by which such value may be estimated most accurately.

Probably the question most frequently asked brokers by clients is, "How much do you think the property is worth?" It is a daily occurrence for the real estate broker to have clients ask about the fair price, fair rental, fair basis for trade, or a proper insurance coverage for property. A broker needs to know how to answer such questions correctly.

To be successful in business, an agent must determine whether time can profitably be spent in trying to sell property at a listing price set by the owner. The agent must keep in mind that in accepting a listing the agent is obligated to put forth best efforts to find a buyer for the property at that price. A seller's unrealistic asking price is a roadblock that can be remedied by a knowledgeable salesperson capable of making a market analysis and using the three approaches to value. Such ability assists the seller to set the most appropriate listing price.

The real estate professional is cautioned, however, not to claim greater appraisal ability or expertise than is actually possessed. Great harm can come to the client and to the professional if significant appraisal mistakes are made. When unable to competently perform an appraisal request, the advice of a professional real estate appraiser should be sought. Licensed or certified appraisers are governed in their competency by the Competency Provision of the Code of Ethics of the Uniform Standards of Professional Appraisal Practice (USPAP), promulgated by the Appraisal Foundation.

THEORETICAL CONCEPTS OF VALUE AND DEFINITIONS

Definition of Appraisal

To appraise means the act or process of developing an opinion of value; an opinion of value. (USPAP, 2000 ed., pg. 10) It may be said that value is the present worth of all rights to future benefits, arising out of property ownership, to typical users or investors. An appraisal report is usually a written statement of the appraiser's opinion of value of an adequately described parcel of property as of a specified date. It is a conclusion which results from the process of research and analysis of factual and relevant data.

Real estate appraising methods are being standardized by virtue of the experience and practice of qualified people in all parts of the country who encounter the same types of valuation problems, and who by various methods and processes succeed in solving them in an equitable manner. It is natural, however, that differences of opinion may exist as to the value of specific parcels of real estate and the means of estimating their value.

Property rights are measurable. Real estate as a tangible thing can be measured. It includes both land and improvements and exists independent of any desire for its possession. To distinguish between its physical aspects and rights in and to real property, the latter are called *property interests* in real estate.

These interests - ownership in fee simple and other lesser interests - have been discussed in preceding chapters.

Property rights in real estate are normally appraised at Market Value. There are many definitions of Market Value, but a good working definition is the most probable price the property would bring if freely offered on the open market with both a willing buyer and a willing seller.

Rights in real property are referred to as "Bundle of Rights," which infers: right to occupy and use; to sell in whole or in part; to bequeath (give away); and, to transfer by contract for a specific period of time (lease). It also implies the right not to take any of these actions.

These rights are limited by: the government's power of taxation; eminent domain; police power (for safety, health and general welfare of the public, such as zoning, building codes); and, right of property to escheat (revert) to the state in the event the owner dies and leaves no heirs.

The rights in a property must be known by the appraiser before making a proper valuation, and the appraiser must also be able to distinguish between personal and real property. Market value is the object of most appraisal assignments, and appraisals mainly are concerned with fee simple estate valuation as opposed to partial interest value.

The widespread need for appraisals is apparent. Everyone uses real estate in one way or another and must pay for its use, which involves a decision about value. Practical decisions concerning value must be based upon some kind of an appraisal or evaluation of real property collateral.

The term evaluation has a special meaning and use for institutional lenders since passage of the Federal Institutions Reform, Recovery, and Enforcement Act (FIRREA). In reality, it is an appraisal, an estimate of value.

Although an appraisal may be transmitted orally, it is usually a written statement of an estimate of value and is referred to as an *appraisal report.*

Traditional Approaches to Value
Basically, there are three approaches to property valuation used by appraisers. Each gives a separate indication of value, yet the approaches are all interrelated and all use market comparison techniques. All three approaches are considered in each complete assignment. However, all three are not always employed, depending upon the property type and the process and report type agreed to by the client and the appraiser.

The approaches to value are: Sales Comparison (or Market Data) Approach; Cost Approach; and Income Capitalization Approach.

The Appraiser's Role in the Real Estate Profession

The appraiser, by reason of professional training, experience, and ethics is responsible for furnishing clients with an objective third party opinion of value, arrived at without pressures or prejudices from the parties involved with the property, such as an owner or lender.

The appraiser has a heavy personal and professional responsibility to be correct and accurate in opinions of value. Otherwise, the appraiser's clients may easily suffer loss and the appraiser's professional reputation may also suffer.

There has been considerable controversy in recent years concerning the appraiser's potential for influencing declining neighborhoods and discrimination in housing. The main thrust of the controversy charges that appraisers have tended to view declining neighborhoods as reducing in value without regard for individual home upgrading and homogeneous neighborhoods as being more stable in value than mixed neighborhoods. It has been claimed that loan appraisals in these declining or mixed areas have been unduly pessimistic and conservative because of these purported appraiser attitudes. This supposed conservatism, it has been declared, leads to further decline because favorable loans are not made.

Appraisers respond that the professional appraiser will only consider the factors actually affecting value, and lenders' policies for granting loans are beyond the appraiser's control. Lenders reply that the appraiser's opinion of value is the main basis for the loan and prudent lending practices must be followed.

In the making of thousands of daily appraisal decisions, there is probably some truth on all sides.

A proper appraisal does not contribute to either problem mentioned above. An accurate appraisal, resulting from the competency of a skilled appraiser, will reflect only the forces affecting value.

True forces affecting value. It is necessary that appraisers be exceptionally sensitive to their roles in accurately assessing the true forces affecting value. In accomplishing this, the appraiser cannot allow the general neighborhood composite of ethnic, religious, or minority populations or the general condition of neighborhood improvement to detract from a clear and objective evaluation of the property appraised on its own merits.

It is also the appraiser's responsibility to keep the appraisals timely in a changing market.

It is no longer prudent to rely solely on past sales of comparable property. The appraiser must use all pertinent data and appraisal methods to insure the appraised value is, in fact, the closest estimate of the price the property would bring if freely offered on the open market.

World events of the late 70's resulted in interest rate and property appreciation spirals to historic highs, dramatic decline in construction, creative financing approaches to generate sales, and extraordinary levels of foreclosure and bankruptcy. Such times required exceptional appraiser sensitivity to the true market forces.

Occasionally appraisers have contributed to individual property problems by failing to understand or recognize contrary market trends.

The professional appraisal associations have responded with increased emphasis on education in current appraisal and financial techniques. The dynamics of such a volatile market require the appraiser to keep abreast of new techniques and market forces. Recognizing this, California statutes enforced by the Office Of Real Estate Appraisers (OREA) require continuing education for licensed and certified appraisers. Those requirements are set forth in the OREA portion at the end of this chapter.

Appraisal Report

An appraisal report sets forth the data, analysis and conclusions of the writer. When put in writing, it protects both appraiser and client. Reports vary in scope and length. The following information should be included and is more specifically outlined in Standards 1 and 2 of the USPAP:

1. **A final value conclusion** is expressed in terms of dollars for the property which is being appraised.

2. **The value conclusion** can be made for any date in the past, and, with some care, for any date in the future. The time of inspection of the physical improvements is generally taken as the date of value unless otherwise informed by either the property owner, owner's attorney, or a court of law. The date of the final writing and delivery of the report is the date of the appraisal, not to be confused with the date of value.

3. **Adequate description of the property.** The street address, including city and state, as well as a complete legal description as set forth by the deed in the County Recorder's Office, should be shown, and the physical structures should be clearly described. The length of this description will depend upon the length and extent of the report.

4. The **latitude of the reasonings** in determining the *value conclusion* will depend upon the type of report and the complexity of the appraisal problem.

5. **Market data, and other factual data.** This includes information on the city and neighborhood which affects the *value conclusion;* information gathered on the site, improvements and the environment of the neighborhood which should be processed by means of one or more of the approaches to value; and, the preliminary estimate of value should be reconciled by means of logic and reasoning in order to arrive at one *value conclusion* for the property. Lengthy details are usually omitted in letter form reports, but appraiser retains the information as backup.

6. **Signature and certification.** Appraisal reports must be signed by the writer and in most instances are preceded by a statement to the effect that the writer has no present or contemplated interest in the property. Requisites of an appraisal are set forth in the USPAP, which was adopted in 1989 by the major appraisal organizations.

Laymen's Terms for Appraisal Reports (USPAP Terminology)

1. **Letter form report.** This type of report is generally used when the client is familiar with the area, and supporting data are not necessary. It consists of a brief description of the property, the type of value sought, the purpose served by the appraisal, the date of value, the value conclusion and the signature of the appraiser. This is known as a Restricted Use Report and is governed by Section 2.2(c) of the USPAP. Specific language is required to put readers on notice that this report type is for a single user for his/her single purpose.

2. **Short form report.** This type of report is normally used by lending institutions, such as banks, insurance companies, saving and loan associations, and governmental agencies. Generally, it consists of simple check sheets or spaces to be filled in by the appraiser. The report varies from two to eight pages in length and includes the pertinent data about the property, with photos, maps, plats and sketches. Today these types of reports are classified as Summary Reports and are governed by Section 2.2(b) of USPAP. This category of report can also be a narrative format, but the data presented will be generally in a summary format with more information than a restricted report.

3. **Narrative report.** This type of report can be a complete document including all pertinent information about the area and the subject property as well as the reasons and computations for the *value conclusion.* It includes: maps, photographs, charts and plot plans. It is written for court cases and out-of-town clients who need all of the factual data. It gives the comprehensive reasoning of the *appraiser* as well as the *value conclusions.* These reports are classified as Self-Contained Reports. They are governed by Section 2.2(a) of USPAP.

Any of these report types could be done on a form or in a narrative format. The contents and the depth of discussion, not the format, define the report type in USPAP terms.

Purposes and Uses of Appraisals

The basic purpose of an appraisal is to estimate a particular value, i.e., market value, check for support of sales price, loan value, investment value, etc. Some of the uses for requiring the estimate of value are:

1. *Transfer of ownership of property.*

    a. An appraisal assists buyers and sellers in arriving at a fair and equitable sales price. An appraisal of physical property may also include an opinion of its age, remaining life, quality or authenticity.

    b. The listing agent needs an estimate of value of the property before accepting a listing from the owner. If the agent can show by means of an appraisal the appraised fair market value of the property, and obtain a listing at that figure, a sale more likely will result. The real estate practitioner should be prepared to demonstrate a knowledge of both comparative and economic values.

    c. Where a trade is involved, appraisals tend to assist in clarifying the opinions of value formed by both parties to the trade.

    d.   Valuations are necessary for the distribution of estate properties among heirs.

2.   *Financing and credit.*

    a.   The lender has an appraisal made of the value of the property to be pledged as security for a mortgage loan.

    b.   Measuring economic soundness of real estate projects involves feasibility studies in relation to financing and credit.

3.   *Appraisal for taxation purposes.*

    a.   Appraisals are needed by governmental bodies to establish the proper relationship between land and improvements for real estate taxes (ad valorem taxation).

    b.   Properties subject to estate taxes must be evaluated for the purpose of levying federal and state taxes.

    c.   Appraisals of income-producing properties are necessary to property owners for the basis of depreciation. Normally, only improvements can be depreciated, not the land. An allocation of the market value between land and improvements is a requisite for accounting and taxation purposes.

4.   *Condemnation actions.*

    a.   With the right of eminent domain being vested in governmental agencies, it is important that properties under condemnation be evaluated at market value to properly estimate purchase price, benefits, and damages to the property being affected.

5.   *Insurance Purposes.*

    a.   Appraisals are based principally upon the cost of replacement. This is important for the purpose of insuring properties for fire insurance.

    b.   Appraisals are useful in setting claims arising from insurance contracts after a property has been destroyed.

6.   *Miscellaneous reasons for appraisals.*

    a.   Catastrophic damage. Establishing fair market value of property before and immediately after the damage.

    b.   Fair rental value for negotiation of leases.

    c.   Appraisals for inheritance and gift tax purposes.

    d.   Fraud cases.

    e.   Damage cases.

    f.   Division-of-estate cases. A distribution of property under the terms of a will, in divorce proceedings, or between rival claimants, frequently requires that the value of the property involved be determined by appraisal.

PRINCIPLES OF VALUATION

A knowledge of basic assumptions, postulates or premises that underlie appraisal methods is essential to an understanding of the purpose, methods and procedures of valuation. The following principles of value influences are the more important for a general understanding of the appraisal process.

Principle of conformity. Holds that maximum value is realized when land uses are compatible and a reasonable degree of architectural harmony is present. Zoning ordinances help set conformity standards.

Principle of change. Real property is in a constant state of flux and change, affecting individual properties, neighborhoods and cities. The appraiser follows trends and influences and is sensitive to changes in conditions that affect the value of real estate. Economic, environmental, government, and social forces affect all markets, especially real estate.

Principle of substitution. This principle is the basis of the appraisal process. Simply stated, value will tend to be set by the cost of acquiring an equally desirable substitute. The value of a property to its owner cannot ordinarily exceed the value in the market to persons generally, when it can be substituted without undue expense or serious delay. In a free market, the buyer can be expected to pay no more, and a seller can expect to receive no less, than the price of an equivalent substitute.

A property owner states that owner's house is worth $95,000. Buyers in the market can obtain a substitute property with the same features and utility for only $90,000. The seller's house, therefore, has a value of approximately $90,000, not $95,000.

Principle of supply and demand. Holds that price varies directly, but not necessarily proportionately, with demand, and inversely, but not necessarily proportionately, with supply. Increasing supply or decreasing demand tends to reduce price in the market. The opposite is also true.

Principle of highest and best use. The best use of a parcel of land, known as its highest, best and most profitable use, is that which will most likely produce the greatest net return to the land over a given period of time. This net return is realized in terms of money or other amenities.

The application of this principle is flexible. It reflects the appraiser's opinion of the best use for the property as of the date of his appraisal. At one period of time, the highest and best use of a parcel of land in a downtown business district might be for the development of an office building; at another time, a parking lot may be the highest and best use.

A single-family house on a commercial lot may not be the highest and best use for the site. A four-unit apartment on multiple zoned land suitable for 30 units is probably not the long-term highest and best use of the land.

It is also useful to understand that highest and best use may not be only economic or profit-making in character. Environmental, aesthetic, and historical considerations are increasingly important in governmental views of highest and best use.

The Appraisal Institute, at Page 244 of the 10th Edition of *The Appraisal of Real Estate,* offers this definition for highest and best use:

"The reasonably probable and legal use of vacant land or an improved property, which is physically possible, appropriately supported, financially feasible, and that results in the highest value."

The first reference in the definition applies to vacant land while the second applies to improved properties. This indicates that there may be two highest and best uses, one with the site vacant and the other as improved. These must be reconciled into a final highest and best use determination for the property being appraised.

Determining highest and best use includes assessing potential buyers' motives, the existing use of the property, potential benefits of ownership, the market's behavior, community or environmental factors, and special conditions or situations which come to bear on appraisal conclusions of value.

Principle of progression. The worth of a lesser-valued object tends to be enhanced by association with many similar objects of greater value (inadequacy or under-improvement).

Principle of regression. The worth of a greater-valued object is reduced by association with many lesser-valued objects of the same type (super adequacy or over-improvement).

Principle of contribution. A component part of a property is valued in proportion to its contribution to the value of the whole property or by how much that part's absence detracts from the value of the whole. Maximum values are achieved when the improvements on a site produce the highest (net) return, commensurate with the investment.

Principle of anticipation. Value is created by anticipated future benefits to be derived from the property. In the Fair Market Value Analysis, appraisers estimate the present worth of future benefits. This is the basis for the income approach to value. Simply stated, the income approach is the analysis of the present worth of projected future net income and anticipated future resale value. Historical data are relevant because they aid in the interpretation of future benefits.

Principle of competition. Competition is created where substantial profits are being made. If there is a profitable demand for residential construction, competition among builders will become very apparent. This could lead to an increase in supply in relation to the demand, resulting in lower selling prices and unprofitable competition, leading to renewed decline in supply.

Principle of balance. Value is created and sustained when contrasting, opposing, or interacting elements are in equilibrium, or balance. Proper mix of varying land uses creates value. Imbalance is created by an *over-improvement* or an *under-improvement*. Balance is created by developing the site to its highest and best use.

Principle of four-stage life cycle. In due course, all material things go through the process of wearing or wasting away and eventually disintegrating. All property is characterized by four distinct stages: *growth, stability, decline, and revitalization.*

Single properties, districts, neighborhoods, etc., tend generally to follow this pattern of growth and decline. It is also evident this process is frequently reversed as neighborhoods and individual properties in older residential areas are renewed and restored.

Revitalization and modernization in inner-city older neighborhoods may result from organized government programs or as a result of changing preferences of individual buyers. Most neighborhoods remain in the mature or stable stage for many years, with decline being hardly noticeable as renewal becomes essentially an ongoing process.

BASIC VALUATION DEFINITIONS

Value Designations

There are many different designations or definitions of value. They may be divided into the following two main classifications:

> *Utility Value*, which is value directed toward a particular use. This frequently is termed *subjective* value and includes valuation of amenities which attach to a property or a determination of value for a specified purpose or for a specific person.

> *Market value*, which represents the amount in money (cash or the equivalent) for which a property can be sold or exchanged in prevailing market conditions at a given time or place as a result of market balancing. It may be based on a "willing buyer" and "willing seller" concept. This is frequently termed the *objective* value, since it is not subject to restrictions of a given project.

Appraisers carefully define the value being sought. Types of values are Liquidation Value, Insurable Value, Investment Value and, of course, Assessed Value (for taxation).

The real estate market sometimes places great importance on real estate financing terms. Market Value might be estimated for specific financing arrangements: seller carry-back, balloon payments, renegotiable mortgages or other "creative" financing techniques.

Market Value Defined

In appraisal practice, the term Market Value is defined by agencies that regulate federal financial institutions in the U.S. That definition is the one found in USPAP and is given as:

> "The most probable price which a property should bring in a competitive and open market under all conditions requisite to a fair sale, the buyer and seller each acting prudently and knowledgeably, and assuming the price is not affected by undue stimulus."

Implicit in this definition is the consummation of a sale as of a specified date and the passing of title from seller to buyer under conditions whereby:

1. buyer and seller are motivated;
2. buyer and seller are well informed or well advised and acting in what they consider their best interest;
3. a reasonable time is allowed for exposure in the open market;

4. payment is made in terms of cash in United States dollars or terms of financial arrangements comparable thereto; and

5. the price represents the normal consideration for the property sold, unaffected by special or creative financing or sales concessions granted by anyone associated with the sale.

(Source: *Uniform Standards of Professional Appraisal Practice,* Appraisal Foundation, 2000 Edition, page 160.)

Legal Definition

The legal definition of Fair Market Value under California law is found in the Code of Civil Procedure, Section 1263.320, as follows:

> "The fair market value of the property is the highest price on the date of valuation that would be agreed to by a seller, being willing to sell but under no particular or urgent necessity for so doing, nor obliged to sell, and a buyer, being ready, willing, and able to buy but under no particular necessity for so doing, each dealing with the other with full knowledge of all the uses and purposes for which the property is reasonably adaptable and available."

Value vs. Price

When reference is made to the value of a property, generally fair market value is meant. Market price is what one might get from the sale of the property in terms of money. Sometimes value and price are the same, most particularly when there is no compulsion to buy or sell. Under other circumstances, there might be a wide difference between the market value of a property and the actual sale price. The appraiser must be careful to consider normal buyers and sellers attitudes for the type of property appraised. The appraiser is estimating actual market value not theoretical value.

The immobility of real estate makes it unique. Theoretically, there are no two parcels exactly alike and therefore no means of making a total comparison between properties. Circumstances of one buyer and one seller affect the sale price of a specific property, whereas the actions of many buyers and sellers of similar type properties determine the going rate for the sale or exchange of property on the open market.

Among the various types of value that have been designated from time to time are book value, tax value, market value, cash value, capital value, speculative value, par value, true value, exchange value, reproduction value, physical value, replacement value, insurance value, investment value, rental value, face value, depreciated value, leasehold value, sound value, sales value and cost value.

The real estate broker should be concerned mostly with the concept of Fair Market Value, or simply market value, for this is the basis upon which most property is generally bought and sold.

Value vs. Cost

Value can be distinguished from "cost" as well as from "price," for neither is necessarily synonymous with value. The principal differences may be explained as follows:

1. Value has to do with the combined factors of present and future anticipated enjoyment or profit. The value sought in the appraisal of property may be said to be the discounted present worth of all desirable things (benefits) which may accrue from a skillful use of it. A conclusion in regard to these things will clearly be a matter of opinion: an intelligent estimate based on a thorough analysis of all available influencing factors and on reasonable and more or less warranted assumptions.

2. Cost represents a measure of past (or prospective) expenditures in money, labor, material or sacrifices of some nature in acquiring or producing the commodity. While cost may be, and frequently is, a factor upon which value is partially based, it need not be, as it does not control present and future value. An example of this fact is the value of an apartment property as compared with an oil well (assuming that the building and drilling costs were the same). The oil well may prove to be a big producer and of great value, or it may prove to be a dry hole and of no value. An apartment building might be costly to build but have little value because of its bad location and high vacancy factor.

3. Price is what one pays for a commodity, regardless of pressure motives or intelligence of the seller or buyer. Usually it is considered to be the amount of money involved in a transaction. Whether we receive in value more or less than what we pay for will depend on the soundness of judgment in the analysis or appraisal of value. Under an efficient market structure, price will usually tend to equal value, varying only as buyers and sellers have unequal knowledge, negotiating skills, or economic strength. Some factors influencing market price (as distinguished from value) are favorable financing, distress sale, forced purchase, uninformed purchaser or seller, misrepresentation of facts by the seller and high pressure sales practices.

Appraisers carefully distinguish between market value, cost and price in refining their appraisal conclusions.

Purposes and Characteristics of Value
The purpose of a valuation or an appraisal is usually indicated in the value concept employed, for example: market value, assessed value, condemnation value, liquidation value, cash value, mortgage loan value, fire insurance value, etc. The purpose of an appraisal frequently dictates the valuation method employed and influences the resulting estimate of value.

Intended use. The intended use of the report has become distinct from the purpose of the appraisal. This relates to how the process has been separated from the writing of the report (Standard 1 vs. Standard 2 in USPAP). The purpose of the appraisal may be, for instance, to help in settling an estate. The intended use of the report may be to communicate the value findings to heirs only, or may include attorneys and/or taxing authorities. The purpose helps to define how the appraisal process will be laid out. The intended use will help to determine which report type is most appropriate for communicating the results of the process.

Four elements of value. There are only four elements of value, all of which are essential. These are utility, scarcity, demand (together with financial ability to purchase), and transferability. None alone will create value.

For example, a thing may be scarce but, if it has no utility, there is no demand for it. Other things, like air, may have utility and may be in great demand, but are so abundant as to have no commercial value. *Utility* is the capacity of a commodity to satisfy a need or desire. To have utility value, real estate should have the ability to provide shelter, income, amenities or whatever use is being sought. Functional utility is an important test for determining value. Likewise, the commodity must be transferable as to use or title to be marketable.

Generally speaking, a commodity will have commercial or marketable value in proportion to its utility and relative scarcity. Scarcity is the present or anticipated supply of a product in relation to the demand for it. Utility creates demand, but demand, to be effective, must be implemented by purchasing power. Otherwise, a person desiring a product cannot acquire it.

Fundamental to the concept of value is the "highest and best use" principle, discussed earlier in this chapter. Location is a most important factor in determining highest and best use. Any analysis to reach a decision as to the "highest and best use" must include consideration as to the future supply and demand for such use within the area and a possible oversupply or undersupply with attendant effect on market demand and value.

FORCES INFLUENCING VALUE

The value of real estate is created, maintained, modified and destroyed by the interplay of the following four great forces:

1. **Environmental and physical characteristics.** Examples of physical characteristics include: quality of conveniences; availability of schools, shopping, public transportation, churches; similarity of land used; and types of physical hazards. Environmental considerations include climate, soil and topography, barriers to future development (oceans, mountains, etc.), transportation systems, and access to other areas/regions.

2. **Social ideals and standards.** Examples of social forces include: population growth and decline; age, marriage, birth, divorce and death rates; and attitudes toward education, recreation, and other instincts and yearnings of mankind.

3. **Economic influences.** Examples of economic forces are: natural resources; industrial and commercial trends; employment trends; wage levels; availability of money and credit; interest rates; price levels; tax loads; regional and community present economic base; new development trends; and rental and price patterns.

4. **Political or government regulations.** Examples of political forces include: building codes; zoning laws; public health measures; fire regulations; rent controls; environmental legislation controlling types of new development; fiscal policies; monetary policies; government guaranteed loans; government housing; and credit controls.

Each and every one of these many physical, social, economic and political factors affect cost, price, and value to some degree. The four forces interweave and each one is in a constant state of change.

Factors Influencing Value

Directional growth. In any estimate of value, attention should be given to "the city directional growth" as well as to "Urban Renewal Plans." The city directional growth refers to the manner and direction in which the city tends to expand.

Properties in the direction of growth or renewal in different sections of the city tend to increase in value, especially if the growth or renewal is steady and rapid.

Location. Location is an exceptionally important value factor because location influences demand for the property. Location must not be described too generally, and is an effective value factor only when it is specifically related to highest and best use. Brokers often claim, "The three most important characteristics for any property are location, location and location."

Utility. Utility includes the capacity to produce. This important factor involves judgment as to the best use to which a given property may be put. Building restrictions and zoning ordinances affect utility.

Size. The width and depth of a parcel of land will often determine the possibilities and character of its use.

Corner influence. Corner sites sometimes have higher unit value than a site fronting on one street only. Disadvantages include loss of privacy, higher cost as off-site improvements cost more and lot maintenance is more expensive, and setbacks may require a smaller size house. Commercial properties benefit from corner sites because of easy access and added exposure.

Shape. Parcels of land of irregular shape generally cannot be developed as advantageously as rectangular lots.

Thoroughfare conditions. The width of streets, traffic congestion, and condition of pavement have an effect on the value of frontage properties and to a lesser degree on other properties in the neighborhood.

Exposure. The south and west sides of business streets are usually preferred by merchants because pedestrians seek the shady side of the street on warm afternoons and merchandise displayed in the windows is not damaged by the sun. This traditional view in older commercial districts is somewhat offset by new architectural concepts (e.g., shopping malls), parking and convenience.

Character of business climate. Larger cities develop residential, shopping, financial, wholesale, and industrial districts.

Plottage or assemblage. An added increment of value when several parcels of land are combined under one ownership to produce greater utility than when the parcels are under separate ownership.

In highly urbanized multiple residential and commercial areas plottage, or assemblage, makes it possible to gain that higher utility. An example of this would be a density bonus for the combining of residential lots. This principle may also apply to light industrial areas.

Topography and character of soil. The bearing qualities of the soil may affect construction costs. Extensive foundations are usually necessary in soft earth. The type and condition of the topsoil affect the growth of grass, plants, shrubs and trees. Value may also be influenced by land contour and grades, drainage and view points.

Obsolescence. Caused by external or economic changes which decrease the functional utility of a property, or by physical deterioration of the property.

Changes in types and methods of construction, style of architecture, or interior arrangements for specific purposes may render a particular building out of date. Changes in the uses of neighboring property may also contribute to the obsolescence of a building. Careful appraisal will include the potential for remodeling, refurbishing or other method to restore value.

Building restrictions and zones. These sometimes operate to depress values and at other times to increase values.

For example, there may be a vacant lot on a residential street which will sell for only $150 a front foot for single family residential use but would sell for $600 per front foot as an apartment site. Or a vacant lot in a zoned area may sell for more per front foot as a business site because of the supply of business sites being restricted by zoning.

Additional Factors Important for Residential Property

When appraising residential property, it is customary to make a direct comparison between the property being appraised (subject property) and comparable properties in the area which have sold recently. This is the market data or "sales comparison approach" method based upon the economic principle of substitution (i.e., the value of a particular property will not generally exceed the cost to purchase a similar, or substitute property which is equally desirable and available).

Gross rent multiplier. An appraiser may also use a technique known as Gross Rent Multiplier (GRM) by comparing actual rentals and sales prices of properties comparable to the subject to get another indication of value by multiplying the monthly rent by an appropriate GRM. If a comparable property rents for $700 a month and sells for $84,000, which is 120 times the gross monthly rental ($84,000 ÷ $700 = 120), the indicated GRM applicable to the subject property is 120.

GRM applies only to *rental* income. When part of a property's income comes from *non-rental sources*, an appraiser will use a similar gross income multiplier (GIM).

Square foot method. In making a preliminary estimate of the value of residential property, it is usual to evaluate the lot and the present value of the building. In California, an estimate of the cost of replacing a building is usually made by the square foot method. The square foot method requires measuring the building and dividing it into rectangles. Multiplying the length by the width of each rectangle will produce the square footage of that segment. The total square footage of the residence is obtained by adding together the square footage of all rectangular segments. The sum obtained thereby is multiplied by an appropriate construction cost per square foot, depending upon the type of construction involved. The result is known as the replacement cost of the residence. Depreciation is then taken from the replacement cost to give the present value of the improvements. The present value added to the land value represents an indication of the value of the subject property. In analyzing depreciation, special attention should be paid to the condition of the building, the exterior finish and roof, the interior fixtures, plans and workmanship, interior decoration, plumbing, heating, and electric fixtures, etc. Particular attention should be given to the inspection of the foundation and the underpinnings of the house in connection with possible termite infestation and soil problems such as subsidence or expansion.

Multi-family dwellings. Trends and standards for residential dwellings vary in the markets, especially for multi-family structures. Appraisers must consider: the layout; adequacy of size; conveniences; safety features and comfort; adaptability for intended use; and cost and ease of maintenance.

Additional Factors Important for Commercial Property
Commercial property is real property acquired for investment. Commercial structures are of many types, sheltering such businesses as shopping centers, banks, service establishments, restaurants, parking lots, retail stores and office buildings. A downtown, regional, or community commercial district is usually clearly defined and located on major streets. Store rentals and business leases are generally based on square footage of rentable area. In many localities the tenant pays, in addition to rent, all property expenses/charges such as taxes, insurance, maintenance, and assessments. Such a lease is a "net" (or, in some communities, a "net, net, net") lease.

Front footage valuations are still applicable in many downtown areas or location. In appraising such property, care must be used to properly evaluate such things as floor plans, utility, relationship of site area to improvements, obsolescence, parking accommodations, ratios of net rentable areas to gross area. Efficiency, safety, structural and design features are also very important, as are energy standards and efficiencies.

Additional Factors Important for Industrial Property
Industrial lands are usually valued in terms of gross buildable area, either by square foot or by acre (e.g., 30 cents a square foot; $13,000 an acre). One of the reasons for valuing industrial land in terms of area is that the parcel is generally all usable. Indeed, optimum efficiency of site, buildings and equipment are vital to the successful operation of industrial properties.

Industrial buildings are generally constructed of concrete or steel, including prefabrications, or tilt-ups. Industrial parks (groups of industrial buildings having similar uses) have grown in importance. These require plenty of parking space, storage facilities, excellent operating layouts, management services, and even room to expand. These properties are frequently designed and equipped to meet needs of specific occupants.

Topography. The topography of undeveloped land is of importance, and consideration should be given to the cost of grading, if required.

Subsoil. The character of the subsoil is frequently overlooked, and yet may be vital. Quicksand, rock, or other detriments may make a certain site unsuitable for a given industry. Drainage may also be an important factor.

Plottage value. There is an added increment of value known as plottage which is gained from combining land parcels in an urban area into a reasonably sized industrial site.

Tract layouts. In the study and valuation of unimproved but potentially valuable industrial lands, it is often necessary to have the assistance of a competent engineer who is familiar with plant and tract layouts.

Additional Factors Important for Agricultural or Farm Lands

Present trends show larger and fewer farms, fewer farm buildings per acre, and fewer family-style operations. The type of buildings an appraiser usually finds on agricultural lands include residences, machine sheds, poultry sheds, multifunctional barns, silos, and various animal shelters. According to some experts in the field, farm buildings contribute less than 20% of the total property value.

One important factor in estimating the value of agricultural land is the nature and long-term trend of costs and prices for the crop grown or intended to be grown. For example, if the property is to be used as a dairy farm the appraiser must consider: whether the soil is suitable for hay and grain; water supply for the cattle and crops; proximity to markets; climatic conditions; labor conditions, etc.

Farm land valuation is highly specialized and often requires the assistance of soil and crop experts and appraisal specialists to evaluate irrigation systems and other equipment and machinery.

ECONOMIC TRENDS AFFECTING REAL ESTATE VALUE

Regional, National and Global Economics

Property values increase, decrease, or remain stable based on the interaction of the four forces influencing value. Appraisers must examine and evaluate these forces.

Economic trends and forces at higher levels (regional, national and international) affect property values at the local level. The real estate appraiser must recognize that the general pattern of statistical analysis that guides in interpreting value influences on a national level should be used in the general analysis of state and regional forces which in turn influence local property values.

An appraiser should follow national and regional economic trends, changes in national income levels, international developments and government financing policies because the greater the severity and duration of any economic swing, the wider and deeper is its influence. Conditions to be observed include: gross national product; balance of payments to other countries; national income levels; employment; price level indexes; interest rates; fiscal and monetary policies; building starts; and credit availability.

Factors Influencing City Growth and Development

An appraiser is constantly concerned with the conditions and prospects of the local economy because the value of local real estate is largely determined by the health of the community, as measured by household purchasing power, population changes, employment diversification and stability, wage and price levels, and area growth potential, including environmental conditions.

Cities are classified generally by the functions that stimulate and determine their potential and growth. These classifications are:

Commercial. Primary source of revenue stems from commercial enterprises. These are usually farming cities, cities located at railroad terminals or on ocean ports.

Industrial. Primary source of revenue is derived from manufacturing and processing of commodities.

Extractive industry. Primary source of revenue comes from natural resources, e.g., mining, fishing and lumber.

Political. Primary source of revenue is government employment.

Recreation and health. Primary source of revenue comes from tourist trade, vacation and health resorts.

Education. The anchor point of these cities is a college or university.

Population Trends
Because of the direct relationship existing between the value of real property and population growth, the appraiser should be concerned with population trends and other demographic factors affecting local population, such as: opportunities for employment; quality of local government; civic and social conditions; demand for goods and services; transportation and living conditions; and, opportunities for education and personal improvement.

Neighborhood Analysis
A neighborhood may be defined as a group of similar land uses which are similarly affected by the operation of the four forces influencing value: utility, scarcity, demand(desire) and effective purchasing power. A common definition for a neighborhood is a grouping together of individuals within the community for similar purposes and interests, whether the reasons be commercial, industrial, residential, cultural or civic. The life cycle of a neighborhood includes growth in desirability, peak desirability, stability for a time, then deterioration. The cycle then tends to turn again as the neighborhood becomes more desirable due to change in use or renewal.

Neighborhood analysis is important because the neighborhood is the setting for the property to be appraised and the property has value, to a large extent, as it contributes to or detracts from the neighborhood.

A neighborhood tends to be a somewhat self-contained community, frequently defined by physical boundaries such as hills, freeways, or major streets and usually with some sense of community. In urban areas, the neighborhood tends to become somewhat blurred due to modern transportation and area-wide cultural, educational, recreational, and commercial services. In analyzing the "neighborhood" of the parcel to be appraised, a good starting point is to ascertain the community identity and boundaries.

After defining, even in vague terms, this community identity, an appraiser will look to common services and features, such as local shopping, street patterns, zoning boundaries, and cultural, religious, educational and recreational services. In short, an appraiser searches the local area by observation and through government and public utility investigation to find the factors most affecting use and value patterns in the area.

Neighborhood analysis also tends to define the best search area for comparable market data. As the appraisal progresses, the appraiser may extend or contract this search area.

Some sources of neighborhood data:

1. U.S. Census tract maps and data (local library or vendors).
2. City and county population demographics (planning departments).
3. City, county, and state street and highway systems (city, county and state road/engineering/highway departments).
4. Local zoning and general planning, including community plans (planning departments).
5. School locations, capacities, policies (local school districts).
6. Public utility services: water, sewer, natural gas, electric power, telephone (local public utility companies and government agencies).
7. City and county economic statistics (local chambers of commerce).
8. Local tax information (county tax assessor).
9. If pertinent, private wells and septic laws (local health departments); national forest/park laws (local forestry and park dept.), etc.

SITE ANALYSIS AND VALUATION

Although the location of the neighborhood and city must be weighed in analysis and valuation of a particular site, the location of the site itself, in relation to the neighborhood, is a very important factor.

Since sites in a neighborhood are not usually uniform in size, shape and other physical and economic characteristics, some are superior to others. It is important that the site be analyzed separately and evaluated in conformity with the principle of highest and best use.

Other reasons to separate the land from the value of an entire property, along with important factors contributing to site value, are discussed on the following pages.

Legal Data of Site Analysis
A. Legal description.
    1. An appraiser must determine the legal property description as set forth by a deed or official record.
    2. The proper legal description to locates the property physically within the neighborhood.
B. Taxes.
    1. A comparison is made between the subject and similar properties to ascertain if the property being appraised has been fairly assessed (assessed value, tax rate and tax total). This comparison of properties is not as useful since the adoption of Proposition 13.

2. The extent of the tax burden will have a bearing upon the desirability of the property, particularly when taxes are out of proportion to income.

C. Zoning and General Plan.

1. Copies of the latest zoning ordinances and general plan should be studied to inform the appraiser as to the present usages to which the land may be developed. Sometimes the highest and best use of land is limited by zoning restrictions.

2. Proposed or contemplated changes in the existing ordinances should be determined, since this could have a bearing upon the valuation of the property. However, zoning by itself does not create value unless there is a demand for the land so zoned.

D. Restrictions and easements.

1. Public and private restrictions and easements affecting the land must be discovered.

2. The restrictions and the types of easements on the property have a direct bearing upon the use and value of the site being appraised.

E. Determination of existence of other interests in property.

1. Life estates.

2. Leases.

3. These partial interests divide property values among the parties involved. This does not mean a mathematical division, but rather a division of the bundle of rights.

Physical Factors Involving the Site

A. The physical features of the site should be compared with typical lots in the neighborhood.

B. Lot values will generally tend to cluster around a "site value,"... the price generally accorded a single, usable, typically-sized parcel of land in the area. Lots larger or smaller will tend to increase or decrease when compared to this usual "site value." A good view will also tend to increase lot value. The effect of topography (drainage, low spots, rock, etc.) can frequently be measured by the cost to cure the problem to make the site usable.

C. Shape of a lot.

1. The utility of the lot is the governing factor in irregular or odd-shaped lots.

2. The total area of the lot is not the most important factor. A 50' x 150' lot containing 7,500 square feet is more valuable than a 25' x 300' lot (also 7,500 sq. ft.) because of utility.

3. Irregular-shaped lots are frequently valued in terms of total site value expressed in dollars rather than in terms of unit values of price per square foot or frontage foot.

D. Topography and soil conditions.

   1. The topography and the type of soil can have an adverse effect upon the site value if it makes building costs higher.

E. Corner influence.

   1. In today's market, it has generally been found that corner single-family lots are not valued appreciably more than inside lots.

   2. Corner lots provide better light and more convenient access.

   3. On the other hand, corner lots result in more traffic noise and trespassing and, if applicable, greater special assessments for streets and lighting.

F. Relation of site to surroundings.

   1. The site must be studied in its relationship to streets, alleys, transportation, and stores.

   2. Does the homesite abut commercial or multi-residential uses?

   3. Is it a key lot looking upon other back yards?

   4. If a corner lot, does a bus line stop at the comer?

G. Availability of public utilities.

H. Title encumbrances and encroachments.

I. Landscaping and underground utilities.

Methods of Site Valuation

A. Sales or market data comparison.

   1. Sales and listings (data) of vacant sites are obtained and compared with the property being valued.

   2. The data should be of comparable properties, including the same zoning and in the same or similar neighborhood. Since people make value, the data gathered should be from areas where the purchasing power or income levels are the same as the subject property.

   3. The sales prices should be investigated to determine whether the price paid was the result of a true open market transaction reflecting fair market value. Listings may also be considered.

   4. Some sources of comparable market data are:

      a. Title insurance company records.

      b. Tax assessor's records.

      c. Recorder's office.

      d. Multiple listing files.

      e. Financial news.

      f. Appraiser's personal files.

   5. The verified market transactions should be compared with the subject parcel as to:

      a. Time.

         (1) Determine if prices have gone up, down, or remained stable from the time of each sale to the date of value.

    (2) A percentage factor or a dollar amount may be applied to the comparable sales in order to arrive at an adjusted price due to the time factor.

  b. Location.

    (1) Determine if the location of each comparable property is superior, equal or inferior to that of the subject property.

    (2) A percentage factor or dollar amount may be applied to the data in order to adjust for the difference in location.

  c. Characteristics of the lots.

    (1) The size, depth, and topography of the other properties are compared with the property being valued.

    (2) A percentage factor or dollar amount is determined for these characteristics and applied to the comparable properties to adjust their prices towards the property being appraised.

  d. The adjusted prices of the comparable properties are then compared and analyzed in order to arrive at an estimate of value for the property under study.

Example. Using only 3 lot sales (the minimum) as a demonstration.

Sale No.	Price	Date	Size (feet)	Square Feet
1	$5,000	October, 1995	50 x 120	6,000
2	$4,750	March, 1996	40 x 130	5,200
3	$5,500	June, 1996	50 x 120	6,000
Subject			50 x 150	7,500

Through investigation, it was found that prices have been increasing approximately 1% a month during the past year.

Sale No. 1 is believed to be located in an area inferior to the subject. This lot would sell for about $500 more if located in the subject's block. Sale No. 2 is located in an area believed to be about $250 better than the subject. Sale No. 3 is also in a superior location, by the same $250 adjustment.

The shape and topography of Sales No. 1 and No. 2 are better than the subject by an amount estimated to be $500 and $100 respectively. Sale No. 3's topography and utility appear about the same as the subject.

Adjustments.

Sale No.	Time	Location	Characteristics	Adjusted $	Adj. $/sq. ft.
1	+$500	+$500	-$500	$5,500	$.92
2	+$240	-$250	-$100	$4,640	$.89
3	+$110	-$250	0	$5,360	$.89

The average adjusted price per square foot of the comparable sales is $.90. Therefore, the subject property has an indicated value as follows:

7,500 square feet x $.90 per square foot = $6,750.

In actual practice, the use of more sales data is advisable in order to arrive at a well-supported adjusted price per square foot.

    e.   If all pertinent factors are considered, the adjusted prices will probably be in a fairly close range. If there is still a wide discrepancy, the appraiser will:

        (1) re-analyze work to find undisclosed pertinent factors;

        (2) reexamine data as being true examples of fair market transactions;

        (3) recompute adjustments to insure accuracy; and

        (4) finally, discard the data or explain the apparent contradictions.

B. Abstraction.

  1.   The abstraction method is used to obtain land value where there are no vacant land sales.

    a.   Sales of houses in the same neighborhood on lots with similar characteristics are obtained.

    b.   An estimate of the cost new of the improvements is made.

    c.   An amount is deducted from cost new for depreciation.

    d.   The depreciated cost of the improvements is deducted from the selling price of the property.

    e.   The difference represents an approximation of land value.

  2.   **Example:**   Appraised lot size is 65' X 100' = 6,500 sq.ft. Sale property is 6,000 sq. ft. lot with a single family residence and sold for $83,000. The sale building has an estimated cost new of $61,000 and an accrued depreciation estimated at $20,000. Land value by abstraction:

Price of sale property $83,000

Less depreciated value of improvements:

    Cost new $61,000

    Less accrued depreciation $20.000

Depreciated value $41,000

Indicated land value $42,000

Divide by lot size .... ÷ 6000 sq.ft.

Indicated lot value/sq.ft. .... $7.00/sq.ft.

Multiply by subject lot size:

65' x 100' = 6,500 sq.ft. ....   x 6,500

Indicated value of lot $45,500

C.   Plot Plan.   For better appraisal reporting, a plot plan can be prepared, with lot dimensions and improvements drawn to scale. It should show walks, driveways and other lot improvements and roof plans of the various structures on the site. The plot, together with pictures of the site, neighboring street and lot improvements are vital for an effective site analysis.

ARCHITECTURAL STYLES AND FUNCTIONAL UTILITY

It is essential for an appraiser to have a working knowledge of building design and construction. Good basic design of both interior and exterior has a decided effect on the marketability of real estate. There is no substitute for appropriate materials and proper proportions and scale. The appraiser should be aware of imitations and new plastic replacements.

To achieve maximum value, architectural style and design should be related to the site. A typical stable neighborhood should be improved with homes of approximately the same size, age and style. A house that has an architectural style extremely foreign to its surroundings tends to encounter difficulty when offered for sale.

Or a home meets resistance in the market because of its style, which places it within a definite age group. Thus, if a certain style of architecture has lost its appeal because public taste has changed, this trend will have an adverse effect on value. Both real estate brokers and appraisers must be familiar with home styles and know the effect on value of misplaced styles. The appraiser must also be alert to resurgence of older properties in public acceptance.

This section: contains brief descriptions of various architectural styles in single family homes; explains how to determine quality of construction; and defines functional utility and its effect on marketability.

Architectural Styles

Colonial. Cape Cod and Cape Ann styles are: generally quite small in size - minimum with good taste; symmetrical-windows balanced on both sides of front door; either one or one and one-half stories with little head room upstairs; fairly steep gable or gambrel roof covered with wood shingles; and exterior of wood siding.

New England Colonial. A square or rectangular, box-like structure having: maximum usable space; symmetrical windows balanced on both sides of front door; either two or two and one-half stories; gable roof covered with wood shingles; exterior of wood generally painted white; and impressive front entrance usually with transom fan of glass above the door.

Dutch Colonial. A moderate-sized home generally not more than 50 feet wide, with a symmetrical front having: an entrance at the center, balanced by the windows; low-sweeping gambrel roof; exterior generally of stone; and either one and one-half story with dormer windows or two and one-half stories with dormer windows.

Georgian and Southern Colonial. These styles have elaborate front entrances with plain or fluted columns; are generally of brick or wood; have prominent gabled roofs, often hipped; are very symmetrical; require large plots of land; large scale, not suitable for a small house; and either two, two and one-half or three stories.

English Elizabethan. This style has gothic refined lines with molded stone around windows and doors; generally of brick, stucco, or stone; steep pitched roof, covered with slate or shingle; usually leaded metal casement windows; and requires a large building site.

English Half-Timber. This style has protruding timber faces with stucco between the faces; lower story of heavy masonry; steep pitched roof; generally two stories; and requires a large lot area.

Regency. A generally symmetrical style with front entrance in center; exterior of brick or stone; shutters on each side of windows; low hipped roof; two stories in height; and octagonal window on second floor over front door.

French Provincial. Usually a large house on a sizable plot, masonry exterior walls with very high roofs; large high windows with long shutters; and one and one-half or two and one-half stories.

French Normandy. Generally has turrets at entry; walls of brick or stone; unsymmetrical; and steep pitched shingle roof.

True Spanish. Enclosed patios; red mission tiled roof; wrought iron decorations; and stucco walls (usually white).

Small California Spanish. Stucco exterior; flat composition roof with mission tile trim in the front; suitable for small lots; no patio; and one story only.

Monterey Spanish. Two stories; stucco (generally white); red mission tiled roof; second story balconies; and decorative iron railings.

Modern and Contemporary. Generally one story; usually flat or low pitched roof; often on concrete slab; large amount of glass; and indoor/outdoor living.

California Bungalow or Ranch House. One story; stucco with wood trim; often on concrete slab; shingle or shake roof; low and rambling; generally attached garage; and indoor/outdoor living.

ROOF TYPES

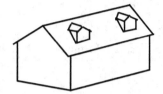

SINGLE DORMERS

SHED DORMER,
or DUSTPAN

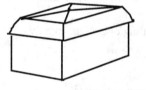

GAMBREL

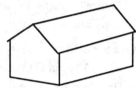

GABLE

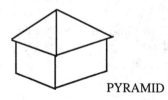

MANSARD

HIP

PYRAMID

FLAT

Building Quality
One of the most important reasons for inspecting a property is to determine its quality of construction and condition. The appraiser must be knowledgeable as to structural details of buildings. All exposed portions of a building should be closely inspected to ascertain the materials used, the present condition, and the type and quality of construction, which may be classified as follows:

A. **Low quality.**
   1.   Competitive low cost house which does not exceed the minimum building codes.

B. **Fair quality.**
   1.   Plain and inexpensive finishes on both interior and exterior.
   2.   Cheap quality finish hardware, lighting fixtures, and heating.
   3.   Generally erected in areas of low purchasing power.
   4.   Typically, stucco exterior, concrete slab floor, composition roof.

C. **Average quality.**
   1.   Meets VA and FHA standards.
   2.   Usually purchased by persons of moderate income.
   3.   Medium standard of construction with some low cost refinements.
   4.   Usually of stucco exterior, hardwood flooring, composition roof or shingle.
   5.   Finish hardware, lighting fixtures and heating of average quality.
   6.   House found in large tract developments.

D. **Good quality.**
   1.   Good architectural design, workmanship and materials.
   2.   Stucco walls with wood and masonry trim, hardwood floors, shingle roofs.
   3.   Usually contains two bathrooms, forced air furnace or equal heating, good quality lighting fixtures and finish hardware.
   4.   Usually has extra built-in equipment in kitchen.

E. **Very good quality.**
   1.   Generally, custom designed by architect.
   2.   Home contains many extra features.
   3.   Stucco walls with extensive wood or masonry trim, hardwood flooring, shake roofs.
   4.   Two or more bathrooms, forced air heating, very good quality finish hardware and lighting fixtures.
   5.   Custom fireplaces.

F. **Excellent quality.**
   1.   Custom designed by architect.

2. Extra features are of the highest quality and design.

3. Stucco walls with redwoods or cedars or other fine woods, stone trim, hardwood, marble and custom carpet floorings, clay tile, slate roofs, copper gutters and so on.

4. A bath with each bedroom, walk-in closets, zoned heating, special wood finishes such as teak, cherry, walnut, etc., designer lighting including recessed art lighting.

5. Custom fireplaces, custom wood libraries, bars, butler's pantries, granite or marble counters in baths and kitchen, gourmet appliances.

Functional Utility

Good architecture is concerned with room layout and functional utility as well as exterior style. A functional analysis of a property measures the conveniences and economy in the use of the property. The combined factors of usefulness and desirability have an effect on a property's marketability. The degree of its functional utility is important in any consideration of its marketability. Thus, marketability is the ultimate test of functional utility.

Functional Utility Checklist

A. **Building.**

1. Living room.
   a. Adequacy of floor and wall space for proper placement of furniture.
   b. Circulation - should not have to pass through long living room to reach other parts of the house.
   c. Fireplace should be away from the traffic flow.
   d. Wall spaces - adequate for furniture arrangements.

2. Dining room or area.
   a. Ease of access to kitchen.
   b. Size of room or area governed by overall size of house.
   c. Best if room is nearly square.

3. Bedrooms.
   a. Master bedroom should be of adequate size (minimum 10' x 12').
   b. Other bedrooms (minimum 9' x 10').
   c. Cross ventilation should be provided.
   d. Located away from family areas and kitchen for privacy.
   e. Should not have to go through one bedroom to enter another.
   f. Closet space should be adequate (minimum depth 2 feet; minimum area 6 square feet).
   g. Proximate to full bath facilities.

4. Kitchen.
   a. Workspace should be ample and efficient in plan.
   b. Equipment should be centrally located to eliminate unnecessary foot travel.

    c.   Walls, ceilings and floors should be of easily maintained materials.

    d.   Adequate provision should be made for proper lighting and ventilation.

    e.   Kitchen should be conveniently located in relation to dining areas and family room.

    f.   Kitchen should have an exterior entrance.

    g.   Laundry facilities should be adjacent to kitchen.

5.   Bathrooms.

    a.   Proper location with respect to other rooms.

    b.   If only one bathroom exists, it should be located off the central hall.

    c.   Bathroom should not open directly into kitchen or living room.

    d.   Adequate ventilation - exterior window or automatic exhaust fan is necessary.

    e.   Floors, walls, and ceilings easily cleaned and maintained.

6.   Closets and storage.

    a.   At least one clothes closet per bedroom.

    b.   Adequate linen closet space.

    c.   Storage closets should be centrally located.

    d.   A storage area should be provided near the laundry equipment.

    e.   Exterior storage necessary if there is only a carport.

B. **Site.**

1.   Construction should be related to the size of the building site.

2.   The house should be so located on the land that it relates to the building site or "belongs."

3.   Adequate front, rear and side yards are necessary for light and privacy. Yards may be clustered in planned unit developments.

4.   A private service yard for drying clothes and storage of refuse should be convenient to the kitchen.

5.   Entrance to the garage should be convenient and readily accessible.

6.   Proper landscaping.

7.   Recreational and garden facilities.

8.   Adequate yard improvements.

Broker's Guidelines for Considering Physical Characteristics of Real Property for FHA Insurance Purposes

A. **Visual appeal of property.** How well will the property as a whole retain its market appeal?

1.   Exterior design of structures.

    a.   Visual appeal based upon the probability of continuing market acceptance.

      b. Certain architectural styles are short-lived in their acceptance and become obsolete.

2. Setting.

      a. Measures the property's appeal in the market because of terrain, accessory buildings, walks, landscaping.

      b. The dwelling and surroundings should present a pleasing and unified composition.

3. Interior design of dwelling.

      a. The interior design should exhibit simplicity of treatment, harmony in proportions and refinement in design.

      b. Interior permanent features should be up-to-date and of adequate construction.

B. **Livability of property.** The degree of usefulness, convenience and comfort which the property affords is determined by:

1. Site utilization.

      a. Considers all aspects of the site and its arrangements as these affect the livability of the entire property.

      b. The lot characteristics including size, shape, topography, orientation and natural advantages are considered.

2. Dwelling space utilization. Consideration is given to the size and efficient distribution of space within the structure.

3. Room characteristics. Consideration is given to the size and proportion of the rooms in relationship to the overall area of the dwelling. The following factors are considered:

      a. Room orientation.

      b. Circulation.

      c. Privacy.

      d. Closet and storage space.

      e. Kitchen efficiency.

      f. Service facilities.

      g. Insulation.

C. **Natural light and ventilation.** The effect of natural light and natural ventilation on the desirability, livability and healthfulness is considered.

1. The proper amount or ratio of natural light to room area should be maintained.

2. Ventilation of all rooms is studied to measure its effect on desirability of the dwelling.

3. Cross ventilation desirable in all bedrooms.

D. **Structural quality.** The quality of structural design, materials, and workmanship is determined for the dwelling. The component elements to be considered are as follows:

1. Foundations.
2. Wall construction.
3. Partitions.
4. Floor construction.
5. Ceiling construction.
6. Roof construction.

E. **Resistance to elements and usage.** A determination is made as to the resistance of the dwelling to the effects of weather, decay, corrosion, fire, and deterioration. Consideration is given to three categories:

1. Lot improvements.
   a. How is the soil protected from erosion?
   b. Is the land properly graded so that the structure is not damaged by water?
   c. The yard improvements such as walks and walls should be of adequate materials.
2. The building exterior. Analysis is made with reference to the resistance of the exterior of the building to the effects of the elements.
3. Building interior. Consideration is given to the resistance of interior surfaces and materials to determine wear and tear and deterioration.

F. **Suitability of mechanical equipment.** Measures the extent that the equipment contributes to the desirability and appeal of the dwelling through convenience, economy, and comfort. Consideration is given to:

1. Plumbing system.
2. Heating system.
3. Electric system.
4. Supplementary equipment.

THE APPRAISAL PROCESS AND METHODS

Over time, well defined ground rules have been developed by professional appraisers to arrive at an estimate of value. This orderly, systematic procedure is known as the appraisal process. Not every step is used every time or necessarily in the same order. However, this comprehensive check list for the appraisal process should serve to give a better understanding of the importance of properly evaluating the various elements that influence market value and market price.

Overview of the Appraisal Process

As governed by Standard 1 of USPAP, the orderly steps and considerations of the appraisal process are designed to answer two questions:

What is highest and best use? and

What is this use worth?

To reach a legitimate conclusion:

A. Define the problem.

1. Identification of the property to be evaluated.

    a. Complete mailing address (including city and state).

    b   Complete legal description (by lot, block and tract number, including county where recorded; by metes and bounds descriptions; or by the government survey system).

2. Description of use of property to be appraised.

    a. Vacant lot.

    b. Single-family residential.

    c. Multi-family residential.

    d. Special purpose (commercial, etc.)

3. Interests to be appraised.

    a. Which of the bundle of rights are to be evaluated? Rights affect value because they set the limits within which the property may be used.

    b. An appraisal estimates the value of the rights of ownership, not merely the physical land and its improvements.

    c. The extent of the research and the valuation opinion will vary depending upon which of the following rights are involved:

        (1) Fee Simple (complete ownership).

        (2) Easement across property.

        (3) Lessor's or lessee's interest.

        (4) Mineral Rights.

        (5) Miscellaneous interests.

4. Purpose and intended use of the valuation determine the types of information to be gathered and processed, such as:

    a. Fair value for sale of a home.

    b. Value for mortgage loan purposes.

    c. Value for insurance purposes.

    d. Value for condemnation proceedings.

    e. Miscellaneous purposes and functions.

5. Date of value is generally the date of the last inspection of the property, although it may be any time in the past. Prospective values may be rendered, such as for proposed developments where "future sales" are projected and discounted to present value.

B. Make a preliminary survey of neighborhood, site and data required for appraisal.

    1. Make a preliminary estimate of the highest and best use of the subject property.

        a. Analysis of the site and improvements. Is it a proper improvement? Does the improvement meet the test? Take inventory of important site utilities and building construction features.

    b.   Analysis of the neighborhood. What are the boundaries and what services are available?

  2. The type of property determines the variety of specific data needed.

    a.   For a single-family home, emphasis will be placed on data concerning similar lots and improvements.

    b.   For a four-plex, emphasis will be placed on data concerning small multi-family units.

  3. A definite plan facilitates the gathering of necessary data as indicated from the preliminary survey.

C. Collect other general and specific data. The value of a property is affected by demand and by purchasing power available. Data should be obtained on population trends, income levels, and employment opportunities. A number of sources should be investigated.

  1. General data are obtained from government publications, newspapers and magazines.

  2. Regional data (metropolitan area) are obtained from monthly bank summaries, regional planning commissions, and government agencies.

  3. Community data (city) are obtained from the Chamber of Commerce, planning commission, city government, banks and savings and loan associations, and real estate boards.

  4. Neighborhood data, obtained from personal inspection, real estate practitioners and builders active in the area, include:

    a.   Age and appearance of the neighborhood.

    b.   Hazards and adverse influences.

    c.   Percentage build-out.

    d.   Contemplated development.

    e.   Proximity to schools, business, recreation, etc.

  5. Obtain comparable market data, such as sales and listing prices, from:

    a.   Assessor's records and county recorder's office.

    b.   Title insurance and trust companies.

    c.   Real estate boards and local real estate offices.

    d.   Property owners in the neighborhood.

    e.   Appraiser's/other appraisers' data bases.

  6. Collect and analyze data regarding the subject property's improvements from:

    a.   Assessor's office for age and other nonconfidential information.

    b.   City building department.

    c.   Contractors in area.

    d.   Personal inspection of improvements.

D. Analyze the data to conclude what is the highest and best use and the estimated worth of this use. As discussed later in this chapter, the following are the three approaches to value which will be used:

   1. Sales Comparison Approach, formerly known as the Market Data Approach. Study of value as indicated by the prices of recent sales and reliable listings of properties similar to the appraised property.

   2. Cost Approach. Study of value by adding the value of the land, if vacant, to the cost new, less accrued depreciation, of improvements

   3. Income Approach. Study of value of the property as an income stream as it would be sold in the open market.

E. Make final estimate of defined value and write the report. The form and extent of the report will depend upon the purpose, type of property, and request of the client.

The Departure Provision

The Departure Provision sets forth the portions of the USPAP Standards that can be left out or departed from in the appraisal process. Care must always be given in departing from the full appraisal process, since the analysis not undertaken may have a material impact on the final value conclusion. In addition to Standard 1 and the Departure Provision, there is Statement 7 and Advisory Opinions 11, 12, 13 and 15 which provide additional valuable guidance in developing a proper appraisal process. These can all be found in the current edition of USPAP.

METHODS OF APPRAISING PROPERTIES

There are three approaches to consider in making a market value estimate. These approaches are:

Sales comparison approach. Recent sales and listings of similar type properties in the area are analyzed to form an opinion of value.

Cost approach. This approach considers the value of the land, assumed vacant, added to the depreciated cost new of the improvements. This is considered a substitute or alternative to buying an existing house.

Income approach. The estimated potential net income of real property is capitalized into value by this approach.

Not only does each parcel of real estate differ in some respects from all other properties, but there are many different purposes for which an appraisal may be made. Each variation of purpose could result in a considerable, yet logical, variation of estimated value. For example the nature of the property, whether noninvestment, investment or service; the purpose of the purchase, whether for use, investment or speculation; and the purpose of the appraisal, such as for sale, loan, taxation, insurance and the like, all constitute matters which will influence the proper methods of appraisal approach and the final result reached by the appraisal.

Consequently, the first step in any appraisal procedure is to have a clear understanding of the purposes for making the appraisal and the value to be sought. The adequacy and reliability of available data also are determining factors in the selection of the approaches to be employed. A lack of certain pertinent or up-to-date information may well eliminate an otherwise possible approach. When this is the case, it is not considered a departure from USPAP, since the approach was considered but not workable.

In other instances, proper procedures may only call for an appropriate discounting of conclusions drawn from such data. Thus, based on its adaptability to the specific problem, one method is subsequently the focus of the analysis and the other approach methods may not be employed. This is considered a limited appraisal and a departure from USPAP Standard 1.

In most appraisals, all three approach methods will ordinarily have something to contribute. Each approach method is used independently to reach an estimated value. Then, as a final step, by applying to each separate value a weight proportionate to its merits in that particular instance, conclusions are reached as to one appropriate value. This procedure is known as reconciliation.

THE SALES COMPARISON APPROACH

This approach, formerly known as the market data comparison approach, is most generally adaptable for use by real estate brokers and salespersons. It lends itself well to the appraisal of land, residences and other types of improvements which exhibit a high degree of similarity, and for which a ready market exists. The principle of substitution is the basis of this approach. The buyer should not pay more for a property than the cost of acquiring a comparable substitute property. An analysis of market data is necessary in all three approaches to value.

The mechanics of the market comparison approach involve the use of sales and market data of all kinds in order to compare closely the property being appraised with other similar properties which have recently been sold or are offered for sale as to time of the sales, location of the sales and physical characteristics of the improvements. The sources used for determining value include actual sales prices, listings, offers, rents and leases, as well as an analysis of economic factors affecting marketability.

Sources of Data
Sales or market data are obtained from many sources including:

Appraiser's own files. Information gathered on previous assignments might provide information for the present appraisal.

Public records. The county assessor's office keeps a record of all sales transactions recorded within the county. This information is kept confidential for the assessor's own use, but an owner can obtain needed information about owner's property from the assessor's office. The date of recording of any deed may be obtained from the recorder's office. The exact legal description as well as legal seller and buyer can be obtained from an inspection of the deed (or facsimile). The documentary transfer tax applies on all transfers of real property located in the county. Notice of payment is entered on the face of the deed or on a separate paper filed with the deed. Tax is computed at the rate of 55 cents for each $500 of consideration or fraction thereof. If a portion of the total price paid for the property is exempt because a lien or encumbrance remains on the property, this fact must be stated on the deed or on a separate paper filed with the deed.

Multiple listing offices, fellow appraisers or brokers. Information on listings, offerings, and sales may frequently be obtained from real estate multiple listing facilities, real estate offices or by appraisers familiar with the area.

Legal property owner, sellers or buyers. When viewing comparable sales and other pertinent data in an area, additional information is solicited by interviewing property owners living in the neighborhood. The appraiser should try to confirm the sales price and circumstances of the sale with buyer, seller and/or broker. If informed of the appraiser's purpose, parties will usually verify and explain the sale.

Classified ads and listings. Ads are a source of information on properties currently being offered for sale. If possible, the appraiser's name should be on the mailing list of banks, savings and loan, and other institutions selling properties.

Listing prices may often indicate the probable top market value of a specific property while bid prices may normally indicate the lowest probable value. Both are subject to variation based on motivation, but a reasonable number of properties falling into this category will provide a bracket within which a current fair value may be found. Offers are likely to approach market value more closely than are listings. However, an offer to purchase is not usually a matter of common knowledge.

The Procedure

The procedure used in the sales comparison approach method is to systematically assemble data concerning comparable properties which are as "like-kind" to the subject as possible in regard to: neighborhood location; size (a comparable number of bedrooms and baths); age; architectural style; financing terms and general price range. The greater the number of good comparable data used, the better the result, provided a proper analysis is made. The approach is based on the assumption that property is worth what it will sell for in the absence of undue stress, and if reasonable time is given to find a buyer. For this reason, the appraiser should look behind sales and transfers to ascertain what influences may have affected sales prices, particularly if only a few comparisons are available.

Proper comparisons between like properties are ideally based on an actual inspection. Inspections should determine: the condition of improvements at time of sale, not as of date of inspection; room arrangement and room count so that the utility of the data may be compared to the subject property; yard improvements and their influence upon the sales price; the sales price (from buyer, seller or broker), to determine if the sale was an arm's length or open market transaction; size and topography of the lot. For nearly comparable properties, negative (downward) adjustments should be imposed for the subject's poor repair, freakish design, existing nuisances, etc. Conversely, positive adjustments should be made for the subject's superior design, view, special features, better condition, higher quality of materials, landscaping, and the like.

Unless the sales being compared are of recent date, consideration must also be given to adjusting values in keeping with the economic trend of the district and the worth of the dollar. Financing terms receive value adjustment considerations, e.g., for favorable existing assumable financing, or perhaps seller-assisted financing.

Units and elements of comparison. The common units of comparison used by appraisers in the sales comparison approach are property components that can readily be used for comparison purposes: square footage; number of rooms; and number of units. Elements of comparison are characteristics in either the property or the transaction itself that cause prices to vary. These principal elements of comparison are financing terms, time (the market conditions at the time of the sale), sale conditions (no pressures/arm's length), location, physical characteristics, and income (if any) from the property.

Using the appropriate units and elements of comparison for the subject and each comparable, the appraiser assigns an estimated adjusted amount (dollar or percentage) for each difference found in the items of comparison (number of bathrooms, view, square footage, financing, forced sale). An adjusted price is thus established for each comparable property that should realistically reflect what the subject would sell for in the current market. The less comparable properties are then eliminated from consideration and greatest weight is given to the comparable sales most similar to the property being appraised. Through this judgment or reconciliation process, the appraiser arrives at the final estimate of value for the subject property.

Advantages. Some advantages of using the sales comparison approach are:

1. It is the most easily understood method of valuation and in most common practice among real estate brokers and salespersons.

2. It is particularly applicable for appraisal purposes involving the sale of single family residences and loan arrangements therewith. These make up the great bulk of real estate transactions.

Disadvantages. Some disadvantages of the comparison approach method are:

1. Locating enough "nearly alike" properties which have recently sold or been listed.

2. Adjusting amenities to make them comparable to the subject property. The greater the amount of adjustment or number of adjustments, the less reliable the comparable becomes.

3. Older sales become less reliable in a changing market.

4. Occasional difficulty confirming transaction details.

5. Limitations in rapidly changing economic conditions and periods of high inflation and interest rates, when property appreciation rates may cause hazardous value conclusions.

Application of the Procedure - Residential Sales

Like properties are always compared. The more current the data the better. The suggested order for making unit and element comparisons is in this sequence:

1. finance terms

2. time (market conditions)

3. sale conditions

4. location

5. physical characteristics

6. other (e.g., special considerations for income property)

The steps.

1. Research the market for *bona fide* "like-kind" recent market data. Select data. Verify.

2. Select the appropriate units and elements of comparison. Adjust the sales price of each comparable (or eliminate it from consideration). The adjustment is always made to the comparable, not to the subject property.

3. Each comparable will have its own value indication. Eliminate the less comparable properties. Set out comparison results in chart or grid form. Using judgment and experience, reconcile or correlate the adjusted sales prices of the comparables and, by giving greatest weight to the sale that is most compatible to the subject property, assign an estimated value to the subject. Do not average the adjusted sales prices of the comparables. Reconciliation is a judgment process. It is not mechanical.

Example. Assume that the house to be appraised is a 2,400 square foot, 5-year old, single-family tract home located two blocks from the beach, with a fair view, stucco, 10 rooms, 4 bedrooms, 3 baths, 3 car garage. It is in good condition.

Prices have been increasing at 1% a month. The appraiser has selected from the neighborhood comparables which are equal in most of their financing and physical characteristics, except as shown on the rating chart. The value or sales price for the subject property is determined as shown on the chart below.

Adjust sales prices to indicate the appraised parcel value by subtracting the adjustment if the appraised parcel (subject) is inferior to the comparable and by adding the adjustment if the subject is superior to the comparable.

SALES COMPARISON DATA APPRAISAL RATING GRID – SINGLE-FAMILY RESIDENCE TRACT HOME

Elements/Units	Comparables			Subject
	Data 1	Data 2	Data 3	
Sales Price	$164,000	$176,000	$178,000	?
Adjustments				
Financing Terms	Normal	Normal	Normal	Normal
Conditions of Sale ...	Normal	Normal	Normal	Normal
Time (Sale Date).....	June, 1995	Nov., 1995	April, 1996	Aug., 1996
Adjustment 1%/mo	+$22,960	+$15,840	+$7,120	
Distance to Beach ...	1 Block	3 Blocks	4 Blocks	2 Blocks
Adjustment	*(inferior) -$6,000	*(superior) +$2,000	*(superior) +$4,000	
Garage.....................	Equal	Equal	Equal	Equal
Age..........................	Equal	Equal	Equal	Equal
Rooms	Equal	Equal	Equal	Equal
Bathrooms...............	Equal	Equal	Equal	Equal
View........................	None	Some	Fine	Fair
Adjustment	*(superior) +$4,000	*(superior) +$1,000	*(inferior) -$6,000	
Square footage	2,400	2,430	2,390	2,400
Adjustment	0	0	0	
Net Adjustments ...	$20,960	$18,840	$5,120	
Adjusted Sale Price .	$184,960	$194,840	$183,120	
Indicated Value				$185,000

* Inferior means the subject property is inferior to the comparable in this regard. Superior means the opposite. Subtract the adjustment if the subject property is inferior to the comparable property. Add the adjustment if the subject property is superior to the comparable property.

Reconciliation: Data 2 is close to the subject property in size, location, and view although not as good as the subject. Data 3 is the latest sale, but has the greatest difference in view and location. Data 1 is the oldest sale but is most useful for confirming the indication of value. Indicated value: $185,000.

COST APPROACH

The Cost Approach views value as the combination of:

the value of the land as if vacant; and

the cost to reconstruct the appraised building as new on the date of value, less the accrued depreciation the building suffers in comparison with a new building.

The principle of substitution applies: i.e., value tends to be set by the price of an equivalent substitute. In the Cost Approach, the substitute is the cost of reconstructing the present building on a vacant site.

The total cost of the land as if vacant, plus the reconstruction cost new of the building with all direct and indirect expenses and profit, and before deduction of depreciation, will tend to set the upper limit of value. In this view, the cost new can be used as a benchmark for measuring the other approaches.

The Procedure in Brief
1. Estimate the value of the land as though vacant and available for development to its highest and best use.
2. Estimate the replacement or reproduction cost of the existing improvements as of the appraisal date.
3. Estimate the amount of accrued depreciation to the improvements from all causes (physical deterioration and/or functional or external obsolescence).
4. Deduct the amount of the accrued depreciation from the replacement cost new to find the estimate of the depreciated value of the improvements.
5. Add the estimated present depreciated value for the improvements to the value of the land. The result is an indication of the value for the subject property.

Cost New Bases
The Cost Approach views the value of the building at its cost of reconstruction as new on date of value. There are three bases of reconstruction cost as new:

1. Historic Cost indexed to Cost New;

2. Reproduction Cost New; and

3. Replacement Cost New. Each basis has value to a cost-as-new study, but terms should not be confused.

Historic cost indexed to cost new. Historic Cost is the actual cost of the building when originally constructed, yesterday or fifty years ago. By use of price indices from building or engineering cost services, or from the original building contractor, Historic Cost can be "indexed" to Cost New on date of value. Indexed Historic Cost can be very useful if the building is fairly new and/or it is so unique that it is the only reliable value base. The advantage of Indexed Historic Cost is the accuracy of employing actual building costs. The disadvantage is that the older the costs are the less reliably they can be indexed. When considering Indexed Historic Costs, the appraiser should be certain that historic costs were normal costs at time of construction and that historic costs, as indexed, will accurately reflect Cost New on date of value.

Reproduction cost new is the cost, on date of value, of constructing a replica of the appraised building. This is a replica in actual design and materials. In this method, the cost-as-new estimate is made as if looking at plans of an exact duplicate of the present building. The advantage of Reproduction Cost New is the greater accuracy of duplicating the building in actual design and materials. The disadvantage is that advances in building construction and methods, materials and design make cost estimates of obsolete building construction very difficult and wildly distorted for materials no longer reasonably available or requiring large amounts of hand labor. Reproduction Cost New is most useful for study of refined methods of depreciation, unique construction, and occasional legal requirements for court testimony.

Replacement cost new views the building as if reconstructed with modern methods, design and materials that would most closely replace the use of the appraised building. For example, an older brick warehouse would be constructed today with concrete block or tilt-up cast slab construction. The advantage of Replacement Cost New is the ready availability of accurate current costs, and a better understanding by all parties of modern methods, design and materials. The disadvantage is the subjective decisions of proper current replacement materials and design for older construction. In actual practice, the Replacement Cost New is the most frequently used Cost Approach base.

Steps in the Cost Approach

A. An estimate is made as to the land's current market value, assumed vacant and available for improvement to its highest and best use. Land value is usually based on a market approach utilizing comparable market data of similar sites in the area.

B. An estimate is made of the cost new of reconstructing the buildings and other improvements.

  1. The appraiser selects the proper cost new base:

      a. *Historic Cost* of appraised building indexed to cost new on date of value.

      b. *Reproduction Cost* of duplicating the replica of the appraised building using original materials and design on date of value.

      c. *Replacement Cost* of replacing the use and facility of the appraised building using modern materials, methods, and design on date of value.

  2. The appraiser completes property inspection, description, measurement, inventory, and plot plan of appraised building improvements and equipment, with notes regarding type, style, quality, and condition of building materials, workmanship and condition.

  3. The appraiser selects appropriate method of cost new estimating.

      a. The **Square-Foot Method** is the most common method used by appraisers on the West Coast to estimate the cost of construction. The property being appraised is compared with similar structures where costs are known, and which have been reduced to units per square foot of floor area. Standard type buildings whose costs are known are broken down to a cost per square foot of floor area. The building being appraised is compared with the most comparable standard building and its cost per square foot is used for the subject property. Adjustments must be made for size of building, and various exterior and interior features. Though adjustments cannot be made for many variables, this method, in most instances, is accurate enough for the real estate appraiser. The square-foot method can be used and applied faster than any other estimate.

b.   The *Cubic-Foot Method* is similar to the square-foot method, except the cubic contents of buildings are compared instead of the square footage of the floor area. This method is most popular in the Eastern United States. If used properly, it is more accurate than the square foot method, since the height as well as area of the building is taken into consideration. This method is most often used for industrial or warehouse buildings.

c.   The *Quantity Survey Method* involves a detailed estimate of all labor and materials for each component of the building. Items such as overhead, insurance, and contractor's profit must be added to direct costs. This is a very accurate but time-consuming method to arrive at costs. Because of the detail and time required, this method is seldom used, except by building contractors and professional cost estimators.

d.   The *Unit-in-Place Cost Method* entails calculation of the cost of units of the building as installed. The total costs of walls in place, heating units, roof, etc. are obtained on a square foot basis, including labor, overhead, and profit. This is a detailed, accurate method generally used for checking on new construction units. It is seldom used by appraisers because specialized knowledge is necessary to gather all elements of unit costs.

4.   The appraiser investigates cost sources and estimates cost-as-new of all buildings and improvements. Costs must be measured accurately. They are classified as direct (hard) costs and indirect (soft) costs. Indirect costs are usually associated with the administration of the project while direct costs are expenditures for labor, equipment and materials, overhead and profit.

a.   Cost sources:

(1)   Costs of comparable buildings under construction.

(2)   Owners, builders, and/or contractors of comparable buildings.

(3)   The contractor of original building, if available.

(4)   Published cost services (usually handbooks providing current comprehensive cost data, by local areas and general construction types).

(5)   Professional cost estimators.

b.   The appraiser completes the cost estimate to include all:

(1)   Direct expenses of construction such as labor, materials and equipment and engineering for the building, site preparation, street and utility work, landscaping, etc.

(2) Indirect expenses such as legal, title, appraisal and feasibility study fees, licenses, permits, *ad valorem* taxes during construction, demolition and removal costs, inspections, insurance during construction, financing charges, accounting, etc.

(3) Developers' overhead, supervision, and profit; for planning, construction, and sale of the project to "turnkey" condition (that is, completely ready for a new purchaser/occupant) and selling costs.

C. The appraiser estimates the accrued depreciation and deducts from cost-as-new estimate. This amount must be deducted from the cost-as-new to determine the present value of the improvements. The difficulties of correctly estimating depreciation tend to increase with the age of the improvement. Experience and good judgment are among the necessary qualifications for making a realistic estimate of proper depreciation. There is no justification in assuming that improvements necessarily depreciate at a rate corresponding to their age.

D. The appraiser adds the land value to depreciated value of improvements for indicated value by Cost Approach.

DEPRECIATION

In connection with the appraisal of real property, depreciation is defined as "loss in value from any cause." It is customarily measured by estimating the difference between the current replacement or reproduction cost new and the estimated value of the property as of the date the property was appraised.

Contrasting with depreciation is *appreciation* of value from inflation or special supply and demand forces relating to the specific property. Appreciation may reduce or offset entirely a normally anticipated decrease of value due to depreciation.

Depreciation includes all of the influences that reduce the value of a property below its cost new. The principal influences are often grouped under three general headings and subdivided as follows:

1. Physical deterioration resulting from:
   a. Wear and tear from use;
   b. Negligent care (sometimes termed "deferred maintenance");
   c. Damage by dry rot, termites, etc.; or
   d. Severe changes in temperature.

2. Functional obsolescence resulting from:
   a. Poor architectural design and style;
   b. Lack of modern facilities;
   c. Out-of-date equipment;
   d. Changes in styles of construction;
   e. Construction methods and materials obsolete by current standards; or
   f. Changes in utility demand such as desire for master bath or more garage space.

3. External obsolescence resulting from adverse environmental and economic influences outside the property itself, such as:

   a. Misplacement of improvement (not typical for neighborhood);

   b. Zoning and/or legislative restrictions;

   c. Detrimental influence of supply and demand; or

   d. Change of locational demand.

The first two categories of accrued depreciation are considered to be inherent within the property and may be curable or incurable. The third category is caused by factors external to the property and is almost always incurable.

Appraisal and Income Tax Views - "Book" vs. Actual Depreciation

It is important to understand that "depreciation" is a word with two meanings: one for the appraiser and another for the owner concerned with tax position.

Book depreciation. Depreciation, for the owner's income tax position, is "book" depreciation, a mathematical calculation of steady depreciation from owner's original purchase price or cost basis. This "book" depreciation allows the owner to recover the cost of the investment over the "useful life" of the improvement. It accrues annually and is an income tax deduction. In this sense, the owner's accountant sees depreciation as a deduction from gross income.

Frequently, "book" depreciation results in negative gross income, at least on paper. The building seems to be losing value faster than the income replaces it. This gives the owner a "paper loss" that can be offset against other income. This "paper loss" or "tax shelter" is a motivating factor for purchase or exchange of many income properties.

"Book" depreciation is:

1. an allowable deduction from cost for accounting or income tax purposes;

2. determined by owner's policy and to meet IRS requirements; and

3. deducted from owner's original (historic) cost.

"Book value" is the current value for accounting purposes of an asset expressed as original cost plus capital additions minus accumulated depreciation, based on the method used for the computation of depreciation over the useful life of the asset for income tax purposes. Depreciation is allowed on improvements only, not land.

The book value of the property may be ascertained at any given time by adding the depreciated value of the improvement to the allocated value of the land.

Actual depreciation. The "book" depreciation from owner's original cost is not the depreciation normally considered by the appraiser. The appraiser looks not to owner's original cost, but cost new on date of value. From this current cost new, the appraiser deducts the estimate of accrued *actual* (not book) depreciation. Depreciation (loss in value) is estimated only for improvements.

Actual depreciation used by appraisers is:

1. loss in value;

2. determined by market data, observed condition, etc.; and

3. deducted from current reconstruction cost new.

Because accountants and appraisers select rates of depreciation for different purposes, accruals for book and actual depreciation vary considerably. While both estimators may use the same period as to the remaining economic life of the property and may also use the same method, additional considerations may affect the resultant rate. Whereas the accountant may be restricted because of accounting conventions, the appraiser is under no such restrictions.

The real estate agent who is determining values should understand the necessity for following proper appraisal procedures and should not rely on book values either to estimate accrued depreciation or for future depreciation accruals.

Methods of Calculating Accrued Depreciation

Accrued depreciation is depreciation which has already occurred up to the date of value. Remainder depreciation is depreciation which will occur in the future. Accrued depreciation may be classified either as curable or incurable. The measure between curable and incurable is economic feasibility. It is possible to physically restore or cure most depreciation such as by expensive restoration of old homes. However, in most circumstances, cure of deficiencies is measured by the economic gain (increased rents) compared with the cost of the cure. Three methods of estimating accrued depreciation are discussed next.

Straight line or age-life method is depreciation which occurs annually, proportional to the improvement's total estimated life.

For example, an improvement with an estimated total life of 50 years would be said to depreciate at an equal rate of 2 percent per year. (2 percent x 50 years equals 100 percent depreciation.)

The effective age of the building is generally used instead of the actual age. Effective age is the age of a similar and typical improvement of equal usefulness, condition and future life expectancy. For example, if a building is actually 25 years of age but is well maintained and would sell for as much as adjoining 20-year-old properties, it would be said to have an effective age of 20 years.

The straight line method is: easy to calculate; used by the Internal Revenue Service; and easily understood by the lay person.

However, in actuality, buildings do not depreciate in a straight line at a stated percentage each year, but will vary according to maintenance and demand for the type of structure.

The **cost-to-cure** or observed condition method (breakdown method) involves:

1. Observing deficiencies within and without the structure and calculating their costs to cure. The cost to cure is the amount of accrued depreciation which has taken place.

2. Computing an amount for physical deterioration or deferred maintenance for needed repairs and replacements.

3. Determining and assigning a dollar value to functional obsolescence due to outmoded plumbing fixtures, lighting fixtures, kitchen equipment, etc.

4. Measuring functional obsolescence which cannot economically be cured (e.g., poor room arrangements and outdated construction materials) and calculating the loss in rental value due to this condition.

5. Calculating external obsolescence (i.e., caused by conditions outside the property) and determining the loss of rental value of the property as compared with a similar property in an economically stable neighborhood. The capitalized rental loss is distributed between the land and the building.

This is the most refined method of examining complex causes and cures of depreciation. However, it can be difficult to calculate minor or obscure depreciation accurately. Also, measurement by rental loss is sometimes difficult to substantiate.

A **combination** of the straight line and cost-to-cure methods may be used to:

• determine the normal depreciation as if the property is not suffering from undue depreciation; and,

• add any excess deterioration and obsolescence.

For example: a house is 20 years old and has a remaining life estimated at 40 years for a total life of 60 years, thus depreciating at a rate of 1.67 percent a year. Effective age due to condition estimated at 15 years.

Cost New $105,000

1. Normal deterioration:

   1.67 percent x 15 years = 25 percent

   25 percent x $105,000 = ... $26,250

2. Excessive physical deterioration:

   New roof, exterior painting $5,000

3. Functional obsolescence, curable:

   Modernize bathroom $3,900

4. Functional obsolescence, incurable:

   Poor room arrangement results in rental loss of
   $40 per month when compared to normal house.

   Monthly gross multiplier 100.

   100 x $40 a month = ... $4,000

5. External obsolescence:

   Estimated monthly rent of subject if located
   in ideal neighborhood (after curing physical
   and functional deficiencies) $1,000

   Estimated rental loss due to external

   causes $50

   Yearly rental loss is 12 x $50 = $600

   Capitalization rate applicable to properties
   in ideal neighborhood (ratio of annual
   rent to value) = 10.5 percent

Capitalized rental loss:

$600 ÷ 10.5 percent = $5,700

Ratio of land to building value:
in ideal neighborhood, land 30 percent,
building 70 percent.

Economic obsolescence:

70 percent x $5,700 .... $3,990

TOTAL ESTIMATED DEPRECIATION $43,140

DEPRECIATED VALUE OF HOUSE $61,860

Reproduction or replacement cost method. The subject property is improved with a duplex, two detached garages, a covered porch for each unit and common driveway and walk.

Measurements and current cost replacement figures for the improvements are as follows:

Each unit of duplex is 25' x 35' @ $55.00 per sq. ft.

Each detached garage is 21' x 25' @ $20.00 per sq. ft.

Each covered porch is 6' x 10' @ $14.00 per sq. ft.

Driveway is 20' x 100' @ $2.40 per sq. ft.

Walk is 3' x 40' @ $2.40 per sq. ft.

The improvements are now 12 years old and it is determined that such improvements have a remaining economic life of 38 years. The current lot value, by comparison, is $45,000.00. Depreciation computations are based on the use of the straight line method.

What is the replacement cost new and, using the cost approach method, what is the present value of this property?

Each duplex unit (25' x 35' x $55.00) x 2 .... $96,250.00

Each detached garage (21' x 25' x $20.00) x 2 .... 21,000.00

Each covered porch (6' x 10' x $14.00) x 2 .... 1,680.00

Driveway (20' x 100' x $2.40) 4,800.00

Walk 3' x 40' x $2.40 .... 288.00

Improvements – Total Replacement Cost New......................... 124,018.00

Depreciation:

12 yrs. + 38 yrs. = 50 yrs. life of improvements when new

100 ÷ 50 = 2 percent annual depreciation rate, or recapture rate.

12 yrs. x 2 percent = 24 percent total depreciation to date.

124,018 x 24 percent = Total depreciation in value to date.......... 29,764.00

Total value of improvements less depreciation $94,254.00

Plus lot value. 45,000.00

Total Current Value by Replacement Cost Approach......... $139,254.00

Market data method. A comparative method is frequently used in residential appraisals where the property being appraised can be compared with market data of buildings of similar type and condition.

1. From the sales price of a comparable residential property, deduct an estimate of land value.

2. From the resulting total comparable improvement value, deduct the estimated contributory value of secondary improvements and landscaping.

3. The result is the value of the comparable main residence at its total depreciated value in place.

4. Divide this main residence value by the residence square footage. This yields depreciated unit value.

5. By multiplying the appraised building square footage by the unit value of the comparable residence, the total indicated depreciated value is found for the appraised residence.

Sales price of comparable property $180,000
Less estimated land value .... - 55,000
Improvement Value 125,000
Less estimated value of secondary improvements
    and landscaping .... - 23,000
Value of comparable residence 102,000
Divide by area of comparable residence .... ÷ 2,900 sq.ft.
Depreciated unit value of comparable residence .... $35.17/sq.ft.
Multiply by size of appraised residence .... x 2,850 sq.ft.
Indicated depreciated value in place of appraised
    residence $100,234

Advantage of the Market Data Method: This method is the most accurate measure of depreciation from the market.

Disadvantage of the method: It is sometimes difficult to obtain truly comparable market data and occasionally difficult to accurately estimate land value and secondary improvement value for deductions for main residence value indication.

Age-life method using effective age. House has an actual physical age of 25 years with a remaining life of 25 years, thus depreciating at the rate of 2 percent a year. It is the opinion of the appraiser that the subject house is of the same condition and utility as similar houses that are only 20 years of age. Therefore, the house has been assigned an effective age of 20 years.

The accrued depreciation would thus be 20 years times 2 percent or 40 percent.

Calculated cost new $120,000
Accrued depreciation (40 percent x $120,000) 48,000
Depreciated value of improvement. 72,000

Plus land value   50,000
Indicated value by cost approach $122,000

Measuring physical deterioration. A store building has a remaining useful life of 30 years and an effective age of 20 years. Present reproduction cost for the structure is $230,000. The roof is 75% deteriorated. A new roof will cost $10,000. The air conditioning and heating systems are 40% depreciated. Their installed cost new is $8,000. What is the total amount of physical deterioration?

The building, under the straight-line or age-life method, is 40% depreciated (100% ÷ 50 = 2% x 20 years effective age = 40%). This 40% depreciation to the building is to be applied to the amount of the building's reproduction cost less the depreciation already taken on the other components.

Depreciation to roof (.75 x $10,000) $7,500
Depreciation to air conditioning and heater (.40 x $8,000) $3200
Depreciation to rest of building (.40 x $212,000) $84,800
Total physical deterioration $95,500

Income approach - future depreciation. Future depreciation is loss in value which has not yet occurred but will come in the future and is of significance in the capitalization of income method, which will be discussed next. In the income approach to valuation, depreciation is based on the remaining economic or useful life, during which time provision is made for the recapture of the value of improvements. It is the return "of" the investment, as differentiated from the return (interest and profits) "on" the invested capital. Under the income approach, this depreciation is usually measured by one of two methods: straight-line or sinking fund.

In straight-line depreciation, a definite sum is deducted from the income each year during the total estimated economic life of a building to replace the capital investment. If the appraiser estimates that a building will have a remaining life of 25 years, this method provides that 1/25 or 4 percent of the building's value be returned annually as a deduction from net income.

The sinking fund method also includes a fixed annual depreciation deduction from income, but with yearly reserves from such funds deposited into a sinking fund which, with compound interest, will offset the depreciated value of the structure and be collectible at the end of the building's useful life. Accruals for future depreciation to replace the capital investment are in addition to and essentially different from both maintenance charges and reserves for periodic replacement of curable depreciation.

Should there be any estimated salvage value to the improvement at the end of its economic life, this amount need not be returned through the annual depreciation charge under either the straight-line or the sinking-fund method.

INCOME (CAPITALIZATION) APPROACH

The income approach is concerned with the present worth of future benefits (the income stream) which may be derived from a property. This method is important in the valuation of income-producing property, although it can rarely be relied on as the only approach. An important consideration in this approach is the *net* income which a fully informed person using good management can expect to receive during the remaining useful life of the improvement. An alternative, using *gross* income and the Gross Rent Multiplier (GRM) is explained later in this chapter.

The process of calculating the present worth of a property on the basis of its capacity to continue to produce an income stream is called *capitalization*. The capitalization approach is based primarily on the appraisal concepts of comparison, substitution and anticipation.

Appraiser's and Owner's Viewpoints
A real estate professional will understand that there are several differences in the owner's and appraiser's viewpoints on income property.

An owner purchases income property as an investment, based on personal desires and tax position. The owner frequently views the investment as equity in a financed property. "Equity" is the owner's down payment or the difference between the loan amount and the value or price of the property. The owner calculates the payments on the loan as an expense of owning the property, and deducts from income tax the interest paid on the loan and the "book" depreciation from the purchase price or cost basis. The owner can deduct only actual expenses, not reserves for future expenses, and can compute gross income only from income actually collected (or owed), not just projected. The owner looks for a profitable resale or exchange at a higher price or favorable tax position. In most cases, the appraiser will ignore these personal considerations.

The appraiser reconstructs expense and income into amounts the well-informed investor would anticipate, without specific regard for personal equity, spendable income, or tax consequences. Using methods outlined below, an appraiser analyzes an income property to ascertain its value to the market *generally,* i.e., the Fair Market Value.

Capitalization
Capitalization is the mathematical process of estimating the present value of income property based on the amount of anticipated annual net income it will produce. Capitalization converts the future income stream into an indication of present worth of property. There are several methods of capitalizing net income. Our discussion will deal with the *direct* method.

There are four types of capitalization (cap) rates used in the appraisal process:

- The *interest rate* is the rate of return *on* invested capital. It is the same as the yield rate or risk rate. It does not include any provision for the return *of* investment capital.

- The *recapture rate* is the rate at which invested funds are being returned to the owner.

- The *capitalization rate* is derived from the interest rate and the recapture rate.

- The *overall rate* is derived from the relationship between net income and value for the total property and theoretically provides in one rate for both return on, and recapture of, the capital investment. The overall cap rate is an income rate.

Any interest in income producing property can be valued using this rate but appraisers apply it most commonly to fee simple estates.

Capitalization rates may be estimated by several methods:

market or sales data;

band of investment (uses a weighted average rate by combining a rate for mortgage loan money and a rate for investor's equity); or

summation (has very limited use - involves building up a "safe" interest rate based on various risk/investment factors).

Of course, the market or sales data method involves an appraiser's systematic comparison of recent sales of similar properties. The appraiser analyzes each comparison property's sales price, rents, expenses, net income and cap rate, makes needed adjustments and selects an appropriate indicated overall cap rate for the property being appraised. This rate represents both the return *on* and the return *of* the investment. To ensure reliability of the selected rate, the appraiser uses judgment and experience to make certain the comparables and the subject property have similar age, physical, location, income, expense and risk characteristics.

Capitalization rate formula. The capitalization rate is a combination of the interest rate (return on the investment) and the recapture rate (return on the investment in improvements). If only the land produces income, the cap rate and interest rate are the same. However, when improvements contribute to the income production, a provision must be made for recapture of the value of the improvements before the end of their economic life. Land has no limited economic life; it will never wear out and thus will always be able to produce income. The building is a wasting asset and cannot be used indefinitely.

The most common method of providing for recapture of the investment in the improvements is the "straight line" method, with the building value recaptured in equal annual installments. The recapture rate is computed by dividing the remaining economic life of the improvements into 100%. Thus, the annual recapture rate for a building with an estimated remaining economic life of 40 years is 2.5% (100% ÷ 40). If the remaining economic life is 25 years, the recapture rate is 4%.

To find the indicated value of income property, divide the net annual income by the capitalization rate:

$$\text{Net Annual Income} \div \text{Capitalization Rate} = \text{Property Value}$$

or

$$I \div R = V$$

If any two factors in this formula are known, the third can be obtained.

$$I = R \times V$$

and

$$R = I \div V$$

INCOME APPROACH PROCESS

The main steps to calculate value by capitalizing income are:

Determine the net annual income;

Select the appropriate cap rate by market comparisons; and

Capitalize the income (divide the net annual income by the cap rate).

Determining Net Annual Income

The procedures for determining net annual income are:

Estimate potential gross income the property is capable of producing.

Deduct from potential gross income an annual allowance for vacancy factor and rent collection loss. The remainder is called "effective" gross income or adjusted gross income.

Deduct from adjusted gross income the estimated probable future annual expenses of operation (fixed expenses, variable expenses, reserves for replacements for building components or short-lived items) to obtain the net income of the investment property.

Income and expenses. The potential gross income used is the expected future income. In many cases, the immediate past or current income may be an indicator of future income. However, reliance solely upon past or current income is incorrect. The income to use is the one which the purchaser and seller anticipate over the remaining productive life of the improvement, as adjusted for foreseeable economic changes.

Income estimates. The gross income estimate for an income property is the potential or anticipated gross income from all sources (market rents, services, parking space fees and rentals, and coin-operated equipment, etc.). Gross income is estimated as of the date of the appraisal. Contract rent is the actual, or contracted, rent received from the property. Market rent is the rent the property should bring in the open market at the date of appraisal. Rents and vacancy factors and collection losses are based on current market rent data. The appraiser uses his/her judgment of the area in arriving at an allowance for vacancy and collection losses.

Rent data is obtained from the subject property's rent schedule and the appraiser's review of rents from similar recent sales in the area. Individual apartments or units of the comparables are compared with the subject property, using square footage, number of bedrooms, or similar items of comparison. It is assumed management for all properties is adequate. Cost of deferred maintenance or repairs is an adjustment item.

Market rent schedules and expenses are usually maintained on a monthly basis. Both must be converted to an annual basis.

Expenses must be realistic. The operating expenses (all expenditures necessary to produce income) are to be deducted from the effective gross income to find the net operating income expected from the property. The appraiser must use caution in extracting expense information from owner's operating statement as some items included on the operating statement, such as principal and interest payments on mortgages and depreciation allowance for income tax purposes, must be disregarded by the appraiser as not being allowable expense items.

These non-allowables may include entertainment expenses and other items of personal expense, and capital improvement expenditures. Since most operating statements are prepared by accountants for tax and accounting purposes, appraisers usually must reconstruct them to properly forecast annual expenses.

Expenses are generally classified as being one of the following:

Fixed expenses. These are incurred annually with relatively little change from year to year. They are to be paid whether the property is fully occupied or not. These items include taxes, insurance, licenses and permits.

Variable expenses. These expenses are incurred continually in order to maintain and give service to the property. They are variable depending upon the extent of occupancy and include items such as utilities, management fees, security, costs of administration, maintenance and repairs for structures, grounds and parking area maintenance, contracted services (e.g., rubbish removal) and payroll.

Reserves for replacements. This is an annual allowance for replacing worn out equipment and building components, such as stoves, carpets, draperies, roof covering.

Selecting the Cap Rate

The appraiser selects an appropriate overall capitalization rate ("present worth" factor) after market analysis of similar properties. This rate provides for return of invested capital plus a return on the investment).

The rate is dependent upon the return which investors will actually demand before they will be attracted by such an investment. The greater the risk of losing the investment, the higher will be the accompanying rate as determined in the market for such properties. By analyzing market prices, the rate can be approximated at any given time.

A variation of only 1 percent may make a substantial difference in the capitalized value of the income.

For example, based on an annual net income of $30,000, and a capitalization rate of 6 percent, the capitalized property valuation would be $500,000 (income ÷ rate). Capitalizing this same income at a rate of 7 percent would result in a value of only $428,500 (rounded).

Capitalizing Net Annual Operating Income

The final step after having determined the net annual income and the capitalization rate is to capitalize the income. This may be merely the mathematical calculation of dividing the income by the rate if the income is considered to be in perpetuity.

For example, the valuation of property which has an assumed perpetual annual net income of $30,000 and a capitalization rate of 5 percent is $600,000. The lower the rate, the greater the valuation, and the greater the assumed security of the investment. So-called annuity tables are used in capitalizing incomes for fixed periods of varying duration.

As stated earlier, an important element in all capitalization rates is provision for a return of the investment on the improvements to the property during their remaining economic life. This may be called an amortization of such investments. It may be provided for by straight-line depreciation, which recovers a definite sum every year for the period of years estimated to be the economic life of the improvement, at the end of which time the cost of improvement will be accrued. It may also be provided for by other methods, such as establishing "sinking funds" or a declining balance depreciation. These are more technical procedures which are used by professional appraisers.

INCOME APPROACH APPLIED

Using procedures just discussed, here are two examples for finding estimated value using the income approach.

1. How much should an investor pay for a 10 unit apartment house, 24 years old, estimated fair market rent per unit being $500 per month. Indicated vacancy factor is 7%. Acceptable cap rate is 8 percent. Fixed expenses are: taxes of $3,200 and insurance of $860. Operating expenses are: management - $3,960; utilities - $1200; waste removal - $600; reserves for replacement - $1,700.

Gross Scheduled Income (Annual)			$60,000
(10 x $500 x 12 = $60,000)			
Less Income Loss Due to Vacancy Factor			4,200
(.07 x $60,000 = $4,200)			
Effective Gross Income			55,800
Less Expenses			
Fixed			
Taxes	$3,200		
Insurance	860		
Total		$4,060	
Operating			
Management	3,960		
Utilities	1,200		
Waste Removal	600		
Total		5,760	
Reserves for Replacement			
Roof	800		
Painting	500		
Carpeting	400		
Total		1,700	
SUBTRACT TOTAL OF EXPENSES			-11,520
NET OPERATING INCOME (NOI)			$44,280

Capitalization Rate Furnished By Owner is 8%.

Using formula $I \div R = V$

$44,280 \div .08 = $553,500

Indicated Value (rounded)	$555,000

2. A small commercial building has rental income of $27,650 annually and
    suffers vacancy/collection losses of 5%. Expenses include: taxes–$3,780;
    utilities–$850; roof reserve–$1,500; insurance–$1,100; maintenance–$2,000;
    repainting and fixture reserve–$500; and management–$2,000. The appraiser
    finds similar properties have cap rates ranging from 8.75% to 9.37%. Based on
    this market data the appraiser selects an indicated overall capitalization rate
    for the subject property of 9%. Using the Income Approach, what is the
    indicated value of the property?

Gross scheduled Income (Annual)		$27,650
Less Vacancy and Collection Loss (5%)		1,383
Effective Gross Income		26,267
Less Expenses		
Fixed		
Taxes	$3,780	
Insurance	1,100	
Operating		
Maintenance	2,000	
Utilities	850	
Management	2,000	
Reserve for Replacements		
(Roof, Repainting and Fixtures)	2,000	
Subtract Total Expenses		-11,730
Net Operating Income (NOI)		14,537
Indicated Overall Capitalization Rate 9%		
$14,537 ÷ .09 = $161,522		
Indicated Total Value by Income Approach		$161,522
Round Value to		$161,500

RESIDUAL TECHNIQUES

Suppose vacant land returns net income of $6000 a year and the applicable interest
rate for this type of real property is 7 percent. Using the income method, the
property has a value of $85,715 ($6,000 ÷ .07).

However, income from improved property is the result of the contribution of both
land and buildings. The buildings have limited economic life and their value must
be recaptured over their remaining economic life. Income attributable to land is
deemed perpetual.

There are three methods to capitalize income from improved property. They are
each a "residual technique" because capitalization is applied to the residual
(leftover or unknown) net income attributable to the property as a whole, to the
building, or to the land. The appropriate technique would be selected based on
market data. The same net income figure applies in all three methods.

Property Residual Technique
This is the simplest method of capitalizing the net income from improved property
because the property is valued as a single unit (used when the value of neither land

nor improvements can be estimated independently). The property's total net income is capitalized directly at an overall rate developed from the market data, comparing similar income producing properties which are also similar in the way net income is estimated.

Example. The net income generated from real property is $32,000 annually and the overall cap rate selected from the market data approach is 9%. What is the value of the property?

Income ÷ Rate = Value

$32,000 ÷ .09 = Value

Value = $355,556

Building Residual Technique

If the value of the land is known and the value of the building is unknown, the property's value may be determined by the building residual technique. This technique allocates the net income of the property to both land and building. The procedure is:

1. Multiply the known land value by the applicable interest (i.e., return) rate on the land to determine the income attributable to land only.

2. Deduct income to the land from total net income to determine the balance ("residue") of the net income which represents the portion of the income attributable to/earned by the building

3. Capitalize the building's income at the overall cap rate (interest rate plus recapture rate) to derive the value of the building.

4. Add the capitalized value of the building to the land value to arrive at the value of the whole property.

Example. An appraiser estimates that a 60 unit apartment building has an estimated remaining economic life of 25 years. The annual net income of the property is forecast at $216,000. On the basis of several comparables, an appraiser estimates that the land value is $60,000 and the applicable rate of interest for this type of investment property is 8%. What is the indicated value of the property by the income approach?

Annual net income of property		$216,000
Less interest on $60,000 land value at 8%		4,800
Net income attributable to building		$211,200
Interest rate	8%	
Recapture rate	4%	
Cap rate	12%	
Indicated building value ($211,200 ÷ .12)		$1,760,000
Land value (by comparison)		60,000
Indicated property value		$1,820,000

Land Residual Technique

If the building value is known and the land value is unknown and cannot be determined separately, the value of the property as a whole may be estimated by using the land residual technique. The land residual technique is similar to the building residual technique except that the appraiser must first find the income attributable to the improvements and the residue (balance) of the income is then attributable to the land. The procedure is:

1. Multiply the known improvement value by the applicable building capitalization rate (interest rate plus recapture rate) to determine the income attributable to the building only.

2. Deduct income to the building from the total net income to determine the residue (balance) of the net income attributable to/earned by the land.

3. Capitalize the land's income at the interest rate only (since it is not necessary to recapture the permanent land value) to derive the value of the land.

4. Add the capitalized value of the land to the building value to arrive at the value of the whole property by the land residual technique.

Example. Same facts as the building residual technique example above.

Annual net income of property	$216,000
Less income attributable to building ($1,760,000 x .12)	211,200
Net income attributable to land	4,800
Indicated land value ($4,800 ÷ .08)	60,000
Building value	1,760,000
Property value indicated by land residual technique	$1,820,000

Finding the Overall Cap Rate - Example

A property sells for $250,000. Building value is $190,000. Remaining economic life is 25 years. Annual net income from building is $28,000. What is the interest rate for the building? What is the overall cap rate?

Recapture rate is 4% (100% ÷ 25).

Building's net income	$28,000
Recapture of building (.04 x $190,000)	$7,600
Net income after recapture	$20,400

Interest rate = $20,400 ÷ $190,000 = .1074 or 10.74%

The overall cap rate is the sum of the interest rate and recapture rate:

Interest Rate = 10.74%
Recapture Rate = 4%
Therefore, the Overall Cap Rate = 14.74%

YIELD CAPITALIZATION ANALYSIS

Now preferred over the residual techniques discussed above, yield capitalization analysis is a method of converting economic benefits of ownership into present value by discounting each anticipated benefit at an appropriate yield rate, or by developing an overall capitalization rate that explicitly reflects the required yield rate and anticipated changes in income and/or value, if any. The *yield rate* is a rate of return on capital. This method simulates typical investor assumptions by using formulas that calculate the present value of future economic benefits based on specified rate of return requirements.

The future economic benefits that are typically considered in this analysis are periodic cash flows and reversion. The procedure used to convert these future economic benefits into present value is called *discounting,* and the required rate of return (or yield rate) is referred to as the *discount rate.* The discounting procedure is based on the assumption that the investor will receive an adequate rate of return *on* the investment, plus return *of* the capital invested. Unlike direct capitalization using market-extracted rates, the method and timing of the returns on and of capital are explicit in yield capitalization analysis. This valuation method can be used to value the fee simple interest in a property, or any property interest for which all future economic benefits can be estimated.

The most common form of yield capitalization analysis is called *discounted cash flow analysis.* In this valuation technique, each anticipated future economic benefit of ownership of the property or property interest being valued must be estimated. Next, each benefit is discounted to present value using a discount rate that reflects the risk associated with the characteristics of the investment. This rate cannot be extracted directly from sales (as can an overall capitalization rate), but must be based on market attitudes and expectations for rates of return for similar assets. Yield rates inherently include a safe, risk-free rate, along with premiums to compensate the investor for the added risk, illiquidity, and burden of management associated with the specific investment. The safe rate included in the yield rate includes an inflationary expectation for the anticipated term of the investment. The discounting process can be performed using formulas and factors obtained from financial tables, or by using financial calculators or personal computers.

The following discounted cash flow analysis example summarizes the application of yield capitalization analysis to a simple real estate problem. The property to be appraised is expected to produce a first-year net operating income of $100,000, which is expected to increase at 3 percent per year over a seven-year holding period. At the end of the holding period, it is anticipated that the property can be sold for $1,000,000 net of sales expenses. The appropriate yield rate for this investment is concluded to be 13 percent. The following table shows the anticipated cash flows, along with the present value factors and the calculated present value of each year's cash flow.

Discounted Cash Flow Analysis

	Year 1	Year 2	Year 3	Year 4	Year 5	Year 6	Year 7
Net oper income	$100,000	$103,000	$106.090	$109,273	$112,551	$115,927	$119,405
Reversion							$1,000,000
Total inc	$100,000	$103,000	$106,090	$109,273	$112,551	$115,927	$1,119,405
Present val factor	x 0.8850	x 0.7831	x 0.6931	x 0.6133	x 0.5428	x 0.4803	x 0.4521
Present value	$88,500	$80,659	$73,531	$67,017	$61,093	$55,680	$475,859

TOTAL PRESENT VALUE: $902,339; rounded to $900,000.

(The present value factors in this analysis were calculated using a financial calculator, but could have been obtained from a set of financial tables.)

GROSS RENT MULTIPLIER

Value is the present worth of all rights to future benefits. The rights being obtained through the payment of rents are the use of the physical structure as well as the intangibles (amenities or satisfactions). Income properties such as large apartments and commercial stores are purchased for the income stream they produce, whereas single-family homes are purchased for shelter plus the satisfaction (amenities of home ownership).

Standard capitalization techniques used for income producing properties do not measure intangibles such as pride of ownership and other amenities found in home ownership.

This indirect method of capitalization, the gross rental multiplier, will measure the market value of the combination of intangibles and tangibles found in single family and small income properties.

The gross rent multiplier is found by dividing the sales price of a house or other small income property by its monthly rent. For example: a $90,000 sales price divided by a monthly rent of $600 results in a gross rent multiplier of 150. If homes in the area were selling at prices equivalent to 150 times the monthly rental, then the 150 multiplier would apply to other comparable homes in the area.

Method of Approach In Using the Gross Rent Multiplier

1. Determine the fair or economic rent of the property being appraised by comparison with similar rental properties.
2. The gross rent multipliers of the sales one investigates are calculated by dividing the sales prices by the monthly rents.
3. The rent multipliers may then be tabulated showing how these properties varied from the subject property: i.e., better or poorer.
4. The gross rent multipliers are *not* averaged to arrive at one final multiplier. Rather,
    a. each property and its multiplier is compared to the subject property as to fair rent obtainable, location, size, condition, utility, and amenities; and
    b. after proper analysis, a judgment is made as to the appropriate gross rent multiplier.
5. The appraiser multiplies the selected gross rent multiplier by the fair rental of the subject property. The product is the value estimate.
6. Discounted Cash Flow Analysis (DCF) is a technique of income analysis which has grown to be a prominent method in recent years. It is defined as: "The procedure in which a discount rate is applied to a set of projected income streams and a reversion. The analyst specifies the quantity, variability, timing, and duration of the income streams as well as the quantity and timing of the reversion and discounts each to its present value at a specified yield rate. DCF analysis can be applied with any yield capitalization technique and may be performed on either a lease-by-lease or aggregate basis." (*Dictionary of Real Estate Appraisal*, 3rd edition, by the Appraisal Institute) For further study of

this method, the reader is advised to seek additional education, as this is a rather technical process subject to misuse and abuse if not properly taught.

SUMMARY

It may be said that all three appraisal approaches to value (Cost, Sales Comparison, and Income Capitalization) should be considered and used when appropriate to the property type. The results are reconciled into one final estimate of value. As independent approaches, the sales comparison method is the most widely used. Investment property is frequently appraised by the income capitalization method, while the replacement cost method best lends itself to special purpose properties or newer properties.

The purpose of the appraisal will have a definite bearing in determining the method of valuation. For example, if the purpose is sale, purchase, exchange or condemnation, the value concept sought is current market value.

Reconciliation of the three indications of value derived through the market data, cost and income approaches leads to the final estimate of value or final value conclusion, which is the final step in the appraisal process. Reconciliation is a method of interpreting the data which have been gathered throughout the entire appraisal process into one final value conclusion. The primary facts which are analyzed and brought together are the estimates of value arrived at by reason of the three approaches to value.

Each approach to value results in only a preliminary estimate or an indicated value of the property. The indications resulting from each of the approaches give a range within which the final value conclusion lies. The result obtained by each of the methods of valuation will not be the same due to the many variables which are encountered, but they generally are within range of each other.

A thorough review of each of the approaches is made in order to narrow the range of preliminary answers. If the results from one particular approach appear to be at a great divergence from the other two, each phase of this approach should be reconsidered to account for the difference.

Greater weight, however, is generally given to one of the approaches over the other two, based on the quality of data in each.

The final conclusion of value is not an average of the three approaches to value. After giving full consideration to each approach, the appraiser uses judgment and reasoning to arrive at one conclusion. The greatest confidence is placed in the approach which seems to produce the most reliable solution to the specific appraisal problem, realizing that it must be reasonable and capable of being supported convincingly.

The final value conclusion should not be reported in odd dollars and cents. If the final answer approximates $1,000, the answer could be rounded to the nearest $100; if $10,000, to the nearest $500; if $50,000, to the nearest $1,000 or more.

APPRAISAL OF MANUFACTURED HOMES (MOBILEHOMES)

The appraisal of mobilehomes attached to foundations on individual lots relies on the approaches outlined for other residential properties. The appraiser needs a technical understanding of mobilehome construction for differences in cost studies. The market data approach works best in this appraisal effort.

Mobilehome coaches in parks are on rental spaces or fee-owned spaces in a mobilehome park subdivision. Again, the general principles of real property appraisal apply, except the appraiser needs the technical background in coach construction to best evaluate quality and features.

In many respects, the appraisal of a mobilehome on a fee-owned space is similar to residential condominium appraisal. This includes consideration of homeowners association services and fees as well as CC&Rs covering operation of the park and space improvement requirements.

Mobilehome appraisal is becoming another specialized opportunity in the appraisal profession. This is particularly true in the expanded market for mobilehomes as low and moderate income housing.

EVALUATING THE SINGLE FAMILY RESIDENCE AND SMALL MULTI-FAMILY DWELLINGS

This section outlines basic premises which must be considered in making an appraisal of a single family residence and emphasizes some important factors to be weighed. It points out the differences that will be encountered between appraising new and used homes, and shows appraisal differences between a small multi-family dwelling and a single family home.

New Residence

Neighborhood analysis.
A. Factors which make up the neighborhood must be determined and analyzed.
    1. Type of occupants.
        a. Income level.
        b. Representative age groups and family sizes.

    2. Type of improvement.
        a. Is there a mixture of uses (e.g., single family, apartments, etc.)?
        b. What is the age bracket of the improvements?
        c. What is the price range of typical houses in the area?

    3. Neighborhood trend.
        a. Are there detrimental factors present which might tend to depress the market?
        b. Is the trend away from single family houses to multi-family, commercial or industrial uses?
        c. Is the neighborhood in a transitional stage from owner occupied homes to tenant occupancy?
        d. Are there advantageous factors which indicate an increasing market demand or price level?

    4. Changes in land use.
        a. Zoning and restrictions.
        b. Street and highway pattern.
        c. Transportation.

      d.   Any encroachments?

      e.   Is utility increased? Decreased?

5.   Community services.
      a.   Commercial.
      b.   Recreational.
      c.   Educational.
      d.   Cultural.
      e.   Governmental.

Inspection of property.

A.   Relationship of the improvements to site.
    1.   The house, including outbuildings, should have a harmonious appearance on the site.
      a.   Is the house too large for the site?
      b.   Is the house properly oriented on the lot to take advantage of climatic conditions?
      c.   Overbuilt? Underbuilt?

B.   Exterior of house.
    1.   Determine the quality of construction. Inspect:
      a.   Foundation.
      b.   Walls.
      c.   Roof.

    2.   Determine the resistance to wear and tear and the action of the elements.
      a.   Are there adequate gutters and drainspouts to take the water away from buildings?
      b.   Are there satisfactory roof overhangs to protect the windows and walls?

    3.   Measure the exterior dimensions of the buildings in order to obtain their areas.

    4.   Examine and describe yard improvements for purposes of estimating their value.

C.   Interior of house.
    1.   Determine the quality of the building.
      a.   Durability of building.
      b.   Arrangement of floor plan and layout of space.
      c.   Attractiveness of design.
      d.   Grade and quality of materials used.
      e.   Adequacy of heating, cooking, electrical, and plumbing equipment.

    2.   Measure or take note of room sizes and placement of windows for adequate light and ventilation.

    3.   Determine if the traffic pattern is functionally proper.

    4.   Does the home have all the modern conveniences necessary for a new house in its price class?

Verification through public records.

A. Public records should be checked to verify the following about the property being appraised:
    1. Proper legal description.
    2. Correct street address.
    3. Size/dimensions of the lot.
    4. Location of the lot with respect to the nearest cross street.
    5. Any easements, restrictions or other reservations or interests affecting the property.
    6. The assessed value and taxes of the property.
    7. Any changes in zoning or street pattern.

B. Transfer of title of similar properties.
    1. Sales of single family vacant lots should be obtained and verified.
    2. Sales of improved single family residences within the same neighborhood should be recorded.

Inspection of comparable sales.

A. Vacant lots or improved similar properties should be inspected.

B. Similar or dissimilar features as compared to the subject property are recorded and the selling price, terms and reasons for sale or purchase must be verified by the seller or buyer.

Application of approaches to value.

A. Cost approach to value.
    1. From the information gathered in the inspection and the size, quality and cost classification, an estimate of cost is made of all improvements on the land.
    2. The land value is estimated from information gathered in the record search of vacant parcels.
    3. In the majority of instances, if the improvements are new and the highest and best use of the land, the estimate of value by means of the cost approach is equal to land value plus the new improvement costs.

B. Sales Comparison or market approach to value.
    1. The sales of similar type houses are compared to the subject as to time, location and physical characteristics.
    2. Necessary adjustment must be made between the sales and the subject.
    3. A preliminary estimate of value by means of the comparative approach is obtained.

C. Income approach to value.
    1. The economic rent of the subject is estimated by means of experience and comparison.
    2. Gross monthly multipliers of similar type properties are gathered and analyzed in order to arrive at one multiplier to apply to the subject.
    3. DCF may be applied for such properties as new condominium projects, subdivisions or any property with a variable type income over the holding period of the investment.
    4. A preliminary estimate of value by means of the income approach is obtained.

D. Reconciliation of the approaches.
1. Each approach is weighed and compared.
2. With a new property it will generally be found that the cost approach will carry the greatest weight in the correlation.
3. If the new subject property were located within a tract of similar type houses, market comparison would be given the most weight in the reconciliation.
4. After weighing all of the factors involved, one final value reconciliation for the property is set forth.

Older Residence

Neighborhood analysis. In addition to the points covered under new residence, the following should be carefully considered when dealing with an older property in a built-up neighborhood:
A. Neighborhood trend.
1. A check should be made to determine if proposed zoning changes are being considered by the local government.
2. Contemplated changes might indicate that the best use of the subject is no longer thought to be for single family housing.

B. Inspection of property. In addition to the items covered under the new residence, consideration should be given to the following:
1. A more careful inspection is made of the premises.
   a. Note effects of dry rot and termites.
   b. Look for deferred maintenance.
   c. Inspect roof and attic for signs of water leaks.
   d. Check foundation for settling.
2. Room arrangement and functional utility.
   a. An older home is more likely to have an out-of-date floor plan.
   b. The livability or utility is often obsolete as compared to a newly designed structure.
3. Wiring and plumbing.
   a. Is the home underwired for today's electrical appliances? Particular attention should be given to the kitchen.
   b. Are the plumbing lines being affected by encrustation? Will they have to be replaced shortly?
   c. Are the plumbing fixtures in the kitchen and bathrooms adequate and in good working condition?
4. Heating plant and/or air conditioning unit.
   a. Is unit(s) sufficient for size and quality of house?
   b. What would be entailed to install a new or more efficient unit? Would it be feasible?

C. Application of approaches. Each approach may be used in valuing an older property. The primary difference between valuing a new and old home is in the determination of depreciation as part of the cost approach.
1. Consideration must be given to the inspection of the home in order to help the appraiser reach an opinion as to the effective age to be assigned.

2. Physical curable deterioration must be calculated with care.
3. Study must be made to determine if a functional item may be treated as curable or incurable.
4. Items of economic depreciation will be more prevalent in an older neighborhood than a newer one.

Definition of small multi-family dwelling.
A. In most instances, a small multi-family dwelling refers to a property which contains more than one but less than six living units. These units may be one of the following:
1. Double bungalow or duplex.
2. Triple bungalow or triplex.
3. Small courts or numerous houses on a lot.
4. Flats or small apartments.

Reasons for purchasing residential properties.
A. There are three categories of residential properties.
1. Single family homes.
2. Small multi-family dwellings.
3. Income producing multi-family dwellings.

B. Single family homes.
1. Primary concern is given to amenities of home ownership.
2. Cost of ownership is of secondary importance.
3. Pride of location and architectural appeal is given consideration before purchasing.

C. Small multi-family dwellings are purchased for a combination of home ownership and income.
1. Location, architectural attractiveness, and the amenities of ownership are given strong consideration by a purchaser.
2. Income is of secondary importance.
3. Typically, a buyer hopes to be able to reduce the cost of living by obtaining some rental income to decrease expenses.
4. The income received tends to offset real estate taxes, insurance, and maintenance costs.
5. In some instances, rental income will also cover mortgage payments on the property.
6. Usually, the owner of a small multi-family dwelling must do all management work.

D. Income producing multi-family dwelling.
1. Large multi-family dwellings (above 10 to 15 units) are purchased primarily for the income stream to be produced.
2. The net income or spendable income is the most important item considered by the buyer.
3. Amenities of ownership have little influence in the buying decision.

E. Other reasons for purchase.
1. Hedge against inflation.
2. Means of forced saving.
3. Chance for appreciation in value due to increasing demand in the area.

Appraisal procedure.

A. Small multi-family units are appraised approximately the same as single family homes.

B. Cost factors, depreciation and estimates of land value are calculated in the same manner as with single family homes.

C. Small units cannot be considered as true income producing units. Therefore, in most instances, monthly gross multipliers are used instead of an income approach to value.

D. The market comparison approach differs to some extent from the comparative approach as used with homes.

　　1. Less emphasis is placed on attempting to measure pride of ownership and amenities.

　　2. The comparison approach can be refined to a greater degree.

　　　　a. Comparisons may be made on a per unit basis.

　　　　b. Comparison can be made on a per room basis.

　　3. The appeal of the units from a renter's standpoint must be considered.

　　4. The location factor as it relates to transportation and shopping may be given greater consideration than with a single family home.

Amenities of multi-family dwellings.

A. Factors and amenities considered important by tenants of multi-family dwellings.

　　1. Distance from employment centers.

　　2. Public transportation.

　　3. Distance to good shopping.

　　4. Distance to parks and recreation.

　　5. Distance from nuisances.

　　6. Rent levels.

　　7. Pride of ownership.

　　8. Adequacy of off-street parking.

B. Factors considered important by the owner.

　　1. Police and fire protection, rubbish collection.

　　2. Vacancy rates in the area.

　　3. Amount of taxes.

TYPICAL OUTLINE FOR WRITING THE SINGLE FAMILY RESIDENCE NARRATIVE APPRAISAL REPORT

A. Title Page:

　　1. "A market value appraisal of the single family residence known as (Address)."

　　2. Name of client.

　　3. The name and address of the appraiser

B. Table of Contents:
    1. Preface.
    2. Body of report.
    3. Addenda section.

C. Letter of Transmittal:
    1. Date.
    2. Name and address of addressee.
    3. Salutation.
    4. Authorization.
    5. Legal description or reference thereto.
    6. Purpose of appraisal, including type of value estimated.
    7. Date of evaluation.
    8. Reference to following report of _____ pages, including _____ exhibits as well as limiting conditions, factors considered and reasoning employed in arriving at the final conclusion of fair market value.
    9. Estimate of value (written and numbered).
    10. Certification of appraiser.
    11. Signature.

D. Summary of Salient Facts and Conclusions:
    1. Recap of pertinent information such as value estimate, date of value, purpose of appraisal, etc.

E. Premise Section:
    1. Statement of intended use of the appraisal report.
    2. Statement of limiting conditions on which the appraisal is based, including full definition of value as estimated in report.

F. Regional, City and Neighborhood Analysis:
    1. Pertinent features.
    2. Economic factors.
    3. Significant trends.

G. General Property Information:
    1. Record or legal owner.
    2. Legal description.
    3. Legal address.
    4. Location.

H. Site Analysis:
    1. Description of parcel:
        a. Size and shape.
        b. Topography and surface drainage.
        c. Soils including subsoil (foundational).
        d. Access.
        e. Landscaping, etc.

    2. Street improvements and utilities.

    3. Deed restrictions and zoning.

    4. Assessed valuation and tax information.

5. Current use and adaptability.

6. Highest and best use.

I. Improvement Analysis:
1. Basic description:
   a. Type and date of construction.
   b. Architectural form.
   c. Number of rooms.

2. Summary of square foot areas:
   a. Residence.
   b. Garage.
   c. Other structures, walks and drives.

3. Exterior description:
   a. Foundation and sub-structure.
   b. Exterior treatment.
   c. Roof design and cover.
   d. Porches.

4. Interior description:
   a. Room descriptions (space allotment; floor, walls and ceiling finish; built-ins and fixtures).

5. Mechanical Equipment:
   a. Heating and air conditioning.
   b. Electrical.
   c. Miscellaneous - garbage disposal, etc.

6. Miscellaneous Improvements:
   a. Outbuildings.
   b. Patios and walks.
   c. Landscaping.

J. Analysis and Valuation:
1. Statement of problem.
2. Methods of appraisal.
3. Investigation.

K. Estimate of Land Value:
1. By market data approach.

2. By sales abstraction.

3. Economic approaches:
   a. As percentage of annual income classification.
   b. As percentage of total property value.

4. Reconciliation of various approaches.
5. Final estimate of land value.

L. The Cost Approach:
1. Reproduction cost estimate:
   a. Justification.

2. Estimate of accrued depreciation:
   a. Physical deterioration with justification: curable and incurable.
   b. Functional Obsolescence with justification: curable and incurable.

3. Economic obsolescence with justification.

4. Depreciated reproduction cost.

5. Addition of estimated land value.

6. Value indicated by cost approach.

M. The Market Data Approach:
   1. Market data presentation including statement of source and verification:
      a. Summary of pertinent data (sales and listings).

   2. Analysis of market data:
      a. Factors of adjustment.

   3. Application of adjusted market data factors:
      a. Comparison by various common denominators: e.g., ratio of sales price to living area; ratio sales price to number of rooms.
      b. Direct property comparison.

   4. Reconciliation of indications using reliability coefficients.

   5. Value indicated by market data approach.

N. The Income Approach:
   1. Seldom employed in analysis of single family residential property.

   2. Justified gross rent multiplier of neighborhood.

   3. Justified fair rental estimate for subject.

   4. Indicated value by income approach.

O. Reconciliation and Discussion of Value Estimates:
   1. State values estimated by three separate approaches.

   2. Analysis:
      a. Major, but not exclusive, weight to approach that:
         Is most closely related to purpose of the appraisal;
         Is most appropriate for property classification concerned;
         Has greatest amount of supporting data;
         Most accurately reflects attitude of typical purchaser; and
         Is most sensitive to current trends.

   3. State final value conclusions:
      a. Suggested arbitrary separation:
         Land; and
         Improvements.

P. Addenda Section:
   1. Market data.
   2. Market data map.

3. Plots, maps, pictures, charts, statistical and factual data pertinent to the value estimate and necessary as supporting evidence not included in body of report.

Q. Appraiser's Qualifications.

CONCLUSION

In concluding this information on concepts, valuation and appraisal techniques, let us wave three warning flags. It is to be noted that there are subtle differences between *valuation* and *appraising*. The first is broader, tends to be economic in origin and emphasizes theory; the latter refers more to practice, methods and techniques. Next, anyone can make an appraisal, even a lay person, but the *worth* of an appraisal report is determined by the experience, knowledge, qualifications, and motives of the person behind it. Finally, let us not be deceived by any broad statement that appraising is an exact science. It is a science as is any of the other social sciences, but people and property cannot be appraised with the exactness and accuracy reached by the mathematical and physical sciences.

ADDITIONAL PRACTICE PROBLEMS

The following are some additional practice problems with suggested solutions.

Applying the Income (Capitalization) Approach

1. A 50 unit apartment building and lot are being appraised. The 30 two-bedroom units rent for $600 and the 20 one-bedroom units rent for $475 monthly, which rent is comparable to market rent in the area. Vacancy and collection losses are estimated to be 5% of potential gross income. The parking structure and laundry facility contribute an additional estimated $1,200 income per month. What is the property's (land and building) total estimated annual effective gross income?

Solution.

30 x $600 = $18,000 x 12 = ...	$216,000
20 x $475 = $9,500 x 12 = ...	114,000
Apartment rental income.	$330,000
Plus other income: $1200 x 12 = ...	14,400
Potential Gross Annual Income	$344,400
Less 5% vacancy/collection loss	-17,220
Total annual effective gross income	$327,180

2. The owner's operating statement shows the following annual expenses:

FIXED EXPENSES

Real Property Taxes	$7,200
Insurance	2,200
License	200
Capital Improvements	22,000
Depreciation	10,000
	$41,600

OPERATING EXPENSES

Water	$9,000

Gas and Electricity	6,000
Pool Service	4,800
Gardening Maintenance	1,200
Entertainment Expenses	750
Building Maintenance	10,000
Resident Manager Salary	12,000
Refuse Service	1,200
	$44,950

RESERVES FOR REPLACEMENTS

Appliances, carpets, drapes	$6,000
Building components	4,000
	$10,000

TOTAL EXPENSES.................................. .... $96,550

After reconstructing owner's statement (determining proper allowable expense items), what is property's annual estimated net income?

Solution.

Deduct $32,000 (Capital Improvements and Depreciation) from fixed expenses and $750 (Entertainment Expense) from operating expense, as being improper deductions.

From problem #1, the effective annual gross income is	$327,180
EXPENSES	
FIXED	$9,600
OPERATING	44,200
REPLACEMENT RESERVES	10,000
TOTAL EXPENSES	- 63,800
ESTIMATED ANNUAL NET INCOME OF PROPERTY	$263,380

3. The appraiser determined a proper overall capitalization rate for the above property is 9.5%. What is the estimated property value?

Solution.

$263,380 net income ÷ .095 cap rate = $2,772,421 estimated property value.

4. Suppose the net income of the property is only $189,000 and similar properties are valued at $1,929,000. What is the indicated overall cap rate?

Solution.

$189,000 (Income) ÷ $1,925,000 (Value) = 9.8% overall cap rate.

5. Given, based on comparative sales technique:

Sale price of an income property	$230,000
Building value	$170,000
Remaining estimated life of building	40 years
Annual net income of property	$23,500

What is the indicated interest rate for the property?

Solution.

(Improved properties have both an interest rate and a recapture rate included in the capitalization rate. The recapture rate applies only to the improvements, while the interest rate applies to both land and improvements.)

Estimated net income before recapture	$23,500
Recapture for building:	
100% ÷ 40 yrs. = 2.5% x $170,000	$4,250
Net income after building recapture	$19,250

Interest Rate = $19,250 ÷ $230,000 = 8.3%

6A. Building Residual Technique Problem (Land value known; building value unknown.)

Assume the following:

Annual net income from the whole property	$14,000
Land value	$42,000
Recapture rate for building (25 yrs remaining economic life) ..	4%
Interest rate	8%

What is (1) the building value and (2) the property value?

Solution.

Net income of property	$14,000
Income attributable to land: $42,000 x .08 = ...	$3,360
Income attributable to building	$10,640

Capitalization rate: 12% (8% + 4%)

Formula: Present Value = Net income ÷ Capitalization Rate

Therefore, Indicated value of building = $10,640 ÷ .12 = ...	$88,667
Plus land value	$42,000
Indicated property value by building residual technique	$130,667
	($130,700 rounded)

6B. Land Residual Technique Problem (Building value known; land value unknown.)

Assume the same figures as above in building residual technique problem, except building value is $88,700 and land value is unknown.

What is (1) land value and (2) property value?

Solution.

Net income	$14,000
Less income attributable to improvements ($88,700 x .12)	-$10,644
Income attributable to land	$3,356
Indicated value of land = $3,356 ÷ .08 = $41,950 (rounded)	$42,000
Add improvement value	$88,700
Indicated property value by land residual technique	$130,700

7A. Assume that comparisons show comparable single-family houses in a neighborhood rent for about $380 per month and sell for an average of $45,600. What is the indicated gross rent multiplier for a subject property in this neighborhood?

Solution.
Formula: sales price ÷ gross monthly rent = gross rent multiplier
Therefore, $45,600 ÷ $380 = 120
The gross rent multiplier is 120

7B. Suppose that, when compared to other rentals, the above property lost $24 per month rental income due to poor kitchen location. What is the estimated depreciation attributable to incurable functional obsolescence?

Solution.
120 x $24 = $2,880

THE OFFICE OF REAL ESTATE APPRAISERS

Background
In 1989, Congress passed the Financial Institutions Reform, Recovery and Enforcement Act (FIRREA), commonly known as the "Savings and Loan Bailout Bill." Title XI of FIRREA contains the *Real Estate Appraisal Reform Amendments* which require each state to establish a program to license and certify real estate appraisers who perform appraisals for federally related transactions. Title XI additionally requires states to adhere to real estate appraiser qualifications criteria set by the Appraiser Qualifications Board (AQB) of The Appraisal Foundation.

Office of Real Estate Appraisers
In response to FIRREA, in 1990 the California Legislature enacted the Real Estate Appraisers' Licensing and Certification Law (Business and Professions Code Section 11300, et seq.) This law created the Office of Real Estate Appraisers (OREA), which was organized in early 1991. OREA regulates real estate appraisers by issuing licenses and investigating complaints of illegal or unethical activity by licensed appraisers.

Real Estate Appraiser Licenses
There are four levels of licensing for real estate appraisers in California. Listed below are the requirements for each of the four levels.

1. **Certified General Real Estate Appraiser** — Certified general appraisers may appraise any type of real property.)

    Education — At least 180 hours of appraisal related education covering these specific topics which are required by AQB:

    • Influences of Real Estate Value
    • Legal Considerations in Appraisal
    • Types of Value
    • Economic Principles
    • Real Estate Markets and Analysis
    • Valuation Process
    • Property Description
    • Highest and Best Use Analysis
    • Appraisal Statistical Concepts

- Sales Comparison Approach
- Site Value
- Cost Approach
- Income Approach, including
  Estimation of income and expenses
  Operating expense ratios
  Gross rent multiplier analysis
  Direct Capitalization
  Cash flow estimates
  Measures of cash flow
  Discounted cash flow analysis
- Valuation of Partial Interests
- Appraisal Standards and Ethics (USPAP) (15 hours, minimum.)
- Narrative Report Writing

Experience — At least 3,000 hours of acceptable appraisal experience, of which at least 1,500 hours must be in appraising non-residential properties. The experience must have been obtained over a minimum of 30 months. Experience may be obtained in any of the following categories:

- Fee and staff appraisal
- Ad valorem tax appraisal
- Review of an appraisal (400 hours maximum.)
- Appraisal analysis
- Real estate counseling
- Highest and best use analysis
- Feasibility analysis/study
- Setting forth opinions of value of real property for tax purposes
- Assisting in the preparation of appraisals (400 hours maximum.)
- Real estate valuation experience such as that of a real estate lending officer or real estate broker.

Examination — Successful completion of the AQB endorsed Uniform State Certified General Real Property Appraiser Examination.

2. **Certified Residential Real Estate Appraiser** — Certified residential appraisers may appraise *any* one-to-four unit residential property, and non-residential property with transaction value up to $250,000.

Education — At least 120 hours of appraisal related education covering these specific topics which are required by AQB:

- Influences of Real Estate Value
- Legal Considerations in Appraisal
- Types of Value
- Economic Principles
- Real Estate Markets and Analysis
- Valuation Process
- Property Description

- Highest and Best Use Analysis
- Appraisal Statistical Concepts
- Sales Comparison Approach
- Site Value
- Cost Approach
- Income Approach, including
  Estimation of income and expenses
  Operating expense ratios
  Gross rent multiplier analysis
  Direct Capitalization
- Valuation of Partial Interests
- Appraisal Standards and Ethics (USPAP) (15 hours maximum.)
- Narrative Report Writing

Experience — At least 2,500 hours of acceptable appraisal experience. The experience must have been obtained over a minimum of 30 months. Experience may be obtained in any of the following categories:

- Fee and staff appraisal
- Ad valorem tax appraisal
- Review of an appraisal (400 hours maximum.)
- Appraisal analysis
- Real estate counseling
- Highest and best use analysis
- Feasibility analysis/study
- Setting forth opinions of value of real property for tax purposes
- Assisting in the preparation of appraisals (400 hours maximum.)
- Real estate valuation experience such as that of a real estate lending officer or real estate broker.

Examination — Successful completion of AQB endorsed Uniform State Certified Residential Real Property Appraiser Examination.

3. **Residential License** — Residential licensed appraisers may appraise any one-to-four unit residential property with a transaction value up to $1 million, and non-residential property with a transaction value up to $250,000.)

Education — At least 90 hours of appraisal related education covering these specific topics which are required by AQB:

- Influences of Real Estate Value
- Legal Considerations in Appraisal
- Types of Value
- Economic Principles
- Real Estate Markets and Analysis
- Valuation Process
- Property Description
- Highest and Best Use Analysis
- Appraisal Statistical Concepts

- Sales Comparison Approach
- Site Value
- Cost Approach
- Income Approach
  Estimation of income and expenses
  Operating expense ratios
  Gross rent multiplier analysis
- Valuation of Partial Interests
- Appraisal Standards and Ethics (USPAP) (15 hours maximum.)

Experience — At least 2,000 hours (1,000 hours for holder of a valid California real estate broker license) of acceptable appraisal experience. Experience may be obtained in any of the following categories:

- Fee and staff appraisal
- Ad valorem tax appraisal
- Review appraisal
- Appraisal analysis (400 hours maximum.)
- Real estate counseling
- Highest and best use analysis
- Feasibility analysis and study
- Setting forth opinions of value of real property for tax purposes
- Assisting in the preparation of appraisals (400 hours maximum.)
- Real estate valuation experience as a real estate lending officer or real estate broker.

Examination — Successful completion of AQB endorsed Uniform State Residential Licensed Real Property Appraiser Examination.

4. **Trainee License** — (Trainee licensed appraisers must work under the technical supervision of a state licensed appraiser. They may assist on any appraisal which falls under the scope authorized for the supervising appraiser.)

Education — 15 hours of instruction related to the Uniform Standards of Professional Appraisal Practice, covering these specific topics which are required by AQB:

- Influences of Real Estate Value
- Legal Considerations in Appraisal
- Types of Value
- Economic Principles
- Real Estate Markets and Analysis
- Valuation Process
- Property Description
- Highest and Best Use Analysis
- Appraisal Statistical Concepts
- Sales Comparison Approach
- Site Value
- Cost Approach

- Income Approach, including
  Estimation of income and expenses
  Operating expense ratios
  Gross rent multiplier analysis
- Valuation of Partial Interests
- Appraisal Standards and Ethics (USPAP) (15 hours maximum.)

Experience — No experience is required for the Trainee License. To accumulate appraisal experience, trainees must work under the technical supervision of a state licensed appraiser.

Examination — Successful completion of AQB endorsed Uniform State Residential Licensed Real Property Appraiser Examination.

Terms of Licenses

Real estate appraiser licenses are valid for two years, however, continuing education requirements are submitted every four years.

Renewal Requirements

All licensed appraisers must meet the following continuing education requirements for license renewal:

Hours. At least 14 hours per year of OREA approved continuing education.

Required topics. Included in the required hours, appraisers must complete at least 7 hours of instruction on the Uniform Standards of Professional Appraisal Practice, and the 4-hour course entitled "Federal and State Laws and Regulations." In lieu of the four-hour course, a certification indicating that the appraiser has used and understands the material may be submitted.

OREA's Enforcement Division

The Enforcement Division is OREA's investigative and enforcement arm. It promotes professionalism in the industry by providing consumers and businesses with protection against unlawful and fraudulent conduct by appraisers. This is accomplished through the examination of past conduct of applicants for licensure, the investigation of complaints and, where appropriate, the initiation of proceedings to deny licenses or impose disciplinary sanctions. Subject to various administrative safeguards and the review and approval of the Chief Deputy Director and the Director, the Division may seek to deny, restrict or revoke a license and/or impose a fine of up to $10,000 for any violation of state law applicable to licensed appraisers.

Additional Information

For additional information, write or phone OREA at:

Office of Real Estate Appraisers
1755 Creekside Oaks Drive, Suite 190
Sacramento, CA 95833-3646
(916) 263-0722

Web site address:

www.orea.ca.gov

18 Taxation and Assessments

NOTE: *Unless otherwise indicated, all statutory references in this chapter are to the California Revenue and Taxation Code.*

Questions concerning taxes and assessments are raised in most real estate transactions. Taxation is an indirect yet significant controlling device affecting estimates of value. It is important for those engaged in the real estate business to know the variety of taxes and their effect on property transfers. Discussion of the specific taxes mentioned in this chapter is for reference purposes only and should not be relied upon as a substitute for professional advice. Full consideration may involve retaining the services of accounting, legal and tax specialists. There are many categories of property that may be exempt from taxation. The county assessor should be consulted for a determination in this area.

Federal, state and local governments tax real property. Local governments assess taxes directly on the property, such as *ad valorem* property taxes, special assessments and transfer taxes. Most state governments have an income tax. The federal and state governments tax property indirectly through the taxation of ordinary and capital gain on income earned from real estate. Federal and state governments also tax property indirectly when it is transferred through an estate or gift to others, i.e., estate and gift taxes.

Taxes may act as a deterrent to many individuals desiring to acquire or dispose of real property. Unless tax benefits and burdens and tax planning alternatives are seriously considered by persons contemplating the purchase or sale of real estate, the anticipated benefits of ownership may not be realized, and losses may be sustained.

PROPERTY TAXES

Property taxes are levied according to the value *(ad valorem)* of the property as of the date acquired, or the date of completion of any new construction. Generally, the more valuable the property and/or the more current its acquisition or construction date, the higher the tax. Property taxes and subventions represent the largest single source of income for local governments. Approximately half of California's one hundred million acres are owned by governments and therefore exempt from property taxation.

All property within the jurisdiction of a taxing authority is taxable unless specifically exempt.

California's Property Taxes

In June of 1978, California voters approved Proposition 13, amending the State Constitution so that the maximum annual tax on real property is limited to one percent of "full cash value" (market value) plus a maximum of two percent annual inflation factor based on the Consumer Price Index (CPI), as calculated by the California Department of Industrial Relations. (Sections 51 and 110.1) An additional sum is allowed to pay for indebtedness on affected property approved by voters prior to the passage of Proposition 13. Also, selected new indebtedness is allowed, only by a two-thirds vote of the residents affected.

Property Tax Liens

Property taxes become liens against real property on January 1 of the year preceding the fiscal year (July 1 - June 30) for which the taxes are levied. One-half the taxes on real property are due on November 1 and payable without penalty until 5 p.m. (or close of business, whichever is later) on December 10. The second half is due on February 1 and is delinquent if not paid by 5 p.m. (or close of business, whichever is later) on April 10. If either December 10 or April 10 falls on a Saturday, Sunday, or legal holiday, the time of delinquency is extended until 5 p.m. (or close of business, whichever is later) on the next business day. A ten percent penalty applies to an installment that becomes delinquent. If the second installment is delinquent, the tax collector adds a charge to place the property on the delinquent roll.

The Morgan Property Taxpayers' Bill of Rights

The Morgan Property Taxpayers' Bill of Rights (Section 5900, et seq.) and the related amendment to subdivision (e) of Section 408 require that the assessor allow, upon request of an assessee (or his/her designated representative), inspection and copying of documents, including an auditor's work papers, relating to the appraisal and assessment of assessee's property. Further information concerning taxpayers' rights relating to the assessment, audit, and collection of property taxes in this state may be obtained from the State Board of Equalization, Taxpayers' Rights Advocate's Office, P.O. Box 942879, Sacramento, CA 94279-0070. Telephone: (916) 324-2798. FAX: (916) 323-3319.

Establishing Values

Operating under constitutional provisions and statutes, assessors have established real property values as follows:

No change in parcel since February 28, 1975. If the parcel has not been further improved with structures and has not been sold or transferred since February 28, 1975, the assessor has established a base value for the parcel and then has applied an inflation rate to that base year value not to exceed 2% per year. Thus, the base year value is locked in place and cannot be changed unless there is a change in ownership or new construction.

Parcel sold/changed ownership since February 28, 1975. If a parcel has sold or otherwise changed ownership since February 28, 1975, its *new base year* value as of the date of change of ownership is enrolled for the following lien date and can be adjusted upward by up to 2% each year.

New construction. If the improvement on the parcel was newly constructed since February 28, 1975 and the parcel remained in the same ownership prior to and after the construction, only the added "new construction" receives a new base year value. The land may have one base year for valuation purposes while the improvements constructed may have another. Only if the improvement is completed in the same assessment year that the parcel is purchased would the land and improvement have the same base year. "New construction" could also apply to land that has been significantly altered.

There are certain improvements which have been excluded from the definition of "new construction" for purposes of reappraisal:

1. water conservation equipment for agricultural use;

2. fire detection or extinguishing systems or modification for fire-related egress;

3. modification for access by disabled person; and

4. seismic retrofitting

5. normal maintenance and repair

Parcel further improved since February 28, 1975 (or since constructed, sold or transferred). If the parcel has been further improved (e.g., by an addition or swimming pool) since February 28, 1975 (or since constructed, sold or transferred), it has a 1975 base value year (or year of sale, construction or transfer) and an additional base year value on the new improvement.

Change in Ownership Exclusions. There are a number of exclusions from change in ownership and consequent reappraisal, some of which are described as follows:

1. Acquiring "comparable" replacement property for original property taken by a governmental agency in eminent domain actions, per Section 68.

2. Replacing property destroyed by disaster. Section 69 requires comparable replacement property to be acquired or newly constructed within 3 years of property substantially damaged or destroyed by governor-declared disaster. Section 69.3 permits counties to enact ordinances allowing such replacement property transfers from other counties. Section 70 requires that reconstructed property that is substantially equivalent to damaged property is not reassessed "new construction."

3. Transferring the principal residence and first one million dollars of full cash value of real property between parents and their children pursuant to Section 63.1, provided that a claim for the exclusion is filed with the assessor within 3 years of the date of transfer or within 6 months after the date of mailing of the notice of supplemental or escape assessment.

4. Transferring the base year value of one's home (original property) to a replacement property for persons over 55 or disabled persons who sold their original property pursuant to criteria in Section 69.5.

6. Transferring real property to a spouse per Section 63, or transferring real property into a trust where the trustor/transferor is the sole present beneficiary of the trust or the trust is revocable by the trustor pursuant to subdivision (d) of Section 62.

7. Transferring real property to a partnership or other legal entity by maintaining exactly the same proportional interests of the transferors and transferees, resulting solely in a change in the method of holding title, under Section 62(a)(2).

Reduction of value. Assessors must recognize declines in value. Under Section 51, the "taxable value" is the lower of the base year value (compounded annually) or the full cash value (defined in Section 110) whichever is less. It may be necessary for the property owner to expressly bring the decline in value to the assessor's attention. The county board of equalization is required to hear applications for reduction in assessment.

Exemptions
There are numerous properties that are assessed but are partially or totally tax-exempt, as well as some kinds of real and tangible business and personal property that are neither assessed nor taxed. Under Section 218, the homeowner's exemption of the first $7,000 of full value applies to each residential property that is owner-occupied on the lien date and meets other qualifying tests. (This includes an owner-occupied unit in a multiple unit residential structure, an owner-occupied condominium, cooperative apartment, or unit in a duplex). Once claimed, the homeowner's exemption remains in effect until terminated. Each homeowner is responsible for notifying the assessor that the property is no longer eligible for exemption . An escape assessment plus a 25 percent penalty and interest may result from failure to notify the assessor of the ineligibility.

Section 205 provides an exemption of up to $4,000 of full value of any property subject to property tax (real, personal, boats, planes, etc.) owned by qualifying veterans or the unmarried spouses of deceased veterans. This exemption results in a tax savings of up to $40. The limitations are that it cannot apply to a property on which the homeowner's exemption has been successfully claimed. And for a non-home owning veteran to qualify, there is a personal wealth cap of $5,000 for an unmarried veteran and $10,000 for a married veteran.. In computing the $5,000 or $10,000 property limitation, one-fourth of the assessed value of the taxable property and the full value of nontaxable property is used. Section 205.5 provides an exemption for disabled veterans and/or their unmarried surviving spouses, as follows: depending on veteran's income and extent of disability (resulting from injury or disease incurred during military service), a disabled veteran may receive an exemption of $40,000, $60,000, $100,000, or $150,000 of the full cash value of his/her residence. The county assessor can provide application forms and other information regarding the disabled veteran's exemption.

All growing crops, fruit, and nut-bearing trees less than four years old and grapevines less than three years old are exempt. Properties held or exclusively used for human burial or owned by nonprofit entities, including certain nursery and kindergarten-to-12th grade schools, hospitals, churches, nonprofit private schools and colleges are exempt. Timber is no longer subject to property tax, but owners pay a yield tax on downed or felled timber. However, timberland remains taxable. Public open-space lands used solely for recreation are also exempt.

Supplemental Assessments
New procedures for enrolling adjustments to assessed valuations of real property have been used by assessors since 1983. Prior to the enactment of the supplemental assessment system, when a change in ownership or completed new construction occurred, increases in base year value were often delayed from 4 to 16 months, resulting in an unwarranted reduction in taxes for some, with a proportionate (and inequitable) shift of the tax burden to others.

The Legislature solved this inequity through Sections 75, et seq., under which assessors appraise at its full cash value real property which has changed ownership or is newly constructed as of the date of the event. Added taxes become due on the date the change in ownership occurs or the new construction is completed. This is done by issuing a supplemental assessment to be added to a supplemental tax roll. The value determined becomes the new base year value of the transferred or newly-constructed property. Just as for regular assessments, there are appeal procedures for protesting supplemental assessments.

If reassessment takes place between January 1st and May 31st, inclusive, two supplemental assessments are made (and the taxpayer receives two supplemental bills). A reassessment occurring between June 1st and December 31st, inclusive, generates only one supplemental assessment.

If a property changes ownership more than once during an assessment year, or if there are multiple completion dates for new construction during an assessment year, or any combination of transfers and construction, a supplemental assessment is made for each occurrence.

Supplemental assessment of property that has decreased in value results in the auditor issuing a partial refund of taxes paid in advance. The refund is sent to the new owner, not the original taxpayer.

New construction is excluded from supplemental assessment (under the "builder's inventory exclusion – Section 75.12) if the owner will not occupy but intends to market the improvement, and has so notified the assessor in writing prior to commencement of construction. When the newly-constructed improvements are transferred, leased or rented, a supplemental assessment is made as of that date.

County assessors are generally alerted to changes in ownership and construction starts through recorded documents and permits. When the assessor determines that an ownership change or new construction completion has occurred, the assessor:

1. places the supplemental assessment information on the roll;

2. notifies the auditor, who places an appropriate notation on the current roll or on a separate document kept with the roll; and

3. sends a prescribed notice of supplemental assessment to the assessee.

The notice includes the new base year property value, the taxable value appearing on the current roll and/or roll being prepared, information concerning the assessee's right to review and to appeal the supplemental assessment, and the procedure for filing a claim of exemption. If the property has decreased in value and the supplemental assessment is a negative amount, the notice will advise the assessee that a refund will be made.

Filing a Change in ownership Statement. Section 480 requires that any person acquiring any interest in real property or a manufactured home taxed as real property must file a change in ownership statement with the county recorder or assessor. The change in ownership statement must be filed either at the time of recording, or if the transfer is not recorded, within 45 days of the date of the change in ownership. Failure to file a change in ownership statement within 45 days from the date of a written request by the assessor will result in a penalty of one hundred dollars or ten percent of the taxes applicable to the new base year value, whichever is greater.

If the transfer is occasioned by a death, and probate is not involved, the transferee (or trustee, if applicable) has 150 days from the date of the death to file the change in ownership statement. If the property is subject to probate, the statement must be filed prior to or at the time the inventory and appraisal are filed with the court.

Sections 480.3 and 480.4 require that county assessors and recorders make available to property buyers a "Preliminary Change of Ownership Report" form. This form is to be completed by the buyer prior to transfer of the property. If a document evidencing a change of ownership is presented to the recorder for recordation without the concurrent filing of this preliminary change of ownership report, the recorder may charge an additional recording fee of twenty dollars.

Statute of limitations on Escape and Supplemental Assessments. Section 532 provides assessors a four-year statute of limitations for the enrollment of escape assessments, and Section 75.11 (d) allows assessors four years to enroll supplemental assessments.

In both cases, the statute of limitations for making escape and supplemental assessments does not begin to run until a change in ownership statement is filed. Where, for example, a change in ownership occurred in 1992, and a change in ownership statement reporting it was filed, the assessor has only four years from 1992 to enroll escape and supplemental assessments. If the change in ownership statement reporting it was not filed, then assessor must enroll escape and supplemental assessments for all of the years since 1992, including the year of discovery. The assessor's statute of limitations does not commence until the statement is filed.

If non-reporting occurs because of a fraudulent act or omission, the penalty of 75 percent of the additional assessed value under Section 504 is added to the escape and supplemental assessments. The supplemental assessment must be made within six years, on or before the sixth July 1, and the escape assessment must be levied six years after the July 1 of the year in which the property escaped taxation.

Postponement (Sections 20581, et seq.)
Senior citizens (62 years of age or older) and persons who are blind or disabled may defer payment of taxes on their residences. To qualify, an individual must own and occupy the home, have at least a 20% equity in the property (using the assessor's full value as the standard), and have a yearly total household income of $24,000 or less ($34,000 for those who filed in 1983). If married, only one spouse need qualify.

In applying the law, a lien in favor of the State of California is placed against the property and an interest rate determined by the rate earned by the Pooled Money Investment Fund is charged. The postponed taxes and interest are not recovered until the property is sold.

Complete information about the deferral program is available from the State Controller's Office at P.O. Box 953, Sacramento, CA 95812. The toll free telephone number is 1-800-952-5661.

Tax Sale (Sections 3351 - 3972)
County tax collectors, not assessors, are charged with the responsibility of administering the law pertaining to the sale of all properties that are "tax-

defaulted" because five or more years have passed since the property taxes were paid. The tax collector is required by law to attempt to sell within two years all properties which have become tax defaulted and subject to the power to sell. The tax collector may sell properties to any person at a public auction or under special circumstances, to adjoining property owners at a sealed bid sale. The minimum price at which property may be sold at public auction is the sum of all taxes, penalties, costs and fees as defined.

The minimum bid has to be approved by the County Board of Supervisors. After authorization by the State Controller, the tax collector publishes or posts the required notices, setting the date of sale. At the sale, the amount of the highest bid must be paid in cash or negotiable paper, or any combination thereof which the tax collector specifies. Upon completion of the tax sale, the purchaser receives a tax deed conveying title free of all encumbrances of any kind existing before the sale, except those shown in Section 3712.

If a tax-defaulted property is unusable because of size, location, or other conditions, the tax collector may sell it at a sealed bid sale to contiguous property owners at a price established by the tax collector.

Buyers of tax-defaulted properties may include taxing agencies, revenue districts, and certain non-profit organizations. In the case of residential property, the sale to a non-profit organization is conditioned upon the rehabilitation and subsequent sale of the property to low-income persons. In the case of vacant property, the non-profit organization must either construct a residential building on the property and sell the property to low-income persons or dedicate the vacant property to public use.

Redemption (Sections 4101, et seq.)
Tax-defaulted real property may be redeemed upon payment of taxes, interest, costs and redemption penalties. Redemption payment is made to the county tax collector, who then issues a certificate of redemption as evidence of payment.

Delinquent taxes, costs, interest and penalties may be paid in five annual installments if the *current* taxes are paid.

If the property has not been redeemed within five years after the initial declaration of default, the property will become subject to the tax collector's power to sell. The right of redemption terminates at the close of business on the last business day prior to the date a tax collector's auction begins. If the property is not sold, the right of redemption is revived. If the property is redeemed, the tax collector will execute and record a "Rescission of Notice of Power to Sell Tax-Defaulted Property."

TAXATION OF MOBILEHOMES

Mobilehomes and manufactured homes are subject to local property taxation under prescribed circumstances.

Under Section 18551 of the Health and Safety Code there are four principal prerequisites for transforming a mobilehome into real property:

1. obtaining a building permit;

2. attaching the mobilehome to an approved foundation;

3. recording a document reflecting that the mobilehome has been affixed to an approved foundation system; and

4. obtaining a certificate of occupancy.

A mobilehome installed on a foundation system is deemed a fixture or improvement to the real property.

Section 5802 provides that the base year value of a mobilehome converted from the vehicle license fee to local property tax shall be its full cash value on the lien date for the fiscal year in which it is first enrolled.

After a mobilehome is attached to a foundation system, the Department of Housing and Community Development (HCD) must cancel the registration. Title is thereafter recorded with the county recorder and ownership is transferred accordingly. Removal of the mobilehome from the foundation is prohibited unless the following conditions are met:

1. all persons having title to any estate or interest in the real property consent to the removal; and

2. 30 days prior to removal, the owner of the mobilehome notifies HCD and the local assessor of its intended removal.

HCD must be given written evidence of the consent to removal by all persons having title or interest in the real property. HCD will then require the owner to obtain a transportation permit or mobilehome registration, whichever it deems appropriate. Once removed from the foundation and the HCD license fee is paid, the mobilehome is personal property and the assessor will remove it from the real property tax roll.

SPECIAL ASSESSMENTS

Special assessments are levied for the cost of specific local improvements such as streets, sewers, irrigation, and drainage. Special assessments may be due periodically to improvement districts or be levied only once by the city or county for a particular work or improvement.

The liens created by special assessments are usually equal in priority to general tax liens.

Self-governing districts may be the source of special assessments. Activated under state law by the local city or county or by vote of the residents, the district becomes a separate legal entity governed by a board of directors.

A district issues bonds to finance particular improvements such as water distribution systems, drainage structures, irrigation works, or parking facilities. To pay off the bonds, the district has the power to assess all lands included in the district on an ad valorem basis. This assessment is a lien on the land until paid. The lien has priority over private property interests and can be foreclosed by sale similar to a tax sale.

Benefit Assessments

Rather than establishing a separate district for the purpose of constructing an improvement, the city or county may establish an "improvement area" and assess the lands contained therein on the basis of benefits to be received from the proposed improvement. A benefit assessment is often included on the property tax bill.

Benefit assessments are distinguished from special assessments chiefly by the differences in the assessment base. However, there are other distinguishing characteristics. Benefit assessments are generally not considered to be deductible as a tax on either California or federal income tax returns. There is a distinction made in federal tax regulations between an assessment to finance improvements and an assessment to finance maintenance. Only the latter is deductible.

The purposes for which benefit assessments are levied include lighting, flood control, transit, police protection, fire protection, county service areas and paramedics.

CERTAIN ASSESSMENT STATUTES

Since 1885, California has enacted numerous statutes relating to special taxes and assessments and to the formation of assessment districts throughout the state. The following are among the important assessment acts.

Vrooman Street Act

Passed in 1885, this act conferred authority on city councils to grade and finish streets, construct sewers, etc., within municipalities or counties. It provides for an election and the issuance of bonds secured by special funds collected under tax levy. It also provides for the acquisition of public utilities by the municipality or county.

A property owner may arrange for street grading according to official specifications and secure a reduction in the amount of the assessment.

Street Improvement Act of 1911

This act is utilized more than any other for street improvements in this state. Assessments are due in equal installments during the term of the bonds. The local legislative body determines the rate of interest on the bonds. The amount of assessment appears on the tax bill as a lien against the property. It may be partially or wholly prepaid at any time, including prior to issuance of the bonds.

The Improvement Bond Act of 1915

Under the terms of this act, a public agency can issue bonds to finance subdivision street improvements. Bonds usually carry a maximum of 6 percent interest. Owners of affected property bear the cost to redeem the bond. Under certain circumstances, an improvement district cannot issue bonds until the California Districts Securities Commission has approved the project.

Mello-Roos

The Mello-Roos Community Facilities Act of 1982 provides for a wider variety of facilities and services than other improvement bond acts and has no requirement that such improvements will specifically benefit individual properties. Although a Mello-Roos assessment is secured by a lien against the property and the maximum tax rate approved may be greater than what will be needed to retire the bonds, the principal amounts of the bonds are not tied to any specific parcels. As such, Mello-Roos is on the order of a general property tax levy for general fund benefits and is not appropriate for inclusion in the land value of the parcels. The amount of any unpaid assessment(s) will not appear on the property tax bill, but will be separately levied and collected. Civil Code Section 1102.6b requires that a seller of one to four dwelling units disclose a Mello-Roos assessment.

FEDERAL TAXES

Federal Estate Tax

An estate tax return must be filed within nine months after a decedent's death. Generally, for citizens or residents of the United States whose death occurred after 1987, there will be no tax liability unless the combined value of the decedent's gifts during their lifetime and the gross estate exceed $600,000.

Gross estate. The gross estate includes the value of all property in which the decedent had an interest at the time of death, plus certain property interests transferred before death. If the decedent was a citizen or a resident, this includes all of the decedent's property, regardless of where it is located.

Various deductions, such as mortgages, funeral and administrative expenses, debts and fees are made to calculate the taxable estate. For a discussion of the basic concepts of both the Federal Estate and Gift Tax, see Publication 559, Tax Information for Survivors, Executors, and Administrators. It may be obtained from the U.S. Government Printing Office.

Property owned by the decedent. Property included in the gross estate generally includes all property beneficially owned by the decedent and transmitted at death according to the provisions of a will or by local law if there is no will. It includes tangible and intangible property interests: real property, stocks, bonds, furniture, personal effects, jewelry, works of art, interest in a business either in the form of a proprietorship or a partnership, cash surrender value of life insurance, and notes and other evidences of indebtedness held by the decedent. The value of the decedent's interest in any income tax refund is included. The value of the property in the gross estate is not reduced by any dower or courtesy interest, or a statutory interest in lieu of such interest.

Estate tax return. The IRS form is due 9 months after the date of death. Extensions may be granted but they cannot total more than 6 months. An extension does not, however, extend the time for payment of the tax.

The fact that a return is due does not mean that there is a "taxable estate." For example, any property that is transferred to the surviving spouse through the estate is excluded from the taxable estate of the decedent.

Federal Tax Liens

Any unpaid Internal Revenue Code tax becomes a lien on all property and rights to property of the taxpayer, including property or rights to property acquired after the lien arises. A federal tax lien is not valid against purchasers, holders of security interests (e.g., mortgages or mechanics' liens) and judgment lien creditors until a notice of lien has been filed in the proper place. Even though a notice of lien has been filed, it is not valid against certain classes of creditors (known as "Super Priorities") defined in Section 6323(b) of the Internal Revenue Code. With respect to real property, the notice must be filed with the county recorder.

In addition to the general tax lien, the Internal Revenue Code provides for special liens for estate and gift taxes. At the date of the decedent's death, an unrecorded estate tax lien attaches to every part of the gross estate and continues for a period of ten years. An estate tax lien is valid against most purchasers and transferees. (If the estate elects to pay the tax in installments for up to fifteen years, the lien is recorded.)

An unrecorded gift tax lien attaches to all gifts made during the calendar year. If the gift tax is not paid by the donor, the donee becomes personally liable for the tax. The gift tax lien extends for ten years from the time the gifts were made.

Federal Gift Tax and the Unified Credit

This tax applies to completed voluntary transfers by an individual of any type of property for less than an adequate and full consideration in money or money's worth.

If a gift is a transfer of a present interest, there is an annual exclusion of $10,000. If a gift exceeds $10,000 in a year, a return is due. If the gift is a transfer of a future interest (i.e., any interest that is to commence in use, possession, or enjoyment at some future time), the exclusion does not apply and a return is due.

Two types of "indirect" transfers are no longer considered gifts and no return is due. These include any amount paid on behalf of an individual:

1. as tuition to an educational organization; or

2. to any person who provides medical care.

The due date of the Federal Gift Tax Return is April 15 of the year following the gift. Any extension of time granted for filing the form 1040 applies to the return. Any compliance questions should be referred to a tax advisor or the local IRS office.

Even though a return may be due, there may not be a tax liability. For example, transfers between spouses are not taxable gifts. Also, donors may make large transfers and use their Unified Credit rather than pay the gift tax. The Unified Credit is a dollar for dollar offset against the tax. It was phased in as follows:

Year	Unified Credit	Equivalent Amt. of Gift	Year	Unified Credit	Equivalent Amt. of Gift
1981	47,000	175,000	1985	121,800	400,000
1982	62,800	225,000	1986	155,800	500,000
1983	79,300	275,000	1987	192,800	600,000
1984	96,300	325,000			

This means that after 1986 a person can make a one-time transfer of $610,000 to an individual without paying any gift tax. The first $10,000 will be absorbed by the annual exclusion and the $600,000 by the Unified Credit. A return would still be required.

To the extent the Unified Credit is used to offset a gift tax liability, it is unavailable for offset in settlement of the transferor's estate tax liability.

Social Security Tax
The federal government operates a retirement pay program. Self-employed persons are generally covered also. This program, commonly known as "social security," requires quarterly contributions by almost all employers.

Federal Insurance Contributions Act (FICA) withholdings are employee contributions to social security and medicare. An employee's FICA tax rate is 7.65%. The social security tax portion is applied to wages up to a certain amount (e.g., $65,400 for 1997). The medicare portion applies to all wages.

Unemployment Tax
This federal tax is applicable only to those employers who:

1. pay wages of $1,500 or more during any calendar quarter; or

2. employ at least one individual for some portion of at least one day of each of at least 20 weeks during the calendar year or the preceding calendar year.

There are also specific requirements for those individuals employing agricultural or domestic workers.

DOCUMENTARY TRANSFER TAX

Section 11911 allows a county or city to adopt a documentary transfer tax to apply to transfers of real property located in the county. Notice of payment is entered on the face of the deed or on a separate paper recorded with the deed.

The tax is computed at the rate of 55 cents for each $500 of consideration or fraction thereof. If a portion of the total price paid for the property is exempt because a lien or encumbrance remains on the property, this fact must be stated on the deed or on a separate paper filed with the deed. Certain types of property transfers, such inter vivos gifts, transfers by reason of death, or proportional transfers into a partnership owned by the same individual or entity, are exempt from documentary transfer tax.

A city within a county which has adopted a transfer tax may also adopt its own transfer tax ordinance with the tax amount fixed at one-half the rate charged by the county. The county collects the total tax in the amount recited above but turns half the amount collected over to the city.

Some cities collect transfer taxes in excess of the amounts provided in Section 11911. In part, the authority for this may lie in the distinction between charter cities and general law cities. A concerned party should contact the recorder's office for the status of a particular city's transfer tax levy.

STATE TAXES

Inheritance Tax

The inheritance tax law was repealed as the result of the passage of Proposition 6 at the election held on June 8, 1982. The new estate law (below) is effective for estates of decedents who died after January 1, 1987.

Gift Tax

The gift tax law was also repealed as the result of the passage of Proposition 6 at the election held on June 8, 1982. The repeal is effective as to all gifts made after June 7, 1982.

Estate Tax

Proposition 6 also enacted the California estate tax. The purpose of this tax is to take advantage of a provision in federal law which allows the estate to claim a credit against the federal estate tax for death taxes paid to the state. The tax is fixed in the maximum amount that the federal government will allow as a credit for estate taxes paid to the state. Therefore, this tax does not cost the estate anything because if the amount were not paid to the state it would have to be paid to the federal government.

A California Estate Tax Return is required to be filed with the State Controller for the estate of every decedent whose date of death is after January 1, 1987, if a Federal Estate Tax Return is required to be filed. The return is due and any tax liability is payable on or before nine months after the date of death. There is a late filing penalty of 5% of the amount of the tax due for each month or portion thereof up to a maximum of 25%. This penalty can be waived for good cause. If an extension to file has been granted by the Internal Revenue Service for the filing of the Federal Estate Tax Return, a like extension will be given for the California return. In addition to the late filing penalty, interest at the rate of 12 percent per annum is chargeable on payments not made within nine months after the decedent's death.

MISCELLANEOUS TAXES

Sales and Use Tax

The California State Sales Tax is imposed upon retailers for the privilege of selling tangible personal property at retail. The retailer is liable for this tax whether or not collected from customers.

The Use Tax is imposed upon the storage, use, or other consumption of tangible personal property purchased or leased under certain conditions from a retailer. Use Tax is the liability of the purchaser and that liability is not extinguished until the tax is paid to the state unless it was paid to, and a receipt for the tax was obtained from, a retailer who is registered with and authorized by the state to collect the tax from the purchaser. Sales or Use Tax also applies to certain leases of tangible personal property under specific conditions. The State Board of Equalization administers these taxes.

A real estate broker may be concerned with the tax on sale of personal property. The tax applies to transfers of buildings which are not considered occasional sales under the law if, pursuant to the contract of sale, the buildings are to be severed by the seller. If the contract of sale requires they be severed by the purchaser, the transaction is not taxable as a sale of tangible personal property. The tax may also apply to the value of machinery, equipment and fixtures that do not constitute occasional sales, when included with the sale of a building.

Where a business which required a seller's permit is being sold, the purchaser may be held liable as a successor for tax owed by the seller. If there is any question, sufficient money should be held in escrow to cover possible sales tax liability until a tax clearance is received from the State Board of Equalization.

Real Estate Broker and Mobilehome Sales

A real estate broker who sells mobilehome s as a retailer is required to hold a seller's permit and report to the Board of Equalization the sales or use tax applicable to these transactions. When such a broker sells a new mobilehome for occupancy as a residence, the broker is classified as a retailer-consumer and is required to declare and pay tax on 75% of the broker's purchase price of the mobilehome . Unattached furnishings and other items that are not part of the mobilehome unit remain subject to tax at the full retail selling price unless otherwise exempt.

A real estate broker who sells *used* mobilehome s as a retailer is also required to hold a seller's permit. The application of tax to sales of used mobilehome s depends on whether the unit is subject to property tax or is exempt, but sales tax would apply to any accessory items sold that are not a component part of the mobilehome unit. For mobilehome units sold that are not subject to property tax, sales tax applies. When a real estate broker acts as agent only, the purchaser is subject to use tax. If the mobilehome is subject to property tax, neither the sales or use tax applies.

Any questions should be referred to the nearest office of the Board of Equalization.

Unemployment Insurance Tax

The California Unemployment Insurance (UI) Code requires contributions by employers for a national system of unemployment insurance. Employers must also pay an employment training tax (ETT) and withhold state personal income tax (PIT) and disability insurance (DI) from employees' wages.

Real estate salesperson and broker exclusion. Services performed as real estate salespersons and brokers are excluded from covered employment for purposes of UI, ETT, DI and PIT withholding, if all of the following conditions are met:

1. The individual must be a licensed real estate broker or salesperson;
2. Substantially all of the remuneration paid to the individual is based on sales or other output rather than by the number of hours worked by the individual; and
3. There is a written contract between the individual performing the services and the person for whom the services are performed; which contract provides that, for purposes of state taxes, the individual performing the services will not be treated as an employee.

Real estate salespersons and brokers who are employees under common law rules and whose services are *not* excluded, are subject to UI, ETT, DI and state PIT withholding. For further information about services in excluded employment or in determining if an individual is an employee or an independent contractor, contact the Employment Development Department.

State Tax Lien Law

Under applicable State law, any tax liabilities which become due and payable, including penalties and interest, together with any costs, constitute an enforceable State tax lien on all real property located in this State. However, the lien is not valid against:

1. a successor in interest of the taxpayer without knowledge of the lien;

2. a holder of a security interest;

3. a mechanic's lienor; or

4. a judgment lien creditor where the right, title, or interest was acquired prior to the recording of the State tax lien.

(Government Code Sections 7150-7229)

California worker's compensation law. An employer's statutory liability toward an employee injured on the job is covered by worker's compensation insurance. While not technically a tax, it is included in this section because it does involve payments by the employer. This insurance provides for weekly benefit payments to employees unable to work as the result of an industrial injury or illness, as well as payment of all medical and hospital costs in connection therewith.

Since California law is very specific about which employees must be covered, employers should be familiar with Sections 3351-3700 of the California Labor Code. Problems are most likely to arise in the areas of independent contractors and part-time employees. Additional information about the law and coverage can be obtained from State Compensation Insurance Fund.

ACQUISITION OF REAL PROPERTY

Tax planning is a key consideration in an analysis of the potential returns and risks of a real estate project. Investors usually seek to:

1. shelter income from taxes; or

2. generate losses to shelter other earned income; or

3. obtain favorable capital gains treatment at disposition.

The manner in which an investor acquires real property can contribute to one or more of these goals.

Recent tax reforms have tended to eliminate most acquisition tax write-offs (e.g., prepaid interest) and there are probably few immediate tax effects resulting from the mere acquisition of property. However, the method of acquisition usually has important tax consequences at sale or other disposition of the property.

Title might be taken through a corporation or individually as community property, joint tenancy or tenancy in common. Corporate ownership permits dealers to segregate their investment property from their stock in trade and establish the true nature of each type of property. On the other hand, individual ownership allows greater maneuverability if future plans are uncertain because the property can later be transferred to a corporation tax-free.

If the taxpayer is in a relatively low tax bracket, individual taxes, particularly for a married person, will be less than corporate taxes on a given amount of income. Although joint tenancy ownership will simplify processing on death and reduce probate costs, the transfer of joint tenancy property cannot be controlled by will and the half not included in the decedent's gross estate does not receive a step-up in basis.

Adjusted Tax Basis

One of the most important factors in determining the amount of ultimate gain or loss on a transaction is the "adjusted tax basis" of property, based on its original acquisition price. Property purchased has a basis equal to the purchase price paid, adjusted for various items over the life of the property (e.g., depreciation). Property received as a gift has a basis of the donor's cost (or market value at date of gift if this is lower and taxpayer desires to claim a loss). The beginning basis of property acquired from a decedent is generally the fair market value at the date of death.

Tax Planning

The subject of income taxation in connection with real estate sales frequently arises in the context of ex-post reporting of the facts. In most instances, once a tax related choice is made, it cannot be altered at the time of filing a tax return. It is then too late to think about tax planning.

The price of a property may be less important than the financial or tax position of the buyer or seller for purposes of developing acquisition and/or disposition strategies. Tax planning should start in the pre-acquisition stage. Real estate has historically enjoyed a favorable position in both federal and state income tax laws, but receipt of the available benefits requires tax awareness during the events leading up to acquisition and continuing through the entire period of ownership.

Broker's role. There are many subtleties in the tax laws relating to real estate income. Unless a real estate broker is also an income tax investment counselor, the broker should never offer tax advice but should urge clients to consult a real estate tax attorney, certified public accountant or other qualified person.

INCOME TAXATION

Federal Income Tax

While the Tax Reform Act of 1986 reduced most tax rates and simplified the rate structure, certain real property tax benefits were changed or repealed. The 60% deduction for long-term capital gain was repealed and capital gain was treated as ordinary income and taxed at a rate no higher than 28%. Mortgage interest also became subject to different rules that could limit its deductibility, especially if the home was refinanced, or a second mortgage, home equity loan, or line of credit was obtained. The rules regarding depreciation also changed, so that all tangible property placed in service after December 31, 1986 was subject to the modified acceleration cost recovery system (MACRS).

The Taxpayer Relief Act of 1997 changed the overall capital gains tax rate. The top rate for high income earners was lowered from 28 percent to 20 percent. The lowest bracket was reduced from 15 percent to 10 percent. The new rates apply to assets sold after May 6, 1997.. Investment property owners will experience slightly different treatment regarding depreciation recapture under the new tax bill than in previous years. The difference between the purchase price and selling price (profit) of a property will enjoy the lower overall capital gains tax rate, but any gains due to depreciation recapture will be taxed at 25 percent. Individual taxpayers will need to consult their tax specialist to determine the application of the new law to their investments.

Passive activity losses and credits. Before the Tax Reform Act of 1986, taxpayers, with some limitation, could use deductions from one activity to offset income from any other activity. Similarly, most tax credits generated in one activity could be used to offset tax on income from any of the taxpayer's other activities.

In response to concerns that extensive tax shelter activity was unfair, Congress enacted the passive activity loss (PAL) rules.

After 1986, income was separated into three categories: non-passive income, portfolio income, and passive income. As a result of these PAL rules, taxpayers generally cannot offset non-passive or portfolio income with losses from passive activities. Nor can they offset taxes on such income with credits from passive activities. The new law does contain exceptions for certain activities, including rental real estate, and also has phase-in rules for some losses.

A passive activity generally is any activity involving the conduct of any trade or business in which you do not *materially participate*. In addition, any rental activity is a passive activity regardless of whether you materially participate. For this purpose, a rental activity generally is an activity the income from which consists of payments principally for the use of tangible property, unless substantial services are performed in connection therewith. A taxpayer materially participates in an activity if the taxpayer is involved on a regular, continuous, and substantial basis in the operation of the activity.

At-risk rules extended to real property. The at-risk rules have been extended to apply to the holding of real property. The at-risk rules place a limit on the amount of deductible losses from certain activities often described as tax shelters. Until 1987, activities associated with holding of real property (other than mineral property) were not subject to the at-risk rules.

The at-risk rules apply to losses incurred through real property placed in service after 1986. In the case of an interest in an S corporation, a partnership, or any other pass-through entity acquired after 1986, the at-risk rules apply to real estate activities regardless of when the entity placed the property in service.

In general, any loss from an activity subject to the at-risk rules is allowed only to the extent of the total amount the taxpayer has at-risk in the activity at the end of the tax year. A taxpayer is considered at risk in an activity to the extent of cash and the adjusted basis of other property the taxpayer contributed to the activity and certain amounts borrowed for use in the activity.

A taxpayer is not considered at risk for amounts protected against loss through nonrecourse financing. Nonrecourse financing is financing for which the taxpayer is not personally liable. However, an exception applies to qualified nonrecourse financing secured by real property used in an activity of holding real property. *Qualified nonrecourse debt* is debt for which no one is personally liable and that is:

1. borrowed by the taxpayer with respect to the activity of holding real property;

2. secured by real property used in the activity;

3. not convertible from a debt obligation to an ownership interest; and

4. a loan from, and guaranteed by, any federal, state, or local government, or borrowed by the taxpayer from a qualified person.

A *qualified person is* a person who actively and regularly engages in the business of lending money. The most common example is a bank. A qualified person is not:

1. a person related to the taxpayer (except as described later);

2. the seller of the property, or a person related to the seller;

3. a person who receives a fee due to the taxpayer's investment in the real property, or a person related to that person.

A person related to the taxpayer may be a qualified person if the nonrecourse financing is commercially reasonable and on substantially the same terms as loans involving unrelated persons.

Depreciation

Depreciation is a deductible periodic accounting charge that represents the recovery of capital investment over the useful life of property used in a trade or business or other income producing activity. Land is not included, as it does not depreciate.

For depreciable properties acquired prior to January 1, 1981, the principal methods for computing depreciation are straight-line, declining balance and sum-of-the-years' digits.

For depreciable properties acquired on and after January 1, 1981 and before August 1, 1986, depreciation is computed under a method called accelerated cost recovery system (ACRS), permitting cost recovery over much shorter periods.

The Modified Accelerated Cost Recovery System (MACRS) must be used to depreciate property placed into service after 1986. Taxpayers need to consult their tax advisors for more information on any changes in the depreciation schedules that have been effected since 1986.

Appraisal and income tax concepts. Depreciation for tax purposes is to be distinguished from depreciation for appraisal purposes. In appraisal practice, depreciation is loss in *value* due to any cause, including functional obsolescence or physical deterioration. For income tax purposes, depreciation is an annual deduction from taxable income in recognition of the fact an asset may become economically obsolete or wear out physically and the owner has the right to recover his investment.

Improvements to real property are depreciable for income tax purposes if they are used in business or held for the production of income and have a determinable life longer than one year.

Even if a taxpayer does not take a deduction for depreciation, the basis of the property is reduced by the amount of the depreciation. Upon sale, the government charges the taxpayer with the full amount of depreciation the taxpayer could have taken.

Home Mortgage Interest Deduction

For years beginning after 1987, the rules for deducting mortgage interest have been modified. The amount of interest a taxpayer may deduct depends on the date, amount, and use of the loan.

In general, the interest on any loan obtained before October 14, 1987 and secured by a main or second home is fully deductible.

If a taxpayer obtained a first loan after October 13, 1987 to buy, build, or substantially improve a main or second home, interest is deductible on the first $1 million of principle ($500,000 if married filing separately). Interest is deductible on up to $100,000 of junior loan(s) secured by a taxpayer's main or second home.

For more information, see IRS Publication 936, *Limits on Home Mortgage Interest Deduction.*

Mortgage Credit Certificates

State and local governments sometimes issue mortgage credit certificates (MCCs). Under any such program, MCCs may be issued until a total dollar amount set by the state or local government is reached. An MCC allows a borrower to use mortgage interest as a credit against income tax, making it easier for a low or moderate income person to qualify for a loan for acquisition, qualified rehabilitation, or qualified home improvement of a residence.

Disposition of Real Property - Tax Effects

The characterization and tax treatment of a sale of real property depend upon the use to which the transferor put the property.

Sales or exchanges must be reported to the Internal Revenue Service on Form 1099-S, *Statement for Recipients of Proceeds from Real Estate Transactions.*

Capital gain is the taxable profit derived from the sale of a capital asset (generally, that property of a taxpayer other than inventory). The gain is calculated as the sales price reduced by the adjusted basis, expenses of sale, and closing costs. Adjusted basis is the original tax basis of the property adjusted for capital improvements, depreciation and fixing-up expenses.

The capital gains deduction was repealed for tax years beginning after 1986. However, net capital gains generally will be taxed at a rate no higher than 28%.

Special rules - sale of personal residence. Until the passage of the Taxpayer Relief Act of 1997, a taxpayer was only permitted to postpone the gain on sale of principal residence by way of a one time only $125,000 exemption on the sale of his/her principal residence if the taxpayer was age 55 or older and had resided in the home for at least three of the last five years. The principal residence replacement rule required the taxpayer to purchase another principal residence of equal or greater value and use it within two years before or after sale of the previous principal residence. The original gain was not recognized at the time of sale but was used to reduce the cost basis of the new house

The Taxpayer Relief Act of 1997 granted a $500,000 capital gains tax exclusion to couples and a $250,000 exclusion to single filers, who sell their principal residence. The bill specified that:

The "rollover" and "over 55" requirements were repealed.

Individuals must have lived in the house for two of the last five years. For purposes of the exclusion, on sales after September 30, 1988, taxpayers who are mentally or physically incapacitated are treated as occupying the principal residence while they are in nursing homes or similar care facilities, as long as the principal residence is actually occupied for periods aggregating at least one year of the applicable five-year period. The facility must be licensed by a state or political subdivision to care for individuals in such condition. [Internal Revenue Code §121(d)(7)]

The sales transaction must have taken place after May 6, 1997.

Sellers and buyers who signed a binding contract between May 7, 1997 and August 5, 1997 could apply either the old or new law into their transaction.

The new law gives buyers more options because they are no longer forced to purchase new homes of equal or greater value. Individuals who meet the requirements can sell their homes every two years and still qualify. In addition, individuals who marry someone who has already taken the "over 55" exclusion, or individuals forced to sell because of an emergency, like a job transfer or large medical bills, will be able to use the new exclusion. The new plan does not allow taxpayers to deduct losses on the sale of their property from their income tax. Individuals will need to consult their own tax advisor to determine how to apply the new law to their particular tax situation.

Tax-free exchanges. Property may be disposed of by exchange rather than sale. Some exchanges qualify as tax-free. If the exchange does not qualify as tax-free, it is treated in all respects as a sale.

To qualify as a tax-free exchange, the properties must be "like kind" in nature or character, not in use, quality or grade. The "like-kind" rules give parties a relatively high degree of flexibility: a farm may be exchanged for a store building; vacant land for an apartment building; a rental house for a vacant parcel. Personal use real property does not qualify. If a tax-free exchange has been made, neither gain nor loss is recognized at the time of the exchange, but is deferred by attributing to the property received the same cost basis as that of the property transferred. The holding period of the new property includes that of the old parcel.

Complications arise when like-kind property received is accompanied by cash or other assets ("boot"). When boot is received, gain is recognized but losses are still excluded from recognition. The taxable gain is the lesser of the value of "boot" received or the gain realized on the exchange. The result may be a fully taxable or a partially tax-free exchange.

For example: A taxpayer exchanges a fourplex with a depreciated cost basis of $190,000 for a duplex worth $194,000 plus $2,000 cash. The taxpayer's gain is

$6,000, but only a portion of this gain, the $2,000 boot, is recognized and taxable at the time of the exchange. The remaining $4,000 of gain is not recognized at this time but is postponed by leaving the cost basis of the new property at $190,000. Upon sale of the duplex, the taxpayer must recognize the $4,000 of former gain.

If one of the properties exchanged is encumbered by mortgage debt, the debt relief is treated as boot received. If both properties are encumbered, the debts are netted for purpose of determining the amount and assignment of boot.

Of course, the principal difficulty in effecting a tax-free exchange is finding suitable properties and investors. Usually, two real estate investors are not interested in each other's property and a multi-party exchange must be arranged.

The tax rule which requires an owner to carry over the basis of the old property as the basis for the new property is a problem when exchanging pre-1981 properties for post-1981 properties. Special rules apply to exchanges of pre-accelerated cost recovery system (ACRS) and post-ACRS properties. To avoid this problem, it may be better to sell the pre-1981 property and purchase the post-1981 property with the proceeds.

Installment sales. Taxpayers selling real property and receiving one or more payments in a later year or years must report the sale as an installment sale unless the taxpayer specifically elects otherwise.

By selling on multi-year terms, a taxpayer avoids bunching gain/income in the year of sale. Rather, recognition of gain is deferred by spreading it over a number of tax years.

The installment sale method may be used for any kind of real estate, including vacant land. The taxable part of installment payments is calculated by applying to each payment the profit percentage realized on the full transaction. This percentage is found by dividing the realized profit on the sale by the full contract price. IRS instructions should be followed for determining this percentage based on the contract price, selling price, gross profit and payments received.

Example: Real property is sold for $200,000; unadjusted basis is $132,000; selling costs are $8,000. Installment payments of $50,000 are to be made in the year of sale and in each of the next three years.

Contract price (selling price............................ $200,000

Less: Selling costs and unadjusted basis .... -140,000

Gross Profit.. $60,000

Gross Profit Percentage = $60,000 ÷ $200,000 = 30%

For the year of sale and each of the following three years, a profit of $15,000 (30% of $50,000) is reported.

Leases. Rent is taxable to the lessor as ordinary income and, for non-residential property, deductible as a business expense to the lessee. Payments by a lessee on execution of a lease may be either advance rent or a security deposit. If the former, a (non-residential) lessee has a deduction and the lessor must report the payment as income in the year paid. A security deposit remains the property of the lessee until default/forfeiture. If forfeited, the deposit is deductible by the lessee and is income to the lessor. If the lessor pays the lessee interest on the deposit, the lessee has reportable income.

If the lessee receives lease cancellation payments from the lessor, they are treated as being in exchange for the sale of the lease to the lessor. If the lease is not a capital asset, the income is ordinary income to the lessee. The lessor is treated as making an expenditure for the acquisition of a property right. The lessor's payment must be capitalized and added to the basis of the property. If the lessor receives lease cancellation payments from the lessee, the lessor has ordinary income and the lessee treats the expenditure as a current business expense.

A lessor or lessee's costs of procuring a lease (i.e., commissions, legal fees, and title expenses) must be prorated over the life of the lease. It should always be remembered that losses and expenses of lessees of residential property are considered personal and not deductible.

State Income Tax

California income tax law is patterned after the federal law. Interpretations of the federal law by the Treasury Department and the courts are usually followed in the administration of similar provisions of the California law.

Tax Credits Related to Real Estate

Residential solar energy credit. The last year a residential solar (or wind) energy state income tax credit could be claimed was 1987. Any unused credit remaining after the 1988 taxable year may be carried forward and used without restriction.

Commercial solar energy credit. California allows a credit equal to 12% of the costs paid or incurred for installing a solar energy system used for commercial purposes. The installation of the solar energy system must have occurred on or after January 1, 1987. Solar energy system means solar energy devices used to perform one (or more) of the following functions: water heating; space conditioning; production of electricity; heat processing; and solar mechanical energy.

Energy conservation. The last year an individual, bank, corporation, estate or trust could claim a state income tax credit for the cost of energy conservation measures installed on the premises of owned or leased single family residences was 1986. However, credit carryovers are allowed.

Residential rental and farm sales credit. California allows individuals a credit of 3 percent (3%) of their net capital gains from the sale or exchange of California residential rental or farm property held for more than one year but not more than five years, or 4 1/2% for such assets held more than five years.

Low-income housing credit. California followed federal law in allowing a credit for a percentage of costs incurred in constructing or rehabilitating low-income rental housing. Qualified residential rental projects were placed in service after 1986 and before 1990 and had to have either:

1. 20% or more of the combined residential units in the project occupied by families with incomes of 50% or less than area median income; or

2. 40% or more of the combined residential units occupied by families with incomes of 60% or less than area median income.

Restrictions apply on the amount of rent that may be charged to families occupying low-income units.

19 Subdivisions and Other Public Controls

If communities were allowed to grow without public controls, development would likely be accompanied by many problems: improper lot design and physical improvements; inadequate streets and parking facilities; insufficient water supplies; lack of adequate police and fire protection; deterioration of air quality; excessive noise; and inadequate utility services.

Through state laws, local master plans, zoning laws and building codes, cities and counties strive to achieve livability and protection of land values.

This chapter discusses the subdivision laws and related controls.

BASIC SUBDIVISION LAWS

The two basic California subdivision laws are the Subdivision Map Act (Government Code Sections 66410, et seq.) and the Subdivided Lands Law (Sections 11000 - 11200 of the Business and Professions Code; hereinafter, the Code).

Subdivision Map Act
The Subdivision Map Act sets forth the conditions for approval of a subdivision map and requires enactment of subdivision ordinances by which local governments have direct control over the types of subdivision projects to be undertaken and the physical improvements to be installed. This act has two major objectives:

1. To coordinate a subdivision's design (lots, street patterns, rights-of-way for drainage and sewers, etc.) with the community plan; and

2. To insure that the subdivider will properly complete the areas dedicated for public purposes, so that they will not become an undue burden upon the taxpayers of the community.

The Subdivision Map Act is discussed in detail later in this chapter.

Subdivided Lands Law
The Real Estate Commissioner (hereinafter, the Commissioner), administers the Subdivided Lands Law to protect purchasers from fraud, misrepresentation, or deceit in the initial sale of subdivided property.

With a few important exceptions, no subdivision can be offered for sale in California until the Commissioner has issued a subdivision public report. A public report includes important information and disclosures concerning the subdivision offering.

The Commissioner does not issue the public report until the subdivider has met all statutory requirements, including financial arrangements to assure completion of improvements and facilities included in the offering and a showing that the lots or parcels can be used for the purpose for which they are being offered.

SUBDIVISION DEFINITIONS

There are some differences and some similarities between the concept "subdivision" under the Subdivided Lands Law and the Subdivision Map Act. The common part of the definition for "subdivision" is "division of improved or unimproved land for the purpose of sale or lease or financing whether immediate or future."

The main differences or similarities are:

Subdivided Lands Law	*Subdivision Map Act*
5 or more lots or parcels............................	2 or more lots or parcels
improved standard residential subdivisions within city limits exempted.......................	included
a "proposed division" is included..............	"proposed division" not included
no contiguity requirement	land must be contiguous units
160 acre and larger parcels designated as such by government survey are excepted..	no exception for 160 acre and larger parcels
community apartments included	same
condominiums included	same
stock co-operatives included	not included unless 5 or more existing dwelling units converted
leasing of apartments, offices, stores or similar space in apartment building, industrial building or commercial building excepted	same
long term leasing of spaces in mobilehome parks or trailer parks included...................	leasing or financing of mobilehome parks or trailer parks not included
undivided interests included......................	not included
expressly zoned industrial or commercial subdivisions are exempt............................	included
agricultural leases included.......................	not included
time-shares included	not included
limited-equity housing cooperatives, with some exemptions, per Section 11003.4 of the Code	not included

FUNCTIONS IN LAND SUBDIVISION

This section discusses the functions of various agencies and individuals important to the subdivision process.

Private Professional Services

Typically, a subdivider will employ a team of specialists (market research analyst, tax planner, land planner, engineer, land surveyor, architect, attorney, and real estate broker) to provide valuable assistance in cost analysis, feasibility, and determination of the appropriateness of the intended land use and physical design.

Planning Commission

The California Government Code provides that the legislative body of each city and county shall, by ordinance, assign responsibility for the jurisdiction's planning program to the legislative body itself, the planning commission, the planning department, or some combination of these. Typically, local governments have, in addition to their legislative council or board, a planning department and a planning commission. Creation of a planning commission is required of counties, but is optional for cities.

Most of a planning commission's work is related to developing and maintaining the jurisdiction's general plan and reviewing and making recommendations to the legislative body on zoning and development proposals.

The planning commission's responsibility for maintenance of the general plan is underscored by the state requirement that the commission consider any general plan proposal or modification prior to action by the legislative body. By local ordinance, the planning commission reviews and makes recommendations to the legislative body on zoning proposals, subdivision and parcel maps, use permits, variances, and other development permits in furtherance of the general plan goals and policies.

Subdivision regulation is one of the major legislative and administrative tools for implementing the general plan. Government Code Section 66473.5 bars local agencies from approving a tentative map where the subdivision has been found inconsistent with the adopted general plan or any specific plan. In 1975, the Attorney General interpreted this requirement to mean that any city or county that had not adopted a general plan including the required elements set forth below could not approve subdivision maps. Other findings required by the law relate to the site's suitability, wildlife habitat and public health. The governing body may also deny approval of a map if it finds that waste discharges would exceed requirements established by the appropriate regional water quality control board.

Another major tool for implementing the local general plan is zoning. By law, the adoption and implementation of a zoning ordinance must be consistent with the adopted general plan. Charter cities are exempted from this consistency requirement although, in many instances, individual city charters include a similar stipulation.

By statute, a general plan must include the following seven elements: land use; circulation pattern; housing; conservation; open space; noise; and safety.

Lending Agencies

Because of the vital role played by financing in the success of a subdivision, the subdivider will endeavor to include the proper safeguards to insure appropriate financing. The subdivider and the engineer must be just as familiar with the requirements of the lending agencies as with those of local, state and federal control agencies. General requirements and land development standards of the FHA are described in detail in the bulletin entitled *Neighborhood Standards* (Land Planning Bulletin Ill), published by the FHA. The bulletin offers a great deal of valuable information about proper standards of design. Also it usually contains special notes relating to local conditions and requirements. A copy may be obtained from the appropriate area office. Offices are located in Sacramento, San Francisco, Los Angeles, San Diego and Santa Ana.

Title Company

After the land to be subdivided has been acquired, the title company will issue a preliminary guaranty showing the names of the persons required to sign the subdivision map as specified by the Subdivision Map Act. The title company also provides the preliminary report required by the Department of Real Estate (DRE).

One of the main services offered by many title companies is subdivision processing. They will develop much of the documentation DRE requires, notable exceptions being management documents and the homeowner association budget.

In addition to the standard title policy coverage, many lenders require affirmative insurance on encroachments, priority over possible mechanics' liens, and certain possessory and survey matters. Most California land title companies make these coverages available, but arrangements should be made before work on the subdivision is started.

COMPLIANCE AND GOVERNMENTAL CONSULTATION

Subdividers and their professional consultants must be thoroughly familiar with the state laws and also with the subdivision control ordinance in the particular community. Numerous differences exist in the various local subdivision ordinances because of a great diversity in types of communities and conditions throughout the state.

To be fully aware of the current requirements of the Commissioner, a subdivider should consult with DRE during the planning stage of a subdivision.

The federal government plays an important role in the financing of home building through its mortgage insurance program. If a developer wants a subdivision offering to include government insured or guaranteed financing, timely consultations may be necessary with the Federal Housing Administration, the Veterans Administration and any other appropriate agencies.

TYPES OF SUBDIVISIONS

Standard

A standard subdivision is a subdivision with no common or mutual rights of either ownership or use among the owners of the lots.

Common Interest

Purchasers in a common interest subdivision own or lease a separate lot, unit, or interest, along with an undivided interest or membership interest in the common area of the entire project. Normally, an association of the owners manages the common area. Condominiums, planned developments, stock cooperatives, community apartment projects and timeshare projects are types of common interest subdivisions.

A **condominium** consists of an undivided interest in common in a portion of real property coupled with a separate interest in space called a unit, the boundaries of which are described on a recorded final map, parcel map, or condominium plan in sufficient detail to locate all boundaries thereof. The description of the unit may refer to: (i) boundaries described in the recorded final map, parcel map, or condominium plan; (ii) physical boundaries, either in existence, or to be constructed, such as walls, floors, and ceilings of a structure or any portion thereof; (iii) an entire structure containing one or more units; or (iv) any combination thereof. The portion or portions of the real property held in undivided interest may be all of the real property, except for the separate interests, or may include a particular three-dimensional portion thereof, the boundaries of which are described on a recorded final map, parcel map, or condominium plan. An individual condominium may include, in addition, a separate interest in other portions of the real property. A condominium may, with respect to the duration of its enjoyment, be (1) an estate of inheritance or perpetual estate; (2) an estate for life; or (3) an estate for years, such as a leasehold or a subleasehold.

Typically, an owner of a condominium owns in fee simple the air space in which the particular unit is situated and an undivided interest in common in certain other defined portions of the whole property involved. An association and its elected governing board perform the management functions.

A **planned development** is defined in Civil Code Section 1351 (k) as consisting of parcels owned separately and lots or areas owned in common and reserved for the use of some or all of the individual lot owners. Generally, an owner's association provides management, maintenance and control of the common areas and has the power to levy assessments and enforce obligations which attach to the individual lots.

A **stock cooperative** is defined in Section 1351 (m) of the Civil Code as a corporation which is formed or availed of primarily for the purpose of holding title to improved real property, either in fee simple or for a term of years. All or substantially all of the shareholders receive a right of exclusive occupancy of a portion of the real property, which right is transferable only concurrently with the transfer of the share(s) of stock.

Most stock cooperative projects are of the apartment house type, operated by a board of directors and including community recreation facilities. The homeowners' governing association is usually a nonprofit mutual benefit corporation.

A **limited equity housing cooperative** is a corporation which meets the criteria of a stock cooperative and complies with the requirements of Section 33007.5 of the Health and Safety Code. To assure that limited equity housing cooperatives provide decent housing for low and moderate income families, the Health and Safety Code mandates the following conditions:

1. The corporation holds title as a nonprofit public benefit corporation pursuant to the Corporations Code **OR** the corporation holds title (or a leasehold of at least 20 years) subject to conditions which will result in reversion to a public or charitable entity upon dissolution/termination.

2. Any resale of a unit shall not exceed the sum of the original consideration paid by the first occupant, the value of any authorized improvement to the unit and an increment based upon an inflation factor, not to exceed 10% per year.

3. The "corporate equity" can only be applied for the benefit of the corporation or a charitable purpose.

4. The management documents for the corporation can be amended only by a vote of at least 2/3 of the owners.

Section 11003.4 (b) of the Code exempts a limited equity housing cooperative from the requirements of the Subdivided Lands Law under the following conditions:

1. At least 50% of the development cost (or $100,000, whichever is less) is financed singly or in combination by governmental agencies listed in Section 11003.4 (b)(1) **OR** the property was purchased from the Department of Transportation for development of the cooperative and is subject to a regulatory agreement approved by the Department of Housing and Community Development for the term of the permanent financing, whatever the source of the financing.

2. No more than 20% of the total development cost of a limited equity mobilehome park (or 10% of any other type of limited equity housing cooperative) is provided by purchasers.

3. A regulatory agreement provides for: (a) assurances of completion of common areas and facilities; (b) governing instruments for the organization and operation of the cooperative by the members; (c) an adequate budget for maintenance and management of the cooperative; (d) distribution of a report to any prospective purchaser, detailing the financial status of the cooperative and the rights and obligations of members.

4. The agency which signs the regulatory agreement is satisfied that the governing documents [as specified in Section 11003.4 (b)(4)] provide adequate protection for the rights of cooperative members.

5. The attorney for the recipient of the financing or subsidy shall provide to the agency signing the regulatory agreement a legal opinion that the cooperative meets the requirements of Section 33007.5 of the Health and Safety Code and the conditions for exemption set forth in Section 11003.4 (b) of the Code.

Residents sometimes form a limited equity housing cooperative to purchase a mobilehome park.

In a **community apartment project**, a purchaser receives an undivided interest in the land coupled with the right of exclusive occupancy of an apartment located thereon. The owners elect a governing board which operates and maintains the project.

A **time-share project** involves long-term rights to use real property for short-term use periods into which the offering has been divided (e.g., the right to use a dwelling unit for two weeks of each year for the next 10 years). In some cases, a time-share purchaser receives an undivided interest in the real property (a time-share estate) as well as the periodic use right. Or, a purchaser may acquire only a right to use (a time-share use). In either case, the right to use may be specified (e.g., the first two weeks in July), or set on a first reserved, first served basis.

Section 11004.5 of the Code provides that the terms "subdivided lands" and "subdivision" include a time-share project, as defined in Section 11003.5, consisting of 12 or more time-share estates or time-share uses. To qualify, time-share uses must have terms of five years or more, or terms of less than five years which also include options to renew.

An offering of (12 or more) time-share use rights, whether or not assignable or irrevocable, in real property other than structural dwelling places does not constitute a subdivision. A time-share estate offering of 12 or more interests in real property other than structural dwelling places (e.g., campgrounds and recreational vehicle parks) is a subdivision.

A developer of a time-share subdivision located outside of California, but within the United States, must obtain a permit pursuant to Section 10250, et seq. of the Code before offering the time-share interests in California.

(A real estate license is required of a person negotiating in this state, for another and for compensation, the sale of *any* time-share interest. This position is consistent with a Court of Appeal decision which declared that memberships in a club conferring time-share use rights in condominiums constituted interests in real property which the court characterized as being in the nature of a lease.)

Undivided Interest
A partial/fractional interest in an entire parcel of land is called an undivided interest. The land itself has not been divided, but its ownership has been divided.

The creation, for sale, lease, or financing, of five or more undivided interests in land, whether or not improved, constitutes a subdivision and a public report is required prior to marketing the interests. Section 11000.1(b) of the Code provides for several exemptions, including purchase of the undivided interests by people related by blood or marriage or by ten or fewer persons who: are informed concerning the risks of ownership; are not purchasing the property for resale; and waive the protections offered by the Subdivided Lands Law.

COMPLIANCE WITH THE SUBDIVIDED LANDS LAW

The Subdivided Lands Law is designed to protect purchasers from misrepresentation, deceit and fraud in subdivision sales. This is accomplished in two ways: by making it illegal to commence sales until DRE determines that the offering meets certain affirmative standards and issues a public report; and by disclosing in the public report pertinent facts about the property and the terms of the offering.

Affirmative Standards

Affirmative standards deal with two major aspects of the proposed subdivision offering:

1. suitability for intended use; and

2. fair dealing regarding the sale or lease of the offering.

The Subdivided Lands Law requires that the Commissioner deny issuance of a public report if the offering is not suitable for the use proposed by the subdivider. The suitability test is, of course, paramount in residential offerings. These must include vehicular access, a potable water source, available utilities, offsite improvements, etc.

To insure fair dealing and receipt of the subdivision interest for which the purchaser has bargained, the affirmative standards include: the security of buyer's deposit money; satisfactory arrangements to clear mechanic's liens; release of the interest from any blanket encumbrance (mortgage lien); and conveyance of proper title.

Disclosures in Public Report

The public report discloses significant information about the subdivision. Disclosures in the public report may alert consumers to any negative aspects of the offering (e.g., unusual present or future costs; hazards or adverse environmental factors; unusual restrictions or easements; necessary special permits for improvements; unusual financing arrangements).

Filing Notice of Intention/Application

Before subdivided land can be offered for sale or lease, a Notice of Intention must be filed with the Commissioner. The Notice of Intention is combined with a Questionnaire and Application and must be completed on forms provided by DRE. The questionnaire is specifically designed to obtain pertinent details about all aspects of the offering.

Usually, the owner files the application for public report. Anybody filing on behalf of the owner must furnish DRE with the owner's written authorization to do so.

Use of Public Report

A copy of the public report must be delivered to a prospective purchaser, who must have time to read the report before any offer is made to purchase or lease a lot or interest covered by the report. The prospective purchaser will sign a receipt for the report on a form approved by the Commissioner. The subdivider must retain the receipt for three years for the Commissioner's inspection.

As stated in a notice required to be posted in the sales office, the subdivider must, upon request, give a copy of the public report to any member of the public.

Violations - Penalties

In addition to disciplinary actions which may be imposed by the Commissioner against licensees for violations of the Subdivided Lands Law, anyone who willfully violates or fails to comply with Sections 11010, 11010.1, 11010.8, 11013.1, 11013.2, 11013.4 11018.2, 11018.7, 11019 or 11022 of the Code shall be guilty of a public offense punishable by a maximum fine of not to exceed $10,000, or up to one year's confinement in county jail or in state prison or by both fine and imprisonment.

The district attorney of each county in the state is charged with prosecuting violators.

Questionnaire Requirements
DRE has developed questionnaires to elicit subdivision information. Some responses to a questionnaire will be in the form of documentation. Other information can be filled in from the subdivider's records.

Subdivision Filing Fees
Maximum fees for filing applications under the Subdivided Lands Law are prescribed by statute. The Commissioner may, by regulation, prescribe fees lower than the statutory maximums when it has been determined that the lower fees are sufficient to offset costs and expenses to administer the Subdivided Lands Law. The Commissioner must hold a hearing at least once each year to consider subdivision filing fees.

A person interested in current fees should contact either the Sacramento or Los Angeles Subdivision Office.

Where to File
Subdivision filings must be made at the DRE district office responsible for the area where the subdivision is located. There are subdivision offices in Sacramento and Los Angeles.

Filings for undivided interest subdivisions, certain qualified limited-equity housing cooperatives and time-share offerings must be made at the Sacramento office.

Questionnaire Forms - Contents
DRE has developed different questionnaires for standard subdivisions, common interest subdivisions, time-shares, and stock cooperatives.

Some of the areas common to the questionnaires are:

1.   on- or off-site conditions which may affect the intended use of the land;

2.   provisions for essential utilities, such as water, electricity, and sewage disposal;

3.   on-site improvements, existing or proposed;

4.   the condition of title, including any restrictions or reservations affecting building, use or occupancy;

5.   the terms and conditions of sales or lease;

6.   the ability of the subdivider to deliver the interest contracted for;

7.   the method of conveyance; and

8.   any representations of "guarantees" or "warranties" made as part of a sales program.

Exceptions

A Notice of Intention and Application is not required for a standard subdivision within city limits if the lots are to be sold improved with completed residential structures and other improvements necessary for occupancy, or with financial arrangements, satisfactory to the city, to secure completion of those other improvements, provided the subdivider has complied with Sections 11013.1, 11013.2 and 11013.4 of the Code.

Also excepted are:

- subdivisions expressly zoned for, and limited in use to, commercial and industrial purposes; and,

- subdivided land offered for sale or lease by a state agency, including the University of California, a local agency, or other public agency.

Filing Packages

When filing for a final public report, a subdivider may choose one of three methods, each relating to the level of completeness of the filing package.

Minimum filing package method. This is the basic method. This filing must meet all the minimum requirements itemized in the questionnaire, including payment of the appropriate fee and appending of the supporting documents. If a package submitted fails to satisfy the minimum filing requirements, the application, package and fee are returned to the applicant with no processing by DRE. Satisfying the minimum requirements enables DRE to: (a) process the filing for issuance of a "normal" preliminary public report, if requested to do so; and (b) within 15 days after receipt of the filing package, notify the subdivider whether (1) the filing also satisfies *Substantially Complete Filing Package* requirements or (2) will be held in a pending file until the filing is made substantially complete by additional information or documentation listed on the Quantitative Deficiency Notice.

Substantially complete application method. This method requires the applicant to satisfy all quantitative requirements for the Minimum Filing Package plus furnish virtually all other documentation needed to issue the final public report, except the recorded map, recorded CC&Rs, certain bonds, etc. Once the filing is substantially complete, qualitative processing begins and DRE must, within 20 days for a standard subdivision or 60 days for a common interest subdivision, provide the applicant with a Qualitative Deficiency Notice listing any substantive corrections to be made in the filing package.

Totally complete filing method. This method requires that the initial package submitted be certified by the subdivider to be complete and correct as originally filed. If it is, DRE can expedite issuance of the final public report.

Preliminary Public Report

A subdivider wishing to begin a marketing effort prior to the issuance of a final public report may request a preliminary public report based on the submission of a qualifying minimum application filing package. A preliminary public report does not provide the same disclosures as a final report and only allows the subdivider to accept reservations from potential purchasers. Reservation money must be fully refundable and kept in an escrow.

Preliminary public reports have a one-year term and may be renewed.

Amended Public Report
If during the life (five years) of a final public report, the subdivision offering undergoes a "material change" (e.g., change of ownership, change in purchase money handling procedure, change in use, etc.), the subdivider must apply for an amended public report.

Renewed Public Report
If at the end of five years the subdivision is not sold out, the subdivider can apply for a renewal of the final public report for an additional five-year term.

Conditional Public Report
An applicant for an original, renewed, or amended final public report may also apply for a conditional public report authorizing the subdivider to enter into binding contracts for the sale of lots or units even though the project has not yet completely qualified for issuance of a final public report. DRE may issue a conditional public report under the circumstances described in Section 11018.12 of the Code and Commissioner's Regulation 2790.2.

HANDLING OF PURCHASERS' DEPOSIT MONEY

Common to all types of subdivision filings are the requirements for the handling of the purchasers' deposit money as set forth in Sections 11013, 11013.1, 11013.2 and 11013.4 of the Code.

Blanket Encumbrance
A blanket encumbrance exists when more than one lot in a subdivision is made security for the payment of a trust deed note or other lien or encumbrance.

When, as is usually the case, there is no agreement for unconditional release of individual parcels from a blanket encumbrance, the owner or subdivider must comply with one of the following conditions:

1. Impoundment of the purchase money, in an escrow depository acceptable to the Commissioner, until a proper release is obtained from the blanket encumbrance or one of the parties defaults and there is a determination as to disposition of the money or the owner or subdivider orders the return of the money to the purchaser or lessee.

2. Title is placed in trust, under an agreement acceptable to the Commissioner, until a proper release from the blanket encumbrance is obtained and the trustee conveys title to the purchaser. This alternative is not practical if the lots are to be sold by real property sales contract.

3. The subdivider furnishes a bond to the State of California in an amount and subject to such terms as the Commissioner may approve. The bond must provide for the return of purchase money if a proper release from the blanket encumbrance is not obtained.

The Commissioner may approve other methods which protect purchasers' payments until receipt of title or other interest contracted for.

No Blanket Encumbrance
Even if a subdivision is not subject to a blanket encumbrance, the deposit money of the purchaser must be impounded in an escrow or trust account unless the subdivider elects an alternative method.

The most common alternative to impounding is an acceptable bond to the State of California to assure return of the deposit money if the seller does not deliver title within the time specified in the contract. Note that a bond cannot be used to secure reservation deposits taken under a preliminary public report.

As in the case of a subdivision subject to a blanket encumbrance, the Commissioner is given discretionary power to approve alternative plans submitted by subdividers which assure adequate protection of purchasers' deposits.

Impound Requirements - Real Property Sale Contracts
A real property sales contract is defined in Section 2985 of the California Civil Code as an agreement wherein one party agrees to convey title to real property to another party upon the satisfaction of specified conditions and which does not require conveyance of title within one year from the date of formation of the contract.

When lots in a subdivision are to be sold using contracts of sale, the subdivider will usually convey the subdivision in trust as detailed in Commissioner's Regulation 2791.9. This is an acceptable alternative under Section 11013.2(d) or Section 11013.4(f) of the Code.

COVENANTS, CONDITIONS AND RESTRICTIONS

Subdividers, mortgage lenders, government agencies, and home buyers need a means of assurance that the nature of a subdivision will remain unchanged. The mechanism most commonly used in California to assure this protection is a document known as the Declaration of Covenants, Conditions and Restrictions, (CC&Rs). Conveyances are made subject to CC&Rs.

The traditional purpose of deed restrictions has been to control land use by requiring structures to be a certain size, or by restricting types of use.

The importance of restrictions has shifted to a broader purpose as the number of common interest developments has increased. CC&Rs are used not only to control land use, but to prescribe the very nature of the common interest subdivision; to provide for maintenance of the project; to set down rules for behavior of persons; and as a vehicle for raising money for maintenance, repair and replacement of the project's components.

Restrictions may be set out in the deed to the land, which is frequently the case when the restrictions are quite simple. When the CC&Rs are complex, as they usually are for a common interest subdivision, they are best set out in a separate document. There are technical requirements to be met if the CC&Rs are to be effective. Therefore, developers usually hire experienced lawyers to draft CC&Rs.

Common interest subdivisions almost invariably have a homeowners' association to carry out the mandates of the CC&Rs. Pursuant to the Subdivided Lands Law, the Commissioner has adopted regulations that require reasonable arrangements in CC&Rs and the other governing instruments for a common interest subdivision.

Often, a title report will disclose that a parcel of land is subject to restrictions recorded years before. An attorney should examine them to discover whether their provisions will hinder the intended development. There are frequently set-back provisions, limits on density and other provisions which cannot be eliminated.

ADDITIONAL PROVISIONS

Material Changes

Any material change in the subdivision itself, or in the program for marketing the subdivision interests, or its handling after the filing of the Application and Questionnaire is made or the public report is issued must be reported to the Commissioner. This not only includes physical changes, such as changing the lot or street lines, but any new condition or development which may affect the utility or value of the subdivision or the terms of the offering. Basically, a material change is anything that results in the public report or questionnaire not reflecting the true facts/conditions of the subdivision offering.

Changes in contracts, deeds, etc., used in the sale of lots or units in a subdivision may constitute a material change to be reported to the Commissioner. The purpose of reporting is to enable the Commissioner to revise the public report and to set forth the true conditions existing in the subdivision after any material change has occurred or take other action as warranted.

For a limited time after subdivision sales begin, amendments to the management documents of common interest subdivisions are invalid without the prior written consent of the Commissioner, if the change would affect an owner's rights to ownership, possession or use in any material way. (Code Section 11018.7)

The owner of a (non-exempt) subdivision must report to the Commissioner the sale of five or more parcels or units to a single purchaser.

Failure to report material changes not only violates the law but may also furnish a basis for rescission of purchases through court action.

Special Districts

If the subdivision lies wholly or partially within a special district such as a community services district, resort improvement district, county water district or similar public or semi-public district, which has the power to tax, issue general obligation bonds, and raise money by other means, for the purpose of financing, acquiring, constructing, maintaining or operating improvements for the subdivision or for the purpose of extending public or other services to this subdivision, the subdivider will submit a Special Assessment District and Special Improvement District Questionnaire identifying the district, the amount and term of indebtedness, the effect on the tax rate and the total assessment and annual assessment per lot, unit or parcel in the subdivision. This same questionnaire elicits similar information about districts empowered to levy "special taxes." The inquiry is not concerned with school districts, irrigation districts, fire protection districts or similar districts *not* formed for the particular purpose of providing services to this and connected projects.

Special Regulations for Common Interest Subdivisions

A number of regulations specify the documents and statements required for a planned development, community apartment, stock cooperative, or condominium project. These requirements are set forth in Sections 2792.1 through Section 2792.32 of the Commissioner's Regulations. Examples include "reasonable arrangements" for:

1.   levying regular and special assessments against each owner;

2.   the governing body's distribution of annual financial and budget information to all members;

3.   members' meetings, voting rights, governing body powers, inspection of the association's books and records; and,

4.   establishing maintenance and reserve funds.

Environmental Impact Reports

An environmental impact report (EIR) may be required by local government prior to approval of the map for the subdivision.

A subdivision developer should determine as early as possible (preferably prior to filing a tentative map) whether an EIR will be required for the project.

The California Coastal Act

The California Coastal Act allows local governments to adopt programs for coastal conservation. Generally, the Coastal Zone runs the length of the state from the sea inland about 1,000 yards, with wider spots in coastal estuarine, habitat and recreational areas. A subdivider planning to develop a tract of land within the Coastal Zone must obtain a coastal development permit or an exemption.

Mineral, Oil and Gas Subdivisions

The definition of mineral, oil and gas subdivisions covers division of land into parcels of any size, even when each parcel created is 160 acres or more in size. No public report on a mineral, oil or gas subdivision has been issued for a number of years.

Advertising Criteria

Guidelines for subdividers in the advertising and promotion of subdivisions are contained in Section 2799.1 of the Commissioner's Regulations. These guidelines are applicable in determining whether advertising for sale or lease of subdivision interests is false or misleading within the meaning of those terms defined in Sections 10140, 10177(c), 11022 and 17500 of the Code.

Nothing contained in these standards shall limit the authority of the Commissioner to take formal action against an owner, subdivider or agent for the use of false or misleading advertising of a type not specifically described in these guidelines.

The DRE publication *Guidelines for Subdivision Advertising* (R/E 631) contains advertising requirements and prohibitions. RE 631 may be obtained from the DRE's Sacramento Subdivision Office

Desist and Refrain Orders

If the Commissioner finds that a person is violating any provision of the Subdivided Lands Law or the pertinent regulations or if the further sale or lease of lots in a given subdivision would constitute grounds for denial of the issuance of a public report, the Commissioner may order the immediate cessation of such violations or the immediate termination of selling or leasing of the property by the issuance of an Order to Desist and Refrain (D & R) from such activity.

When the Commissioner issues a D & R, the person named therein has the right, within 30 days after its receipt, to file a written request for a hearing to contest the order. The Commissioner must assign the request to conduct a hearing to the Office of Administrative Hearings. If the hearing is not commenced within 15 days after receipt of the request or on the date to which it is continued by mutual agreement, or if the decision of the Commissioner is not rendered within 30 days after completion of the hearings, the D & R is deemed vacated.

Out-of-State Subdivisions

A developer who wishes to offer in California subdivision interests (other than in a time-share) located outside of California but within the United States must register the project with DRE and include certain disclaimers in advertising and sales contracts.

A developer who wishes to offer in California subdivision interests located outside the United States is not required to register with DRE but must include a disclaimer in advertising and sales contracts.

Basically, the disclaimers mentioned above state that DRE has not examined the offering and urge a prospective purchaser to seek the advice of an attorney who is familiar with real estate and development law in the state or country where the subdivision is located.

As discussed earlier, a developer of an out-of-state (but within the United States) time-share subdivision must obtain a permit from DRE before offering the subdivision interests in California.

GROUNDS FOR DENIAL OF PUBLIC REPORT

If grounds exist, the Commissioner will deny issuance of a public report and no offerings or sales can be made until the subdivider has remedied the unsatisfactory conditions and the report is issued.

The grounds for denial are listed in Section 11018 of the Code.

Section 11018.5 applies only to common interest subdivisions and lists standards which, if met, mandate issuance of the public report if there are no other grounds for denial. Grounds for denial include the failure to meet these standards.

A subdivider objecting to an order of denial may request a hearing pursuant to Section 11018.3 of the Code.

SUBDIVISION MAP ACT

The following is a discussion of the requirements of the Subdivision Map Act (Government Code Section 66410, et seq.).

A "subdivision" is, with a few exceptions, any division of contiguous land for the purpose of sale, lease or financing. Condominium projects, community apartments, and the conversion of five or more existing dwelling units to a stock cooperative are included.

Generally, the subdivider must prepare a map for approval by the local government agency.

PRELIMINARY PLANNING CONSIDERATIONS

The local jurisdiction, usually through its planning department, must find that a proposed subdivision is in conformance with the applicable general and specific plans for the area. The local agency must deny approval of a subdivision project if it finds that the site is not physically suitable for the proposed development. Water, drainage, soil and sewerage problems can limit the feasibility of a subdivision.

Natural Features
The subdivider and local agency must consider the impact of the proposed subdivision on trees, streams, lakes, ponds and views. Potential for significant adverse effects on the environment will occasion review of the project under the Environmental Quality Act.

Soils Report
A preliminary soils report, prepared by a registered California civil engineer and based upon adequate test borings, is required for every subdivision for which a final map is required, and may be required by local ordinance for other subdivisions. The law does provide for a waiver by the city or county under certain conditions. When a soils report has been prepared, that fact should be noted on the final map with the date of the report and the name of the engineer.

Neighboring Property
The local agency must disapprove a subdivision if it finds that the subdivision or the improvements are likely to cause serious public health problems. Undesirable surroundings can also be detrimental to the success of a new residential subdivision. If the adjacent site is a residential development, planners must study its general character and design. The design characteristics, building techniques, and street layout should blend and be compatible with those planned for the new subdivision. Noxious industrial uses, 24-hour factory operations, noises, fumes, railroad yards, and similar factors render a residential subdivision on the adjoining property highly undesirable. Cemeteries, penal institutions, mental institutions, dairy farms, fuel storage tanks, and many other types of land use may also render a neighboring site undesirable for residential development.

The developer should check with the local planning commission, the Division of Highways, the Federal Aviation Agency, and the California Division of Aeronautics regarding location of proposed industries, factories, freeways, or airport facilities.

Drainage

Local jurisdictions have adopted master plans for drainage and requirements for grading of subdivisions and installation of drainage facilities to protect purchasers from the hazards of uncontrolled runoff of storm waters, erosion, deposits of silt and debris, and flooding. The developer must consider the cost and feasibility of these measures.

The local agency may issue a flood hazard and drainage report on any subdivision proposed within its jurisdiction.

Flood Hazard

When a flood hazard is found to exist, the flood hazard report will describe the degree and the frequency of flood hazard using the following terminology:

1. Degree of Hazard

Inundation: Ponded water, or water in motion, of sufficient depth to damage property due to the mere presence of water or the depositing of silt.

Flood: Flowing water having sufficient velocity to transport or deposit debris, to scour the surface soil, or to dislodge or damage buildings. It also indicates erosion of the banks of watercourses.

Possible Flood: Possible flood hazard of uncertain degree.

Sheet Overflow: Overflow of water in minor depths, either quiescent or flowing, at velocities less than those necessary to produce serious scour. This type of overflow is a nuisance rather than a menace to the property affected.

Ponding of Local Storm Water: Standing water in local depressions. Originates on or in the vicinity of the property and due to the condition of the ground is unable to reach a street or drainage course.

2. Frequency

Frequent: Flooding which may occur, on average, more than once in 10 years.

Infrequent: Flooding which may occur once in 10 years or more.

Remote: Flooding which is dependent upon conditions which do not lend themselves to frequency analysis, such as break of levee, obstruction of a channel, etc.

Alquist-Priolo Earthquake Fault Zoning Act

This law (Public Resources Code Sections 2621, et seq.) is designed to control development in the vicinity of hazardous earthquake faults.

On official maps, the State Geologist delineates earthquake fault zones around traces of potentially active faults. The zones are usually one quarter of a mile in width.

The maps may be consulted at any district office of the California Division of Mines & Geology or at the county assessor or recorder's office.

Real estate licensees who are involved in property transactions located near special studies zones should obtain information about that zone.

Section 2621.9 of the Public Resources Code provides that any person who is acting as an agent for a seller of real property which is located within a delineated earthquake fault zone, or the seller if acting without an agent, shall disclose to any prospective purchaser the fact that the property is located within a delineated earthquake fault zone.

The developer of a subdivision lying within a delineated earthquake fault zone and subject to the Subdivision Map Act must obtain special approval by a city or county in accordance with policies and criteria established by the State Mining and Geology Board.

Sewage Disposal

County and/or city engineers will determine if it is feasible to connect the proposed subdivision to existing sewage facilities. This will depend mainly on the capacity, location, and the type of disposal used. If there is no existing system, the developer must plan for an alternative: typically septic tank systems approved by the local health officer or by the State Department of Health Services if there is no health officer. The subdivision engineer must conduct careful soil analysis and percolation tests.

Water Supply

For a residential subdivision, the subdivider must ascertain the feasibility of connecting to an existing public water supply. Normally, the utility company determines the required size of connections to supply an area and to provide for future extensions.

The developer must consider the quantity of water needed for a given site, the population served and average daily use for all purposes, along with maintenance of pressure at fire hydrants.

If there is no local water company, the subdivider must investigate alternate sources. The creation of a special water district is one possibility.

Water quality must meet the standard of the local health department or the State Department of Health Services.

In response to concern for the quality, conservation, control, and utilization of the state's water resources, the Legislature enacted the *Porter-Cologne Water Quality Control Act* (Water Code Sections 13000 et seq.), which is administered by nine regional control boards within the State Water Quality Control Board. The following provision (Section 13266 of the Water Code) is of particular importance to subdividers:

> Pursuant to such regulations as the regional board may prescribe, each city, county, or city and county shall notify the regional board of the filing of a tentative subdivision map, or of any application for a building permit which may involve the discharge of waste, other than discharges into a community sewer system and discharges from dwellings involving five-family units or less.

Other Utilities

The developer must arrange telephone, gas, and electricity service to the site.

The developer should consult with the city or county engineer and with the power company regarding the necessity or desirability of a street lighting system.

The Public Utilities Commission has mandated that undergrounding be used for all extensions of electricity and telephone service in residential subdivisions.

Dedication of Streets and Easements

The local government may require the dedication of sufficient land in the subdivision for streets, alleys, public utility easements, drainage easements, access easements (e.g., for public access to adjacent shoreline) and bicycle paths.

Public Parks and Recreational Facilities

The governing body of a city or county may enact ordinances requiring the subdivider to make contributions for public parks or recreational facilities. The contributions may be in the form of land or money. If the subdivision contains fifty or fewer parcels or units, the subdivider may be required to pay a dollar amount proportionate to the number of parcels in the proposed tract.

If there are more than fifty parcels in the subdivision, the local ordinance may require dedication of a portion of the property for public use as a park or other recreational facility. There is no provision for reimbursement to the subdivider for the cost of acquisition or improvements to the parcel or parcels dedicated for public use. Industrial subdivisions are exempt from these requirements.

Dedication of School Sites

Under the provisions of the Map Act and the School Facilities Act, the local ordinance may require dedication of land for public schools. The requirement for dedication must be imposed at the time of approval of the tentative map. The school district must, within 30 days after the requirement has been imposed, agree to accept the dedication. Absent timely agreement, the requirement terminates automatically.

The school district accepting dedication of the land pays for it at its original cost to the subdivider, plus the sum of the cost of improvements, interest, taxes and any other costs which had been incurred in maintenance of the site.

An ordinance of this nature is applicable only to a subdivider who has owned the land for less than ten years prior to filing a tentative map.

Airport within Subdivision

A developer may consider including aircraft landing facilities, particularly in a remote planned development. Under certain conditions, the Division of Aeronautics may not require a permit but the facility must still meet certain minimum standards. The developer should contact the Division of Aeronautics at the beginning of project planning.

Preapplication Conferences

The developer and the planning commission technical staff may consider the above items in conferences *before* preparation of a tentative map. Obviously, a coordinated beginning will save time in securing subdivision approval and may avoid costly changes in the subdivision set-up.

BASIC STEPS IN FINAL MAP PREPARATION AND APPROVAL

1. Feasibility analysis of subdivision, based on economics, location and physical survey.

2. Preliminary discussions to learn requirements of agencies having jurisdiction over the project.

3. Preparation of tentative map (copy sent to coastal commission if project is in coastal zone).

4. Tentative map submitted to local jurisdiction (e.g., planning commission, city clerk) and, if applicable, government loan agency (e.g., FHA).

5. Copy of approved tentative map sent to DRE with application for public report.

6. Preparation and signing of final map.

7. Final map submitted to planning commission and government loan agency.

8. Approved final map recorded.

9. Copy of approved final map sent to DRE.

TYPES OF MAPS

For the most part, the Subdivision Map Act requires tentative and final maps for subdivisions which create five or more parcels, five or more condominiums, a community apartment project containing five or more interests, or the conversion of a dwelling into a stock cooperative of five or more dwelling units. The exceptions are included in Government Code Section 66426.

Generally, the Subdivision Map Act requires a tentative map and a parcel map if a final map is not required. Government Code Section 66428 includes exceptions and waivers to the parcel map requirement.

TENTATIVE MAP PREPARATION

A tentative map usually shows the design of the proposed subdivision and the existing topographic conditions. Design includes street alignment, proposed grades and widths, alignment and widths of easements and rights-of-way for drainage and sanitary sewers, and minimum lot area and width. To the extent possible, the design of the subdivision must also provide for future passive (i.e., natural) heating and cooling. This requirement does not apply to condominiums converted from existing structures. Many jurisdictions require that a tentative map be based upon an accurate or final survey by a registered civil engineer, licensed land surveyor, or professional planner. (The survey for a *final* map must be the product of either a registered civil engineer or licensed surveyor.)

The local subdivision ordinance usually stipulates that the tentative map contain:

1. A legal description sufficient to define the boundaries of the proposed tract;

2. The locations, names, and existing widths of all adjoining highways, streets, and ways;

3.   The proposed use of the property;

4.   The width and proposed grades of all highways, streets and ways within the proposed subdivision;

5.   The width and approximate location of all existing and proposed easements for roads, drainage, sewers and other public utility purposes;

6.   The tentative lot layout and dimensions of each lot;

7.   The approximate locations of all areas subject to inundations or storm water overflow and the locations, widths, and direction of flow of all watercourses;

8.   The source of water supply;

9.   The proposed method of sewage disposal;

10. The proposed public areas, if any; and

11. The approximate contours when topography controls street layout.

TENTATIVE MAP FILING

Processing the Map
After preparing a tentative map and meeting prefiling requirements, a subdivider files the map with the planning department, the clerk of the city council or the board of supervisors, as the particular jurisdiction requires. Typically, a large jurisdiction will have a planning department which will study the map and report on the design and improvements of the proposed tract. The road department, health department, flood control district, parks and recreation department, the local school authority and the city or county surveyor will also review the map. A city or county adjacent to the area in which the proposed tract is located may desire to make recommendations regarding map approval. If the tract is bounded or traversed by a state highway, the District Engineer of the Division of Highways of the State Department of Transportation will also review the map. If the subdivision lies in the Coastal Zone, as defined in Section 30103 of the Public Resources Code, the local jurisdiction will send a copy of the tentative map to the California Coastal Zone Conservation Commission. The notified officials study the map with regard to their special concerns and report their findings to the planning department. The reports may recommend approval, conditional approval, or disapproval. The subdivider may meet with representatives of all interested departments to discuss the proposed tract and the conditions recommended for approval. After review by its technical staff, the local jurisdiction schedules a public hearing on the map.

Basis for Approval or Denial
The local jurisdiction will not normally approve a tentative map unless the proposed design and improvements conform to the applicable general and specific plans, including acceptable population density, physical suitability, and health and environmental considerations. In many cases, approval is conditioned upon changes to the development plan.

Appeal
The subdivider has 10 days from the date of any adverse action with respect to a tentative map to file an appeal.

Upon the filing of an appeal, the local jurisdiction must set the matter for a hearing to be held within 30 days after the appeal is filed and render its decision within 10 days after the hearing.

If the legislative body fails to act on the appeal within the time periods mentioned above, the tentative map is deemed approved insofar as it complies with the Subdivision Map Act and the local ordinance. However, the local ordinance may give interested persons the right to file a complaint and have it heard by the governing body.

Vesting Tentative Maps and Development Agreements

Section 66498.1 of the Government Code provides that a subdivider can obtain approval of a *vesting* tentative map with certain rights to proceed with development in substantial compliance with specified ordinances, policies and standards in effect at the time that map is approved.

Another way to secure development rights is by agreement between the developer and the local jurisdiction (Government Code Sections 65864, et seq.). Entering into a development agreement is a discretionary act.

FINAL MAP

Prior to expiration of a tentative map, a subdivider must prepare and record a final map.

Taxes and Assessments

Before filing a final map, a subdivider must file with the clerk of the governing body a certificate showing that no liens against the tract exist for unpaid state, county, municipal, or local taxes or special assessments collected as taxes. Taxes or special assessments which are a lien that are not yet payable are excepted but the developer must file a certificate showing an estimate of the amount of these taxes or special assessments and a bond or cash deposit to insure payment.

Improvements

Prior to approval of a final map, the subdivider must improve or agree to improve portions of land to be used for public or private streets, highways, and easements necessary for vehicular traffic and drainage. The developer must secure with a bond or cash deposit any agreement to make these improvements. The developer and the local jurisdiction may contract to begin proceedings for creation of a special assessment district for the financing and construction of the improvements. The developer must secure the contract with a performance bond or cash deposit.

Final Map Filing

A developer may file a final map for approval after meeting all conditions and having all certificates signed.

Provided a final map meets the requirements of the Map Act and of the local subdivision ordinance, the local jurisdiction will approve it at its next meeting after the filing unless the subdivider and the governing body agree to a time extension for some final corrections to the map.

Final Map Recordation

After the local jurisdiction approves a final map, it is accepted for recordation. A copy is transmitted by the clerk of the appropriate governing body to the recorder. At the time of recordation, the subdivider must furnish a certificate of title establishing that the parties consenting to recordation are those having record title interest in the land.

PARCEL MAP

A parcel map, prepared by or under the direction of a registered civil engineer or licensed land surveyor, must include:

1.   the boundaries of the land included within the subdivision;

2.   the streets;

3.   each parcel, numbered or otherwise designated;

4.   a certificate, signed and acknowledged by all parties having any record title interest in the real property subdivided, consenting to the preparation and recordation of the parcel map.

A parcel map must satisfy any additional requirements of the local subdivision ordinance.

OTHER PUBLIC CONTROLS

The basic regulation of the housing and construction industries is accomplished by three laws: the State Housing Law (Health and Safety Code Section 17910, et seq.); local building codes; and the Contractors' State License Law (Business and Professions Code Section 7000, et seq.).

State Housing Law

The State Housing Law, administered by the Codes and Standards Division of the Department of Housing and Community Development, provides minimum construction and occupancy requirements for dwellings.

Construction regulations under this statewide act are handled by local building inspectors, while occupancy and sanitation regulations are enforced by local health officers. Typical procedure for new construction or building alterations requires initial application to the local building inspector for a building permit.

The application must be accompanied by plans, specifications, and plot plan. After examination of the application and accompanying exhibits and revision where necessary, the corrected application is approved and a building permit is issued. No construction or alterations can be commenced prior to issuance of a building permit.

Local Building Codes

In 1970, the Legislature amended the State Housing Law to make the Uniform Housing Code, Uniform Building Code, Uniform Plumbing Code, Uniform Mechanical Code, and National Electric Code applicable in lieu of local building codes. The law now provides that the Regulations of the Commission of Housing and Community Development under the State Housing Law shall impose substantially the same requirements as the most recent edition of these codes.

Local government retains only the power to determine local use zoning requirements, local fire zones, building setback, side and rear yard requirements and property line requirements. (Health and Safety Code Section 17922(b)). Local variances are permitted only if based on an express finding that local conditions make them reasonably necessary. Materials and design which comply with the uniform codes but are determined in fact to be unsafe (for example "pigtailing" copper to aluminum wire) may be prohibited by the local authorities.

In 1969, by the California Factory Built Housing Law (Health & Safety Code Section 19960 et seq.), the Legislature provided for regulation of factory built housing by the Department of Housing and Community Development. The standards must be reasonably consistent with the most recent editions of the uniform codes mentioned above. Local governments may elect by ordinance to take over the function of in-plant inspections within their territorial limits in accordance with the standards set by the commission.

Local government supervises on-site installation of factory built housing.

Contractors' State License Law
Under the Contractors' State License Law, every person who engages in the business of a contractor in this state must be licensed by the Contractors' State License Board. Licensing exemptions exist only for public entities, public utilities, oil and gas operations, certain construction operations related to agriculture, minor work not exceeding $300, and an owner's own work unless the owner intends to offer the property for sale within one year of completion.

Contractors must meet certain experience and knowledge qualifications and must post a bond or cash deposit to the State of California for the benefit of persons damaged by the contractor.

A contractor is subject to being disciplined by the Contractors' State License Board, which may result in the suspension or revocation of the license. Grounds for discipline include: abandoning a project; diverting funds to a different project or for a different purpose; departing from plans and specifications; violation of work safety provisions or of building laws and regulations; and a material breach of contract.

Note: Various FHA, VA or Cal-Vet requirements regulate housing and construction. These programs require, as a prerequisite to participation, that the house involved meet elaborate Minimum Property Requirements (MPRs). In some instances, MPRs are more demanding than either the State Housing Law or local building codes.

HEALTH AND SANITATION

The sanitary condition of all housing is subject to control by health authorities. While the State Department of Health Services controls statewide enforcement of health measures, the local health officer actually enforces state and local health laws and uses the Department of Health Services as an advisory agency.

Proper drainage, sewage disposal, and water supply are crucial health and sanitation considerations. The local health officer may stop a development if there are problems in these areas.

EMINENT DOMAIN

The power of eminent domain permits the government to take private property for public use. The United States and California Constitutions require "just compensation" for such a taking. Not all government activity which may reduce or entirely destroy the value of property is a "taking." For example, zoning or health regulations which prohibit an owner from using a property for a certain purpose or in a certain manner may make the property much less valuable but, usually, no compensation is paid. Where governmental regulation or impositions on the use or development of land denies all economically beneficial or productive use of the land, the regulatory action constitutes a taking requiring compensation.

The federal government, states, cities, counties, improvement districts, public utilities, public education institutions, and similar public and semi-public bodies may all exercise the power of eminent domain and almost always have the power to obtain the property in question for fair market value. The government can take property within several weeks of advance notice, before any price is paid or even determined, upon depositing an estimated price in court and getting a court order.

Examples of public uses are streets, irrigation, railroads, electric power, public housing, and off street parking.

Compensation
The use of the power of eminent domain is often referred to as condemnation. The main issue in almost all condemnation cases is the amount of "just compensation." Most courts have ruled that fair market value is just compensation.

Severance Damage
Condemnation of a *portion* of a parcel of land may result in a loss in value of the remaining parcel. Normally, the government must compensate the owner for this severance damage.

Benefits affected by severance are either general or special. A highway benefits all who use it, including the condemnee. This general benefit is not an offset against severance damages. Conversion of the remainder of an agricultural parcel to commercial usage because the severed portion is used for a government office building is an example of a special benefit/increase in value which may be an offset against severance damages due from the government.

Procedure
Negotiations with the property owner usually precede formal condemnation action by a public body. If negotiations are successful, the property is purchased rather than condemned. If negotiations are unsuccessful, the public body files a formal proceeding in court against the property owner.

If the government abandons a condemnation action, the property owner may recover legal expenses reasonably and necessarily incurred, including attorney fees, appraisal fees, and fees for the service of other experts.

Inverse Condemnation
If a public work results in damage to property, the owner may initiate a suit as an inverse condemnation action. An inverse condemnation action may also result if a

public entity, having commenced an eminent domain proceeding, does not diligently attempt to serve the complaint and the summons within 6 months.

Inverse Condemnation for Governmental Regulation

Government regulation of the use and development of real estate does not usually result in the "taking" or condemnation of the real estate by the government without compensation as inverse condemnation. However, in certain instances, where the governmental regulation is excessive in nature, the land owner may have an action against the government for inverse condemnation. Where governmental regulation or impositions on the use or development of land denies all economically beneficial or productive use of the land, the regulatory action constitutes a taking that would require payment of compensation. However, it is the rare instance that all of the legal factors result which legally establish that a government regulatory action constitutes such a taking. There are also many procedural requirements that must be met before a landowner can validly assert that a governmental regulation actually constitutes such a taking without compensation.

WATER CONSERVATION AND FLOOD CONTROL

California law provides that an individual's water rights do not exceed the amount reasonably required for beneficial use.

The courts refer water rights litigation to the State Water Resources Control Board for investigation, report, and/or hearing and preliminary determination, subject to final court decision. (Water Code Section 2000, et seq.)

Surface water rights are dependent to some extent upon whether or not the surface water is flowing in a defined channel. A defined channel is any natural watercourse, even though dry during a good portion of the year. If water flows across the surface of the earth without being contained within any defined channel, the landowner below may not obstruct it in such a manner as to flood the owner above. Also, a landowner above may not divert or concentrate such waters upon the landowner below by artificial structures, such as ditches or streets in a subdivision.

Again, if water is flowing in a defined channel, a landowner may not obstruct or direct such water. A local flood control district, however, may grant a permit for such diversion if properly approved disposal methods are provided. Waters overflowing a defined channel are considered floodwaters and a landowner may protect property by reasonable methods.

Cities, counties and specially created districts may incur indebtedness for the construction of flood control works. Assessments on the parcels within the area will repay the indebtedness.

Mutual Water Company

Water users may organize a mutual water company in order to secure an ample water supply at a reasonable cost. The company must file articles of incorporation with the Secretary of State.

In most cases, the stock is made appurtenant to the land; that is, each share of stock is attached to a particular portion of land and cannot be sold separately. This enables the company to plan its distribution more easily and prevents speculation in shares.

No cash dividends are declared by these companies, but credits are given to water users if surpluses occur. On the other hand, assessments may be levied if operating revenues are not sufficient or special improvements are voted by the directors. Directors are elected by stockholders. The directors usually employ one paid officer, the secretary, who supervises the clerical help and advises stockholders regarding their water problems.

If the domestic water supply for a subdivision is to be provided by a mutual water company, the application for a public report on the subdivision must include the information, representations and assurances prescribed by Corporations Code Section 14312 on a form prescribed by the Real Estate Commissioner.

Public Utilities
Public utilities are corporations which have powers of a public nature, such as the power of condemnation, to enable them to discharge their duties for the public benefit. They are subject to the regulations and control of the Public Utilities Commission.

Special Water Districts
Water districts, while state agencies, are not part of the state government as such. Such districts have been historically divided into two groups: (1) those which protect or reclaim the land from water; and (2) those which bring water to the land. Some districts of each type have been given powers of the other type. Water districts may also be classified as existing under general or special laws, the former typically being an enabling act for the voluntary formation of districts and their government, while the latter either create or provide for the creation of one district and its government.

Sometimes the district law, though general in form, is so modeled to fit a particular situation that it may be said to be special in fact. This is true of the Metropolitan Water District Act, originally enacted in 1927, under which only the Metropolitan Water District of Southern California operates, and of the County Water Authority Act, originally enacted in 1943, under which only the San Diego County Water Authority operates. Both acts contemplate the wholesaling of water to cities and districts included in either a metropolitan water district or a county water authority.

Among the types of districts are:

    California water districts,

    California water storage districts,

    County water districts,

    County waterworks districts,

    Drainage districts,

    Irrigation districts,

    Public utility districts, and

    Reclamation districts.

Water Pollution Control

Water pollution control for the State is governed by the Porter-Cologne Water Quality Control Act (Water Code Section 13000 et seq.). This act establishes a State Water Resources Control Board and nine regional water quality control boards. This act provides a comprehensive scheme for controlling discharge of effluents which may affect the quality of water. This regulation has frequently involved property owners in regulation or clean up of spills from septic tanks, underground oil and gasoline storage tanks and other sources which leach materials into the groundwater.

INTERSTATE LAND SALES FULL DISCLOSURE ACT

Subdividers of large subdivisions to be sold interstate should contact HUD's Interstate Land Sales Registration Division (ILSRD) for a determination as to whether they are subject to ILSRD jurisdiction.

20 Planning, Zoning, and Redevelopment

THE NEED FOR PLANNING

Early American cities were relatively compact by today's standards. Their land areas were limited primarily by how far people could walk in going about their daily activities. As time progressed, urban populations surged due to industrialization and immigration. As city centers became overcrowded, housing conditions declined, sanitary systems were rendered inadequate, and there was a lack of parks and open space. Some cities turned into very unpleasant and unhealthy places to live.

In the 1880's with the coming of mechanized transportation (chiefly the electric trolley on rails), many people moved to cleaner, less congested suburban areas. Land speculation flourished and urban sprawl went unchecked. Sprawl intensified when automobiles became widely available. The development of the automobile was paralleled by advancing techniques in road construction, bridge building, tunneling, reinforced concrete construction, fireproofing and electric elevators. Cities not only expanded farther out, but also grew upward.

By the beginning of the twentieth century, civic leaders perceived the need for improving their urban environments. City planning, which had existed for centuries, took on added importance in what became known as the "City Beautiful" movement. The City Beautiful movement stressed public works and civic improvements as a way of making cities more livable.

About the same time, city development plans gained prominence. City plans evolved into "comprehensive plans": expressions of community goals and values covering the planning needs of both public and privately owned land.

The comprehensive plans contain proposals and policies addressing the numerous components of an urban area's physical development. These proposals and policies are a rational response to the problems inherent in urbanization.

GENERAL PLANS

In California, comprehensive plans are known as "general plans." By state law, every city and county must adopt its own general plan for long-term physical development. The plan must cover a local government's entire planning area. At a minimum, a planning area includes all land subject to the local government's jurisdiction and "any land [outside the city's or county's] boundaries which in the planning agency's judgment bears relation to its planning." (California Government Code Section 65300). The general plan is extremely important because all land use decisions of the city or county must be consistent with the general plan. It has been described by California courts as being "a constitution for all future developments."

State law also requires that each local general plan address a comprehensive list of development issues falling under seven major categories or "elements." These include: land use; circulation; housing; conservation; open space; noise; and safety.

Depending upon the jurisdiction's location, its general plan may also be required to address elements such as coastal development and the protection of mineral resources. In addition, the general plan may include other concerns such as recreation, historic preservation, public services, and hazardous waste management. The general plan, together with all its elements and parts, must constitute an integrated, internally consistent and compatible statement of development policies for a planning area.

Preparation

Typically, general plans are arranged according to the following four basic components:

1. background data on and analysis of the local economy, existing and projected demographics (the characteristics of human population such as size, growth, density, distribution and vital statistics), existing land use, projected land use needs, existing and projected environmental conditions, and the capacities of public facilities and services (e.g., sewer, water, and storm drainage systems, highways, transit, police and fire protection, and schools);

2. a statement of goals and development policies based on the analysis of data that guides community development decision making;

3. diagrams that reflect and support the general plan's statement of development policies (e.g., planned land uses, circulation, noise level contours); and

4. a program of measures that will be subsequently adopted to implement the general plan (e.g., proposed rezonings, specific plans, public works and other capital improvements, public financing techniques, etc.).

Some general plans are developed as a single document for the entire jurisdiction, while others are composed of a combination of documents such as a jurisdiction-wide policy plan and a series of area or community plans, which together cover the entire jurisdiction. Individual general plan formats differ from jurisdiction to jurisdiction based on local conditions, needs, and philosophy.

Similarly, local conditions and preferences dictate who actually prepares a general plan document. Each local planning agency is ultimately responsible for developing a plan. Some planning departments prepare their plans in-house, while others assign all or part of the work to consultants or other planning agencies.

Hearings - Adoption or Denial

Once the plan is written, the planning commission holds at least one public hearing on the document. The commission then forwards the plan with recommendations for local action to the local legislative body, which also conducts at least one public hearing and then either adopts or denies the plan by resolution. In some charter cities, the planning commission may be authorized to take final action on the plan without holding a public hearing.

Importance of the General Plan

A general plan is the basis for fitting together in organized relationships a myriad of individual development projects. It is the rationale behind a city's or county's development regulations and decisions; a statement of local values that sets forth the future direction of community development. It helps eliminate inefficient resource allocations associated with random or untimely development. Finally, a general plan promotes fairness in the development entitlement process by discouraging capricious decision making.

Until fairly recently, general plans were idealistic and inspirational, but had little legal effect. Community development decisions such as rezonings, subdivision map approvals, and public works projects were not required to be consistent with the plan.

Legislation, court decisions and legal opinions have established the general plan as the local constitution for a community's physical development. State law now requires that zoning ordinances of general law cities and Los Angeles be consistent with the general plan. In addition, every city and county in the state, except Los Angeles, is prohibited by state law from approving a subdivision map proposal unless the map is found to be consistent with the general plan. Furthermore every city and county, including Los Angeles, must deny a subdivision map proposal which the city or county finds to be inconsistent with the general plan. A court decision in 1980 established that public works of all cities and counties must be consistent with the plan.

A 1984 California Appellate Court decision held that a local government may not grant a conditional use permit if the general plan inadequately addresses pertinent state-mandated issues. Other decisions of the late 1970's and the 1980's have also prohibited various development projects due to the inadequacy of local general plans. Consequently, it is now in the best interests of real estate licensees, developers, local governments, and the public to make sure that general plans are legally adequate and that their implementing actions meet the consistency requirements.

Amendment to General Plans
Amendments to mandatory elements of general plans are limited to no more frequently than four times during any calendar year. Although most amendments are initiated by city or county planning agencies, an amendment may be initiated in any manner specified by the local legislative body. Additionally, amendment by initiative measure has been upheld by the California Supreme Court. However, such an initiative-based general plan amendment must conform with all substantive requirements imposed on general plan amendments. If a development agreement is in effect, its terms supersede amendments to the general plan.

General Plan Implementation
Zoning is one of the best known and most frequently used tools for carrying out a general plan's land use proposals. Subdivision regulations, property tax incentives, land banking, transfer of development rights programs, etc. also enact a general plan's land use policies. As noted earlier, however, general plans are comprehensive. They address development issues that go beyond land use, such as traffic circulation, public works, public safety, and water reclamation. Implementation techniques, including specific plans, public finance measures, and capital improvement programs tackle more than just land use planning issues. The following is a discussion of two of the more popular implementation tools: specific plans and zoning.

After a municipality has adopted a general plan, it may prepare *specific plans* to systematically implement the general plan. Specific plans usually pertain to a particular development site or sub-area of the general plan's planning territory. They contain a text and a diagram or diagrams detailing development specifications for, among other things, land use and supporting infrastructure. They may also include phasing programs which coordinate the timing of development with the general plan's long-term outlook. Specific plans have a program of implementation measures (e.g., proposed rezonings, public works, and public finance). Specific plans may take the form of: detailed planning policy documents; zoning-like land use regulations that take the place of zoning; urban development and design guidelines; capital improvement programs; and combined policy and regulatory programs for guiding and controlling urban development.

Although expensive to prepare and sometimes difficult to administer, specific plans are increasingly popular general plan implementation tools. Although specific plans contain planning provisions, they are not part of the general plan, nor should they be confused with area or community plans which are sub-units of a general plan. As in the case of a zoning ordinance, a specific plan is subordinate to and must conform to the general plan. However, zoning, public works, tentative subdivision maps, parcel maps, and development agreements must be consistent with an applicable specific plan. With regard to the hierarchy of planning documents, a specific plan falls somewhere between the general plan and some of the most common general plan implementation mechanisms. Specific plans have two distinct advantages over other general plan implementation tools:

- They bring together in one document many of the factors necessary for successfully developing a land use project.

- By matching proposed land uses with infrastructure, they help eliminate costly over or undersizing of public utilities and streets.

Zoning

Most California cities and counties have adopted ordinances that divide their jurisdictions into land use districts or zones. Within each zone a specific set of regulations control the use of land. There are often zones for single-family residences, multi-family dwellings, commercial uses, industrial activities, open space or agriculture and, sometimes, mixed uses.

The authority for local zoning is derived from the police power in Article XI, Section 7 of the California Constitution. State law augments the authority by setting forth minimum standards and procedures for exercising zoning regulations. This provides cities and counties with a great deal of local discretion in controlling land use. Nevertheless, zoning, as a police power action, is invalid unless it rationally promotes the public health, safety, and welfare.

A zoning ordinance consists of a map and a text. The map identifies and delineates the boundaries of the various zones within a city or county. The text specifies zoning ordinance amendment and administrative procedures, and sets forth the characteristics of each zoning category such as: permitted land uses; land uses that require conditional use permits; minimum parcel sizes; building height limitations; lot coverage limits; building setback standards; and housing unit and building densities.

While the nature of zoning ordinances is fairly well known to the general public, the relationship of zoning to the general plan may not be as apparent. A zoning ordinance may appear to duplicate the general plan, as both are concerned with land use. The zoning ordinance and the general plan each have texts setting forth development standards. Both also have community land use maps and map-like diagrams.

However, zoning ordinances are very different from the general plan. The general plan covers a much wider range of land use issues and looks much further into the future of a land use area. The general plan is policy-oriented, setting forth in general terms the context in which site-by-site decisions are made. A zoning ordinance regulates land use from the viewpoint of the individual project site. Therefore, a zoning ordinance is merely one of a variety of measures used to implement the general plan. The general plan provides an overall perspective of the community-wide consequences of individual rezonings which are commonly initiated by local governments following an amendment or revision of the general plan. Rezonings are sometimes necessary for maintaining zoning ordinance consistency with the general plan, although they are more commonly initiated by individual property owners or developers.

Zoning is inherently inflexible. With the exception of "charter cities," all cities and counties are subject to the same basic zoning procedures and statutory requirements (including mandatory noticed public hearings before a local planning commission and city council or board of supervisors). Zoning standards must also be applied uniformly, while at the same time recognizing that different land parcels have their own particular characteristics. Over the years, a variety of methods have evolved to make zoning more responsive and accommodating to the many unique circumstances involving land use. "Floating zones," special purpose overlay or combining zones, mixed-use development, building block zoning and planned unit developments exemplify some of these techniques.

Typically, different categories of uses are established within a particular zoning district. These are most often primary permitted uses, conditional uses and accessory uses. Permitted uses are those allowed as a matter of right within the district. Conditional uses are those not allowed as a matter of right, but which may be allowed by special permit from a local administrative body usually after a public hearing as to the propriety thereof. The agency can impose conditions on the proposed use, thus using greater flexibility in applying the zoning criteria. Accessory uses are uses incidental to a primary use permitted within the zoning district.

Zoning measures often establish various criteria with respect to types of uses, and also various aspects of the types of uses allowed, such as building heights, minimum lot sizes, set-backs from property lines, open space requirements, ratio of building floor areas to size of the lot, and other such criteria.

Planned unit development or planned development is a type of zoning classification. (This terminology also describes certain land development techniques.) As a zoning mechanism, planned unit development designation applies to the development of land as a unit where it is desirable to apply zoning regulations in a more flexible manner than those pertaining to other, more specific zoning classifications, and to grant diversification in the location of structures and other site qualities. The planned development zoning process is implemented by the local government's review and approval of a master plan or "precise" plan for the designated area. Approval usually includes various detailed planning and development conditions to implement the precise plan.

If a property owner desires to use property in a manner not permitted under the applicable comprehensive zoning ordinance he may seek the administrative relief of a variance or conditional use permit or the legislative relief of an amendment to the zoning ordinance. Such a rezoning or zoning amendment would have to be consistent with the applicable general or specific plan. If the use sought is not consistent with the general or specific plan, then an amendment of the general or specific plan would also have to be obtained.

Zoning and Use Variances
Sometimes the size, irregular shape, surroundings, unusual topography, or location of a parcel of land is such that a use of the property cannot meet a zoning standard, such as a side-yard setback. This prevents the owner from enjoying the development privileges available to other property owners in the same vicinity and zone. The disadvantaged land owner may apply to the city or county for a waiver of the strict application of a zoning standard (or standards) to his/her property. If granted, the waiver or "zoning variance" provides the property owner with the same, but not additional, development privileges as neighboring parcels in the same zone.

In California, counties and general law cities are prohibited by state law from granting use variances that authorize a land use not otherwise permitted in a zone. For instance, if retail sales are prohibited in a single family residential zone, a zoning variance may not waive the restriction.

Conditional Use Permits
Zoning ordinances often list special land uses that are authorized in a zone subject to the granting of a conditional use permit or special use permit. Land uses requiring such permits are usually potentially incompatible with other activities existing in the zone. The proposed land use can create spillover effects such as noise, traffic congestion, or air pollution that adversely affect the public's health, safety, or welfare. Conditional use permits may authorize the use as long as the project proponents agree to abide by conditions that alleviate the spillover effects. If the project owner fails to comply with the conditions, the local government may revoke the permit. A conditional use permit is said to run with the land in that its provisions usually apply despite a change in ownership of the project site.

California Environmental Quality Act of 1970 (CEQA)
The California Environmental Quality Act of 1970 (CEQA) plays a major role in planning, zoning and other land-use permitting decisions by government agencies. A primary purpose of CEQA is to provide procedures and information to ensure that governmental agencies will consider and respond to the environmental effects of their proposed decisions. The state has adopted CEQA Guidelines to implement the CEQA process.

CEQA and the CEQA Guidelines affect planning whenever city or county officials exercise their judgment or discretion in approving, conditionally approving, or denying a development project which has the potential for creating a significant impact on the environment. Examples of discretionary projects include: adoption or amendment of general plans, specific plans, and zoning ordinances; granting of conditional use permits or zoning variances; approvals of tentative subdivision maps or parcel maps; and development agreement approvals. Ministerial projects, such as final subdivision maps and most building permits, are not subject to CEQA; nor are projects which are specifically exempted by state law and regulations.

One of the first CEQA-related steps in the processing of a discretionary project proposal is the preparation of an *initial study*. This study is a preliminary investigation and analysis, prepared by the lead government agency, of the project's potential for significant adverse effects on the environment. The initial study identifies the type of environmental document that will be necessary for evaluating the project.

If it is determined that the proposal will not have a significant adverse effect, the city or county prepares a *negative declaration* prior to making a decision on the development. As a means of expediting the review and approval process, under appropriate circumstances, the local agency can issue a "mitigated" negative declaration. A mitigated negative declaration is useful where the initial study has identified potentially significant effects on the environment, but revisions to the project have been made or are agreed to which will avoid or mitigate the potential effects to a point where no significant effect on the environment would occur. The permit approvals for the project would have to provide for measures which implement the specific mitigation measures.

If, however, the project may potentially cause one or more significant effects, the city or county must prepare and certify an *environmental impact report* (EIR) prior to the development decision. An EIR identifies a project's significant, cumulative, and unavoidable environmental impacts, cites mitigation measures, and discusses project alternatives, including "no project." An EIR goes through two stages: draft and final. The draft EIR is prepared by the lead government agency and sets forth a variety of information on various issues required by the statute and Guidelines. It is circulated for public review and intra-agency consultation. After public review of the draft EIR, the lead agency must prepare written responses to comments on the environmental impact of the proposed project. The city or county must mitigate significant impacts by incorporating feasible changes or alterations into the project which avoid or substantially lessen the impacts. If one or more significant effects are unavoidable, the project may be approved only if the city or county decision-makers adopt a *statement of overriding considerations*. This statement allows decision-makers to balance a project's social and economic benefits against its environmental consequences. It is an indication of the elected official's environmental, social, and economic priorities with regard to the project.

Speeding Up Routine Matters
To reduce the workload of the local planning commission and legislative body, communities may authorize zoning administrators, zoning boards, or boards of zoning adjustment to handle many of the routine permits and appeals. These hearing bodies enable the local planning commission and city council or board of supervisors to spend more time on substantive planning policy and regulatory

issues. Known as California's Permit Streamlining Act (commencing at California Government Code Section 65920), this change also quickens the planning pace by setting use permits and variances. The Subdivision Map Act and the California Environmental Quality Act also specify time limits.

REDEVELOPMENT

Community Redevelopment Law (Health and Safety Code Sections 33000, et seq.) authorizes a local government to adopt an ordinance subject to referendum to establish a redevelopment agency for the purpose of correcting blighted conditions in a project area within its territorial jurisdiction. A project area for redevelopment is not restricted to buildings, improvements, or lands which are detrimental to the public health, safety, or welfare, but may also consist of an entire area in which such conditions predominate. A project may also include lands, buildings, or improvements which are not detrimental to the public health, safety or welfare, but whose inclusion is found necessary for the effective redevelopment of the area of which they are a part.

The fundamental purposes of redevelopment include: the expansion of the supply of low and moderate income housing; the expansion of employment opportunities for jobless, underemployed, and low-income persons; and the development of an environment for the social, economic, and psychological growth and well-being of all citizens. To ensure that these objectives are met, the law provides special redevelopment financing and land use control authority. The use of this authority may affect the title, resale, and use of properties within a redevelopment project area. Under some circumstances, redevelopment powers and controls may extend to low- and moderate income housing developed, with agency assistance, outside of redevelopment project areas. Housing is the only activity a redevelopment agency may aid outside redevelopment areas.

In most instances, the city or county's elected officials function as the community redevelopment agency board of directors for the jurisdiction. For legal purposes, the redevelopment agency has status separate from that of the jurisdiction in which it is established. The agency can sue and be sued; acquire property by eminent domain; dispose of property; construct public improvements; borrow money from any public or private source; and engage in a wide range of government and development activities mandated by redevelopment law. Enforcement of redevelopment law occurs through public monitoring of agency planning functions and annual reports, and civil legal challenges to perceived violations of state or federal requirements.

Housing Powers, Responsibilities, and Activities of Redevelopment Agencies
A community redevelopment agency (CRA) must replace, or cause to be replaced, low and moderate income housing which is lost as a result of redevelopment activities. Replacement must be accomplished within four years of the destruction, removal, rehabilitation or development of a dwelling unit. The agency must also provide relocation benefits to households or businesses displaced as a result of its activities.

Prior to 1988, properties developed or assisted by a CRA were subject to affordability requirements that were often contained in written agreements, and which were to be part of resale and leasing arrangements. The agency monitors these arrangements for continuing compliance. Beginning in 1988, affordability requirements on CRA units must be enforced through covenants, conditions, and restrictions in recorded deeds.

Funding Redevelopment Projects

Most redevelopment projects are funded through the issuance of tax allocation bonds secured by anticipated property tax revenues. This procedure, called *tax increment financing*, allows the CRA to receive any increases in project area property taxes which are a direct result of redevelopment activities. Tax allocation bonds are not obligations of the city or any public entity other than the CRA. They can be issued by a CRA without voter approval. Before issuing bonds to be secured by tax increments, the taxes being realized from all property within the designated redevelopment area are calculated and recorded. This tax base, plus an equivalent portion of the annual reassessments permitted under state law, continue to be allocated to the county and any other taxing entities entitled to property taxes from the area. Property tax increments resulting from redevelopment activities which may not begin to flow until two or three years after the project becomes active are allocated back to the CRA to pay for debts incurred to accomplish redevelopment of the project area.

Expenditure of tax increments. All CRAs, unless exempted under the law, must set aside not less than twenty percent (20%) of their tax increments in a special fund for low and moderate income housing. (See Health and Safety Code Sections 50052.5, 50093, and 50105.) In carrying out this mandate, the agency may exercise any or all of its powers, including the following: acquire and improve land or building sites; construct, acquire or rehabilitate buildings or structures; donate land to private or public persons or entities; provide subsidies to or for the benefit of low or moderate income households; develop land, pay principal and interest on bonds, loans, advances, other indebtedness, or pay financing and carrying charges; and maintain the community's supply of mobilehomes.

Although tax increments are the major source of redevelopment financing, there are other tools available to CRAs, such as general obligation lease revenue and mortgage revenue bonds; transient occupancy taxes; and shares of sales taxes generated within the project area.

21 Brokerage

Brokerage as a Part of the Real Estate Business

Overall, the real estate business consists of the production, marketing and financing of real property.

Real estate brokerage involves *agency* directed, *for compensation*, primarily toward the sale, exchange, lease, rental, financing, or managing of real property or a business opportunity.

Other Specialists

Real estate brokers deal frequently with other specialists in the real estate business: appraisers, surveyors, engineers, financial institutions, title companies, escrow agents, architects, contractors, pest control inspectors, credit reporting agencies, attorneys, and accountants. A broker should establish and maintain good working relationships with these fellow professionals.

Operations

With regard to the sale of real property, brokerage operations may be divided into several elements:

1. securing listings (developing an inventory) through leads, referrals, and direct canvassing;

2. prospecting for buyers through various forms of advertising;

3. negotiating or bringing together a "meeting of the minds" of buyer and seller;

4. assisting in whatever manner necessary with closing (transfer of the property by the required instruments).

Typically, brokerage firms compete for listings and cooperate with other brokers who desire to find buyers for the listings.

Office Size - Management

A small office will conduct its operations successfully only if the broker is a good salesperson *and* manager. The medium-sized firm is customarily manned by a "sales manager broker." In a large office, the broker generally has only executive and administrative duties. This broker-owner employs one or more sales managers and an office staff. Whatever the office size, a broker must maintain proper records and documents and be certain that the office is well organized.

Career Building

A person considering a career in real estate brokerage should be aware of the following:

1. Other selling experience is valuable, but selling real estate is different because:

    a. The product is more complex and individualized.

    b. The sales period is longer and more tedious, requiring patience and effort.

    c.   The broker must be familiar with and fulfill many legal requirements.

    d.   Real estate is usually the largest single purchase a buyer will ever make.

2.   The broker must have in-depth knowledge of the city and district in which the broker seeks to operate.

3.   The broker must know the specific product being marketed: its value; its construction; its neighborhood; and the type of buyer who will be attracted.

4.   A real estate brokerage is very closely identified with the person running it. As Emerson said, "A business is the lengthening shadow of the man." A broker should be established in the community and active in civic affairs.

The Broker and the New Salesperson

Office and personal characteristics crucial to the success of a new salesperson are:

- The broker is available for consultation and makes certain that the salesperson is trained, informed and up-to-date.

- The broker has an organizational chart and plan. The salesperson's position and duties are clear. The broker must constantly evaluate the salesperson's attitude, knowledge, transaction documents, and production.

Specialization

Residential selling probably accounts for more than 75 percent of sales made by the typical realty office. After making a good start in general home selling, the licensee may wish to specialize and become an expert in only one particular area of brokerage, such as:

1.   homes of a defined district of the city, usually within 10 or 15 miles of the office;

2.   homes within a certain price range;

3.   residential rentals; and

4.   specific types of property: farm, commercial, industrial, multiple units, motels, business opportunities, franchising, tract homes or mobilehomes.

If a licensee wishes to leave general brokerage after acquiring extended experience, consideration may be given to becoming one of the following:

- licensed appraiser;
- real estate investment counselor;
- subdivider;
- builder;
- property manager;
- mortgage loan correspondent or agent;
- syndicator;
- franchise investment specialist;
- commercial/industrial property leasing agent; or
- business opportunities specialist.

A Broker's Related Pursuits

A broker may be engaged in related pursuits which we might term the allied functions. The broker may: be licensed to appraise property on a fee basis; act as an adviser or consultant in real estate investment; operate a property insurance business; or offer notary public services.

Subdividing/developing. A real estate broker might select the production function of real estate and become a producer or manufacturer by taking "raw" land and converting it into higher priced land to suit the needs of the community. The broker-developer may construct dwellings or commercial buildings upon the subdivided land or even develop an entire community. Once these products have been completed, the broker-developer may then proceed to market them through other agents or through the broker's own organization. For this specialization in real estate, the broker must have a suitable contractor's license or work with or for a licensed contractor and comply with subdivision laws.

Notary functions. Often a broker provides notary services as a convenience to clients and as a service intended for the general public.

A notary must keep a sequential journal of notarial acts and be certain that the person whose signature on a document is to be acknowledged personally appears before the notary and provides acceptable forms of identification. An acknowledged signature is supposed to provide protection for individuals who rely on the notary's act. This protection will not be considered trivial by an individual who must rely on it while enforcing a contract in court.

Effective January 1, 1996, Government Code Section 8206 requires that a notary public's journal include the right thumb print of a person signing a deed, quitclaim deed, or deed of trust affecting real property. (The statute specifies alternatives if the right thumb print is not available.) Government Code Section 8211 sets forth maximum fees for various notarial functions.

Insurance. Most property insurance is sold through specialized insurance agencies. It is common, nevertheless, for the larger real estate brokerage offices to represent insurance companies in placing policies. Insurance is a natural feeder business or extra source of income for the real estate broker who taps the lead at its source: sales transactions originating in the broker's office.

A real estate broker who also acts in the capacity of an insurance agent is acting as the agent of the insurance underwriter and is governed by the carrier's instructions. It is incumbent upon the agent to secure competitive rates and charge the client no more than the latter could obtain in the open market. Of course, the client should always have the opportunity of selecting his or her own source of insurance.

PROFESSIONALISM

Staying Informed - Disclosures

Real estate licensees must keep current with changing real estate laws, technological changes, and trends impacting the broad field of real estate.

To illustrate, consider the ever-increasing responsibilities imposed upon real estate licensees and their principals under various disclosure laws. (See also Chapter 22.)

For example, Civil Code Section 2956 requires that in sales of residential property containing not more than four units, when the seller carries back purchase money financing, the licensee ("arranger of credit") must provide a detailed written disclosure to the buyer and seller with respect to the credit transaction.

Civil Code Section 2079 sets forth the duty of a broker in a sales transaction of one to four dwelling units (including a manufactured home) to conduct a reasonably competent and diligent visual inspection of accessible areas of the property and disclose to the prospective purchaser all facts affecting the value or desirability of the property revealed by the broker's investigation. This law also applies to lease options, ground leases of land with one to four dwelling units and real property sales contracts.

Civil Code Section 2079.14 requires disclosure of real estate agency relationships.

Civil Code Section 1102.3 requires that, except under certain specifically defined situations, a seller of one to four dwelling units must provide the prospective transferee with a written disclosure statement covering such items as appliances, structural defects and modifications, possible easements, flooding, drainage, soil problems, and whether additions, structural modifications or other repairs or alterations are in compliance with the Building Code. The disclosure must be delivered to the prospective transferee as soon as practicable before the transfer of title. The required form includes space for the results of the inspection by the agent(s).

Finally, the general laws of agency require a real estate agent to disclose to his or her principal any material fact the agent knows (or should know) which will affect the principal's decisions in a transaction. In this regard, a good policy is: when in doubt, *disclose*.

MOBILEHOME SALES

This section discusses a real estate licensee's involvement in sales of mobilehomes. As to a mobilehome's status as real or personal property, see page 413. If a mobilehome is real property, Business and Professions (B & P) Code Section 10131 (a) is a real estate broker's authorization to negotiate a sale of the real property/mobilehome, with transfer effected by grant deed.

Sections 10131.6, 10131.7 of the B & P Code apply when a real estate licensee negotiates the sale of a mobilehome which is personal property.

Section 10131.6 provides that a real estate broker may list and sell a mobilehome if it has been registered under Part 2 (commencing with Section 18000) of Division 13 of the Health and Safety Code. This means that the mobilehome must be registered with the Department of Housing and Community Development (HCD). Section 10131.6 also prohibits a broker from maintaining a place of business where two or more mobilehomes are displayed and offered for sale unless the broker is also licensed as a mobilehome dealer.

Section 10131.7 prohibits the following:

- advertising or offering for sale in any manner any mobilehome unless it is either in place on a lot rented or leased for human habitation within an established mobilehome park (and the advertising or offering for sale is not contrary to any terms of a contract between the seller of the mobilehome and the owner of the mobilehome park), or the mobilehome is otherwise located, pursuant to a local zoning ordinance or permit, on a lot where its presence has been authorized or its continued presence and such use would be authorized for a total and uninterrupted period of at least one year;

- licensee's failure to withdraw an advertisement of a mobilehome within 48 hours after receipt of notice that the mobilehome is no longer available for sale, lease or exchange;

- representing a mobilehome as new;

- incorporation into the selling price of either an amount for licensing (except where buyer and seller agree to proration of the fee) or an amount for transfer of title of the mobilehome unless the licensee paid the fee in order to avoid late payment penalties;

- representation that a mobilehome is capable of being transported on California highways if the mobilehome does not meet all of the equipment requirements applicable to mobilehomes of Division 12 (commencing with Section 24000) of the Vehicle Code; failure to disclose any material fact respecting those equipment requirements;

- advertising or otherwise representing that no down payment is required in connection with the sale of a mobilehome when a down payment is in fact required and the buyer is advised or induced to finance the down payment with a separate loan; and

- failure to properly endorse, date, and deliver the certificate of ownership or certificate of title of the mobilehome to HCD (unless demanded in writing by the buyer) and deliver the registration card to the buyer.

Permit for Movement

A permit is required for moving a mobilehome over a public highway (Section 35790 of the Vehicle Code). The permit must be obtained from either the Department of Transportation or the local authority with respect to highways under its jurisdiction. The permit may be issued on a special or annual basis. Whenever a mobilehome is to be moved, licensees should contact HCD to insure that all laws and regulations pertaining to the move are followed.

Transferring Title (personal property)

Requirements for transferring title and registering a mobilehome with HCD are set forth in Section 18100.5, et seq., of the Health and Safety Code. Upon registration, HCD must issue a certificate of title to the registered owner or lienholder.

A real estate broker engaging in used mobilehome sales must, not later than the end of the tenth calendar day after the sale of a mobilehome that is subject to registration, give written notice of the transfer to the headquarters office of HCD on a form prescribed by that department.

All persons who acquire or release an interest in a mobilehome must notify HCD within 20 days of the date of acquisition or release (Health and Safety Code Section 18100.5). Both the transferor and transferee must sign the certificate of title. HCD will amend the registration and certificate card and provide a copy to all lienholders.

The transferee must also file a change of ownership statement with the county assessor.

Additional Information

Section 10147.5 Notice. The notice regarding the negotiability of the amount or rate of commission is applicable to the sale of mobilehomes, whether the mobilehome is real or personal property.

Out-of-state mobilehomes. Mobilehomes which are purchased out-of-state and brought into California are treated, for tax purposes, in the same manner as if they were originally registered in California. For example, if the mobilehome was sold new on or after June 30 1980, it will (unless excepted) be taxed as personal property. There are potential registration problems relating mainly to documenting ownership and out-of-state registration. Licensees should refer to Health and Safety Code Section 18075.5 et seq., for a detailing of the documentation necessary to register an out-of-state mobilehome in California.

Escrow. Unless performing acts which require a vehicle dealer's license, a real estate licensee is not required to use a third party escrow holder when selling a mobilehome.

When preparing escrow instructions, proration of usual items such as ground rent or taxes is permissible. If buyer and seller agree, the license fee may also be prorated.

If an escrow is used, the sale is complete upon the close of escrow. When no escrow is used, the sale is completed when the buyer has signed a purchase contract or security agreement and has taken possession of the mobilehome. Regardless of whether or not an escrow is used, the provisions of Health and Safety Code Sections 18100.5 and 18101 must be followed to effect a transfer of title and to perfect a security interest.

Mobilehome trailer parks. Licensees should review the Mobilehome Residency Law, Sections 798, et seq., of the Civil Code and the Mobilehome Parks Act, Sections 18200, et seq., of the Health and Safety Code.

22 BASIC CONTRACT PROVISIONS AND DISCLOSURES IN A RESIDENTIAL REAL ESTATE TRANSACTION

A residential real estate sale transaction usually begins at the time a broker obtains an agency contract in the form of a listing from the property owner. If a buyer is found, the transaction proceeds through several closings:

Closing the sale. Buyer and seller agree as to terms. The deposit receipt form/contract is fully executed. This is the result of sales effort and negotiation.

Legal closing. Title insurance or title evidence has been furnished and escrow has the funds necessary to cash out the seller's equity, less expenses. All instruments necessary to transfer title are executed and recorded. Transfer of title and transfer of money are thought of as simultaneous acts.

Financial closing. Financial closing is closely related to legal closing but with more emphasis upon the settlement function or mechanics: i.e., the actual disbursement of funds by checks and a written accounting to all parties. In a complicated transaction involving new financing, there may be not only buyer and seller, but several old lenders and a new lender to be taken into consideration. To show that instructions of the escrow have been fully performed, the escrow holder will prepare settlement statements for the principals.

A BASIC TRANSACTION

An owner (the seller) of a single family residence (the property) in California wishes to sell the property.

The seller enters into an Exclusive Authorization And Right To Sell Agreement (the listing) with a California real estate broker (the listing broker).

Prior to entering into the listing, the broker gives the seller an agency disclosure form. This requirement is discussed later in this chapter and, more completely, in Chapter 10.

The listing provides that it will be placed into a multiple listing service and the listing broker can cooperate/share the commission if another broker (the selling broker) finds a buyer for the property.

The selling broker finds a buyer purportedly ready, willing and able to purchase the property. An offer (preceded by an agency disclosure form) is made, negotiated, and accepted so that a meeting of the minds is reflected in a real estate purchase contract and receipt for deposit (the contract). The contract includes confirmation of the agency relationships.

The transaction, grounded in the sale closing negotiated by the listing and selling brokers, proceeds to legal and financial closing.

This chapter examines the provisions of a listing agreement and a contract involved in such a transaction and the required disclosures.

A BASIC LISTING

The Exclusive Authorization and Right to Sell is a listing for sale of one or more specifically described parcels of real property. (This is one of several different types of listing agreements.) The phrase "right to sell" means "right to find a buyer." It does *not* authorize the broker to sign transaction documents for the seller. Prior to signing the listing agreement, the seller should be given the agency disclosure form. See Chapter 10.

Term
An exclusive listing must have a definite term. The term of the listing ends at midnight on a specified day. If the listing is intended to be for a certain number of weeks or months, the termination date should be determined with care to avoid misunderstanding.

Description of the Property
The description of the property should be as exact as possible to satisfy the statute of frauds. Accuracy of description avoids any doubt of enforcement of the listing on that ground.

Terms of Sale
The minimum requirement for setting forth the terms of sale, where cash is acceptable to the seller, is to express the price in cash.

Complications may arise when the seller demands assumption of the existing loan or loans, or indicates a willingness to pay part of the assumption fees or new set-up charges if the buyer assumes the existing loan or refinances with the existing lender. Such terms of sale should be spelled out in detail.

If the sale may be financed by a VA or FHA loan, the listing will include details of the seller's conditions with respect to the payment of points.

Where a first loan can be assumed and the seller is willing to carry secondary financing, the specific terms of the proposed secondary financing will be set forth.

The Broker's Authority
A listing authorizes the broker to:

- place a "for sale" sign on the property;

- place the property in a multiple listing service;

- cooperate with subagents or buyer's agents; and

- accept on the seller's behalf a prospective buyer's good faith deposit toward the purchase price.

The Broker's Duty

In return for the exclusive rights granted by the owner, the broker agrees to use due diligence in attempting to find a suitable buyer and negotiate a sale. Thus, the listing is a bilateral contract.

The listing states that the right of the broker is "irrevocable." Basically, this means that it cannot be revoked by either party without the other's consent. However, if there is a breach of contract (e.g., failure of the broker to use due diligence), the contract may be subject to rescission.

Broker's Compensation

The compensation clause in an exclusive right to sell listing will be specific and unequivocal. It will state simply that the broker is entitled to the compensation, expressed either as a percentage of the purchase price or a dollar amount, if the property is sold by the broker, by another broker, or by the seller during the term of the listing or any extension of it. It also obligates the seller to pay the compensation if, without the consent of the broker, the owner withdraws the property from sale or in some other way makes it unmarketable during the term of the listing or any extension thereof.

A listing's "safety clause" will designate a period of time after expiration of the listing during which the broker's compensation is protected if the owner personally sells to someone who physically entered and was shown the property or who wrote an offer on the property. For this clause to be effective, the broker must, either before or within the time specified in the agreement, notify the owner in writing of the names of the prospective buyers with whom the broker has negotiated during the listing term.

Negotiability of Commission

In the sale of residential property of not more than four units, including a mobilehome, Business and Professions Code Section 10147.5 requires that the listing (or whatever document initially establishes the broker's right to a commission, or increases the amount or rate of the commission) contain, in not less than 10-point boldface type, the following provision before the compensation clause:

Notice: The amount or rate of real estate commissions is not fixed by law. They are set by each broker individually and may be negotiable between the seller and broker.

A broker cannot use a listing form in which the amount or rate of compensation is preprinted or otherwise inserted prior to negotiation with the seller.

Personal Property

The listing will specify the items of personal property included in the purchase price. For example:

Sales price to include all screens, blinds, curtain rods, drapes, patio furniture, swimming pool equipment and supplies, outdoor potted plants, and outdoor statuary.

Multiple Listing Service (MLLES)) **and Internet**
A paragraph may provide that the listing will be submitted to a designated MLLES where information about the property will be disseminated to members, who may also solicit potential buyers for the property. The MLLES and broker often are also have a service to advertise the property on the internet.

Deposit
This clause authorizes the agent to accept a certain deposit to be applied toward the purchase price.

Other Provisions
Home protection plan. Informs seller of the availability of such coverage.

Keybox. Authorizes the agent to place a key repository on the listed property.

Sign. Authorizes placement of broker's "for sale" sign on the property.

Equal housing opportunity clause. This clause is *prima facie* evidence of nondiscriminatory intent. The proof of compliance is, of course, that the parties act in the spirit of the declaration.

Arbitration. This provision, if initialed by the broker individually, or by the broker's authorized associate licensee, and all sellers, constitutes an agreement to refer all disputes or claims "in law or equity" arising out of the listing or any resulting transaction to binding arbitration.

Attorney's fees. In the event of any legal action to resolve a dispute, this clause provides that the prevailing party will be paid reasonable attorney's fees.

Additional terms. Additional provisions could include: date for possession; rent if possession is delivered on a date other than closing day; repairs to be made by owner; and termite work. Also, if the seller has a prospect which the seller personally located, the seller may wish to exclude a sale to that person from seller's obligation to pay a commission.

Change of price or terms. A change of price or terms of a listing should never be made on the face of the original contract, but rather on a price change or extension form.

Owner's signature. All owners must sign the listing. If the property is owned by a partnership or a corporation, the proper officials must sign.

Agent's signature. When the listing is signed by an authorized licensee member of the broker's staff or by the broker himself, it becomes a (bilateral) contract. Broker (or broker's agent) must give the seller a copy of the agreement.

Single Agency
Single agency brokerage firms have become more common since the Agency Relationship Disclosure law was enacted. Special listing forms exist.

A Buyer-Broker agreement such as the "Buyer Representation Agreement" or the "Exclusive Authorization to Locate Property" will contain many clauses similar to those in a seller-broker exclusive listing. Cooperation between brokers representing sellers only and buyers only should be conducted with full disclosure of the nature and terms of the cooperation and understanding of the compensation split, if any. In order to avoid disputes with the buyer, the broker should be particularly careful in describing the property the broker is engaged to locate and when the commission will be deemed earned. Changes in the buyer's specifications should be made in writing and a complete "paper trail" maintained throughout the transaction.

PURCHASE CONTRACT AND RECEIPT FOR DEPOSIT

This section discusses provisions which comprise a comprehensive Residential Real Estate Purchase Contract and Receipt for Deposit. When completed with the terms and other information relative to the buyer's attempt to purchase the property, it is an offer. When the seller [or seller or buyer after counter offer(s)] communicates unqualified acceptance, it is a contract. In this discussion, we refer to the document as the deposit receipt, offer, or contract.

Date and Place of Buyer's Offer

This is the date and place the deposit receipt is signed by the (prospective) buyer. This is *not* the date used to measure temporal compliance with any of the performance provisions of the contract. Those time constraints flow from the date a contract is formed by receipt of communication of acceptance.

The Full and Correct Name of the Buyer

This will include the buyer's marital status (single person, husband and wife, unmarried, widow or widower). If the buyer is a corporation, include the state where the corporation is chartered. If buyer is a general partnership, include the names of the partners. If buyer is a limited partnership, include the name of the general partner. If the buyer is a real estate licensee, disclose that fact. It is not necessary to include the manner in which buyer will take title. That will be taken care of in escrow.

Description of the Property

The property description must be adequate for a court to identify it: street address, map book, page and parcel, or other legal description.

Purchase Price and Terms

The offer must state unmistakably the total purchase price offered and the terms to which the buyer is willing to commit (e.g., all cash, new loan, or loan assumption). The total purchase price will *not* include the buyer's closing costs and any costs associated with obtaining financing.

Financing

The contract will contain a financing contingency unless the buyer is paying all cash or specified there is no loan contingency. That is, the loan(s) necessary for closing will be described and buyer will agree to act diligently to obtain the financing. There will be a time limitation for this to occur. If, in spite of buyer's diligent attempt, the stated financing is not obtained within the allotted time, the buyer must either cancel the contract or remove the financing contingency and proceed with the transaction.

Deposit

The offer will detail the form (cash, personal or cashier's check, promissory note, or money order), amount and disposition of buyer's deposit. Disposition means deposit of the funds into escrow or into the broker's trust account in a bank or other recognized depository in this state not later than three business days after receipt of the funds by the broker or by the broker's salesperson. If a check is used, the offer may require that the check be held after acceptance of the offer.

Time Constraints

The offer will require delivery of acceptance by a date certain. If this does not occur, the offer is revoked and the deposit must be returned.

The contract will require that buyer and seller deliver instructions to the escrow holder within a certain number of days after acceptance of the offer.

The contract will require that escrow close within a certain number of days after acceptance of the offer.

The contract will state that time is of the essence of the agreement and the time for performance can be extended or otherwise modified only by a writing signed by both buyer and seller.

Title and Vesting

The contract will state that title will vest as directed by the buyer in instructions to the escrow holder. As there can be significant legal and tax implications, a real estate licensee should urge a buyer to seek competent advice regarding the manner of taking title.

The contract will typically require transfer by grant deed, with mineral, oil and water rights if currently owned by the seller.

The contract will state that title must be free of financing liens except as provided in the contract and will be subject to all other encumbrances, easements, covenants, conditions, and restrictions, etc. shown in the preliminary title report. Title will also be subject to any other exceptions disclosed to, or discovered by, the buyer prior to closing unless the buyer disapproves in writing of a particular exception.

The contract will designate which party must pay for a preliminary title report and a policy of title insurance.

Prorations

Typically, the contract will require that certain expenses of ownership be paid current as of the date of close of escrow, to become the buyer's responsibility thereafter. These include:

- real property taxes (including supplemental taxes) and assessments;
- if applicable, homeowners' association assessments;
- premiums on insurance assumed by buyer; and
- payments on bonds assumed by buyer.

If the property is a rental, the rent will be prorated so that any prepaid rent for time on and after the date of close of escrow will be credited to the buyer.

Transfer Taxes/Fees
The contract will fix responsibility for the county transfer tax, the city transfer tax (if any) and any homeowners' association transfer fee.

Occupancy and Possession
The contract will include a paragraph in which the buyer designates whether he/she will occupy the property as a principal residence. The contract will further require delivery of possession (keys, etc.) on a date certain, usually the date escrow closes. If the seller is to remain in possession after close of escrow or if the buyer is to take possession prior to close of escrow, such possession should be by appropriate written agreement.

Buyer's Inspection of the Property
Acceptance of the property's condition is a contract provision, subject to inspections to be conducted at buyer's expense. The buyer must communicate approval of the property's condition or request the seller make repairs or take other actions The buyer and seller then have a certain period of time to negotiate buyer's requests. If the seller is willing to correct the items, the transaction proceeds. If the seller is unable or unwilling to correct the items, the buyer must either proceed with the transaction or cancel the contract.

Condition of the Property
The Property is usually sold in its condition on the date of acceptance of the contract. The buyer still has the right to inspect the property and request that the seller make repairs. The seller remains obligated to disclose known material defects, however.

Smoke Detector(s)
The contract may reiterate state laws that require that dwelling units be equipped with smoke detectors approved by the State Fire Marshall. In an existing dwelling, there must be a battery operated smoke detector outside each sleeping area. As of August 14, 1992, new construction (or an addition, alteration or repair that exceeds $1,000 and requires a permit or includes addition of a sleeping room) must include smoke detectors in each bedroom and at a point centrally located *outside* the bedroom(s). In new construction, the smoke detector(s) must be hard-wired, with battery back-up. The seller must give the buyer written certification of smoke detector compliance, as required by Health and Safety Code Section 13113.8. This may be done in the contract or in a separate writing. Certain transactions are exempt from this requirement, as set forth in Health and Safety Code Section 13113.8(d). These exemptions are nearly identical to those set forth below relative to the provision of a Transfer Disclosure Statement.

Water Heater Bracing
The contract may set forth the seller's duty to see that each water heater is braced, anchored or strapped, in accordance with the California Plumbing Code, to resist falling or horizontal displacement during an earthquake. As indicated in Health and Safety Code Section 19211, the seller must give the buyer written certification of compliance in the contract, the Homeowner's Guide to Earthquake Safety

(discussed below), in the Transfer Disclosure Statement, or in some other transaction document.

Retrofit

The contract should assign responsibility for any retrofitting required, upon sale, by the local government. This could include installation of low flow shower heads and gallon restricted flush toilets.

Governmental Compliance

The contract may include the seller's representation that he/she has no knowledge of any notice of violation of any building, zoning, fire, or health laws, regulations or ordinances. If the seller has such knowledge, disclosure must be made. Further, the contract may include the seller's covenant to notify the buyer if the seller receives a notice of violation.

Fixtures

Subject to specific exclusions made part of the contract, the buyer is entitled to all fixtures. Fixtures are items attached permanently (e.g., by cement, plaster, bolts, screws, or nails) to what is permanent (walls, etc.). Examples are electrical, lighting, plumbing and heating fixtures, fireplace inserts, solar systems, built-in appliances, window coverings, TV antennas, air conditioners, and in-ground landscaping.

Personal Property

The buyer is entitled to only that personal property listed in the contract. This could include any large outside potted plants, as these are ordinarily not fixtures.

Home Warranty Plans

The contract may remind seller and buyer of the availability of home warranty plans. If a plan is to be purchased, the contract will detail the duration, maximum cost, provider, and responsibility for payment.

Septic/Sewer/Well Systems

As applicable, the contract should specify responsibility for inspection and any needed repair of the septic system and testing of the well for potability and production. If local law requires connection to a sewer system, the contract must assign this responsibility. Of course, these items must be completed prior to close of escrow.

Pest Control

The contract will specify whether or not a pest control inspection is to be performed and, if so, at whose expense and may specify who must pay for any work required so that a registered structural pest control company can issue a written certification that the property is free of evidence of active infestation in the accessible areas. Lenders may require issuance of a certification prior to funding. If the contract provides that some of the required work will be completed at seller's expense after close of escrow, that provision may also require that the seller deposit funds into escrow, to be disbursed when the buyer has received a written certification.

A copy of the structural pest control inspection report (and other pest control documents required by Civil Code Section 1099) must be delivered to the buyer as soon as practical before transfer of title, provided the report is a condition affecting the transfer or financing of the property. If more than one licensee is acting as an agent in the transaction, the selling agent must deliver the documents, unless the seller has given written instructions to another licensee acting as agent in the transaction to make the delivery. The responsible broker shall maintain a record of action taken to effect compliance. (Commissioner's Regulation 2905)

Rental Property

If applicable, an addendum to the contract should state that the buyer takes the property subject to the rights of existing tenants. The contract can help ensure that the rental situation undergoes a smooth transition by requiring that:

- the seller, within a stated period of time, give the buyer copies of the rental agreement/lease, the current income and expense statement, and any notices sent to the tenants;

- the seller cannot make any changes to the rental agreement/lease without the buyer's consent;

- the seller must give the buyer written statements from the tenants confirming the salient aspects of the tenancy and that no defaults exist; and

- the seller must transfer to the buyer, through escrow, any unused tenant deposits.

Repairs and Final Inspection

The contract may provide that all required repairs will be performed in a skillful manner with materials of comparable quality to the original and, unless otherwise agreed in writing, be completed prior to close of escrow. The buyer can be given the right to inspect the property prior to close of escrow to confirm both the repairs and that the property is otherwise in the same condition as when the contract was formed.

Sale of Buyer's Property

If applicable, the contract will provide that buyer is not obligated to complete the transaction unless buyer closes escrow on the sale of his/her property, as described. The contract may then afford the seller two options:

- to continue to offer the property for sale and to accept another offer. If this happens, the contract will provide that the buyer must, in writing and within a stated period of time, remove this contingency and the loan contingency of there is one. If the buyer does not do this, the transaction is terminated.

- to continue to market the property for back-up offers only.

Property Destruction or Damage

The contract may assign the risk of loss due to destruction or damage to the property which is not the fault of either buyer or seller. If the contract does not, then damage or destruction prior to close of escrow is the seller's problem. An exception to this would be damage or destruction occurring after buyer takes possession but before escrow closes (i.e., buyer moved in as a tenant).

Multiple Listing Service

The contract may give the brokers authorization to report the terms of the transaction to any MLS, to be published and distributed to other parties on terms approved by the MLS.

Equal Housing Opportunity

The contract may inform the parties that the property is sold in compliance with federal, state and local anti-discrimination laws. It is illegal to discriminate on the basis of race, color, religion, sex, handicap, familial status, or national origin.

Mediation/Arbitration of Disputes

The parties may agree to mediate all disputes and claims before resorting to arbitration or court action. A mediator is impartial and may facilitate resolution of a dispute but cannot impose a settlement. However, mediation can result in a binding settlement document signed by seller and buyer. For mediation which is not successful, the contract may afford the option of proceeding to arbitration. An arbitration, conducted in accordance with the rules of either the American Arbitration Association (AAA) or Judicial Arbitration and Mediation Services, Inc. (JAMS), results in a binding decision.

Liquidated Damages

If separately signed or initialed by both seller and buyer, the liquidated damages paragraph is activated and provides that if the seller proves that the buyer breached the contract:

1. The seller is released from the obligation to sell the property to the buyer.
2. The amount of the liquidated damages is limited to the buyer's deposit, to a maximum of 3% of the purchase price.

The liquidated damages provision must be printed in at least 10-point bold type or in contrasting red print in at least 8-point bold type.

If the deposit was increased after the initial offer/acceptance, the buyer and seller must, if the amount of the increase is to be subject to liquidated damages, sign a separate liquidated damages agreement covering the increased deposit.

Attorney's Fees

The contract may provide that the prevailing party in any action, proceeding or arbitration between buyer and seller is entitled to reasonable attorney's fees and costs. This provision may include an exclusion if the prevailing party commenced the action, proceeding or arbitration without first attempting mediation.

Offer and Acceptance - Contract

In order to form a binding contract, the seller must accept the buyer's offer, without modification, and communicate that acceptance to the buyer before a specified expiration date.

If the seller finds unacceptable some element(s) of the offer, the seller may make a counteroffer, giving the buyer a certain time to accept. These negotiations will culminate in either a stalemate or a contract. If a contract is reached, the result will be either breach or transfer of the property.

The acceptance clause may include the seller's agreement to compensate the listing and selling broker's:

* on recordation of the deed;

- upon seller's default; or
- upon buyer's default (a stated portion of any damages seller recovers from buyer, after first deducting title and escrow expenses and any costs of collection).

DISCLOSURES

The following are important disclosure requirements which attach primarily to the sale of residential real property of one-to-four units.

Real Estate Transfer Disclosure Statement
Many facts about a residential property affect its value and desirability. These include:

- age, condition, and any defects or malfunctions of the structural components and/or plumbing, electrical, heating, or other mechanical systems;

- easements, common driveways, or fences;

- room additions, structural alterations, repairs, replacements, or other changes, especially those made without required building permits;

- flood, drainage, settling or soil problems on or near the property;

- zoning violations, such as nonconforming uses or insufficient setbacks;

- homeowners' association obligations and deed restrictions or "common area" problems;

- citations against the property or lawsuits against the owner or affecting the property;

- neighborhood noise or nuisance problems; and

- location of the property within a known earthquake zone.

California Civil Code Section 1102.3 requires that a seller of real property consisting of one-to-four residential dwelling units deliver to prospective buyers a specified written disclosure statement concerning the condition of the property. The disclosure covers matters within the personal knowledge of the seller and the agent, and matters based on a reasonably diligent inspection of the property. This requirement extends to any transfer by sale, exchange, installment land sale contract, lease with an option to purchase, any other option to purchase, or ground lease coupled with improvements. The following transfers are exempt:

- transfers required to be preceded by delivery to the prospective transferee of a subdivision public report or where a public report is not required because the offering of subdivided land satisfies all the criteria in Business and Professions Code Section 11010.4;

- transfer pursuant to a court order;

- transfer to a mortgagee by a mortgagor who is in default; transfer by a foreclosure sale, or pursuant to a power of sale, after such default;

- transfer by a fiduciary in the administration of a decedent's estate, guardianship, conservatorship or certain transfers from a trust;

- transfer from one co-owner to another;

- transfer to a spouse or to a person or persons in the lineal line of consanguinity;

- transfer between spouses resulting from a judgment of dissolution of marriage or of legal separation or from a property settlement agreement incidental to such a judgment;

- transfer by the State Controller of unclaimed property;

- transfer resulting from failure to pay taxes; and

- transfer to or from any governmental entity.

The required disclosure must be delivered to the prospective buyer as soon as practicable before transfer of title, or before the execution of the contract in the case of a lease option, sales contract, or ground lease coupled with improvements. If any disclosure or amended disclosure is delivered after execution of the offer by the buyer, the buyer has three days after delivery in person or five days after delivery by deposit in the United States mail to terminate the offer or agreement to purchase by delivering a written notice of termination to the seller or to the seller's agent.

The obligation to prepare and deliver disclosures is imposed upon the seller and the seller's agent and any agent acting in cooperation with such agent. If more than one real estate agent is involved in the transaction, (unless otherwise instructed by the seller) the agent obtaining the offer is required to deliver the disclosures to the prospective buyer. If the disclosure is based on a report or opinion of an expert, such as a contractor or structural pest control operator, the seller and the agent may be protected from liability for any error as to the item covered by the report or opinion.

The required disclosures are set forth in Civil Code Section 1102.6.

Local Option Disclosure Statement
Civil Code Section 1102.6a permits any city or county to require an additional disclosure statement focusing on some local condition which may materially affect a buyer's use and enjoyment of residential property. The statute uses the example of adjacent land zoned for timber production and perhaps subject to harvest.

Mello-Roos Disclosure
The Mello-Roos Community Facilities Act of 1982 authorizes the formation of community facilities districts, the issuance of bonds, and the levying of special taxes thereunder to finance designated public facilities and services. Civil Code Section 1102.6b requires that a seller of a property consisting of one-to-four dwelling units subject to the lien of a Mello-Roos community facilities district make a good faith effort to obtain from the district a disclosure notice concerning the special tax and give the notice to a prospective buyer. The same exemptions apply as for delivery of a Real Property Transfer Disclosure Statement.

Smoke Detector Statement of Compliance
See discussion above under "DEPOSIT RECEIPT/CONTRACT."

Disclosure Regarding Lead-Based Paint Hazards
Many housing units in California still contain lead-based paint, which was banned for residential use in 1978. Lead-based paint can peel, chip, and deteriorate into contaminated dust, thus becoming a lead-based paint hazard. A child's ingestion of the lead-laced chips or dust may result in learning disabilities, delayed development or behavior disorders.

The federal Real Estate Disclosure and Notification Rule (the Rule) requires that owners of "residential dwellings" built before 1978 disclose to their agents and to prospective buyers or lessees/renters the presence of lead-based paint and/or lead-based paint hazards and any known information and reports about lead-based paint and lead-based paint hazards (location and condition of the painted surfaces, etc.). The Rule defines a residential dwelling as a single-family dwelling or a single-family dwelling unit in a structure that contains more than one separate residential dwelling unit, and in which each such unit is used or occupied, or intended to be used or occupied, in whole or in part, as the residence of one or more persons.

Properties affected by the Rule are termed target housing. Target housing does *not* include pre-1978 housing which is:

- sold at a foreclosure sale (but a subsequent sale of such a property *is* covered);

- a "0-bedroom dwelling" (e.g., a loft, efficiency unit or studio);

- a dwelling unit leased for 100 or fewer days (e.g., a vacation home or short-term rental), provided the lease cannot be renewed or extended;

- housing designated for the elderly or handicapped, unless children reside there or are expected to reside there;

- leased housing for which the requirements of the Rule have been satisfied, no pertinent new information is available, and the lease is renewed or renegotiated;

- rental housing that has been inspected by a certified inspector and found to be free of lead-based paint. (The Rule allows use of state certified inspectors only until a federal certification program or a federally accredited state certification program is in place.)

Sellers (and lessors) of units in pre-1978 multifamily structures will have to provide a buyer (or lessee) with any available records or reports pertaining to lead-based paint and/or lead-based paint hazards in areas used by all the residents (stairwells, lobbies, recreation rooms, laundry rooms, etc.). If there has been an evaluation or reduction of lead-based paint and/or lead-based paint hazards in the entire structure, the disclosure requirement extends to any available records or reports regarding the other dwelling units.

The federal Environmental Protection Agency (EPA) publishes a pamphlet titled *"Protect Your Family From Lead In Your Home."* This pamphlet describes ways to recognize and reduce lead hazards. The Rule requires that a seller (or lessor) of target housing deliver this pamphlet to a prospective buyer (or tenant) before a contract is formed. If this is done after that time the buyer has the right to cancel the contract.

The Rule requires that a seller of target housing offer a prospective buyer ten days to inspect for lead-based paint and lead-based paint hazards. This 10-day inspection period can be increased, decreased, or waived by written agreement between buyer and seller. The Rule does not require a seller to pay for an inspection or to remove any lead-based paint/hazards, but merely gives a buyer the opportunity to have the property inspected. A list of State-certified lead inspectors and contractors is available by calling the California Department of Health Services at (800) 597-LEAD.

The Rule further requires that the seller's (or lessor's) lead-based paint/lead-based paint hazards disclosures, a Lead Warning Statement, and the buyer's (or lessee's) acknowledgment of receipt of the information, offer of inspection period (or waiver of same) and the EPA pamphlet be included in an attachment to the contract. Seller (or lessor), buyer (or tenant) and agent must sign and date the attachment. The retention period, for sellers (or lessors) and agents, of this document is three years from completion of the sale (or from commencement of the lease/rental).

A real estate agent must ensure that:

- his or her principal (seller or lessor) is aware of the disclosure requirements;
- the transaction documentation includes the required notifications and disclosures;
- the buyer or lessee/renter receives the EPA pamphlet; and,
- in the case of a sale, the buyer is offered an opportunity to have the property inspected for lead-based paint and lead-based paint hazards. In the case of a sale, "agent" does not include one who represents only the buyer and receives compensation only from the buyer.

Violation of the Rule may result in civil and/or criminal penalties.

To obtain the essential compliance information, a person may call the EPA at 1-800-424-LEAD.

California's environmental hazards pamphlet. As discussed above, in California a seller (with a few exceptions) of residential real property comprising one-to-four dwelling units must give the buyer a Real Estate Transfer Disclosure Statement. The statement must include environmental hazards of which the seller is aware. The listing and selling agents must inspect the property and disclose to the buyer material facts, including environmental hazards (e.g., lead-based paint), which may affect the value or desirability of the property. Further, the seller or the seller's agent can give the buyer (of any real property) a pamphlet titled *"Environmental Hazards: A Guide for Homeowners, Buyers, Landlords, and Tenants."* If the buyer receives the pamphlet, neither the seller nor agent is required to say more about environmental hazards (again, assuming no awareness of such a problem).

Disclosures Regarding State Responsibility Areas
The Department of Forestry and Fire Protection (the Department) has produced maps identifying rural lands classified as state responsibility areas. In a state responsibility area, the state (as opposed to a local or federal agency) has the

primary financial responsibility for the prevention and extinguishing of fires. Maps of these state responsibility areas and any changes (including new maps to be produced every five years) are to be provided to assessors in the affected counties.

If a seller knows that the property is located in a state responsibility area or the property is included on a map given by the Department to the county assessor, the seller must disclose the possibility of substantial fire risk and that the land is subject to certain preventative requirements. (Public Resources Code Section 4291 lists the requirements.) Notices of the location of the maps will be posted at the offices of the county recorder, county assessor, and the county planning commission.

With the agreement of the Director of Forestry and Fire Protection, a county may, by ordinance, assume responsibility for *all* fires, including those occurring in state responsibility areas. Absent such an ordinance, the seller of property located in a state responsibility area must disclose to the buyer that the state is *not* obligated to provide fire protection services for any building or structure unless such protection is required by a cooperative agreement with a county, city, or district.

These disclosures must be made on the Natural Hazard Zone Disclosure Statement.

Disclosure of Ordnance Location
Federal and state agencies have identified certain areas once used for military training which may contain live ammunition. A seller of residential property located within one mile of such a hazard must, pursuant to Civil Code Section 1102.15, give the buyer written notice as soon as practicable before transfer of title. This obligation depends upon the seller having actual knowledge of the hazard. The exemptions which pertain to delivery of the Real Property Transfer Disclosure Statement apply also to this requirement.

Disclosure of Geological Hazards and Earthquake Fault Zones
Pursuant to the Alquist-Priolo Earthquake Fault Zoning Act, the State Geologist is in the process of identifying areas of the state susceptible to "fault creep" and delineating these areas on maps prepared by the State Division of Mines and Geology.

A seller of real property situated in an earthquake fault zone, or the agent of the seller and any agent acting in cooperation with such agent, must disclose to the buyer that the property is or may be situated in an earthquake fault zone. This disclosure must be made on the Natural Hazard Zone Disclosure Statement,

In addition, the Seismic Safety Commission has developed a Homeowner's Guide to Earthquake Safety for distribution to real estate licensees and the general public. The guide includes information on geologic and seismic hazards for all areas, explanations of related structural and nonstructural hazards, recommendations for mitigating the hazards of an earthquake, and a statement that safety or damage prevention cannot be guaranteed with respect to a major earthquake and that only precautions such as retrofitting can be undertaken to reduce the risk. The Seismic Safety Commission has also developed a Commercial Property Owner's Guide to Earthquake Safety.

If a buyer receives a copy of the Homeowner's Guide (or, if applicable, the Commercial Property Owner's Guide), neither the seller nor the broker are required to provide additional information regarding geologic and seismic hazards. Sellers and real estate licensees must, however, disclose that the property is in an earthquake fault zone and the existence of known hazards affecting the real property being transferred.

Delivery of a booklet is required in the following transactions:

1. Transfer of any real property improved with a residential dwelling built prior to January 1, 1960 and consisting of one-to-four units any of which are of conventional light-frame construction (Homeowner's Guide); and,

2. Transfer of any masonry building with wood-frame floors or roofs built before January 1, 1975 (if residential, both guides; if commercial property, only the Commercial Guide).

In a transfer subject to item 1 above, the following aspects of the structure and any corrective measures taken, which are within the seller's actual knowledge, must be disclosed to a prospective buyer:

*   absence of foundation anchor bolts;

*   unbraced or inappropriately braced perimeter cripple walls;

*   unbraced or inappropriately braced first-story wall or walls;

*   unreinforced masonry perimeter foundation;

*   unreinforced masonry dwelling walls;

*   habitable room or rooms above a garage; and

*   water heater not anchored, strapped, or braced.

Certain exemptions apply to the obligation to deliver the booklet when transferring either a dwelling of one-to-four units or a *reinforced* masonry building. These exemptions are essentially the same as those that apply to delivery of the Real Estate Transfer Disclosure Statement.

Environmental Hazard Disclosures

The Real Estate Transfer Disclosure Statement includes disclosure of hazardous substances, materials, or products including, but not limited to, asbestos, formaldehyde, radon gas, lead-based paint, fuel or chemical storage tanks, and contaminated soil or water.

(Lessees or renters of real property who know or suspect that a release of a hazardous substance has occurred or may occur on or beneath the property are required to provide written notice of that condition to the property owner or lessor. Failure of the lessee or renter to provide written notice to the property owner or lessor may subject the lessee or renter to actual damages and/or civil penalties.)

The Department of Real Estate, the Department of Toxic Substances Control, and the Office of Environmental Health Hazard Assessment have developed a booklet to be used for the purpose of educating and informing consumers on environmental hazards which may be located on and affect real property. The booklet, titled *Environmental Hazards: A Guide for Homeowners, Buyers, Landlords, and Tenants* identifies common environmental hazards, describes the risks involved with each, discusses mitigation techniques, and provides lists of publications and sources from which consumers can obtain more detailed information. Hazards discussed in the booklet are asbestos, radon, lead, and formaldehyde. The booklet also provides general information on hazardous wastes and the use and disposal of hazardous household products.

If the booklet is provided to a prospective buyer of real property, neither the seller nor a real estate agent involved in the sale has a duty to provide further information concerning such hazards, other than lead, unless the seller or licensee has actual knowledge of the existence of environmental hazards on or affecting the subject property.

Energy Conservation Retrofit and Thermal Insulation Disclosure

State law prescribes a minimum energy conservation standard for all new construction without which a building permit may not be issued. Local governments also have ordinances that impose additional energy conservation measures on new and/or existing homes. Some local ordinances impose energy retrofitting as a condition of the sale of an existing home. The requirements of the various ordinances, as well as who is responsible for compliance, may vary among local jurisdictions. The existence and basic requirements of local energy ordinances should be disclosed to a prospective buyer by the seller and/or the seller's agent and any cooperating agent.

Federal law requires a "new home" seller to disclose in every sales contract the type, thickness, and R-value of the insulation which has been or will be installed in the house.

Special Flood Hazard Area Disclosure and Responsibilities of FEMA

Flood Hazard Boundary Maps identify the general flood hazards within a community. They are also used in flood plain management and for flood insurance purposes. Flood Hazard Boundary Maps developed by the Federal Emergency Management Agency (FEMA) in conjunction with communities participating in the National Flood Insurance Program (NFIP) delineate areas within the 100-year flood boundary termed "special flood zone areas." Also identified are areas between 100 and 500-year levels termed "areas of moderate flood hazards" and the remaining areas above the 500-year level termed "areas of minimal risk."

A seller of property located in a special flood hazard area, or the seller's agent and any cooperating agent, must disclose that fact to the buyer and that federal law requires flood insurance as a condition of obtaining financing on most structures located in a special flood hazard area. Since the cost and extent of flood insurance coverage may vary, the buyer should contact an insurance carrier or the intended lender for further information. The disclosure must be made on the Natural Hazard Zone Disclosure Statement.

Local Requirements Resulting from City and County Ordinances

Residential properties located in cities and counties throughout California are typically subject to specific local ordinances relating to occupancy, zoning and use, building code compliance, and fire, health and safety code regulations. Whether such matters must be investigated when they are not within the personal knowledge of the seller or the agent may depend on the circumstances. Civil Code Section 2079.3 provides that the listing and selling agents' duty to inspect does not include areas off the site of the property or public records or permits concerning the title or use of the property in the absence of special circumstances.

Foreign Investment in Real Property Tax Act

Federal law requires that a buyer of real property must withhold and send to the Internal Revenue Service (IRS) 10% of the gross sales price if the seller of the real property is a "foreign person." The primary grounds for exemption from this requirement are: the seller's nonforeign affidavit and U.S. taxpayer I.D. number; a qualifying statement obtained through the IRS attesting to other arrangements resulting in collection of, or exemption from, the tax; or the sales price does not exceed $300,000 and the buyer intends to reside in the property.

Because of the number of exemptions and other requirements relating to this law, it is recommended that the IRS be consulted for more detailed information. Sellers and buyers and the real estate agents involved who desire further advice should also consult an attorney, CPA, or other qualified tax advisor.

Notice and Disclosure to Buyer of State Tax Withholding on Disposition of California Real Property

In certain California real estate sale transactions, the buyer must withhold 3 1/3% of the total sale price as state income tax and deliver the sum withheld to the State Franchise Tax Board. The escrow holder, in applicable transactions, is required by law to notify the buyer of this responsibility.

A buyer's failure to withhold and deliver the required sum may result in the buyer being subject to penalties. Should the escrow holder fail to notify the buyer, penalties may be levied against the escrow holder.

Transactions to which the law applies are those in which:

- The seller shows an out of state address, or sale proceeds are to be disbursed to a financial intermediary of the seller;
- The sales price exceeds $100,000; and,
- The seller does not certify that he/she is a resident of California or that the property being conveyed is his/her personal residence, as defined in Section 1034 of the Internal Revenue Code. (Note: If the seller is a corporation, the certification would be that the corporation has a permanent place of business in California.)

For further information, contact the Franchise Tax Board.

Furnishing Controlling Documents and a Financial Statement

The owner (other than a subdivider) of a separate interest in a common interest development (community apartment project, condominium project, planned development, or stock cooperative) must provide a prospective buyer with the following:

- a copy of the governing documents of the development;

- should there be an age restriction not consistent with Civil Code Section 51.3, a statement that the age restriction is only enforceable to the extent permitted by law and specifying the applicable provisions of law;

- a copy of the most recent documents of the homeowners' association, including financial statements, budgets and insurance information required under Civil Code Section 1365;

- a written statement from the association specifying the amount of the current regular and special assessments as well as any unpaid assessment, late charges, interest, and costs of collection which are or may become a lien against the property; and,

- information regarding any approved change in the assessments or fees which is not yet due and payable as of the disclosure date.

Notice Regarding the Advisability of Title Insurance

In an escrow for a sale (or exchange) of real property where no title insurance is to be issued, the buyer (or both parties to an exchange) must receive and sign the following notice as a separate document in the escrow:

"IMPORTANT: IN A PURCHASE OR EXCHANGE OF REAL PROPERTY, IT MAY BE ADVISABLE TO OBTAIN TITLE INSURANCE IN CONNECTION WITH THE CLOSE OF ESCROW SINCE THERE MAY BE PRIOR RECORDED LIENS AND ENCUMBRANCES WHICH AFFECT YOUR INTEREST IN THE PROPERTY BEING ACQUIRED. A NEW POLICY OF TITLE INSURANCE SHOULD BE OBTAINED IN ORDER TO ENSURE YOUR INTEREST IN THE PROPERTY THAT YOU ARE ACQUIRING."

This requirement is also of interest to a real estate broker conducting an escrow pursuant to the exemption set forth in Financial Code Section 17006(a)(4).

Visual Inspection

The real estate agent representing a seller of residential property consisting of one to four dwelling units (or a manufactured home) and any cooperating agent each have the duty to conduct a reasonably competent and diligent visual inspection of the property and to disclose to a prospective buyer all material facts affecting value, desirability, and implicitly intended use.

The required inspection does not include areas not reasonably accessible. If the real property is a dwelling unit in a condominium, planned development, or a stock cooperative, the visual inspection need only include the unit involved and not the common area. It also does not include investigation of areas off the site of the property or public records and permits in the absence of special circumstances.

Nothing in the law relieves a buyer of the duty to exercise reasonable care to protect himself/herself, including the facts that are known to or within the reasonably diligent attention and observation of the buyer.

An agent's certification of performing the required visual inspection is contained in the Real Estate Transfer Disclosure Statement. This requirement does not apply if the sale is made pursuant to a subdivision public report or the sale is exempt from the public report requirement pursuant to Business and Professions Code Section 11010.4, *provided* that the property has not been previously occupied.

(See also Chapter 10.)

Agency Relationship Disclosure

To clarify relationships between buyers and sellers and real estate brokers, the law requires persons acting as agents in certain residential real estate transactions to make statutorily prescribed written disclosures concerning the agency roles intended. This requirement applies to transactions involving the sale or exchange of certain estates (including leases of more than one year) in residential real property of from one-to-four dwelling units, as well as the sale or exchange of mobilehomes occurring through a real estate agent. The seller should receive the agency disclosure before signing the listing agreement.

Principals and agents may modify and change the agency relationship(s) between the parties by written consent of all of the parties to the transaction. The required agency disclosure form is set forth in Civil Code Section 2079.16.

(See also Chapter 10.)

No Disclosure Required for Manner/Occurrence of Death; Affliction of Occupant with AIDS

No cause of action arises against an owner or the owner's agent (or any cooperating agent) when selling, leasing, or renting real property and failing to disclose to the buyer, lessee, or renter the following:

• the manner or occurrence of an occupant's death upon the real property if the death occurred more than 3 years prior to the transferee's offer to purchase, lease, or rent the property; or

• that an occupant of the property was afflicted with, or died from, Acquired Immune Deficiency Syndrome (AIDS).

Note that the controlling statute does not change the law relating to disclosure of any other physical or mental condition or disease of an occupant or the physical condition of the property. Further, the statute will not protect the owner or agent(s) from misrepresentation if the buyer asks a direct question concerning deaths occurring on the real property.

Disclosure of Sale Price Information

Within one month after the close of escrow for the transfer of title to real property (or the sale of a business opportunity) through a real estate agent(s), the agent(s) must inform the buyer and seller in writing of the selling price. In the case of an exchange, the information on the selling price is required to include a description of the property and the amount of added money consideration, if any.

If a transaction is closed through an authorized third party escrow holder, a closing statement from said escrow holder will be regarded as compliance with the requirements of this law.

Seller Financing Disclosure Statement

Some sellers of residential properties participate in financing the sale of their homes by extending credit to the buyer in the form of a seller "carry-back." This is usually in the form of a promissory note secured by a deed of trust. To ensure adequate disclosure and to prevent abuses involving some of these seller-assisted financing plans, the state legislature enacted a disclosure law which applies to real estate transactions involving residential dwellings of not more than four units if the seller extends credit to the buyer through a written agreement which provides for either a finance charge or more than four payments of principal and interest (or interest only), not including the down payment.

Written disclosures required by this law are the responsibility of the *arranger of credit*. An *arranger of credit* is defined as a person who is not a party to the transaction (except as noted below), but is involved in negotiation of the credit terms and completion of the credit documents, and who is compensated for arranging the credit or for facilitating the transaction. A real estate broker may be deemed an arranger of credit. The duty to provide the disclosures also applies to an attorney or a real estate licensee who is a principal in the transaction.

Disclosures pursuant to this law are *not* required to be given to a buyer or seller who is entitled to receive (in connection with the credit being extended) a disclosure under any of the following :

- Federal Truth-in-Lending Act;

- Real Estate Settlement Procedures Act (RESPA);

- A mortgage loan disclosure statement (Business and Professions Code Section 10240) or a lender/purchaser disclosure statement (Business and Professions Code Section 10232.4); or

- Section 25110 of the Corporations Code or exemption therefrom relating to the sale of qualified securities under permit or exempt securities or transaction.

The disclosure statement required by this law must be delivered as soon as possible before the execution of any note or security document. The statement must be signed by the arranger of credit and the buyer and seller, who are each to receive a copy. Should there be more than one arranger of credit, the arranger obtaining the offer from the buyer is responsible for making the disclosure unless another person is designated in writing by the parties to the transaction.

The disclosure statement will include comprehensive information about the financing, cautions applicable to certain types of financing, and suggestions of procedures which will protect the parties during the term of the financing. The disclosures include:

- identification of the note, or credit, or security document and the property which is or will become the security;

- a copy of the note, or credit, or security document, or a description of the terms of these documents;

- the terms and conditions of each encumbrance recorded against the property which shall remain as a lien or is an anticipated lien which will be senior to the financing being arranged;

- a warning about the hazards and potential difficulty of refinancing and, should the existing financing or the financing being arranged involve a balloon payment, the amount and due date of any balloon payment and a warning that new financing may not be available;

- an explanation of the possible effects of an *increase* in the amount owed due to negative amortization as a result of any variable or adjustable-rate financing being arranged;

- if the financing being arranged involves an all-inclusive trust deed (AITD), a statement of the possible penalties, discounts, responsibilities, and rights of parties to the transaction with respect to acceleration and/or prepayment of a prior encumbrance as the result of the creation and/or refinancing of the AITD;

- if the financing involves an AITD or a real property sales contract, a statement identifying the party to whom payments will be made and to whom such payments will be forwarded, and if the party receiving and forwarding the payments is not a neutral third party, a warning that the principals may wish to designate a neutral third party;

- a complete disclosure about the prospective buyer, including credit and employment information along with a statement that the disclosure is not a representation of the credit worthiness of the prospective buyer; or, a statement that no representation regarding the credit worthiness of the prospective buyer is being made;

- a warning regarding possible limitations on the seller's ability, in the event of foreclosure, to recover proceeds of the sale financed;

- a statement recommending loss payee clauses be added to the property insurance policy to protect the seller's interest and advising of the existence or the availability of services which will notify the seller if the property taxes are not paid;

- a statement suggesting or acknowledging that the seller should file or has filed a request for notice of delinquency and a request for notice of default in case the buyer fails to pay liens senior to the financing being arranged;

- a statement that a title insurance policy has been or will be obtained and furnished to the buyer and seller insuring their respective interests, or that the buyer and seller should each obtain title insurance coverage;

- a disclosure whether the security documents for the financing being arranged have been or will be recorded, and what might occur if the documents are not recorded; and,

- information as to whether the buyer is to receive any *"cash back"* from the sale, including the amount, source, and purpose of the cash refund.

The requirement of a seller financing disclosure statement also applies to transactions by real property sales contracts (as defined in Civil Code Section 2985) and to leases with option-to-purchase provisions where the facts demonstrate intent to transfer equitable title. If the extension of credit is subject to a balloon payment, a balloon payment notice is to be included on the face of the promissory note or other evidence of debt.

An arranger of credit must inform the seller that a buyer who intends to occupy the real property involved may have the right to homeownership counseling in the event of a default in the mortgage payments. The collector of the payments, whether the seller or a loan servicing agent, has the duty to inform the defaulting homeowner of the availability of such counseling. Loss of or reduced ability to make payments on a residence may entitle the homeowner to the aforementioned counseling. The duty to inform a defaulting homeowner of the availability of counseling is operative regardless of the nature of the credit transaction or the presence of an arranger of credit.

Water Heater Bracing
See discussion above under "DEPOSIT RECEIPT/CONTRACT

23 Trust Funds

Real estate brokers and salespersons receive trust funds in the normal course of doing business. They receive these funds on behalf of others, thereby creating a fiduciary responsibility to the funds' owners. Brokers and salespersons must handle, control and account for these trust funds according to established legal standards. While compliance with these standards may not necessarily have a direct bearing on the financial success of a real estate business, non-compliance can result in unfavorable business consequences. Improper handling of trust funds is cause for revocation or suspension of a real estate license, not to mention the possibility of being held financially liable for damages incurred by clients.

This chapter discusses the legal requirements for receiving and handling trust funds in real estate transactions as set forth in the Real Estate Law and the Regulations of the Real Estate Commissioner. It describes the requisites for maintaining a trust fund bank account and the precautions a licensee should take to ensure the integrity of the account. It explains and illustrates the trust fund record keeping requirements under the Business and Professions Code and the Commissioner's Regulations.

The discussions and examples in this chapter involve real property sales and property management trust account transactions. Other types of real estate activities involving trust funds, although subject to the same laws and regulations, may also have to comply with additional legal and regulatory requirements. While these other types of transactions may require records significantly different from those illustrated, the record keeping fundamentals still apply.

GENERAL INFORMATION

Trust Funds and Non-Trust Funds

Since trust funds must be handled in a special manner, a licensee must be able to distinguish trust funds from non-trust funds. Trust funds are money or other things of value that are received by a broker or salesperson on behalf of a principal or any other person, and which are held for the benefit of others in the performance of any acts for which a real estate license is required. Trust funds may be cash or non-cash items. Some examples are; cash; a check used as a purchase deposit (whether made payable to the broker or to an escrow or title company); a personal note made payable to the seller; or even an automobile's "pink slip" given as a deposit.

The discussions in this chapter pertain to real estate trust funds received by licensees, and not to non-trust funds such as real estate commissions, general operating funds, and rents and deposits from broker-owned real estate. These other types of funds, as long as not commingled with trust funds, are not subject to the Real Estate Law and Commissioner's Regulations. It should be noted, however, that under certain circumstances the Department of Real Estate does have the jurisdiction to look into transactions involving non-trust funds.

Why a Trust Account?

A trust account is set up as a means to separate trust funds from non-trust funds. Although it can certainly be argued that keeping trust funds in a trust account will not prevent a dishonest broker from misusing the funds, separating client's funds from the broker's own funds provides a better physical and accounting control over the trust funds.

An important reason for designating a trust fund depository as a trust account is the protection afforded principals' funds in situations where legal action is taken against the broker or if the broker becomes incapacitated or dies. Trust funds held in a true trust account cannot be "frozen" pending litigation against the broker or during probate.

Trust funds also have better insurance protection if deposited into a trust account. The general counsel of the FDIC, in an opinion in 1965, held that funds of various owners which are placed in a custodial deposit (trust account) in an insured bank will be recognized for insurance purposes to the same extent as if the owners' names and interests in the account are individually disclosed on the records of the bank, provided the trust account is specifically designated as custodial and the name and interest of each owner of funds in the account are disclosed on the depositor's records. Each client with funds deposited in a trust account maintained with a federally insured bank is insured by the FDIC up to $100,000, as opposed to just $100,000 for the entire account, as long as the regulatory requirements are met.

Trust Fund Handling Requirements

A typical trust fund transaction begins with the broker or salesperson receiving trust funds from a principal in connection with the purchase or lease of real property. According to Business and Professions Code Section 10145, trust funds received must be placed into the hands of the owner(s) of the funds, into a neutral escrow depository, or into a trust account maintained pursuant to Commissioner's Regulation 2832 not later than three business days following receipt of the funds by the broker or by the broker's salesperson.

An exception to this rule is *when* a check is received from an offeror in connection with an offer to purchase or lease real property. As provided under Commissioner's Regulation 2832, a deposit check may be held uncashed by the broker until acceptance of the offer if the following conditions are met:

1.   the check by its terms is not negotiable by the broker, or the offeror has given written instructions that the check shall not be deposited or cashed until acceptance of the offer; and

2.   the offeree is informed, before or at the time the offer is presented for acceptance, that the check is being held.

If the offer is later accepted, the broker may continue to hold the check undeposited only if the broker receives written authorization from the offeree to do so. Otherwise, the check must be placed, not later than three business days after acceptance, into a neutral escrow depository or into the trust fund bank account or into the hands of the offeree if both the offeror and offeree expressly so provide in writing.

According to Business and Professions Code Section 10145, a real estate salesperson who accepts trust funds on behalf of the broker under whom he or she is licensed must immediately deliver the funds to the broker or, if directed *to do so* by the broker, place the funds into the hands of the broker's principal or into a neutral escrow depository or deposit the funds into the broker's trust fund bank account.

A *neutral escrow depository*, as used in Business and Professions Code Section 10145, means an escrow business conducted by a person licensed under Division 6 (commencing with Section 17000) of the Financial Code or by any person described in subdivisions (a)(1) and (a)(3) of Section 17006 of the Financial Code.

Identifying the Owner(s) of Trust Funds

A broker must be able to identify who owns the trust funds and who is entitled to receive them, since these funds can be disposed of only upon the authorization of that person. The person entitled to the funds may or may not be the person who originally gave the funds to the broker or the salesperson. In some instances the party entitled to the funds will change upon the occurrence of certain events in the transaction. For example, in a transaction involving an offer to buy or lease real property or a business opportunity, the party entitled to the funds received from the offeror (prospective buyer or lessor) will depend upon whether or not the offer has been accepted by the offeree (seller or landlord).

Prior to the acceptance of the offer, the funds received from the offeror belong to that person and must be handled according to his/her instructions. If the funds are deposited in a trust fund bank account, they must be maintained there for the benefit of the offeror until acceptance of the offer. Or, as discussed in the previous section, if the offeror wishes, his/her check may be held uncashed by the broker as long as he/she gives written instructions to the broker to do so and the offeree is informed before or at the time the offer is presented for acceptance that the check is being so held.

After acceptance of the offer, the funds shall be handled according to instructions from the offeror and the offeree as follows:

- An offeror's check held uncashed by the broker before acceptance of the offer may continue to be held uncashed after acceptance of the offer, only upon written authorization from the offeree. [Commissioner's Regulation 2832(d)]

- The offeror's check may be given to the offeree only if the offeror and offeree expressly so provide in writing. [Commissioner's Regulation 2832(d)]

- All or part of an offeror's purchase money deposit in a real estate sales transaction shall not be refunded by an agent or subagent of the seller without the *express written permission* of the offeree to make the refund.

TRUST FUND BANK ACCOUNTS

General Requirements

Trust funds, such as a purchase money deposit check, received by a licensee that are not forwarded directly to the broker's principal or to a neutral escrow depository or for which the broker does not have authorization to hold uncashed must be deposited to the broker's trust fund bank account. (Business and Professions Code Section 10145)

Business and Professions Code Section 10145 and Commissioner's Regulation 2832 require that a trust account meet the following criteria:

1. designated as a trust account in the name of the broker as trustee;

2. maintained with a bank or recognized depository located in California; and

3. not an interest-bearing account for which prior written notice can, by law or regulation, be required by the financial institution as a condition to withdrawal (except as noted in the discussion below of "Interest-Bearing Accounts").

A broker may have an out-of-state trust account if the account is insured by the Federal Deposit Insurance Corporation (FDIC) and is used to service first loans for the types of note owners/investors specified in Section 10145(a)(2) of the Business and Professions Code.

Trust Account Withdrawals

According to Commissioner's Regulation 2834, withdrawals from the trust account may be made only upon the signature of one or more of the following:

1. the broker in whose name the account is maintained;

2. the designated broker-officer if the account is in the name of a corporate broker;

3. if specifically authorized in writing by the broker, a salesperson licensed to the broker; or

4. if specifically authorized in writing by the broker who is a signatory of the trust account, an unlicensed employee of the broker covered by a fidelity bond at least equal to the maximum amount of trust funds to which the employee has access at any time.

No arrangement under which a person named in items 3 or 4 is authorized to make withdrawals from a broker's trust fund relieves an individual broker or the broker-officer of a corporate broker licensee from responsibility or liability as provided by law in handling trust funds in the broker's custody.

Interest-Bearing Accounts

A trust fund bank account normally may not be interest-bearing. A broker may, however, at the request of the owner of trust funds, or of the principals to a transaction or series of transactions from whom the broker has received trust funds, deposit the funds into an interest-bearing account in a bank or savings and loan association if all of the following requirements of Business and Professions Code Section 10145(d) are met:

1. The account is in the name of the broker as trustee for a specified beneficiary or specified principal of a transaction or series of transactions.

2. All of the funds in the account are covered by insurance provided by an agency of the federal government.

3. The funds in the account are kept separate, distinct, and apart from funds belonging to the broker or to any other person for whom the broker holds funds in trust.

4. The broker discloses the following information to the person from whom the trust funds are received and to any beneficiary whose identity is known to the broker at the time of establishing the account:

   • the nature of the account;

   • how the interest will be calculated and paid under various circumstances;

   • whether service charges will be paid to the depository and by whom; and

   • possible notice requirements or penalties for withdrawal of funds from the account.

5. No interest earned on funds in the account shall inure directly or indirectly to the benefit of the broker or to any person licensed to the broker, even if the funds' owners would permit such an arrangement.

6. In an executory sale, lease, or loan transaction in which the broker accepts funds in trust to be applied to the purchase, lease, or loan, the parties to the contract shall have specified in the contract or by collateral written agreement the person to whom interest earned on the funds is to be paid or credited.

The only other situation where a real estate broker is allowed to deposit trust funds into an interest-bearing account occurs when the broker is acting as an agent for a financial institution which is the beneficiary of a loan. In this case the broker may, pursuant to Commissioner's Regulation 2830.1, deposit and maintain funds received from or for the account of an obligor (borrower) into an interest-bearing trust account in a bank or savings and loan association in order to pay interest on an impound account to the obligor in accordance with Section 2954.8 of the Civil Code, as long as the following requirements are met:

1. The funds received from or for the account of the obligor are for the future payment of property taxes, assessments or insurance relating only to a property containing a one-to-four family residence.

2. The account is in the name of the broker as trustee.

3. All of the funds in the account are covered by insurance provided by an agency of the federal government.

4. All of the funds in the account are funds held in trust by the broker for others.

5. The broker discloses to the obligor how interest will be calculated and paid.

6. No interest earned on the trust funds shall inure directly or indirectly to the benefit of the broker or to any person licensed to the broker.

Commingling Prohibited

Funds belonging to a licensee may not be commingled with trust funds. Commingling is strictly prohibited by the Real Estate Law. It is grounds for the revocation or suspension of a real estate license pursuant to Business and Professions Code Section 10176(e).

Commingling occurs when:

1. Personal or company funds are deposited into the trust fund bank account. *Except for what is provided in Section 2835 of the Commissioner's Regulations as noted below, this* is a violation of the law even if separate records are kept.

2. Trust funds are deposited into the licensee's general or personal bank account rather than into the trust fund account. In this case the violation is not only commingling, but also handling trust funds contrary to Business and Professions Code Section 10145. It is also grounds for suspension or revocation of a license under Business and Professions Code Section 10177(d).

3. Commissions, fees, or other income earned by the broker and collectible from the trust account are left in the trust account for more than 25 days from the date they were earned.

A common example of commingling is depositing rents and security deposits on broker-owned properties into the trust account. As these funds relate to the broker's properties, they are not trust funds and, therefore, may not be deposited into the trust fund bank account. Likewise, the broker may not make mortgage payments and other payments on broker-owned properties from the trust account even if the broker reimburses the account for such payments. Conducting personal business through the trust account is strictly prohibited and is a violation of the Real Estate Law.

Commissioner's Regulation 2835 provides that the following situations do not constitute "commingling" for purposes of Business and Professions Code Section 10176(e):

(a) The deposit into a trust account of reasonably sufficient funds, not to exceed $200, to pay service charges or fees levied or assessed against the account by the bank or financial institution where the account is maintained.

(b) The deposit into a trust account maintained in compliance with item (d) below of funds belonging in part to the broker's principal and in part to the broker when it is not reasonably practicable to separate such funds, provided the part of the funds belonging to the broker is disbursed not later than 25 days after the deposit and there is no dispute between the broker and the broker's principal as to the broker's portion of the funds. When the right of a broker to receive a portion of trust funds is disputed by the broker's principal, the disputed portion shall not be withdrawn until the dispute is settled.

(c) The deposit into a trust account of broker-owned funds in connection with mortgage loan activities as defined in subdivision (d) or (e) of Section 10131 of the Business and Professions Code or when making, collecting payments on, or servicing a loan which is subject to the provisions of Section 10240 of the Business and Professions Code provided:

(1) The broker meets the criteria of Section 10232 of the Business and Professions Code.

(2) All funds in the account which are owned by the broker are identified at all times in a separate record which is distinct from any separate record maintained for a beneficiary.

(3) All broker-owned funds deposited into the account are disbursed from the account not later than 25 days after their deposit.

(4) The funds are deposited and maintained in compliance with item (d) below.

(5) For this purpose, a broker shall be deemed to be subject to the provisions of Section 10240 of the Business and Professions Code if the broker delivers the statement to the borrower required by Section 10240.

(d) The trust fund account into which the funds are deposited is maintained in accordance with the provisions of Section 10145 of the Business and Professions Code, the Commissioner's Regulations, and the provisions of Title 10, California Code of Regulations, Section 260.105.30.

To summarize, a real estate broker's personal funds may be in the trust account in the following two specific instances:

1. Up to $200 to cover checking account service fees and other bank charges such as check printing charges and service fees on returned checks. Trust funds may not be used to pay for these expenses. (The preferred practice, however, is for the broker to have the bank debit his/her own *personal* account for any trust account fees and charges.)

2. Commissions, fees, and other income earned by a broker and collectible from trust funds may remain in the trust account for a period not to exceed 25 days. Regulation 2835 recognizes that it may not always be practical to disburse the earned income immediately upon receipt. For instance, a property management company may find it too burdensome to collect its management fee every time a rent check is received and deposited to the trust account. Therefore, as long as the broker disburses the fee from the trust account within 25 days after deposit there is no commingling violation. Note, however, that income earned *shall not* be taken from trust funds received *before* depositing such funds into the trust bank account. Also, under no circumstances may the broker pay personal obligations from the trust fund bank account even if such payments are a draw against commissions or other income. The broker must issue a trust account check to himself/herself for the total amount of the income earned, adequately documenting such payment, and then pay personal obligations from the proceeds of that check.

Trust Fund Liability

Trust fund liability arises when funds are received from or for the benefit of a principal. The aggregate trust fund liability at any one time for a trust account with multiple beneficiaries is equal to the total *positive* balances due to all beneficiaries of the account at the time. Note that beneficiary accounts with negative balances are not deducted from other accounts when calculating the aggregate trust fund liability.

Funds on deposit in the trust account must always equal the broker's aggregate trust fund liability. If the trust account balance is *less* than the total liability a *trust fund shortage* results. Such a shortage is in violation of Commissioner's Regulation 2832.1, which states that the written consent of every principal who is an owner of the funds in the account shall be obtained by a real estate broker prior to each disbursement if such a disbursement will reduce the balance of the funds in the account to an amount less than the existing aggregate trust fund liability of the broker to all owners of the funds. Conversely, if the trust account balance is *greater* than the total liability, there is a *trust fund overage* and the broker may be in violation of Business and Professions Code Section 10176(e) for commingling.

A trust fund discrepancy of any kind is a serious violation of the Real Estate Law. Many real estate licenses have been revoked after a DRE audit disclosed a trust account shortage. To ensure that the balance of the trust account always equals the trust fund liabilities, a broker should implement the following procedures:

1. Deposit intact and in a timely manner to the trust account all funds that are not forwarded to escrow or to the funds' owner(s) or which are not held uncashed as authorized. This practice, required under Commissioner's Regulation 2832, lessens the risk of the funds being lost, misplaced, or otherwise not deposited to the trust account. A licensee is accountable for all trust funds received whether or not they are deposited. DRE auditors have seen numerous cases where trust funds received were properly recorded on the books but were never deposited to the trust account.

2. Maintain adequate supporting papers for any disbursement from the trust account. Record the disbursement accurately in both the Bank Account Record and the Separate Beneficiary Record. The broker must be able to account for all disbursements of trust funds. Any unidentified disbursement will cause a shortage.

3. Disburse funds from a beneficiary's account only when the disbursement will not result in a negative or deficit balance (negative accountability) in the account. Many trust fund shortages are caused by disbursements to a beneficiary in excess of funds received from or for account of that beneficiary. The excess disbursements are, in effect, paid out of funds belonging to other beneficiaries. A shortage occurs because the balance of the trust fund bank account, even if it is a positive balance, is less than the broker's liability to the other beneficiaries.

4. Ensure that a check deposited to the trust fund account has cleared before disbursing funds against that check. This applies, for example, when a broker who has deposited an earnest money check for a purchase transaction has to return the funds to the buyer because the offer is rejected by the seller. A trust fund shortage will result if the broker issues the buyer a trust account check and the buyer's deposit check bounces or for some reason fails to clear the bank.

5. Keep accurate, current and complete records of the trust account and the separate record for each beneficiary. These records are essential to ensure that disbursements are correct.

6. On a monthly basis, reconcile the cash record with the bank statement and with the separate record for each beneficiary or transaction.

Summary - Maintaining Trust Account Integrity

In summary, to maintain the integrity of the trust fund bank account, a broker must ensure that:

1. his/her personal or general operating funds are not commingled with trust funds;

2. the balance of the trust fund account is equal to the broker's trust fund liability to all owners of the funds; and

3. the trust fund records are in an acceptable form and are current, complete and accurate.

ACCOUNTING RECORDS

General Requirements

An important aspect of the broker's fiduciary responsibility to the client is the maintenance of adequate records to account for trust funds received and disbursed. This is true whether the funds are deposited to the trust fund bank account, sent to escrow, held uncashed as authorized under Commissioner's Regulation 2832, or released to the owner(s) of the funds. These records:

1. provide a basis upon which the broker can prepare an accurate accounting for clients.

2. state the amount of money the broker owes the account beneficiaries at any one time. (This is especially important when there are a large number of transactions.)

3. prove whether or not there is an imbalance in the trust account. Some brokers audited by DRE have disagreed that their trust accounts had a shortage or an overage in the amount disclosed by the audit, but could not provide documentation to support their position.

4. guarantee that beneficiary funds deposited in the trust account will be insured up to the maximum FDIC insurance coverage.

There are two types of accounting records that may be used for trust funds: columnar records in the formats prescribed by Commissioner's Regulations 2831 and 2831.1; and records other than columnar that are in accordance with generally accepted accounting practices *which include details specified in subdivision (a) of the Regulations and are in a format that will readily enable tracing and reconciliation in accordance with Section 2831.2.* Regardless of the type of records used, they must include the following information:

1. all trust fund receipts and disbursements, with pertinent details, presented in chronological sequence;

2. the balance of the trust fund account, based on recorded transactions;

3. all receipts and disbursements affecting each beneficiary's balance, presented in chronological sequence; and

4. the balance owing to each beneficiary or for each transaction.

Either manually produced or computerized accounting records are acceptable. The type and form of records appropriate to a particular real estate operation as well as the means of processing transactions will depend on factors such as the nature of the business, the number of clients, the volume of transactions, and the types of reports needed. For example, manual recording on columnar records might be satisfactory for a broker handling a small number of transactions, while a computerized system might be more appropriate and practical for a large property management operation.

Columnar Records

A broker may decide to use the columnar records prescribed by Commissioner's Regulations 2831 and 2831.1. The records required will depend on whether the trust funds received are deposited to the trust account or are forwarded to an escrow depository or to the owner of the funds. These records are:

1. Columnar Record of All Trust Funds Received and Paid Out - Trust Fund Bank Account (DRE form RE 4522);

2. Separate Record for Each Beneficiary or Transaction (DRE form RE 4523); and

3. Record of All Trust Funds Received - Not Placed in Broker's Trust Account (DRE form RE 4524).

The first two records are required when trust funds are received and deposited to the trust fund bank account.

The third record is required when trust funds received are not deposited to the trust account, but are instead forwarded to the authorized person(s).

If the trust fund account involves clients' funds from rental properties managed by the broker, the Separate Record for Each Property Managed (DRE form RE 4525) may be used in lieu of the Separate Record for Each Beneficiary or Transaction.

A broker who has an escrow division pursuant to Financial Code Section 17006(a)(4) must keep the above mentioned records for escrow funds. (Commissioner's Regulation 2951)

Record of All Trust Funds Received and Paid Out - Trust Fund Bank Account

This record is used to journalize all trust funds deposited to and disbursed from the trust fund bank account. At a minimum, it must show the following information in columnar form: date funds were received; name of payee or payor; amount received; date of deposit; amount paid out; check number and date; and the daily balance of the trust account.

All transactions affecting the trust account are entered in chronological order on this record regardless of payee, payor or beneficiary. If there is more than one trust fund bank account, a different columnar record must be maintained for each account, pursuant to Commissioner's Regulation 2831.

Separate Record for Each Beneficiary or Transaction

This record is maintained to account for funds received from or for the account of each beneficiary, or for each transaction, and deposited to the trust account. With this record, the broker can ascertain the funds owed to each beneficiary or for each transaction. The record must show the following in chronological order: date of deposit; amount of deposit; name of payee or payor; check number; date and amount; and balance of the individual account after posting transactions on any date.

A separate record must be maintained for each beneficiary or transaction from whom the broker received funds that were deposited to the trust fund bank account. If the broker has more than one trust account, each account must have its own set of beneficiary records so that they can be reconciled with the individual trust fund bank account record required by Commissioner's Regulation 2831.2.

Record of All Trust Funds Received - Not Placed in Broker's Trust Account

This record is used to keep track of funds received and not deposited to a trust fund bank account. In this situation, the broker is handling the funds and must keep records of same. Examples are:

1. earnest money deposits forwarded to escrow;

2. rents forwarded to landlords; and

3. borrowers' payments forwarded to lenders.

This record must show the date funds were received, the form of payment (check, note, etc.), amount received, description of property, identity of the person to whom funds were forwarded, and date of disposition. Trust fund receipts are recorded in chronological sequence, while their disposition is recorded in the same line where the corresponding receipt is recorded.

Transaction folders usually maintained by a broker for each real estate sales transaction showing the receipt and disposition of undeposited checks are not acceptable alternatives to the Record of Trust Funds Received But Not Deposited to the Trust Fund Bank Account.

An exception to this record keeping requirement is provided in Commissioner's Regulation 2831(e), which states that a broker is not required to keep records of checks made payable to service providers, including but not limited to escrow, credit and appraisal services, when the total amount of such checks for any transaction does not exceed $1,000. However, a broker shall retain for three years copies of receipts issued or obtained in connection with the receipt and distribution of such checks and, upon request of the Department or the maker of the checks, a broker must account for the receipt and distribution of the checks.

Separate Record for Each Property Managed

This record is similar to, and serves the same purpose as, the Separate Record for Each Beneficiary or Transaction. It does not have to be maintained if a separate record is already used for a property owner's account. The Separate Record for Each Property Managed is useful when the broker wants to show some detailed information about a specific property being managed.

OTHER ACCOUNTING SYSTEMS AND RECORDS

A broker may use trust fund records not in the columnar form as prescribed by Commissioner's Regulations 2831 and 2831.1. Such records must be in accordance with generally accepted accounting principles *and must include detail specified in subdivision (a) of these Regulations and be in a format that will readily enable tracing and reconciliation in accordance with Section 2831.2.* Whether prepared manually or by computer, they must include at least the following:

1. A *journal* to record in chronological sequence the details of all trust fund transactions.

2. A *cash ledger* to show the bank balance as affected by the transactions recorded in the journal. The ledger is posted in the form of debits and credits. (In some cases the cash ledger may be combined with the journal.)

3. A *beneficiary ledger* for each of the beneficiary accounts to show in chronological sequence the transactions affecting each beneficiary's account, as well as the balance of the account.

To comply with generally accepted accounting principles, there must be one set of journal, cash ledger, and beneficiary ledger for each trust fund bank account.

Journal

A journal is a daily chronological record of trust fund receipts and disbursements. A single journal may be used to record both the receipts and the disbursements, or a separate journal may be used for each. To meet minimum record keeping requirements, a journal must:

1. Record all trust fund transactions in chronological sequence.

2. Contain sufficient information to identify the transaction such as the date, amount received or disbursed, name of or reference to payee or payor, check number or reference to another source document of the transaction, and identification of the beneficiary account affected by the transaction.

3. Correlate with the ledgers. For example, it should show the same figures that are posted, individually or in total, in the cash ledger and in the beneficiary ledgers. The details in the journal must be the basis for posting transactions on the ledgers and arriving at the account balances.

4. Show the total receipts and total disbursements regularly, at least once a month.

Cash Ledger

The cash ledger shows, usually in summary form, the periodic increases and decreases (debits and credits) in the trust fund bank account and the resulting account balance. It can be incorporated into the journal or it can be a separate record, for example a general ledger account. If a separate record is used, the postings must be based on the transactions recorded in the journal. The amounts posted on the ledger must be those shown in the journal.

Beneficiary Ledger

A separate beneficiary ledger must be maintained for each beneficiary or transaction or series of transactions. This ledger shows in chronological sequence the details of all receipts and disbursements related to the beneficiary's account, and the resulting account balance. It reflects the broker's liability to a particular beneficiary. Entries in all these ledgers must be based on entries recorded in the journal.

RECORDING PROCESS

Keeping complete and accurate trust fund records is easier when specific procedures are regularly followed. The following procedures may be useful in developing a record keeping routine:

1. Record transactions daily in the trust fund bank account and in the separate beneficiary records.

2. Use consistently the same specific source documents as a basis for recording trust fund receipts and disbursements. (For example, receipts pertaining to real estate resales will be recorded based on the Real Estate Contract and Receipt for Deposit form, and disbursements will always be recorded based on the checks issued from the trust account or debit notices from the bank.)

3. Calculate the account balances on all applicable records at the time entries are made.

4. Reconcile the records monthly to ascertain that transactions are properly recorded on both the bank account record and the applicable subsidiary records.

5. *Reconcile the trust records to the trust account bank statement on a monthly basis to ascertain that amounts per the bank are in agreement with amounts per the trust fund records.*

6. If more than one trust fund bank account is maintained, keep a different set of properly labeled columnar records (cash record and beneficiary record) for each account.

RECONCILIATION OF ACCOUNTING RECORDS

Purpose

The trust fund bank account record, the separate beneficiary or transaction record, and the bank statement are all interrelated. Any entry made on the bank account record must have a corresponding entry on a separate beneficiary record. By the same token, any entry or transaction shown on the bank statement must be reflected on the bank account record. This applies to columnar as well as to other types of records.

The accuracy of the records is verified by reconciling them at least once a month. Reconciliation is the process of comparing two or more sets of records to determine whether their balances agree. It will disclose whether the records are completed accurately.

For trust fund record keeping purposes, two reconciliations must be made at the end of each month:

1. reconciliation of the bank account record (RE 4522) with the bank statement; and,

2. reconciliation of the bank account record (RE 4522) with the separate beneficiary or transaction records (RE 4523).

Reconciling the Bank Account Record With the Bank Statement

The reconciliation of the bank account record with the bank statement will disclose any recording errors by the broker or by the bank. If the balance on the bank account record agrees with the bank statement balance as adjusted for outstanding checks, deposits in transit, and other transactions not yet included in the bank statement, there is more assurance that the balance on the bank account record is correct. Although this reconciliation is not required by the Real Estate Law or the Commissioner's Regulations, it is an essential part of any good accounting system.

Reconciling the Bank Account Record With the Separate Beneficiary or Transaction Records

This reconciliation, which is required by Commissioner's Regulation 2831.2, will substantiate that all transactions entered on the bank account record were posted on the separate beneficiary or transaction records. The balance on the bank account record should equal the total of all beneficiary record balances. Any difference should be located and the records corrected to reflect the correct bank and liabilities balances. Commissioner's Regulation 2831.2 requires that this reconciliation process be performed monthly except in those months when there is no activity in the trust fund bank account, and that a record of each reconciliation be maintained. This record should identify the bank account name and number, the date of the reconciliation, the account number or name of the principals or beneficiaries or transactions, and the trust fund liabilities of the broker to each of the principals, beneficiaries or transactions.

Unexplained Trust Account Overages

When a broker performs a reconciliation pursuant to Commissioner's Regulation 2831.2, the broker may find an unexplained overage. An unexplained overage is defined as funds in a real estate broker's trust account which exceed the aggregate trust fund liability of such account where the broker is unable to determine the ownership of such excess funds.

Unexplained trust account overages are trust funds and unless the broker can establish the ownership of such funds, the funds must be maintained in the broker's trust fund account or in a separate trust fund account established to hold such funds.

Unexplained trust account overages may not be used to offset or cover shortages that may exist otherwise in the broker's trust account.

A broker must keep a separate record of unexplained trust account overages including a separate subsidiary ledger to record the potential trust fund liability. Such records must include the date of recording and the date on which such funds became an unexplained trust account overage. A broker holding unexplained trust account overages must perform a monthly reconciliation of such funds in accordance with Commissioner's Regulation 2831.2.

Suggestions for Reconciling Records

The following is a general discussion on how to perform the trust account reconciliations.

1. Before performing the reconciliations, record all transactions up to the cut-off date in both the bank account record and the separate beneficiary or transaction records.

2. Use balances as of the same cut-off date for the two records and the bank statement.

3. For the bank account reconciliation, calculate the adjusted bank balance from the bank statement and from the bank account record. (Brokers commonly err by calculating the adjusted bank balance based solely on the bank statement, ignoring the bank account record. While they may know the correct account balances, they may not realize their records are incomplete or erroneous.)

4. Keep a record of the two reconciliations performed at the end of each month, along with the supporting schedules.

5. Locate any difference between the three sets of accounting records. A difference can be caused by:

    - not recording a transaction
    - recording an incorrect figure
    - erroneous calculations of entries used to arrive at account balances
    - missing beneficiary records
    - bank errors.

DOCUMENTATION REQUIREMENTS

Activities and Related Documents

In addition to accounting records, the Department of Real Estate requires that the broker maintain all documents prepared or obtained in connection with any real estate transaction handled. Here is a list of typical activities and the corresponding documentation.

Activity	Documentation
1. Receiving trust funds in the form of:	
Purchase deposits from buyers	• Real estate purchase contract and receipt for deposit, signed by the buyer
Rents and security deposits from tenants	• Collection receipts
Other receipts	• Collection receipts
2. Depositing trust funds	• Bank deposit slips
3. Forwarding buyers' checks to escrow	• Receipt from title/*escrow* company and copy of check
4. Returning buyers' checks	• Copy of buyer's check signed and dated by buyer, signifying buyer's receipt of check

5. Disbursing trust funds	• Checks issued
	• Supporting papers for the checks, such as invoices, escrow statements, billings, receipts, etc.
6. Receiving offers and counteroffers from buyers and sellers	• Real estate purchase contract and receipt for deposit, signed by respective parties
	• Agency disclosure statement
	• Transfer disclosure statement
7. Collecting management fees from the trust fund bank account	• Property management agreements between broker and property owners. (Note: If only one trust fund check is issued for management fees charged to various property owners, there should be a schedule or listing on file showing each property and amount charged, and the total amount, which should agree with the check amount.)
	• Cancelled checks
8. Reconciling bank account record with separate beneficiary records	• Record of reconciliation

ADDITIONAL REQUIREMENTS - DOCUMENTS

The following is an additional requirement of the Real Estate Law and the Commissioner's Regulations relating to the preparation and management of real estate transaction documents.

Person Signing Contract to be Given Copy

Under Business and Professions Code Section 10142, any time a licensee prepares or has prepared an agreement authorizing or employing that licensee to perform any acts for which a real estate license is required or when the licensee obtains the signature of any person to any contract pertaining to such services or transaction, the licensee must deliver a copy of the agreement to the person signing it at the time the signature is obtained. Examples of such documents are listing agreements, real estate purchase contract and receipt for deposit forms, addenda to contracts, and property management agreements.

AUDITS AND EXAMINATIONS

Because of the importance of trust fund handling, the Commissioner has an ongoing program of examining brokers' records. As necessary, audited licensees are made aware of deficiencies in trust fund handling and record keeping. If an audit discloses actual trust fund imbalances or money handling procedures which may cause monetary loss, appropriate disciplinary proceedings are initiated.

Section 10148 of the Business and Professions Code provides that a real estate broker shall retain for three years copies of all listings, deposit receipts, canceled checks, trust records, and other documents executed by or obtained by the broker in connection with any transaction for which a real estate broker license is required. The retention period shall run from the date of the closing of the transaction or from the date of the listing if the transaction is not consummated. After notice, such books, accounts and records shall be made available for examination, inspection and copying by the Commissioner or a designated representative during regular business hours, and shall, upon the appearance of sufficient cause, be subject to audit without further notice, except that such audit shall not be harassing in nature.

SAMPLE TRANSACTIONS

To demonstrate the record keeping requirements discussed in this chapter, we have simulated trust account records for typical real estate transactions occurring over a thirty-day period. To set the stage, let us assume that James Adams, a real estate broker, owns and operates a one-man real estate office specializing in residential sales and property management. Broker Adams has one trust fund bank account. We will look at the trust account activity for this office for the month of May, *2000*.

The use of columnar records to record these transactions is illustrated in Exhibits 1 - 10 at the end of this chapter. As previously discussed, a broker may use other types of records as long as they meet generally accepted accounting standards.

2000	*TRANSACTIONS*
May 1	Opened a trust account with First County Bank, and deposited $100 of his own money to cover bank service charges.
May 1	Entered into agreements to manage the following rental properties:

	Address	*Owner's Name*	*Number of Units*
a.	1538 South Ave. Anycity, CA	T. Eddie	1
b.	3490 Tower St. Anycity, CA	L. Stewart	4
c.	9152 High Way Anycity, CA	W. Allen	4
d.	2351-2353 Kingston Way Anycity, CA	S. Manly	2
e.	7365 Meadow Cir. Anycity, CA	J. Bird	1

May 3	Deposited the following rents received from tenants of managed properties:

	Property	Tenant's Name	Rent Received
a.	1538 South Ave.	B. Hamns	$600
b.	3490 Tower St., Unit 1	R. Robertson	350
c.	2351 Kingston Way	I. Warren	450
			$1,400

May 5   Received a $2,000 check payable to broker from Mr. and Mrs. Dennis White as deposit for their offer to buy a house at 615 Lake Drive, Anycity, owned by Mr. and Mrs. Richard J. Jensen. Buyers' offer instructed broker to hold the check uncashed until their offer was accepted by the Jensens.

May 5   Received and deposited $750 from T. Sundance representing rent of $500 for September 5 to 30, and $250 security deposits for 7365 Meadow Circle.

May 5   Was notified by the Jensens that they accepted the offer on their property.

May 6   Deposited the $2,000 check from Mr. and Mrs. White.

May 8   Obtained an exclusive listing to sell a six-plex at 915 Galaxy St., Anycity, owned by R. Jays.

May 9   Received $1,000 from W. Allen, owner of 9152 High Way, to cover anticipated expenses for the property. Amount was deposited the same day.

May 10   Issued the following checks to pay for various expenses connected with the managed properties:

Check No.	Payee	Purpose	Amount
1001	ABC Mortgage Co.	Mortgage payment for 1538 South Ave.	$450
1002	Anycity Treasury	Utilities for 1538 South Ave.	35
1003	Professional Cleaners	Cleaning for 3490 Tower St.	55
1004	Mr. Handyman	Minor repairs on 2351 Kingston	25
		TOTAL	$565

May 14   Received a $4,000 check from B. Sun, payable to Title Escrow Company, with an offer to buy the 915 Galaxy property.

May 15   Received R. Jays' acceptance of the buyer's offer on 915 Galaxy Street.

May 16   Delivered the $4,000 check from B. Sun to Title Escrow Company.

May 19   Issued check number 1005 for $2,000 to First Title Co. for account of Mr. and Mrs. White, buyers of the 615 Lake Drive property.

May 22   Received an offer and a $3,000 check as deposit from R. Olive to buy a single family house at 31009 Technology Street owned by T. Evans.

May 24   Returned R. Olive's check after seller rejected the offer.

May 31   Charged property management fees to the following accounts and issued check number 1006 for $330 payable to himself:

Property Owner	Management Fee
T. Eddie	$45
L. Stewart	100
W. Allen	80
S. Manly	60
J. Bird	45
Total	$330

May 31   Sent statement of account to each owner of the managed properties.

Background Information

James Adams keeps four types of columnar records:

1. Record of all Trust Funds Received and Paid Out - Trust Fund Bank Account (hereinafter referred to as "Bank Account Record"). This record is required under Commissioner's Regulation 2831 for each trust account a broker has.

2. Record of all Trust Funds Received - Not Placed in Broker's Trust Account (hereinafter referred to as "Record of Undeposited Receipts"). This is required under Commissioner's Regulation 2831.

3. Separate Record For Each Beneficiary or Transaction (hereinafter referred to as "Separate Beneficiary Record"). This is required under Commissioner's Regulation 2831.1.

4. Separate Record For Each Property Managed (hereinafter referred to as "Separate Property Record"). This serves the same purpose as the Separate Beneficiary Record.

To illustrate the recording process, listed below are the entries made on the books by James Adams as well as the documents prepared or obtained as support for each transaction. The actual entries are shown on the forms/exhibits at the end of this chapter.

Note that:

- Each entry to any record shows all the pertinent information of the transaction, such as the date, name of payee, name of payor, amount, check number, etc.

- The daily *bank balance* is computed and posted on the Account Record after recording the transactions.

- The balance owing to the client is computed and posted on the Beneficiary Record or Separate Property Record, after posting transactions.

- Any entry made on the Bank Account Record has a corresponding entry on a Beneficiary Record or a Separate Property Record, and vice versa.

- All records except the Record of Undeposited Receipts show entries in chronological sequence regardless of transaction type. The Record of Undeposited Receipts shows the disposition of a trust fund in the same line as the receipt is entered, rather than in chronological sequence.

Step-By-Step Narrative of Trust Account Entries
(Actual recording shown on Exhibits 1 - 10 at end of chapter.)

Transaction Date	Documentation	Entries
May 1	Deposit slip prepared by broker.	Record the deposit on: 1. The Bank Account Record. Balance is $100. (**Exh. 1**) 2. A newly prepared Separate Beneficiary for James Adams. Balance is $100. (**Exh. 2**)
May 1	Management agreements signed by property owners and broker.	No entries needed since there was no receipt nor disbursement of trust funds.
May 3	Collection receipts Nos. 2, 3 and 4 issued to B. Hamns, R. Robertson, and I. Warren, respectively.	Record the $1,400 receipt on: 1. The Bank Account Record. New balance is $1,500. (**Exh. 1**) 2. Newly prepared Separate Beneficiary Records for: T. Eddie - balance is $600 (**Exh. 4**) L. Stewart – bal. is $350 (**Exh. 5**) S. Manly - balance is $450 (**Exh. 6**)
May 5	Real Estate Purchase Contract and Receipt for Deposit signed by Mr. and Mrs. White. Collection receipt No. 1 issued to the Whites.	Enter transaction on the Record of Undeposited Receipts. (**Exh. 3**) No Separate Beneficiary Record is necessary since the check was not deposited.

Transaction Date	Documentation	Entries
May 5	Collection receipt No. 5 issued to T. Sundance. Receipt showed that $500 of the $750 was for rent and the other $250 was for security deposit.	Record the $750 deposit on: 1. The Bank Account Record. (**Exh. 1**) 2. Separate Beneficiary Records for: J. Bird - Sundance's Security Deposit, bal. is $250. (**Exh. 7**) J. Bird - balance is $500. (**Exh. 8**) (Since security deposits will be accounted to the tenant in the future, James Adams keeps a separate record for deposits. Total liability to the owner is the sum of the two records - one for security deposits, another for rents and other transactions.)
May 5	Real Estate Contract and Receipt for trust funds were received for Deposit signed by Mr. and Mrs. Jensen.	No entries were made since no trust funds were received or disbursed.
May 6	Deposit receipt prepared by broker.	Record $2,000 deposit on: 1. Bank Account record. New balance is $4,250. (**Exh. 1**) 2. A newly prepared Separate Beneficiary Record - Mr. and Mrs. White/Mr. and Mrs. Jensen. Account balance is $2,000. (**Exh. 9**) 3. Record of Undeposited Receipts. (**Exh. 3**) Shows disposition of check previously entered on the record.
May 8	Exclusive Listing Agreement signed by sellers and broker.	
May 9	Collection receipt No. 6 issued to W. Allen.	Record receipt on: 1. The Bank Account Record. New balance is $5,250. (**Exh. 1**) 2. A newly prepared Separate Beneficiary Record - W. Allen. Balance is $1,000. (**Exh. 10**)

Transaction Date	Documentation	Entries
May 10	Checks issued by broker. Supporting papers for each check.	Record disbursements on: 1. Bank Account Record. New Balance is $4,685. **(Exh. 1)** 2. Separate Beneficiary Records for: T. Eddie - New balance is $115. **(Exh. 4)** L. Stewart - New balance is $295. **(Exh. 5)** S. Manly - New balance is $425. **(Exh. 6)**
May 14	Real Estate Purchase Contract and Receipt for Deposit signed by B. Sun.	Record receipt on the Record of Undeposited Receipts. **(Exh. 3)**
May 15	Real Estate Purchase Contract and Receipt for Deposit signed by R. Jays.	No entry was needed since there was no receipt or disbursement of funds.
May 16	Receipt issued by Title Escrow Company.	Note disposition of check on the Record of Undeposited Receipts. **(Exh. 3)**
May 19	Check issued by broker. Receipt issued by First Title Company.	Record disbursements on the: 1. Bank Account Record. New balance is $2,685. **(Exh. 1)** 2. Separate Beneficiary Record - Mr. and Mrs. White/Mr. and Mrs. Jensen. New balance is $0. **(Exh. 9)**
May 22	Real Estate Purchase Contract and receipt for Deposit signed by R. Olive.	
May 24	Real Estate Purchase Contract and Receipt for Deposit rejected by T. Evans.	Post the return of check on the Record of Undeposited Receipts. **(Exh. 3)**

Transaction Date	Documentation	Entries
May 31	List showing the breakdown of the check amount, showing the charge to each owner.	Record disbursements on the: 1. Bank Account Record. New balance is $2,685. (**Exh. 1**) 2. Separate Beneficiary Records for:

	New Owners	Balance
	T. Eddie	$70
	L. Stewart	$195
(NOTE: A list is	W. Allen	$920
necessary as support for	S. Manly	$365
a check disbursement	J. Bird	$455

(NOTE: A list is necessary as support for a check disbursement chargeable to a number of beneficiaries. Posting the entries on the separate records without such a list is not sufficient.)

After recording the daily transactions, the next step in the trust fund accounting process is the reconciling of records at the end of the month. James Adams prepared reconciliation schedules by comparing the bank balance on the Bank Account Record with the bank statement balance (the bank reconciliation) and also with the total of the Separate Beneficiary Records balances (the reconciliation report).

The bank statement and reconciliations are shown on the next two pages.

FIRST COUNTY BANK   STATEMENT
MAIN BRANCH
5 Main Avenue
ANYCITY, CA 90002

PAGE 1 of 1

DATE OF THIS STATEMENT 05/31/00

JAMES ADAMS
TRUST ACCOUNT
8310 ORANGE AVENUE
ANYCITY, CA 90002

CHECKING ACCT. 123456   CUSTOMER SINCE 1995

SUMMARY: PREVIOUS STATEMENT BALANCE ON 04/30/00 ..... 00.00
TOTAL OF 5 DEPOSITS FOR 5,250.00
TOTAL OF 4 CHECKS FOR 2,540.00
TOTAL OF 1 OTHER DEBIT FOR 7.00
STATEMENT BALANCE ON 05/31/00 .... 2,703.00

CHECKS/ OTHER DEBITS	CHECKS	CHECK NUMBER	DATE POSTED	AMOUNT
		1001	5/14	450.00
		1002	5/16	35.00
		1003	5/16	55.00
		1005	5/21	2,000.00

	OTHER DEBITS DATE POSTED			AMOUNT
	05/31	SERVICE CHARGE		7.00

DEPOSITS/ OTHER CREDITS	DEPOSITS		DATE POSTED	AMOUNT
			5/1	100.00
			5/5	1,400.00
			5/5	750.00
			5/6	2,000.00
			5/9	1,000.00

DAILY BALANCE	DATE	AMOUNT	DATE	AMOUNT
	5/1	100.00	5/14	4,800.00
	5/5	2,250.00	5/16	4,710.00
	5/6	4,250.00	5/21	2,710.00
	5/9	5,250.00	5/31	2,703.00

James Adams
Bank Reconciliation
First County Bank
May 31, 2000

Balance per bank statement, 5/31/00		$2,703.00
Add deposits in transit		-0-
Less outstanding checks:		
check #1004	$25.00	
#1006	330.00	<355.00>
Adjusted bank balance, 5/31/00		$2,348.00
Balance per books, 5/31/00		$2,355.00
Less May bank service charge		<7.00>
Adjusted balance, 5/31/00		$2,348.00

James Adams
Reconciliation Report
First County Bank
Account No. 123456
May 31, 2000

Beneficiary	*Balance*
James Adams (Broker)	$93.00
W. Allen	920.00
J. Bird	250.00
J. Bird	455.00
T. Eddie	70.00
S. Manly	365.00
L. Stewart	195.00
Total per subsidiary records	$2,348.00

(Agrees with bank account record balance.)

QUESTIONS AND ANSWERS REGARDING TRUST FUND
REQUIREMENTS AND RECORD KEEPING

Q. Are security deposits on rental units the property of the owner or should they
be held in trust by the broker for the tenant?

A. *They are trust funds. As such, control and disbursement of the security
deposits are at the instruction of the property owner.*

Q. Am I permitted to wait until checks deposited to my trust account have cleared
before I issue a trust check to fund a customer's check?

A. *Although the Real Estate Law is silent on this, good business practice dictates
that you wait until a customer's check deposited to your trust account has
cleared prior to the issuing of your trust check as a refund.*

Q. How should I handle an earnest money check which is to be deposited into
escrow upon acceptance of the offer?

A. *Such a check may be held until the offer is accepted and then placed in escrow
but only when directed to do so by the buyer, provided you disclose to the
seller the fact the check is being held in uncashed form. In such cases, it is
good practice to include such a provision in the deposit receipt. You must keep
a columnar record of the receipt of the check, the name of the escrow company
and the date the check was forwarded to the escrow.*

Q. As a broker-owner of rentals, do I have to put security deposits in a trust
account?

A. *Money you receive on your own property is received as a principal, not as an
agent. As such, these are not trust funds and should not be placed in the trust
account.*

Q. Must I keep a deposit receipt signed only by the buyer and rejected by the
seller?

A. *Yes. Such a record must be maintained for three years.*

Q. May I maintain one trust fund account for both collections from my property
management business and deposits on real estate sales transactions?

A. *Since property management funds usually involve multiple receipt of funds and
several monthly disbursements, it is suggested that separate trust fund
accounts be maintained for property management funds and earnest money
deposits. However, all trust funds can be placed in the same trust fund account
as long as separate records for each trust fund deposit and disbursement are
maintained properly and the account is not an interest-bearing account.*

Q. If the buyer and seller decide to go directly to escrow and the buyer makes out a check to the escrow company and hands it directly to the escrow clerk, do I have to maintain any records of this check?

A. *No. You must maintain records only of trust funds which pass through your hands for the benefit of a third party.*

Q. How long must I keep deposit receipts?

A. *Deposit receipts must be maintained for three years.*

SUMMARY

We might say this chapter presents the three R's of trust funds: Responsibility, Requirements and Records.

It is a real estate broker's responsibility to protect clients' funds at all times and keep clients fully informed of the nature and disposition of all trust funds.

To aid brokers in carrying out this responsibility, the Real Estate Commissioner's Regulations include requirements concerning trust funds. A real estate broker also needs to meet other requirements from a practical business point of view. To protect clients' funds adequately and in the business-like fashion expected, the broker must keep accurate records.

COLUMNAR RECORD OF ALL TRUST FUNDS RECEIVED AND PAID OUT
TRUST FUND BANK ACCOUNT

2000 (yr.) Date Received	From Whom Received or To Whom Paid	Description	Received Amount Received	Reference	Date of Deposit	XX	Paid Out Amount Paid Out	Check Number	Date of Check	XX	D-B-Bank Account
5-1-00	James Adams	Open TA Account	100.00		5-1-00						100.00
5-3	B. Harms	Rent: 1538 South Ave.	600.00	#2	5-3						700.00
5-3	R. Robertson	Rent: 3490 Tower St., Unit 1	350.00	#3	5-3						1,050.00
5-3	I. Warren	Rent: 2351 Kingston Way	450.00	#4	5-3						1,500.00
5-5	T. Sundance	Rent: $500; Dep. $250.									
		7365 Meadow Circle	750.00	#5	5-5						2,250.00
5-5	Mr. & Mrs. Dennis White	Deposit: 615 Lake Drive	2,000.00		5-6						4,250.00
5-9	W. Allen	Owner Contribution	1,000.00	#6	5-9						5,250.00
	ABC Mortgage Co.	Mtg. Pmt. 1538 South Ave.					450.00	1001	5-10		4,800.00
	Anycity Treasury	Utilities 1538 South Ave.					35.00	1002	5-10		4,765.00
	Professional Cleaners	Cleaning: 3490 Tower St.					55.00	1003	5-10		4,710.00
	Mr. Handyman	Repairs: 2351 Kingston					25.00	1004	5-10		4,685.00
	First Title Co.	Deposit: 615 Lake Drive					2,000.00	1005	5-19		2,685.00
	James Adams	Mgmt. Fees: See Schedule					330.00	1006	5-30		2,355.00
	First County Bank	May Bank Service Charge					7.00	DM	5-31		2,348.00

EXHIBIT 1

RE 4522 (Rev. 2-99)

SEPARATE RECORD FOR EACH BENEFICIARY OR TRANSACTION
FOR CLIENT'S FUNDS PLACED IN TRUST FUND BANK ACCOUNT

Identification Of Transaction *(names, addresses, account numbers, etc.)*

James A. Adams

Trust Fund Balance - Broker

Description	Discharge Of Trust Accountability For Funds Paid Out			Trust Accountability For Funds Received		Account Balance
	Date of Check	Check Number	Amount	Date of Deposit	Amount	
Open TA Account				5-1-00	100.00	100.00
May '00 Bank Service Charge	5-31-00	SM	7.00			93.00

RE 4523 (Rev. 2/94)   **EXHIBIT 2**

RECORD OF ALL TRUST FUNDS RECEIVED — NOT PLACED IN BROKERS TRUST ACCOUNT
(Include Notes and Uncashed Checks Taken As Deposits)

20XX (yr) Date Received	Form of Receipt (Cash, note, etc.)	Amount	Received From	Description of Property or Other Identification	Disposition of Funds (To escrow, principal, trust account, or returned)	Date Deposited
5-5-00	check	2,000.00	Mr. & Mrs. Dennis White	615 Lake Drive	To Trust Account upon acceptance	5-6-00
5-14	check	4,000.00	B. Sun	915 Galaxy	To Title Escrow Company	5-16
5-22	check	3,000.00	R. Olive	31009 Technology Street	Returned to Buyer	5-24

RE 4524 (Rev. 2-99)

EXHIBIT 3

SEPARATE RECORD FOR EACH PROPERTY MANAGED

T. Eddie

6439 Alvera Way, Anycity

1538 South Ave. Anycity

B. Hanns

Deposit:	$
Monthly Rent	$
Commission:	$
Leases	$
Collection:	$
Management:	$

Date	Received From or Paid To	Description	Receipt/ Check No.	Amount Received	Date Deposited	Amount Disbursed	Balance
5-3-00	B. Hanns	Rent - May 00	#2	600.00	5-3-00		600.00
5-10	ABC Mortgage Co...	Mortgage Payment	1001			450.00	150.00
5-10	Anycity Treasury	Utilities	1002			35.00	115.00
5-31	James Adams	Management Fee	1006			45.00	70.00

RE 4525 (Rev. 2/94)

EXHIBIT 4

SEPARATE RECORD FOR EACH PROPERTY MANAGED

L. Stewart
10037 Airline Place, Anycity
3490 Tower St., Anycity
R. Robertson

	$
Deposit	$
Monthly Rent	$
Commission	$
Limits	$
Collection	$
Management	$

Date	Received From or Paid To	Description	Receipt/ Check No.	Amount Received	Date Deposited	Amount Disbursed	Balance
5-3-00	R. Robertson	Rent - May 00	#3	350.00	5-3-00		350.00
5-10	Professional Cleaners	Cleaning	1003			55.00	295.00
5-31	James Adams	Management Fee	1006			100.00	195.00

RE 4525 (Rev. 2/94)

EXHIBIT 5

SEPARATE RECORD FOR EACH PROPERTY MANAGED

S. Manly
950 Crosswoods Rd., Anycity
2351 Kingston Way, Anycity
I. Warren

	$
Deposit	$
Monthly Rent	$
Commission	$
Lease	$
Collection	$
Management	$

Date	Received From or Paid To	Description	Receipt/ Check No.	Amount Received	Date Deposited	Amount Disbursed	Balance
5-3-00	I. Warren	Rent - May 00	#4	450.00	5-3-00		450.00
5-10	Mr. Handyman	Repairs	1004			35.00	425.00
5-31	James Adams	Management Fee	1006			60.00	365.00

RE 4525 (Rev. 2-94)

EXHIBIT 6

SEPARATE RECORD FOR EACH PROPERTY MANAGED

J. Bird

882 Flight Lane, Anycity

7365 Meadow Circle, Anycity

T. Sundance

Security Deposit

		Deposit	$
		Monthly Rent	$
		Commission	$
		Lease	$
		Collection	$
		Management	$

Date	Received From or Paid To	Description	Receipt/ Check No.	Amount Received	Date Deposited	Amount Disbursed	Balance
5-5-00	T. Sundance	Deposit	#5	250.00	5-5-00		250.00

RE 4525 (Rev. 2/94)

EXHIBIT 7

SEPARATE RECORD FOR EACH PROPERTY MANAGED

J. Bird

882 Flight Lane, Anycity

7365 Meadow Circle, Anycity

T. Sundance

					Deposit	$
					Monthly Rent	$
					Commission	$
					Lease	$
					Collection	$
					Management	$

Date	Received From or Paid To	Description	Receipt/ Check No.	Amount Received	Date Disbursed	Amount Disbursed	Balance
5-5-00	T. Sundance	Rent - May 2000	#5	500.00	5-5-00		500.00
5-31	James Adams	Management Fees	1006			45.00	455.00

RE 4525 (Rev. 2/94)

EXHIBIT 8

**SEPARATE RECORD FOR EACH BENEFICIARY OR TRANSACTION
FOR CLIENTS FUNDS PLACED IN TRUST FUND BANK ACCOUNT**

IDENTIFICATION OF TRANSACTION *(names, addresses, account numbers, etc.)*

Mr. & Mrs. Whte/Mr. & Mrs. Jensen

RE: 615 Lake Drive, Anycity

DESCRIPTION	DISCHARGE OF TRUST ACCOUNTABILITY FOR FUNDS PAID OUT			TRUST ACCOUNTABILITY FOR FUNDS RECEIVED		ACCOUNT BALANCE
	Date of Check	Check Number	Amount	Date of Deposit	Amount	
Purchase Deposit				5-6-00	2,000.00	2,000.00
Deposit to Title Co.	5-19-00	1005	2,000.00			- 0 -

RE 4523 (Rev. 5/94)   **EXHIBIT 9**

SEPARATE RECORD FOR EACH PROPERTY MANAGED

W. Allen

43 River Lake Drive, Anycity

9152 High Way, Anycity

Deposit	$
Monthly Rent	$
Commission:	$
Leases	$
Collection	$
Management	$

Date	Received From or Paid To	Description	Receipt/ Check No.	Amount Received	Date Deposited	Amount Disbursed	Balance
5-9-00	W. Allen	Owner Contribution	#6	1,000.00	5-9-00		1,000.00
5-31	James Adams	Management Fees	1006			80.00	920.00

EXHIBIT 10

RE 4525 (Rev. 2/94)

Property management is a specialty in which real estate brokers manage homes and duplexes as well as large projects such as office and industrial complexes, shopping centers, apartment houses, and condominiums.

Reasonable knowledge and understanding of the general principles and responsibilities relating to this field is appropriate for all brokers and salespersons.

Knowledge of agency, contracts, fair housing, rentals and leases satisfies a considerable portion of property management requirements. Additional knowledge is required in business administration, marketing, purchasing, extensions of credit, accounting, advertising, insurance, repairs and maintenance, taxation and public relations. The Institute of Real Estate Management (IREM), a professional organization of persons involved in property management, is dedicated to the improvement of the operational and ethical standards of its members.

Professional Organization

In 1933, to foster professionalism and provide a source of management experience data, a group of property management firms organized the Institute of Real Estate Management (IREM). To be a member, a property management firm was required to certify that it would adhere to the following guidelines:

1. Maintain separate bank accounts for its own funds and for the funds of its clients, with no commingling;

2. Carry a satisfactory fidelity bond on all of its employees whose duties involved the handling of funds; and,

3. Refrain from taking discounts or commissions from purchases, contracts, or other expenditures of clients' funds without full disclosure to, and permission from, the property owner.

Beyond the adoption of standards of practice, IREM also set fixed principles of qualification.

In 1938, IREM's founders realized that the focus of professionalism must be on the individual because firms and corporations could not be qualified as having "ability." A firm, John Jones & Company for example, might be qualified to manage property so long as John Jones was its administrative head. But when John Jones retired, died or sold the firm, the character of its management might change completely. It was obvious only the "man" or "woman" in management could be certified to be a qualified property manager.

Having agreed upon this fundamental thesis, the members of IREM undertook to reorganize into a truly professional society, with membership restricted to individuals. Now, individuals meeting the educational and experience requirements are designated as Certified Property Managers[©] (CPM[©]). A lesser degree of training and on-site experience qualifies an individual as an Accredited Residential Manager[©] (ARM[©]). A firm that meets IREM's guidelines and utilizes at least one CPM[©] can be designated as an Accredited Management Organization[©] (AMO[©]).

Property Managers and Professional Designations

There are three types of property managers: the individual property manager, the individual building manager, and the resident manager.

The individual property manager is usually a real estate broker who manages properties for various owners or an owner. The property manager may be a member of a small property management firm and devote full time to property management; or, he may own his own firm; or, he may be one of a number of property management specialists in a large real estate organization. Some property managers are asset managers and make the same types of decisions that an owner would relative to change of use, refinancing and sale. Asset managers frequently supervise other CPM$^\circledR$s.

The individual building manager may be employed by a property manager or directly by an owner, and usually manages a single large property.

The resident manager may be employed by a real estate broker or a managing agent or an owner to manage an apartment building on a part or full-time basis.

The training, experience and number of units managed determine the individual property or building manager's qualification for the CPM$^\circledR$ designation. To qualify for the ARM$^\circledR$ designation, size of the property as well as training and experience are again criteria.

Functions of a Property Manager

The many and varied duties of a property manager require the skills of a business executive, decorator, salesperson, parking lot attendant, gardener, housekeeper, information center, accountant, banker, doctor, lawyer, social director, psychologist, marriage counselor, baby sitter, bookkeeper, rent collector, maintenance expert, security officer, keeper of the keys, telephone operator, messenger service, and complaint department. The manager must also be soft-spoken, fast-moving, poised, quick-thinking, non-tiring, ever-available, mechanical-minded, all-knowing and never-ailing. This "expert" knows how to visit without visiting, sell without selling, see without judging, hear without repeating - and all without having time for an uninterrupted meal.

The property manager has a dual responsibility: to the owner or client who is interested in the highest return from the property; and to the tenants, who are interested in the best value for their money, including reasonable safety measures and compliance with fair housing laws.

The property manager must promptly rent the property/units at the highest market rent possible, keep operational and other costs within budget, and preserve and enhance the physical value and prestige of the property.

SPECIFIC DUTIES OF THE PROPERTY MANAGER

Here are some of the specific duties a property manager must perform:

1. Establish the rental schedule that will bring the highest yield consistent with good economics.

2. Merchandise the space and collect the rent.

3. Create and supervise maintenance schedules and repairs.

4. If applicable, insure independent contractor status.

5. Set up payroll system for all employees.

6. Develop a tenant/resident relations policy.

7. Supervise employees and develop employee policies, including an Injury Prevention Plan.

8. Maintain proper records and make regular reports to the owner.

9. Qualify and investigate a prospective tenant's credit.

10. Prepare and execute leases.

11. Obtain decorating specifications and secure estimates.

12. Hire, instruct, and maintain satisfactory personnel to staff the building(s).

13. Audit and pay bills.

14. Advertise and publicize vacancies through selected media and broker lists.

15. Recommend alterations and modernization as the market dictates.

16. Inspect vacant space frequently.

17. Keep abreast of the times and competitive market conditions.

18. Obtain and pay insurance premiums and taxes.

19. Be knowledgeable about and comply with applicable Federal, State and local laws.

Rent Schedule

In establishing the rental schedule, the property manager must make a thorough neighborhood analysis by doing a market survey of rents for comparable buildings. Rent levels, generally, are established on the basis of scarcity and comparability of values. The manager must know the building thoroughly, assess its values objectively, then survey all of the "competition" buildings in whatever limits the manager sets for the neighborhood. The manager must then analyze:

1. The character of the buildings and amenities of the neighborhood.

2. Economic level, family size, and age groups.

3. Trends in number of occupants per unit.

4. Availability of transportation, recreation, shopping, churches, and schools.

5. Physical aspects as well as lot coverage.

6. The breadth and growth of local industries.

7. Population growth trends.

8. Personal income range, financial capacity, and stability of income.

9. Growth and expansion of the community.

10. Condition of the housing market in terms of inventory on the market, sales price range, new construction, and vacancy.

After a thorough analysis, the property manager will prepare a rent schedule that will bring the maximum income obtainable, consistent with good economics.

Merchandising the Space

All of the activities relating to property management are useless unless the property manager knows how to effectively merchandise the space available for rent. Various methods of merchandising include: business cards, newspaper ads, signs on the property, radio and television advertising, brochures and fliers, billboard advertising, business contacts, and tenant referrals.

When a prospective qualified tenant responds to advertising, the property manager must make every effort to secure the tenant for the vacant property, as advertising can be very expensive. A sound property maintenance program is very important. Rental properties showing the wear and tear of the previous occupants will discourage a prospective tenant.

Maintenance and Purchasing Operations

The property manager must establish and maintain sound policies for the maintenance of the building and purchasing of supplies and services. However, if all of the building's income is used for expenditures, leaving the owner no profit, the dissatisfied owner will seek the services of another property manager.

It is the responsibility of the property manager to routinely inspect the building and know its current, as well as deferred maintenance needs. The property manager should have access to skilled specialists for repair and maintenance work, unless the resident manager is personally skilled to perform necessary repairs. In either case, the property manager must correct the building's repair/maintenance problems as soon as they are discovered. It is less expensive to make repairs immediately than to delay action and allow the problem to worsen. Ongoing preventive maintenance to reduce the need for large maintenance expenditures should be the goal of all property managers. This approach makes good sense and, ultimately, provides more profit for the owner.

The property manager must also supervise all purchasing operations, with the emphasis on obtaining the best value possible for the owner's money.

Tenant Relationships

Tenants want to get the most they can for their rental dollar and feel safe in their surroundings. The property manager must set policies which will give tenants the most benefits commensurate with a proper return to the owner. Effort expended for tenant retention will result in more satisfied residents and increased profits for the owner. Here, the manager has to use experience and courtesy as well as psychology.

Manager as Employer

The property manager employs almost all the people working on the premises and provides for their instruction and supervision. The manager must know the "what, how and when" of each employee's job.

The success or failure of the management operation often depends on the property manager's ability to choose, train, direct and retain personnel. An effective staff will keep vacancies and maintenance costs at a minimum, thus contributing to the project's profitability.

Vacancies

There are many reasons why a rental space might be unintentionally vacant: improper rent required; space not ready to rent; resident manager not "selling" effectively; an inattentive manager; poor resident retention program; unappealing facade or public areas; no traffic or lookers; and high vacancy factor in area.

Successful managers are continually alert to these factors and make appropriate adjustments in marketing strategies and personnel where indicated.

Reports to Owner

The property manager must set up and maintain proper records, making regular reports to the owner that are easily understandable and that cover all operations. It is also recommended that the property manager provide not only a monthly accounting to the property owner, but also a detailed annual statement. By means of such annual statements, the property manager can assess the fluctuations of income and expense and formulate future rental, maintenance and employee policies.

EARNINGS

Management fees can be either a flat amount per month, a percentage of the gross rents collected, or a combination of the two. Property managers usually base their fees on a percentage of the gross rents collected. This may vary from 3 percent on large structures to as high as 20 percent on individual houses or small buildings. In some resort areas with high turnover rates and short terms of occupancy, as much as 50 percent of the gross rent is charged as a fee for renting a property. In addition to the fees collected on rentals, the property manager frequently receives additional compensation for the renewal of leases and for supervising major repairs or alterations.

Salaries for supervisors in a management company, resident managers, and office building managers depend largely upon local conditions and vary with geographical areas of the country, size of the city, and the size of the building. Additionally, care must be taken to comply with the minimum wage law.

Management Contract

It is good business practice for a property manager to have a written contract with the property owner which clearly sets forth the responsibilities of both parties. This should include the terms and period of the contract, the policies pertaining to the management of the premises, management fees, and the authority and powers that are given by the owner to the agent. Standard management agreement forms are available covering the management of rental properties. Building managers should have a special agency contract drawn up by a qualified legal adviser.

As an agent, the property manager is subject to all of the legal restrictions generally imposed upon an agent, as well as those specifically included in the contract. Such obligations include good faith and loyalty to the principal, performance of all duties with skill, care and due diligence, full disclosure of all pertinent facts, avoidance of commingling of funds, and refraining from personal profits without the principal's full knowledge and consent. The agent must be familiar with the laws concerning real estate licensing, contracts, agency, fair housing, employment, property protection, and tenant/landlord relationships.

The preparation of leases, tax reports and other matters may involve legal and accounting services beyond the province of the property manager. In such cases, professional counsel should be obtained. On the other hand, it is the property manager who normally engages maintenance workers, contractors, subcontractors, and others. The property manager must get the full name, address, and proper tax identification numbers from all such individuals. When and if their annual compensation meets or exceeds the taxable amount, the proper IRS 1099 form must be sent to these individuals and to the appropriate governmental agencies.

ACCOUNTING RECORDS FOR PROPERTY MANAGEMENT

A property manager must have knowledge of accounting procedures and cost accounting. The broker will need to maintain complex trust account records and make regular reports to the owner.

The maintenance of an adequate trust fund accounting system is necessary due to the fiduciary relationship between the real estate broker and the property owner. An accurate record must be kept of all trust funds passing through the broker's hands. The property manager must comply with the laws and regulations concerning trust accounts and records. This subject is discussed in Chapter 23.

Volume of business will determine the number of bookkeeping records needed. The small office requires simple records. The larger operation with office assistants and added sales personnel will almost certainly require more elaborate record keeping methods.

The responsibility for trust fund records is placed on the property management broker. An outside accountant should be retained periodically for review of the accounting system.

Firms doing a large volume of business and having a sales force may wish to consider the possibility of bonding the unlicensed office assistants so that they can legally handle clients' funds. Corporations and many limited partnerships may impose this bonding requirement and require individual bonding rather than a "blanket bond." The accountant may be able to consider various aspects of the accounting system and to devise methods to assist the broker in keeping control of the trust funds.

25 DEVELOPERS OF LAND AND BUILDINGS

The development of real estate provides a portion of the inventory that a real estate broker utilizes in his or her business. Just as any retailer or wholesaler must stock adequate inventories of their products, the real estate broker stocks listings of real property. The broker constantly replaces sold or expired listings with new listings, some of which may come from developers.

Real estate developers usually function in a larger business "arena" than do real estate brokers. Developers "manufacture" residential, commercial or industrial sites, either as vacant lot subdivisions or as improved or partially improved subdivisions. Their goal is to supply the type and price range of product that will satisfy the market.

In the course of business, a developer:

- carries inventory of raw, semi-finished and finished products, often for lengthy periods and for several widely separated, ongoing projects;
- uses personal funds or negotiates loans from land sellers, joint venture partners or financial institutions; and
- assumes large risks because of land planning uncertainties and possible misjudgment of the market which result in delays and losses due to interest payments, carrying charges, overhead, and other costs.

Some developers specialize in converting raw land to finished lots, suitable for builders to buy and begin construction of off-site as well as on-site improvements. Often the land developer will also install the principal off-site improvements and infrastructure. Other developer-builders plan and complete the entire subdivision from raw land through construction and sale of homes.

SUBDIVIDING

A subdivider must understand the potential difficulties involved in subdividing and the market for the project. The development plan must take into account state and local government regulation (e.g., the Subdivided Lands Law, the Subdivision Map Act, the California Environmental Quality Act, zoning, and local general and specific plans).

Often, zoning and planning preconditions drastically reduce the potential of a property. Before a developer or builder purchases property, he or she should consult with the local planning agency and private land use specialists to evaluate the likelihood of final approval of a project.

A developer will use civil engineers, construction engineers, soil engineers, land use planners, building architects, landscape architects, contractors, attorneys, title companies, bankers, real estate analysts, market researchers, and cost accountants to formulate a plan consisting of the following:

1. physical layout of tract in engineered detail;

2. land use processing and approval schedule;

3. amenities to be provided;

4. initial financing and continuing financing until the last sale;

5. advertising and sales promotion.

To determine if the project will yield adequate profit, the developer must calculate:

1. cost of the land;

2. cost of government fees;

3. cost of off-site improvements (e.g., water mains, sewers, streets, gutters, curbs, sidewalks, and street lighting);

4. survey, legal, marketing, financing and office/overhead costs; and,

5. the likely retail sales price(s) of the lots.

The developer's educated guess at the rate at which the lots will sell (the absorption rate) will impact the marketing, financing, and overhead costs, all adjusted for anticipated inflation.

The sum of all costs and expenses of the project is subtracted from the *realistic* estimate of the retail sales price of the lots to derive the estimated (pre-tax) profit.

A developer may subdivide a large tract of land pursuant to a phased master plan designed to meet the anticipated demand/absorption rate. These projects are more complex, with master governing restrictions and more obstacles to state and local approval.

A broker may gain initial experience in subdividing by becoming involved in a more limited aspect of the process. An owner of acreage might engage the broker as a subdivider, with the broker arranging the services of skilled consultants (civil engineer, land planner, land use attorney, etc.) to accomplish subdivision of the land. The broker and land owner may form a partnership: one contributing capital and land, the other management and marketing.

DEVELOPER-BUILDER

Development and building requires financing for land acquisition, land use approval and subdividing, construction, marketing, and carrying of inventoried properties until they are sold. A developer-builder may find it desirable to set up specialized subsidiary companies with separate financing needs: one company to hold title and subdivide the property; another to conduct building operations; and another for sales and marketing.

Subdividing and building is a cyclical business. High productivity and profit may be followed by a period of depressed sales. The cost of land, unpredictability of land use approvals, credit availability, interest rates, and inflation are all important factors.

Developers must find ways to build affordable homes despite increases in:

- demands from local agencies as conditions for approval of projects;

- wages;

- cost of building supplies; and,

- energy conservation and other building code requirements.

Some cost-saving options are:

- precut or prefabricated materials;

- use of fewer skilled craftsmen through standardization of jobs;

- complete on-site assembly of prefabricated units; and,

- reduction of land cost per home through increased density (e.g., planned development/cluster home and condominium projects).

Even though production efficiency has increased, total construction costs have risen with inflation and the demands of the consumer for more amenities.

Furthermore, a potential home builder needs to be aware of the risk that defective construction can lead to legal claims from purchasers. This liability can endure for up to ten years after the home is completed.

HOME CONSTRUCTION

The details of home construction methods, special installations, price and quality of materials are not generally within the scope of the real estate licensee's role. There are, however, some general areas with which the licensee should be familiar. Responses to some of the following questions will vary from community to community.

1. What styles of architecture are common in your community and how are they identified?

2. What are the approximate per square foot costs of homes of varying quality within your community?

3. Can you identify the different types and styles of windows with respect to location, function, materials and operating mechanisms?

4. What kinds of floor materials are available? What is the cost differential? What are the qualities of durability and comparative costs of maintenance?

5. What are the materials most commonly used on the exterior surface of a house and what are the relative costs of installation and upkeep?

6. What are the different types of heating/cooling systems for a home and their relative costs of installation and operation?

7. What are current insulation standards for windows, roof, walls, and underfloor areas? What types of materials are commonly used?

8. What can be done to prevent termites, dry rot and other fungus and insect infestations?

9. What are the most desirable roof pitches and roofing materials? Can you distinguish a hip roof from a gable roof? What types of roofing materials are permitted in the community?

10. What window coverings and window systems are available to prevent excess sun infiltration?

11. What are some common concerns about floor plans and specific rooms?

12. What kinds of materials are approved for use in the water and plumbing systems?

13. What kinds of materials are approved for use in electrical systems? What are some common devices that protect against overloading the system?

14. What is the condition of the soil on which the house is built? Is structural integrity jeopardized by filled ground? Slide conditions? Expansive soil?

15. What restrictions, if any, run with the property?

A home builder needs to be aware of the risk that defective construction of a home can lead to legal claims from the purchasers of homes. This potential liability can endure for up to 10 years after the home is completed.

26 Business Opportunities

The statutory merger of the real estate and business opportunity licenses occurred in 1966. Since then, a real estate license is required to engage as an agent in the sale or lease of business opportunities.

Definition
The Real Estate Law defines "business opportunity" as the sale or lease of the business and goodwill of an existing business enterprise or opportunity.

The sale of a business opportunity may involve the sale of only personal property. Typical transactions involve retail stores, automotive service businesses, restaurants, cocktail lounges, bakeries, manufacturing facilities, distribution and services businesses, etc. The sale almost always includes the inventory, fixtures, non-competition agreement, lease assignment, and goodwill. If real property is involved in the sale, the agent usually treats the sale of the business and sale of the land/building as two separate and concurrent transactions with two concurrent and contingent escrows.

Agency
In most business opportunity transactions, the real estate licensee will be acting as a dual agent, with the informed consent of the principals. Thus, the licensee is in a fiduciary relationship with both the buyer and seller.

The real estate broker must obtain the written authorization of the owner of the business property before he or she may obtain the signature of a prospective buyer on a procuring cause agreement. Failure to do so is grounds for revocation or suspension of the agent's license under Business and Professions Code Section 10176(j).

Small Businesses and the Small Business Administration
The Small Business Administration (SBA), a federal agency, assists small businesses through various financial and counseling programs. In establishing loan qualifying criteria, the SBA has developed *size* standards governing eligibility. Depending on the type of business (manufacturing, wholesaling, retailing, service, construction, or agriculture), the standard of eligibility is based either on the number of employees or on the annual gross sales of the business. Interested persons should contact the SBA for current criteria, loan amounts, etc.

Form of Business Organization
Legal and tax considerations generally enter into a buyer's decision regarding the legal form of business organization. Sole proprietorship, corporation, partnership, limited liability company, syndicate, and franchise are examples.

It is estimated that about 75% of American businesses operate as sole proprietorships. About 16% are corporations. However, corporate enterprises earn over 70% of the total income.

The sole proprietorship is the simplest form of business opportunity. Corporations are governed by officers, directors, and shareholders (owners), and the business is conducted under authority of its articles of incorporation, bylaws, resolutions and policies. Organizers must comply with the legal requirements of the state in which the corporation is established.

Form of Sale

The usual form of transfer for small businesses is a sale of assets for individual owners and a sale of assets or stock when a corporate owner is involved. (Transfer of partnership interests, corporate mergers, etc., are other examples of forms of sale.) Tax factors often influence the form of sale.

The transfer of ownership of a corporate small business by sale of all corporation stock may require that the agent negotiating the sale have a broker-dealer securities license issued by either the California Department of Corporations or the Securities and Exchange Commission. However, a real estate broker who has a listing for the sale of the *assets* of a corporation is entitled to a commission if the parties decide on the sale of the stock in the corporation, provided it is a sale of all of the outstanding stock. Regarding the sale of stock of a corporation, see Section 260.204.1 of the California Code of Regulations.

In a sale of assets, a buyer assumes no obligations of the business unless by specific agreement. The seller's liabilities and creditors' claims are generally cleared up in escrow. In a sale of stock, with the parties intending that the corporation remain the owner of the business with the same assets and liabilities as before the sale, the shareholders of the corporation sell and assign their stock to the new shareholders.

Why an Escrow?

The use of an escrow holder specializing in business bulk transfers is advisable for all business opportunity transactions. It is the escrow holder's responsibility to insure that both the obligations and benefits of the Bulk Sales Law (Commercial Code Section 6101, et seq.) and, if applicable, the Secured Transactions statutes (Commercial Code Section 9101, et seq.) concerning personal property transfers and security devices have been met and/or obtained.

Pursuant to the written instructions of the principals, the escrow holder:

- conducts lien searches;
- publishes, records, and mails to the tax collector the appropriate Notice(s) to Creditors of Bulk Transfer;
- obtains the designated tax releases from the government agencies who could otherwise impose successor tax liability upon the buyer; and,
- acts as a general "clearing house" depository for funds, documents, instruments and delivery of same at close of escrow, at which time the escrow holder provides an accounting.

(It should be noted that the Internal Revenue Service does not give tax clearances. In some sections of California, a tax lien insurance policy is available to protect a buyer against a future or undisclosed tax lien.)

Buyer's Evaluation

A buyer should be given an opportunity to evaluate all material aspects of the seller's business, including:

- liens and liabilities that affect the business (because of possible successor liability);

- the lease terms and conditions;

- the recent past and the present financial history of the business;

- the present and probable future risks involved with ownership; and,

- the probable future income stream (assuming effective management by buyer)

Although the buyer has a responsibility to exercise "due diligence" in evaluating the business opportunity, the agent should advise the buyer to seek the advice of a competent accountant and attorney.

Motives of Buyers and Sellers

Most purchasers expect to buy a business with either a good earnings record or a good earnings potential. Few people buy businesses with heavy loss records or at the price of assuming the seller's obligations. While real property always retains some value, a defunct business has little or no value. A broker must exercise reasonable care in screening potential buyers and keep in mind the seller's motives in selling and the buyer's motives in buying.

A seller's motives might include: retirement; burnout; poor health; a move to another city; imminent bankruptcy; or a desire to quit business and work for others. A buyer's motives could include: wants to be boss; desires more income; lacks skills or training for employment; retiring to a second career; buying "a dream"; or expanding an existing on-going business.

Counseling the Buyer

A broker may be asked to counsel a business opportunity buyer. Particular care should be taken to ensure that counseling statements are not construed as legal advice or as representations or warranties concerning the future of a specific business.

Normally, the broker and prospective buyer discuss the buyer's background and whether he/she has experience in the business being investigated. Other important topics include:

1. the amount of money the buyer can invest, including the money necessary for start-up costs, (beginning inventory, deposits with utilities, licenses and permits, lease payment, advertising, etc.);

2. where additional funds, if needed, may be borrowed;

3. credit extensions that can be expected from suppliers;

4. the opinions of any accountant, attorney, or banker who has consulted with the buyer and whether or not the broker will be coordinating the purchase with them;

5. the reasonableness of the buyer's net income expectations;

6. the possibility of unexpected expenses or losses; and,

7.   the likelihood that the current financial statement (balance sheet) and earnings statement (profit and loss) of the business and the buyer's financial statement will be adequate to obtain a direct loan from a bank or a loan through the SBA.

Especially with a novice buyer, the broker should anticipate being questioned in detail about all phases of owning the subject business.

A broker should be aware of the taxable events involved as a result of a transfer of a business. Particular care should be taken to ensure that counseling statements are not taken as legal or tax advice. The principals in the transaction should further be advised to seek legal and tax advice.

A new tax law went into effect January 2000 which adversely affects the seller who takes a note for part of the purchase price of the business. It applies to an asset sale as opposed to a corporate sale and where one is on the accrual method of accounting. The new law in general provides that the total dollar amount of the note to the seller is taxable all at once, even if the proceeds are to be received in installments over several years. This is a drastic change from previous law. It is incumbent on the licensee to direct the seller to discuss this matter with his or her accountant at the time of the listing. The new law may affect each taxpayer differently, depending upon their tax situation.

Additionally, in the sale of assets of a business, great care must be taken on how to allocate the consideration, i.e.; furniture, fixtures, equipment, non-compete agreement, goodwill, inventory, consulting agreements, lease, leasehold interests, employment contracts. The allocation of the items may have important tax consequences for the parties.

Satisfying Government Agencies
The broker should also be prepared to inform the purchaser of the various federal, state and local governmental agencies which the purchaser should contact for required permits, licenses, and clearances. Such agencies include:

- Internal Revenue Service (for employer identification number in connection with federal withholding taxes, etc.);

- State Board of Equalization (for sales tax permit, bond and sales tax deposit);

- State Department of Benefit Payments (state payroll tax withholding);

- State Department of Industrial Relations (workers' compensation insurance and California Occupational Safety and Health Act); and

- County and Municipal Agencies (licenses and permits, such as the business license).

Listings
Listings should be taken with great care after evaluating the business location, operation and the seller's records and financial statements (profit and loss statements, balance sheets and business tax statements for at least the last three years). The seller, or seller's accountant or attorney, should cooperate in furnishing the broker with income and expense records and copies of leases, insurance policies, inventory records for resale items, equipment, furniture, sales tax reports, IRS schedules, etc., so that the agent can evaluate the quality of the business and its income stream to arrive at a fair market price and listing terms with the seller. A

seller is often cautious about disclosing books and records to a buyer since a prospective purchaser could be a competitor or person not acting in good faith. If there is great resistance by the seller in accepting the broker's evaluation of a fair and realistic sales price and if reasonable value is not represented in the seller's demand for a higher listing price and terms, the listing should probably be turned down.

After the agent has reviewed the seller's basic records and evaluated the other aspects of the business, the broker and owner determine the listing price and terms to meet the owner's selling objectives.

In negotiating a listing, the licensee must remember the responsibility for making a full disclosure of and accurately detailing all information material to the business being sold - information furnished by the seller. Where shares of stock are involved, the law imposes a duty upon the broker to verify, within certain limitations, the accuracy and completeness of such information. This obligation is referred to as the duty of due diligence. Therefore, the owner's motive for selling is important. If the owner isn't making a success of the business and appears to be distorting or manipulating records, or "padding" statements to the broker, the broker must point out that failure to accurately disclose material facts concerning the business or "padding" of statements are material misrepresentations constituting fraud. The broker must not participate in such a transaction.

Preparing the Listing

The sale of a business opportunity should begin with an exclusive authorization to sell agreement, adequately and properly completed by the agent. Often with the advice of attorneys, experienced brokers and their associations have devised forms which serve as a checklist to avoid overlooking essential provisions for the protection of the parties. The broker should make sure that the form used applies to the transaction at hand, or amend the form. Specialized forms are the general rule.

Most authorizations to sell will provide room for a good deal more information about the property than would be necessary in listing a residence. The authorization may well contain:

- conditions and terms under which the business will be sold;
- duration of listing extensions;
- financing;
- how and when the business can be shown;
- name and address of seller's accountant;
- pending citations, if any, from government agencies against the business and/or owner that would prevent the selling or transferring of any licenses and/or permits;
- health and welfare and paid vacation provisions, etc., for employees, if there is a union contract in force;
- legality of any structural changes made (check to see if all necessary permits have been issued, final inspections made and jobs approved);
- days (and hours) of the week business is open or closed;
- number of employees;

- square footage of business area and parking area;
- dba of business, if any, and whether it is properly registered;
- name of the business if it is to be included as consideration;
- gross income and average per month; and,
- list of average expenses per month.

A business opportunity broker must ensure that all representations concerning a business are those of the owner or seller. A broker may be liable for any personal representations or projections that he or she makes.

The agent must inform the seller that the seller must have all equipment purchased and used in the operation of the business in working order on the day the buyer takes possession, unless the listing agreement and purchase agreement provide otherwise. It is also the seller's responsibility to see that necessary clearances from governmental agencies are secured. The seller should understand clearly that any sale will be subject to the buyer receiving all required licenses, permits and clearances.

When sales and/or social security and unemployment taxes are involved in the transaction, the agent must remind the seller (and see that the purchase agreement provides) that no funds are to be released to seller from escrow until such time as seller has provided the escrow holder clearances from the State Board of Equalization and the Department of Benefit Payments. Remember, the buyer can be held responsible for the unpaid taxes of buyer's predecessor ("successor's tax liability") up to the amount buyer paid to purchase the business. Sales tax must also be paid on the fixtures and furniture. The tax must be paid by the buyer to the seller, and the state will collect it from the seller, normally through escrow.

The seller must also be apprised that the buyer will have the right to inspect the business records of income and expense and in most cases will make the offer to purchase contingent upon the later inspection and approval of the records. The seller should also be informed of escrow costs and of any other fees the seller will be expected to pay. In most cases, the seller and buyer share the closing costs equally.

Establishing Value

There is no magic formula for estimating the equitable "saleable price" of a business. Some brokers draw from their own experience and ability to understand business accounting and devise initial price guides. These should be used only as rough guides.

When a broker has developed a price guide for use as a starting point in listing negotiations, the broker will find out by market comparison and careful examination of economic data that market prices of like businesses in the same general area vary considerably. Some of the factors making for this variation are differences in location, net earnings, hours of operation of the business, terms and conditions of lease, number of employees, etc. Other major factors in adjusting any price guide are the age, appearance and usefulness of furniture, fixtures and equipment, and the exterior and interior physical appearance of the business.

To arrive at an estimate of value, a business opportunity agent will examine the following:

1. Operating statements and business tax statements for the last three years. Sometimes a formal reconstruction of the records may be necessary to arrive at an "adjusted net profit." The adjusted net profit may reflect certain discretionary expenses which a new owner may not have.

2. Intangible assets being purchased, including goodwill, location, fictitious business name (dba), and the seller's covenant not to compete.

3. Aspects of the lease: renewable or extendible on reasonable terms; new lease or assignment; lessor's consent.

4. Financing: availability; suitability of assets (including real property, if applicable) as security for a bank or other loan.

5. The business opportunity's compliance with all applicable laws and regulations.

6. Employees; insurance; hours of operation needed to produce income; management problems; labor costs.

7. Zoning; parking; pedestrian and vehicular access; compatibility of neighboring businesses; square footage/future expansion possibilities.

8. Current ratio of operating expenses to gross income; seller's return on investment; seller's current assets, liabilities, and cash flow; consistency of profitability.

9. Comparison with similar businesses being offered for sale.

10. Written appraisal report from expert, if necessary.

Note that it is inevitable that there will be differences of opinion as to the appraised value of a business opportunity. The appraisal of a business opportunity is difficult because of the wide diversity of types of businesses and the fact that the amount of "goodwill" is difficult to quantify.

Some brokers become value specialists in their own right in specific types of business opportunities.

The final appraised value will be the best coordination of (1) the quality of the business investment and (2) the current market price for that type of business opportunity. Where the business is large and complex, the agent should advise the seller to have it appraised by a reputable specialist.

Valuation Methods

A number of valuation methods and statistical models exist for estimating the value of a business. Two common methods are: (1) capitalizing value based on estimated annual profit and the desired rate of return of the investment; and (2) evaluating the fixed assets and inventory being purchased.

A business opportunity broker who prepares a pro forma budget or statement of projected income should be aware that these documents may be construed as a representation or warranty. The broker may be held liable to the buyer for such statements. A business opportunity broker should deal only with the factual, historic operation of a business as reflected in existing records, and avoid any representations concerning future income.

Lease

If there is a lease involved, what is its status? Will the landlord permit the present lease to be assigned, and, if so, under what terms and conditions? Is a sublease possible and preferable to a new lease? If the present lease has only a few years left, is a new lease for a longer term possible and under what terms and conditions? Will the lessor demand payment of a bonus for a new lease and, if so, who will pay it? What is the lessor's name and address and who is to be held responsible for dealing with the lessor regarding a new lease or the transferring or extension of the present lease? If it is a percentage lease, how is the payment and accounting of same to be handled? The buyer should reimburse the seller through escrow for any prepaid rent and/or security money on the lease. The broker should carefully read any lease which is part of the transaction, and note all pertinent facts therein before quoting what broker believes to be facts to a buyer. It is likely that the buyer will need competent legal advice in this regard.

Goodwill

The goodwill of a business has monetary value, which the law protects. Goodwill is the expectation of continued public patronage.

Some factors to be considered in establishing a value for goodwill are:

1. History of sales and profits with greater weight given to the most current figures.

2. Length of time a business has been established in its present location.

3. Location and whether or not, with a few changes, the volume of business can be increased.

4. The present and protected future situation regarding competition. If a business has a location or license which amounts to a monopoly, it is possible to obtain a premium for goodwill. (As to a liquor license, there may be a limit on the valuation of goodwill.)

5. Purchase of the business name. If the name has become well known and has a good reputation for quality, service, dependability, etc., the goodwill value of the name is a definite asset and should be reflected in the price.

6. The seller's agreement not to compete, within legal limitations.

7. The characteristics of the business in reference to customer traffic (both foot and automobile), repeat business, and personality/ability of the owner and key personnel.

Fictitious Business Name

Not later than 40 days after commencing business in California under a fictitious business name, a business entity is required to file a fictitious business name statement with the county clerk in the county where the principal place of business is located (or with the Clerk of Sacramento County if there is no place of business located in this state).

Under the provisions of Section 17900 of the Business and Professions Code, a fictitious business name is one which does not include the surname of the individual or suggests the existence of additional owners. A partnership (or other association of persons) name that does not include the surname of each general partner or suggests the existence of additional owners is fictitious. In the case of a corporation, any name other than the one stated in the Articles of Incorporation is also considered fictitious. Names that suggest the existence of additional owners include such words as "Company," "& Company," "& Son," "& Sons," "& Associates," and "Brothers."

Within 30 days after a fictitious business name statement has been filed it must be published once a week for four successive weeks in a newspaper of general circulation in the county where the principal place of business is located. Where a new statement is required because the prior statement has expired, the new statement need not be published unless there has been a change in the information required in the expired statement.

An affidavit showing the publication of the statement shall be filed with the county clerk within 30 days after the completion of the publication.

A fictitious business name statement expires at the end of five years from December 31 of the year in which it was filed in the office of the county clerk, unless, prior to its expiration, a statement of abandonment of the fictitious business name described in the statement has been filed.

Franchising

Franchising is a business plan under which a business firm (franchisor) agrees to provide a purchaser-investor (franchisee) the right to engage in the business of offering, selling or distributing goods or services under a marketing plan or system prescribed by the franchisor, for a franchise fee.

Franchising allows investors to benefit from the expert management, assistance, special training, and marketing and promotional know-how of the franchisor while being self-employed.

A few examples of franchises are food service operations, hotels and motels, convenience stores, and drug stores.

There are many risks to consider in purchasing a franchise. Many poorly conceived, inefficient, noncompetitive, product-deficient franchisors have failed.

The Franchise Investment Law (Section 31000, et seq. of the Corporations Code) is designed to provide a prospective purchaser with full and adequate disclosure of all material terms of the franchise agreement. These disclosures will be contained in an offering prospectus which must be delivered to a prospective purchaser at least 10 business days prior to the effect of any binding franchise agreement, or at least 10 business days before the receipt of any consideration, whichever occurs first. To find out if a franchise is registered in California, call the California Department of Corporations Index Section.

The three categories of persons authorized to sell franchises under Section 31210 of the Corporations Code are:

1. A person identified in an application registered with the Commissioner of Corporations for an offering of a franchise in California.

2. A person licensed as a real estate broker or a real estate salesperson.

3   A person licensed by the Commissioner of Corporations as a broker-dealer or agent under the Corporate Securities Law of 1968.

Thus, a real estate broker, real estate salesperson, broker-dealer or agent can sell franchise interests without being identified in the registration application, while a person identified in the registration application can sell the franchise interest even though not licensed as a real estate broker, real estate salesperson, broker-dealer or agent.

Before becoming involved in franchising, a real estate licensee should possess a professional knowledge of the entire system and be familiar with the type of problems likely to be encountered by an owner of a franchise business.

BULK SALES AND THE UNIFORM COMMERCIAL CODE

Division 6 of the Uniform Commercial Code (UCC) pertains to bulk sales. A bulk sale is a sale, not in the ordinary course of the seller's business, of more than half of the seller's inventory and equipment (as measured by *value* on the date of the bulk sale agreement).

Public Notice

When the owner of an enterprise whose principal business is the sale of merchandise desires to effect a bulk sale, the buyer must give public notice to the seller's creditors by:

1. recordation of a notice in the Office of the County Recorder (of the county or counties in which the property to be sold is located) at least 12 business days before the bulk sale is to be consummated, or the sale, if by auction, is to commence;

2. publication of the notice at least once in a newspaper of general circulation published in the judicial district in which the property is located and in the judicial district in which the chief executive office of the seller, or, if the chief executive office is not in California, the principal business office in California, is located, if in either case there is one, and if there is none, then in a newspaper of general circulation in the county embracing such judicial district. Notice must be published at least 12 business days before the bulk sale is to be consummated or the sale by auction is to be commenced.

3. sending a copy of the notice by registered or certified mail at least 12 business days before the bulk sale is to be consummated or the sale by auction is to be commenced to the county tax collector in the county or counties in which the property to be transferred is located.

The notice to creditors shall state:

*   that a bulk sale will be made;

- the names and business addresses of the seller and, except in the case of a sale at auction, the buyer, and all other business names and addresses used by the seller within the last three years so far as known to the buyer;

- the location and general description of the property to be sold;

- the place, and the date on or after which the bulk sale is to be consummated; and,

- whether or not the bulk sale is subject to UCC Section 6106.2 (consideration is $2,000,000 or less, substantially all cash or cash plus an obligation to pay the balance in the future), and, if so, the information required by subdivision (f) of Section 6106.2 (the name and address of the person with whom claims may be filed and the last date claims may be filed, which is the last business day before the date of the bulk sale).

Sale at Public Auction
If the sale will be at a public auction, the notice must also state that fact, the name of the auctioneer, and the time and place of the auction.

Escrows
In any case where a bulk sales notice subject to the requirements of Division 6 of the Uniform Commercial Code provides for an escrow, the transferee (buyer) must deposit the full purchase price or consideration (not necessarily cash) with the escrow holder. If there is no escrow, then the transferee must apply the consideration as required by law.

If the seller disputes any filed creditor's claim, the escrow holder will withhold the amount of the claim and notify the creditor. The creditor has 25 days from the mailing of the notice to attach the funds. If not attached, escrow holder pays the funds to the seller, or to other creditors.

If, at the time for closing the escrow, the amount of money deposited is insufficient to pay in full all creditors' claims, the escrow holder must delay the closing, give notice to the creditors of the deficiency within the specified time limit, and distribute the cash consideration and any installment payments in strict compliance with the priorities established by law.

Escrow may not make any payments for fees and commissions prior to closing.

Effect of Noncompliance
The principal purpose of the bulk transfer law is to afford the creditors of a business an opportunity to satisfy their claims before the owner can sell the assets and vanish with the proceeds.

When the statutory filing and publication requirements are not met, the buyer is liable to creditors who hold valid claims based on transactions or events occurring before the bulk transfer. Creditors must take action within one year of the date of transfer of possession to satisfy their claims, unless the transfer was concealed, in which case action may be brought within one year after its discovery by the creditor.

In an auction sale, the auctioneer is responsible for giving the statutory notice. If an auction sale does not comply with the statutory requirements, the auctioneer becomes personally liable to the transferor's creditors for the sums owed to them by the debtor.

The provisions of Division 6 of the Uniform Commercial Code do not apply to certain transactions, including: transfers made to create or modify a security interest; assignments for the benefit of all the transferor's creditors; sale by executors, administrators, receivers, trustees in bankruptcy or any public officer under judicial process; or transfer of property exempt from execution.

Compliance with Division 6 does not exclude compliance with other applicable statutes, such as the transfer of liquor licenses under the Alcoholic Beverage Control Act (Business and Professions Code, Sections 23000, et seq.) and the Uniform Fraudulent Transfer Act (Civil Code Sections 3439, et seq.).

Uniform Commercial Code (Division 9)

Division 9 of the UCC (entitled "Secured Transactions, Sales of Accounts, Contract Rights and Chattel Paper") establishes a unified and comprehensive scheme for regulation of security transactions in *personal property* and fixtures, superseding statutes on chattel mortgages, conditional sales, trust receipts, assignment of accounts receivable and others in this field.

Division 9 applies to a transaction in any form which is intended to create a security interest in personal property.

There are a number of transactions excepted from this coverage. It is not applicable to real property security transactions, although a security interest in an obligation secured by real property (a note secured by real property pledged to secure another note) is covered.

A transaction subject to Division 9 might also be subject to one or more of the following:

1.   The Unruh Act (retail installment sales - Civil Code Sections 1801, et seq.);

2.   Automobile Sales Finance Act (Civil Code, 2981, et seq.);

3.   Industrial Loan Law (Financial Code, 18000, et seq.);

4.   Pawnbroker Law (Financial Code, 21000, et seq.);

5.   Personal Property Brokers Law (Financial Code, 22000, et seq.); and

6.   Consumer Finance Lenders Law (Financial Code, 24000, et seq.).

The UCC provides for a simplified filing system by means of a "financing statement" to perfect security interests provided for under the code. Local filing in the county recorder's office is permitted only for specific types of transactions. In all other cases, financing statements (Form UCC-1) are to be filed with the Secretary of State. See also Chapter 14.

CALIFORNIA SALES AND USE TAX PROVISIONS

The Sales and Use Tax Law is relevant to the transfer of a retail business which sells tangible personal property. Of particular importance are:

- a "clearance receipt" confirming payment of state and local sales taxes so that the buyer is protected from "successor's liability";

- releases or subordination agreements covering sales tax liens against real or personal property; and,

- the tax liability on that portion of the sale price allocated to the personal property to be used in the business.

Successor's Liability

In the sale of a business opportunity or stock of goods, the buyer must hold back enough of the selling price to cover any outstanding tax liability.

The successor's liability extends to taxes incurred with reference to the operation of the business by the seller or any former owner.

The purchaser of the business or stock of goods will be released from further obligation to withhold funds from the purchase price if he obtains a certificate from the Board of Equalization stating that no taxes, interest, or penalties are due from the seller or any previous owner.

The liability is enforced by service of a notice of successor liability. The successor may petition the Board of Equalization for reconsideration of the liability.

ALCOHOLIC BEVERAGE CONTROL ACT

The sale of a business involving an alcoholic beverage license is a specialty all to itself and is subject to laws which are constantly being changed.

Regulation

Pursuant to the Alcoholic Beverage Control Act (the ACT - Division 9 of the Business and Professions Code), the Department of Alcoholic Beverage Control (ABC) issues licenses authorizing the sale of alcoholic beverages. The ABC has the authority, for good cause, to deny, suspend or revoke an alcoholic beverage license.

The ABC issues alcoholic beverage licenses to qualified adult persons, partnerships, and corporations for use at approved locations. The ABC investigates each applicant and may refuse to issue a license to any person who has violated the Act, has a disqualifying criminal record, or attempts to conceal an arrest record. The location may be disapproved if it is in the immediate vicinity of a school, church, or public playground or if there is an over-concentration of alcoholic beverage licenses in the area or if licensure may create or aggravate a police problem. Most ABC application investigations take approximately 45 - 60 days.

A license issued for a specific location must be placed in use within 30 days of the date of issuance. If the premises are still under construction, the ABC will hold the license in safekeeping for not more than 6 months unless cause for further delay can be established.

Transfer of License - Posting of Notice

Like an applicant for license issuance, an applicant for transfer of a license must post the premises with a notice of application to sell alcoholic beverages. Local officials and private parties may protest the proposed transfer and the license cannot be transferred while a valid protest is pending or on appeal. Further, the ABC may decline to transfer a license if disciplinary action is pending against the transferor.

No one should make any investment upon the assumption that an alcoholic beverage license will be transferred. An applicant for license transfer may be able to obtain a temporary operating permit. However, it may not be prudent for the seller to give possession of the business for operation under a temporary permit.

Notice to County Recorder and Escrow Requirement
Before filing a license transfer application with the ABC, the applicant and current licensee must file a notice of intended transfer with the county recorder and establish an escrow. Escrow may not release any consideration before the ABC approves transfer of the license. Then, transfer of the business will occur simultaneously with transfer of the license.

27 Mineral, Oil and Gas Brokerage

History

Prior to 1943 there was much speculation in the sale and leasing of mineral, oil and gas lands, particularly during the depression period from 1933 to 1939. While it may seem strange that people invested in such highly speculative ventures during that period, it is explained that they were desperation investments. Many persons gambled their last resources in hope of gaining huge profits.

During the period mentioned, it was estimated that approximately 1,000 oil and gas salespersons were actively engaged in every section of the state. They confined their sales to parcels in newly created oil and gas subdivisions for the most part. While most oil and gas subdivisions were located in California, lands and leases in Texas, Oklahoma, Illinois, New Mexico, Wyoming, Montana and various other states were offered. While these lands were believed to have some potential for oil and gas production, the possibilities were rather remote. In most cases, purchasers of interests lost the entire amount invested.

A statewide drive was undertaken in 1943 to end these activities. This was accomplished by the Department of Real Estate (the Department) with the assistance of district attorneys, the Attorney General, Department of Corporations and local police departments. Many promoters were convicted of grand theft and about 600 operators lost their real estate licenses as a result of formal hearings or failure to renew because of circumstances.

MINERAL, OIL AND GAS REGULATION

The 1943 legislation required persons engaging in business as mineral, oil and gas brokers or salespersons within this state to secure a Mineral, Oil and Gas (M.O.G.) license from the Department. In 1967, due to the declining appeal of these types of transactions, the mineral, oil and gas salesperson license was discontinued. However, the broker classification was retained. Licensed real estate brokers were not required to have an M.O.G. license if the transfer of a mineral, oil or gas interest was "purely incidental" to the sale, lease or exchange of real property. If not, a real estate licensee was required to obtain a special M.O.G. permit in order to engage in not more than ten mineral, oil or gas transactions in a year.

In 1984, the licensing laws for mineral, oil and gas brokers were further simplified to conform them to those relating to real estate brokers, and to eliminate the bonding and quarterly report requirements.

1994 - NO SEPARATE LICENSE REQUIREMENT

Since January 1, 1994, an M.O.G. broker license is no longer required to allow anyone who is a licensed real estate broker or salesperson to engage in M.O.G. transactions. Those who hold M.O.G. licenses may continue to do so, and may renew their licenses, but no new M.O.G. licenses are issued. Instead, the definition of a real estate broker has been expanded to include mineral, oil and gas transactions.

Transactions Requiring a Real Estate License

A real estate broker, or a salesperson duly employed by a broker, may now solicit, negotiate and broker the sale, purchase or exchange of mineral, oil or gas property. A licensee may also solicit borrowers or lenders, negotiate loans, service loans, lease, rent and collect rents or royalties relating to M.O.G. properties.

A real estate license is also required to assist or offer to assist another in filing an application for the purchase or lease, or to locate or enter upon mineral, oil or gas property owned by the state or federal government.

Persons who act as principals in the purchase, lease or taking of an option on mineral, oil or gas land or property must obtain a real estate license if the purpose of the transaction is to then sell, exchange. lease, sublease or assign a lease on all or part of the property to another. Any person acting as a principal who offers mining claims for sale or assignment must also have a real estate license.

Exempt Transactions

A real estate broker's license is not required to engage in the following activities with respect to a mineral, oil or gas property:

- acting as a depository under an oil and/or gas lease if it is not for the purpose of a sale;

- engaging in a transaction subject to a court order;

- engaging in the business of drilling for or producing oil or gas, or in the business of mining for or producing minerals;

- negotiating leases or agreements between owners of mineral, oil or gas lands, leases, or mineral rights, and specified production businesses, or entering into leases or agreements with owners on behalf of such production businesses; and

- dealing with mineral rights or land, other than oil or gas rights or land, as the owner of the rights or land.

Mineral, Oil and Gas is a Technical Field

Mineral, oil and gas brokerage is a specialized branch of the general real estate brokerage business. The primary prerequisites for success are a broad knowledge of the elementary principles of geology relating to this field and sound knowledge of the fundamentals of real estate practice and ethics.

A person interested in focusing on M.O.G. transactions should develop a working knowledge of the technical subject matter with particular emphasis upon the functions and duties of a real estate broker as they relate to practice in the field of mineral, oil and gas brokerage.

Study References

Given the nature of this *Reference Book* and the relatively few persons specializing in this field, an extended discussion of mineral, oil and gas subject areas is not warranted. There are a number of geology text books available in bookstores, including *California's Changing Landscapes* by Gordon B. Oakeshott, which focus on the geology of California.

Considerable information concerning the oil and gas fields of this state, their structural conditions, importance, quality of oil or gas produced, etc., may be obtained in various publications of the California Division of Oil, Gas, and Geothermal Resources of the Department of Conservation. The Division of Mines and Geology of that Department also has publications and resources of value regarding mineral, mining, and geological matters.

Mineral Oil and Gas Subdivisions

Mineral, oil and gas subdivisions are those created for the sale, lease or financing of 5 or more speculative parcels of land for mineral, oil or gas purposes. The subdivision laws apply and there is no exemption for lots of 160 acres or more. The property may be located in California or in any other state. If the developer proposes to make sales in this state, the Department assumes jurisdiction.

No mineral, oil or gas subdivisions have been filed with the Department for a number of years, perhaps because of the stringent conditions which must be met under the law and the widespread prospecting activities of the major oil companies. Anyone interested in filing a mineral, oil or gas subdivision with the Department may obtain details from the Subdivisions Technical Section in Sacramento.

INTEREST COMPUTATION AND TABLES

Simple interest computation involves multiplying the principal (amount of note) by the selected interest rate and the product or result is the interest for one year. Remember, the interest rate (.06 or .09 for example) is a decimal and two points are to be marked off from the right.

There are 12 months in a year or 365 days. This latter figure makes for an awkward denominator. As a result, as an acceptable business practice, we assume 12 months of 30 days each, and 360 days to a year.

To avoid long computations which may involve cumbersome fractions, it is common to use prepared computations in the form of interest tables which show the base as $1, $100 or $1,000 for a variety of interest and time periods. From the interest table, we determine the factor and multiply it by the amount involved if it exceeds or is less than the base of the table. The following illustrates the different methods and short cuts.

Long Conventional Method
1. What is the interest on $4,650 for 75 days at 10 percent?
2. What is the interest on $4,650 for 1 year, 4 months and 10 days at 10 percent?

Answer:
1. 4650 x .10 x 75/360 = $96.88
2. 4650 x .10 x {360 + 120 + 10} or 490/360 = $632.92

(proper fraction for periods if less than 1 year; improper fraction for periods of more than 1 year)

Use of Interest Tables Method
1. Same problem
    Look in table on next page for 30 days at 10 percent

factor is	8.3340	= 30
factor is	8.3340	= 30
factor for 15 days	4.1670	= 15
	20.8350	75 days

    $4,650 = $4.65 per $1,000
    Multiply $4.65 x 20.8350 = $96.88

2. Table not complete to show higher factors, but it could be done this way:

30 day factor	8.3340	
	x 16	(16 months)
	133.3440	
	2.7780	(10 days)
	136.1220	factor for 1 year, 4 months and 10 days at $1,000

Therefore, 136.1220 x 4.65 (number of thousands) = $632.92 interest.

CHAPTER TWENTY-EIGHT

INTEREST TABLE FIGURED ON $1,000
360 Days to the Year

Days	5%	6%	7%	8%	9%	10%
1	$0.1389	$0.1667	$0.1944	$0.2222	$0.2500	$0.2778
2	0.2778	0.3333	0.3889	0.4444	0.5000	0.5556
3	0.4167	0.5000	0.5833	0.6666	0.7500	0.8334
4	0.5556	0.6667	0.7778	0.8888	1.0000	1.1112
5	0.6944	0.8333	0.9722	1.1111	1.2500	1.3890
6	0.8333	1.0000	1.1667	1.3333	1.5000	1.6668
7	0.9722	1.1667	1.3611	1.5555	1.7500	1.9446
8	1.1111	1.3333	1.5556	1.7777	2.0000	2.2224
9	1.2500	1.5000	1.7500	2.0000	2.2500	2.5002
10	1.3889	1.6667	1.9444	2.2222	2.5000	2.7780
11	1.5278	1.8333	2.1389	2.4444	2.7500	3.0558
12	1.6667	2.0000	2.3333	2.6666	3.0000	3.3336
13	1.8056	2.1667	2.5278	2.8888	3.2500	3.6114
14	1.9444	2.3333	2.7222	3.1111	3.5000	3.8892
15	2.0833	2.5000	2.9167	3.3333	3.7500	4.1670
16	2.2222	2.6667	3.1111	3.5555	4.0000	4.4448
17	2.3611	2.8333	3.3055	3.7777	4.2500	4.7226
18	2.5000	3.0000	3.5000	4.0000	4.5000	5.0004
19	2.6389	3.1667	3.6944	4.2222	4.7500	5.2782
20	2.7778	3.3333	3.8889	4.4444	5.0000	5.5560
21	2.9167	3.5000	4.0833	4.6666	5.2500	5.8338
22	3.0556	3.6667	4.2778	4.8888	5.5000	6.1116
23	3.1944	3.8333	4.4722	5.1111	5.7500	6.3894
24	3.2222	4.0000	4.6667	5.3333	6.0000	6.6672
25	3.4722	4.1667	4.8611	5.5555	6.2500	6.9450
26	3.6111	4.3333	5.0555	5.7777	6.5000	7.2228
27	3.7500	4.5000	5.2500	6.0000	6.7500	7.5006
28	3.8889	4.6667	5.4444	6.2222	7.0000	7.7784
29	4.0278	4.8333	5.6389	6.4444	7.2500	8.0562
30	4.1667	5.0000	5.8333	6.6666	7.5000	8.3340

TABLE OF MONTHLY PAYMENTS
TO AMORTIZE $1,000 LOAN

Years	5%	5.5%	6.0%	6.5%	7.0%	7.5%	8.0%	8.5%
5	18.88	19.11	19.34	19.57	19.81	20.04	20.28	20.52
6	16.11	16.34	16.58	16.81	17.05	17.30	17.54	17.78
7	14.14	14.38	14.61	14.85	15.10	15.34	15.59	15.84
8	12.66	12.90	13.15	13.39	13.64	13.89	14.14	14.40
9	11.52	11.76	12.01	12.26	12.51	12.77	13.02	13.28
10	10.61	10.86	11.11	11.36	11.62	11.88	12.14	12.40
11	9.87	10.12	10.37	10.63	10.89	11.15	11.42	11.69
12	9.25	9.51	9.76	10.02	10.29	10.56	10.83	11.11
13	8.74	8.99	9.25	9.52	9.79	10.06	10.34	10.62
14	8.29	8.55	8.82	9.09	9.36	9.64	9.92	10.20
15	7.91	8.17	8.44	8.72	8.99	9.28	9.56	9.85
16	7.58	7.85	8.12	8.40	8.63	8.96	9.25	9.55
17	7.29	7.56	7.84	8.12	8.40	8.69	8.99	9.29
18	7.04	7.31	7.59	7.87	8.16	8.45	8.75	9.06
19	6.81	7.08	7.37	7.65	7.95	8.25	8.55	8.86
20	6.60	6.88	7.17	7.46	7.76	8.06	8.37	8.68
21	6.42	6.70	6.99	7.29	7.59	7.90	8.21	8.53
22	6.26	6.54	6.84	7.13	7.44	7.75	8.07	8.39
23	6.11	6.40	6.69	7.00	7.30	7.62	7.94	8.27
24	5.97	6.27	6.56	6.87	7.18	7.50	7.83	8.16
25	5.85	6.15	6.45	6.76	7.07	7.39	7.72	8.06
26	5.74	6.04	6.34	6.65	6.97	7.30	7.63	7.96
27	5.64	5.94	6.24	6.56	6.88	7.21	7.55	7.88
28	5.54	5.84	6.16	6.48	6.80	7.13	7.47	7.81
29	5.45	5.76	6.08	6.40	6.73	7.06	7.40	7.75
30	5.37	5.68	6.00	6.33	6.66	7.00	7.34	7.69
35	5.05	5.38	5.71	6.05	6.39	6.75	7.11	7.47
40	4.83	5.16	5.51	5.86	6.22	6.59	6.96	7.33

TABLE OF MONTHLY PAYMENTS
TO AMORTIZE $1,000 LOAN

Years	9.0%	9.5%	10.0%	10.5%	11.0%	11.5%	12.0%	12.5%
5	20.76	21.01	21.25	21.49	21.74	21.99	22.25	22.50
6	18.03	18.28	18.53	18.78	19.04	19.29	19.55	19.81
7	16.09	16.35	16.61	16.86	17.12	17.39	17.65	17.92
8	14.66	14.92	15.18	15.44	15.71	15.98	16.25	16.53
9	13.55	13.81	14.08	14.35	14.63	14.90	15.18	15.47
10	12.67	12.94	13.22	13.49	13.78	14.06	14.35	14.64
11	11.97	12.24	12.52	12.80	13.09	13.38	13.68	13.98
12	11.39	11.67	11.96	12.24	12.54	12.83	13.13	13.44
13	10.90	11.19	11.48	11.78	12.08	12.38	12.69	13.00
14	10.49	10.79	11.09	11.38	11.69	12.00	12.31	12.63
15	10.15	10.45	10.75	11.05	11.37	11.68	12.00	12.33
16	9.85	10.15	10.46	10.77	11.09	11.41	11.74	12.07
17	9.59	9.90	10.22	10.53	10.85	11.18	11.51	11.85
18	9.37	9.68	10.00	10.32	10.65	10.98	11.32	11.66
19	9.17	9.49	9.82	10.14	10.47	10.81	11.15	11.50
20	9.00	9.33	9.66	9.98	10.32	10.66	11.01	11.36
21	8.85	9.18	9.51	9.85	10.19	10.54	10.89	11.24
22	8.72	9.05	9.39	9.73	10.07	10.42	10.78	11.14
23	8.60	8.93	9.28	9.62	9.97	10.33	10.69	11.05
24	8.49	8.83	9.18	9.52	9.88	10.24	10.60	10.97
25	8.40	8.74	9.09	9.44	9.80	10.16	10.53	10.90
26	8.31	8.66	9.01	9.37	9.73	10.10	10.47	10.84
27	8.23	8.58	8.94	9.30	9.67	10.04	10.41	10.79
28	8.16	8.52	8.88	9.25	9.61	9.99	10.37	10.75
29	8.10	8.46	8.82	9.19	9.57	9.94	10.32	10.71
30	8.05	8.41	8.78	9.15	9.52	9.90	10.29	10.67
35	7.84	8.22	8.60	8.98	9.37	9.76	10.16	10.55
40	7.71	8.10	8.49	8.89	9.28	9.68	10.09	10.49

OTHER SHORTCUT METHODS
FOR COMPUTING SIMPLE INTEREST

4%   Multiply the principal by number of days; cut off right-hand figure and divide by 9.

5%   Multiply by number of days and divide by 72.

6%   Multiply by number of days; cut off right-hand figure and divide by 6.

7%   Compile the interest for 6% and add 1/6.

8%   Multiply by number of days and divide by 45.

9%   Multiply by number of days; cut off right-hand figure and divide by 4.

10%   Multiply by number of days and divide by 36.

BANKERS 12%-30 DAY/6%-60 DAY INTEREST
COMPUTATION METHOD

(Using 360 day year)

To find interest on any principal amount for 30 days at 12%, or for 60 days at 6%, simply move the decimal point in the principal amount two places to the left.

Therefore, the interest amount on $8432.67 at 12% for 30 days is $84.33.

Likewise, the interest amount on $8432.67 at 6% for 60 days is $84.33

(Since 12% per annum is 1% a month, and 1% of any number is the hundredth part of it, then by pointing off two places from the right of a number, it is in effect divided by 100.)

What is the interest on $7397.64 at 9% for 69 days?

Interest @ 6% for 60 days = $73.98 (move decimal two places to left)
Interest @ 3% for 60 days = 36.99 (1/2 of 6% amount)
Interest @ 9% for 60 days = 110.97

We still need 9 days more interest:

6 days = 1/10 of 60 days:	6 days	= 11.09	(1/10 of $110.97)
3 days = 1/2 of 6 days	3 days	= 5.55	(1/2 of $11.09)
	9 days	= 16.64	

Therefore, interest @ 9% for 69 days = $110.97 + $16.64 = $127.61

FORMULAS

Three-Variable Formulas

In three-variable formulas, each variable is a function of the other two.

Income Formula

Income = Rate x Value

$$I = R \times V$$
$$R = I \div V$$
$$V = I \div R$$

Property Tax Formula

Tax = Assessed Value x Rate

$$T = A \times R$$
$$A = T \div R$$
$$R = T \div A$$

Percentage Formula

Percentage = Rate x Base

$$P = R \times B$$
$$R = P \div B$$
$$B = P \div R$$

Commission Formula

Commission = Sale Price x Rate

$$C = S \times R$$
$$S = C \div R$$
$$R = C \div S$$

Area Formula

Area = Length x Width

$$A = L \times W$$
$$L = A \div W$$
$$W = A \div L$$

LINEAR AND SPATIAL MEASUREMENTS
AS USED IN APPRAISING AND LAND DESCRIPTIONS

Common Linear Measurements

One foot = 12 inches
One yard = 3 feet or 36 inches
One rod = 16 1/2 feet or 5 1/2 yards
One furlong = 40 rods
100 feet = 6.6 rods
One mile = 5,280 feet; 1,760 yards; 320 rods; or 80 chains

Surveyors' Measurements

1 link = 7.92 inches
1 rod = 25 links
1 chain = 4 rods or 66 feet
(These are the old surveyors' measurements. Modern surveyors use a steel tape or what is called an engineer's chain which is 100 feet long with links of one foot. Thus, a mile measured by a modern steel tape chain is 52.8 chains.)

Spatial or Area Measurements (Length x Width)

1 square foot = 144 square inches
1 square yard = 9 square feet
1 square rod = 30 1/4 square yards
1 acre = 10 square chains; 160 square rods; 4,840 square yards; 43,560 square feet

(An acre is an odd and inconsistent measurement. It is supposed to have been the amount of land that a farmer could plow in a day with oxen and the old wooden plow. As a square, it is approximately 208.71 feet on a side.)

A section = 1 square mile or 640 acres
A township = 36 square miles
A quarter section = 160 acres
Area of a square or rectangle = length x width in unit of linear measurement used
Area of a triangle = base x 1/2 height

Cubic Measurement (Length x Width x Height)
1 cubic foot = 1,728 cubic inches.
1 cubic yard = 27 cubic feet.

SOME METRIC EQUIVALENTS

Lengths	Areas
one foot = 0.3048 meter	one square foot = 0.0929 sq. meter
one yard = 0.9144 meter	one square yard = 0.836 sq. meter
one mile = 1.6093 kilometers or 1609 meters	one acre = 4068.8 sq. meters
one meter = 39 inches	one square mile = 259 hectares or 2.59 sq. km.
one kilometer = 3281 feet or .62 miles or 1000 meters	one square meter = 10.76 sq. feet
	one hectare = 2.47 acres or 10,000 sq. meters

29 Glossary

ABATEMENT OF NUISANCE — Extinction or termination of a nuisance.

ABSOLUTE OWNERSHIP — See *FEE SIMPLE ESTATE.*

ABSTRACT OF JUDGMENT — A condensation of the essential provisions of a court judgment.

ABSTRACT OF TITLE — A summary or digest of all transfers, conveyances, legal proceedings, and any other facts relied on as evidence of title, showing continuity of ownership, together with any other elements of record which may impair title.

ABSTRACTION — A method of valuing land. The indicated value of the improvement is deducted from the sale price.

ACCELERATED COST RECOVERY SYSTEM — The system for figuring depreciation (cost recovery) for depreciable real property acquired and placed into service after January 1, 1981. (ACRS)

ACCELERATED DEPRECIATION — A method of cost write-off in which depreciation allowances are greater in the first few years of ownership than in subsequent years. This permits an earlier recovery of capital and a faster tax write-off of an asset.

ACCELERATION CLAUSE — A condition in a real estate financing instrument giving the lender the power to declare all sums owing lender immediately due and payable upon the happening of an event, such as sale of the property, or a delinquency in the repayment of the note.

ACCEPTANCE — The act of agreeing or consenting to the terms of an offer thereby establishing the "meeting of the minds" that is an essential element of a contract.

ACCESS RIGHT — The right of an owner to have ingress and egress to and from owner's property over adjoining property.

ACCESSION — An addition to property through the efforts of man or by natural forces.

ACCRETION — Accession by natural forces, e.g., alluvium.

ACCRUED DEPRECIATION — The difference between the cost of replacement new as of the date of the appraisal and the present appraised value.

ACCRUED ITEMS OF EXPENSE — Those incurred expenses which are not yet payable. The seller's accrued expenses are credited to the purchaser in a closing statement.

ACKNOWLEDGMENT — A formal declaration made before an authorized person, e.g., a notary public, by a person who has executed an instrument stating that the execution was his or her free act. In this state an acknowledgment is the statement by an officer such as a notary that the signatory to the instrument is the person represented to be.

ACOUSTICAL TILE — Blocks of fiber, mineral or metal, with small holes or rough-textured surface to absorb sound, used as covering for interior walls and ceilings.

ACQUISITION — The act or process by which a person procures property.

ACRE — A measure of land equaling 160 square rods, or 4,840 square yards, or 43,560 square feet, or a tract about 208.71 feet square.

ACTUAL AUTHORITY — Authority expressly given by the principal or given by the law and not denied by the principal.

ACTUAL FRAUD — An act intended to deceive another, e.g., making a false statement, making a promise without intending to perform it, suppressing the truth.

ADJUSTABLE RATE MORTGAGE (ARM) — A mortgage loan which bears interest at a rate subject to change during the term of the loan, predetermined or otherwise.

ADJUSTMENTS — In appraising, a means by which characteristics of a residential property are regulated by dollar amount or percentage to conform to similar characteristics of another residential property.

ADMINISTRATOR — A person appointed by the probate court to administer the estate of a deceased person who died intestate. (Administratrix, the feminine form.)

AD VALOREM — A Latin phrase meaning "according to value." Usually used in connection with real estate taxation.

ADVANCE — Transfer of funds from a lender to a borrower in advance on a loan.

ADVANCE COMMITMENT — The institutional investor's prior agreement to provide long-term financing upon completion of construction; also known as a "take-out" loan commitment.

ADVANCE FEES — A fee paid in advance of any services rendered. Sometimes unlawfully charged in connection with that illegal practice of obtaining a fee in advance for the advertising of property or businesses for sale, with no intent to obtain a buyer, by persons representing themselves as real estate licensees, or representatives of licensed real estate firms.

ADVERSE POSSESSION — A method of acquiring title to real property through possession of the property for a statutory period under certain conditions by a person other than the owner of record.

AFFIANT — One who makes an affidavit or gives evidence.

AFFIDAVIT — A statement or declaration reduced to writing sworn to or affirmed before some officer who has authority to administer an oath or affirmation.

AFFIDAVIT OF TITLE — A statement, in writing, made under oath by seller or grantor, acknowledged before a Notary Public in which the affiant identifies himself or herself and affiant's marital status certifying that since the examination of title on the contract date there are no judgments, bankruptcies or divorces, no unrecorded deeds, contracts, unpaid repairs or improvements or defects of title known to affiant and that affiant is in possession of the property.

AFFIRM — To confirm, to aver, to ratify, to verify. To make a declaration.

AGENCY — The relationship between principal and the principal's agent which arises out of a contract, either expressed or implied, written or oral, wherein the agent is employed by the principal to do certain acts dealing with a third party.

AGENT — One who acts for and with authority from another called the principal.

AGREEMENT — An exchange of promises, a mutual understanding or arrangement; a contract.

AGREEMENT OF SALE — A written agreement or contract between seller and purchaser in which they reach a "meeting of minds" on the terms and conditions of the sale. The parties concur; are in harmonious opinion.

AIR RIGHTS — The rights in real property to the reasonable use of the air space above the surface of the land.

ALIENATION — The transferring of property to another; the transfer of property and possession of lands, or other things, from one person to another.

ALIENATION CLAUSE — A clause in a contract giving the lender certain rights in the event of a sale or other transfer of mortgaged property.

ALLODIAL TENURE — A real property ownership system where ownership may be complete except for those rights held by government. Allodial is in contrast to feudal tenure.

ALLUVIUM — The gradual increase of the earth on a shore of an ocean or bank of a stream resulting from the action of the water.

ALTA OWNER'S POLICY — An owner's extended coverage policy that provides buyers and owners the same protection the ALTA policy gives to lenders.

ALTA TITLE POLICY — (American Land Title Association) A type of title insurance policy issued by title insurance companies which expands the risks normally insured against under the standard type policy to include unrecorded mechanic's liens; unrecorded physical easements; facts a physical survey would show; water and mineral rights; and rights of parties in possession, such as tenants and buyers under unrecorded instruments.

AMENITIES — Satisfaction of enjoyable living to be derived from a home; conditions of agreeable living or a beneficial influence from the location of improvements, not measured in monetary considerations but rather as tangible and intangible benefits attributable to the property, often causing greater pride in ownership.

AMORTIZATION — The liquidation of a financial obligation on an installment basis; also, recovery over a period of cost or value.

AMORTIZED LOAN — A loan to be repaid, interest and principal, by a series of regular payments that are equal or nearly equal, without any special balloon payment prior to maturity. Also called a Level Payments Loan.

ANNUAL PERCENTAGE RATE — The relative cost of credit as determined in accordance with Regulation Z of the Board of Governors of the Federal Reserve System for implementing the Federal Truth in Lending Act.

ANNUITY — A sum of money received at fixed intervals, such as a series of assured equal or nearly equal payments to be made over a period of time, or it may be a lump sum payment to be made in the future. The installment payments due to the landlord under a lease is an annuity. So are the installment payments due to a lender.

ANTICIPATION, PRINCIPLE OF — Affirms that value is created by anticipated benefits to be derived in the future.

APPELLANT — A party appealing a court decision or ruling.

APPRAISAL — An estimate of the value of property resulting from an analysis of facts about the property. An opinion of value.

APPRAISER — One qualified by education, training and experience who is hired to estimate the value of real and personal property based on experience, judgment, facts, and use of formal appraisal processes.

APPROPRIATION OF WATER — The taking, impounding or diversion of water flowing on the public domain from its natural course and the application of the water to some beneficial use personal and exclusive to the appropriator.

APPURTENANCE: That which belongs to something, but not immemorially; all those rights, privileges, and improvements which belong to and pass with the transfer of the property, but which are not necessarily a part of the actual property. Appurtenances to real property pass with the real property to which they are appurtenant, unless a contrary intention is manifested. Typical appurtenances are rights-of-way, easements, water rights, and any property improvements.

APPURTENANT — Belonging to; adjunct; appended or annexed to. For example, the garage is appurtenant to the house, and the common interest in the common elements of a condominium is appurtenant to each apartment. Appurtenant items pass with the land when the property is transferred.

APR — See ANNUAL PERCENTAGE RATE.

ARCHITECTURAL STYLE — Generally the appearance and character of a building's design and construction.

ARTICLES OF INCORPORATION — An instrument setting forth the basic rules and purposes under which a private corporation is formed.

ASSESSED VALUATION — A valuation placed upon a piece of property by a public authority as a basis for levying taxes on the property.

ASSESSMENT — The valuation of property for the purpose of levying a tax or the amount of the tax levied. Also, payments made to a common interest subdivision homeowners- association for maintenance and reserves.

ASSESSOR — The official who has the responsibility of determining assessed values.

ASSIGNMENT — A transfer to another of any property in possession or in action, or of any estate or right therein. A transfer by a person of that person's rights under a contract.

ASSIGNMENT OF RENTS — A provision in a deed of trust (or mortgage) under which the beneficiary may, upon default by the trustor, take possession of the property, collect income from the property and apply it to the loan balance and the costs incurred by the beneficiary.

ASSIGNOR — One who assigns or transfers property.

ASSIGNS, ASSIGNEES — Those to whom property or interests therein shall have been transferred.

ASSUMPTION AGREEMENT — An undertaking or adoption of a debt or obligation primarily resting upon another person.

ASSUMPTION FEE — A lender's charge for changing over and processing new records for a new owner who is assuming an existing loan.

ASSUMPTION OF MORTGAGE — The taking of a title to property by a grantee wherein grantee assumes liability for payment of an existing note secured by a mortgage or deed of trust against the property, becoming a co-guarantor for the payment of a mortgage or deed of trust note.

ATTACHMENT — The process by which real or personal property of a party to a lawsuit is seized and retained in the custody of the court for the purpose of acquiring jurisdiction over the property, to compel an appearance before the court, or to furnish security for a debt or costs arising out of the litigation.

ATTEST — To affirm to be true or genuine; an official act establishing authenticity.

ATTORNEY IN FACT — One who is authorized by another to perform certain acts for another under a power of attorney; power of attorney may be limited to a specific act or acts or be general.

AVULSION — A sudden and perceptible loss of land by the action of water as by a sudden change in the course of a river.

BACKFILL — The replacement of excavated earth into a hole or against a structure.

BALANCE SHEET — A statement of the financial condition of a business at a certain time showing assets, liabilities, and capital.

BALLOON PAYMENT — An installment payment on a promissory note - usually the final one for discharging the debt - which is significantly larger than the other installment payments provided under the terms of the promissory note.

BARGAIN AND SALE DEED — Any deed that recites a consideration and purports to convey the real estate; a bargain and sale deed with a covenant against the grantor's act is one in which the grantor warrants that grantor has done nothing to harm or cloud the title.

BASE AND MERIDIAN — Imaginary lines used by surveyors to find and describe the location of private or public lands. In government surveys, a base line runs due east and west, meridians run due north and south, and are used to establish township boundaries.

BASIS — (1) *Cost Basis*—The dollar amount assigned to property at the time of acquisition under provisions of the Internal Revenue Code for the purpose of determining gain, loss and depreciation in calculating the income tax to be paid upon the sale or exchange of the property. (2) *Adjusted Cost Basis*—The cost basis after the application of certain additions for improvements, etc., and deductions for depreciation, etc.

BEARING WALL — A wall or partition which supports a part of a building, usually a roof or floor above.

BENCH MARK — A monument used to establish the elevation of the point, usually relative to Mean Sea Level, but often to some local datum.

BENEFICIARY — (1) One entitled to the benefit of a trust; (2) One who receives profit from an estate, the title of which is vested in a trustee; (3) The lender on the security of a note and deed of trust.

BEQUEATH — To give or hand down by will; to leave by will.

BEQUEST — Personal property given by the terms of a will.

BETTERMENT — An improvement upon property which increases the property value and is considered as a capital asset as distinguished from repairs or replacements where the original character or cost is unchanged.

BILL OF SALE — A written instrument given to pass title of personal property from vendor to the vendee.

BINDER — An agreement to consider a down payment for the purchase of real estate as evidence of good faith on the part of the purchaser. Also, a notation of coverage on an insurance policy, issued by an agent, and given to the insured prior to issuing of the policy.

BLANKET MORTGAGE — A single mortgage which covers more than one piece of real property.

BLIGHTED AREA — A district affected by detrimental influences of such extent or quantity that real property values have seriously declined as a result of adverse land use and/or destructive economic forces; characterized by rapidly depreciating buildings, retrogression and no recognizable prospects for improvement. However, renewal programs and changes in use may lead to resurgence of such areas.

BLOCKBUSTING — The practice on the part of unscrupulous speculators or real estate agents of inducing panic selling of homes at prices below market value, especially by exploiting the prejudices of property owners in neighborhoods in which the racial make-up is changing or appears to be on the verge of changing.

BONA FIDE — In good faith; without fraud or deceit; authentic.

BOND — Written evidence of an obligation given by a corporation or government entity. A surety instrument.

BOOK VALUE — The current value for accounting purposes of an asset expressed as original cost plus capital additions minus accumulated depreciation.

BREACH — The breaking of a law, or failure of duty, either by omission or commission.

BROKER — A person employed for a fee by another to carry on any of the activities listed in the license law definition of a broker.

BROKER-SALESPERSON RELATIONSHIP AGREEMENT — A written agreement required by the regulations of the Real Estate Commissioner setting forth the material aspects of the relationship between a real estate broker and each salesperson and broker performing licensed activities in the name of the supervising broker.

B.T.U. — British thermal unit. The quantity of heat required to raise the temperature of one pound of water one degree Fahrenheit.

BUILDING CODE — A systematic regulation of construction of buildings within a municipality established by ordinance or law.

BUILDING LINE — A line set by law a certain distance from a street line in front of which an owner cannot build on owner's lot. A setback line.

BUILDING, MARKET VALUE OF — The sum of money which the presence of that structure adds to or subtracts from the value of the land it occupies. Land valued on the basis of highest and best use.

BUILDING RESTRICTIONS — Zoning, regulatory requirements or provisions in a deed limiting the type, size and use of a building.

BUNDLE OF RIGHTS — All of the legal rights incident to ownership of property including rights of use, possession, encumbering and disposition.

BUREAU OF LAND MANAGEMENT — A federal bureau within the Department of the Interior which manages and controls certain lands owned by the United States.

BUSINESS OPPORTUNITY — The assets for an existing business enterprise including its goodwill. As used in the Real Estate Law, the term includes "the sale or lease of the business and goodwill of an existing business enterprise or opportunity."

BUYDOWN — See SUBSIDY BUYDOWN.

BUYER'S MARKET — The condition which exists when a buyer is in a more commanding position as to price and terms because real property offered for sale is in plentiful supply in relation to demand.

BYLAWS — Rules for the conduct of the internal affairs of corporations and other organizations.

CAL-VET PROGRAM — A program administered by the State Department of Veterans Affairs for the direct financing of farm and home purchases by eligible California veterans of the armed forces.

CC&Rs — Covenants, conditions and restrictions. The basic rules establishing the rights and obligations of owners (and their successors in interest) of real property within a subdivision or other tract of land in relation to other owners within the same subdivision or tract and in relation to an association of owners organized for the purpose of operating and maintaining property commonly owned by the individual owners.

CCIM — Certified Commercial Investment Member.

CPM© — Certified Property Manager, a designation of the Institute of Real Estate Management.

CAPITAL ASSETS — Assets of a permanent nature used in the production of an income, such as land, buildings, machinery and equipment, etc. Under income tax law, it is usually distinguishable from "inventory" which comprises assets held for sale to customers in ordinary course of the taxpayer's trade or business.

CAPITAL GAIN — At resale of a capital item, the amount by which the net sale proceeds exceed the adjusted cost basis (book value). Used for income tax computations. Gains are called short or long term based upon length of holding period after acquisition. Usually taxed at lower rates than ordinary income.

CAPITALIZATION — In appraising, determining value of property by considering net income and percentage of reasonable return on the investment. The value of an income property is determined by dividing annual net income by the Capitalization Rate.

CAPITALIZATION RATE — The rate of interest which is considered a reasonable return on the investment, and used in the process of determining value based upon net income. It may also be described as the yield rate that is necessary to attract the money of the average investor to a particular kind of investment. In the case of land improvements which depreciate, to this yield rate is added a factor to take into consideration the annual amortization factor necessary to recapture the initial investment in improvements. This amortization factor can be determined in various ways — (1) straight-line depreciation method, (2) Inwood Tables and (3) Hoskold Tables. (To explore this subject in greater depth, the student should refer to current real estate appraisal texts.)

CAP RATE — See LIFE OF LOAN CAP.

CASEMENT WINDOWS — Frames of wood or metal which swing outward.

CASH FLOW — The net income generated by a property before depreciation and other noncash expenses.

CAVEAT EMPTOR — Let the buyer beware. The buyer must examine the goods or property and buy at his or her own risk, absent misrepresentation.

CERTIFICATE OF ELIGIBILITY — Issued by Department of Veterans Affairs - evidence of individual's eligibility to obtain VA loan.

CERTIFICATE OF REASONABLE VALUE (CRV) — The Federal VA appraisal commitment of property value.

CERTIFICATE OF TAXES DUE — A written statement or guaranty of the condition of the taxes on a certain property made by the County Treasurer of the county wherein the property is located. Any loss resulting to any person from an error in a tax certificate shall be paid by the county which such treasurer represents.

CERTIFICATE OF TITLE — A written opinion by an attorney that ownership of the particular parcel of land is as stated in the certificate.

CHAIN — A unit of measurement used by surveyors. A chain consists of 100 links equal to 66 feet.

CHAIN OF TITLE — A history of conveyances and encumbrances affecting the title from the time the original patent was granted, or as far back as records are available, used to determine how title came to be vested in current owner.

CHANGE, PRINCIPLE OF — Holds that it is the future, not the past, which is of prime importance in estimating value. Change is largely result of cause and effect.

CHARACTERISTICS — Distinguishing features of a (residential) property.

CHATTEL MORTGAGE — A claim on personal property (instead of real property) used to secure or guarantee a promissory note. (See definition of Security Agreement and Security Interest.)

CHATTEL REAL — An estate related to real estate, such as a lease on real property.

CHATTELS — Goods or every species of property movable or immovable which are not real property. Personal property.

CHOSE IN ACTION — A personal right to something not presently in the owner's possession, but recoverable by a legal action for possession.

CIRCUIT BREAKER — (1) An electrical device which automatically interrupts an electric circuit when an overload occurs; may be used instead of a fuse to protect each circuit and can be reset. (2) In property taxation, a method for granting property tax relief to the elderly and disadvantaged qualified taxpayers by rebate, tax credits or cash payments. Usually limited to homeowners and renters.

CLOSING — (1) Process by which all the parties to a real estate transaction conclude the details of a sale or mortgage. The process includes the signing and transfer of documents and distribution of funds. (2) Condition in description of real property by courses and distances at the boundary lines where the lines meet to include all the tract of land.

CLOSING COSTS — The miscellaneous expenses buyers and sellers normally incur in the transfer of ownership of real property over and above the cost of the property.

CLOSING STATEMENT — An accounting of funds made to the buyer and seller separately. Required by law to be made at the completion of every real estate transaction.

CLOUD ON TITLE — A claim, encumbrance or condition which impairs the title to real property until disproved or eliminated as for example through a quitclaim deed or a quiet title legal action.

CODE OF ETHICS — A set of rules and principles expressing a standard of accepted conduct for a professional group and governing the relationship of members to each other and to the organization.

COLLATERAL — Marketable real or personal property which a borrower pledges as security for a loan. In mortgage transactions, specific land is the collateral. (See definition of Security Interest.)

COLLATERAL SECURITY — A separate obligation attached to contract to guarantee its performance; the transfer of property or of other contracts, or valuables, to insure the performance of a principal agreement.

COLLUSION — An agreement between two or more persons to defraud another of rights by the forms of law, or to obtain an object forbidden by law.

COLOR OF TITLE — That which appears to be good title but which is not title in fact.

COMMERCIAL ACRE — A term applied to the remainder of an acre of newly subdivided land after the area devoted to streets, sidewalks and curbs, etc., has been deducted from the acre.

COMMERCIAL LOAN — A personal loan from a commercial bank, usually unsecured and short term, for other than mortgage purposes.

COMMERCIAL PAPER — Negotiable instruments such as promissory notes, letters of credit and bills of lading. Instruments developed under the law of merchant.

COMMISSION — An agent's compensation for performing the duties of the agency; in real estate practice, a percentage of the selling price of property, percentage of rentals, etc. A fee for services.

COMMITMENT — A pledge or a promise or firm agreement to do something in the future, such as a loan company giving a written commitment with specific terms of mortgage loan it will make.

COMMON AREA — An entire common interest subdivision except the separate interests therein.

COMMON INTEREST SUBDIVISION — Subdivided lands which include a separate interest in real property combined with an interest in common with other owners. The interest in common may be through membership in an association. Examples are condominiums and stock cooperatives.

COMMON LAW — The body of law that grew from customs and practices developed and used in England "since the memory of man runneth not to the contrary."

COMMON STOCK — That class of corporate stock to which there is ordinarily attached no preference with respect to the receipt of dividends or the distribution of assets on corporate dissolution.

COMMUNITY PROPERTY — Property acquired by husband and/or wife during a marriage when not acquired as the separate property of either spouse. Each spouse has equal rights of management, alienation and testamentary disposition of community property.

COMPACTION — Whenever extra soil is added to a lot to fill in low places or to raise the level of the lot, the added soil is often too loose and soft to sustain the weight of the buildings. Therefore, it is necessary to compact the added soil so that it will carry the weight of buildings without the danger of their tilting, settling or cracking.

COMPARABLE SALES — Sales which have similar characteristics as the subject property and are used for analysis in the appraisal process. Commonly called "comparables", they are recent selling prices of properties similarly situated in a similar market.

COMPARISON APPROACH — A real estate comparison method which compares a given property with similar or comparable surrounding properties; also called market comparison.

COMPETENT — Legally qualified.

COMPETITION, PRINCIPLE OF — Holds that profits tend to breed competition and excess profits tend to breed ruinous completion.

COMPOUND INTEREST — Interest paid on original principal and also on the accrued and unpaid interest which has accumulated as the debt matures.

CONCLUSION — The final estimate of value, realized from facts, data, experience and judgment, set out in an appraisal. Appraiser's certified conclusion.

CONDEMNATION — The act of taking private property for public use by a political subdivision upon payment to owner of just compensation. Declaration that a structure is unfit for use.

CONDITION — In contracts, a future and uncertain event which must happen to create an obligation or which extinguishes an existent obligation. In conveyances of real property conditions in the conveyance may cause an interest to be vested or defeated.

CONDITION PRECEDENT — A qualification of a contract or transfer of property, providing that unless and until a given event occurs, the full effect of a contract or transfer will not take place.

CONDITION SUBSEQUENT — A condition attached to an already-vested estate or to a contract whereby the estate is defeated or the contract extinguished through the failure or non-performance of the condition.

CONDITIONAL COMMITMENT — A commitment of a definite loan amount for some future unknown purchaser of satisfactory credit standing.

CONDITIONAL ESTATE — Usually called, in California, Fee Simple Defeasible. An estate that is granted subject to a condition subsequent. The estate is terminable on happening of the condition.

CONDITIONAL SALE CONTRACT — A contract for the sale of property staffing that delivery is to be made to the buyer, title to remain vested in the seller until the conditions of the contract have been fulfilled. (See definition of Security Interest.)

CONDOMINIUM — An estate in real property wherein there is an undivided interest in common in a portion of real property coupled with a separate interest in space called a unit, the boundaries of which are described on a recorded final map, parcel map or condominium plan. The areas within the boundaries may be filled with air, earth, or water or any combination and need not be attached to land except by easements for access and support.

CONDOMINIUM DECLARATION — The document which establishes a condominium and describes the property rights of the unit owners.

CONFESSION OF JUDGMENT — An entry of judgment upon the debtor's voluntary admission or confession.

CONFIRMATION OF SALE — A court approval of the sale of property by an executor, administrator, guardian or conservator.

CONFISCATION — The seizing of property without compensation.

CONFORMITY, PRINCIPLE OF — Holds that the maximum of value is realized when a reasonable degree of homogeneity of improvements is present. Use conformity is desirable, creating and maintaining higher values.

CONSERVATION — The process of utilizing resources in such a manner which minimizes their depletion.

CONSIDERATION — Anything given or promised by a party to induce another to enter into a contract, e.g., personal services or even love and affection. It may be a benefit conferred upon one party or a detriment suffered by the other.

CONSTANT — The percentage which, when applied directly to the face value of a debt, develops the annual amount of money necessary to pay a specified net rate of interest on the reducing balance and to liquidate the debt in a specified time period. For example, a 6% loan with a 20 year amortization has a constant of approximately 8 1/2%. Thus, a $10,000 loan amortized over 20 years requires an annual payment of approximately $850.00.

CONSTRUCTION LOAN — A loan made to finance the actual construction or improvement on land. Funds are usually dispersed in increments as the construction progresses.

CONSTRUCTIVE EVICTION — Breach of a covenant of warranty or quiet enjoyment, e.g., the inability of a lessee to obtain possession because of a paramount defect in title or a condition making occupancy hazardous.

CONSTRUCTIVE FRAUD — A breach of duty, as by a person in a fiduciary capacity, without an actual fraudulent intent, which gains an advantage to the person at fault by misleading another to the other's prejudice. Any act of omission declared by law to be fraudulent, without respect to actual fraud.

CONSTRUCTIVE NOTICE — Notice of the condition of title to real property given by the official records of a government entity which does not require actual knowledge of the information.

CONTIGUOUS — In close proximity.

CONTOUR — The surface configuration of land. Shown on maps as a line through points of equal elevation.

CONTRACT — An agreement to do or not to do a certain thing. It must have four essential elements — parties capable of contracting, consent of the parties, a lawful object, and consideration. A contract for sale of real property must also be in writing and signed by the party or parties to be charged with performance.

CONTRIBUTION, PRINCIPLE OF — A component part of a property is valued in proportion to its contribution to the value of the whole. Holds that maximum values are achieved when the improvements on a site produce the highest (net) return, commensurate with the investment.

CONVENTIONAL MORTGAGE — A mortgage securing a loan made by investors without governmental underwriting, i.e., which is not FHA insured or VA guaranteed. The type customarily made by a bank or savings and loan association.

CONVERSION — (1) Change from one legal form or use to another, as converting an apartment building to condominium use. (2) The unlawful appropriation of another's property, as in the conversion of trust funds.

CONVEYANCE — An instrument in writing used to transfer (convey) title to property from one person to another, such as a deed or a trust deed.

COOPERATIVE (apartment) — An apartment building, owned by a corporation and in which tenancy in an apartment unit is obtained by purchase of shares of the stock of the corporation and where the owner of such shares is entitled to occupy a specific apartment in the building. In California, this type of ownership is called a "stock cooperative."

CORNER INFLUENCE TABLE — A statistical table that may be used to estimate the added value of a corner lot.

CORPORATION — An entity established and treated by law as an individual or unit with rights and liabilities, or both, distinct and apart from those of the persons composing it. A corporation is a creature of law having certain powers and duties of a natural person. Being created by law it may continue for any length of time the law prescribes.

CORPOREAL RIGHTS — Possessory rights in real property.

CORRECTION LINES — A system for compensating inaccuracies in the Government Rectangular Survey System due to the curvature of the earth. Every fourth township line, 24 mile intervals, is used as a correction line on which the intervals between the north and south range lines are remeasured and corrected to a full 6 miles.

CORRELATION — A step in the appraisal process involving the interpretation of data derived from the three approaches to value (cost, market and income) leading to a single determination of value. Also frequently referred to as "reconciliation."

CO-SIGNER — A second party who signs a promissory note together with the primary borrower.

COST APPROACH — One of three methods in the appraisal process. An analysis in which a value estimate of a property is derived by estimating the replacement cost of the improvements, deducting therefrom the estimated accrued depreciation, then adding the market value of the land.

COTENANCY — Ownership of an interest in a particular parcel of land by more than one person; e.g. tenancy in common, joint tenancy.

COVENANT — An agreement or promise to do or not to do a particular act such as a promise to build a house of a particular architectural style or to use or not use property in a certain way.

CRAWL HOLE — Exterior or interior opening permitting access underneath building, as required by building codes.

CRE — Counselor of Real Estate, Member of American Society of Real Estate Counselors.

CREDIT — A bookkeeping entry on the right side of an account, recording the reduction or elimination of an asset or an expense, or the creation of or addition to a liability or item of equity or revenue.

CURABLE DEPRECIATION — Items of physical deterioration and functional obsolescence which are customarily repaired or replaced by a prudent property owner.

CURRENT INDEX — With regard to an adjustable rate mortgage, the current value of a recognized index as calculated and published nationally or regionally. The current index value changes periodically and is used in calculating the new note rate as of each rate adjustment date.

CURTAIL SCHEDULE — A listing of the amounts by which the principal sum of an obligation is to be reduced by partial payments and of the dates when each payment will become payable.

DAMAGES — The indemnity recoverable by a person who has sustained an injury, either in his or her person, property, or relative rights, through the act or default of another. Loss sustained or harm done to a person or property.

DATA PLANT — An appraiser's file of information on real estate.

DEBENTURE — Bonds issued without security, an obligation not secured by a specific lien on property.

DEBIT — A bookkeeping entry on the left side of an account, recording the creation of or addition to an asset or an expense, or the reduction or elimination of a liability or item of equity or revenue.

DEBT — That which is due from one person or another; obligation, liability.

DEBTOR — A person who is in debt; the one owing money to another.

DECLINING BALANCE DEPRECIATION — A method of accelerated depreciation allowed by the IRS in certain circumstances. Double Declining Balance Depreciation is its most common form and is computed by using double the rate used for straight line depreciation.

DECREE OF FORECLOSURE — Decree by a court ordering the sale of mortgaged property and the payment of the debt owing to the lender out of the proceeds.

DEDICATION — The giving of land by its owner to a public use and the acceptance for such use by authorized officials on behalf of the public.

DEED — Written instrument which when properly executed and delivered conveys title to real property from one person (grantor) to another (grantee).

DEED IN LIEU OF FORECLOSURE — A deed to real property accepted by a lender from a defaulting borrower to avoid the necessity of foreclosure proceedings by the lender.

DEED OF TRUST — (See Trust Deed.)

DEED RESTRICTIONS — Limitations in the deed to a property that dictate certain uses that may or may not be made of the property.

DEFAULT — Failure to fulfill a duty or promise or to discharge an obligation; omission or failure to perform any act.

DEFEASANCE CLAUSE — The clause in a mortgage that gives the mortgagor the right to redeem mortgagor's property upon the payment of mortgagor's obligations to the mortgagee.

DEFEASIBLE FEE — Sometimes called a base fee or qualified fee; a fee simple absolute interest in land that is capable of being defeated or terminated upon the happening of a specified event.

DEFENDANT — A person against whom legal action is initiated for the purpose of obtaining criminal sanctions (criminal defendant) or damages or other appropriate judicial relief (civil defendant).

DEFERRED MAINTENANCE — Existing but unfulfilled requirements for repairs and rehabilitation. Postponed or delayed maintenance causing decline in a building's physical condition.

DEFERRED PAYMENT OPTIONS — The privilege of deferring income payments to take advantage of statutes affording tax benefits.

DEFICIENCY JUDGMENT — A judgment given by a court when the value of security pledged for a loan is insufficient to pay off the debt of the defaulting borrower.

DELEGATION OF POWERS — The conferring by an agent upon another of all or certain of the powers that have been conferred upon the agent by the principal.

DEPOSIT RECEIPT — A term used by the real estate industry to describe the written offer to purchase real property upon stated term and conditions, accompanied by a deposit toward the purchase price, which becomes the contract for the sale of the property upon acceptance by the owner.

DEPRECIATION — Loss of value of property brought about by age, physical deterioration or functional or economic obsolescence. The term is also used in accounting to identify the amount of the decrease in value of an asset that is allowed in computing the value of the property for tax purposes.

DEPTH TABLE — A statistical table that may be used to estimate the value of the added depth of a lot.

DESIST AND REFRAIN ORDER — An order directing a person to stop from committing an act in violation of the Real Estate Law.

DETERMINABLE FEE — An estate which may end on the happening of an event that may or may not occur.

DEVISE — A gift or disposal of real property by last will and testament.

DEVISEE — One who receives a gift of real property by will.

DEVISOR — One who disposes of real property by will.

DIRECTIONAL GROWTH — The location or direction toward which the residential sections of a city are destined or determined to grow.

DISCOUNT — To sell a promissory note before maturity at a price less than the outstanding principal balance of the note at the time of sale. Also an amount deducted in advance by the lender from the nominal principal of a loan as part of the cost to the borrower of obtaining the loan.

DISCOUNT POINTS — The amount of money the borrower or seller must pay the lender to get a mortgage at a stated interest rate. This amount is equal to the difference between the principal balance on the note and the lesser amount which a purchaser of the note would pay the original lender for it under market conditions. A point equals one percent of the loan.

DISCRETIONARY POWERS OF AGENCY — Those powers conferred upon an agent by the principal which empower the agent in certain circumstances to make decisions based on the agent's own judgment.

DISINTERMEDIATION — The relatively sudden withdrawal of substantial sums of money savers have deposited with savings and loan associations, commercial banks, and mutual savings banks. This term can also be considered to include life insurance policy purchasers borrowing against the value of their policies. The essence of this phenomenon is financial intermediaries losing within a short period of time billions of dollars as owners of funds held by those institutional lenders exercise their prerogative of taking them out of the hands of these financial institutions.

DISPOSABLE INCOME — The after-tax income a household receives to spend on personal consumption.

DISPOSSESS — To deprive one of the use of real estate.

DOCUMENTARY TRANSFER TAX — A state enabling act allows a county to adopt a documentary transfer tax to apply on all transfers of real property located in the county. Notice of payment is entered on face of the deed or on a separate paper filed with the deed.

DOCUMENTS — Legal instruments such as mortgages, contracts, deeds, options, wills, bills of sale, etc.

DONEE — A person who receives a gift.

DONOR — A person who makes a gift.

DOUBLE DECLINING BALANCE DEPRECIATION — (See *DECLINING BALANCE DEPRECIATION*.)

DRAW — Usually applies to construction loans when disbursement of a portion of the mortgage is made in advance, as improvements to the property are made.

DUAL AGENCY — An agency relationship in which the agent acts concurrently for both of the principals in a transaction.

DUE ON SALE CLAUSE — An acceleration clause granting the lender the right to demand full payment of the mortgage upon a sale of the property.

DURESS — Unlawful constraint exercised upon a person whereby he or she is forced to do some act against his or her will.

EARNEST MONEY — Down payment made by a purchaser of real estate as evidence of good faith. A deposit or partial payment.

EASEMENT — A right, privilege or interest limited to a specific purpose which one party has in the land of another.

ECONOMIC LIFE — The period over which a property will yield a return on the investment over and above the economic or ground rent due to land.

ECONOMIC OBSOLESCENCE — A loss in value due to factors away from the subject property but adversely affecting the value of the subject property.

ECONOMIC RENT — The reasonable rental expectancy if the property were available for renting at the time of its valuation.

EFFECTIVE AGE OF IMPROVEMENT — The number of years of age that is indicated by the condition of the structure, distinct from chronological age.

EFFECTIVE DATE OF VALUE — The specific day the conclusion of value applies.

EFFECTIVE INTEREST RATE — The percentage of interest that is actually being paid by the borrower for the use of the money, distinct from nominal interest.

EMINENT DOMAIN — The right of the government to acquire property for necessary public or quasi-public use by condition; the owner must be fairly compensated and the right of the private citizen to get paid is spelled out in the 5th Amendment to the United States Constitution.

ENCROACHMENT — An unlawful intrusion onto another's adjacent property by improvements to real property, e.g. a swimming pool built across a property line.

ENCUMBRANCE — Anything which affects or limits the fee simple title to or value of property, e.g., mortgages or easements.

EQUITY — The interest or value which an owner has in real estate over and above the liens against it. Branch of remedial justice by and through which relief is afforded to suitors in courts of equity.

EQUITY BUILD-UP — The increase of owner's equity in property due to mortgage principal reduction and value appreciation.

EQUITY PARTICIPATION — A mortgage transaction in which the lender, in addition to receiving a fixed rate of interest on the loan acquires an interest in the borrower's real property, and shares in the profits derived from the real property.

EQUITY OF REDEMPTION — The right to redeem property during the foreclosure period, such as a mortgagor's right to redeem within either 3 months or 1 year as may be permitted after foreclosure sale.

EROSION — The wearing away of land by the act of water, wind or glacial ice.

ESCALATION — The right reserved by the lender to increase the amount of the payments and/or interest upon the happening of a certain event.

ESCALATOR CLAUSE — A clause in a contract providing for the upward or downward adjustment of certain items to cover specified contingencies, usually tied to some index or event. Often used in long term leases to provide for rent adjustments, to cover tax and maintenance increases.

ESCHEAT — The reverting of property to the State when heirs capable of inheriting are lacking.

ESCROW — The deposit of instruments and/or funds with instructions with a third neutral party to carry out the provisions of an agreement or contract.

ESCROW AGENT — The neutral third party holding funds or something of value in trust for another or others.

ESTATE — As applied to real estate, the term signifies the quantity of interest, share, right, equity, of which riches or fortune may consist in real property. The degree, quantity, nature and extent of interest which a person has in real property.

ESTATE OF INHERITANCE — An estate which may descend to heirs. All freehold estates are estates of inheritance, except estates for life.

ESTATE FOR LIFE — A possessory, freehold estate in land held by a person only for the duration of his or her life or the life or lives of another.

ESTATE FROM PERIOD TO PERIOD — An interest in land where there is no definite termination date but the rental period is fixed at a certain sum per week, month, or year. Also called a periodic tenancy.

ESTATE AT SUFFERANCE — An estate arising when the tenant wrongfully holds over after the expiration of the term. The landlord has the choice of evicting the tenant as a trespasser or accepting such tenant for a similar term and under the conditions of the tenant's previous holding. Also called a tenancy at sufferance.

ESTATE AT WILL — The occupation of lands and tenements by a tenant for an indefinite period, terminable by one or both parties.

ESTATE FOR YEARS — An interest in lands by virtue of a contract for the possession of them for a definite and limited period of time. May be for a year or less. A lease may be said to be an estate for years.

ESTIMATE — A preliminary opinion of value. Appraise, set a value.

ESTIMATED REMAINING LIFE — The period of time (years) it takes for the improvements to become valueless.

ESTOPPEL — A legal theory under which a person is barred from asserting or denying a fact because of the person's previous acts or words.

ETHICS — That branch of moral science, idealism, justness, and fairness, which treats of the duties which a member of a profession or craft owes to the public, client or partner, and to professional brethren or members. Accepted standards of right and wrong. Moral conduct, behavior or duty.

ET UX — Abbreviation for "et uxor." Means "and wife."

EVICTION — Dispossession by process of law. The act of depriving a person of the possession of lands in pursuance of the judgment of a court.

EXCEPTIONS — Matters affecting title to a particular parcel of real property which are included from coverage of a title insurance policy.

EXCHANGE — A means of trading equities in two or more real properties, treated as a single transaction through a single escrow.

EXCLUSION — General matters affecting title to real property excluded from coverage of a title insurance policy.

EXCLUSIVE AGENCY LISTING — A listing agreement employing a broker as the sole agent for the seller of real property under the terms of which the broker is entitled to a commission if the property is sold through any other broker, but not if a sale is negotiated by the owner without the services of an agent.

EXCLUSIVE RIGHT TO SELL LISTING — A listing agreement employing a broker to act as agent for the seller of real property under the terms of which the broker is entitled to a commission if the property is sold during the duration of the listing through another broker or by the owner without the services of an agent.

EXECUTE — To complete, to make, to perform, to do, to follow out; to execute a deed, to make a deed, including especially signing, sealing and delivery; to execute a contract is to perform the contract, to follow out to the end, to complete.

EXECUTOR — A man named in a will to carry out its provisions as to the disposition of the estate of a deceased person. (A woman is executrix.)

EXECUTORY CONTRACT — A contract in which something remains to be done by one or both of the parties.

EXPENSES — Certain items which appear on a closing statement in connection with a real estate sale.

FACADE — The front of a building, often used to refer to a false front and as a metaphor.

FAIR MARKET VALUE. This is the amount of money that would be paid for a property offered on the open market for a reasonable period of time with both buyer and seller knowing all the uses to which the property could be put and with neither party being under pressure to buy or sell.

FANNIE MAE — An acronymic nickname for Federal National Mortgage Association (FNMA).

FARMERS HOME ADMINISTRATION — An agency of the Department of Agriculture. Primary responsibility is to provide financial assistance for farmers and others living in rural areas where financing is not available on reasonable terms from private sources.

FEDERAL DEPOSIT INSURANCE CORPORATION — (FDIC) Agency of the federal government which insures deposits at commercial banks, savings banks and savings and loans.

FEDERAL HOME LOAN MORTGAGE CORPORATION — An independent stock company which creates a secondary market in conventional residential loans and in FHA and VA loans by purchasing mortgages.

FEDERAL HOUSING ADMINISTRATION — (FHA) An agency of the federal government that insures private mortgage loans for financing of new and existing homes and home repairs.

FEDERAL LAND BANK SYSTEM — Federal government agency making long term loans to farmers.

FEDERAL NATIONAL MORTGAGE ASSOCIATION — (FNMA) "Fannie Mae" a quasipublic agency converted into a private corporation whose primary function is to buy and sell FHA and VA mortgages in the secondary market.

FEDERAL RESERVE SYSTEM — The federal banking system of the United States under the control of central board of governors (Federal Reserve Board) involving a central bank in each of twelve geographical districts with broad powers in controlling credit and the amount of money in circulation.

FEE — An estate of inheritance in real property.

FEE SIMPLE DEFEASIBLE — An estate in fee subject to the occurrence of a condition subsequent whereby the estate may be terminated.

FEE SIMPLE ESTATE — The greatest interest that one can have in real property. An estate that is unqualified, of indefinite duration, freely transferable and inheritable.

FEUDAL TENURE — A real property ownership system in which ownership rests with a sovereign who may grant lesser interests in return for service or loyalty. This is in contrast to allodial tenure.

FHLMC — See FEDERAL HOME LOAN MORTGAGE CORPORATION.

FIDELITY BOND — A security posted for the discharge of an obligation of personal services.

FIDUCIARY — A person in a position of trust and confidence, as between principal and broker; broker as fiduciary owes certain loyalty which cannot be breached under the rules of agency.

FIDUCIARY DUTY — That duty owed by an agent to act in the highest good faith toward the principal and not to obtain any advantage over the latter by the slightest misrepresentation, concealment, duress or pressure.

FILTERING — The process whereby higher-priced properties become available to lower income buyers.

FINANCIAL INTERMEDIARY — Financial institutions such as commercial banks, savings and loan associations, mutual savings banks and life insurance companies which receive relatively small sums of money from the public and invest them in the form of large sums. A considerable portion of these funds are loaned on real estate.

FINANCING PROCESS — The systematic 5 step procedure followed by major institutional lenders in analyzing a proposed loan, which includes — filing of application by a borrower; lender's analysis of borrower and property; processing of loan documentation; closing (paying) the loan; and servicing (collection and record keeping).

FINANCING STATEMENT — The instrument which is filed in order to give public notice of the security interest and thereby protect the interest of the secured parties in the collateral. (See definition of Security Interest and Secured Party.)

FIRST MORTGAGE — A legal document pledging collateral for a loan (See "mortgage") that has first priority over all other claims against the property except taxes and bonded indebtedness. That mortgage superior to any other.

FIRST TRUST DEED — A legal document pledging collateral for a loan (See "trust deed") that has first priority over all other claims against the property except taxes and bonded indebtedness. That trust deed superior to any other.

FISCAL CONTROLS — Federal tax revenue and expenditure policies used to control the level of economic activity.

FISCAL YEAR — A business or accounting year as distinguished from a calendar year.

FIXITY OF LOCATION — The physical characteristic of real estate that subjects it to the influence of its surroundings.

FIXTURES — Appurtenances attached to the land or improvements, which usually cannot be removed without agreement as they become real property; examples — plumbing fixtures, store fixtures built into the property, etc.

FORECLOSURE — Procedure whereby property pledged as security for a debt is sold to pay the debt in event of default in payments or terms.

FORFEITURE — Loss of money or anything of value, due to failure to perform.

FRANCHISE — A specified privilege awarded by a government or business firm which awards an exclusive dealership.

FRAUD — The intentional and successful employment of any cunning, deception, collusion, or artifice, used to circumvent, cheat or deceive another person whereby that person acts upon it to the loss of property and to legal injury. (Actual Fraud — A deliberate misrepresentation or representation made in reckless disregard of its truth or its falsity, the suppression of truth, a promise made without the intention to perform it, or any other act intended to deceive.)

FRAUDS, STATUTE OF — (See Statute of Frauds.)

"FREDDIE MAC" — (See FEDERAL HOME LOAN MORTGAGE CORPORATION.)

FREEHOLD ESTATE — An estate of indeterminable duration, e.g., fee simple or life estate.

FRONTAGE — A term used to describe or identify that part of a parcel of land or an improvement on the land which faces a street. The term is also used to refer to the lineal extent of the land or improvement that is parallel to and facing the street, e.g., a 75-foot frontage.

FRONT FOOT — Property measurement for sale or valuation purposes; the property measured by the front linear foot on its street line—each front foot extending the depth of the lot.

FRONT MONEY — The minimum amount of money necessary to initiate a real estate venture, to get the transaction underway.

FROSTLINE — The depth of frost penetration in the soil. Varies in different parts of the country. Footings should be placed below this depth to prevent movement.

FULLY INDEXED NOTE RATE — As related to adjustable rate mortgages, the index value at the time of application plus the gross margin stated in the note.

FUNCTIONAL OBSOLESCENCE — A loss of value due to adverse factors from within the structure which affect the utility of the structure, value and marketability.

FUTURE BENEFITS — The anticipated benefits the present owner will receive from the property in the future.

GABLE ROOF — A pitched roof with sloping sides.

GAIN — A profit, benefit, or value increase.

GAMBREL ROOF — A curb roof, having a steep lower slope with a flatter upper slope above.

GENERAL LIEN — A lien on all the property of a debtor.

GIFT DEED — A deed for which there is no consideration.

GOODWILL — An intangible but salable asset of a business derived from the expectation of continued public patronage.

GOVERNMENT NATIONAL MORTGAGE ASSOCIATION — An agency of HUD, which functions in the secondary mortgage market, primarily in social housing programs. Commonly called by the acronymic nickname "Ginnie Mae" (GNMA).

GOVERNMENT SURVEY — A method of specifying the location of parcel of land using prime meridians, base lines, standard parallels, guide meridians, townships and sections.

GRADE — Ground level at the foundation.

GRADUATED LEASE — Lease which provides for a varying rental rate, often based upon future determination; sometimes rent is based upon result of periodical appraisals; used largely in long-term leases.

GRADUATED PAYMENT MORTGAGE — Providing for partially deferred payments of principal at start of loan. (There are a variety of plans.) Usually after the first five years of the loan term the principal and interest payment are substantially higher, to make up principal portion of payments lost at the beginning of the loan. (See Variable Interest Rate.)

GRANT — A technical legal term in a deed of conveyance bestowing an interest in real property on another. The words "convey" and "transfer" have the same effect.

GRANT DEED — A limited warranty deed using the word "grant" or like words that assures a grantee that the grantor has not already conveyed the land to another and that the estate is free from encumbrances placed by the grantor.

GRANTEE — A person to whom a grant is made.

GRANTOR — A person who transfers his or her interest in property to another by grant.

GRATUITOUS AGENT — A person not paid by the principal for services on behalf of the principal, who cannot be forced to act as an agent, but who becomes bound to act in good faith and obey a principal's instructions once he or she undertakes to act as an agent.

GRID — A chart used in rating the borrower risk, property and the neighborhood.

GROSS INCOME — Total income from property before any expenses are deducted.

GROSS MARGIN — With regard to an adjustable rate mortgage, an amount expressed as percentage points, stated in the note which is added to the current index value on the rate adjustment date to establish the new note rate.

GROSS NATIONAL PRODUCT (GNP) — The total value of all goods and services produced in an economy during a given period of time.

GROSS RATE — A method of collecting interest by adding total interest to the principal of the loan at the outset of the term.

GROSS RENT MULTIPLIER — A number which, times the gross income of a property, produces an estimate of value of the property. Example — The gross income from an unfurnished apartment building is $200,000 per annum. If an appraiser uses a gross multiplier of 7%, then it is said that based on the gross multiplier the value of the building is $1,400,000.

GROUND LEASE — An agreement for the use of the land only, sometimes secured by improvements placed on the land by the user.

GROUND RENT — Earnings of improved property credited to earnings of the ground itself after allowance is made for earnings of improvements; often termed economic rent.

HABENDUM CLAUSE — The "to have and to hold" clause which may be found in a deed.

HEIR — One who inherits property at the death of the owner of the land, if the owner has died without a will.

HIGHEST AND BEST USE — An appraisal phrase meaning that use which at the time of an appraisal is most likely to produce the greatest net return to the land and/or buildings over a given period of time; that use which will produce the greatest amount of amenities or profit. This is the starting point for appraisal.

HIP ROOF — A pitched roof with sloping sides and ends.

HOLDER IN DUE COURSE — One who has taken a note, check or bill of exchange in due course:

1. before it was overdue;
2. in good faith and for value; and
3. without knowledge that it has been previously dishonored and without notice of any defect at the time it was negotiated to him or her.

HOLDOVER TENANT — Tenant who remains in possession of leased property after the expiration of the lease term.

HOMESTEAD — **(exemption)** — A statutory protection of real property used as a home from the claims of certain creditors and judgments up to a specified amount.

HOUSING FINANCIAL DISCRIMINATION ACT OF 1977 (Holden Act) — California Health and Safety Code Section 35800, et seq., designed primarily to eliminate discrimination in lending practices based upon the character of the neighborhood in which real property is located. (See Redlining.)

HUD — The Department of Housing and Urban Development which is responsible for the implementation and administration of U.S. government housing and urban development programs.

HUNDRED PERCENT LOCATION — A city retail business location which is considered the best available for attracting business.

HYPOTHECATE — To pledge a thing as security without the necessity of giving up possession of it.

IMPERATIVE NECESSITY — Circumstances under which an agent has expanded authority in an emergency, including the power to disobey instructions where it is clearly in the interests of the principal and where there is no time to obtain instructions from the principal.

IMPOUNDS — A trust type account established by lenders for the accumulation of borrowers funds to meet periodic payment of taxes, FHA mortgage insurance premiums, and/or future insurance policy premiums, required to protect their security. Impounds are usually collected with the note payment. The combined principal, interest, taxes and insurance payment is commonly termed a PITI payment.

INCOME (CAPITALIZATION) APPROACH — One of the three methods of the appraisal process generally applied to income producing property, and involves a three-step process— (1) find net annual income, (2) set an appropriate capitalization rate or "present worth" factor, and (3) capitalize the income dividing the net income by the capitalization rate.

INCOMPETENT — One who is mentally incompetent, incapable; any person who, though not insane, is, by reason of old age, disease, weakness of mind, or any other cause, unable, unassisted, to properly manage and take care of self or property and by reason thereof would be likely to be deceived or imposed upon by artful or designing persons.

INCORPOREAL RIGHTS — Nonpossessory rights in real estate, a rising out of ownership, such as rents.

INCREMENT — An increase. Most frequently used to refer to the increase of value of land that accompanies population growth and increasing wealth in the community. The term "unearned increment" is used in this connection since values are supposed to have increased without effort on the part of the owner.

INDEMNITY AGREEMENT — An agreement by the maker of the document to repay the addressee of the agreement up to the limit stated for any loss due to the contingency stated on the agreement.

INDENTURE — A formal written instrument made between two or more persons in different interests, such as a lease.

INDEPENDENT CONTRACTOR — A person who acts for another but who sells final results and whose methods of achieving those results are not subject to the control of another.

INDORSEMENT — The act of signing one's name on the back of a check or note, with or without further qualification.

INITIAL NOTE RATE — With regard to an adjustable rate mortgage, the note rate upon origination. This rate may differ from the fully indexed note rate.

INITIAL RATE DISCOUNT — As applies to an adjustable rate mortgage, the index value at the time of loan application plus the margin less the initial note rate.

INJUNCTION — A writ or order issued under the seal of a court to restrain one or more parties to a suit or proceeding from doing an act which is deemed to be inequitable or unjust in regard to the rights of some other party or parties in the suit or proceeding.

INSTALLMENT NOTE — A note which provides for a series of periodic payments of principal and interest, until amount borrowed is paid in full. This periodic reduction of principal amortizes the loan.

INSTALLMENT REPORTING — A method of reporting capital gains by installments for successive tax years to minimize the impact of the totality of the capital gains tax in the year of the sale.

INSTALLMENT SALES CONTRACT — Commonly called contract of sale or "land contract." Purchase of real estate wherein the purchase price is paid in installments over a long period of time, title is retained by seller, and upon default by buyer (vendee) the payments may be forfeited.

INSTITUTIONAL LENDERS — A financial intermediary or depository, such as a savings and loan association, commercial bank, or life insurance company, which pools money of its depositors and then invests funds in various ways, including trust deed and mortgage loans.

INSTRUMENT — A written legal document; created to effect the rights of the parties, giving formal expression to a legal act or agreement for the purpose of creating, modifying or terminating a right. Real estate lenders' basic instruments are — promissory notes, deeds of trust, mortgages, installment sales contracts, leases, assignments.

INTEREST — A portion, share or right in something. Partial, not complete ownership. The charge in dollars for the use of money for a period of time. In a sense, the "rent" paid for the use of money.

INTEREST EXTRA LOAN — A loan in which a fixed amount of principal is repaid in installments along with interest accrued each period on the amount of the then outstanding principal only.

INTEREST ONLY LOAN — A straight, non-amortizing loan in which the lender receives only interest during the term of the loan and principal is repaid in a lump sum at maturity.

INTEREST RATE — The percentage of a sum of money charged for its use. Rent or charge paid for use of money, expressed as a percentage per month or year of the sum borrowed.

INTERIM LOAN — A short-term, temporary loan used until permanent financing is available, e.g., a construction loan.

INTERMEDIATION — The process of pooling and supplying funds for investment by financial institutions called intermediaries. The process is dependent on individual savers placing their funds with these institutions and foregoing opportunities to directly invest in the investments selected.

INTERPLEADER — A court proceeding initiated by the stakeholder of property who claims no proprietary interest in it for the purpose of deciding who among claimants is legally entitled to the property.

INTERVAL OWNERSHIP — A form of timeshare ownership. (See Timeshare Ownership.)

INTESTATE — A person who dies having made no will, or one which is defective in form, is said to have died intestate, in which case the estate descends to the heirs at law or next of kin.

INVOLUNTARY LIEN — A lien imposed against property without consent of an owner; example — taxes, special assessments, federal income tax liens, etc.

IRREVOCABLE — Incapable of being recalled or revoked, unchangeable.

IRRIGATION DISTRICTS — Quasi-political districts created under special laws to provide for water services to property owners in the district; an operation governed to a great extent by law.

JOINT NOTE — A note signed by two or more persons who have equal liability for payment.

JOINT TENANCY — Undivided ownership of a property interest by two or more persons each of whom has a right to an equal share in the interest and a right of survivorship, i.e., the right to share equally with other surviving joint tenants in the interest of a deceased joint tenant.

JOINT VENTURE — Two or more individuals or firms joining together on a single project as partners.

JUDGMENT — The final determination of a court of competent jurisdiction of a matter presented to it; money judgments provide for the payment of claims presented to the court, or are awarded as damages, etc.

JUDGMENT LIEN — A legal claim on all of the property of a judgment debtor which enables the judgment creditor to have the property sold for payment of the amount of the judgment.

JUNIOR MORTGAGE — A mortgage recorded subsequently to another mortgage on the same property or made subordinate by agreement to a later-recorded mortgage.

JURISDICTION — The authority by which judicial officers take cognizance of and decide causes; the power to hear and determine a cause; the right and power which a judicial officer has to enter upon the inquiry.

LACHES — Delay or negligence in asserting one's legal rights.

LAND — The material of the earth, whatever may be the ingredients of which it is composed, whether soil, rock, or other substance, and includes free or unoccupied space for an indefinite distance upwards as well as downwards.

LAND CONTRACT — A contract used in a sale of real property whereby the seller retains title to the property until all or a prescribed part of the purchase price has been paid. Also commonly called a conditional sales contract, installment sales contract or real property sales contract. (See REAL PROPERTY SALES CONTRACT for statutory definition.)

LAND AND IMPROVEMENT LOAN — A loan obtained by the builder-developer for the purchase of land and to cover expenses for subdividing.

LANDLORD — One who rents his or her property to another. The lessor under a lease.

LATE CHARGE — A charge assessed by a lender against a borrower failing to make loan installment payments when due.

LATER DATE ORDER — The commitment for an owner's title insurance policy issued by a title insurance company which covers the seller's title as of the date of the contract. When the sale closes the purchaser orders the title company to record the deed to purchaser and bring down their examination to cover this later date so as to show purchaser as owner of the property.

LATERAL SUPPORT — The support which the soil of an adjoining owner gives to a neighbor's land.

LEASE — A contract between owner and tenant, setting forth conditions upon which tenant may occupy and use the property and the term of the occupancy. Sometimes used as an alternative to purchasing property outright, as a method of financing right to occupy and use real property.

LEASEHOLD ESTATE — A tenant's right to occupy real estate during the term of the lease. This is a personal property interest.

LEGAL DESCRIPTION — A land description recognized by law; a description by which property can be definitely located by reference to government surveys or approved recorded maps.

LESSEE — One who contracts to rent, occupy, and use property under a lease agreement; a tenant.

LESSOR — An owner who enters into a lease agreement with a tenant; a landlord.

LEVEL-PAYMENT MORTGAGE — A loan on real estate that is paid off by making a series of equal (or nearly equal) regular payments. Part of the payment is usually interest on the loan and part of it reduces the amount of the unpaid principal balance of the loan. Also sometimes called an "amortized mortgage" or "installment mortgage."

LEVERAGE — The use of debt financing of an investment to maximize the return per dollar of equity invested.

LIEN — A form of encumbrance which usually makes specific property security for the payment of a debt or discharge of an obligation. Example — judgments, taxes, mortgages, deeds of trust, etc.

LIFE ESTATE — An estate or interest in real property, which is held for the duration of the life of some certain person. It may be limited by the life of the person holding it or by the life of some other person.

LIFE OF LOAN CAP (CAP RATE) — With regard to an adjustable rate mortgage, a ceiling the note rate cannot exceed over the life of the loan.

LIMITATIONS, STATUTE OF — The commonly used identifying term for various statutes which require that a legal action be commenced within a prescribed time after the accrual of the right to seek legal relief.

LIMITED PARTNERSHIP — A partnership consisting of a general partner or partners and limited partners in which the general partners manage and control the business affairs of the partnership while limited partners are essentially investors taking no part in the management of the partnership and having no liability for the debts of the partnership in excess of their invested capital.

LINTEL — A horizontal board that supports the load over an opening such as a door or window.

LIQUIDATED DAMAGES — A sum agreed upon by the parties to be full damages if a certain event occurs.

LIQUIDATED DAMAGES CLAUSE — A clause in a contract by which the parties by agreement fix the damages in advance for a breach of the contract.

LIQUIDITY — Holdings in or the ability to convert assets to cash or its equivalent. The ease with which a person is able to pay maturing obligations.

LIS PENDENS — A notice filed or recorded for the purpose of warning all persons that the title or right to the possession of certain real property is in litigation; literally "suit pending;" usually recorded so as to give constructive notice of pending litigation.

LISTING — An employment contract between principal and agent authorizing the agent to perform services for the principal involving the latter's property; listing contracts are entered into for the purpose of securing persons to buy, lease, or rent property. Employment of an agent by a prospective purchaser or lessee to locate property for purchase or lease may be considered a listing.

LIVERY OF SEISIN (SEIZIN) — The appropriate ceremony at common law for transferring the possession of lands by a grantor to a grantee.

LOAN ADMINISTRATION — Also called loan servicing Mortgage bankers not only originate loans, but also "service" them from origination to maturity of the loan through handling of loan payments, delinquencies, impounds, payoffs and releases.

LOAN APPLICATION — The loan application is a source of information on which the lender bases a decision to make the loan; defines the terms of the loan contract, gives the name of the borrower, place of employment, salary, bank accounts, and credit references, and describes the real estate that is to be mortgaged. It also stipulates the amount of loan being applied for and repayment terms.

LOAN CLOSING — When all conditions have been met, the loan officer authorizes the recording of the trust deed or mortgage. The disbursal procedure of funds is similar to the closing of a real estate sales escrow. The borrower can expect to receive less than the amount of the loan, as title, recording, service, and other fees may be withheld, or can expect to deposit the cost of these items into the loan escrow. This process is sometimes called "funding" the loan.

LOAN COMMITMENT — Lender's contractual commitment to make a loan based on the appraisal and underwriting.

LOAN-TO-VALUE RATIO — The percentage of a property's value that a lender can or may loan to a borrower. For example, if the ratio is 80% this means that a lender may loan 80% of the property's appraised value to a borrower.

MAI — Member of the Appraisal Institute. Designates a person who is a member of the American Institute of Real Estate Appraisers.

MARGIN OF SECURITY — The difference between the amount of the mortgage loan (s) and the appraised value of the property.

MARGINAL LAND — Land which barely pays the cost of working or using.

MARKET DATA APPROACH — One of the three methods in the appraisal process. A means of comparing similar type properties, which have recently sold, to the subject property. Commonly used in comparing residential properties.

MARKET PRICE — The price paid regardless of pressures, motives or intelligence.

MARKET VALUE — The highest price in terms of money which a property will bring in a competitive and open market and under all conditions required for a fair sale, i.e., the buyer and seller acting prudently, knowledgeably and neither affected by undue pressures.

MARKETABLE TITLE — Title which a reasonable purchaser, informed as to the facts and their legal importance and acting with reasonable care, would be willing and ought to accept.

MATERIAL FACT — A fact is material if it is one which the agent should realize would be likely to affect the judgment of the principal in giving his or her consent to the agent to enter into the particular transaction on the specified terms.

MECHANIC'S LIEN — A lien created by statute which exists against real property in favor of persons who have performed work or furnished materials for the improvement of the real property.

MERIDIANS — Imaginary north-south lines which intersect base lines to form a starting point for the measurement of land.

MESNE PROFITS — Profit from land use accruing between two periods as for example moneys owed to the owner of land by a person who has illegally occupied the land after the owner takes title, but before taking possession.

METES AND BOUNDS — A term used in describing the boundary lines of land, setting forth all the boundary lines together with their terminal points and angles. Metes (length or measurements) and Bounds (boundaries) description is often used when a great deal of accuracy is required.

MILE — 5,280 feet.

MINOR — A person under 18 years of age.

MISPLACED IMPROVEMENTS — Improvements on land which do not conform to the most profitable use of the site.

MISREPRESENTATION — A false or misleading statement or assertion.

MOBILEHOME — As defined in Business and Professions Code Section 10131.6(c), "mobilehome" means a structure transportable in one or more sections, designed and equipped to contain not more than two dwelling units to be used with or without a foundation system. "Mobilehome" does not include a recreational vehicle, as defined in Section 18010.5 of the Health and Safety Code, a commercial coach, as defined in Section 18012 of the Health and Safety Code, or factory-built housing, as defined in Section 19971 of the Health and Safety Code.

MODULAR — A system for the construction of dwellings and other improvements to real property through the on-site assembly of component parts (modules) that have been mass produced away from the building site.

MOLDINGS — Usually patterned strips used to provide ornamental variation of outline or contour, such as cornices, bases, window and door jambs.

MONETARY CONTROLS — Federal Reserve tools for regulating the availability of money and credit to influence the level of economic activity, such as adjusting discount rates, reserve requirements, etc.

MONUMENT — A fixed object and point established by surveyors to establish land locations.

MORATORIUM — The temporary suspension, usually by statute, of the enforcement of liability of debt. Temporary suspension of development or utilities connections imposed by local government.

MORTGAGE — An instrument recognized by law by which property is hypothecated to secure the payment of a debt or obligation; a procedure for foreclosure in event of default is established by statute.

MORTGAGE BANKER — A person whose principal business is the originating, financing, closing, selling and servicing of loans secured by real property for institutional lenders on a contractual basis.

MORTGAGE CONTRACTS WITH WARRANTS — Warrants make the mortgage more attractive to the lender by providing both the greater security that goes with a mortgage, and the opportunity of a greater return through the right to buy either stock in the borrower's company or a portion of the income property itself.

MORTGAGE GUARANTY INSURANCE — Insurance against financial loss available to mortgage lenders from private mortgage insurance companies (PMICs).

MORTGAGE INVESTMENT COMPANY — A company or group of private investors that buys mortgages for investment purposes.

MORTGAGE LOAN DISCLOSURE STATEMENT — The statement on a form approved by the Real Estate Commissioner which is required by law to be furnished by a mortgage loan broker to the prospective borrower of loans of a statutorily-prescribed amount before the borrower becomes obligated to complete the loan.

MORTGAGEE — One to whom a mortgagor gives a mortgage to secure a loan or performance of an obligation; a lender or creditor. (See definition of secured party.)

MORTGAGOR — One who gives a mortgage on his or her property to secure a loan or assure performance of an obligation; a borrower.

MULTIPLE LISTING — A listing, usually an exclusive right to sell, taken by a member of an organization composed of real estate brokers, with the provisions that all members will have the opportunity to find an interested buyer; a cooperative listing insuring owner property will receive a wider market exposure.

MULTIPLE LISTING SERVICE — An association of real estate agents providing for a pooling of listings and the sharing of commissions on a specified basis.

MUTUAL SAVINGS BANKS — Financial institutions owned by depositors each of whom has rights to net earnings of the bank in proportion to his or her deposits.

MUTUAL WATER COMPANY — A water company organized by or for water users in a given district with the object of securing an ample water supply at a reasonable rate; stock is issued to users.

NARRATIVE APPRAISAL — A summary of all factual materials, techniques and appraisal methods used by the appraiser in setting forth his or her value conclusion.

NEGATIVE AMORTIZATION — Occurs when monthly installment payments are insufficient to pay the interest accruing on the principal balance, so that the unpaid interest must be added to the principal due.

NEGOTIABLE — Capable of being negotiated, assignable or transferable in the ordinary course of business.

NET INCOME — The money remaining after expenses are deducted from income; the profit.

NET LEASE — A lease requiring a lessee to pay charges against the property such as taxes, insurance and maintenance costs in addition to rental payments.

NET LISTING — A listing which provides that the agent may retain as compensation for agent's services all sums received over and above a net price to the owner.

NOMINAL INTEREST RATES — The percentage of interest that is stated in loan documents.

NOTARY PUBLIC — An appointed officer with authority to take the acknowledgment of persons executing documents, sign the certificate, and affix official seal.

NOTE — A signed written instrument acknowledging a debt and promising payment, according to the specified terms and conditions. A promissory note.

NOTE RATE — This rate determines the amount of interest charged on an annual basis to the borrower. Also called the "accrual rate", "contract rate" or "coupon rate."

NOTICE — (l) *Actual Notice* - Express or implied knowledge of a fact. (2) *Constructive notice* - A fact, imputed to a person by law, which should have been discovered because of the person's actual notice of circumstances and the inquiry that a prudent person would have been expected to make. (3) *Legal Notice*—Information required to be given by law.

NOTICE OF NONRESPONSIBILITY — A notice provided by law designed to relieve property owner from responsibility for the cost of unauthorized work done on the property or materials furnished therefor; notice must be verified, recorded and posted.

NOTICE TO QUIT — A notice to a tenant to vacate rented property.

NOVATION — The substitution or exchange of a new obligation or contract for an old one by the mutual agreement of the parties.

NULL AND VOID — Of no legal validity or effect.

OBSOLESCENCE — Loss in value due to reduced desirability and usefulness of a structure because its design and construction become obsolete; loss because of becoming old-fashioned and not in keeping with modern needs, with consequent loss of income. May be functional or economic.

OFFER TO PURCHASE — The proposal made to an owner of property by a potential buyer to purchase the property under stated terms.

OFFSET STATEMENT — Statement by owner of property or owner of lien against property setting forth the present status of liens against said property.

OPEN-END MORTGAGE — A mortgage containing a clause which permits the mortgagor to borrow additional money after the loan has been reduced without rewriting the mortgage.

OPEN HOUSING LAW — Congress passed a law in April 1968 which prohibits discrimination in the sale of real estate because of race, color, or religion of buyers.

OPEN LISTING — An authorization given by a property owner to a real estate agent wherein said agent is given the nonexclusive right to secure a purchaser; open listings may be given to any number of agents without liability to compensate any except the one who first secures a buyer ready, willing and able to meet the terms of the listing, or secures the acceptance by the seller of a satisfactory offer.

OPINION OF TITLE — An attorney's written evaluation of the condition of the title to a parcel of land after examination of the abstract of title.

OPTION — A right given for a consideration to purchase or lease a property upon specified terms within a specified time, without obligating the party who receives the right to exercise the right.

ORAL CONTRACT — A verbal agreement; one which is not reduced to writing.

ORIENTATION — Placing a structure on its lot with regard to its exposure to the rays of the sun, prevailing winds, privacy from the street and protection from outside noises.

OSTENSIBLE AUTHORITY — That authority which a third person reasonably believes an agent possesses because of the acts or omissions of the principal.

OVERIMPROVEMENT — An improvement which is not the highest and best use for the site on which it is placed by reason of excess size or cost.

OWNERSHIP — The right of one or more persons to possess and use property to the exclusion of all others. A collection of rights to the use and enjoyment of property.

PACKAGE MORTGAGE — A type of mortgage used in home financing covering real property, improvements, and movable equipment/appliances.

PARAMOUNT TITLE — Title which is superior or foremost to all others.

PARTICIPATION — Sharing of an interest in a property by a lender. In addition to base interest on mortgage loans on income properties, a percentage of gross income is required, sometimes predicated on certain conditions being fulfilled, such as a minimum occupancy or percentage of net income after expenses, debt service and taxes. Also called equity participation or revenue sharing.

PARTIES (PARTY) — Those entities taking part in a transaction as a principal, e.g., seller, buyer, or lender in a real estate transaction.

PARTITION — A division of real or personal property or the proceeds therefrom among co-owners.

PARTITION ACTION — Court proceedings by which co-owners seek to sever their joint ownership.

PARTNERSHIP — A decision of the California Supreme Court has defined a partnership in the following terms — "A partnership as between partners themselves may be defined to be a contract of two or more persons to unite their property, labor or skill, or some of them, in prosecution of some joint or lawful business, and to share the profits in certain proportions." A voluntary association of two or more persons to carry on a business or venture on terms of mutual participation in profits and losses.

PARTY WALL — A wall erected on the line between two adjoining properties, which are under different ownership, for the use of both properties.

PAR VALUE — Market value, nominal value.

PATENT — Conveyance of title to government land.

PAYMENT ADJUSTMENT DATE — With regard to an adjustable rate mortgage, the date the borrower's monthly principal and interest payment may change.

PAYMENT CAP — With regard to an adjustable rate mortgage, this limits the amount of increase in the borrower's monthly principal and interest at the payment adjustment date, if the principal and interest increase called for by the interest rate increase exceeds the payment cap percentage. This limitation is often at the borrower's option and may result in negative amortization.

PAYMENT RATE — With respect to an adjustable rate mortgage, the rate at which the borrower repays the loan—reflects buydowns or payment caps.

PENALTY — An extra payment or charge required of the borrower for deviating from the terms of the original loan agreement. Usually levied for being late in making regular payment or for paying off the loan before it is due, known as "late charges" and "prepayment penalties."

PERCENTAGE LEASE — Lease on the property, the rental for which is determined by amount of business done by the lessee; usually a percentage of gross receipts from the business with provision for a minimum rental.

PERIMETER HEATING — Baseboard heating, or any system in which the heat registers are located along the outside walls of a room, especially under the windows.

PERIODIC INTEREST RATE CAP — With respect to an adjustable rate mortgage, limits the increase or decrease in the note rate at each rate adjustment, thereby limiting the borrower's payment increase or decrease at the time of adjustment.

PERSONAL PROPERTY — Any property which is not real property.

PHYSICAL DETERIORATION — Impairment of condition. Loss in value brought about by wear and tear, disintegration, use and actions of the elements; termed curable and incurable.

PLAINTIFF — In a court action, the one who sues; the complainant.

PLANNED DEVELOPMENT — A subdivision consisting of separately owned parcels of land together with membership in an association which owns common area. Sometimes the owners of separate interests also have an undivided interest in the common area.

PLANNED UNIT DEVELOPMENT — (PUD) A term sometimes used to describe a planned development. A planning and zoning term describing land not subject to conventional zoning to permit clustering of residences or other characteristics of the project which differ from normal zoning.

PLANNING COMMISSION — An agency of local government charged with planning the development, redevelopment or preservation of an area.

PLAT (of survey) — A map of land made by a surveyor showing the boundaries, buildings, and other improvements.

PLEDGE — The depositing of personal property by a debtor with a creditor as security for a debt or engagement.

PLEDGEE — One who is given a pledge or a security. (See definition of Secured Party.)

PLEDGOR — One who offers a pledge or gives security. (See definition of debtor.)

PLOTTAGE — A term used in appraising to designate the increased value of two or more contiguous lots when they are joined under single ownership and available for use as a larger single lot. Also called assemblage.

PLOTTAGE INCREMENT — The appreciation in unit value created by joining smaller ownerships into one large single ownership.

POINTS — See Discount Points.

POLICE POWER — The right of the State to enact laws and enforce them for the order, safety, health, morals and general welfare of the public.

POWER OF ATTORNEY — A written instrument whereby a principal gives authority to an agent. The agent acting under such a grant is sometimes called an attorney in fact.

POWER OF SALE — The power of a mortgagee or trustee when the instrument so provides to sell the secured property without judicial proceedings if a borrower defaults in payment of the promissory note or otherwise breaches the terms of the mortgage or deed of trust.

PREFABRICATED HOUSE — A house manufactured and sometimes partly assembled before delivery to building site.

PREFERRED STOCK — A class of corporate stock entitled to preferential treatment such as priority in distribution of dividends.

PREPAID ITEMS OF EXPENSE — Prorations of prepaid items of expense which are credited to the seller in the closing escrow statement.

PREPAYMENT — Provision made for loan payments to be larger than those specified in the note.

PREPAYMENT PENALTY — The charge payable to a lender by a borrower under the terms of the loan agreement if the borrower pays off the outstanding principal balance of the loan prior to its maturity.

PRESCRIPTION — The means of acquiring incorporeal interests in land, usually an easement, by immemorial or long continued use. The time is ordinarily the term of the statute of limitations.

PRESUMPTION — An assumption of fact that the law requires to be made from another fact or group of facts found or otherwise established in the section.

PRIMA FACIE — Latin meaning first sight, a fact presumed to be true until disproved.

PRINCIPAL — This term is used to mean the employer of an agent; or the amount of money borrowed, or the amount of the loan. Also, one of the main parties in a real estate transaction, such as a buyer, borrower, seller, lessor.

PRINCIPAL NOTE — The promissory note which is secured by the mortgage or trust deed.

PRIOR LIEN — A lien which is senior or superior to others.

PRIORITY OF LIEN — The order in which liens are given legal precedence or preference.

PRIVATE MORTGAGE INSURANCE — Mortgage guaranty insurance available to conventional lenders on the first, high risk portion of a loan (PMI).

PRIVITY — Mutual relationship to the same rights of property, contractual relationship.

PRIVITY OF CONTRACT — The relationship which exists between the persons who are parties to a contract.

PROCURING CAUSE — That cause originating from a series of events that, without break in continuity, results in the prime object of an agent's employment producing a final buyer; the real estate agent who first procures a ready, willing, and able buyer for the agreed upon price and terms and is entitled to the commission.

PROGRESS PAYMENTS — Scheduled, periodic, and partial payment of construction loan funds to a builder as each construction stage is completed.

PROGRESSION, PRINCIPLE OF — The worth of a lesser valued residence tends to be enhanced by association with higher valued residences in the same area.

PROMISSORY NOTE — Following a loan commitment from the lender, the borrower signs a note, promising to repay the loan under stipulated terms. The promissory note establishes personal liability for its payment. The evidence of the debt.

PROPERTY — Everything capable of being owned and acquired lawfully. The rights of ownership. The right to use, possess, enjoy, and dispose of a thing in every legal way and to exclude everyone else from interfering with these rights. Property is classified into two groups, personal property and real property.

PROPERTY MANAGEMENT — A branch of the real estate business involving the marketing, operation, maintenance and day-to-day financing of rental properties.

PRO RATA — In proportion; according to a certain percentage or proportion of a whole.

PRORATION — Adjustments of interest, taxes, and insurance, etc., on a pro rata basis as of the closing or agreed upon date. Fire insurance is normally paid for three years in advance. If a property is sold during this time, the seller wants a refund on that portion of the advance payment that has not been used at the time the title to the property is transferred. For example, if the property is sold two years later, seller will want to receive 1/3 of the advance premium that was paid. Usually done in escrow by escrow holder at time of closing the transaction.

PRORATION OF TAXES — To divide or prorate the taxes equally or proportionately to time of use, usually between seller and buyer.

PROXIMATE CAUSE — That cause of an event which, in a natural and continuous sequence unbroken by any new cause, produced that event, and without which the event would not have happened. Also, the procuring cause.

PUBLIC RECORDS — Records which by law impart constructive notice of matters relating to land.

PUBLIC TRUSTEE — The county public official whose office has been created by statute to whom title to real property in certain states, e.g., Colorado, is conveyed by Trust Deed for the use and benefit of the beneficiary, who usually is the lender.

PURCHASE AND INSTALLMENT SALEBACK — Involves purchase of the property upon completion of construction and immediate saleback on a long-term installment contract.

PURCHASE OF LAND, LEASEBACK AND LEASEHOLD MORTGAGES — An arrangement whereby land is purchased by the lender and leased back to the developer with a mortgage negotiated on the resulting leasehold of the income property constructed. The lender receives an annual ground rent, plus a percentage of income from the property.

PURCHASE AND LEASEBACK — Involves the purchase of property by buyer and immediate leaseback to seller.

PURCHASE MONEY MORTGAGE OR TRUST DEED — A trust deed or mortgage given as part or all of the purchase consideration for real property. In some states the purchase money mortgage or trust deed loan can be made by a seller who extends credit to the buyer of property or by a third party lender (typically a financial institution) that makes a loan to the buyer of real property for a portion of the purchase price to be paid for the property. In many states there are legal limitations upon mortgagees and trust deed beneficiaries collecting deficiency judgments against the purchase money borrower after the collateral hypothecated under such security instruments has been sold through the foreclosure process. Generally no deficiency judgment is allowed if the collateral property under the mortgage or trust deed is residential property of four units or less with the debtor occupying the property as a place of residence.

QUANTITY SURVEY — A highly technical process in arriving at cost estimate of new construction and sometimes referred to in the building trade as the "price take-off" method. It involves a detailed estimate of the quantities of raw material (lumber, plaster, brick, cement, etc.,) used as well as the current price of the material and installation costs. These factors are all added together to arrive at the cost of a structure. It is usually used by contractors and experienced estimators.

QUARTER ROUND — A molding that presents a profile of a quarter circle.

QUIET ENJOYMENT — Right of an owner or tenant to the use of the property without interference of possession.

QUIET TITLE — A court action brought to establish title; to remove a cloud on the title.

QUITCLAIM DEED — A deed to relinquish any interest in property which the grantor may have, without any warranty of title or interest.

RADIANT HEATING — A method of heating, usually consisting of coils, or pipes placed in the floor, wall, or ceiling.

RANGE — A strip or column of land six miles wide, determined by a government survey, running in a north-south direction, lying east or west of a principal meridian.

RANGE LINES — A series of government survey lines running north and south at six-mile intervals starting with the principal meridian and forming the east and west boundaries of townships.

RATE ADJUSTMENT DATE — With respect to an adjustable rate mortgage, the date the borrower's note rate may change.

RATIFICATION — The adoption or approval of an act performed on behalf of a person without previous authorization, such as the approval by a principal of previously unauthorized acts of an agent, after the acts have been performed.

READY, WILLING AND ABLE BUYER — One who is fully prepared to enter into the contract, really wants to buy, and unquestionably meets the financing requirements of purchase.

REAL ESTATE — (See Real Property.)

REAL ESTATE BOARD — An organization whose members consist primarily of real estate brokers and salespersons.

REAL ESTATE INVESTMENT TRUST — (See REIT).

REAL ESTATE SETTLEMENT PROCEDURES ACT (RESPA) — A federal law requiring the disclosure to borrowers of settlement (closing) procedures and costs by means of a pamphlet and forms prescribed by the United States Department of Housing and Urban Development.

REAL ESTATE SYNDICATE — An organization of investors usually in the form of a limited partnership who have joined together for the purpose of pooling capital for the acquisition of real property interests.

REAL ESTATE TRUST — A special arrangement under Federal and State law whereby investors may pool funds for investments in real estate and mortgages and yet escape corporation taxes, profits being passed to individual investors who are taxed.

REAL PROPERTY — In the strict legal sense, land appurtenances, that which is affixed to the land, and that which by law is immovable. It usually refers to the "bundle of rights" inherent in ownership.

REAL PROPERTY LOAN LAW — Article 7 of Chapter 3 of the Real Estate Law under which a real estate licensee negotiating loans secured by real property within a specified range is required to give the borrower a statement disclosing the costs and terms of the loan and which also limits the amount of expenses and charges that a borrower may pay with respect to the loan.

REAL PROPERTY SALES CONTRACT — An agreement to convey title to real property upon satisfaction of specified conditions which does not require conveyance within one year of formation of the contract.

RECAPTURE — The process of recovery by an owner of money invested by employing the use of a rate of interest necessary to provide for the return of an investment; not to be confused with interest rate, which is a rate of return on an investment.

RECONVEYANCE — The transfer of the title of land from one person to the immediate preceding owner. This instrument of transfer is commonly used to transfer the legal title from the trustee to the trustor (borrower) after a trust deed debt has been paid in full.

RECORDING — The process of placing a document on file with a designated public official for public notice. This public official is usually a county officer known as the County Recorder who designates the fact that a document has been presented for recording by placing a recording stamp upon it indicating the time of day and the date when it was officially placed on file. Documents filed with the Recorder are considered to be placed on open notice to the general public of that county. Claims against property usually are given a priority on the basis of the time and the date they are recorded with the most preferred claim going to the earliest one recorded and the next claim going to the next earliest one recorded, and so on. This type of notice is called "constructive notice" or "legal notice".

REDEEM — To buy back; repurchase; recover.

REDEMPTION — Buying back one's property after a judicial sale.

REDLINING — A lending policy, illegal in California, of denying real estate loans on properties in older, changing urban areas, usually with large minority populations, because of alleged higher lending risks without due consideration being given by the lending institution to the credit worthiness of the individual loan applicant.

REFINANCING — The paying-off of an existing obligation and assuming a new obligation in its place. To finance anew, or extend or renew existing financing.

REFORMATION — An action to correct a mistake in a deed or other document.

REHABILITATION — The restoration of a property to satisfactory condition without drastically changing the plan, form or style of architecture.

REIT — A Real Estate Investment Trust is a business trust which deals principally with interest in land—generally organized to conform to the Internal Revenue Code.

RELEASE CLAUSE — A stipulation that upon the payment of a specific sum of money to the holder of a trust deed or mortgage, the lien of the instrument as to a specifically described lot or area shall be removed from the blanket lien on the whole area involved.

RELEASE DEED — An instrument executed by the mortgagee or the trustee reconveying to the mortgagor or trustor the real estate which secured the loan after the debt has been paid in full.

REMAINDER — An estate which takes effect after the termination of the prior estate, such as a life estate. A future possessory interest in real estate.

REMAINDER DEPRECIATION — The possible future loss in value of an improvement to real property.

RENEGOTIABLE RATE MORTGAGE — A loan secured by a long term mortgage which provides for renegotiation, at pre-determined intervals, of the interest rate (for a maximum variation of five percent over the life of the mortgage.)

REPLACEMENT COST — The cost to replace a structure with one having utility equivalent to that being appraised, but constructed with modern materials and according to current standards, design and layout.

REPRODUCTION COST — The cost of replacing the subject improvement with one that is the exact replica, having the same quality of workmanship, design and layout, or cost to duplicate an asset.

RESCISSION — The cancellation of a contract and restoration of the parties to the same position they held before the contract was entered into.

RESCISSION OF CONTRACT — The abrogation or annulling of contract; the revocation or repealing of contract by mutual consent by parties to the contract, or for cause by either party to the contract.

RESERVATION — A right retained by a grantor in conveying property.

RESERVES — 1) In a common interest subdivisions, an accumulation of funds collected from owners for future replacement and major maintenance of the common area and facilities. 2) With regard to mortgage loans, an accumulation of funds, collected by the lender from the borrower as part of each monthly mortgage payment, an amount allocated to pay property taxes and insurance when they are due.

RESPA — (See Real Estate Settlement Procedures Act.)

RESTRICTION — A limitation on the use of real property. Property restrictions fall into two general classifications—public and private. Zoning ordinances are examples of the former type. Restrictions may be created by private owners, typically by appropriate clauses in deeds, or in agreements, or in general plans of entire subdivisions. Usually they assume the form of a covenant, or promise to do or not to do a certain thing.

RETROSPECTIVE VALUE — The value of the property as of a previous date.

RETURN — Profit from an investment; the yield.

REVERSION — The right to future possession or enjoyment by a person, or the person's heirs, creating the preceding estate. (For example, at the end of a lease.)

REVERSIONARY INTEREST — The interest which a person has in lands or other property, upon the termination of the preceding estate. A future interest.

RIGHT OF SURVIVORSHIP — The right of a surviving tenant or tenants to succeed to the entire interest of the deceased tenant; the distinguishing feature of a joint tenancy.

RIGHT OF WAY — A privilege operating as an easement upon land, whereby the owner does by grant, or by agreement, give to another the right to pass over owner's land, to construct a roadway, or use as a roadway, a specific part of the land; or the right to construct through and over the land, telephone, telegraph, or electric power lines; or the right to place underground water mains, gas mains, or sewer mains.

RIGHT, TITLE AND INTEREST — A term used in deeds to denote that the grantor is conveying all of that to which grantor held claim.

RIPARIAN RIGHTS — The right of a landowner whose land borders on a stream or watercourse to use and enjoy the water which is adjacent to or flows over the owners land provided such use does not injure other riparian owners.

RISK ANALYSIS — A study made, usually by a lender, of the various factors that might affect the repayment of a loan.

RISK RATING — A process used by the lender to decide on the soundness of making a loan and to reduce all the various factors affecting the repayment of the loan to a qualified rating of some kind.

SALE AND LEASEBACK — A financial arrangement where at the time of sale the seller retains occupancy by concurrently agreeing to lease the property from the purchaser. The seller receives cash while the buyer is assured a tenant and a fixed return on buyer's investment.

SALE-LEASEBACK-BUY-BACK — A sale and leaseback transaction in which the leaseholder has the option to buy back the original property after a specified period of time.

SALES CONTRACT — A contract by which buyer and seller agree to terms of a sale.

SALVAGE VALUE — In computing depreciation for tax purposes, the reasonably anticipated fair market value of the property at the end of its useful life and must be considered with all but the declining balance methods of depreciation.

SANDWICH LEASE — A leasehold interest which lies between the primary lease and the operating lease.

SASH — Wood or metal frames containing one or more window panes.

SATISFACTION — Discharge of a mortgage or trust deed from the records upon payment of the debt.

SATISFACTION PIECE — An instrument for recording and acknowledging payment of an indebtedness secured by a mortgage.

SCRIBING — Fitting woodwork to an irregular surface.

SEAL — An impression made to attest the execution of an instrument.

SECONDARY FINANCING — A loan secured by a second mortgage or trust deed on real property. These can be third, fourth, fifth, sixth mortgages or trust deeds, on and on ad infinitum.

SECTION — Section of land is established by government survey, contains 640 acres and is one mile square.

SECURED PARTY — This is the party having the security interest. Thus the mortgagee, the conditional seller, the pledgee, etc., are all now referred to as the secured party. (Uniform Commercial Code.)

SECURITY AGREEMENT — An agreement between the secured party and the debtor which creates the security interest. (Uniform Commercial Code.)

SECURITY INTEREST — A term designating the interest of the creditor in the property of the debtor in all types of credit transactions. It thus replaces such terms as the following — chattel mortgage; pledge; trust receipt; chattel trust; equipment trust; conditional sale; inventory lien; etc., according to Uniform Commercial Code usage.

SEISIN (SEIZIN) — Possession of real estate by one entitled thereto.

SELLER'S MARKET — The market condition which exists when a seller is in a more commanding position as to price and terms because demand exceeds supply.

SEPARATE PROPERTY — Property owned by a married person in his or her own right outside of the community interest including property acquired by the spouse (1) before marriage, (2) by gift or inheritance, (3) from rents and profits on separate property, and (4) with the proceeds from other separate property.

SEPTIC TANK — An underground tank in which sewage from the house is reduced to liquid by bacterial action and drained off.

SERVICING LOANS — Supervising and administering a loan after it has been made. This involves such things as — collecting the payments, keeping accounting records, computing the interest and principal, foreclosure of defaulted loans, and so on.

SET BACK ORDINANCE — An ordinance requiring improvements built on property to be a specified distance from the property line, street or curb.

SEVERALTY OWNERSHIP — Owned by one person only. Sole ownership.

SHARED APPRECIATION MORTGAGE — A loan having a fixed rate of interest set below the market rate for the term of the loan which also provides for contingent interest to be paid to the lender on a certain percentage of appreciation in the value of the property against which the loan is secured upon transfer or sale of the property or the repayment of the loan.

SHERIFF'S DEED — Deed given by court order in connection with sale of property to satisfy a judgment.

SIMPLE INTEREST — Interest computed on the principal amount of a loan only as distinguished from compound interest.

SINKING FUND — Fund set aside from the income from property which, with accrued interest, will eventually pay for replacement of the improvements.

SLANDER OF TITLE — False and malicious statements disparaging an owner's title to property and resulting in actual pecuniary damage to the owner.

SPECIAL ASSESSMENT — 1) Legal charge against real estate by a public authority to pay cost of public improvements such as street lights, sidewalks, street improvements. 2) In a common interest subdivision, a charge, in addition to the regular assessment, levied by the association against owners in the development, for unanticipated repairs or maintenance on the common area or capital improvement of the common area.

SPECIAL POWER OF ATTORNEY — A written instrument whereby a principal confers limited authority upon an agent to perform certain prescribed acts on behalf of the principal.

SPECIAL WARRANTY DEED — A deed in which the grantor warrants or guarantees the title only against defects arising during grantor's ownership of the property and not against defects existing before the time of grantor's ownership.

SPECIFIC PERFORMANCE — An action to compel performance of an agreement, e.g., sale of land as an alternative to damages or rescission.

SREA — Society of Real Estate Appraisers.

STANDARD DEPTH — Generally the most typical lot depth in the neighborhood.

STANDBY COMMITMENT — The mortgage banker frequently protects a builder by a "standby" agreement, under which banker agrees to make mortgage loans at an agreed price for many months into the future. The builder deposits a "standby fee" with the mortgage banker for this service. Frequently, the mortgage broker protects self by securing a "standby" from a long-term investor for the same period of time, paying a fee for this privilege.

STATUTE OF FRAUDS — A state law, based on an old English statute, requiring certain contracts to be in writing and signed before they will be enforceable at law, e.g.. contracts for the sale of real property, contracts not be performed within one year.

STATUTORY WARRANTY DEED — A short term warranty deed which warrants by inference that the seller is the undisputed owner, has the right to convey the property, and will defend the title if necessary. This type of deed protects the purchaser in that the conveyor covenants to defend all claims against the property. If conveyor fails to do so, the new owner can defend said claims and sue the former owner.

STRAIGHT LINE DEPRECIATION — A method of depreciation under which improvements are depreciated at a constant rate throughout the estimated useful life of the improvement.

STRAIGHT NOTE — A note in which a borrower repays the principal in a lump sum at maturity while interest is paid in installments or at maturity. (See Interest Only Note.)

SUBAGENT — A person upon whom the powers of an agent have been conferred, not by the principal, but by an agent as authorized by the agent's principal.

SUBDIVISION — A legal definition of those divisions of real property for the purpose of sale, lease or financing which are regulated by law. For examples see — California Business and Professions Code Sections 11000, 11000.1, 11004.5; California Government Code Section 66424; United States Code, Title 15, Section 1402(3).

"SUBJECT TO" A MORTGAGE — When a grantee takes title to real property subject to a mortgage, grantee is not responsible to the holder of the promissory note for the payment of any portion of the amount due. The most that grantee can lose in the event of a foreclosure is grantee's equity in the property. (See also "assumption of mortgage".) In neither case is the original maker of the note released from primary responsibility. If liability is to be assumed, the agreement must so state.

SUBLEASE — A lease given by a lessee.

SUBORDINATE — To make subject to, or junior or inferior to.

SUBORDINATION AGREEMENT — An agreement by the holder of an encumbrance against real property to permit that claim to take an inferior position to other encumbrances against the property.

SUBPOENA — A legal order to cause a witness to appear and give testimony.

SUBROGATION — Replacing one person with another in regard to a legal right or obligation. The substitution of another person in place of the creditor, to whose rights he or she succeeds in relation to the debt. The doctrine is used very often where one person agrees to stand surety for the performance of a contract by another person.

SUBSIDY BUYDOWN — Funds provided usually by the builder or seller to temporarily reduce the borrower's monthly principal and interest payment.

SUBSTITUTION, PRINCIPLE OF — Affirms that the maximum value of a property tends to be set by the cost of acquiring an equally desirable and valuable substitute property, assuming no costly delay is encountered in making the substitution.

SUM OF THE YEARS DIGITS — An accelerated depreciation method.

SUPPLY AND DEMAND, PRINCIPLE OF — In appraising, a valuation principle starting that market value is affected by intersection of supply and demand forces in the market as of the appraisal date.

SURETY — One who guarantees the performance of another — Guarantor.

SURPLUS PRODUCTIVITY, PRINCIPLE OF — The net income that remains after the proper costs of labor, organization and capital have been paid, which surplus is imputable to the land and tends to fix the value thereof.

SURVEY — The process by which a parcel of land is measured and its area is ascertained.

SYNDICATE — A partnership organized for participation in a real estate venture. Partners may be limited or unlimited in their liability. (See real estate syndicate.)

TAKE-OUT LOAN — The loan arranged by the owner or builder developer for a buyer. The construction loan made for construction of the improvements is usually paid in full from the proceeds of this more permanent mortgage loan.

TAX — Enforced charge exacted of persons, corporations and organizations by the government to be used to support government services and programs.

TAX DEED — The deed given to a purchaser at a public sale of land held for nonpayment of taxes. It conveys to the purchaser only such title as the defaulting taxpayer had.

TAX-FREE EXCHANGE — The trade or exchange of one real property for another without the need to pay income taxes on the gain at the time of trade.

TAX SALE — Sale of property after a period of nonpayment of taxes.

TENANCY IN COMMON — Co-ownership of property by two or more persons who hold undivided interest, without right of survivorship; interests need not be equal.

TENANT — The party who has legal possession and use of real property belonging to another.

TENANTS BY THE ENTIRETIES — Under certain state laws, ownership of property acquired by a husband and wife during marriage, which property is jointly and equally owned. Upon depth of one spouse it becomes the property of the survivor.

TENTATIVE MAP — The Subdivision Map Act requires subdividers to submit initially a tentative map of their tract to the local planning commission for study. The approval or disapproval of the planning commission is noted on the map. Thereafter, a final map of the tract embodying any changes requested by the planning commission is required to be filed with the planning commission.

TENURE IN LAND — The mode or manner by which an estate in lands is held. All rights and title rest with owner.

TERMITES — Ant-like insects which feed on wood and are highly destructive to wooden structures.

TERMITE SHIELD — A shield, usually of noncorrodible metal, placed on top of the foundation wall or around pipes to prevent passage of termites.

TESTATOR — One who makes a will.

THIRD PARTY — Persons who are not parties to a contract which affects an interest they have in the object of the contract.

THRESHOLD — A strip of wood or metal beveled on each edge and used above the finished floor under outside doors.

TIDELANDS — Lands that are covered and uncovered by the ebb and flow of the tide.

TIME IS OF THE ESSENCE — A condition of a contract expressing the essential nature of performance of the contract by a party in a specified period of time.

TIME-SHARE ESTATE — A right of occupancy in a time-share project (subdivision) which is coupled with an estate in the real property.

TIME-SHARE PROJECT — A form of subdivision of real property into rights to the recurrent, exclusive use or occupancy of a lot, parcel, unit, or segment of real property, on an annual or some other periodic basis, for a specified period of time.

TIME-SHARE USE — A license or contractual or membership right of occupancy in a timeshare project which is not coupled with an estate in the real property.

TITLE — Indicates "fee" position of lawful ownership and right to property. "Bundle of Rights" possessed by an owner. Combination of all elements constituting proof of ownership.

TITLE INSURANCE — Insurance to protect a real property owner or lender up to a specified amount against certain types of loss, e.g., defective or unmarketable title.

TITLE REPORT — A report which discloses condition of the title, made by a title company preliminary to issuance of title insurance policy.

TITLE THEORY — Mortgage arrangement whereby title to mortgaged real property vests in the lender. Some states give greater protection to mortgage lenders and assume lenders have title interest. Distinguished from Lien Theory States.

TOPOGRAPHY — Nature of the surface of land; topography may be level, rolling, mountainous. Variation in earth's surface.

TORRENS TITLE — System of title records provided by state law (no longer used in California)

TORT — Any wrongful act (not involving a breach of contract) for which a civil section will lie for the person wronged.

TOWNHOUSE — One of a row of houses usually of the same or similar design with common side walls or with a very narrow space between adjacent side walls.

TOWNSHIP — In the survey of public lands of the United States, a territorial subdivision six miles long, six miles wide and containing 36 sections, each one mile square, located between two range lines and two township lines.

TRADE FIXTURES — Articles of personal property annexed by a business tenant to real property which are necessary to the carrying on of a trade and are removable by the tenant.

TRADE-IN — An increasingly popular method of guaranteeing an owner a minimum amount of cash on sale of owner's present property to permit owner to purchase another. If the property is not sold within a specified time at the listed price, the broker agrees to arrange financing to personally purchase the property at an agreed upon discount.

TRANSFER FEE — A charge made by a lending institution holding or collecting on a real estate mortgage to change its records to reflect a different ownership.

TRUST ACCOUNT — An account separate and apart and physically segregated from broker's own funds, in which broker is required by law to deposit all funds collected for clients.

TRUST DEED — Just as with a mortgage this is a legal document by which a borrower pledges certain real property or collateral as guarantee for the repayment of a loan. However, it differs from the mortgage in a number of important respects. For example, instead of there being two parties to the transaction there are three. There is the borrower who signs the trust deed and who is called the trustor. There is the third, neutral party, to whom trustor deeds the property as security for the payment of the debt, who is called the trustee. And, finally, there is the lender who is called the beneficiary, the one who benefits from the pledge agreement in that in the event of a default the trustee can sell the property and transfer the money obtained at the sale to lender as payment of the debt.

TRUSTEE — One who holds property in trust for another to secure the performance of an obligation. Third party under a deed of trust.

TRUSTOR — One who borrows money from a trust deed lender, then deeds the real property securing the loan to a trustee to be held as security until trustor has performed the obligation to the lender under terms of a deed of trust.

TRUTH IN LENDING — The name given to the federal statutes and regulations (Regulation Z) which are designed primarily to insure that prospective borrowers and purchasers on credit receive credit cost information before entering into a transaction.

UNDERIMPROVEMENT — An improvement which, because of its deficiency in size or cost, is not the highest and best use of the site.

UNDERWRITING — Insuring something against loss; guaranteeing financially.

UNDUE INFLUENCE — Use of a fiduciary or confidential relationship to obtain a fraudulent or unfair advantage over another's weakness of mind, or distress or necessity.

UNEARNED INCREMENT — An increase in value of real estate due to no effort on the part of the owner; often due to increase in population.

UNIFORM COMMERCIAL CODE — Establishes a unified and comprehensive method for regulation of security transactions in personal property, superseding the existing statutes on chattel mortgages, conditional sales, trust receipts, assignment of accounts receivable and others in this field.

UNIT-IN-PLACE METHOD — The cost of erecting a building by estimating the cost of each component part, i.e., foundations, floors, walls, windows, ceilings, roofs, etc., (including labor and overhead).

URBAN PROPERTY — City property; closely settled property.

USURY — On a loan, claiming a rate of interest greater than that permitted by law.

UTILITIES — Refers to services rendered by public utility companies, such as — water, gas, electricity, telephone.

UTILITY — The ability to give satisfaction and/or excite desire for possession. An element of value.

VACANCY FACTOR — The percentage of a building's space that is not rented over a given period.

VALID — Having force, or binding force; legally sufficient and authorized by law.

VALLEY — The internal angle formed by the junction of two sloping sides of a roof.

VALUATION — Estimated worth or price. Estimation. The act of valuing by appraisal.

VA LOAN — A loan made to qualified veterans for the purchase of real property wherein the Department of Veteran's Affairs guarantees the lender payment of the mortgage.

VALUE — Present worth of future benefits arising out of ownership to typical users/investors.

VARIABLE INTEREST RATE — (VIRs or VMRs, Variable Mortgage Rates.) An interest rate in a real estate loan which by the terms of the note varies upward and downward over the term of the loan depending on money market conditions.

VENDEE — A purchaser; buyer.

VENDOR — A seller.

VENEER — Thin sheets of wood.

VERIFICATION — Sworn statement before a duly qualified officer to correctness of contents of an instrument.

VESTED — Bestowed upon someone; secured by someone, such as title to property.

VOID — To have no force or effect; that which is unenforceable.

VOIDABLE — That which is capable of being adjudged void, but is not void unless action is taken to make it so.

VOLUNTARY LIEN — Any lien placed on property with consent of, or as a result of, the voluntary act of the owner.

WAINSCOTING — Wood lining of an interior wall; lower section of a wall when finished differently from the upper part.

WAIVE — To relinquish, or abandon; to forego a right to enforce or require anything.

WARRANTY OF AUTHORITY — A representation by an agent to third persons that the agent has and is acting within the scope of authority conferred by his or her principal.

WARRANTY DEED — A deed used to convey real property which contains warranties of title and quiet possession, and the grantor thus agrees to defend the premises against the lawful claims of third persons. It is commonly used in many states but in others the grant deed has supplanted it due to the modern practice of securing title insurance policies which have reduced the importance of express and implied warranty in deeds.

WASTE — The destruction, or material alteration of, or injury to premises by a tenant.

WATER TABLE — Distance from surface of ground to a depth at which natural groundwater is found.

WEAR AND TEAR — Depreciation of an asset due to ordinary usage.

WILL — A written, legal declaration of a person expressing his or her desires for the disposition of that person's property after his or her death.

WRAP AROUND MORTGAGE — A financing device whereby a lender assumes payments on existing trust deeds of a borrower and takes from the borrower a junior trust deed with a face value in an amount equal to the amount outstanding on the old trust deeds and the additional amount of money borrowed.

X — An individual who cannot write may execute a legal document by affixing an "X" (his/her mark) where the signature normally goes. Beneath the mark a witness then writes the person's name and signs his or her own name as witness.

YARD — A unit of measurement 3 feet long.

YIELD — The interest earned by an investor on an investment (or by a bank on the money it has loaned). Also, called return.

YIELD RATE — The yield expressed as a percentage of the total investment. Also, called rate of return.

ZONE — The area set off by the proper authorities for specific use; an area subject to certain restrictions or restraints.

ZONING — Act of city or county authorities specifying type of use to which property may be put in specific areas.

A

Abandonment, 145
Abstract of title, 110
Acceleration and due-on-sale clauses, 260
Acceptance of offer, 122, 480
Accession, 144
Accounting-trust funds, 507
Accredited Management Organization,
    (AMO), 537
Accredited Residential Manager©, 537
Accretion, 144
Acknowledgment (of deed, etc.), 80, 150-151
Acknowledgment, recorded instruments not
    requiring, 80
Acquisition of real estate, 142
Actual authority of agent, 194
Actual fraud, 123, 221-223
Actual notice, 79
Adjustable rate mortgage (ARM), 256, 323
Adjustments and prorations at closing, 239,
    256, 482
Administrative hearings, 17-18
Administrative Procedure Act, 17
Administrator of decedent's estate, 143
Ad valorum taxation, 407
Advance fee, 3, 305
Advances, loan, 264, 309
Adverse possession, 145
Advertising:
    advance fees, 305
    consumer credit, 322
    escrow services, 160-163
    false advertising, 19
    mobilehome sales, 472
    mortgage loan and trust deed brokerage,
        307-309, 323
    subdivisions, 444
    Truth in Lending Act, 244
Age discrimination, 25, 236
Agency (see also brokers, commissions,
    licensing, listing agreements)
    generally, 191-220
    agency involving more than one broker,
        201, 209
    agency relationship disclosure and
        confirmation, 198-199, 478
    agent as principal acting on own account,
        214
    agent's authority, 194
    associate licensee (agent's agent) 217
    attorney in fact, 196
    broker-salesperson relationship, 217
    broker's duty to inspect property and
        disclose facts, 204
    business opportunity agency, 547
    buyer ready, willing and able, 209
    commingling of funds, 19, 198, 221
    commission disputes, 219
    compensation, agent's right to, 129, 208-
        209
    contraqcts, agent's liability for
        performance, 206
    cooperating broker/subagents, 209
    copies of contracts to be given to signers,
        142, 206, 514
    corporate broker, 8, 217
    creation of agency, 191
    deposit money or check, handling of,
        137, 196-97
    duties to principals, 202
    duties to third parties, 205
    dual agency (two principals), 19, 200
    emergency authority, 195
    employment contract, 208-209
    escrow holder's agency relationship, 159
    fair and honest dealing, 203
    fiduciary duty, 198, 202-205
    fraud, actual or constructive, 123, 221
    gratuitous agent, 194
    inspection of property and disclosure of
        facts by broker, 204, 472, 485
    liability insurance, 205
    listings, generally, (see Listing
        Agreements)
    material fact,disclosure of, 200, 203-205
    misrepresentation, 22, 206
    multiple listing service, 193
    net listing, 140
    open listing, 140
    option and listing, 215
    options, 139, 215
    ostensible (implied) agency, 193
    ostensible authority, 195-196
    power of attorney, 196
    probate sale, 212
    procuring cause of sale, 208-209
    promissory note, acceptance of, 197
    property management agreement, 541
    public property sales, 213
    puffing, 207
    ratification of unauthorized acts, 196
    reasonable care and skill, 203, 217
    salespersons, broker resonsibility for,
        205, 217
    secret profit, 19, 205
    selling agent and listing agent, 198-199
    subagents/cooperating brokers, 193, 217
    termination or revocation of agency, 19,
        211
    torts, 206
    warranty of authority, 205
Agreement to purchase. See Deposit Receipt
    and Contracts
Agricultural land, 170-171
Airspace rights, 72
Alcoholic beverage license, 559
Alienation, 146
All-inclusive trust deed, 255
Alluvion, 144-145
Alquist-Priolo Earthquake Fault Zoning Act,
    447

A.L.T.A. (American Land Title Assn.)
policy, 111, 306
Alternative financing, 256
American Institute of Real Estate Appraisers,
434
Amortization, 277-282
Annual percentage rate (APR), 275, 316,
323-324
Anticipation, principle of, 338
Apartment management, 538
Appraisal and valuation:
generally 331-406
agricultural land, 346
appraisal methods and procedure, 360
appraisal report and uses, 335
appreciation, 372
architecture and construction, 353
assemblage value, 343
balance, principle of, 338
book value, 373
building quality, 356
building residual technique, 384
business opportunities, 560
capitalization rate (income approach),
379-381
change, principle of, 337
commercial property, 345
competition, principle of, 338
conformity, principle of, 337
contribution, principle of, 338
cost approach, 372
definitions, 331
departure (from USPAP) provision, 363
depreciation, 278, 372-374
fair market value, 339
FHA loan appraisal, 358
functional obsolescence, 344
functional utility, 353-357
gross rent multiplier (GRM), 344, 388
highest and best use, 337
income (capitalization) approach, 379-
381
industrial property, 346
location, 343
market data (sales) comparison approach,
364, 377
market value, 339
mobilehomes/manufactured homes, 389
narrative report, 395
neighborhood analysis, 347
obsolescence, 344, 372
Office of Real Estate Appraisers, 402
overimprovement, 338
physical deterioration, 372
plottage value, 343, 346
progression, principle of, 338
quantity survey, 371
recapture rate, 379
reconciliation and final conclusion, 368,
389
regression, principle of, 338
replacement cost, 369-370
report, 334
reproduction cost, 370
residual techniques, 384
sales (market data) comparison approach,
364-368, 377
salvage value, 378
site analysis, 348
soil analysis, 343
square foot method, 344
straight line depreciation, 474
substitution, principle of, 337
supply and demand, 231, 337
underimprovement, 338
uniform standards of professional
appraisal practice (USPAP), 331
unit-in-place cost, 371
utility value, 339
VA loan appraisal, 289, 291
Valuation, definition and principles, 339
value conclusion, 333
yield capitalization analysis, 386
Appreciation, 372
Appurtenant easement, 72, 96
Arbitration/mediation of contract disputes,
484
Architecture, (see also Construction) 353-
355
Arranger of credit, 253, 472
Assemblage value, 343
Assessments, special, 443
Assignment of contract, 130
Assignment of debt, 258
Assignment of lease, 182
Assignment of rents, 264
Assumption of loan, 261, 318
Attachment, 94
Attorney in fact, 196
Attorney's fees, 271
Auction sale, business goods, 557
Authorization to sell. See Listing
Agreements
Avulsion, 144

B

Balance, principle of, 338
Balloon payment, 278
Base line and meridian, 74-75
Beneficiary, 162
Beneficiary statement, 162
Benefit assessments, 415
Bilateral contract, 130
Blanket trust deed encumbrance, 254, 441
Blockbusting, 20
Board of Education (local) property sales,
213
Board of Equalization, State, 550
Bond, surety (escrow), 297
Borrower. See loans
Branch office license, 15, 21

Breach of contract, 133-135
Brokers and brokerage (see also Agency, Licensing, Salespersons)
  advance fee, 3, 305, 325
  brokerage business, generally, 469
  business opportunities, 469
  career development, 469
  codes of ethics, 50
  compensation. See Commissions
  commission dispute, 219
  continuing education, 14
  corporate broker, 8
  deposit dispute, 196, 219
  disciplinary action, 17
  escrow handling, 164, 474
  franchising, 555
  insurance business, 471
  investment trusts, 329
  legal advice, unlawfully giving, 222
  lending own funds, 311
  loan servicing, 309
  mineral, oil and gas (MOG) land, 13, 444, 561-563
  mobilehome sales, 470
  mortgage loan negotiation/arranging credit, 305, 494
  notary services, 152, 471
  professionalism, 171
  property management, 537-542
  real estate boards, 47
  referral to escrow or title company, 22,
  salespersons, employment and supervision of, 20-29, 470
  salespersons, termination or discharge of, 16, 22, 29
  specialization, 470
  tax advice, unlawfully giving, 422
  trust deed sales, 306-307
  trust fund records, 507-511
  violations of law, 17, 126, 221-223
  wage withholding, 420
  workers' compensation, 218, 421
Building. See construction
Building manager, 538
Bulk sales/transfers, 556
Bundle of Rights, 71-72, 332
Business and Professions Code violations, 18-21
Business loan, 547
Busness opportunity listing, 550
Business opportunities:
  generally, 300, 547-60
  alcoholic beverage sale license, 559
  auction sale, 557
  Board of Equalization seller's permit, 550
  bulk transfers, 556
  business listing, 550
  covenant not to compete, 554
  definition, 547
  escrow, 548-557

  financing statement, 302, 550
  franchising, 555
  government permits, leases, etc., 550
  goodwill, 553
  lease, 554
  net lease, 345
  personal property security transactions, 300
  sales and assets, 550
  sales and use tax, 552, 559
  small business, 547
  successor's tax liability, 559
Buydown of interest rate, 286, 322
Buyer ready, willing, and able, 208
Buyer's responsibilities at closing, 160, 163, 165-166

C

California Assn. Of Real Estate Brokers (CAREB) 49
California Assn. Of REALTORS (CAR) 48,
California Land Title Assn. (CLTA) 112
Cal-Vet loan. See Veterans' loans.
Campgrounds, 437
Capital gain, 421, 424, 425-427
Capitalize (lease cancellation payment), 427
Certificate of corporate status, 8
Certificate of reasonable value, 289-291
Certificate of qualification - foreign corporation, 8
Certificate of title, 110
Certified Property Manager (CPM)$^\circ$, 537
Chain of title, 109
Change, principle of, 337
Check, post-dated, 197
Chose in action, 73
City planning, zoning, and redevelopment, 459-464
Civil code violations, 204-222
Civil rights laws, 20-29, 204, 236
Closing of sale. See Escrows.
Closing of loan, 239
Closing (settlement) statements, 163, 474
Cloud on the title, 83, 87, 155
Coastal zone, 444
Codes of ethics, 50
Collateral, 302
Collateralized junior mortgage, 252
College real estate courses, 6, 10
Combination trust, 330
Commercial Code, Uniform, 300, 556
Commercial loans, 297
Commercial property, 345, 440
Commingling of funds, 19, 198, 503
Commissioner of Real Estate. See Real Estate Commissioner.
Commissions and compensation (see also Agency)
  generally, 129, 208-219, 220
  amount, negotiability of, 209, 477

board of education sales, 213
commingling with deposit funds, 19, 198
damages when buyer breaches contract, 133
deposit receipt provisions, 142, 210-211, 479-485
division of commission, 209
escrow referral fee, 165
kickbacks and unearned fees, 352
listing agreement provisions, 192-194
mortgage loan negotiation, 311
probate sales, 144, 212
public property sales, 213
safety period, 477
unlawful payment or receipt, 216
unlicensed persons, 3, 21, 216
written contract, 127
Common interest subdivisions, 435
Common Law, English, 71, 149
Community apartment project, 436
Community property, 84, 135, 147
Community redevelopment agencies, 466
Compensation. See Commissions
Competition principle of, 338
Completion, notice of, 92
Compound interest, 275
Concurrent ownership, 82
Condemnation, 187, 455-456
Conditional use permit, 464
Condition precedent or subsequent, 147
Condominiums, 435
Conformity, prnciple of, 337
Consideration, 127, 150
Constant annual percentage rate, 278
Construction: (See also Subdivisions and land development.)
  Architectural style and building design, 353-356
  construction loans, 249, 295
  contractor licensing, 454
  diversion of funds, 221
  general contractor, unlicensed, 126
  housing and construction laws, 453
  installment contract, 253
  kickbacks, 221
  materialmen, 89
  mechanic's liens, 81, 87, 90, 92-95
  notice of cessations, completion or non-responsibility, 92-95
Constructive eviction, 176-176
Constructive fraud, 123, 206
Constructive notice, 79
Consumer credit contract, 245
Consumer loans, 330
Consumer protection, 17-29, 203-205, 485, 594-595
Continuing education requirements, 14
Contractor. See Construction
Contracts:
  acceptance of offer, 122
  aliens, 117

assignment of contract, 130
bilateral or unilateral contract, 115
broker-salesperson contract, 217
broker, unlicensed, 126
Commissions. See Commissions and Conpensation
condition precedent or subsequent, 120, 147
consideration, 127, 135
convicts, 117
copies to be furnished by agent, 142, 514
counteroffer, 122
damages for breach of contract, 133
death of seller, 138
definition and classification of contracts, 115
deposit money, 137, 196-197, 219
deposit receipt contract. See Deposit Receipt
duress, 125
executory or executed contract, 116
forfeiture clause, 138
fraud, actual or constructive, 123
genuine assent, 123
husband and wife, 135
illusory or nonillusory offer, 121
implied or expressed contract, 115
incompetent persons, 117
injunction, 134
interpretation and performance, 129
invalid or unenforceable contract, 146
lawful object, 125
limited liability corporation, 118
listing contract. See Listing Agreement
land contract, 298
material facts, 201, 208
menace, 125
minors, emancipated or unemancipated, 116-117
misrepresentation, 18, 124, 126
mistake of fact or law, 124
mutual consent, 120
novation, 131
offer and acceptance, 120, 122
options, 139
oral or written contract, 127, 168
parol evidence, 130
partnership, 118
performance and discharge, 130
persons capable of contracting, 116
power of attorney, 196
rescission, 133
signatures, 19
specific performance, 134
statute of frauds, 127
statute of limitations, 131
tender, 142
termination or revocation of offer, 121
time, lapse of, 131
undue influence, 125
unenforceable contract, 110

Uniform Vendor and Purchaser Risk Act, 138
unilateral or bilateral contract, 115, 193
usurious interest provision, 126
void or illegal contract, 116
voidable or unenforceable contract, 110
written or oral contract, 127
Contribution, principle of, 338
Controlled escrow, 166
Conventional loan, 247
Conversion of funds, 19
Corporate broker, 8-10, 12-14
Corporation, 119
Cost basis, 422, 426
Counteroffer, 122
County planning commission, 459
County recorder, 79
Covenant not to compete, 126, 554
Covenants, conditions, and restrictions (CC&Rs), 29, 98, 442
Creative financing, 252
Credit advertising, 322
Credit analysis, 231
Credit life or disability insurance, 312
Crops, 72

D

Damages, liquidated, 137, 197, 482
DBA (doing business as) or fictitious name, 9-15, 554
Debt condition statement, 272
Debt-to-equity ratio, 279
Deceased persons:
Administrator of estate, 119, 138, 144
deeds, 154
estate taxes, 419
income tax effect of will, 415
intestate succession, 110, 144
joint tenancy - right of survivorship, 84
probate sales, 212
purchase contract - death of seller, 138
wills, 143
Declaration of restrictions, 97-100
Declaratory relief action, 147
Declared homestead, 101-107
Dedication, public, 146
Deeds (see also Title, Trust Deeds)
acknowledgment, 150
dates, 151
delivery and acceptance, 154
gift deed, 156
grant deed, 155
habendum clause, 150
names in deeds, 153
property description, 121
quitclaim deed, 155
reconveyance deed, 156, 250
recordation, 79, 150, 153
restrictions in deeds, 99
sheriff's deed, 156, 266

special limitation, 147
tax deed, 413
trustee's deed, 270
void or voidable deed, 156-157
warranty deed, 155
Deed of Trust. See Trust Deeds
Default on loan, 156, 262-265
Default on tax, 413
Deficiency judgment, 263
Department of Real Estate. See Real Estate Department.
Deposit money, 137, 196-97, 218, 480
Deposit receipt (purchase) contracts (see also contracts)
generally 142, 479
acceptance of offer, 122, 484
agency relationship disclosure, 198-99, 478, 494
arbitration of contract dispute, 478, 484
attorney's fees, 478
ballon payment clause, 253
buyer's financing and terms of payment, 479
cancellation, 163
commission provision, 477
compensation of agent if no prior listing, 210
contingent on sale of other property, 483
counteroffer, 484
death of seller, effect of, 138
deposit, 137, 196-197, 219, 480
energy conservation retrofitting, 491
escrow holder designation, 166
exchange agreement, 425-426
fixtures, 482
flood hazard disclosure, 491
foreign/nonforeign status of seller, 492
geological inspection and disclosure, 489
home protection policy for buyer, 482
inspection of property, 481-483, 493
liquidated damages, 484
Mello Roos disclosure, 486
option contracts, 139
personal property, 477
possession by buyer before closing or seller after closing, 481
property condition statement, 485
property description, 479
property destruction or damage, 483
proration clause, 480
repairs clause, 483
security deposit (rental property), 170, 173
seller financing statement, 494
smoke detectors, 481, 487
structural pest control inspection and report, 482
time is of the essence, 480
title condition - report and insurance, 480
transfer disclosure statement, seller's, 485

Uniform Vendor and Purchaser Risk Act (damage to property before closing), 138, 483
warranty re condition of appliances utilities, etc., 481
water heater bracing, 481
Depository Institutions Deregulation and Monetary Control Act (1980), 226
Depreciation. See Appraisal and valuation.
Desist and refrain orders, 18, 445
Developer-builder, 543-545
Disabled persons' property tax postponement, 410
Disciplinary action, 17
Disclosure requirements:
   generally, 475-485
   adjustable (variable) rate mortgage, 256, 314-320
   agency relationship, 200, 494
   broker acting on own account, 21, 214
   closing costs, 161-162, 479
   copies of contracts, 142, 514
   dual agency, 19, 200
   due on sale clause, 258-261
   environmental hazards, 487-488, 490
   flood hazard, 491
   geologic hazard, 489
   inspection of sale property by agent, 204, 485
   landlord to tenant, 190
   late charges, 317
   lead-based paint, 487
   listing and option, 139
   loan assumptions, 318
   material facts, 203-204, 207
   Mello-Roos, 486
   mortgage loan disclosure statement, 310
   postdated check or promissory note accepted as deposit, 197
   prepayment penalty, 317
   RESPA (Real Estate Settlement Procedures Act), 495
   seller-assisted financing, 252, 494
   subdivision public report, 438
   supplemental assessment and tax bill, 410
   transfer disclosure statement, 205, 485
   Truth in Lending Act/Regulation Z, 314
Discount points, 275-277
Discount rate, Federal Reserve, 230, 277
Discrimination:
   age discrimination, 25
   blockbusting, 20, 29
   civil rights clause in listing agreement, 478
   complaint resolution and administrative hearings, 17-18
   deed restrictions, 97
   Equal Credit Opportunity Act, 236
   fair housing laws, 26-27
   financial discrimination (redlining) 28, 236
   notice of discrimination restriction, 100
   panic selling, 20, 29
   race not a material fact, 204
   rental housing, 28, 539
Dishonest dealing, 19
Documentary transfer tax, 418, 481
Dominant tenement, 96
Drainage and flood control, 417, 456
Dual agency, 19, 200
Due-on-sale clause, 258-261

E

Earnest money deposit, 137, 196-197
Earthquake fault zones, 447, 489
Easement by prescription, 97, 145
Easements, 72, 96
Easton v. Strassburger, 204
Education, real estate, 6, 8, 10, 11, 14, 17
Effective interest rate, 276
Egress and ingress, 96
Emblements, 72
Eminent domain, 147, 455
Employer-employee relationship, 217
Employment taxes and employer withholding, 218
Employment training tax (ETT), 420
Encroachments, 101
Encumbrances, 87
Endorsement, 245-246
Energy conservation, 289, 428
Engineer, land planning and development, 449
Environmental impact report (EIR), 444, 464
Equitable title/ownership, 155
Equity trust, 330
Escheat (reversion), 147
Escrow companies and agents, licensing and regulation of, 159-161
Escrows and Closing
   generally, 159-166
   agency status of escrow holder, 159
   basic escrow principles and procedures, 160-163
   beneficiary statement, 162
   bilateral or unilateral escrow instructions, 161
   broker as escrowholder, 164
   broker's relationship to escrowholder, 165
   business opportunity bulk sales, 556
   cash reconciliation statement, 163
   closing defined, 475
   controlled escrow (developer's interest in company), 166
   deposit placed in escrow, 196-197
   documentary transfer tax, 418
   escrow defined, 159
   escrow holder, selection of, 160, 166
   escrowholder's duties and responsibilities, 160-161

fire insurance policy, 162
interest, 244
loan disclosure statement, 313-320
mobilehome sales, 472-474
neutral escrow depository, 480
opening of escrow, 159-162, 165
personal property transactions, 300, 477, 556
possession by buyer before closing or seller after closing, 481
prorations and adjustments, 163, 239, 480
recording, 163
rents, proration or adjustment of, 171, 239, 483
RESPA (Real Estate Settlement Procedures Act), 226, 240
structural pest control report, 162, 482
termination of escrow, 163
title search, 162
uniform settlement statements, 163, 475
Estate Tax, 416-419
Estates, freehold, 67
Estates, less-than-freehold, 72 See also Lease.
Estoppel, equitable, 147
Eviction, 172, 189
Examination, Real Estate. See Licensing examinations.
Exchange of property, 298, 426
Exclusive agency listing, 141
Execution sale, 108, 147
Executor of estate, 119
Executory contract, 116
Exemptions from real estate license requirement, 4

F

Factory-built housing, 454
Fair housing laws, 27, 204, 236, 478
Fair market value, 339, 364, 389
False promise, 19
Federal Deposit Insurance Corp. (FDIC), 231
Federal Home Loan Mortgage Corp. (FHLMC), 232-233
Federal Housing Administration (See also FHA Loan.), 232, 281
Federal National Mortgage Assn. (FNMA), 232
Federal Reserve, 230
Federal Trade Commission (FTC), 245, 324
Fee simple estate, 71
Fees, real estate license and examination, 13
FHA loan (see also Loan, Real Property, Veterans' Loans)
generally, 281-83, 358-360
adjustable rate mortgage, 282
assumability, 261
condominiums, 281
direct endorsement, 283
downpayment, 282
fixed rate loan, 282
graduated payment loan, 282
growing equity mortgage, 282
interest rates, 244-253
lending institutions, 281
lending institutions, approved, 281
low-income buyers, 284
maximum loan amount, 282
mobilehomes/manufactured homes, 283
mortgage insurance premium (MIP), 282
multifamily rental housing, 284
negative amortization, 282
points, discount, 282
prepayment, 282
property improvement loan, 283
refinancing, 255
substitution of liability, 290
urban renewal, 284
veterans' terms, special, 281
FHLMC (Federal Home Loan Mortgage Corporation) 233
Fictitious business name (DBA), 9, 15, 554
Fiduciary relationship, 202
Final map, 452
Finance (see also Lenders, Mortgages, Trust Deeds)
alternative financing, 256
deregulation, 226
economy, national, 228-229
government agencies and programs, 281
investment trusts, 329
loan process, 235
mortgage market, primary and secondary, 231-232
mortgage money supply and demand, 231
mortgages and trust deeds, 246
nonmortgage financing, 297, 327
promissory notes, 243
syndicates, 327
Financial closing, 475
Financial discrimination in housing (redlining), 28
Financing statement (Commercial Code), 301, 558
Fingerprinting of license applicants, 4
Fire insurance, 162
Fixed rate mortgage, 227
Fixtures, 73, 145
Flexible loan insurance program (FLIP), 255
Flooding and drainage, 447
Foreclosure, 265-271
Foreign seller/investor, 492
Forfeiture, 147
Forgery, 222
Franchising, 555
Frauds, Statute of, 127, 165
Freddit mac (Federal Home Loan Mortgage Corp), 233
FSLIC (Federal Savings and Loan Insurance Corp), 231

Functional obsolescence, 357, 372

G

Garn-St. Germain Depository Institutions Act of 1982, 260
General plan, city or county, 459
Gift deed, 146, 156
GI loan. See Veterans Loans
Ginnie Mac/CNMA)Government National Mortgage Assn), 233
Goodwill, 554
Grant deed, 155
Gratuitous agent, 194
Gross estate, 415
Gross rent multiplier, 388
Guarantee of title, 110

H

Habendum clause, 150
Habitability, warranty of, 177-178
Handicapped (disabled) persons, 27-29
Hard money loan, 305
Hearings, Administrative, 445
Highest and best use, 357
Holder in due course, 244
Holographic will, 143
Home equity sales contracts, 271
Home mortgage interest deduction, 425
Home protection plan for buyer, 482
Homeowners' association, 442
Homestead declaration and exemption, 101, 103
Housing and Urban Development (HUD) 281
Housing discrimination (sales, rentals), 26-27
Housing financial discrimination (loans), 28
Housing, low-income or low-rent, 428, 466
Husband and wife. See Married Persons.

I

Implied contract, 115
Implied easement, 96
Implied warranty, 155
Improvement bonds, districts, and assessments, 414
Improvements in error, 145
Income approach (appraisal) 378-88
Income tax:
    generally, 422-428
    at-risk rules, 423
    boot, 426
    capital gain, 425
    cost basis, 422, 426
    depreciation, 424
    energy conservation credit, 428
    exchange, tax-free, 426
    federal estate tax, 416
    federal income tax, 422, 424
    federal tax liens, 417
    foreign investors, 492
    home mortgage interest deduction, 425
    installment sales, 427
    leases, 427
    low-income housing credit, 428
    mobilehomes, 414, 420
    mortgage credit certificates (MCCs), 425
    passive activity losses and credits, 423
    property taxes and liens, 408
    social security tax, 418
    solar energy system credit, 428
    state income tax, 419, 428, 421
    supplemental assessments, 414-416
    tax planning, 422
    Tax Reform Act of 1997, 425
    tax sale, 413
    wage withholding, 417, 420
Incompetence, 20
Incompetent persons, 117
Independent contractor, 217
Index to interest rate changes for adjustable loan, 316-319
Indorsement, 244
Industrial property, 345, 440
Ingress and egress, 96
Inheritance tax, 417
Installment construction contract, 253
Installment note, 243
Installment land sale contract (real property sales contract), 243, 253, 427
Installment sale - income taxation of, 427
Institute of Real Estate Management (IREM), 537
Institutional lenders, 231
    Instruments affecting title, recording of, 83-87
Instruments, negotiable, 243
Insurance:
    appraisals, 336
    broker as insurance agent, 471
    credit life or disability insurance, 317
    escrow adjustments, 162
    fire insurance, 162
    liability insurance professional, 205
    mortgage insurance (FHA), 282
    private mortgage insurance (PMI), 234,
    title insurance, 110
Inter vivos trust, 261
Interest-only mortgage, 254
Interest proration, 268
Interpleader action, 131, 138, 271
Interstate land sales, 458
Intestate succession, 144
Inverse condemnation, 455
Investment trust, real estate (REIT), 330

J-K

Joint tenancy, 84
Judgments, 94
Judicial foreclosure and sale, 265
Junior lienholder, 252

Junior (secondary) financing, 249, 262
Keybox, real estate agent's, 478

L

Land, 72
Land contract (real property sales contract), 298
Land descriptions:
　generally. 71-78
　government lots, 78
　informal description, 784
　lot and block description, 77
　metes and bounds, 76
　property description in contract; in deed, 121, 150
　township and section, 74
　survey map, 78
Land planning and development. See Subdivisions and land development.
Landlocked parcel, easement to, 97
Landlord and tenant. See Lease.
Late payment charges, 312
Laws, California:
　Administrative Procedure Act, 187
　Alcoholic Beverage Control Law, 559
　Alquist-Priolo Earthquake Fault Zoning Act, 447
　Bulk Sales Law, 556
　Coastal Act, 444
　Contractors State License Law, 454
　Corporate Securities Law, 223
　Environmental Quality Act, Calif. (CEQA), 464
　Factory Built Housing Law, 454
　Fair Employment and Housing Act, 27
　Franchise Investment Law, 20, 555
　Housing Financial Discrimination Act, 28
　Housing Law, State, 453
　Limited Partnership Act, Revised, 328
　Mortgage Foreclosure Consultants Law, 272
　Permit Streamlining Act, 466
　Porter-Cologne Water Quality Act, 448
　Real Property Loan Law, 310
　Recording Act, 79
　Sales and Use Tax Law, 558
　Subdivided Lands Law, 3, 431-432
　Subdivision Map Act, 431-32
　Uniform Commercial Code, 558
　Uniform Vendor and Purchaser and Risk Act, 138
　Unruh Civil Rights Act, 26
Laws, Federal:
　Civil Rights Act of 1968, 29
　Equal Credit Opportunity Act, 236
　Foreign Investment in Real Property Tax Act, 492
　Interstate Land Sales Full Disclosure Act, 458

Real Estate Settlement Procedures Act (RESPA), 226, 240
Tax Equity and Fiscal Responsibility Act (TEFRA), 219
Truth in Lending Simplification and Reform Act, 244
Lease:
　generally, 167-190
　abandonment, 187
　assignment (transfer) of lease, 182
　assignment of rents, 262
　basic requirements, 168
　breach, remedies, 186
　business lease, 554
　community apartment project, 436
　covenants and conditions, 170, 186
　contract specifics, 169
　default, 188
　destruction of premises, 184
　discrimination, 25
　dual legal nature, 167
　eviction, 176
　extension, 171
　foreclosed lien, lease senior in priority to, 270
　injury liability, 180
　late charge, 172
　leasehold estates, types of, 167
　maintenance and repairs by landlord, 175-179
　mobilehome parks, 432, 436
　notice to quit, 189
　oral and written agreements, 167
　owner's disclosure of information, 190
　periodic tenancy, 167
　personal property of tenant, 190
　possession and quiet enjoyment, 175-176
　prepaid rental listing service (PRLS), 17
　recording, 169
　renewal, 171
　rent, 171
　rights and obligations, 170
　security deposit, 173
　surrender of premises, 187
　sublease, 182
　tenancy at sufferance, 167
　tenancy at will, 167
　term of lease, 170
　termination of lease, 183, 189
　unlawful detainer action, 189
　warranty of habitability, implied, 177
Lease-purchase (leaseback), 298
Legal advice (illegal practice of law), v, 222-23
Legal description of property, 74
Lenders and Lending Institutions: (see also Loans, Savings and Loan Associations)
　generally, 231-235
Leverage, 279
Liability insurance, 218
Liability, substitution of, 258, 289

License examination (see also Licensing)
generally, 33-38
applications and fees, 4
college courses, prerequisite, 6, 10
content and weighting, 34
nonwaiverable, 4
preparing for examination, 33
question construction, 37
reexamination, 4
rules, subversion, 34
study questions and problems, 37
Licensing:
addresses, 9, 14
applications, 4
branch office, 15
broker, 5
broker officer of corporation, 8
broker's qualifying experience, 6
child support obligors, 12
college courses prerequisite, 6, 10
continuing education, 14
corporate licenses, 8, 10
equivalent experience, 6
exemptions, 4
fees, 13
fictitious business name (DBA), 9, 15
fingerprinting, 4
late renewal, 13
MOG (mineral, oil and gas) broker's
license, 13
non-California residents, 16
partnerships, 13
place of business, 16
prepaid rental listing service (PRLS), 17
renewals, 11, 13
restricted licenses, 13
salesperson, 10
term of license, 5
unlicensed person performing acts
requiring a license, 3, 21, 216
Liens: (See also Mortgages; Trust deeds)
generally, 87-95
attachments, 94
design professional, 94
execution sale, 147
homestead exemption, 101-103
judgments, 94
lis pendens, 88
mechanic's lien, 81, 87
recording and priority, 80
tax liens, 407, 415, 419
termination, 93
voluntary or involuntary lien, 87
Life estate, 71
Limited equity housing cooperative, 435
Limited Liability Corporation, 118
Limited partnership, 328
Liquidated damages, 134, 197, 484
Liquidity, 278
Liquor license, 559
Lis pendens, 88, 263

Listing agreements (see also Agency,
Commissions, Contracts)
generally, 140
agency realtionship disclosure, 198-202
arbitration of contract disputes, 134, 197,
484
business opportunity listing, 550
civil rights clause, 478
compensation provisions, 141, 194, 477
exclusive agency listing, 140, 192
exclusive authorization and right to sell,
141, 192, 476
exchange agreement, 298, 425
keybox authorization, 478
mobilehome listing, 472
multiple listing, 49, 141, 193
net listing, 140, 192
open listing, 140, 192
option and listing, 139
personal property included in sale, 477
property description, 74-78, 191
safety clause, 477
termination date, 19, 192
Loans, business, 547
Loans, commercial, 297
Loans, personal property, 300
Loans, real property: (see also FHA Loan,
Lenders, Mortgages, Trust Deeds,
Veteran's Loans)
generally, 476-478
acceleration and due-on-sale clauses, 259
adjustable rate mortgage (ARM), 256,
318-319, 322
advertising, 307, 322
all inclusive trust deed, 255
alternative financing, 256-297
amortization, 282
annual percentage rate (APR), 275, 316
application, 235, 305
appraisal, 238, 336
assignment of debt, 258
assumption, 261, 318-319
balloon payment, 253, 312
beneficiary statement, 162, 272
blanket encumbrance, 254, 444
borrower information, 236
buydown of interest rate, 322
cap on ARM rate increase, 282
closing of loan, 239
collateralized junior mortgage, 252
computerized loan origination, 240
construction loans, 249, 295
conventional loans, 231
credit analysis, 237-238
debt-to-equity ratio, 279
default and foreclosure, 262
deficiency judgment, 248
development loans, 434, 441, 467
disclosure statement, 308-310
discount points, 277, 279, 289
due-on-sale clause, 259-260

effective interest rate, 276, 323
Federal Housing Administration, loans
    insured by; see FHA loans
finance charges, 315
fixed-rate mortgage, 227
flexible loan insurance program (FLIP),
    255
FNMA below-market interest program,
    232
graduated payment adjustable mortgage
    (GPAM), 256
hard money loan, 254
holder in due course, 245
home improvement loan, 234, 245
impounds, 272
inflation index for ARM interest rate
    adjustments, 320-321
interest-only mortgage, 254
junior trust deeds, 252
late payment charge, 317
leverage, 279
lien priorities, 259
liquidity, 278
loan committee, 238
loan-to-value ratio, 234, 238
mobilehomes/manufactured homes, 283,
    286
negative amortization, 282
nominal interest, 276
offset statement, 259
open-end trust deed, 254
package trust deed, 162, 254
payoff demand statement, 239
piggyback mortgage, 254
pledged savings account mortgage, 255
prepayment, 317
private lenders, 253
promissory note, 243, 246
property information, 236
purchase money loan, 249, 252
reconveyance, 250
refinancing, 255, 319
release clause, 254
renegotiable rate mortgage (RRM), 227,
    257
rescission period, 3-day, 321
RESPA requirements, 240
reverse annuity mortgage (RAM), 257
rollover mortgage (ROM), 257
satisfaction or full payment of debt, 249
secondary financing, 249
security interest, 243-246, 317
seller-assisted financing, 252, 494
servicing, 242, 309
shared appreciation mortgage (SAM),
    257
straight loan, 243
subordination agreement, 249
swing mortgage, 255
take-out loan, 253
tandem mortgage, 254

teaser rate (ARM), 323
Truth-in-Lending Law and Regulation Z,
    313
unimproved land, 320
usury law and exemptions, 126, 253, 306
variable rate mortgage (VRM), 227, 316-
    319, 322
VA loan (guaranteed by Veterans
    Administration) See Veterans loans
wrap-around mortgage, 255
Local government planning, 459
Long-term lease, 297
Lot and block property description, 74
Low income housing, 233, 284, 428, 466

M

Manufactured homes, See Mobilehomes
Maps:
    assessor's map, 78
    earthquake fault zone maps, 447
    final subdivision map, 452
    parcel map, 453
    survey map, 78
    tentative subdivision map, 450
Market data approach (appraisal) 339, 366-
    368
Marketable title, 109, 135-136
Married persons:
    community property, 82-84, 147
    contracts and deeds, 135, 153
    emancipated minors, 117
    homestead laws, 101
    joint tenancy, 82-84
    separate property, 81-82
    signatures on contracts, 135
Material fact, 203-204, 207
Materialmen, 89
Mechanic's liens, 89-93
Meridian and base line, 74-75
Mesne profits, 133
Metes and bounds, 75
Mexican land grants, 149
Mineral, oil and gas (MOG) broker licensing,
    12, 562
Mineral, oil and gas lands, 13, 444, 561
Minimum property requirements (MPRs),
    454
Minors, contracts and conveyances, 116, 150
Misrepresentation, 19, 136, 203-206
Mistake of fact or law, 125
Mobilehome parks, 474
Mobilehomes/manufactured homes:
    generally, 3, 389, 413, 420, 472
    broker as seller/agent, 420, 473
    escrows, 474
    financing (FHA, VA, etc.), 281, 284
    homestead exemption for affixed
        mobilehome, 103
    moving requirements, 473
    out-of-state purchases, 474

property taxation, 413
registration, 413, 473
removal from foundation, 473
sales and use tax, 419
transfer of title, 473
transforming to real property, 414
Moral turpitude, 20
Mortgage bankers (mortgage companies), 232
Mortgage insurance companies (MICs), private, 234
Mortgage loan brokerage, 305
Mortgage loan disclosure statement, 310
Mortgage trust, 330
Mortgages (see also Loans, Finance, Trust Deeds)
generally, 225-281
default and foreclosure, 262, 271
deficiency judgment, 248
foreclosure consultants, 271
judicial sale, 265
junior mortgages, 252, 259
power of sale, 262-266
recording and lien priorities, 80, 259
redemption, right of, 248, 264
reinstatement of debt after default, 248, 264
servicing, 242, 308
trust deeds compared to mortgages, 247, 251
types of mortgages, 254-257
Multiple listing service (MLS), 49, 141, 193, 478
Mutual consent, 120-123
Mutual water company, 456

N

Names in title documents, 153
Narrative appraisal report, 395
National Assn. Of Real Estate Brokers (NAREB), 66-69
National Assn. Of REALTORS (NAR), 51-65
Negative amortization, 256
Negative declaration, 465
Negative fraud (nondisclosure), 203
Negligence, 20
Negotiable instruments, 129, 243-245
Net listing, 140, 192
Neutral escrow depository, 480, 499, 501
Nominal damages, 133
Notary public, 152, 471
Note, promissory, 197, 243
Notice, actual or constructive, 79
Notice of cessation, 92
Notice of completion, 92
Notice of default, 267
Notice of nonresponsibility, 93
Notice of Sale, 268

Notice, preliminary 20-day (mechanic's lien), 91
Novation, 131

O

Obsolescence, 344
Offer, 120, 123
Offer to purchase. See Deposit Receipt, Contracts
Office of Real Estate Appraisers, 402
One-form-of-action rule, 262
Open-end trust deed, 254
Options, 139, 215
Ostensible (implied) agency, 193
Overriding trust deed, 255, 496
Ownership of real property (See also Title.), 81

P

Panic selling, 20
Parcel map, 453
Parks, dedication for, 449
Parol evidence, 130
Partition action, 82
Partnerships, 118, 328
Payoff, demand for, 162
Perpetual estate, 71
Personal property, 73, 303, 477, 482
Planning commission, local, 460
Points, discount, 277, 286, 289
Police power, 1
Post dated check, 197
Power of attorney, 196
Power of sale, 266
Prepaid rental listing service (PRLS), 17
Prepayment of loan, 312
Prescription, easement by, 145
Primary mortgage market, 231
Principal and agent. See Agency
Principle and interest, 274-277
Private lenders, 253
Private mortgage insurance, 234
Probate, 144
Procuring cause of sale, 141, 208
Professional associations, 47, 538
Progression-regression, principle of, 338
Promissory note, 197
Property appraisal and valuation, 331-406
Property classification and description, 71-78, 137, 191
Property condition disclosure statement, 204, 471, 485
Property management, 542
Property ownership. See Title
Property taxes and assessments:
generally, 407-429
benefit assessments, 415
change in ownership, 409-411
documentary transfer tax, 418

homeowner's exemption, 410
lien date, 408
liens, 408, 416, 452
Mello Roos, 416
mortgage interest deduction, 425
mobilehomes/manufactured homes, 413-414
postponement for disabled persons and senior citizens, 412
Proposition 13 limitations, 407
redevelopment project funding, 466
special assessments and districts, 414-416
supplemental assessment and bill, 410
tax rate and bill, 407
tax deed, 413
tax sale and redemption, 412-413
veterans' exemptions, 410
Prorations, 163, 480
Public administrator of decedent's estate, 119, 212
Public report, subdivision, 2, 438
Public utilities, 457
Public works, 90
Purchase agreements. See Deposit Receipts
Purchase-lease, 298

Q

Qualifying (designated) broker for corporate license, 8-10, 219
Questionnaire, subdivision, 439-440
Quiet title action, 146
Quit, notice to, 189
Quitclaim deed, 155

R

Racial discrimination. See Discrimination
Range and Township, 74-76
Real Estate Advisory Commission, 3
Real estate agents. See Agency, Brokers and Brokerage, Licensing, Salespersons
Real estate boards, 47
Real Estate Commissioner:
    generally, 2-5
    audit or inspection of broker's trust account records, 514
    desist and refrain orders, 18, 445
    disciplinary action, 1, 17
    investigations and hearings, 17-18
    regulations, 18, 437, 442
    subdivision approvals, 2, 30, 431
Real Estate, Department of (see also Licensing, Examinations)
    generally, 3-5
    brokers arranging loans to file annual report, 308-309
    office addresses and telephone numbers, iii
    publications, 30
    Recovery Account, 31

Real estate education:
    continuing education, 14
    courses required for licensing, 6, 10
    elective courses, 6, 10
    home study/corresondence, 6-14
    private vocational schools, 6
Real estate investment trust (REIT), 329
Real Estate law, hostory and scope of, 1-5
Real Estate Law - violations, 17-30
Real estate licenses. See Licensing, Brokers and Salespersons
Real estate loan. See Loans, Real Property, FHA Loan, Veteran" Loans
Real estate purchase agreements. See Deposit Receipts, Contracts
Real Estate Settlement Procedures Act, (RESPA), 226, 240
Real estate syndicates, 297, 327
Real property distinguished from personal property, 73, 300
Real property loans secured by. See Loans
Real property sales contract (installment land sale), 3, 210, 223, 298, 427
Realtist, 49, 66-69
REALTOR, 26, 47-48, 51-66
REALTOR associate, 51
Recapture rate, 379
Reconveyance deed, 156, 250
Recording of title documents, 79, 153
Recordkeeping requirements, 21
Recovery Account, 31
Recreational vehicle parks, 432, 437
Redemption, 264, 413
Redevelopment agency, 466
Redlining (housing financial discrimination) 26-28, 236
Refinancing, 255, 319
Regression and progression, principles of, 338
Regulation Z (truth in lending), 226, 240
Regulations of Real Estate Commissioner, 25
Reinstatement of loan, 264
REIT (Real Estate Investment Trust), 300
Release clause, 251
Release of liability (VA loan), 290-292
Reliction, 145
Rent (See also Lease.), 170
Rent schedule, 539
Rental property management, 537-538
Rescission of contract, 133
Rescission period, 3-day (loans), 321
Resident manager, 8, 538
RESPA (Real Estate Settlement Procedures Act), 226, 240, 495
Restrictions in deeds, 97, 100
Reverse anunity mortgage, (RAM), 257
Reversion, 147, 332
Revocation of offer, 121
Revocation or suspension of license, 18-25, 547
Riparian property, 145

Rollover mortgage (ROM), 257
Roof leaks, warranty by seller against, 479
Roof types, 355

S

Sale financing, 254
Sale leaseback, 298
Sales and use tax, 419, 421
Sales comparison approach (appraisal), 332, 339, 364
Sales contract, installment. See Real Property Sales Contract, 298
Salespersons (see also Agency, Brokers, Commissions, Licensing)
  generally, 10-12, 21-25, 34
  broker-salesperson employment contract, 217
  broker's supervision and liability, 20
  career development, 469
  commission and deposit disputes, 219
  corporate employment, 9
  discharge or transfer of employment, 16
  education, continuing, 14
  education prerequisite to licensure, 6, 10
  employee or independent contractor, 217-218
  employment status re social security, unemployment insurance, workers' compensation, income tax status and withholding, 218
  license application, 11
  license examination, 10, 33
  partnership employment, 13
  public liability, 218
  qualifying experience for broker license, 5
Salvage value, 378
SBA (Small Business Administration) loan, 547
School district property sales, 213
School site dedication, 449
Secondary (junior) financing, 252
Secret profit, 19, 205
Section and township, 74-76
Security agreement (personal property), 300, 558
Security deposit, 173, 483
Security instrument, 243, 300
Seller-assisted financing, 252, 494
Seller acceptance of offer, 122
Seller's rental agreement with buyer, 481
Senior citizens:
  homestead exemption amount, 101
  housing developments, age-restricted, 26
  income tax exclusion of gain on sale of residence, 425-426
  property tax postponement, 412
  reverse annuity mortgage (RAM), 257
  social security, 418
Separate (sole) ownership, 82

Separate property of spouse, 84
Septic tanks and percolation (subdivisions), 448
Servient tenement, 96
Settlement charges, 163-165
Settlement statements, 240, 294, 313
Severance damage, 455
Sewage disposal (subdivisions), 448
Sheriff's deed, 156
Small Business Administration (SBA) loan, 547
Smoke detectors, 481
Social Security, 418
Soil test and report, 446
Sole ownership, 82-84, 118
Sole proprietor of business, 117, 547
Source and use of funds, 281-282
Special assessment and improvement districts, 443
Special Studies Zones, 447, 489
Specific performance, 134
Specific plan (local planning agency), 459-460
Standard pplicy of title insurance, 109
State income tax laws, 419
Statute of frauds, 127, 165
Statute of limitations, 131-133
Straight loan, 253
Straight note, 243
Streets in subdivisions, 449-450, 452
Structural pest control inspection, report, certification, 162
Subagent, 201
Subdivided Lands Law: (see also Subdivision Map Act, Subdivisions and Land Development)
  generally, 2, 430-431, 458, 543-546
  application and questionnaire (public report), 439
  blanket encumbrance, release of parcels from, 441
  bond to secure deposit moneys, 441
  common interest subdivisions, 435-444
  condominium project, 435
  covenants, conditions, and restrictions (CC&Rs), 442
  definition and types of subdivisions, 434, 437
  denial of public report, 445
  deposit money handling, 441-442
  desist and refrain orders, 445
  disciplinary action, 17-25
  disclosure of consumer information, 438
  exempt subdivisions, 440
  filing procedures and fees, 438-39
  homeowners' association, 443
  improvement districts and assessments, 413
  material changes in offering, 443
  mobilehome (manufactured home) parks, 432

MOG (mineral, oil and gas) subdivisions, 444
Notice of intention, 440
out-of-state subdivisions, 445
planned developments, 435
public report, 438
real property sales (installment) contracts, 243, 298, 427
standard subdivision, 434
time-share project, 437
title company report, 434, 528-529
undivided interests subdivision, 437
violations of law and penalties, 438-439
Subdivision Map Act (see also Subdivided Lands Law, Subdivision and Land Development)
generally, 431-458, 543-546
airport facilities, 449
appeal procedure, 445
approval of final map at local level, 453
costal zone, 444
dedication of land for parks, schools, streets, 449
definition of subdivision, 432
earthquake fault zones, 447
environmental impact report, 444
final map, 450-453
flood control and drainage, 447
improvement districts and special assessments, 443
neighboring property, noise, etc., 446
mutual water company, 456
parcel map, 453
planning commission (or advisory agency), local, 433
sewers or septic tanks, 448
soil test and report, 446
streets and easements, 449
survey map, 450
tentative map, 450
utility line (telephone and power) undergrounding, 448
vesting tentative map, 450
water quality and supply, 448
Subdivisions and land development:
building codes, local, 431
city and county planning, 433
community redevelopment agency (CRA), 466
conditional use permits, 464
Contractor's License Law, 454
eminent domain (condemnation) law, 147, 455
environmental impact report or negative declaration, 444, 464
fair housing laws, 26, 27
FHA/VA standards, 281-283, 291-296, 358-360
Financing generally, 204-257, 281-296, 297-300,
general plan, city or county, 446, 459
health and sanitation, 454
housing and construction laws, 453
initial study, 460
Interstate Land Sales Full Disclosure Act, 458
local planning commission or advisory agency, 433
Permit Streamlining Act, 466
public utilities, 448-457
sewage disposal, 448
specific plan, 459
variances, 464
water companies and districts, 456-457
water quality and supply, 448, 458
zoning, 461-462
Subjective value, 339
Sublease, 182
Subordinate encumbrances, 252-253, 259
Subordination agreement, 81
Substitution of liability, (assumed loan), 259
Substitution, principle of, 237
Succession, 144
Successor's tax liability, 552-558
Sufferance, estate at, 167
Supplemental assessment and tax bill, 410
Supply and demand, 231, 337
Surrender of premises, 187
Survey of land. See Land descriptions.
Survivorship (joint tenancy), 78, 84
Suspension or revocation of license, 18-24
Syndicates, real estate, 297, 327

T

Take out loan, 320
Tandem mortgage, 254
Tax liens (subdivisions), 81-84. 293. 559
Tax sale, 412
Taxation (see also Income Tax, Property Tax)
generally, 407-430
deductability of benefit assessments, 415
disability insurance, state, 218
documentary transfer tax, 418
employment training tax (ETT), 419
estate tax, 416
federal taxes, 416-417, 422
foreign seller tax withholding, 492
gift tax, 417
inheritance tax, 417-419
Mello Roos, 416
mobilehome/manufactured home, 413, 420
personal income tax, See income tax 219
real property taxes, 408
redemption, 413
sales and use tax, 419-421
social security tax (FICA), 418
successor's tax liability, 552, 558
supplemental assessments, 410

unemployment insurance tax, 219, 418, 420
workers' compensation, 213, 421
tax sale, 412
Tenancy in common, 82
Tenancy, joint, 82
Tenant and landlord. See Lease.
Tender, 142
Tentative map, 450-452
Termite inspection. See Structural pest control inspection.
Theft, 221
Time-is-of-the-essence clause, 480
Time share project, 437, 445
Title (see also Deeds, Liens, Title instruments)
generally, 87, 243, 246, 257
abstract of title, 110
accession, 144
adverse possession, 93, 97, 145
after-acquired title, 99, 155
alienation by court action, 146
chain of title, 109
cloud on title, 87, 155
community property, 84, 144-147
dedication, 449
encumbrances, 87
equitable title, 156
escheat (reversion), 147
estate of inheritance, 72
foreign-language documents, 80
gift, 146
grant deed, 155
income tax consequences, 422
intestate succession, 144
involuntary transfers (legal action), 146
joint tenancy, 82-85
legal title, 155
liens, 87
marketable title, 109
mobilehomes, 472
names in title instruments, 153
ownership, forms of, 80-87
partition action, 82
partnership, tenancy in, 86
probate, 145
public dedication, 449
quiet-title action, 146
quitclaim deed, 155
recording of title documents, 79, 153, 163
recording, time of, 80
severance, 83
sole owner/separate property, 81-82
succession, 144
survivorship, 83
tenancy in common, 82
transfer of title, 146
unities of interest, title, time, possession, 82-83
voluntary encumbrance, 87
will, acquisition by, 143
Title insurance:
generally, 109-113
American Land Title Assn. (ALTA) standard policy, 111
California Land Title Assn. (CLTA) standard policy, 112
anti-rebate law, 112
companies, 112
guarantee of title, 110
preliminary title report for lender, 162, 236
search and report, 109, 162
Torrens land registration system, 113
Torts, 206-208
Township, range and section, 74-76
Trade and professional associations, 47-50
Trade name, misuse of, 20
Trailer parks, 474
Transfer disclosure statement, seller's, 204, 485
Transfer of real property, 143-147
Transfer tax, documentary, 418, 481
Trust deeds (see also Mortgages, Loans, Finance)
generally, 155, 246-254
compared to mortgages, 246-247
debt condition statement, 272
default and foreclosure, 262, 265
deficiency judgment, 248-263
equity purchasers, 271
foreclosure consultants, 271
junior trust deeds, 252
one-action rule, 262
partial payment, 269
power of sale (trustee's sale), 266-271
purchase money trust deeds, 262-263
reconveyance, 250
recording and lien priority, 80, 239
reinstatement of debt after default, 264
sale or exchange of trust deeds by broker, 253
trustee's sale (power of sale), 266
types of trust deeds, 246, 251-252
Trust funds (see also Agency, Broker)
generally, 155, 246-251, 499, 535
accounting records, 507
advance fees, 305
beneficiary ledger, 508-510
broker's initial handling of funds received, 499, 500-502
brokers trust account, 500-507
cash ledger, 510
clearance of deposited check before withdrawing funds, 506, 524
check held uncashed, 500
commingling, 19, 503-505
conversion, 19
definition of trust funds, 499
examination or audit of records by Commissioner, 514

forms, trust fund records, 526-535
insurance on trust account, 500
interest-bearing account, 502-503
journal, 510
liability, 499, 505-506
neutral escrow depository, 501
ownership of funds, 501
overages, handling, 512
reconciliation reports, 511-512
record of trust funds received and paid
out, 508, 511
record of trust funds received but not
placed in trust account, 509
separate record for each beneficiary or
transaction, 508
separate record for each property
managed, 509
transaction examples, 515-525
withdrawal of funds, 502
Trust, real estate investment (REIT), 300
Truth in Lending Act, 244, 313

U

Undivided interests, subdivisions, 437
Undue influence, 125
Unemployment insurance, 218
Uniform Commercial Code, 301
Uniform Settlement Statement. See RESPA
Uniform Vendor and Purchaser Risk Act,
138
Unilateral contract, 193
Unlawful detainer action, 189-190
Unlawful practice of Law, 222
Unruh Civil Rights Act, 26
Urban renewal (FHA loan) 284
Use tax, sales and, 419-421
Usury, 126, 253, 306
Utility value, 342

V

VA loan. See Veterans' Loans
Valuation of property. See Appraisal and
Valuation
Variable (adjustable rate) mortgage (VRM),
316
Variance, zoning, 464
Verbal (oral) agreements, 127
Veterans Administration, 232
Veterans Affairs, Department of, 232, 284
Veterans' loans:
Cal-Vet Loan (Calif. Veterans Farm and
Home Purchase Program):
generally, 291-296
application, 294
construction loan, 295
eligibility, 291-292
interest rate, 292
insurance, 296
mobilehomes, 291
prepayment, 295
refinancing, 294
secondary financing, 295
subsequent loan, 295
transferability to another property,
245
FHA loan special terms for veterans, 251
SBA (Small Business Administration)
547
VA loan (United States Department of
Veterans Affairs):
generally, 284-291
appraisal, 289-291
assumability, 287-289
automatic loan commitment, 291
certificate of reasonable value (CRV),
289
condominiums, 284-288
delinquency, default, and
supplemental servicing, 290
disability release, 289
downpayment, 289
eligibility, 285
energy conservation improvements,
289
fixed rate mortgage, 227
funding fee, 286
graduated payment mortgage (GPM),
256
lending agencies, 284, 291
interest rate maximum, 286
minimum property requirements,
(MPRs), 291
mobilehomes/manufactured homes,
286
origination fee, 311
points, discount, 289
prepayment, 289
refinancing, 284, 287
release of liability, 289
restoration of entitlement, 290
Veterans' property tax exemption, 410
Violations of law, 18, 123-126
Vocational schools, private, 6
Void or voidable contracts, 116
Void or voidable deeds, 156-157
Voluntary encumbrance, 87

W-Z

Warranty deed, 155
Warranty implied in grant deed, 155
Warranty of agent's authority, 205
Warranty of habitability by landlord,
implied, 177-178
Warranty of seller re appliances, roof,
utilities, 481
Water:
costal zone, 444
drainage and flood control, 447
mutual water company, 445, 457

quality and supply, 448
riparian property, 144
sanitation, 448
special districts, 443
water table, 620
Wellenkamp v. Bank of America, 260
Wills, 143
Withholding, 420, 492
Work of improvement, 89-90, 92-94
Workers' compensation, 217-218, 421
Worthless security, 262
Wrap-around mortgage, 255, 496
Writ of execution, 108, 147
Yield tables and analysis, 278, 280
Zoning, 97, 101, 337-393, 436-455, 459-464